THE **BRITAIN GUIDE** 2000

AA

A Colourful and
Comprehensive Guide
to Britain's Heritage and
Leisure Attractions

Produced by   AA Publishing

This edition published October 1999

© The Automobile Association 1999. The Automobile Association retains the copyright in the current edition © 1999 and in all subsequent editions, reprints and amendments to editions

Mapping is produced by the Cartographic Department of The Automobile Association. Maps © The Automobile Association 1999

Directory compiled by the AA's Hotel and Touring Services Department and generated from the AA's establishment database

Cover artwork by   Sue Climpson, Whitchurch, Hampshire
Colour repro by   Microset Graphics Ltd, Basingstoke
Printed and bound
in Italy by   Rotolito, Lombarda

Advertisement production: Karen Weeks
                               direct line 01256 491545

A CIP catalogue record for this book is available from the British Library

Published by AA Publishing, which is a trading name of Automobile Association Developments Limited whose registered office is Norfolk House, Priestley Road, Basingstoke, Hampshire RG24 9NY, Registered number 1878835.

ISBN 0749522445

Cover images provided by   AA Picture Library

THE BRITAIN GUIDE 2000

CONTENTS

HOW TO USE THIS GUIDE

THE DIRECTORY

The directory is arranged in countries: England, Northern Ireland and the Republic of Ireland are listed in alphabetical location order within each county. Scotland and Wales are listed in alphabetical location within regions - the counties that comprise each region are listed below the region heading. Each county or region has an introductory page, and within each county or region a town, village, or item of regional interest has been highlighted with a half page feature. These features may mention places, landmarks or streets which do not have an entry in the directory.

OPENING DATES

quoted in the guide are inclusive - for instance, where you see Apr-Oct, that place will be open from the beginning of April to the end of October.

PRICES

quoted are, as far as possible, those which are expected to be in force in 2000. However, some establishments have been unable to give us their projected prices and for those we have given 1999 prices prefixed by an asterisk. If no price is quoted, you should check with the establishment concerned before you visit. Places which are open 'at all reasonable times' are usually free, and a number of the places which do not charge admission at all may ask for a voluntary donation.

DIRECTIONS

are given after the address of each establishment or attraction and have been provided by the places of interest themselves.

Map references for establishments can be found in the index (page 413). These are based on the National Grid, and can be used with the Atlas which begins on page 399, or with any AA or Ordnance Survey atlas. If a place was a late entry to the guide, it may have a map reference but not be highlighted on the atlas in this guide.

See page 7 for a key of Symbols and Abbreviations used in this guide.

Chatsworth House, Derbyshire

EXERCISE YOUR IMAGINATION

IMAGINE THIS:
A land dedicated to the imagination of children. A land of over 40 rides, attractions and live shows. Where children can earn a licence at the Driving school. Where you can marvel at the miniature world of Miniland, ride the thrilling coaster in the Dragon Knights Castle or get wet and wild at the Extreme Team Challenge. That land is LEGOLAND®. Call for information 0990 04 04 04...

LEGO
LEGOLAND®
W I N D S O R

LEGOLAND Windsor
is open daily from 13th March
to 31st October, 10 am to 6 pm.

KEY OF SYMBOLS AND ABBREVIATIONS

SYMBOLS

In order to give you as much information as possible in the space available, we have used the following symbols in the guide:

	ENGLISH	**FRANÇAIS**	**DEUTSCH**	**ITALIANO**	**ESPAÑOL**
☎	Telephone number	Numéro de téléphone	Telefonnummer	Numero telefonico	Número telefónico
📄	Fax number				
♿	Suitable for visitors in wheelchairs	Les invalidens fauteuils roulants pourrant y accéder	Für Rollstuhltahrer zugänglich	Accessibile agli handicappeti	Acondicionado para visitantes en silla de reudas
*	Indicates 1999 price	Prix 1999	1999 Preise	Indica i prezzi del 1999	Indica los precios de 1999
🅿	Parking at Establishment	Stationnement à l'établissement	Parken an Ort und Stelle	Parcheggio in loco	Aparcamiento en el establecimiento
🅿	Parking nearby	Stationnement tout près	Parken in der Nähe	Parcheggio nelle vicinanze	Aparcamiento cerca del
☕	Refreshments	Rafraîchissements	Erfrischungen	Snack-bar	Refrescos
✕	Restaurant	Restaurant	Restaurant	Ristorante	Restaurante
🐕	No dogs	Chiens non permis	Hundeverbot	Cani non accettati	Se prohiben los perros
🚌	No coaches	Les groupes en cars pas admis	Keine Reisebusgesellschaften	Non si accettano comitive in pullman	Non se admiten los grupos de viajeros en autobús
⚜	Cadw (Welsh Historic Monuments)	Cadw Monument ancien (Pays de Galles)	Cadw Historiches Gebaude (Walisland)	Cadw Monumento storico (Galles)	Cadw Monumento histórico (Gales)
⛫	English Heritage	English Heritage	English Heritage	English Heritage	English Heritage
🌿	National Trust	National Trust	National Trust	National Trust	The National Trust
🌿	National Trust for Scotland	National Trust en Ecosse	National Trust in Schottland	National Trust per la Scozia	The National Trust de Escocia
▌	Historic Scotland				

ABBREVIATIONS

In the same way, we have abbreviated certain pieces of information:

	ENGLISH	**FRANÇAIS**	**DEUTSCH**	**ITALIAN**	**ESPAÑOL**
BH	Bank Holidays	Jours fériés	Bankfeiertage	Festività nazionale	Días festivos (bancos y comercio)
PH	Public Holidays	Jours fériés	Feiertage	Festività nazionale	Días festivos
Etr	Easter	Pâques	Ostern	Pasqua	Semana Santa
ex	except	sauf	ausser	eccetto	excepto
IR£	Irish punts	Punts irlandais	Punts Irisch	Punts irlandesi	Punts irlandeses
Free	Admission free	Entrée gratuit	Freier eintritt	Ingresso gratuito	Entrada gratuita
£1	Admission £1	Entrée £1	Eintritt £1	Ingresso £1	Entrada £1
ch 50p	Children 50p	Enfants 50p	Kinder 50p	Bambini 50p	Niños 50p
ch 15 50p	Children under 15 50p	Enfants de moins de 15 ans 50p	Kinder unter 15 Jahren 50p	Bambini sotto i 15 anni 50p	Los niños de menores de 15 años 50p
Pen	Senior Citizens	Retraites	Rentner	Pensionati	Jubilados
Party	Special or reduced rates for parties booked in advance	Tarifs spéciaux ou réduits pour groupes réservés d'advance	Sondertarife oder Ermässigungen für im voraus bestellte Gesellschaften	Tariffe speciali o ridotte per comitive che prenotano in anticipo	Tarifas especiales o reducidas para los grupos de viajeros que reserven de anternano
Party 30+	Special or reduced rates for parties of 30 or more booked in advance	Tarifs spéciaux ou réduits pour groupes de 30 ou plus réservés d'advance	Sondertarife oder Ermässigungen für im voraus bestellte Gesellschaften von wenigstens 30 Personen	Tariffe speciali o ridotte per comitive di 30 o più persone che prenotano in anticipo	Tarifas especiales o reducidas para grupos de 30 viajeros, o más, que reserven de anternano

CREDIT & CHARGE CARDS are now taken by a number of establishments for admission charges. To indicate which establishments accept credit cards we have used this symbol at the end of the entry:

TELEPHONE NUMBERS have the STD code shown before the telephone number. (If dialling Northern Ireland from England use the STD code, but for the Republic you need to prefix the number with 00353). A number of telephone number changes will take place during the currency of this Guide - please see page 11 for details.

VISITORS WITH DISABILITIES
Visitors with disabilities should look for the wheelchair symbol showing where all or most of the establishment is accessible to wheelchair-bound visitors. We strongly recommend that you telephone in advance of your visit to check the exact details, particularly regarding access to toilet and refreshment facilities. Guide dogs are usually accepted where the establishments show the 'No Dogs' symbol – unless stated otherwise. For the hard of hearing induction loops are indicated.

PHOTOGRAPHY is restricted in some places and there are many where it is only allowed in specific areas. Visitors are advised to check with places of interest on the rules for taking photographs and the use of video cameras.

The Sunken Garden at Hampton Court

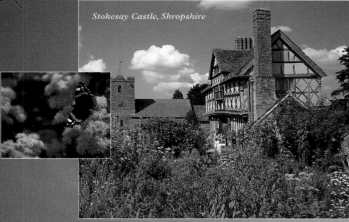

Stokesay Castle, Shropshire

Discover our
eventful
days

From magnificent castles, abbeys and stately homes to hidden gems in beautiful countryside settings, English Heritage properties offer you the real history of England. Taste the excitement of the past as many of our properties come alive with an action packed programme of historic re–enactments, living history, music and drama. With over 400 properties across the country we guarantee an eventful day out.

For a free brochure call us now on 0207 973 3434.

Rievaulx Abbey, Yorkshire

ENGLISH HERITAGE

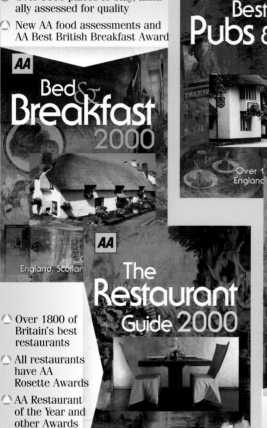

TELEPHONE CODE AND NUMBER CHANGES

From 22 April 2000 there will be new dialling codes beginning with 02 in London, Cardiff, Coventry, Portsmouth, Southampton and right across Northern Ireland. At the same time, all local numbers in these areas will become eight-digit numbers.

PORTSMOUTH AREA
TELEPHONE NUMBER CHANGES

From the 22 April 2000, all dialling codes listed as (01705) will change to (023), followed by an eight-digit local number starting with 92.
For example, (01705) 123456 will become (023) 9212 3456.

SOUTHAMPTON AREA
TELEPHONE NUMBER CHANGES

From the 22 April 2000, all dialling codes listed as (01703) will change to (023), followed by an eight-digit local number starting with with 80.
For example, (01703) 123456 will become (023) 8012 3456.

COVENTRY AREA
TELEPHONE NUMBER CHANGES

From the 22 April 2000, all dialling codes listed as (01203) will change to (024), followed by an eight-digit local number, starting with 76.
For example, (01203) 123456 will become (024) 7612 3456.

CARDIFF AREA
TELEPHONE NUMBER CHANGES

From the 22 April 2000, all dialling codes listed as (01222) will change to (029), followed by an eight-digit local number, starting with 20.
For example, (01222) 123456 will become (029) 2012 3456.

LONDON AREA
TELEPHONE NUMBER CHANGES

From the 22 April 2000, the dialling code for the whole of London will be (020), followed by an eight-digit local number.

For example, (0171) 123 4567 will become (020) 7123 4567,
(0181) 123 4567 will become (020) 8123 4567.

NORTHERN IRELAND
TELEPHONE NUMBER CHANGES

From the 22 April 2000, the dialling code for the whole of Northern Ireland will be (028) followed by an eight-digit local number. There are 32 local conversions to eight-digit numbers, please check with Directory Enquiries. For example, the prefix for Belfast numbers will be 90. (01232) 123456 will become (028) 9012 3456.

In case of difficulty please contact Directory Enquiries.

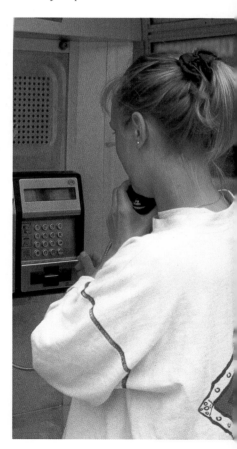

AA Hotel Booking Service

The AA Hotel Booking Service - Now you have a free, simple way to reserve a place to stay for a week, weekend, or a one-night stopover.

Do you want to book somewhere in the Lake District that has leisure facilities; a city-centre hotel in Glasgow with parking facilities, or do you need accommodation near Dover which is handy for the Eurotunnel?

The AA Booking Service can take the hassle out of booking the right place for you.

And if you are touring round the UK or Ireland, simply give the AA Hotel Booking Service your list of overnight stops, and from one phone call all your accommodation can be booked for you.

Telephone 0870 5050505

Office hours
Monday-Friday 9am-6pm
Saturday 9am-1pm
Not available Sundays or Bank Holidays

Full listings of AA recognised accommodation available through the Hotel Booking Service can be found and booked at the AA's Internet Site:

http://www.theaa.co.uk/hotels

Bedfordshire

One of England's smallest counties, Bedfordshire contains the picturesque villages of Woburn and Old Warden, and the large towns of Luton and Bedford. There's plenty of countryside to explore on foot or by bike, and plenty to see and do in Bedfordshire's towns and villages.

For many travellers, Luton is the gateway to London and Eastern England. London Luton Airport offers an increasing number of international flights, but that's not all there is to this bustling town. Once a centre for hat manufacture, Luton has a variety of attractions including gardens, museums, parks and a unique collection of horse-drawn carriages. Not far from the town there stands the magnificent Luton Hoo, a 19th-century house with 1,500 acres of Capability Brown garden and a notable collection of art connected with the Russian royal family.

The county has some charming sights, set among its many small villages. Woburn is one of these, and is known not only for its Abbey and Safari Park, but also its fine Georgian houses and antique shops. Not far from Old Warden, the Swiss Garden is an ideal place for a quiet afternoon. In its ten acre spread there are trees and shrubs from all over the world, as well as islands and ponds and a tiny thatched Swiss cottage.

There is also plenty of history on view. Dunstable boasts the Norman Church of St Peter, with medieval additions that include a 15th-century chancel screen. Ampthill, between Luton and Bedford, is full of fascinating architecture, including Avenue House, and the 14th-century Church of St Andrew, which houses a cannon-ball monument to Richard Nicolls, a local citizen who became the first Governor of Long Island, USA.

EVENTS & FESTIVALS

February
26th-4th March Bedfordshire Festival of Music, Speech & Drama, Corn Exchange, Bedford

March
26th February-4th Bedfordshire Festival of Music, Speech & Drama, Corn Exchange, Bedford

April
22nd-23rd (provisional) St George's Festival, Silsoe

May
27th-28th (provisional) River Festival, Embankment, Bedford

September
tbc Bedfordshire Steam & Country Fayre

October
tbc Bedford Beer Festival, Corn Exchange, Bedford

December
tbc Victorian Christmas Fair, town centre

Top: Bridge over the River Ouse

BEDFORD

Bedford, the county town, straddles the River Ouse and is steeped in history. The town was settled in the 8th century but is best known as the birthplace of Christian preacher and author, John Bunyan (1628-88). Although his work is now celebrated, at the time he was attacked for his non-conformism, and spent over a decade in Bedford's County Gaol. While in prison he wrote Grace Abounding in the Chief of Sinners, *his spiritual autobiography, as well as* Pilgrim's Progress.*

The town also has connections with John Howard, of the Howard League of Penal Reform, and Glenn Miller, who was stationed here with his band during WWII.

▥ AMPTHILL
HOUGHTON HOUSE
(1m NE off A421)

Now a ruin, the mansion was built for Mary Countess of Pembroke, the sister of Sir Philip Sidney. Inigo Jones is thought to have been involved in work on the house, which may have been the original 'House Beautiful' in Bunyan's 'Pilgrim's Progress'.
Times: Open all reasonable times.
🅿 ♿ ▦

▥ BEDFORD
CECIL HIGGINS ART GALLERY & MUSEUM
Castle Ln MK40 3RP (in the centre of the town, just off the Embankment)
☎ 01234 211222   🖹 01234 327149

A recreated Victorian mansion, with the rooms arranged as though the house was lived in. The adjoining gallery has an outstanding collection of ceramics, glass, prints and watercolours.
Times: Open all year, Tue-Sat 11-5, Sun 2-5, BH Mon 2-5. (Closed Mon, Good Fri & 25-26 Dec).
Fee: Free.
🅿 (50 yds) ♿ toilets for disabled shop 🐾 (ex guide dogs)

▥ LUTON
LUTON MUSEUM & ART GALLERY
Wardown Park, Old Bedford Rd LU2 7HA (1m N of Luton town centre)
☎ 01582 546722 & 546739
🖹 01582 546763

A Victorian mansion, with displays illustrating the natural and cultural history, archaeology and industries of the area, including the development of Luton's hat industry, and the Bedfordshire and Hertfordshire Regimental Collections.
Times: Open all year, Tue-Sat 10-5, Sun 1-5 (Closed Xmas, 1 Jan & Mon).
Fee: Free.
🅿 🖵 ♿ (parking adjacent to entrance, lift to 1st floor) toilets for disabled shop 🐾 (ex guide dogs & hearing dogs)

▥ SANDY
RSPB NATURE RESERVE
The Lodge SG19 2DL (1m E, on B1042 Potton Rd)
☎ 01767 680541

The headquarters of the Royal Society for the Protection of Birds. The house and buildings are not open to the public, but there are waymarked paths and formal gardens, and two species of woodpecker, nuthatches and woodland birds may be seen, as may muntjac deer.
Times: Open daily 9am-9pm or sunset.
🅿 ♿ toilets for disabled shop 🐾 *Details not confirmed for 2000* 🐦

⚒ SILSOE
WREST PARK HOUSE & GARDENS
MK45 4HR (three quarters of a mile E off A6)
☎ 01525 860152

The formal gardens designed over 150 years ago form a serene and beguiling setting for this elegant 19th-century mansion.
Times: Open Apr-1 Nov, daily 10-6 (or dusk if earlier).
Fee: £3.20 (ch £1.60).
🅿 💺 ✈ (in certain areas) ♨

⚒ WOBURN
WOBURN ABBEY
MK43 0TP
☎ 01525 290666 📄 01525 290271

Standing in 3000 acres of parkland, this palatial 18th-century mansion was originally a Cistercian Abbey, and the Dukes of Bedford have lived here since 1547. The valuable art collection includes works by Canaletto, Rembrandt, Van Dyck, and Gainsborough. Fourteen state apartments are on view, and the private apartments are shown when not in use by the family. Many special events are held during the year, including Craft Fairs and a De-Havilland Tiger Moth Fly-In (Aug).
Times: Open Jan-20 Mar; Abbey Sat & Sun only 11-4, Deer park 10.30-3.45; 21 Mar-26 Sep; Abbey weekdays 11-4, Sun & BH 11-5; 2-31 Oct Sat & Sun only; Deer Park weekdays 10-4.30, Sun & BH 10-4.45.
Fee: *Abbey & Deer Park £7.50 (ch over 12yrs £3.00, pen £6.50). Family ticket £19-£21.50. Deer Park only car & passengers £5. Motorcycles & passengers £2.
🅿 💺 ♿ (wheelchairs accommodated by prior arrangement) toilets for disabled shop ✈ 🦭

WOBURN SAFARI PARK
Woburn Park MK17 9QN (M1 J13)
☎ 01525 290407 📄 01525 290489

Within the 3000 acres of parkland belonging to Woburn Abbey is 300 acres of safari park. The safari road passes through an African plains area, with eland, zebra, hippos and rhinos, then through well-keepered tiger and lion enclosures, and on past bears and monkeys. The sea lion and parrot shows are popular, there is a pets' corner and special events take place on all Bank Holidays and in the school summer holidays.
Times: Open 6 Mar-31 Oct 10-5.
Fee: £11.50 (ch 3-17 £8.00, pen £8.00).
🅿 ✗ licensed ♿ toilets for disabled shop ✈ 🦭

Berkshire

Berkshire is a narrow county of wide variety, reaching from the edge of London on its eastern boundary to the relative isolation of the Lambourn Downs in the west, containing towns as diverse as Reading and Hungerford, Newbury and Windsor.

EVENTS & FESTIVALS

April
28th April-1st May: CAMRA Real Ale Festival, Kings Meadow, Reading

May
6th-20th: Newbury International Spring Festival
20th May-18th June: Reading Children's Festival
29th: Reading Community Carnival

June
20th May-18th June: Reading Children's Festival
24th-25th: Reading Water Fest
30th June-2nd July: Bracknell Festival

July
20th-22nd: Reading Real Ale & Jazz Festival
28th-30th (provisional): WOMAD world music & arts festival, Reading

August
25th-27th: Reading Festival

September
15th-19th: Windsor Festival

November
4th (provisional): Fireworks Fiesta, Kings Meadow, Reading

Waterways play an important part in Berkshire's character and history, not least the River Thames which forms the county's border with Oxfordshire. The Kennet, a tributary of the Thames that was partially converted into the Kennet and Avon Canal, had a major role in the growth and success of both Reading and Newbury, and flows the length of the county from its source in Wiltshire. Both of these rivers, as well as The Bourne and the River Pang, flow through some of England's prettiest countryside. Part of the charm of these scenes has been preserved in one of Britain's best-loved children's books. Kenneth Graham used the river banks around Cookham as the setting for The Wind in the Willows in 1908. Cookham is also known as the birthplace of artist, Sir Stanley Spencer (1891-1959), whose work includes Christ Carrying the Cross and various religious murals.

Newbury, the county's largest town after Reading, has seen its share of history. Its most famous citizen, Jack of Newbury, (JohnWinchcombe) established the first true factory in England with 200 looms and 1000 employees. In 1513 he led 150 men against the Scots at Flodden in Northumberland. The town saw fighting during the Civil War, when Donnington Castle was ruined. Today, the town is better known for the more peaceful, if no less noisy, sport of horseracing.

Top: Windsor Castle

⛪ BASILDON
BASILDON PARK
Lower Basildon RG8 9NR (7m NW of Reading on W side of A329)
☎ 0118 984 3040   🗎 0118 984 1267

This lovely 18th-century house, built of golden Bath stone, fell into decay in the 20th century, but was rescued and beautifully restored by Lord and Lady Iliffe. The classical front has a splendid central portico and pavilions, and inside there are delicate plasterwork decorations on the walls and ceilings, and an elegant staircase. The Octagon drawing room has fine pictures and furniture, and there is a small formal garden.
Times: House open 1 Apr-1 Nov, Wed-Fri 1-5.30; Sat, Sun & BH Mon 1-5.30 (Closed Good Fri). Park & garden 1-27 Mar, wknds 12-5, otherwise same as house (ex wknds & BH Mon 12-5). 1 Apr-1 Nov 11.30-5.30.
🅿 🍽 ♿ (driven buggy) toilets for disabled shop ✶ (ex in grounds) 🐾 *Details not confirmed for 2000*

BEALE PARK
Lower Basildon RG8 9NH (signposted from M4 J12)
☎ 0118 984 5172   🗎 0118 984 5171

Ornamental pheasants, peacocks, parrots and other birds can be seen here, together with Highland cattle and rare breeds of sheep. There's a craft centre and a children's playground; excellent fishing in season; and numerous events and exhibitions are held during the year. The park's focal point is the mausoleum, built by Mr Child Beale in memory of his parents, surrounded by a large and varied collection of statues, fountains and walks. Please ring for details of special events.
Times: Open daily, Mar-Sep 10-6. Last admission 5pm. Oct-Dec 10-5. Last admission 4pm.
🅿 🍽 ♿ (wheelchair available, parking) toilets for disabled shop ✶ *Details not confirmed for 2000*

⛪ ETON
DORNEY COURT
Dorney SL4 6QP (signposted from M4 J7, via B3026)
☎ 01628 604638   🗎 01628 665772

An enchanting brick and timber manor house (c1440) in a tranquil setting. With tall Tudor chimneys and a splendid great hall, it has been the home of the present family since 1510.
Times: BH Mons in May and preceding Sun 1-4.30 Jul & Aug, Mon-Thu 1-4.30.
Fee: *£4.50 (ch £2.80, under 9yrs free)
🅿 🍽 shop garden centre ✶

⛪ MAIDENHEAD
COURAGE SHIRE HORSE CENTRE
Cherry Garden Ln, Maidenhead Thicket SL6 3QD (off B3206, off A4)
☎ 01628 824848   🗎 01628 828472

You are free to wander around and meet the horses, or take a free tour with a guide who will explain the care and history of these gentle giants of the equestrian world. Dray rides are also available.

Times: Open Mar-Oct, daily 10.30-5. Last admission 4pm.
🅿 🍽 ✗ licensed ♿ (wheelchair available) toilets for disabled shop *Details not confirmed for 2000* 🔔

⛪ NEWBURY
WEST BERKSHIRE MUSEUM
The Wharf RG14 5AS (from London take M4 J13, then Southbound on A34 for 3m, follow signs for town centre.)
☎ 01635 30511   🗎 01635 38535

Situated in two historic buildings in the centre of Newbury, the Cloth Hall built in 1627, and the Granary built in 1720. Apart from local history and archaeology, birds and fossils, the museum displays costume and other decorative art.
Times: Open all year: Apr-Sep, Mon-Fri (Wed during school hols only) 10-5, Sat 10-4.30. Oct-Mar, Mon-Sat (Wed during school hols only) 10-4. (Closed Sun & BHs).
Fee: Free.
🅿 (15yds) ♿ shop ✶ (ex guide dogs)

⛪ RISELEY
WELLINGTON COUNTRY PARK
RG7 1SP (signposted off A33)
☎ 0118 932 6444   🗎 0118 932 6445

350 acres of woodland and meadows, set around a lake in peaceful countryside. The Thames Valley Time Trail traces the development of earth and mineral resources in the area, and there's a collection of farm animals, a deer park and a miniature steam railway. You can also fish, sail, windsurf and row here.

contd.

READING

Reading is one of Berkshire's most vibrant and lively towns, and for all its history certainly hasn't let any grass grow under its feet. There's plenty of nightlife along Friar Street, and a wealth of excellent shopping opportunities at Friar's Walk and the Broad St Mall. The arts are well represented by an important local art and theatre centre in the shape of the aptly-named Hexagon, The Rising Sun Institute which provides more avant-garde entertainment, and the Town Hall Art Gallery and Museum. More sedate pastimes can be pursued by the River Thames which is surrounded by green space and runs behind the railway station out of the centre of town.

Wellington Country Park

Times: Open Mar-Oct, daily 10-5.30.
Fee: *£3.90 (ch £1.90)
🅿 💺 ♿ (fishing platform & nature trail for disabled) toilets for disabled shop 🏷

🏛 WINDSOR

FROGMORE HOUSE
Home Park SL4 1NJ (entrance from B3021)
☎ 01753 831118 (recorded info)
🖹 01753 832290

The present building dates back to 1618, and residents have included Charles II's architect, Hugh May (who built it), Queen Charlotte, Queen Victoria and Queen Mary. An original mural,

discovered only recently during redecoration, can be seen on the stairway.
Times: Open: 6-7 & 20 May 10-7 (last admission 6), 27 May (mausoleum only) 11-4 (last admission 3.30), 11 Aug-1 Oct Tue-Thu (last admission 4).
🅿 shop 🏷 *Details not confirmed for 2000*

HOUSEHOLD CAVALRY MUSEUM
Combermere Barracks, St Leonards Rd SL4 3DN
☎ 01753 755203

One of the finest military museums in Britain, with comprehensive displays of the uniforms, weapons, horse furniture (tack, regalia, etc) and armour used by the Household Cavalry from 1600 to the present day.
Times: Open all year Mon-Fri (ex BH) 9-12.30 & 2-4.30.
Fee: *Free admission, however a donation would be appreciated.
♿ shop 🏷

LEGOLAND WINDSOR
Winkfield Rd SL4 4AY (on B3022 Windsor to Ascot road well signposted from M3 J3 & M4 J6)
☎ 0990 040404 🖹 01753 626300

Set in 150 acres of Windsor Great Park, Legoland Windsor offers over 40 hands-on activities, with rides, themed playscapes and more Lego bricks that you would ever dream possible. The cities of Europe, recreated in Lego, can be seen in Miniland.

Times: Open daily 13 Mar-Oct
Fee: *£16.50(ch 3-15, £13.50, pen £10.50) Groups 20+.
Tickets can be booked in advance by telephoning 0990
040404.
🅿 💷 ✗ licensed ♿ toilets for disabled shop ✖ (ex guide
dogs) 🍽

ST GEORGE'S CHAPEL

SL4 1NJ
☎ 01753 865538 📠 01753 620165

Begun in 1475 by Edward IV, and completed in
the reign of Henry VIII, the chapel is a fine
example of Perpendicular architecture, with large
windows adding to the effect of light and
spaciousness. The fan vaulting on the ceiling is
magnificent, and the chantries, and intricate
carving on the choir stalls, all add to this superb
building.
Times: Open weekdays 10-4, Sun 2-4. (Closed 26 & 27 Apr,
16-19 Jun, 24-25 Dec & occasionally at short notice).
♿ shop ✖ Details not confirmed for 2000

SAVILL GARDEN (WINDSOR GREAT PARK)

Wick Ln, Englefield Green TW20 0UU (via Wick
Ln, Englefield Green. Signposted off A30
between Egham & Virginia Water)
☎ 01753 847518 📠 01753 847536

The 35 acres include woodland plantings,
rhododendrons and azaleas, magnificent rose
beds and herbaceous borders, dry gardens and
temperate houses, fiery autumn colour and
winter interest.

Times: Open all year, daily 10-6 (10-4 Nov -Feb). (Closed 25-
26 Dec & 31 Dec-1 Jan)
Fee: *£3.80 (ch 16 free, pen £3.30). Party 20+.
🅿 💷 ✗ licensed ♿ (wheelchairs available) toilets for
disabled shop (& plant centre) (ex in the garden) 🍽

WINDSOR CASTLE

SL4 1NJ
☎ 01753 831118 📠 01753 832290

Covering 13 acres, this is the official residence of
HM The Queen and the largest inhabited castle in
the world. Begun as a wooden fort by William
the Conqueror, it has been added to by almost
every monarch since. The Upper Ward includes
the State Apartments, magnificently restored
following the fire of 1992, and the Lower Ward is
where St George's Chapel is situated.
  Queen Mary's Dolls House designed for Queen
Mary in the 1920s by Lutyens, is also displayed at
Windsor Castle. Every piece of furniture,
decoration, tableware and equipment is a
perfectly scaled down version of the real thing.
Times: Open all year, daily except 10 April, 15 June & 25-26
Dec. Nov-Feb 10-4 (last admission 3), Mar-Oct 10am-5.30 (last
admission 4).
🅿 (400yds) ♿ (except The Gallery) toilets for disabled shop
✖ Details not confirmed for 2000 🍽

Bristol

Bristol was once one of the South of England's major ports but is now perhaps better known for its contributions to contemporary art and music. It is an ancient city with a modern outlook, and centuries of history are waiting, ready to be explored by the curious visitor

EVENTS & FESTIVALS

January
8th: Friends of Bristol Art Gallery Fanfare for the Millennium, St Georges Hall

April
30th April-1st May: North Somerset Show, Ashton Court

June
10th-11th (provisional): Bristol Motor & Classic Car Show, Ashton Court

July
1st: St Pauls Carnival, St Pauls
2nd week: Bristol Challenger Tennis Trophy, Bristol Lawn Tennis & Squash Club, Redland Green
15th-16th: Bristol Community Festival, Ashton Court
29th-30th: Lloyds TSB Harbour Regatta, Bristol Harbour

August
12th-14th: Bristol Balloon Fiesta, Ashton Court

September
4th-5th: International Kite Festival, Ashton Court

October
tbc: Bristol Sound 2000, various venues

November
24th-1st: December Brief Encounters Short Film Festival, various venues

Top: SS Great Britain

For centuries ships sailed from Bristol to every part of the known world in search of new produce and markets, opening up international trade routes. In 1497 John Cabot (Giovanni Caboto), a Genoese pilot set sail from Bristol and within months had discovered North America. Four centuries later the Cabot Tower was built in commemoration. In 1843 Brunel launched his SS Great Britain, the largest iron ship then built. She now sits, rescued and restored, in the dock where she was built.

The city's cathedral was founded as an Augustinian monastery and contains examples of Norman, early-English, Gothic and Victorian architecture. Other important church buildings include St Mary Redcliffe, which was built and extended in the Middle Ages and carries a massive tower with a 285ft spire.

Post-war rebuilding of the blitz-damaged city centre means that Bristol's current identity is less defined by its history than by its recent contributions to popular culture and art. Redevelopment of the disused dockland has led to the creation of art spaces such as the Arnolfini and the Watershed, which are at the forefront of uncovering new talent. In music the city has left its mark in the shape of innovative dance acts such as Massive Attack, Roni Size, Tricky and Portishead (the last of which are named after a nearby resort overlooking the Bristol Channel).

BRISTOL

BLAISE CASTLE HOUSE MUSEUM
Henbury Rd, Henbury BS10 7QS (4m NW of city, off B4057)
☎ 0117 950 6789 ▤ 0117 959 3475

Built in the 18th century for a Quaker banker, this mansion is now Bristol's Museum of Social History. Nearby Blaise Hamlet is a picturesque estate village, designed by John Nash.
Times: Open Apr-Oct, Sat-Wed, 10-5.
Fee: Free.
Ⓟ ᛭ shop ✈

BRISTOL CITY MUSEUM & ART GALLERY
Queen's Rd BS8 1RL
☎ 0117 922 3571 ▤ 0117 922 2047

Regional and international collections, representing ancient history, natural sciences, and fine and applied arts. Displays include dinosaurs, Bristol ceramics, silver, Chinese and Japanese ceramics. A full programme of Special Exhibitions take place throughout the year. Ring for details.
Times: Open all year, daily 10-5.
Fee: *Prices under review.
Ⓟ (NCP 400 yds) ▆ ᛭ (lift) toilets for disabled shop ✈

HARVEYS WINE MUSEUM
12 Denmark St BS1 5DQ
☎ 0117 927 5036 ▤ 0117 927 5051

Wine cellars which date back to the 1220s. A wonderful collection of wine-related items - silver and porcelain decanter labels, original corkscrews, rare glassware and Bristol Blue. Displays follow the evolution of the wine bottle, and you can either wander through the cellars independantly, or bring a group of friends and take a guided tour, followed by an informal tutored tasting. If you can't get a group together it is usually possible to join another pre-booked tour. Please telephone for further details.
Times: Open all year, Mon-Sat 10-5. Closed Sun & BH.
Fee: *£4 (concessions £3). Family ticket £8.
Ⓟ (5 mins walk) (parking meters) ✗ licensed shop ✈ ◥

JOHN WESLEY'S CHAPEL (THE NEW ROOM)
36 The Horsefair, Broadmead BS1 3JE
☎ 0117 926 4740

The oldest Methodist chapel in the world, built in 1739 and extended in 1748. John Wesley Day is 24 May, special events are held, please telephone for details.
Times: Open all year, Mon-Sat 10-4. (Jan-Feb 11-2.30)
Fee: *Donation requested. £2.50 for guided tour.
Ⓟ (250yds) ᛭ shop ✈ (ex guide dogs)

SS GREAT BRITAIN
Great Western Dock, Gas Ferry Rd BS1 6TY (off Cumberland Rd)
☎ 0117 926 0680 ▤ 0117 925 5788

Built and launched in Bristol in 1843, the SS Great Britain, designed by Isambard Kingdom Brunel, was the first ocean-going, propeller-driven, iron ship in history. After an active life as a cargo ship, liner and troop ship, she was abandoned in the Falkland Islands in 1886. In 1970 what remained of her rusting carcass was towed back to Bristol and she is now being restored to her original 1843 appearance at the Great Western Dock in which she was built.
Times: Open all year daily 10-5.30, 4.30 in winter. (Closed 24 & 25 Dec).
Ⓟ (charged) ▆ ᛭ shop ✈ *Details not confirmed for 2000*
◥

Buckinghamshire

Visitors to Buckinghamshire cannot fail to be enchanted by the majestic sweep of the Chiltern Hills, and fascinated by the history and heritage of the county's many attractive towns and villages.

Richly wooded in the west but mainly windswept and bare near Ivinghoe in the east, the Chilterns extend in a line from Goring in the Thames Valley, across the breadth of Buckinghamshire, to a point near Hitchin in Hertfordshire. Its highest point is the 835ft Coombe Hill near Wendover. Many of the chalk downs are crowned with ancient beech groves. Walkers can get to grips with the Chilterns by walking the North Bucks Way - 30 miles from Wolverton to Chequers near Great Missenden.

Chequers Court plays an important role as the official country residence of the British Prime Minister. It was given to the nation by Lord Lee of Fareham in thanksgiving for the end of World War I. It sits in acres of parkland and fittingly, contains some valuable Cromwellian relics.

Buckinghamshire is famous for its pretty villages and any one of them would make a visit here worthwhile. Not only are they attractive, but many have strong historical connections. Jordan is the site of the most famous of all Quaker Meeting Houses, which was built in 1688. British Prime Minister, Benjamin Disraeli, lived at Hughenden Manor in Hughenden; John Milton, author of Paradise Lost, lived in a cottage near Chalfont St Giles; Florence Nightingale lived at Claydon House near Buckingham; and in the 17th century, Charles II visited his mistress, Barbara Palmer, Countess of Castlemaine, at Dorney Court near Windsor.

EVENTS & FESTIVALS

March
7th Olney Pancake Day

May
1st (provisional) Marlow Millennium Spring Regatta
7th (provisional) Charity Carnival, The Rye, High Wycombe
21st (provisional) Elizabeth Cullum Memorial Challenge, Princes Risborough

June
11th Churches in Bucks Millennium Festival, Aylesbury
17th Marlow Regatta, Higginson Park, Marlow
18th Millennium Musical, Higginson Park, Marlow

July
14th (provisional) Churches Millennium Event, High Wycombe

August
14th (provisional) Asian Arts 2000, The Rye, High Wycombe

September
2nd (provisional) Millennium Wycombe Show
10th (provisional) Thames Valley Grand Prix Raft Race, Marlow
16th (provisional) Marlow Millennium Carnival, Higginson Park, Marlow

Top: Hughenden Manor

AYLESBURY

The county town of Buckinghamshire since the reign of Henry VIII, Aylesbury has a long and varied history which includes the trials of the Great Train Robbers and The Rolling Stones in the 1960s. Local notables include John Hampden, MP for nearby Wendover, an important figure in the Civil War; John Wilkes, (another MP) a contributor to press freedom; the Rothschild family; Roald Dahl, author; and Sir James Clark Ross, who discovered the magnetic North Pole.

Guttmann Sports Centre annually plays host to the World Wheelchair Games.

⛪ AYLESBURY
BUCKINGHAMSHIRE COUNTY MUSEUM
St Mary's Square, Church St HP20 2QP
☎ 01296 331441   📠 01296 334884

Buckinghamshire's largest museum consists of a range of period buildings, and displays are based on eight county-linked themes, including lacemaking, Romans and Celts, jewellery, and fossils. The Art Gallery shows several exhibitions throughout the year, and various special exhibitions also take place, please telephone for

details. Also on site is the Roald Dahl Children's Gallery.
Times: Open all year, Mon-Sat 10-5, Sun & BHs 2-5. (Closed 25-26 Dec). Roald Dahl Children's Gallery as above in school holidays, Mon-Fri 3-5 term time.
P (200 yds) 🍴 ♿ (purpose built restrooms for disabled chair lifts) toilets for disabled shop ✂ *Details not confirmed for 2000* 💬

⛪ BEACONSFIELD
BEKONSCOT MODEL VILLAGE
Warwick Rd HP9 2PL (2.7m M40 J2, 4m M25 J16).
☎ 01494 672919   📠 01494 675284

A miniature world, depicting rural England in the 1930s. A Gauge 1 model railway meanders

MODEL VILLAGE
Warwick Road, Beaconsfield
Bucks HP9 2PL
Tel: 01494 672919
Fax: 01494 675284
Web site: www.bekonscot.org.uk
The oldest model village in the world

By road: Jct16 M25, then Jct2 M40 · By rail: Marylebone/Beaconsfield/Birmingham
Be a giant in a miniature wonderland of make-believe depicting rural England in the 1930s
Open 19 Feb–31 Oct. Adults £4, Children £2.50, Concessions £3
A little piece of history that is forever England

through six little villages, each with their own tiny population.
Times: Open 19 Feb-31 Oct, daily 10-5.
P **⬛** **&** (wheelchair loan) toilets for disabled shop **✕** (ex guide dogs) *Details not confirmed for 2000*

🏛 CHALFONT ST GILES
CHILTERN OPEN AIR MUSEUM
Newland Park, Gorelands Ln HP8 4AD (follow brown signs)
☎ 01494 871117 & 875542
📄 01494 872774

Among the buildings dismantled and brought to the site are a toll house, cart sheds, stables, granaries, a forge, barns, an Iron Age house, a pair of 18th-century cottages and a 1947 prefab. There's a nature trail through the 45 acres of parkland, and an adventure playground.
Times: 27 Mar-30 Oct, Tue-Sun, BH Mon (August daily 10-5)
Fee: *£4.50 (ch 5-16 £2.50, concessions £3.50) Family £13.
P **⬛** **&** (Braille guide books & taped guides available, wheelchairs) toilets for disabled shop

MILTON'S COTTAGE
Dean Way HP8 4JH (0.5m W of A413. 3m N of M40 J2)
☎ 01494 872313

A timber-framed, 16th-century cottage, with a charming garden, the only surviving home in which John Milton lived and worked. He completed *Paradise Lost* and started *Paradise Regained* here. First editions of these works are among the many rare books and artefacts on display.
Times: Open Mar-Oct, Tue-Sun 10-1 & 2-6. Also open Spring & Summer BH.
Fee: *£2 (ch 15 60p). Party 20+.
P **✕** licensed **&** (special parking area closer to cottage) shop
✕

🏛 CLIVEDEN
CLIVEDEN
SL6 0JA (2m N of Taplow)
☎ 01628 605069   📄 01628 669461

The 375 acres of garden and woodland overlook the River Thames, and include a magnificent parterre, topiary, lawns with box hedges, and rose and water gardens. The palatial house, home of the Astors, is now a hotel, 3 rooms only of the house can be visited on certain afternoons.
Times: Open Grounds Mar-2 Nov daily 11-6, Nov-Dec daily 11-4 (Woodlands only 1 Mar-1 Nov). House Apr-Oct, Thu & Sun 3-6 by timed ticket. (Last admission 5.30)
P **✕** licensed **&** (powered vehicle & wheelchairs available) toilets for disabled shop **✕** (ex in woodland) **😺** *Details not confirmed for 2000*

🏛 HIGH WYCOMBE
WYCOMBE LOCAL HISTORY & CHAIR MUSEUM
Castle Hill House, Priory Av HP13 6PX (5mins walk from town centre & 2 mins walk from rail station)
☎ 01494 421895   📄 01494 421897

Situated in an 18th-century house, set in attractive grounds. The displays explore the history of the Wycombe area, focusing on the chair making industry, with interactive displays, and changing exhibitions.
Times: Open all year, Mon-Sat 10-5, Sun (seasonal-please telephone for details). Closed on BHs except special events - ring for details.
Fee: Free.
P **&** toilets for disabled shop **✕** (ex guide dogs)

🏛 HUGHENDEN
HUGHENDEN MANOR
HP14 4LA (1.5m N of High Wycombe, on W side of A4128)
☎ 01494 532580

Benjamin Disraeli, later Earl of Beaconsfield and twice Prime Minister, bought the house in 1847 and lived there until his death in 1881. It still has many of his books and other possessions.
Times: House open 1-30 Mar, Sat & Sun only. Apr-Oct, Wed-Sun & BH Mon 1-5. Last admission 4.30. Gardens same dates as house 12-5. Park open all year. (closed on Good Friday)
P **⬛** **&** (braille leaflet and taped guide) toilets for disabled shop **✕** (ex in park & car park only) **😺** *Details not confirmed for 2000*

🏛 LONG CRENDON
COURTHOUSE
HP18 9AN (2m N of Thame, via B4011)

Probably built as a wool store in the early 1400s, but also used as a manorial courthouse until the late 19th century, this timber-framed building stands out, even in this picturesque village of 16th- and 17th-century cottages. Although the windows and doors have been altered and the chimney stack is Tudor, the magnificent timber roof is original.
Times: Open, Upper storey Apr-Sep, Wed 2-6, Sat, Sun & BH Mons 11-6.
P (street) **✕** **😺** *Details not confirmed for 2000*

🏛 MIDDLE CLAYDON
CLAYDON HOUSE
MK18 2EY (off A413, entrance by North drive only).
☎ 01296 730349   🖥 01296 738511

The rather sober exterior of this 18th-century house gives no clue to the extravagances that lie inside, in the form of fantastic rococo carvings. Ceilings, cornices, walls and overmantels are adorned with delicately carved fruits, birds, beasts and flowers by Luke Lightfoot, and his Chinese room is particularly splendid.
Times: Open 4 Apr-1 Nov: Sat-Wed 1-5pm, Closed Good Friday. Last admission 4.30pm.
🅿 💺 ⅋ (Braille guide) toilets for disabled 🐕 (ex car park)
♨ *Details not confirmed for 2000*

🏛 STOWE
STOWE HOUSE
MK18 5EH
☎ 01280 813164 ext 282
🖥 01280 816070

Set in the National Trust's landscaped gardens, Stowe is a splendid 18th-century mansion. The leading designers of the day were called in to lay out the gardens, and leading architects - Vanbrugh, Gibbs, Kent and Leoni - commissioned to decorate them with garden temples. The house is now a major public school.
Times: Open 22 Mar-11 Apr & 5 Jul-3 Sep. Daily 2-5pm, 12-5pm Sun. May occasionally be closed if booked for private functions. Please ring for confirmation.
Fee: *£2 (ch £1).
🅿 ⅋ shop 🐕 (ex guide dogs) ♨

STOWE LANDSCAPE GARDENS
MK18 5EH (3m NW of Buckingham)
☎ 01280 822850   🖥 01280 822437

One of the supreme creations of the Georgian era, the first, formal layout was adorned with buildings by Vanbrugh, Kent and Gibbs. In the 1730s Kent designed the Elysian Fields in a more naturalistic style, and it's one of the earliest examples of the reaction against formality, which lead to the evolution of the landscape garden.
Times: Open 20 Mar-11 Apr, daily; 12 Apr-4 Jul, Mon, Wed, Fri & Sun; 5 Jul-5 Sep daily; 6 Sep-31 Oct, Mon, Wed, Fri & Sun; 11-23 Dec daily. 10-5 (or dusk if earlier). Last admission 1hr before closing. (Closed 24-26 Dec).
Fee: *£4.50(ch £2.25). Family ticket £11.50
🅿 💺 ⅋ (unsuitable manual wheelchairs, powered batricars available) toilets for disabled shop ♨

🏛 WADDESDON
WADDESDON MANOR
HP18 0JH (gates off A41)
☎ 01296 651211   🖥 01296 651293

Designed by the French architect Destaileur in the 1870s for Baron Ferdinand de Rothschild. The Renaissance style château was conceived as a showcase for the Baron's collection of works of art, which includes Sèvres porcelain as well as portraits by Gainsborough and Reynolds, and works by Dutch and Flemish masters of the 17th century. The wine cellars, which house more than 15,000 bottles of Rothschild wine, are also open to the public. The garden includes a rococo-style aviary, shrubberies and woodland. Many events are organised throughout the year including floodlit openings, wine tastings, garden workshops and collection study days. Please ring 01296 651226 for details.
Times: Open, Grounds & Aviary only, Mar-20 Dec, Wed-Sun & BH Mon 10-5. House 2 Apr-1 Nov, Thu-Sun & BH Mon 11-4, also open Wed in Jul & Aug. Entrance by timed ticket.
🅿 🗙 licensed ⅋ (wheelchairs available braille guide) toilets for disabled shop 🐕 (ex guide dogs in grounds) ♨ *Details not confirmed for 2000* ♨

🏛 WEST WYCOMBE
WEST WYCOMBE PARK
HP14 3AJ (S of A40)
☎ 01628 488675

Set in 300 acres of beautiful parkland, the house was rebuilt in the Palladian style, between 1745 and 1771, for Sir Francis Dashwood. Of particular note are the painted ceilings by Borgnis. The park was laid out in the 18th century and given an artificial lake and classical temples.
Times: Open, House & grounds Jun-Aug, Sun-Thu 2-6. Grounds only 1 Apr-end May, Sun & Wed 2-6 & Etr, May Day & Spring BH Sun & Mon 2-6. Last admission 5.15. Entry by timed tickets on wkdays. Parties must book in advance.
🅿 ⅋ (partial access to ground floor & gardens) 🐕 ♨ *Details not confirmed for 2000*

🏛 WING
ASCOTT
LU7 0PS (0.5m E, on S side of A418)
☎ 01296 688242   🖥 01296 681904

The house, once the property of the de Rothschilds, houses a collection of French and Chippendale furniture, pictures by Hogarth, Gainsborough and Rubens, and an outstanding collection of Oriental porcelain. Outside there are 260 acres of grounds, with many unusual trees, thousands of naturalised bulbs, and a formal garden.
Times: Open: Apr-7 May daily ex Mon 2-6: 13 May-30 Aug Wed & Sun 2-6.
🅿 ⅋ (wheelchairs available) toilets for disabled 🐕 ♨ *Details not confirmed for 2000*

Cambridgeshire

The City of Cambridge is the place that visitors will want to visit most, and who can blame them? It's ancient colleges, air of learning and rich history are guaranteed to be of interest to anyone looking for a special taste of England. Yet there is much more to the county.

EVENTS & FESTIVALS

March
2nd-4th Pageant 2000, Ely Cathedral, 7.30pm, using drama, music & light to celebrate 2000 years of life in Cambridgeshire, Ely

April
8th-9th Daffodil Weekend, Thriplow
30th (provisional) Duxford Air Show, Duxford

June
16th-18th East of England Show, Peterborough
28th-2nd July Wisbech Rose Fair

July
28th-2nd June Wisbech Rose Fair
8th-9th (provisional) Duxford Air Show, Duxford

September
9th-10th (provisional) Duxford Air Show, Duxford

October
15th (provisional) Duxford Air Show, Duxford

Much of Cambridgeshire remains unspoilt and is ideal for exploration. Many of the peat-black Fens have been reclaimed over the centuries, and beautiful rivers such as the Ouse and the Nene, as well as miles of canal, are all perfect for visitors looking for a relaxed pace of life. 750 acres of undrained fenland at Wicken Fen have been retained by the National Trust as a nature reserve.

Walkers are well catered for, with over 3,000 miles of public footpaths to explore. Routes include the Fen Rivers Way, the Hereward Way, and the Nene Way.

But Cambridgeshire isn't all peace and quiet. Peterborough has modern arcades as well as lots of old streets that have been pedestrianised. Huntingdon, Ely, Wisbech, St Neots and St Ives have all retained something of the atmosphere of the English market town, complete with family-run shops and busy market days.

The county also has many connections with important historical figures. Katherine of Aragon is buried in Peterborough's Norman cathedral, Wisbech is home to the Octavia Hill Birth Place Museum, commemorating the life and work of one of the founders of the National Trust, and Lord High Protector Oliver Cromwell was born in Huntingdon.

Top: Peterborough Cathedral

CAMBRIDGE

Cambridge is one of the world's foremost seats of learning, a distinction it shares with Oxford, although it is worth noting that Cambridge's first students were those who had fled from Oxford in the 13th century to avoid being hanged in anti-scholar riots!

Many of the 31 colleges that make up the University can be visited: among them, Peterhouse, the oldest, founded in 1284; Kings, with its famous chapel; and many others, dating from medieval times to the most recent, Robinson, which was added in 1977. The University 'Backs' lining the River Cam are famous for their spring flowers.

CAMBRIDGE

FITZWILLIAM MUSEUM

Trumpington St CB2 1RB

☎ 01223 332900 🖹 01223 332923

The Fitzwilliam is the art museum of the University of Cambridge and one of the oldest public museums in Britain. Exhibits include ancient art and sculpture, pottery, glass, furniture, clocks, armour, ceramics, rugs, coins, medals, and manuscripts as well as masterpieces by painters including Picasso, Monet, Constable and Titian.

Times: Open all year Tue-Sat 10-5, Sun 2.15-5 plus Etr Mon, Spring & Summer BH. (Closed Good Fri, May Day & 24 Dec-1 Jan).

Fee: Free.

P (400 yds) (2hr max, metered) 🍺 ♿ (preferably pre-arranged) toilets for disabled shop ✖ 🐕

SCOTT POLAR RESEARCH INSTITUTE MUSEUM

Lensfield Rd CB2 1ER

☎ 01223 336540 🖹 01223 336549

An international centre for polar studies, including a museum featuring displays of Arctic and Antarctic expeditions, with special emphasis on those of Captain Scott. Other exhibits include Eskimo work and other arts of the polar regions, as well as displays on current scientific exploration. A special exhibition is presented every summer, and public lectures run from October to December and February to April.

Times: Open all year, Mon-Sat 2.30-4. Closed for some public & university hols.

Fee: Free.

P (400mtrs) ♿ shop ✖

UNIVERSITY BOTANIC GARDEN

Cory Lodge, Bateman St CB2 1JF (1.5m S of city centre)

☎ 01223 336265 🖹 01223 336278

Founded in 1762, and transferred to its present site in 1846, the Garden covers 40 acres, with collections of trees and shrubs; botanical groups of herbaceous perennials, and a lake. The glasshouses contain sub-tropical and tropical plants. Features include a Scented Garden and collection of native British plants, and the Gardens hold nine National Collections, including Geranium, Tulip and Alchemilla.

Times: Open all year daily 10-6 (summer), 10-5 (autumn & spring), (10-4) winter. Glasshouses 10-12.30 & 2-3.45. Closed 25-26 Dec. Entry by Bateman St and Station Rd gates on weekdays & by Bateman Street gate only at weekends & BH.

Fee: *£2 (ch & pen £1.50).

P (on street parking bays-pay & display) 🍺 ♿ (scented garden for the visually impaired) toilets for disabled shop ✖ (ex guide dogs)

UNIVERSITY MUSEUM OF ARCHAEOLOGY & ANTHROPOLOGY

Downing St CB2 3DZ

☎ 01223 337733   ▤ 01223 333517

Covering humanity's development from the earliest times throughout the world, with anthropology displays and extensive sections on British archaeology and local archaeology in particular.

Times: Open all year Tues-Sat 2-4.30.(Closed 1 wk Etr, Aug BH & 24 Dec-2 Jan)

Fee: Free.

P (100yds) (severely limited short-term parking) ♿ (lift available) shop ✕

⛪ DUXFORD

DUXFORD AIRFIELD

CB2 4QR (off J10 of M11 on A505)

☎ 01223 835000   ▤ 01223 837267

This former Battle of Britain fighter station, with hangars dating from World War I, is home to most of the Imperial War Museum's collection of military aircraft, armoured fighting vehicles, midget submarines and other large exhibits. Also on display is the Duxford Aviation Society's collection of civil aircraft. Major flying displays are held in summer, and pleasure flights can be taken during summer weekends. Please telephone for details.

Times: Open all year, mid Mar-mid Oct daily 10-6; mid Oct-mid Mar daily 10-4. (Closed 24-26 Dec)

Fee: *£7.20 (pen £5 & students £3.50). Ch under 16yrs free. Parties.

P ▣ ✕ licensed ♿ (wheelchair available-phone in advance) toilets for disabled shop ✕ ➡

⛪ ELY

ELY CATHEDRAL

CB7 4DL

☎ 01353 667735   ▤ 01353 665658

The Octagon Tower of Ely Cathedral can be seen for miles as it rises above the surrounding flat fenland. A monastery was founded on the site by St Etheldreda in 673, but the present cathedral church dates from 1083 and is a magnificent example of Romanesque architecture.

Times: Open daily, summer 7am-7pm, winter 7.30-6 (5pm Sun).

Fee: *£3.50 (concessions £3). Ch free in family group.

P ▣ ✕ licensed ♿ toilets for disabled shop ✕ (ex guide dogs)

THE STAINED GLASS MUSEUM

The Cathedral CB7 4DN (situated inside Ely Cathedral)

☎ 01353 660347   ▤ 01223 327367

Situated in the cathedral, this museum is the only one of its kind in the country. Case exhibits show how stained-glass windows are designed and made, and there is an exhibition of approximately 100 panels dating from the 13th century to the present day, displayed at eye level in back-lit cases. The museum is undergoing

refurbishment and may be closed for one or two months. Please ring to avoid disappointment.

Times: Open daily, Mon-Fri 10.30-4.30, Sat & BH 10.30-5 & Sun 12-6.

Fee: *£2.50 (ch, students & pen £1.50). Party 10+.

P 400yds ▣ shop ✕ (ex guide dogs)

⛪ LINTON

LINTON ZOOLOGICAL GARDENS

Hadstock Rd CB1 6NT (exit M11 at J9/10, situated on B1052 off A604/A1307, signposted)

☎ 01223 891308   ▤ 01223 891308

Conservation and education are the main concerns of this zoo, and the many species of animals and birds are housed in 16 acres of landscaped enclosures as close to their natural habitats as possible. A special education programme enhances and complements the conservation work and includes days when you can meet and touch boa constrictors, as well as other reptiles, bats, parrots and owls.

Times: Open daily 10-6 or dusk (ex 25 Dec). Last admission 1 hour before closing time.

Fee: *£4.50 (ch 2-13 £3.50, pen £4.25).

P ▣ ♿ toilets for disabled shop ✕ ➡

⛪ LODE

ANGLESEY ABBEY

CB5 9EJ (6m NE of Cambridge on B1102 (signposted from A14).)

☎ 01223 811200   ▤ 01223 811200

A medieval undercroft has survived from the priory founded here in 1135, but the house dates mainly from 1600. Thomas Hobson of 'Hobson's Choice' was one of the owners. A later owner was Lord Fairhaven, who amassed the huge collection of pictures, and laid out the beautiful gardens.

Times: Open House: 21 Mar-11 Oct, Wed-Sun & BH Mon 1-5; closed Good Fri. Garden: 21 Mar-1 Nov, Wed-Sun & BH Mon 11-5.30; 6 Jul-13 Sep, daily 11-5.30; Lode Mill: 21 Mar-1 Nov, Wed-Sun & BH Mons 1pm-5pm. Last admission 4.30pm. 'Snowdrop' weekends 7/8, 14/15, 21/22 Feb 11am-4pm.

P ▣ ✕ licensed ♿ (electric buggy, braille guide) toilets for disabled shop garden centre ✕ (ex guide dogs) ✤ *Details not confirmed for 2000* ➡

⛪ PETERBOROUGH

LONGTHORPE TOWER

☎ 01733 268482

The main attraction of this medieval fortified house are the rare wall paintings of religious and educational subjects, which are the finest surviving in Northern Europe.

Times: Open Apr-1 Nov, daily 10-6 (or dusk if earlier). Wknds & BH's 12-5.

✕ ✜ *Details not confirmed for 2000*

Fee: £1.40 (ch 70p).

PETERBOROUGH CATHEDRAL
PE1 1XS (access from A1 juncts with A605 or A47)
☎ 01733 343342 📠 01733 52465

Behind the huge Early English arches and Perpendicular porch of the West Front is one of the finest examples of Norman architecture in the country, with superb examples of early rib-vaulting and a magnificent Norman apse. The painted wooden ceiling dates from 1220.
Times: Open all year, daily 8.30-5.15 (8pm summer)
P (300yds) (no parking within cathedral precincts) ⬛ ♿ (touch & hearing centre, braille guide, ramps to grnd floor) shop ✖ (ex guide dogs or in grounds) *Details not confirmed for 2000* 🔖

▥ WANSFORD
NENE VALLEY RAILWAY
Wansford Station, Stibbington PE8 6LR (A1 west of Peterborough)
☎ 01780 784444 📠 01780 784440

Seven-and-a-half miles of track through the picturesque Nene Valley, and locomotives and rolling stock from Europe and the UK. There's a museum and engine shed, and facilities for the disabled at Wansford, as well as a specially adapted carriage on each train. Please telephone for details of special events.
Times: Open end Feb-Etr, Sun; Apr-June, Sep-end Oct, wknds; May, June & Jul, Wed; Aug, daily ex Mondays, (but inc BH Mondays). Some midweek days at other times.
Fee: *£7.50 (ch £3.50, other concessions £6). Family ticket £17.50.
P ⬛ ♿ (disabled access to trains) toilets for disabled shop 🔖

▥ WIMPOLE
WIMPOLE HALL
SG8 0BW (M11 J12, 8miles SW of Cambridge off A603)
☎ 01223 207257 📠 01223 207838

Although Wimpole Hall is one of the grandest mansions in East Anglia, it is perhaps the 360 acres of parkland that make it unusual, devised and planted by no less than four celebrated landscape designers, Charles Bridgeman, `Capability' Brown, Sanderson Miller and Humphrey Repton. The house dates back to 1640, but was altered into a large 18th-century mansion with a Georgian façade. The chapel has a wonderful painted trompe l'oeil ceiling, and the garden has two restored parterres. Ring for details of special events.
Times: Open 14-Mar-1 Nov, Tue-Thu, Sat & Sun & Good Fri 1-5, BH Sun & Mon 11-5. Also open Fri in Aug 1-5.
P ⬛ ✖ licensed ♿ (braille guide, battery operated vehicle, stairlift) toilets for disabled shop ✖ (ex park only) 🐾 *Details not confirmed for 2000* 🔖

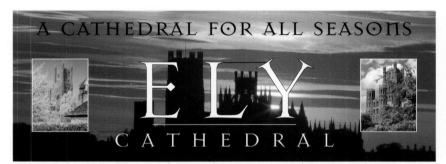

WIMPOLE HOME FARM
SG8 0BW (M11 J12 8m SW of Cambridge
off A603)
☎ 01223 207257 📄 01223 207838

When built in 1794, the Home Farm was one of
the most advanced agricultural enterprises in the
country. The Great Barn, now restored, holds a
display of farm machinery and implements of the
kind used at Wimpole over the past two
centuries. On the farm there are rare breeds of
domestic animals. Please ring for details of
special events.

Times: Open 14 Mar-1 Nov, Tue-Thu & Sat-Sun; daily Aug;
Good Fri & Mon 10.30-5; 3 Nov-6 Mar Sat & Sun 11-4. (Closed
Xmas & New Year).

P ⬛ ✗ licensed & (braille guide) toilets for disabled shop
✗ ✖ *Details not confirmed for 2000* ⬎

⚏ WISBECH
PECKOVER HOUSE & GARDEN
North Bank PE13 1JR
☎ 01945 583463 📄 01945 583463

Peckover House is Georgian, and is named after
a banker who purchased the house in 1777. The
interior has Rococo decoration in plaster and
wood. The two-acre garden is a delightful and
colourful example of Victorian planting, and in
the kitchen garden there are greenhouses with
orange trees still bearing fruit after 250 years.

Times: Open, House, Garden & Tearoom 28 Mar-1 Nov,
wknds, Wed & BH Mon 12.30-5.30pm. Garden only: Apr-Oct,
Mon & Tue & Thur 12.30-5.30.

P (400yds) ⬛ & toilets for disabled ✗ ✖ *Details not
confirmed for 2000*

WISBECH & FENLAND MUSEUM
Museum Square PE13 1ES (on A17)
☎ 01945 583817 📄 01945 589050

Purpose-built in 1847, this museum retains
almost all of its original cases and fittings, and
contains a fine collection of ceramics and *objets
d'art*, as well as local and natural history
displays. Parish Registers, and a collection of
over 14,000 books including early manuscripts,
originally forming the library of the literary
society, are in the town library. There is a
programme of special exhibitions and evening
lectures. A Wisbech Millenium Exhibition will be
held early 2000.

Times: Open all year, Tue-Sat 10-5 (4pm Oct-Mar). Closed
Xmas.

Fee: *Free. (Museum libraries & archives available by
appointment only).

P (100 yds) shop ✗

Cheshire

Bordered by Wales and the metropoli of Liverpool and Manchester, Cheshire has a rich history that can be seen in its wealth of Roman heritage, black and white buildings, and industrial waterways. The county also boasts some beautiful countryside and a strong tradition of floral excellence.

From the invasion of the Romans who made Chester one of their major garrisons, to skirmishes with Norsemen during the Dark Ages, Cheshire has been the scene of many conflicts. The area was also the base for Hugh the Wolf's violent reign in the 11th century, and the setting for the some of the fiercest battles of the Civil War, including the seige of Chester. Clearly, life is less stressful now, but the history of the county is far from forgotten.

Cheshire's canals, part of which form a ring of around 100 miles (151km) of waterways, are the ideal way to explore by foot or by boat. The county has over 200 miles (302 km) of man-made waterways - more than any other county in England - and is a centre for boating holidays. Ellesmere Port has a Boat Museum which has preserved many of the vessels used for both inland and sea travel, from a small weedcutter to a 300-ton coaster. Cheshire's canals also played in important part in the salt and silk industries which contributed to the county's success. The museums detailing these industries are in Northwich and Macclesfield respectively.

Cheshire is full of gardens. From the acres of orangeries and Japanese gardens surrounding the stately homes, to the town parks of Crewe and Congleton, the county is a feast of flowers, lawns and landscaping. Even many private gardens are showpieces of gardening expertise.

EVENTS & FESTIVALS

January
31st Dec-1st Overnight Vigil at Chester Cathedral
2nd Civic Rededication Service, Chester Cathedral

April
28th Pentice Court Procession, parade of Freemen of the City

May
2nd-4th (provisional) Chester Races
13th-14th Chester Carnival
13th Lord Mayor's Show
29th Warrington Horse Show

June
5th-31st July Chester Mystery Plays 2000
9th-11th Ness Botanic Gardens Festival
20th-21st Cheshire Show
24th-25th Midsummer Watch Parade, Chester

July
9th-17th Cheshire Pilgrimage
22nd-25th (provisional) RHS Flower Show, Knutsford

September
6th-10th Flower Festival, Chester Cathedral

November
1st-5th December Chester & District Festival of Trees

Top: The Bridestones, Congleton

CHESTER

Established by the Romans as Fortress Deva some 2000 years ago, Chester has been attracting visitors ever since. The city's defensive walls were built as protection from attacks by the Welsh but have since been partially converted into a leisurely promenade.

Even though the once-important harbour has long ago silted up, Chester has retained much of its vitality and affluence in its role as county town. It was a major force in the Industrial Revolution and has many remnants of that time, including the Eastgate Clock, which was erected in honour of Queen Victoria's jubilee.

BEESTON
BEESTON CASTLE
CW6 9TX (on minor road off A49 or A41)
☎ 01829 260464

This ruined 13th-century stronghold was built by the Earl Ranuf of Chester on a steep and inaccessible hillside. The remains of the inner and outer wards can still be seen and there is an exhibition of the castle's history.
Times: Open all year, Apr-1 Nov, daily 10-6 (or dusk if earlier); 2 Nov-31 Mar daily 10-4.
P shop ✸ (in certain areas) ‖
Fee: £2.80 (ch £1.40).

CHESTER
CHESHIRE MILITARY MUSEUM
The Castle CH1 2DN
☎ 01244 327617   📄 01244 327617

Exhibits from the history of the Cheshire Regiment, Cheshire Yeomanry, 5th Royal Inniskilling Dragoon Guards, and 3rd Carabiniers. Display of the work of George Jones, Victorian battle artist, and an exhibition of life in barracks in the 1950's.
Times: Open all year, daily 10-5 (last entry 4.30pm). (Closed 22 Dec-2 Jan).
Fee: *£1 (ch & pen 50p).
P (within 400yds) & shop

CHESTER CATHEDRAL
Saint Werburgh St CH1 2HU (opposite the town hall)
☎ 01244 324756   📄 01244 341110

Founded as a Benedictine monastery in 1092 on the sites of earlier churches, in 1541 it became the cathedral church of the newly created Diocese of Chester and is an unusually well preserved example of a medieval monastic complex. Restored in the 19th century, the building contains work by Gilbert Scott, Clayton, Pugin and Kempe. There are daily services and visitors are welcome to join in. A summer music festival is held during the last two weeks of July and a flower festival from 6-10 Sept.
Times: Open daily 7.30-6.30 (subject to alteration).
Fee: *Donation of £2 per person requested.
P (multi-storey) ▱ ✕ licensed & (induction loop, tactile model) toilets for disabled shop ✸

CHESTER VISITOR CENTRE
Vicars Ln CH1 1QX (opposite Roman Amphitheatre)
☎ 01244 351609   📄 01244 403188

Over 2000 years of Chester's history, illustrated by a video and a reconstruction of a scene in the Chester Rows during Victorian times. Guided tours depart regularly from the Centre, and there

are working craft shops. Craft fairs take place on Bank Holiday weekends.
Times: Open: Nov-Apr 10-5 Mon-Sat, 10-4 Sun. May-Oct 9-6.30 Mon-Sat, 10-5 Sun & BH.
Fee: Free.
P (200yds) (short stay visitor parking) 🚐 ⚹ (ramped access from Vicars lane) toilets for disabled shop 🍴

CHESTER ZOO
Upton-By-Chester CH2 1LH (2m N of city centre off A41)
☎ 01244 380280 ☐ 01244 371273

The largest zoological gardens in the UK, with 5000 animals in 500 species, Chester Zoo is acclaimed for its conservation work and award winning gardens. There are large outdoor islands for chimps, orang-utans and monkeys; a children's farm; penguin pool; elephant island; and birds of prey. The Bat Cave is the largest enclosure in the world for endangered bat species.
Times: Open all year, daily from 10. Closing times vary with season from 7am high summer to 4.30 winter. (Closed 25 Dec).
P 🚐 ✗ licensed ⚹ (electric scooters-prebooked audio guide for blind) toilets for disabled shop ✗ *Details not confirmed for 2000* 🍴

DEVA ROMAN EXPERIENCE
Pierpoint Ln, (off Bridge St) CH1 1NL (city centre)
☎ 01244 343407 ☐ 01244 347737

Stroll along reconstructed streets experiencing the sights, sounds and smells of Roman Chester.

From the streets of Deva (the Roman name for Chester) you return to the present day on an extensive archeological 'dig', where you can discover the substantial Roman, Saxon and medieval remains beneath the modern city.
Times: Open daily 9-5. Closed 25-26 Dec. New year times to be confirmed.
Fee: *£3.95 (ch £2.25, under 5's free, pen £3.50, student £3.50). Family ticket £11. Group rate £3.
P (200yds) ⚹ shop ✗ (ex guide dogs)

GROSVENOR MUSEUM
27 Grosvenor St CH1 2DD
☎ 01244 402008 ☐ 01244 347587

This award-winning museum tells the story of the Roman army in Chester, and has a reconstructed Roman graveyard full of original tombstones. There are period rooms which date from the 1680s to the 1920s; and a Natural History Gallery.
Times: Open all year, Mon-Sat 10.30-5, Sun 2-5. (Closed Good Fri, 24-26 Dec & 1 Jan).
P (440yds) 🚐 ⚹ shop ✗ *Details not confirmed for 2000* 🍴

🏛 CHOLMONDELEY
CHOLMONDELEY CASTLE GARDENS
SY14 8AH (off A49/A41)
☎ 01829 720383 ☐ 01829 720383

Dominated by a romantic Gothic Castle built in 1801 of local sandstone, the gardens are
contd.

imaginatively laid out with fine trees and water gardens, and have been extensively replanted with rhododendrons, azaleas, cornus, acer and other acid loving plants. There is also a rose and lavender garden, lovely lakeside and woodland walks, and rare breeds of farm animals, inlcuding llamas. Special events are held throughout the year, please telephone for details.
Times: Open Apr-Sep, Wed-Thu, Sun & BH 11.30-5.
Fee: *£3 (ch £1, pen £2.50).
P ⬛ & (disabled car park near tearoom) toilets for disabled shop garden centre

🏛 DISLEY
LYME PARK
SK12 2NX (off A6, 6.5m SE of Stockport)
☎ 01663 762023   🖹 01663 765035

Home of the Legh family for 600 years and the largest house in Cheshire, Lyme Park featured as Pemberley in the BBC's production of Pride and Prejudice. Parts of the original Elizabethan house remain, with 18th and 19th century additions. Set in extensive historic gardens with a lake and also a 1,400 acre park, home to red and fallow deer.
Times: Open - Hall, 29 Mar-31 Oct, 1-5. (Closed Wed/Thur).Telephone for details (01663) 766492. Park all year, Gardens Apr-Oct Fri-Tue 11-5, Wed-Thur 1-5. For winter opening ring for details.
Fee: *House & Garden £4.50; House only £3.50; Garden only £2. Family ticket £12. Park £5.50 per car. Combined family ticket £15.
P ⬛ ✕ licensed & (by arrangement) toilets for disabled shop ✈ (ex park on lead) 🐾

🏛 ELLESMERE PORT
BOAT MUSEUM
South Pier Rd L65 4FW
☎ 0151 355 5017   🖹 0151 355 4079

Occupying a historic dock complex at the junction of the Shropshire Union and Manchester Ship Canals, this museum has more than 60 floating craft, from a small weedcutter to a 300-ton coaster, many of which can be explored. Boat trips are also available. There are indoor exhibitions on canal life and local history, together with period worker's cottages, a

blacksmith's forge and working engines. Many special events and craft courses take place throughout the year.
Times: Open Summer daily 10-5. Winter daily (ex Thu & Fri) 11-4. (Closed 25 & 26 Dec).
Fee: *£5.70 (ch £3.70, pen £4.30, student £4.20). Family ticket £16.50.
P ⬛ & (resources pack for blind & deaf) toilets for disabled shop 🚩

🏛 JODRELL BANK SCIENCE CENTRE & ARBORETUM
JODRELL BANK SCIENCE CENTRE, PLANETARIUM & ARBORETUM
SK11 9DL (A535 Holmes Chapel to Chelford rd)
☎ 01477 571339   🖹 01477 571695

The Lovell telescope is one of the largest fully-steerable radio telescopes in the world, and the Science Centre features exhibitions on space, energy, astronomy and space art. Interactive exhibits help you get to grips with science. Outside, there are 35 acres of beautiful tree-lined walkways in the Arboretum. Ring for details of holiday activities and temporary exhibitions.
Times: Open summer 3rd weekend in Mar-last weekend in Oct, 10.30-5.30: winter Nov-mid Mar. Tue-Sun 11-4.30. (ex 20-26 Dec/New Year).
Fee: *£4.30 (ch £2.10, pen £3) includes Exhibition, Planetarium, Arboretum & Environmental Discovery Centre. Family ticket £12.50. Children under 5 not admitted to the Planetarium.
P ⬛ & (Audio loop, wheelchair loan) toilets for disabled shop ✈ (ex guide dogs)

🏛 KNUTSFORD
TABLEY HOUSE
WA16 0HB (leave M6 J9 onto A556 S towards Chester. Entrance for cars off A5033, 2m W of Knutsford)
☎ 01565 750151   🖹 01565 653230

Home of the Leicester family since 1272, the present magnificent 18th-century mansion has the first great collection of English pictures, furniture by Chippendale, and fascinating family memorabilia. Friendly stewards are available to talk about the Leicester's 700 years at Tabley.
Times: Open Thu-Sun & BH, 2 Apr-31 Oct, 2-5 (last entry 4.30).
Fee: *£4 (ch & students £1.50)
P ⬛ & (Phone administrator in advance for help) toilets for disabled shop ✈

TATTON PARK
WA16 6QN (5m from M6, J19, or M56 J7)
☎ 01625 534400   🖹 01625 534403

Tatton is one of England's most complete historic estates, with gardens and a 1000-acre country park. The centrepiece is the great Georgian mansion, with gardens laid out by Humphrey Repton and Sir Joseph Paxton. More recently, a Japanese garden with a Shinto temple was created. The Tudor Old Hall is the original manor house, where a guided tour is available. There is a regular programme of special events. Please telephone for details.

Times: Open Apr-Sep, Park 10.30-6, Gardens, 10.30-5 Mansion & Farm 12-4. Old Hall (guided tours only), (all ex Park closed Mon ex BH Mon); 1-24 Oct Mansion, Farm & Old Hall wknds only; 25 Oct-Mar, Park 11-5, Gardens 11-4. (Closed Mon & 24-25 Dec), Farm Sun only & Shop 11.30-4. (Last admission 1hr before closure).

Fee: * Mansion £3 (ch 4-15 £2) Family £8; Gardens £3 (ch 4-15 £2) Family £8; Old Hall £3 (ch 4-15 £2) Family £8; Farm & stables £2.50 (ch 15 £1.50) Family £8. Any two attractions £4.50 (ch 4-15 £2.50) Family £12.50.

🅿 (charged) 💷 ♿ (Old Hall & areas of Farm not accessible) toilets for disabled shop garden centre ✈ (ex in Park) 🐕 🍴

🏛 MACCLESFIELD
HARE HILL
SK10 4QB (4m N off B5087)
☎ 01625 828981

The beautiful parkland at Hare Hill also features a pretty walled garden and pergola. There are woodland paths and ponds, and, in late spring, a brilliant display of rhododendrons and azaleas.

Times: Open 3 Apr-30 Oct Wed, Thu, Sat, Sun & BH Mons 10-5.30. Parties by written appointment with the Head Gardener. Special openings (to see rhododendrons & azaleas) 10 May-31 May daily 10-5.30; (Closed Nov-Mar).

Fee: *£2.50 (ch £1.25). £1.50 per car (refundable on entry to garden).

🅿 (charged) ♿ (wheelchair available braille guides) ✈ (ex guide dogs) 🐕

MACCLESFIELD SILK MUSEUM
Heritage Centre, Roe St SK11 6UT (follow brown signs)
☎ 01625 613210 📠 01625 617880

The story of silk in Macclesfield, told through a colourful audio-visual programme, exhibitions, textiles, garments, models and room settings. The Silk Museum is part of the Heritage Centre, which runs a full programme of musical and artistic events throughout the year.

Times: Open all year, Mon-Sat 11-5, Sun & BH Mon 1-5. (Closed Good Fri, 24-26 Dec & 1 Jan)

Fee: *£2.70 (concessions £1.90). Family ticket £7.20 Joint ticket with Paradise Mill £4.75 (concessions £2.70). Family ticket £7.20.

🅿 (50m) 💷 ✗ licensed ♿ (ramps & chairlift) toilets for disabled shop ✈ 🍴

PARADISE MILL
Park Ln SK11 6TJ
☎ 01625 618228

A working silk mill until 1981, with restored looms in their original settings. Knowledgeable guides, many of them former silk mill workers, illustrate the silk production process with the

contd.

help of demonstrations from weavers. Exhibitions and room settings give an impression of working conditions at the mill during the 1930s.

Times: Open all year, BH Mon & Tue-Sun 1-5 (1-4 in winter). (Closed Good Fri, 24-26 Dec & 1 Jan).

Fee: *£2.70 (concessions £1.90). Family ticket £7.20. Joint ticket with Macclesfield Silk Museum £4.75 (concessions £2.70). Family ticket £10.50.

P (400 yds) & shop ✗ ☞

⌂ NESTON
LIVERPOOL UNIVERSITY BOTANIC GARDENS (NESS GARDENS)
Ness Gardens L64 4AY (off A540 near Ness-on-Wirral)

☎ 0151 353 0123 🖹 0151 353 1004

A long association with plant collectors ensures a wide range of plants, providing interest for academics, horticulturists and amateurs alike. There are tree and shrub collections, water and rock gardens, well-stocked herbaceous borders and glasshouses. A regular programme of lectures, courses and special events take place throughout the year for which tickets must be obtained in advance.

Times: Open all year, Nov-Feb, daily 9.30-4; Mar-Oct, daily 9.30-dusk. Closed 25 Dec.

Fee: *£4.30 (ch free admission when accompanied with an adult, concessions £3.80)

P 💷 ✗ licensed & (wheelchair route, induction loop in lecture theatre) toilets for disabled shop garden centre ✈ (ex guide dogs) ☞

⌂ NETHER ALDERLEY
NETHER ALDERLEY MILL
Congleton Rd SK10 4TW (1.5m S of Alderley Edge on E side of A34)

☎ 01625 523012 🖹 68045 527139

Built in the 15th century, this water-mill is much larger inside than it looks. Inside there are tandem overshot water-wheels, original Elizabethan timber work, and Victorian machinery which was restored to full working order in the 1960s after being derelict for 30 years. Wheat is ground occasionally for demonstration purposes, water permitting.

Times: Open 31 Mar-May & Oct, Wed, Sun & BH Mon 1-4.30; Jun-Sep, Tue-Sun & BH Mon 1-5. Parties by arrangement.

Fee: *£2 (ch £1)

P ✗ ⅜

⌂ NORTHWICH
ARLEY HALL & GARDENS
Great Budworth CW9 6NA (5m N)

☎ 01565 777353 & 777284
🖹 01565 777465

Owned by the same family since medieval times, the present Arley Hall is a good example of the early Victorian Jacobean style and contains fine

furniture, plasterwork, panelling and family portraits. The gardens include a walled garden, unique clipped Ilex avenue, herb garden, scented garden and a woodland garden with rhododendrons, azaleas and exotic trees. Antique Fairs are held in March, June and October, also a Garden Festival in June.

Times: Open Etr-Sep, Tue-Sun & BH 11-5. Hall open Tue & Sun only.

Fee: *Gardens, Grounds & Chapel £4 (ch 6-16 £2, pen £3.40) Family ticket £11 Hall £2.50 (ch 6-16 £1.20,pen £2). Party 15+.

P 💷 ✗ licensed & (ramps parking by entrance) toilets for disabled shop garden centre

⌂ SCHOLAR GREEN
LITTLE MORETON HALL
Newcastle Rd CW12 4SD (4m SW of Congleton on A34)

☎ 01260 272018

One of the best examples of half-timbered architecture in England, and was used for the recent TV production of Moll Flanders. By 1580 the house was much as it is today, and the long gallery, chapel and the great hall are very impressive. The garden has a knot garden, orchard and herbaceous borders. Ring for details of special events.

Times: Open 20 Mar-31 Oct, Wed-Sun 11.30-5, BH Mon 1130-5; 6 Nov-19 Dec, weekends 11.30-4.

Fee: *£4.20 (ch £2.10). Joint ticket with Biddulph Grange Gardens £6 (ch £3). Dec free entry to ground floor and garden. Parking £2, refundable on entry to Hall.

P (charged) ✗ licensed & (wheelchair & electric vehicle available, Braille guide) toilets for disabled shop ✈ ⅜ ☞

⌂ STYAL
QUARRY BANK MILL & STYAL COUNTRY PARK
Quarry Bank Mill SK9 4JQ (M56 J5, signposted)

☎ 01625 523012 🖹 01625 539267

Quarry Bank Mill is a Georgian cotton mill that is now a museum of the cotton industry and powered by a waterwheel. Galleries illustrate all aspects of the textile process and the role of factory pioneers. Other attractions include the factory 'colony' nearby with its shop, cottages and chapels, and the apprentice house. The garden is laid out in Victorian utilitarian style.

Times: Mill open all year, Apr-Sep daily 11-6 (last admission 4.30); Oct-Mar Tue-Sun 11-5 (last admission 3.30). Apprentice House & Garden, as Mill opening times during school hols, Tue-Fri 2pm-Mill closing time during school term. Sat & Sun as for Mill. (Closed Mon all year ex BH Mon and school hols). Country Park open daily 8am-dusk.

Fee: *Mill and Apprentice House £5.50 (ch £3.50). Mill £4.20 (ch £3). Family ticket £15. Apprentice House & Garden £3.50 (ch £2.50). Styal Country Park £1.50 per car.

P (charged) 💷 ✗ licensed & toilets for disabled shop ✈ (ex in Park) ⅜ ☞

Cornwall & Isles of Scilly

Cornwall is one of Britain's most striking and majestic counties, and a land of contrasts. While small coastal towns like Mousehole, Mevagissey and Polperro remain largely untouched by time, the resort of Newquay is at the forefront of the European surfing scene.

Unsurprisingly, Cornwall's history is tied to the sea and seafaring, surrounded as it is by the Atlantic on three sides. For a long time the county was a centre for smuggling operations. The seclusion of its many coves and caves were ideal for the shady machinations of customs dodgers right up until the 20th century.

The isolation and ruggedness of the coastal landscape and its inhabitants has offered the perfect challenge for many religious groups and individuals. Some of Britain's earliest Christian churches and communities were started in Cornwall, including St Pirran's Church in Perranporth which was founded in the 6th century by the patron saint of tinners. Like many other missionaries of this time he came from Ireland, and as local tales claim, was not the most sober of ministers. St Columba was another, perhaps more important influence on Christianity in England

As legend has it, Cornwall was once the site of fabled Camelot. High on the cliffs near Tintagel is the ruined castle most strongly connected to King Arthur, although its remains post-date Arthurian lore by some seven centuries. Some local legends state that nearby Camelford was once Camelot.

EVENTS & FESTIVALS

January
31st Jan-12th Feb: Saltash Music, Drama & Speech Festival

February
26th Feb & 2nd-4th Mar: Wadebridge Music & Speech Festival

March
6th-11th: Cornwall County Music Festival, Truro

April
28th April-1st May: Boscastle Beer Festival, Charity Fun Day & Duck Race

May
1st: Padstow 'Obby 'Oss
5th-14th: Daphne du Maurier Festival
27th-29th (provisional): Newquay Surfing Festival

June
16th-25th: Golowan Festival, Penzance
25th: Mevagissey Feast Week

August
24th-28th: British National Championships (surfing), Newquay
26th Aug-2nd Sep: Bude Jazz Festival

October
6th: Callington Honey Fair

Top: Polperro

🏛 BODMIN
MILITARY MUSEUM
The Keep, Victoria Barracks PL31 1EG (on B3268 beside steam railway)
☎ 01208 72810 🖷 01208 72810

The history of a famous County Regiment with fascinating displays of uniforms, weapons, medals, badges and much more. A Centenary exhibition of the Boer War will be held in August.
Times: Open all year Mon-Fri, Sun during Jul & Aug 9-5. Closed Etr & Xmas.
Fee: *£2 (ch 50p). Parties 10+.
🅿 shop

🏛 CALSTOCK
COTEHELE
St Dominick PL12 6TA (2m E of St Dominick)
☎ 01579 351346 🖷 01579 351222

A 15th-century house that contains tapestries, embroideries, furniture and armour; and outside, a beautiful garden on different levels, including a formal Italian style garden, medieval stewpond, dovecote, and an 18th-century tower with lovely views. There is a restored water mill in the valley below, and an outstation of the National Maritime Museum.
Times: Open 27 Apr-Oct, House, daily (ex Fri) 11-5; (11-4.30 Oct). Mill, daily (ex Fri) 1-5.30 (4.30 Oct) - open Fri in Jul & Aug (4.30 Oct). Garden & Shop daily 11-5 (4.30 Oct). Last admission 30 mins before closing. Nov-Mar garden & woodland open daylight hours.
🍴 ✕ licensed ♿ (limited access in garden, braille guide) toilets for disabled shop ✖ (ex guide dogs) ♨ ⬗

🏛 CHYSAUSTER ANCIENT VILLAGE
CHYSAUSTER ANCIENT VILLAGE
(2.5m NW of Gulval, off B3311)
☎ 01736 61889

This fascinating ancient Celtic village, 2000 years old, includes 9 drystone houses ranged along the oldest known village street in England.
Times: Open Apr-1 Nov, daily 10-6 (or dusk if earlier in Oct).
Fee: £1.60 (ch 80p).
🅿 ✖ ⬗

🏛 DOBWALLS
DOBWALLS FAMILY ADVENTURE PARK
PL14 6HD (0.5 N of A38)
☎ 01579 320325 & 321129
🖷 01579 21345

Plenty to do here, with stretches of miniature American railroads to ride - there are steam and diesel locos, and visitors can take the Rio Grande ride through the forests or the Union Pacific route over the prairies. Adventureland - eight action-packed areas filled with adventure play equipment - is another attraction.
Times: Open Etr-Sep, daily 10-6 (last admission 4.30pm). Oct, Sat & Sun only & school half term (check as dates may differ).
🅿 ⬗ ♿ (motorised & manual wheelchairs available) toilets for disabled shop *Details not confirmed for 2000*

🏛 FALMOUTH
PENDENNIS CASTLE
TR11 4LP (1m SE)
☎ 01326 316594

The well preserved granite gun fort and outer ramparts testify to the strength of the coastal fortresses erected in the Tudor period by Henry VIII. It was eventually besieged and captured from the land during the Civil War in the 17th century.
Times: Open all year, Apr-1 Nov, daily 10-6 (or dusk if earlier); 2 Nov-31 Mar, daily 10-4. Closed 24-26 Dec & 1 Jan.
Fee: £3.80 (ch £1.90).
🅿 ♿ shop ✖ (in certain areas) ⬗

🏛 FOWEY
ST CATHERINE'S CASTLE
(0.75m along footpath off A3082)

The ruined stronghold (restored in 1855) was one of the many castles built by Henry VIII to defend the coast.
Times: Open all year, any reasonable time.
⬗

🏛 GWEEK
NATIONAL SEAL SANCTUARY
TR12 6UG (pass RNAS Culdrose & take A3293 & then B3291 to Gweek, the sanctuary is signposted from village)
☎ 01326 221361 & 221874
🖷 01326 221210

Britain's largest seal rescue facility - offering a unique opportunity to learn more about these beautiful creatures. Every year it rescues, rehabilitates and releases around 30 sick or abandoned seal pups.
Times: Open all year, daily from 9am. (Closed 25 Dec).
Fee: *Please call for admission prices.
🅿 ⬗ ♿ (wheelchair available) toilets for disabled shop ✖

🏛 LANHYDROCK
LANHYDROCK
PL30 5AD (2.5m SE of Bodmin, signposted from A30, A38 & B3268)
☎ 01208 73320 🖷 01208 74084

Approached along an avenue of beeches through a wooded park, Lanhydrock looks Tudor, but only the gatehouse, entrance porch and north wing date from the 16th century. The rest, rebuilt after a fire in 1881, gives a vivid picture of life in Victorian times. The `below stairs' sections are fascinating, with a huge kitchen, larders, dairy, bakehouse, cellars, and servants' quarters. The long gallery has a moulded ceiling showing Old Testament scenes, and overlooks the formal gardens with their clipped yews and bronze urns; the higher garden, famed for its magnolias and rhododendrons, climbs the hillside behind the house. Telephone for details of the summer concert.

Times: Open 1 Apr-1 Nov: House daily (ex Mon), but open BH Mon 11-5.30 (11-5 in Oct). Gardens daily from 1st Mar, last admission half hour before closing. Winter Gardens Nov-Feb during daylight hours.

Fee: *House & Grounds £6.40 (ch £3.20). Grounds £3.20 (ch £1.60). Family ticket £16.00. Party £5.50.

P 🍺 ✗ licensed 🕭 (house accessible ex 2nd floor, small lift to 1st floor) toilets for disabled shop garden centre 🐾 (ex on lead in park) 😽 🍹

�🏛 LAUNCESTON
LAUNCESTON CASTLE
☎ 01566 772365

Dominating this old market town is the ruin of the 12th-and 13th-century castle. Built in the early years of the Norman Conquest, it soon became a symbol of the authority of the Earls of Cornwall.

Times: Open Apr-1 Nov, daily 10-6 (or dusk if earlier). Closed 24-26 Dec & 1 Jan.

Fee: £1.60 (ch 80p).

🕭 (outer bailey only) 🐾 ✣

�🏛 MADRON
TRENGWAINTON GARDEN
Penzance TR20 8RZ
☎ 01736 363021   📠 01736 368142

Rhododendrons and magnolias grow in profusion at Trengwainton, along with many plants that are difficult to grow in Britain. The mild climate means that seed collected on expeditions to the Far East and southern hemisphere have flourished to produce a magnificent display in this 20th-century garden.

Times: Open 1 Mar-29 Oct, Sun-Thu also Good Fri 10-5.30. (Mar & Oct 11-5). Last admission 30 mins before closing.

P 🕭 (braille guide) toilets for disabled shop garden centre 😽 *Details not confirmed for 2000* 🍹

�🏛 MARAZION
ST MICHAEL'S MOUNT
TR17 0HT (0.5m S of A394)
☎ 01736 710507 & 710265
📠 01736 711544

Reached on foot by causeway at low tide, or by ferry at high tide in the summer only, St Michael's Mount rises dramatically from the sea, a medieval castle to which a magnificent east wing was added in the 1870s. It is home to Lord St Leven, whose ancestor St John Aubyn aquired it in the 17th century.

Times: Open Apr-30 Oct, Mon-Fri 10.30-5.30. Last admission 4.45. Mar-May special educational visits by prior arrangement, Tue only. The Castle and grounds are open most weekends during the summer season. These are special charity open days and NT members are also asked to pay.

Fee: *£4 Family ticket £11. Party 20+.

P (on mainland) 🍺 ✗ licensed shop (Apr-Oct) 🐾 😽 🍹

⚓ MAWNAN SMITH
TREBAH GARDEN
TR11 5JZ (signposted at Treliever Cross roundabout at junction of A39/A394)
☎ 01326 250448   📠 01326 250781

A 25-acre wooded ravine garden, descending 200 feet from the 18th-century house down to a private cove on the Helford River. The cascading Water Garden has pools of giant koi carp and exotic water plants, winding through two acres of blue and white hydrangeas to the beach. There are glades of huge sub-tropical tree ferns and palms, as well as rhododendrons and many other trees and shrubs. The beach is open to visitors and there are children's trails and activities all year. Please telephone for details of special events.

Times: Open daily 10.30-5 (last admission).

Fee: *Mar-Oct £3.50 (pen £3.20, ch & disabled £1.20, ch under 5 free); Nov-Feb £1 (concessions £1.50). Party 12+.

P ✗ 🕭 (2 wheelchair routes) shop garden centre (only on leads) 🍹

⚓ PENTEWAN
THE LOST GARDENS OF HELIGAN
PL26 6EN (signposted from A390 & B3273)
☎ 01726 845100   📠 01726 845101

The largest garden reclamation project in Britain, covering 80 acres. Four walled gardens are being restored to their former glory including the re-planting of Victorian varieties of fruit and vegetables. Various events are held throughout the year including walks, horticultural events, theatre workshops and educational courses.

Times: Open Mar-Oct daily 10-6 (last admission 4.30pm): winter 10-dusk. Closed 24-25 Dec.

Fee: *£5 (ch 5-15 £2.50, pen £4.50, ch under 5 free). Family £14

P 🍺 🕭 (free loan of wheelchairs) toilets for disabled shop garden centre 🍹

⛏ POOL
CORNISH ENGINES
East Pool TR14 7AW
☎ 01209 216657   ▤ 01209 612142

Impressive relics of the tin mining industry, these great beam engines were used for pumping water from 2000ft down and for lifting men and ore from the workings below ground. The mine at East Pool has been converted into the Cornwall Industrial Heritage Centre.
Times: Open 28 Mar-2 Nov, daily 11-5.
🅿 ♿ shop ✖ (ex guide dogs) ❦ *Details not confirmed for 2000* ☜

⛏ RESTORMEL
RESTORMEL CASTLE
PL22 ODB (1.5m N of Lostwithiel off A390)
☎ 01208 872687

Perched on a high mound surrounded by a deep moat, the huge circular keep of this splendid Norman castle is remarkably well preserved and commands the Fowey Valley.
Times: Open Apr-1 Nov, daily 10-6(or dusk if earlier).
Fee: £1.60 (ch 80p).
🅿 ♿ ✖ ⊞

⛏ ST AUSTELL
CHARLESTOWN SHIPWRECK & HERITAGE CENTRE
Quay Rd, Charlestown PL25 3NJ (1.25m SE A3061)
☎ 01726 69897   ▤ 01726 68025

Charlestown is a small and unspoilt village with a unique sea-lock china-clay port, purpose built in the 18th century. The Shipwreck and Heritage Centre houses the largest display of shipwreck artefacts in the UK, along with local heritage and diving exhibits.
Times: Open Mar-Oct, daily 10-5 (later in high season). Last admission 1 hour before closing.
Fee: *£4.45 (pen, student & disabled £2.95, ch under 14 free if accompanied by paying adult).
🅿 (charged) ▣ ✖ licensed ♿ (ramps) toilets for disabled shop ☜

WHEAL MARTYN CHINA CLAY HERITAGE CENTRE
Carthew PL26 8XG (2m N on B3274)
☎ 01726 850362   ▤ 01726 850362

This museum tells the story of Cornwall's most important present-day industry: china clay production. The open-air site includes a complete 19th-century clayworks, with huge granite-walled settling tanks, working water-wheels and a wooden slurry pump. There is a short audio-visual programme, a working pottery, nature trails and an adventure trail.
Times: Open Apr-Oct, 10-6 (last admission 5pm).
🅿 ▣ ♿ shop *Details not confirmed for 2000* ☜

⛏ ST IVES
BARBARA HEPWORTH MUSEUM & SCULPTURE GARDEN
Barnoon Hill TR26 1AD (M5 to Exeter, A30 to Penzance & St Ives)
☎ 01736 796226   ▤ 01736 794480

Dame Barbara Hepworth lived here from 1949 until her death in 1975, and the house is now a museum displaying sculptures and drawings, photographs, documents and other memorablia. Visitors can also visit her workshops, which house a selection of tools and some unfinished carvings. Please phone for details of special events.
Times: Open all year, Tue-Sun (Mon Jul/Aug) 10.30-5.30, BHs 10.30-5.30 (Closed 24-26 Dec).
Fee: *£3.50. (concessions £1.80)
🅿 (880 yds) ♿ (accessible with assistance) shop ✖ (ex guide dogs)

TATE GALLERY ST IVES
Porthmeor Beach TR26 1TG (M5 to Exeter, then A30 to Penzance & St Ives)
☎ 01736 796226   ▤ 01736 794480

Tate Gallery St Ives offers a unique introduction to modern art, where over 200 works can be seen at any one time in the surroundings and atmosphere which inspired them. The gallery presents changing displays from the Tate Gallery's Collections, focusing on the post-war modern movement St Ives is so famous for. The displays are complemented by a series of exhibitions and artists' projects.
Times: Open all year, Tue-Sun (Mon in Jul-Aug) 10.30-5.30. BHs 10.30-5.30 (Closed 24-25 Dec).
Fee: *£3.90 (concessions £2.30)
🅿 (800yds) ▣ ✖ licensed ♿ toilets for disabled shop ✖ (ex guide dogs)

⛏ ST MAWES
ST MAWES CASTLE
TR2 3AA (on A3078)
☎ 01326 270526

Part of the coastal-defence system built in the reign of Henry VIII, the castle guarded the Fal estuary, together with Pendennis Castle (see Falmouth). A fine example of military architecture, it is of particular interest to military historians, and a further attraction are the delightful gardens surrounding it.

Times: Open Apr-1 Nov, daily 10-6 (or dusk if earlier); 2 Nov-Mar, Fri-Tues 10-4 (closed 1-2pm). Closed 24-26 Dec & 1 Jan.

P & shop ✕ ⌗ *Details not confirmed for 2000*

🏛 SANCREED
CARN EUNY ANCIENT VILLAGE
(1.25m SW, off A30)

Four courtyard houses and several round houses dating from the 1st century BC can be seen at this site. There is also an impressive 'fogou', a subterranean passage leading to a circular chamber which may have served as a hiding place.

Times: Open any reasonable time.

P ⌗

🏛 TINTAGEL
OLD POST OFFICE
PL34 0DB
☎ 01840 770024

A small, 14th-century manor house, tumble-roofed with thick uneven slates, it served as a receiving office for letters from 1844 to 1892.

Times: Open 1 Apr-1 Nov, daily 11-5.30, (Oct 11-5). Last admission 30 mins before closing.

P (opposite) & (braille guide) shop ✕ (ex guide dogs) 🎗
Details not confirmed for 2000

TINTAGEL CASTLE
(on Tintagel Head, 0.5m along uneven track from Tintagel, no vehicles)
☎ 01840 770328

These romantic ruins make a dramatic sight on the edge of the towering cliffs. Associated in popular legend with King Arthur and the magician, Merlin, theories as to its origins abound: a Celtic monastery, the stronghold of Cornish Kings of the Dark Ages, the Durocornovium of the Romans? Whatever the true answer, it remains one of the most spectacular sites in Britain.

Times: Open all year, Apr-1 Nov, daily 10-6 (or dusk if earlier); 2 Nov-Mar, daily 10-4. Closed 24-26 Dec & 1 Jan. (NB – steep climb up steps to reach castle)

Fee: £2.80 (ch £1.40).

P (in village) shop ✕ ⌗

🏛 TORPOINT
ANTONY HOUSE
PL11 2QA (2m NW, off A374 from Trerulfoot rdbt, 2m from Torpoint Ferry)
☎ 01752 812191

A fine, largely unaltered mansion, built in brick and Pentewan stone for Sir William Carew between 1711 and 1721. The stable block and outhouses remain from an earlier 17th-century building. Most of the rooms in the house contain contemporary furniture and family portraits. The grounds include a dovecote and the Bath Pond

House (which may be seen after previous written application).

Times: Open Apr-29 Oct, Tue-Thu & BH Mons (also Sun Jun-Aug), 1.30-5.30. Last admission 4.45.

Fee: *£4. Woodland Garden £2.50. Combined Gardens only £3. Party.

P ▄ & (braille guide) toilets for disabled shop ✕ 🎗 ➤

🏛 TRERICE
TRERICE
TR8 4PG (3m SE of Newquay off A3058 at Kestle Mill)
☎ 01637 875404   🖷 01637 879300

Built in 1571 for Sir John Arundell, this picturesque Elizabethan house has unusual curved and scrolled gables, which may have been influenced by Sir John's stay in the Netherlands. The hall has an imposing window with 576 panes. Throughout the house are plasterwork ceilings, fine furniture and a large clock collection. Ring for details of special events.

Times: Open daily 28 Mar-31 Oct 11-5.30 (ex Tue & Sat), Open every day from 26 Jul-5 Sep. Last admission 30mins before closing.

Fee: *House: £4 (ch £2) Family ticket (2+3) £10. Party.

P ▄ & (braille/large print guides & tape tour) toilets for disabled shop ✕ (ex guide dogs) 🎗 ➤

🏛 TRURO
ROYAL CORNWALL MUSEUM
River St TR1 2SJ (follow A390 towards town centre)
☎ 01872 272205   🖷 01872 240514

Interesting and well-laid out displays on the history of the county, a world-famous collection of minerals, and paintings and drawings, including a number of Old Masters. Other galleries house displays of archaeology, Cornish history, and Egyptian artefacts. Contact the museum for a full programme of temporary exhibitions. A Millennium Exhibition will display 2000 years of Christianity in Cornwall.

Times: Open all year, Mon-Sat 10-5. Library closes 1-2. (Closed BHs).

Fee: *£2.50 (unaccompanied ch 50p, pen & students £1.50)

P (200 yds) ▄ ✕ licensed & (lift, ramps to main entrances) toilets for disabled shop ✕ (ex guide dogs) ➤

🏛 WENDRON
POLDARK MINE AND HERITAGE COMPLEX
TR13 0ER (on B3297)
☎ 01326 573173   🖷 01326 563166

This Cornish tin mine has three levels open to the public; an 18th-century village, museums and a cinema showing a film on the history of Cornish mining. On the surface there are restaurants, shops, gardens and children's amusements. The area around the mine has been laid to lawn and shows the West Country's largest collection of antiquities, including a 40ft beam engine.

Times: Open Etr-Oct, daily 10-5.30 (last admission 4pm)

Fee: *£5.25 (ch 5-15 £3.15 & pen £3.95, ch under 5 free).

P ▄ ✕ licensed & shop (ex grounds) ➤

ZENNOR

It was here, during the First World War, that D H Lawrence finished his classic novel, Women in Love, which seems quite fitting in its way, as the area is well-known for a local legend involving a mermaid who lured a squire's son to his death beneath the sea. A carving of the mermaid can be seen on a bench in the 12th-century church of St Senara. Another local literary inhabitant was Virginia Woolf, who once lived in a local house called the Eagle's Nest. Also on the subject of language, the churchyard at Zennor in the resting place of John Davey, who died in 1891 and is thought to have been the last person to understand Cornish as his native language.

Cumbria

The heart of Cumbria is the massive and majestic Lake District National Park, approximately 1,200 square miles of woodland, hills, lakes, mountains, rivers, and small villages. This means that a visit to Cumbria is basically a visit to some of Britain's finest landscapes.

The highest of the Lake District's peaks is Scafell Pike, which at 3,210ft (978m) is also the highest point in England. Other notable peaks include Scafell itself, Helvellyn towering above Ullswater, Skiddaw looming in the north above Bassenthwaite Lake and the impressive Langdale Pikes towering above the fertile greenery of the Great Langdale valley. In all, there are more than 60 summits above 2,500ft (762m).

At the foot of the mountains are the lakes the district takes its name from. These were scooped out millions of years ago by Ice Age glaciers, and are mostly called 'mere' (Old English) or 'water'. Derwent Water is commonly regarded as the most beautiful of these, and is studded with islands that provide a haven for wildlife. Wast Water is a much more sombre lake, hemmed in by grim mountains and scree slopes, while long and winding Ullswater is perhaps the most spectacular. Windermere is certainly the busiest as well as being the biggest at 10.5 miles (17km) long.

It wasn't until the 18th century that the beauty of the Lake District began to be appreciated by visitors, and it wasn't until the 19th century and the spread of the railways, that people came in large numbers to see it. Now, those wishing to visit may want to come in the spring or autumn, as the area can get very crowded in summer. Fell walking, rock climbing, pony trekking, fishing and touring are major Lake District activities.

EVENTS & FESTIVALS

February
18th-20th First Keswick Film Festival

April
8th (provisional) Damson Day, Kendal
30th-1st May Carlisle & Borders Spring Flower Show

May
14th-21st Keswick Jazz Festival

June
5th Mallerstang Horseshoe & Nine Standards Yomp, Kirkby Stephen
11th Carlisle Carnival, Carlisle

July
8th-9th Lakeland Rose Show, Grange-over-Sands

August
6th (provisional) Grasmere Rushbearing
11th-13th Ambleside Garden Festival & Craft Fair

September
9th Kendal Torchlight Procession

October
14th-15th Outdoor Theatre Project, Keswick

November
6th Carlisle Fireshow, Carlisle Castle

Top: Langdale Pikes

▥ BARROW-IN-FURNESS
Furness Abbey
LA13 0PJ (1.5m NE on unclass road)
☎ 01229 823420

Founded by the wealthy Cistercian Order in the 12th century, the red sandstone abbey is an impressive ruin. Its setting is the beautiful `Glen of Deadly Nightshade' near Barrow. Fine stone carving is displayed in the site museum.

Times: Open all year, Apr-1 Nov, daily 10-6 (or dusk if earlier); 2 Nov-Mar, Wed-Sun 10-4 (closed 1-2). Closed 24-26 Dec & 1 Jan.

Fee: £2.60 (ch £1.30).

🅿 ㊤ ✖ (in certain areas) ♯

▥ BIRDOSWALD
Roman Fort
CA6 7DD (signposted off A69 from Brampton)
☎ 016977 47602/4 🖹 016977 47605

This unique section of Hadrian's Wall is in a lovely setting, overlooking the Irthing Gorge, and is the only point along the Wall where all the components of the Roman frontier system can be found together. Birdoswald isn't just about the Romans, though, it's also about border raids in the Middle Ages, and recent archaeological discoveries. Please ring for details of August Bank Holiday events.

Times: Open Etr-Oct, daily 10-5.30. Winter opening by prior arrangement only.

🅿 ▬ ㊤ (ramp) toilets for disabled shop (not in tea room)
Details not confirmed for 2000 ➘

▥ BRAMPTON
Lanercost Priory
CA8 2HQ (2.5m NE)
☎ 016977 3030

The Augustinian priory was founded around 1166. The nave of the church has survived and is now used as the local parish church, providing a striking contrast with the ruined chancel, transepts and priory buildings.

Times: Open Apr-1 Nov, daily 10-6 (or dusk if earlier).

Fee: £2 (ch £1).

🅿 ㊤ ✖ ♯

▥ BROUGH
Brough Castle
(S of A66)
☎ 0191 261 1585

Standing on the site of the Roman Verterae, the castle, of which the keep and curtain wall remain, was built in the 12th and 13th centuries to replace an earlier stronghold. The later castle also fell into ruin, but was restored in the 17th century.

Times: Open any reasonable time.

🅿 ✖ ♯

▥ BROUGHAM
Brougham Castle
CA10 2AA (1.5m SE of Penrith on minor road off A66)
☎ 01768 62488

On the banks of the River Eden lie the ruins of one of the strongest castles in the region, founded in the 13th century and restored in the 17th by the strong-minded Lady Anne Clifford.

Times: Open Apr-1 Nov, daily 10-6 (or dusk if earlier in Oct).

Fee: £2 (ch £1).

🅿 ㊤ (ex keep) ♯

▥ CARLISLE
Carlisle Castle & Border Regiments Museum
CA3 8UR (city centre, close to station)
☎ 01228 591880 & 532774 (museum)
🖹 01228 21275

This medieval castle has a long history of warfare. An exhibition marks the Jacobite Rising of 1745, when Bonnie Prince Charlie took the castle. It is also the home of the Museum of the King's Own Border Regiment.

Times: Open all year, daily Apr-Sep 9.30-6; Oct-Nov 10-dusk. Winter months 10-4.

Fee: £3 (ch £1.50).

🅿 (400 yds) ㊤ (parking for disabled at Castle) shop ✖ ♯

Carlisle Cathedral
Castle St CA3 8TZ
☎ 01228 535169 & 548151
🖹 01228 547049

Founded in 1122 as a Norman Priory for Augustinian canons. The chancel roof is magnificently decorated and the cathedral features an exquisite east window. Telephone for details of special events.

Times: Open daily throughout the year, Mon-Sat 7.30-6.15, Sun 7.30-5, summer BHs 9.45-6.15, winter BHs, Xmas & New Year 9.45-4.

Fee: *Suggested donation of £2 per adult.

🅿 ✖ licensed ㊤ (disabled parking Radar key for toilet from vestry) toilets for disabled shop ✖ (ex guide dogs)

▥ COCKERMOUTH
Wordsworth House
Main St CA13 9RX
☎ 01900 824805 🖹 01900 824805

William Wordsworth was born here on 7th April 1770, and happy memories of the house had a great effect on his work. The inside staircase, panelling and other features are original. Portraits and other items connected with the poet are displayed. Please ring for details of concerts and other events during the season.

Times: Open Apr-30 Oct, Mon-Fri 10.30-4.30. Also Sats in Jun, Jul & Aug.

Fee: *£3 (ch £1.50). Family ticket £7.50. Party. Ask for details of discount with Dove Cottage,the Wordsworth Museum and Rydal Mount.

🅿 ✖ shop ✖ ♨

⛰ CONISTON

BRANTWOOD
LA21 8AD (2.5m SE off B5285, unclass road.
Regular ferry services from Coniston Pier)
☎ 015394 41396   📇 015394 41263

Brantwood, home of John Ruskin, is a beautifully situated house with fine views across Coniston Water. Inside, there is a large collection of Ruskin paintings and memorabilia, and outside visitors can enjoy delightful nature walks through the Brantwood Estate. Ring for details of exhibitions, and musical and theatrical events.
Times: Open mid Mar-mid Nov, daily 11-5.30. Rest of year, Wed-Sun 11-4.30 (closed 25-26 Dec).
Fee: *House & Estate £4 (ch £1, student £2.50). Family ticket £9.50. Estate only £2.
🅿 🖭 ✗ licensed ♿ toilets for disabled shop (& plant sales) ✈ (ex guide dogs & on grounds) 🍽

RUSKIN MUSEUM
The Institute LA21 8DU (In centre of village of Coniston)
☎ 015394 41164   📇 01539 441132

The Victorian writer John Ruskin lived nearby, and the museum displays watercolours, drawings, letters, sketchbooks and other relics, with portraits of the writer and his circle. There are also minerals and examples of Ruskin Lace, based on a design which he brought back from Italy. Other material relates to the Campbells and their Coniston water speed record bids, slate quarrying, copper mining and sheep husbandry. There are also local connections with writers Beatrix Potter and Arthur Ransome.
Times: Open Etr-mid Nov, daily 10-17.30. Phone for details of winter opening.
Fee: *£3 (ch £1.75). Family ticket £8.50 : Joint ticket to include museum & lake cruise with Coniston launch; £8.50 (ch £4) family ticket £24.50
🅿 (50 yds) ♿ toilets for disabled shop ✈ (ex guide dogs)

STEAM YACHT GONDOLA
Pier Cottage LA21 8AJ
☎ 015394 41288

Launched in 1859, the graceful Gondola worked on Coniston Water until 1937. She came back into service in 1980, and visitors can once again enjoy her silent progress and old-fashioned comfort.
Times: Open Apr-31 Oct to scheduled daily timetable. Trips commence 11 at Coniston Pier; on Sat 12.05. Piers at Coniston, Park-a-Moor at SE end of lake & Brantwood. (Not NT).
Fee: *Ticket prices on application.
🅿 ✈ 🐾

⛰ DALEMAIN

DALEMAIN
CA11 0HB (between Penrith & Ullswater on the A592)
☎ 017684 86450   📇 017684 86223

Originally a medieval pele tower, Dalemain was added to in Tudor times, and the imposing Georgian façade was completed in 1745. It has splendid oak panelling, Chinese wallpaper, Tudor plasterwork and fine period furniture. The tower contains the Westmorland and Cumberland Yeomanry Museum, and there is a countryside collection in the Great Barn. The grounds include a deerpark and gardens with a collection of old fashioned roses. Please telephone for details of special events.
Times: Open 28 Mar-3 Oct, Sun-Thu. 10.30-5, Gardens, Medieval Hall and agricultural & countryside collections. 11-4.
Fee: *House £5 (ch £3) Family £13. Gardens £3. (ch free when accompanied) Party,
🅿 ✗ licensed ♿ (ramp access at entrance, setting down & collection point) toilets for disabled shop garden centre ✈ (ex guide dogs)

🏛 DALTON-IN-FURNESS
SOUTH LAKES WILD ANIMAL PARK
Crossgates LA15 8JR (M6 J36, A590 to Dalton-in-Furness, signed)
☎ 01229 466086 🖷 01229 466086

This zoo park is a unique safari on foot, with many animals wandering free in natural surroundings. Active conservation is practised with partnerships world wide to save animals and their habitata. Walking through, the visitor is surrounded by sounds of the Australian Bush and Indonesian rain forests. Animals include tigers, rhino, apes and monkeys, kangaroo and many other species.
Times: Open all year, daily ex 25 Dec.
Fee: *£6.50 (ch/pen £3.20). Family ticket £16.
🅿 💺 ♿ (most areas accessible) toilets for disabled shop ✖ 🍽

🏛 GRASMERE
DOVE COTTAGE & THE WORDSWORTH MUSEUM
LA22 9SH (S, off A591, immediately before Grasmere village)
☎ 015394 35544 & 35547
🖷 015394 35748

Wordsworth lived at Dove Cottage from 1799 to 1808, and wrote much of his best-known poetry here. The house is kept in its original condition, as described in the journals of his sister Dorothy, and the award-winning museum displays manuscripts, paintings and various items associated with the poet. Wordsworth, his wife and sister, and other members of the family, are buried in the churchyard. Millenium events include a Wordsworth Winter School in February and a Wordsworth Summer Conference in August.
Times: Open daily 9.30-5.30, last admission 5pm. (Closed 11 Jan-7 Feb & 24-26 Dec).
Fee: *£4.50-£4.80 (ch £2.25-£2.40). Reciprocal discount with Rydal Mount Wordsworth House.
🅿 ✖ licensed ♿ toilets for disabled shop ✖ (ex guide dogs) 🍽

🏛 HARDKNOTT CASTLE ROMAN FORT
HARDKNOTT CASTLE ROMAN FORT
(at W end of Hardknott Pass)

Hair-raising hairpin bends on a steep hill are a feature for which Hardknott Pass is famous, and this astonishing Roman fort commands its western end, looking down over Eskdale.
Times: Open any reasonable time. Access may be hazardous in winter.
🅿 ⚙

🏛 HAWKSHEAD
BEATRIX POTTER GALLERY
Main St LA22 0NS
☎ 015394 36355 🖷 015394 36118

An annually changing exhibition of Beatrix Potter's original illustrations from her children's storybooks, housed in the former office of her husband, solicitor William Heelis.
Times: Open Apr-31 Oct & Good Friday Sun-Thu 10.30-4.30 (last admission 4). Admission is by timed ticket including NT members.
Fee: *£2.90 (ch £1.45)
🅿 (300metres) (braille guide) shop ✖ ♿ 🍽 🍽

🏛 HOLKER
HOLKER HALL & GARDENS
Cark in Cartmel, Grange over Sands LA11 7PL (from M6 J36, on A590, signposted)
☎ 015395 58328 🖷 015395 58776

Dating from the 16th century, the new wing of the Hall was rebuilt in 1871 after a fire. It has notable woodcarving and many fine pieces of furniture which mix happily with family photographs from the present day. There are magnificent gardens, both formal and woodland, and the Lakeland Motor Museum, exhibitions, deer park and adventure playground are further attractions. Please ring for details of special events.
Times: Open Apr-30 Oct Sun-Fri 10-6. Last entry to grounds, hall & motor museum 4.30pm.
🅿 💺 ♿ (ramps, handrails) toilets for disabled shop ✖
Details not confirmed for 2000

🏛 KENDAL
ABBOT HALL ART GALLERY
Kirkland LA9 5AL
☎ 01539 722464 🖷 01539 722494

The ground floor rooms of this splendid house have been restored to their former glory, with original carvings and fine panelling. The rooms make a perfect setting for the Gillow furniture and *objets d'art* displayed here, and the walls are hung with paintings by Romney, Gardner, Turner and Ruskin. The gallery has a fine collection of 18th-and 19th-century watercolours of the Lake District, and 20th-century British art, including works by Hepworth, Frink, Nicholson, and Sutherland. Please telephone for details of exhibitions.
Times: Open 11 Feb-22 Dec, Mon-Sun 10.30-5 (reduced hours in winter, Feb, Mar, Nov & Dec) please telephone for details.
Fee: *£2.80 (ch & students £1.25, pen £2.50). Family ticket £6.90.
🅿 💺 ♿ (chair lifts in split level galleries) toilets for disabled shop ✖ 🍽

KENDAL MUSEUM
Station Rd LA9 6BT (opposite railway station)
☎ 01539 721374 🖷 01539 722494

The archaeology and natural history of the Lakes is explored in this popular museum which also features a world wildlife exhibition and a gallery

KESWICK

Keswick is next to Derwent Water and is set among some of Britain's most imposing scenery. The town has some interesting old buildings, and has played host to more than its share of famous writers, including Robert Southey, a 19th-century poet laureate and biographer whose most famous work is undoubtedly the nursery tale, The Three Bears. *His tomb is in the churchyard at nearby Great Crosthwaite. Derwent Water was also the setting for Sir Hugh Walpole's historic 'Herries' novels, and Arthur Ransome's* Swallows and Amazons. *Other literary notables who lived in the area include William Wordsworth, Beatrix Potter, and Alfred Lord Tennyson.*

devoted to author Alfred Wainwright, who was honorary clerk to the museum.

Times: Open Feb-Dec, daily 10.30-5. Reduced hours Feb, Mar. Nov & Dec, 10.30-4.

Fee: *£2.80 (ch, students £1.25, pen £2.50). Family tickets £6.80. Ticket provides reduced entry to Abbot Hall Art Gallery & Museum of Lakeland life & Industry.

🅿 ⅙ (chair lift) toilets for disabled shop ✖

⚏ KESWICK
KESWICK MUSEUM & GALLERY
Fitz Park, Station Rd CA12 4NF (follow brown & white signs)
☎ 017687 73263

A mecca for writers, poets and artists, Keswick's attractions are well illustrated in this museum and gallery. Exhibits include letters, manuscripts and other relics, and the geology collection contains magnificent minerals from the Caldbeck Fells. Fitz Park contains formal gardens and a children's adventure playground. There are monthly exhibitions by local artists and craft workers.

Times: Open Good Fri-Oct, daily 10-4.

Fee: *£1 (ch, pen, students, UB40's & disabled 50p). Party 10+.

🅿 ⅙ (ramp at front entrance) shop ✖ (ex guide & hearing dogs)

MIREHOUSE
CA12 4QE (3m N of Keswick on A591)
☎ **017687 72287** 🖹 **017687 72287**

A walk along the beautiful lake shore will take you past the place where Tennyson wrote much of *Morte d'Arthur*, and inside the 17th-century house portraits and manuscripts of Francis Bacon, Carlyle and, of course, Tennyson, are on display. Outside, there's a lovely walled garden, a wildflower meadow and access to the 10th century church. Mirehouse is the venue for concerts attached to Keswick Jazz Festival at the end of May, and bobbin lace demonstrations are held each Wednesday in June, July and September.

Times: Open Apr-Oct. House: Wed, Sun, (also Fri in Aug) 2-last entry 4.30. Grounds: daily 10.30-5.30. Parties by arrangement Mar-Nov.

Fee: *House & grounds £3.75 (ch £1.80). Grounds only £1.50 (ch 80p). Family ticket £10.50(2 adults & up to 4 children)

🅿 ⬛ ⅙ (notes available listing facilities) toilets for disabled ✖ (ex in grounds on lead)

⚏ LEVENS
LEVENS HALL
LA8 0PD (M6 J36. 5m S of Kendal, on A6)
☎ **015395 60321** 🖹 **015395 60669**

An Elizabethan mansion, built onto a 13th-century pele tower, with fine plasterwork and panelling. The topiary garden, laid out in 1694,

contd.

has been little changed. There is also a steam engine collection.

Times: Open - House & gardens 1 Apr-14 Oct, Sun-Thur. Gardens 10-5. House 12-5. Last admission 4.30. Steam collection 2-5.

Fee: *House & garden £5.30 (ch £2.80), garden only £3.90 (ch £2.10).

🅿 💺 & (ramps within garden) toilets for disabled shop (plants on sale) ✕ (ex guide dogs) 🍽

🏛 NEAR SAWREY
HILL TOP
LA22 0LF (2m S of Hawkshead)
☎ 015394 36269 📠 015394 36118

Beatrix Potter wrote many of her books in this little 17th-century house, which contains her furniture and china.

Times: Open Apr-Oct, Sat-Wed & Good Friday 11-5. Last admission 4.30pm.

Fee: *£3.90 (ch £1.95)

🅿 (braille guide, handling items) shop ✕ 🐾 🍽

🏛 RAVENGLASS
RAVENGLASS & ESKDALE RAILWAY
CA18 1SW (close to the A595)
☎ 01229 717171 📠 01229 717011

A narrow gauge steam railway, laid in the 19th century to carry iron ore from the mines at Boot. It began to carry passengers and then over freight once the mines were closed, and is now a passenger line. The railway runs through beautiful countryside for the seven mile journey from Ravenglass, on the coast, up to Dalegarth. Purpose-built toilets for wheelchair users at Ravenglass, Eskdale and intermediate stations.

Times: Open: trains operate all year. Mar-Nov & between Xmas & New Year, daily; some winter weekends, please enquire . Limited service Jan & Feb except school hols.

Fee: *Return fare £6.50 (ch 5-15 £3.30). Family ticket £15.50

🅿 (charged) 💺 ✕ licensed & (special coaches - prior notice advisable) toilets for disabled shop 🍽

🏛 RYDAL
RYDAL MOUNT
LA22 9LU (1.5m, from Ambleside on A591 to Grasmere)
☎ 015394 33002 📠 015394 31738

The family home of William Wordsworth from 1813 until his death in 1850. The house contains important family portraits, furniture, and many of the poet's personal possessions, together with first editions of his work. In a lovely setting overlooking Windermere and Rydal Water, the gardens were designed by Wordsworth himself. Evening visits for groups can be organised, including a tour of the house and gardens, with poetry readings, wine and gingerbread at a small charge. Please telephone for details of the Daffodil Tour (March-May), and the Coffin Trail

(November-March). The Lake District Summer Festival takes place during August.

Times: Open Mar-Oct daily 9.30-5; Nov-Feb daily (ex Tue) 10-4 (Closed 8 Jan-1 Feb).

Fee: *£3.50 (ch £1, pen & student £3). Garden only £1.50. Party 10+(pre booked groups £2.50). Reciprocal discount ticket with Dove Cottage and Wordsworth House.

🅿 & shop ✕ (ex guide dogs & garden) 🍽

🏛 SEDBERGH
NATIONAL PARK CENTRE
72 Main St LA10 5HL
☎ 015396 20125

At the north-western corner of the Yorkshire Dales National Park, Sedbergh is set below the hills of the Howgill Fells. The rich natural history of the area and the beautiful scenery created a need for this Visitor Centre; maps, walks, guides, local information and interpretative displays can be found here, and there is a full tourist information service.

Times: Open Apr-Nov, daily 10-5.

🅿 (charged) & (accessible with help Radar key scheme) toilets for disabled shop *Details not confirmed for 2000*

🏛 SHAP
SHAP ABBEY
(1.5m W on bank of River Lowther)

Dedicated to St Mary Magdalene, the abbey was founded by the Premonstratensian order in 1199, but most of the ruins are of 13th-century date. The most impressive feature is the 16th-century west tower of the church.

Times: Open any reasonable time.

🅿 & ⚡

🏛 SIZERGH
SIZERGH CASTLE
LA8 8AE (3.5m S of Kendal)
☎ 015395 60070 📠 015395 60070

The castle has a 60-foot high pele tower, built in the 14th century, but most of the castle dates from the 15th to the 18th centuries. There are panelled rooms with fine carved overmantles and adze-hewn floors, and the gardens, laid out in the 18th century, contain the National Trust's largest limestone rock garden.

Times: Open Apr-Oct, Sun-Thu 1.30-5.30; Garden open 12.30. Last admission 5pm.

Fee: *£4.50 (ch £2.20). Family ticket £11.20, Garden £2.20, Party 15+.

🅿 💺 & (wheelchair and powered buggy for use, braille guide etc) toilets for disabled shop ✕ 🐾

🏛 SKELTON
HUTTON-IN-THE-FOREST
CA11 9TH (6m NW of Penrith on B5305 to Wigton, 2.5m from M6 J41)
☎ 017684 84449 📠 017684 84571

A beautiful house, set in magnificent woods which were once part of the medieval forest of Inglewood. The house consists of a 14th-century pele tower with later additions, and contains a fine collection of furniture, portraits, tapestries and china, a 17th-century gallery and cupid staircase. The lovely walled garden is the setting for the large collection of herbaceous plants, and there are 19th-century topiary terraces, a 17th-century dovecote and a woodland walk with impressive specimen trees.

Times: Open, House;12.30-4 Etr wkend, 29 Apr-3 Oct, Thu, Fri, Sun,& BH Mons. Grounds daily (ex Sat) 11-5. Groups any day booked in advance from Apr-Oct.
Fee: *£4 (accompanied ch 7 free, ch £2, students £3). Family ticket £10. Grounds £2.50 (ch free & students £1.50).
🅿 ⬛ 🅱 shop (local products also sold) ✈ (ex grounds on leads)

⛲ TEMPLE SOWERBY
ACORN BANK GARDEN
CA10 1SP (6m E of Penrith on A66)
☎ 017683 61893 📋 017683 61893

A delightful garden of some two and a half acres, which is used to grow an extensive collection of over 180 varieties of medicinal and culinary herbs. Scented plants are grown in the small greenhouse, and a circular walk runs beside the Crowdundle Beck. Please ring for details of special events.
Times: Open 28 Mar-Oct, daily 10-5 (last admission 5pm).
Fee: *£2.30 (ch £1.20). Family ticket £5.80. Party £1.70.
🅿 🅱 toilets for disabled shop ✈ 🐾

⛲ WINDERMERE
LAKE DISTRICT NATIONAL PARK VISITOR CENTRE
LA23 1LJ (on A591, between Windermere and Ambleside)
☎ 015394 46601 & 01539 73126 (minicom) 📋 015394 45555

Set in 32 acres of landscaped gardens and grounds, on the shore of Lake Windermere, this house became England's first National Park Visitor Centre in 1969. It offers exhibitions, audio-visual programmes, lake cruises, an adventure playground and an extensive events programme.
Times: Open Etr to early Nov, 10-5 daily, plus most winter weekends. Grounds & gardens open all year.
Fee: *Free admission but parking charge £4 full day, £3 half day.
🅿 (charged) ⬛ ✕ licensed 🅱 (wheelchairs with accessible trails & routes, lifts) toilets for disabled shop 🍴

WINDERMERE STEAMBOAT MUSEUM
Rayrigg Rd LA23 1BN (500mtr N of Bowness on the A592)
☎ 015394 45565 📋 015394 48769

A unique collection of Victorian and Edwardian steamboats and vintage motorboats. Many are still afloat and in working order, including the oldest steamboat in the world - the S L Dolly of 1850. Displays tell the social and commercial history of England's largest lake, and there are steamboat trips daily, weather permitting. Ring for details of special events.
Times: Open 18 Mar-29 Oct daily, 10-5. Steamboat trips subject to availability & weather.
Fee: *£3.25 (ch £2) Family ticket £8
🅿 ⬛ 🅱 toilets for disabled shop 🍴

Derbyshire

The natural features of this central English county range from the modest heights of the Peak District National Park, where Kinder Scout stands at 2,088 ft (636 m), to the depths of its remarkable underground caverns, floodlit to reveal exquisite Blue John stone.

These underground explorations may extend as far as a mile by boat at Speedwell Cavern, or half a mile by foot at Peak Cavern. Walkers and cyclists will enjoy the High Peak Trail which extends from the Derwent Valley to the limestone plateau near Buxton.

The county is richly endowed with stately homes. Most notably Chatsworth, the palatial home of the Duke and Duchess of Devonshire, with its outstanding collections of paintings, statuary and decorative art. Other gems include Haddon Hall, a well preserved medieval house; the splendid Elizabethan Hardwick Hall, and Kedleston Hall, an exemplary Adam creation.

The spa town of Matlock is the county's administrative centre. Other major towns are industrialised Derby, home of Royal Crown Derby china, and the old coal mining town of Chesterfield, symbolised by the crooked spire of St Mary and All Saints Church. Bargain hunters will enjoy a browse around the huge open air market in Chesterfield on a Monday, Friday and Saturday, or the Flea Market on a Thursday.

Around the villages of Derbyshire, look out for the ancient tradition of well dressing, the decorating of springs and wells - the precious sources of life-sustaining water - with pictures formed from flowers.

Top: Derby Cathedral

BUXTON

Buxton is an elegant former spa town and 'capital' of the Peak District. Its gushing hot springs were discovered by the Romans, but the town's heyday as a spa was in the 18th century, and this is reflected in the classical architecture of lower town and Crescent, where the 18th-century bath houses are preserved, and the old Pump Room now houses the Micrarium.

Buxton is justifiably proud of its beautifully restored Edwardian Opera House, which has a year-round programme of opera, drama, dance and children's shows. It also provides the focus for the Buxton Opera Festival during the last two weeks of July.

⛪ BOLSOVER
BOLSOVER CASTLE
S44 6PR (on A632)
☎ 01246 823349

An enchanting and romantic spectacle, situated high on a wooded hilltop dominating the surrounding landscape, this 17th-century mansion was built on the site of a Norman castle. The keep displays elaborate fireplaces, panelling and wall paintings and there is also an impressive indoor Riding School, also of the 17th century.
Times: Open all year, Apr-1 Nov, daily 10-6 (or dusk if earlier in Oct); 2 Nov-Mar, Wed-Sun 10-4. Closed 24-26 Dec & 1 Jan.
Fee: £3.10 (ch £1.60).
🅿 ♿ (keep not accessible) shop ✖ ⚏

⛪ CALKE
CALKE ABBEY
DE73 1LE (9m S of Derby, on A514)
☎ 01332 863822 📠 01332 865272

This fine baroque mansion dating from the early 18th century was built for Sir John Harpur. Among its treasures are an extensive natural history collection, a magnificent Chinese silk state bed, and a spectacular red and white drawing room. The house stands in extensive wooded parkland and also has walled flower gardens.
Times: Open 1 Apr-1 Nov Sat-Wed (incl BH Mon); House & church 12.45-5.30 Gardens from 11am. Last admission 5pm. Park open all year, Apr-Oct closes 9pm or dusk if earlier, Nov-Mar closes at dusk. House, church & garden closed Sat 15 Aug. Admission to house for all is by timed ticket, obtained on arrival.
🅿 ✖ licensed ♿ (braille guide, hearing system, buggy/wheelchair available) toilets for disabled shop ✖ ⚏
Details not confirmed for 2000

⛪ CASTLETON
BLUE-JOHN CAVERN & MINE
Buxton Rd S33 8WP
☎ 01433 620638 & 620642
📠 01433 621586

A remarkable example of a water-worn cave, over a third of a mile long, with chambers 200ft high. It contains 8 of the 14 veins of Blue John stone, and has been the major source of this unique form of fluorspar for nearly 300 years.
Times: Open all year daily 9.30-6 (or dusk). Guided tours of approx 1hr every 10 mins tour.
Fee: *£4.50 (ch £2.50 pen £3, student £3.50) Family ticket £13. Party.
🅿 shop 🍴

PEAK CAVERN
S33 8WS (on A6187)
☎ 01433 620285

One of the most spectacular natural limestone caves in the Peak District, with an electrically-lit underground walk of about half a mile. Ropes have been made for over 500 years in the 'Grand Entrance Hall', and traces of a row of cottages can be seen. Rope-making demonstrations are included on every tour.
Times: Open Etr-Oct, daily 10-5. Nov-Etr wknds only 10-5
Fee: *£4.75 (ch £2.75, other concessions £3.75). Family ticket £13.
🅿 (charged) shop ☜

PEVERIL CASTLE
Market Place S30 2WX (on S side of Castleton)
☎ 01433 620613

William Peveril, one of William the Conqueror's trusted knights, guarded the King's manors in the Peak from this natural vantage point which commands spectacular views of the Hope Valley. The area is designated a Site of Special Scientific Interest.
Times: Open all year, Apr-1 Nov, daily 10-6 (or dusk if earlier in Oct); 2 Nov-Mar, Wed-Sun 10-4. Closed 24-26 Dec & 1 Jan.
Fee: £2 (ch £1).
shop ✖ ⛫

SPEEDWELL CAVERN
Winnats Pass S33 8WA (off A625, (A625 becomes A6187 at Hathersage) 0.5m W of Castleton Village).
☎ 01433 620512 ▤ 01433 621888

Descend 105 steps to a boat which will take you on a one-mile underground exploration of the floodlit cavern.
Times: Open all year, daily 9.30-5.
Fee: *£5.25 (ch £3.25)
🅿 (charged) shop ☜

TREAK CLIFF CAVERN
S33 8WP (0.75m W of Castleton on A6187)
☎ 01433 620571 ▤ 01433 620519

An underground world of stalactites, stalagmites, flowstone, rock and cave formations, minerals and fossils. There are rich deposits of the rare and beautiful Blue John Stone, and the show caves include the Witch's Cave, Aladdin's Cave and Fairyland Grotto.
Times: Open all year, Mar-Oct daily 9.30-5.30, Nov-Feb daily 10-4. All tours are guided & last about 40 mins.
Fee: *Adults £4.99 (ch5-15 £2.50). Family ticket £13.50.
🅿 ▱ shop ☜

⌂ CHATSWORTH
CHATSWORTH
DE45 1PP (8m N of Matlock on B6012)
☎ 01246 582204 ▤ 01246 583536

Home of the Duke and Duchess of Devonshire, and of one of the richest private collections of fine and decorative arts in the country. There is is a splendid painted hall, and a great staircase leads to the chapel, decorated with statues,

marble and painted walls and ceiling. There are magnificent pictures, furniture and porcelain, and a memorable trompe l'oeil painting of a violin on the music room door. The park was laid out by 'Capability' Brown, but is most famous as the work of Joseph Paxton, head gardener in the 19th century. Notable features include the Cascade and the Emperor Fountain, which sends up a jet of water to 290ft.
Times: Open 18 Mar-1 Nov. House & garden 11-4.30, Farmyard 10.30-4.30
🅿 (charged) ▱ ✖ licensed ♿ (3 electric wheelchairs available for garden) toilets for disabled shop garden centre ✖ (ex park & gardens) *Details not confirmed for 2000* ☜

⌂ CRESWELL
CRESWELL CRAGS VISITOR CENTRE
off Crags Rd S80 3LH (1m E off B6042)
☎ 01909 720378

A deep narrow gorge, pitted with caves and rock shelters, used as seasonal camps by Stone Age hunter-gatherers. Unusual finds from the caves include pieces of decorated animal bone and the remains of extinct animals such as woolly mammoth and hyena. A visitor centre explains the importance of the site, and guided cave tours are organised throughout the year, pre-booking is advised.
Times: Open all year, Feb-Oct, daily, 10.30-4.30; Nov-Jan, Sun only 10.30-4.30.
Fee: *Free (under review). Cave/site tour £2.25 (ch £1.60).
🅿 ♿ (wheelchair loan) toilets for disabled shop

⌂ CRICH
NATIONAL TRAMWAY MUSEUM
DE4 5DP (off B5035)
☎ 01773 852565 ▤ 01773 852326

A mile-long scenic journey through a period street to open countryside with panoramic views. You can enjoy unlimited vintage tram rides, and the exhibition hall houses the largest collection of vintage electric trams in Britain. Ring for details of special events.
Times: Open daily, Apr-Oct 10-5.30 (6.30pm weekends Jun-Aug & BH weekends). Winter, open Sun.
Fee: *£6.50 (ch 4-15 £3.20, pen £5.60). Family ticket £17.60. Winter (Sun only) £3 (ch 4-15 £1.50).
🅿 ▱ ♿ Braille guidebooks, ramps, converted tram, talktype facility toilets for disabled shop ☜

🏛 CROMFORD
CROMFORD MILL
Mill Ln DE4 3RQ (off A6, 3m S of Matlock)
☎ 01629 824297   📠 01629 823256

Sir Richard Arkwright established the world's first successful water-powered cotton spinning mill at Cromford in 1771. The Arkwright Society are involved in a major restoration to create a lasting monument to an extraordinary genius. Guided tours are available, and there is a programme of lectures and visits - ring for details.

Times: Open all year, daily 9-5 (Closed 25 Dec). Guided tours 10-4.

Fee: *Guided tour & exhibitions £2 (ch & pen £1.50). Mill site Free.

P ✗ & toilets for disabled shop

🏛 DENBY
DENBY POTTERY VISITORS CENTRE
Derby Rd DE5 8NX (8m N of Derby, on B6179)
☎ 01773 740799   📠 01773 740749

Guided factory tours show the intricate skills of the potters craft, including throwing, turning, glazing and decorating. The museum illustrates the history of Denby Pottery, and there's a large factory shop selling Denby products. Please check tour times and availabilty prior to arriving at the visitor centre.

Times: Open all year. Full factory tours, Mon-Thu 10.30 & 1. Craftroom only, daily 10-3.15. Visitors Centre Mon-Sat 9.30-5, Sun 10-5.

Fee: *Factory tours £3.75 (ch & pen £2.50). Craftroom only £2.75 (ch & pen £1.75).

P ▣ ✗ licensed & (lift) toilets for disabled shop garden centre ✈ (ex guide dogs) ⬤

🏛 DERBY
DERBY MUSEUM & ART GALLERY
The Strand DE1 1BS
☎ 01332 716659 & 716669
📠 01332 716670

The museum has a wide range of displays, notably of Derby porcelain, and paintings by the local artist Joseph Wright (1734-97). Also antiquities, natural history and militaria, as well as many temporary exhibitions. `Deoraby to Derby - 1000 Years of Achievement' exhibition end Jan-Sep 2000.

Times: Open all year, Mon 11-5, Tue-Sat 10-5, BHs 2-5,Sun telephone for details. (Closed Xmas telephone for details).

Fee: Free.

P (50yds) & (lift to all floors) toilets for disabled shop ✈ (ex guide dogs)

ROYAL CROWN DERBY VISITOR CENTRE

194 Osmaston Rd DE23 8JZ

☎ 01332 712800 & 712841 (tours)

🖷 01332 712863

The the museum traces the history of the company from 1750 to the present day, while the factory tour demonstrates the making of Royal Crown Derby in detail from clay through to the finished hand decorated product. A demonstration studio gives you the opportunity to watch craftspeople at close quarters and try your hand at a variety of different skills.

Times: Open all year, daily. Factory tours twice dauly, booking strongly advised.

Fee: *Visitor centre £2.50 (ch/pen £2). Family &7. Factory tour £5.50 (ch/pen £4.75). Family £16.

🅿 💷 ✗ licensed ⅃ (visitor entry aceesible but not factory tour) toilets for disabled shop ✖ 🖅

🏛 EYAM

EYAM HALL

S32 5QW (in village centre)

☎ 01433 631976 🖷 01433 631603

An intimate 17th-century manor house in the heart of the famous "plague village". Home to the Wrights for 300 years, the Hall offers a glimpse of of domestic history through the eyes of one family, in portraits, furniture, tapestries, costumes and memorabilia. Converted farm buildings house the Eyam Hall Craft Centre. Please telephone for details of musical and theatrical events throughout the season.

Times: Open: House 31 Mar-Oct, Wed,Thu,Sun & BH: first tour 11am, last tour 4.30pm. Craft centre open allyear Tue-Sun 10.30-5.30.

Fee: *£4 (ch £3, pen £3.50). Family ticket £12.50. Party.

🅿 💷 ✗ licensed ⅃ (disabled may enter by special gate, avoiding steps) toilets for disabled shop ✖ (ex guide dogs) 🖅

🏛 HADDON HALL

HADDON HALL

DE45 1LA (1.5 S of Bakewell off A6)

☎ 01629 812855 🖷 01629 814379

Originally held by the illegitimate son of William the Conqueror, Haddon has been owned by the Dukes of Rutland since the 16th century. Little has been added since the reign of Henry VIII, and, despite its time-worn steps, few medieval houses have so successfully withstood the ravages of time.

Times: Open Apr-Sep, 10.30-5, Oct, Mon-Thu 10.30-4.30.

Fee: *£5.50 (ch £3 & pen £4.75). Family ticket £14.75. Party 20+.

🅿 (charged) ✗ licensed ⅃ shop ✖ (ex guide dogs) 🖅

🏛 HARDWICK HALL

HARDWICK HALL

S44 5QJ (2m S M1 Junc 29)

☎ 01246 850430 🖷 01246 854200

Hardwick Hall is celebrated as the creation of Bess of Hardwick, who began the building at 70 after the death of her fourth husband, the Earl of Shrewsbury. The house has a vast area of

windows, which become taller from the ground floor up. The High Great Chamber and the long gallery are hung with tapestries and Cavendish portraits. Some of the needlework is by Mary, Queen of Scots, who was the Earl of Shrewsbury's prisoner for 15 years.

Times: Open 1 Apr-1 Nov Wed, Thu, Sat, Sun & BH Mon 12.30-5. (Closed Good Fri). Last admission 4.30pm. Garden 1 Apr-1 Nov daily 12-5.30. Park all year daily dawn-dusk. Car park gates close 6pm.

🅿 ✗ licensed ⅃ (hearing scheme wheelchair if prebooked) toilets for disabled shop ✖ (ex in park on leads) 🦌 *Details not confirmed for 2000* 🖅

🏛 KEDLESTON HALL

KEDLESTON HALL

DE22 5JH (5m NW of Derby)

☎ 01332 842191 🖷 01332 841972

Kedleston has been the Derbyshire home of the Curzon family for over eight centuries. The original house was demolished at the end of the 17th century. In 1760 Robert Adam built the south front and designed most of the interior including the awe-inspiring marble hall. There are some notable pictures, furniture and china displayed in the house together with an Indian Museum containing the collection accumulated by Lord Curzon, Viceroy of India.

Times: Open - House; 28 Mar-1 Nov, Sat-Wed 1-5.30, last admission 5pm, (closed Good Fri). Garden; same as house but open 11-6. Park; 28 Mar-1 Nov daily 11-6, 2 Nov-20 Dec, Sat & Sun 12-4 (entry charge £2 on Thu/Fri for park only).

🅿 ✗ licensed ⅃ (braille guide, wheelchair, self-drive vehicle) toilets for disabled shop ✖ (ex in park, must be on leads) 🦌 *Details not confirmed for 2000* 🖅

🏛 MATLOCK BATH

THE HEIGHTS OF ABRAHAM COUNTRY PARK & CAVERNS

DE4 3PD (On A6, signposted from M1 J28 & A6. Base station next to Matlock Bath railway station)

☎ 01629 582365 🖷 01629 580279

High on a hill above the village of Matlock Bath are the Grounds of the Heights of Abraham. Until recently the climb to the summit was only for the very energetic, but now alpine-style cable cars provide a leisurely and spectacular way of reaching the top. There are two show caverns, plenty for children to do, and, naturally, superb views.

Times: Open daily Etr-Oct 10-5 (later in high season) for Autumn & Winter opening telephone for details.

Fee: *£6.20 (ch £4.10, pen £5.20). Under 5's free - one per adult.

P (300m) 🍴 ✗ licensed ♿ toilets for disabled shop 🛍

⛪ MELBOURNE
MELBOURNE HALL
DE73 1EN (9m S of Derby on A514)
☎ 01332 862502 🖹 01332 862263

Sir John Coke (Charles I's Secretary of State) bought the lease of Melbourne Hall in 1628 and the house, still owned by his descendants, has been home to two Prime Ministers: Lord Melbourne and Lord Palmerston. The atmosphere is intimate and `lived in', and the glorious formal gardens are among the finest in Britain. Special events are usually held each Sunday afternoon in August.

Times: Open, house daily throughout Aug only (ex first three Mons) 2-5. Prebooked parties by appointment in Aug. Gardens Apr-Sep, Wed, Sat, Sun & BH Mon 2-6.

Fee: *House Tue-Sat (guided tour) £2.50 (ch £1, pen £2), Sun & BH Mon (no guided tour) £2 (ch 75p, pen £1.50). House & Garden (Aug only) £4.50 (ch £2.50, pen £3.50). Garden only £3 (pen £2). Family £8.

P (200 yds) 🍴 ♿ (ramp at garden entrance) shop 🐕 (ex guide dogs)

⛪ MIDDLETON BY WIRKSWORTH
MIDDLETON TOP ENGINE HOUSE
Middleton Top Visitor Centre DE4 4LS (0.5m S from B5036 Cromford/Wirksworth road)
☎ 01629 823204 🖹 01629 825336

A beam engine built in 1829 for the Cromford and High Peak Railway, and its octagonal engine house. The engine's job was to haul wagons up the Middleton Incline, and its last trip was in 1963 after 134 years' work. The visitor centre tells the story of this historic railway.

Times: Open: Information Centre, daily, wknds only winter. Engine House Etr-Oct 1st wknd in month (engine in motion).

Fee: *Static Engine 50p (ch 25p). Working Engine £1 (ch 50p). P (charged) ♿ (ex Engine house) toilets for disabled shop

⛪ RIPLEY
MIDLAND RAILWAY CENTRE
Butterley Station DE5 3QZ (1m N of Ripley on B6179)
☎ 01773 747674 & 749788
🖹 01773 570721

A regular steam-train passenger service runs here, providing the the focal point for the Centre, where the aim is to depict every aspect of the golden days of the Midland Railway and its successors. Exhibits range from the steam locomotives of 1866 to an electric locomotive. There is also a large section of rolling stock spanning the last 100 years. A wide range of special events, including Friends of Thomas the Tank Engine, take place throughout the year.

Times: Open: every weekend from 23rd Jan-7th Nov & 28th Nov-27th Dec, every Wednesday from Apr-Oct (ex 11th June). Daily 30 Mar-11 Apr, 29 May-6 Jun, 20 Jul-6 Sep, 23-31 Oct.

Fee: *£7.95 (ch 5-16 £4, pen £6.50) children under 5 free. Party 15+.

P 🍴 ♿ (special accommodation on trains) toilets for disabled shop 🛍

Devon

EVENTS & FESTIVALS

A county of great contrasts, Devon encompasses wild moorland terrain and rolling farming country dotted with delightful villages. Exmoor extends to the spectacular northern coastline with England's highest cliffs, where there are excellent walks on the hills and coastal footpath.

May
5th-7th Dartmouth Music Festival
7th Blackawton International Festival of Worm Charming,
18th-20th Devon County Show, Exeter
26th-10th June English Riviera Dance Festival, Torquay

June
2nd-16th July Exeter Festival
2nd-5th Appledore Arts Festival
10th-18th Victorian Celebration, Ilfracombe
26th-3rd July Dartmouth Carnival (provisional)
27th May-4th (provisional) Brixham Heritage Festival

July
2nd June-16th Exeter Festival
10th May -3rd Dawlish Arts Festival

August
4th-11th Sidmouth International Folk Festival
24th-26th Port of Dartmouth Royal Regatta
25th-27th Westcountry Hot Air Balloon Fiesta

Top: Pendeen

In the south, stretching from Dartmoor to the seaside resorts of Torbay, is the area alluringly dubbed the 'English Riviera'. The major resorts are Torquay, Paignton and Teignmouth on the south coast, and Ilfracombe on the north. Perhaps more interesting to explore however, are the estuaries of Kingsbridge and Dartmouth, Sidmouth with its elegant seafront, and Salcombe with its flotilla of yachts.

Both Dartmoor and Exmoor have National Park status which preserves them from encroachment. Exmoor is home to the hardy little Exmoor pony and is the only remaining habitat in England for the native red deer. Dartmoor is the largest expanse of untamed country in Southern England, with Dartmoor Forest at its heart.

Devon's main towns are Exeter and Plymouth. The former was badly damaged in World War II, but the cathedral survives. Plymouth has been closely associated with naval history since Sir Francis Drake played his legendary game of bowls before facing the Spanish Armada, but as a centre for shipbuilding and a military base, it was also doomed to devastation by Luftwaffe bombing.

Local products to look out for while visiting Devon, are seafood, cider, clotted cream, Honiton lace and Dartington glass.

⛪ ARLINGTON
ARLINGTON COURT
EX31 4LP (7m NE of Barnstaple, on A39)
☎ 01271 850296 ▤ 01271 850711

Built in 1822, Arlington Court is filled with a fascinating collection of objets d'art: pewter, shells and model ships as well as furniture and costumes from the 19th century. The biggest attraction, however, is the collection of carriages and horsedrawn vehicles. Around the house is a landscaped park grazed by Shetland ponies and sheep. Ring for details of special events.
Times: Open 28 Mar-Oct, Sun-Fri 11-5.30; also Sat of BH wknds. Footpaths through park and woods open 28 Mar-Oct, Sun-Fri 11-5.30; Nov-27 Mar open during daylight hours.
Fee: *House & grounds £5.20. Grounds only £3.20. Parties 15+
🅿 ▆ ✗ licensed ♿ (wheelchairs available - ramped steps at house) toilets for disabled shop ✈ (ex in park) ⅍ ▇

⛪ BICTON
BICTON PARK
East Budleigh EX9 7BJ (2m N of Budleigh Salterton on B3178)
☎ 01395 568465 & 568374
▤ 01395 568465

Fifty acres of gardens, woodland, lakes, ponds and fountains, with an Italian garden and a restored palm house where bananas and other exotica flourish. There are also fuchsia, geranium and temperate houses. A countryside museum contains farm tools, wagons and a cider press, and there's also an adventure playground, and Bicton Woodland Railway.

Times: Open all year 10 Jan-May 10-4, May-Oct 10-6, Oct-24 Dec 10-4.
Fee: £4.95 (ch £2.95, pen £3.95). Family ticket £13.95.
🅿 ▆ ✗ licensed ♿ (adapted carriage on woodland railway, wheelchairs) toilets for disabled shop garden centre ✈ (ex on lead) ▇

⛪ BUCKFASTLEIGH
BUCKFAST ABBEY
TQ11 0EE (off A38 on A384 Dartbridge turn off, follow tourist signs for 0.5m)
☎ 01364 642519 ▤ 01364 643891

The Abbey, founded in 1018, was Dissolved by Henry VIII in the 16th century. Monks returned to the site in 1882 and considered restoration, and in 1907 four monks with little building experience began the work, making the Abbey a religious community once again. The church was built on the old foundations, using local blue limestone and Ham Hill stone, and the modern east window is stunning. The precinct contains several medieval monastic buildings, including the 14th century guest hall which contains an exhibition of the history of the Abbey. Monthly concerts are held here, please telephone for details.
Times: Open all year daily 5.30am-9.30pm. (visitor facilities 9-5.30 (summer) 10-4.30 (winter)
Fee: Free.
🅿 ▆ ✗ licensed ♿ (level site, braille plan, wheelchair available) toilets for disabled shop ✈ ▇

⛪ BUCKLAND ABBEY
BUCKLAND ABBEY
PL20 6EY (off A386 0.25m S of Yelverton, signed)
☎ 01822 853607 ▤ 01822 855448

Originally a prosperous 13th-century Cistercian Abbey, and then home of the Grenville family, Buckland Abbey was sold to Sir Francis Drake in 1581, who lived there until his death in 1596. Several restored buildings house a fascinating exhibition about the abbey's history. Among the exhibits is Drake's drum, which is said to give warning of danger to England.
Times: Open 27 Mar-Oct, daily (ex Thu) 10.30-5.30. Nov-end Mar, Sat & Sun 2-5. (Closed 25-26 Dec & 3 Jan-18 Feb). Last admissions 45mins before closing.
Fee: *Abbey & grounds £4.40 (ch £2.10). Grounds only £2.30 (ch £1). Party 15+. (Car park charge fundable against purchase of admission ticket).
🅿 (charged) ✗ licensed ♿ (wheelchairs & motorised buggy available) toilets for disabled shop ✈ (ex guide dogs) ⅍

🏛 CHUDLEIGH
CANONTEIGN FALLS
EX6 7NT (off A38 at Chudleigh/Teign Valley juntion onto B3193 and follow tourist signs for 3m)
☎ 01647 252434   🖹 01647 52617

A magical combination of waterfalls, woodlands and lakes.
Times: Open all year, mid Mar-mid Nov, daily 10-5.30; Feb Half Term & Winter, Sun only 11-4.
Fee: *£3.75 (ch £2.50 & pen £3.25). Family ticket £11. Party 12+.
🅿 ✕ licensed shop 🦪

🏛 COMPTON
COMPTON CASTLE
TQ3 1TA (off A381 near Marldon)
☎ 01803 872112

A fortified house of the 14th to 16th centuries, Compton has been the home of the Gilbert family for 600 years. The Great Kitchen still has its bread ovens and knife-sharpening marks, and the withdrawing room has squints through which occupants could watch services in the chapel. The towers, portcullis entrances and curtain walls were added in the 16th century, when there were French raids in the area.
Times: Open 29 Mar-28 Oct Mon, Wed & Thu 10-12.15 & 2-5.
Fee: *Castle & garden £2.80
🅿 ✕ 🐾 🦪

🏛 DARTMOUTH
BAYARD'S COVE FORT
TQ6 9AT (on riverfront)

Built by the townspeople to protect the harbour, the remains of the circuar stronghold still stand at the southern end of the harbour.
Times: Open at all reasonable times.
🅿 ✈ (in certain areas) ⧉

DARTMOUTH CASTLE
TQ6 0JN (1m SE off B3205, narrow approach road)
☎ 01803 833588

The castle dates from 1481 and was one of the first to be designed for artillery. It faces Kingswear Castle on the other side of the Dart estuary, and a chain could be drawn between the two in times of war.
Times: Open all year, Apr-1 Nov, daily 10-6 (or dusk if earlier); 2 Nov-Mar, Wed-Sun 10-4. Closed 24-26 Dec & 1 Jan.
Fee: £2.60 (ch £1.30).
🅿 shop ✈ ⧉

WOODLANDS LEISURE PARK
Blackawton TQ9 7DQ (W, off A3122)
☎ 01803 712598   🖹 01803 712680

A beautiful 60-acre park with indoor and outdoor attractions for all the family. The large animal complex and wildlife walkabout has hundreds of animals and birds, and there is an international wildfowl collection and Bee Observatory, as well as rides and children's activities. Live entertainment days in the school holidays, including an Easter Extravaganza.
Times: Open 26 Mar-5 Nov daily, also weekends & school holidays.
🅿 💺 ♿ (ramps) toilets for disabled shop ✈ (ex guide dogs) *Details not confirmed for 2000* 🦪

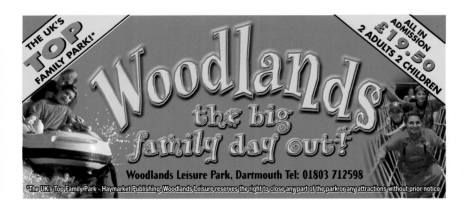

DREWSTEIGNTON

CASTLE DROGO

EX6 6PB (4m S of A30)

☎ 01647 433306 📠 01647 433186

The granite castle is one of the most remarkable designs of Sir Edwin Lutyens, and was built between 1910 and 1930 for Julius Drewe. It is a fascinating combination of medieval might and 20th-century luxury, with its own telephone and hydro-electric systems. The castle stands on a rocky crag overlooking the gorge of the River Teign.

Times: Open 27 Mar-Oct, daily (ex Fri but open Good Fri) 11-5.30. Garden open all year, daily 10.30-5.30 (or dusk if earlier).

Fee: *Castle £5.30. Garden & grounds only £2.50

🅿 💷 ✗ licensed ♿ (wheelchairs available, lift to lower ground floor) toilets for disabled shop garden centre ✖ ♨ 🍴

EXETER

UNDERGROUND PASSAGES

Boots Arcade, High St EX4 3RX

☎ 01392 265858 & 265887

📠 01392 421252

A remarkable medieval water system with an introductory exhibition. Definitely not suitable for those inclined to claustrophobia - and flat shoes are essential. All tours are guided.

Times: Open Jul-Sep and school holidays Mon-Sat 10-5; rest of year Tue-Fri 2-5, Sat 10-5.

🅿 shop ✖ Details not confirmed for 2000

GREAT TORRINGTON

DARTINGTON CRYSTAL

Linden Close EX38 7AN (follow brown tourist signs)

☎ 01805 626262 📠 01805 626263

Tours of the factory are conducted from the safety of viewing galleries, where you can watch the craftsmen carrying out the age-old techniques of glass manufacture and processing. The Visitor Centre has a permanent exhibition tracing the history of glass and crystal over the past 2000 years.

Times: Open all year. Factory & Visitor centre: Mon-Fri 9.30-3.30. (Closed 16 Dec-2 Jan)

Fee: *£3.50 (ch 6-16 £1, pen £2.50). Party.

🅿 💷 ✗ licensed ♿ (special tours available, book in advance) toilets for disabled shop ✖ 🍴

RHS GARDEN ROSEMOOR

EX38 8PH (1m SE of town on B3220)

☎ 01805 624067 📠 01805 624717

Rosemoor is the Royal Horticultural Society's first Regional Garden and Centre, second only to Wisley. The Formal Garden includes 200 varieties of roses, and there's a herb garden, potager, cottage garden, winter garden, alpine terrace and extensive herbaceous borders. Elsewhere are stream and bog gardens, and a large walled fruit and vegetable garden. Contact for details of lectures, demonstrations and garden walks.

Times: Open: Gardens all year; Visitor Centre Apr-Sep 10-6, Oct-Mar 10-5.

🅿 ✗ licensed ♿ (Herb garden for disabled) toilets for disabled shop garden centre ✖ ex guide dogs Details not confirmed for 2000 🍴

KILLERTON HOUSE & GARDEN

KILLERTON HOUSE & GARDEN

EX5 3LE (off B3181)

☎ 01392 881345

Elegant 18th-century house set in an 18 acre garden with sloping lawns and herbaceous borders. A majestic avenue of beech trees runs up the hillside, past an arboretum of rhododendrons and conifers. The garden has an ice house and rustic summer house where the family pet bear was once kept. The main house is furnished with family portraits and period furniture. The Killerton Dress Collection is on display.

Times: Open: House, 13 Mar-Oct, Wed-Mon 11-5.30. Gardens all year, daily from 10.30am.

Fee: *House & grounds £5. Grounds only £3.50.

🅿 💷 ✗ licensed ♿ (wheelchairs & motorised buggy available) toilets for disabled shop garden centre ✖ (ex in park) ♨

KINGSWEAR

COLETON FISHACRE HOUSE & GARDEN

Brownstone Rd, Coleton TQ6 0EQ (3m from Kingswear. Take Ferry Road and turn off at Toll House)

☎ 01803 752466 📠 01803 752466

A beautiful valley garden set on the South Devon coastline, created between 1925 and 1947 by Rupert and Lady Dorothy D'Oyly Carte, who experimented with a wide range of trees and exotic shrubs from around the world. From the formal wall garden and terraces surrounding the house the paths descend the valley and head toward Pudcombe Cove.

Times: Open 7-21 Mar, Sun only 2-5; 27 Mar-Oct, Wed-Fri, Sun & BH Mon 11-4.

Fee: *£4.60 (ch £2.30). Family ticket £11.50.

🅿 💷 (wheelchair available) shop garden centre ✖ (ex guide dogs) ♨

KNIGHTSHAYES COURT

KNIGHTSHAYES COURT

EX16 7RQ (2m N of Tiverton off A396)

☎ 01884 254665 & 257381

📠 01884 243050

This fine Victorian mansion, a rare example of William Burges' work, offers much of interest to all ages. The garden is one of the most beautiful in Devon, with formal terraces, amusing topiary. Pool garden and woodland walks.

Times: House open 27 Mar-Sep, Sat-Thu & Good Fri 11-5.30. Oct, Sat-Wed 11-4.30. Garden 27 Mar-Oct 11-5.30.

Fee: *House & garden £5.20 (ch £2.60). Garden only £3.60 (ch £1.80).

🅿 💷 ✗ licensed ♿ (wheelchairs available, braille & aidio guide) toilets for disabled shop garden centre ✖ (in park) ♨ 🍴

🏛 LYDFORD
LYDFORD CASTLE
EX20 4BH (off A386)

The great square stone keep dates from 1195. It is not built on a mound, as it seems to be, but had earth piled against the walls. The upper floor was a Stannary Court, which administered local tin mines, and the lower floor was used as a prison.

Times: Open all reasonable times.
🅿 ♿

LYDFORD GORGE
EX20 4BH (off A386, between Okehampton & Tavistock)
☎ 01822 820441 & 820320
🖹 01822 820320

The spectacular gorge has been formed by the River Lyd, which has cut into the rock and caused swirling boulders to scoop out potholes in the stream bed. This has created some dramatic features, notably the Devil's Cauldron close to Lydford Bridge. At the end of the gorge is the 90ft-high White Lady Waterfall.

Times: Open 28 Mar-Sep, daily 10-5.30. (Nov-Mar, waterfall entrance only, daily 10.30-3).
Fee: *£3.40
🅿 💺 shop 🐾 🥾

🏛 MORWELLHAM
MORWELLHAM QUAY
PL19 8JL (4m W of Tavistock, off A390. Midway between Gunnislake & Tavistock. Signed)
☎ 01822 832766 & 833808
🖹 01822 833808

Morwellham was the greatest copper port in Queen Victoria's empire. Once the mines were exhausted the port area disintegrated into wasteland, until 1970, when a charitable trust was set up for its restoration. Visitors can ride by electric tramway underground into a copper mine, last worked in 1869. Staff wear Victorian costume, and visitors (including children and dogs!) can try on replica costumes in the Limeburners Cottage. Unspoilt countryside, with riverside and woodland trails, surrounds the museum, and there's also a wildlife nature

reserve sited in marshland, valley and woodland, with bird watching hides and nature trails.
Times: Open all year (ex Xmas wk) 10-5.30 (4.30 Nov-Etr). Last admission 3.30 (2.30 Nov-Etr).
Fee: *£8.50 (ch 5-16 £6, pen & students £7.50). Family ticket £28. Party.
🅿 💺 ✗ licensed (smooth paths, but difficult areas in Victorian village) shop ✕ (ex on lead) 🥾

🏛 NEWTON ABBOT
BRADLEY MANOR
TQ12 6BN (on A381)
☎ 01626 54513

A National Trust property of 70 acres, the 15th-century house and chapel are surrounded by woodland. The River Lemon and a millstream flow through the estate.
Times: Open Apr-Sep, Wed only 2-5; also Thu, 1 & 8 Apr, 16 & 23 Sep.
Fee: *£2.60
🅿 ✕ 🚲 🐾 🥾

TUCKERS MALTINGS
Teign Rd TQ12 4AA (follow brown tourist signs from Newton Abbot rlwy station)
☎ 01626 334734   🖹 01626 330153

The only working malthouse in England open to the public, producing malt from barley for over 30 West Country breweries. Learn all about the process of malting - and taste the end product at the new in-house brewery. Guided tours last over an hour. Special events for 2000 include: Maltings Beer Festival (13-16 April).
Times: Open Etr-Oct, daily 10-4 (Jul-Aug open to 5pm).
Fee: *£4.35 (ch 5-15 £2.75, 16-17 £3.50, pen £3.95). Family ticket £12.25.
🅿 (charged) ♿ toilets for disabled shop 🥾

🏛 OKEHAMPTON
OKEHAMPTON CASTLE
(1m SW of town centre)
☎ 01837 52844

The chapel, keep and hall date from the 11th to 14th centuries and stand on the northern fringe of Dartmoor National Park.
Times: Open all year, Apr-1 Nov, daily 10-6 (or dusk if earlier in Oct). (Closed 24-26 Dec & 1 Jan).
Fee: £2.30 (ch £1.20). 🅿 ♿

🏛 OTTERTON

OTTERTON MILL CENTRE

EX9 7HG (between North Poppleford & Budleigh Salterton)

☎ 01395 568521　📠 01395 568521

Mentioned in the Domesday Book, this water-powered mill grinds wholemeal flour used in the baking of bread and cakes sold on the premises. A gallery houses exhibitions through the summer and autumn, and there are sculpture, pottery, weaving, basket-making and spinning studios. There is a co-operative craft shop, and an annual exibition of furniture from West Country workshops.

Times: Open all year, daily, summer 10.30-5.30; winter 11-4.
Fee: *£1.75 (ch 90p). Party.
🅿 💷 ♿ (free entry to ground floor) shop garden centre 🍴

🏛 OTTERY ST MARY

CADHAY

EX11 1QT (near jct of A30 & B3167)

☎ 01404 812432　📠 01404 812432

A beautiful Tudor and Georgian house, which stands around a courtyard and dates from 1550.

Times: Open Jul-Aug Tue, Wed & Thu. Also Sun & Mon of late spring & late summer BH's. 2-5.30.
Fee: *£4 (ch £2). Party 20+ by appointment.
🅿 ♿ 🐾 (ex guide dogs)

🏛 PAIGNTON

PAIGNTON & DARTMOUTH STEAM RAILWAY

Queens Park Station, Torbay Rd TQ4 6AF

☎ 01803 555872　📠 01803 664313

Steam trains run for seven miles from Paignton to Kingswear on the former Great Western line, stopping at Goodrington Sands, Churston, and Kingswear, connecting with the ferry crossing to Dartmouth. Ring for details of special events.

Times: Open Jun-Sep daily 9-5.30 & selected days Oct & Mar-May.
Fee: *Paignton to Kingswear £6.10 (ch £4.10, pen £5.50). Family £18.50. Paignton to Dartmouth (including ferry) £7 (ch £4.60, pen £6.40). Family £21.50.
🅿 (5mins walk) 💷 ♿ (wheelchair ramp for boarding train) toilets for disabled shop

PAIGNTON ZOO ENVIRONMENTAL PARK

Totnes Rd TQ4 7EU (1m from town centre on A385)

☎ 01803 527936　📠 01803 523457

Paignton is one of Britain's biggest zoos, set in a beautiful and secluded woodland valley, where new enclosures are spacious and naturalistic. A tour will take you through some of the world's threatened habitats, Forest, Savannah, Wetland and Desert, with hundreds of species, many of them endangered and part of conservation breeding programmes. There are regular keeper

contd.

PLYMOUTH

The Pilgrim Fathers, Charles Darwin, Scott of the Antarctic and Captain James Cook, all set sail from Devon's major seaport. The fact that nearly 50 places around the world bear the city's name is testament to the success of many of these travellers.

The Barbican is the historic heart of the city, and its narrow cobbled streets and charming pubs and teashops are pervaded by a sense of its Elizabethan past. The area is still very much alive however, and boasts some excellent shops and galleries, including the vibrant Barbican Centre, a 400-year-old building which houses over 30 shops and two restaurants.

talks and a children's play area, and special events include an annual Easter Egg Safari.

Paignton Zoo

Times: Open all year, daily 10-6 (5pm in winter). Last admission 5pm (4pm in winter). (Closed 25 Dec).
Fee: *£7 (ch 3-15 £4.90, pen £5.40). Family ticket £21.80. Party 15+.
🅿 💺 ✕ licensed ♿ (some steep hills wheelchair loan-booking advisable) toilets for disabled shop ✕ (ex guide dogs) 🍴

🏛 PLYMOUTH
ROYAL CITADEL
(at the end of Plymouth Hoe)
☎ 01752 603300

Probably designed by Sir Thomas Fitz, this magnificent gateway was built for the stronghold begun by Charles II in 1666. Some buildings remain, notably the Guardhouse, Governor's House and Chapel.
Times: Open for guided tours only May-Sep, daily. For security reasons tours may be suspended at short notice.
✕ ♨

SMEATONS TOWER
The Hoe PL1 2NZ
☎ 01752 603300   🖥 01752 256361

This famous lighthouse, a triumph of 18th-century engineering, was built on the treacherous Eddystone rocks fourteen miles out at sea to the south west of Plymouth. It was replaced by a larger lighthouse in 1882, and moved stone by stone to its present site on the Hoe.
Times: Open Good Fri-Sep, 10.30-4.30. Parties by appointment throughout the year.
🅿 (500 yds) ✕

🏛 PLYMPTON
SALTRAM
PL7 1UH (2m W between A38 & A379)
☎ 01752 336546   🖥 01752 336474

This magnificent George II house still has its original contents. The collection of paintings was begun at the suggestion of Reynolds and includes many of his portraits. The saloon and dining room were designed by Robert Adam and have superb decorative plasterwork and period furniture. Set in beautiful surroundings with a shrub garden and 18th-century summer house,

Saltram House has a lovely view of the Plym estuary. Special events take place throughout the year.
Times: Open 27 Mar-Oct, Sun-Thu; House 12-5. Garden & Great Kitchen 10.30-5.
Fee: *£5.70 (ch £2.80). Gardens only £2.70 (ch £1.30). Family £14.20.
🅿 (charged) 💺 ✕ licensed ♿ (wheelchairs available, lift, braille & audio guides) toilets for disabled shop ✕ (ex designated areas) 🐾 🍴

🏛 POWDERHAM
POWDERHAM CASTLE
EX6 8JQ (signposted off A379 Exeter/Dawlish road)
☎ 01626 890243   🖥 01626 890729

Built between 1390 and 1420, this ancestral home of the Earls of Devon was damaged in the Civil War. The house was restored and altered in later times and is set in beautiful rose gardens with views over the deer park to the Exe Estuary. Ring for details of special events.
Times: Open 2 Apr-29 Oct, 10-5.30 (last admission 5pm). (Closed Sat).
Fee: *£5.45 (ch £2.95, pen £4.95). Family ticket £13.85. Party 10+
🅿 💺 ✕ licensed ♿ (ramps) toilets for disabled shop garden centre 🍴

🏛 SALCOMBE
OVERBECKS MUSEUM & GARDEN
Sharpitor TQ8 8LW (2.5m SW of Salcombe and 2m S of Malborough)
☎ 01548 842893   🖥 01548 842530

The garden at Overbecks is stunning when the magnolias are in bloom; but its situation, on the most southerly tip of Devon, allows many exotic plants to flourish; one of the most varied collections in the country is grown here. The Edwardian house displays toys, dolls and a natural history collection, and there is a `secret room' for children in which they can search for "Fred" the friendly ghost.
Times: Open Mar-Jul Sun-Fri 11-5.30; Aug daily 11-5.30; Sep Sun-Fri 11-5.30; Oct Sun-Thu 11-5. Last admission 30 mins before closure. Gardens open all year, 10-8 (or sunset if earlier).
Fee: *Museum & gardens £3.90. Gardens only £2.70.
🅿 (charged) 💺 ♿ (ramp from garden, braille guide) shop ✕ ♿ 🐾 🍴

🏛 SOUTH MOLTON
QUINCE HONEY FARM
EX36 3AZ (3.5m W of A361)
☎ 01769 572401   🖥 01769 574704

The largest bee farm in Britain - view the honey-bees, without disturbing them, in a specially designed building with glass booths and tunnels. Observation hives enable you to see into the centre of the colony and view larvae and newly-hatched bees in the cells of the comb.
Times: Open daily, Apr-Sep 9-6; Oct 9-5; Shop only Nov-Etr 9-5. (Closed 25 Dec-4 Jan).
Fee: *£3 (ch 5-16 £1.60, pen £2.50)
🅿 💺 ♿ toilets for disabled shop ✕ 🍴

🏛 TIVERTON

TIVERTON CASTLE

EX16 6RP

☎ 01884 253200 & 255200

🖹 01884 254200

The original castle, built in 1106 by order of Henry I, was rebuilt late 13th/14th century. It resisted General Fairfax during the Civil War and fell to him when a lucky shot hit the drawbridge chain. Now a private house, the gardens are lovely and there's a fine Civil War armoury.

Times: Open Etr-Jun & Sep, Sun,Thu & BH Mon's only 2.30-5.30; Jul & Aug, Sun-Thu 2.30-5.30.

Fee: *£3 (ch 7-16 £2, under 7 free). Disabled half price if accessing ground floor only)

P ⓑ toilets for disabled shop garden centre ✠ (ex guide dogs)

🏛 TORQUAY

TORRE ABBEY HISTORIC HOUSE & GALLERY

The Kings Dr TQ2 5JX (on sea front, next to Riviera Centre)

☎ 01803 293593   🖹 01803 215948

The Abbey was founded in 1196 as a monastery and later adapted as a country house. It contains mementoes of crime writer Agatha Christie, paintings, sculpture, antiques, and Torquay terracotta pottery. The medieval monastic remains, which include the great barn, guest hall, gatehouse and undercrofts, are the most complete in Devon and Cornwall. Special exhibitions throughout the summer, including a Flower Festival during the 2nd weekend in September.

Times: Open daily Apr-1 Nov, 9.30-6. (Last admission 5pm).

Fee: *£3 (ch 15 £1.50, under 8 free, pen & students £2.50). Family ticket £7.25.

P (100 yds) 🍴 ⓑ shop ✠ (ex guide dogs)

🏛 TOTNES

TOTNES CASTLE

TQ9 5NU (on hill overlooking town)

☎ 01803 864406

A classic example of the Norman motte-and-bailey castle, Totnes dates from the 11th, 13th and 14th centuries. The circular shell-keep,

protected by a curtain wall, gives marvellous views.

Times: Open all year, Apr-1 Nov, daily 10-6 (or dusk if earlier in Oct); 2 Nov-Mar, Wed-Sun 10-4, (closed 1-2). Closed 24-26 Dec & 1 Jan.

Fee: £1.60 (ch 80p).

P (70yds) ✿

TOTNES MUSEUM

70 Fore St TQ9 5RU (Totnes town centre)

☎ 01803 863821

A four-storey, partly timbered house, complete with connecting gallery to a kitchen/buttery block, dating from about 1575. It is now a museum, featuring furniture, domestic objects, toys, dolls, costumes and archaeology. One room is dedicated to Charles Babbage who invented the ancestor of modern computers. There are changing displays of contemporary art and craft from the Totnes area. Please enquire about a range of events for children.

Times: Open Etr-30 Oct, Mon-Fri & BHs 10.30-5, Sat group bookings only.

Fee: *£1.50 (ch 5-16 50p).

P (440yds) ⓑ Personal guided tours available shop ✠ (ex small dogs)

🏛 YEALMPTON

NATIONAL SHIRE HORSE CENTRE

PL8 2EL (On A379, Plymouth to Kingsbridge)

☎ 01752 880268   🖹 01752 881014

A 60-acre farm, with more than 40 Shire horses. Not only can you see the heavy horses and their foals, but a variety of other creatures as well. There is a butterfly house as well as a craft centre. Falconry displays take place daily (at 1pm and 3.30pm), and there are parades of the Shire horses (at 11.30 and 2.30). Children are well catered for, with a pets area, cart rides and an adventure playground.

Times: Open 1 May-31 Sep.

Fee: *£3.95 (ch £2.75, pen £3.40).

P 🍴 ✕ licensed ⓑ toilets for disabled shop

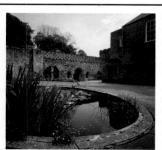

Dorset

One of England's most picturesque counties, Dorset has such a wealth of history, stunning scenery and coastal attractions on offer that one is spoilt for choice when visiting it, and it seems a shame that so many people simply drive through it on their way somewhere else.

EVENTS & FESTIVALS

February
4th-5th: Beerex 2000 Real Ale Festival, Dorchester

April
28th: Dorchester Festival of Music & Arts
30th-1st May: International Beach & Kite Festival, Weymouth

May
28th: Vintage & Classic Vehicle Rally, Lodmoor Country Park, Weymouth
29th: Trawler Race & Water Carnival, Weymouth

July
15th: International Maritime Modelling Festival, Weymouth
15th: Royal Naval Air Station Yeovilton International Air Day
16th: Tolpuddle Martyrs Rally & Festival, Tolpuddle
22nd-30th: RNLI Lifeboat Week, Lyme Regis

August
4th-6th National Sand Soccer Festival, Weymouth Beach
4th: Sidmouth International Folk Festival
11th: Weymouth Sailing Regatta
16th: Weymouth Carnival
30th: Great Dorset Steam Fair, Tarrant Hinton

September
17th: Beaulieu to Weymouth Vintage & Classic Car Rally

Top: Shaftesbury

Possibly the county's most famous landmark is the Cerne Abbas giant, a 180-foot high depiction of a naked man with a club, visible for miles around. However, those visiting this important remnant of Dorset's distant past shouldn't pass by Cerna Abbas itself, which contains a centuries-old church, and the remains of a 10th-century Abbey.

Rural Dorset has retained a great deal of the charm and tranquillity of England before the Industrial Revolution. All of the market towns in this area (Gillingham, Blandford Forum, Stalbridge, Shaftesbury and Sturminster Newton) are well worth seeing. Shaftesbury is one of England's oldest towns and is the site of an abbey founded by Alfred The Great. The area around these towns, - known as 'Hardy Country', after Thomas Hardy, the 19th-century novelist, - has been designated an Area of Outstanding Natural Beauty, and includes Cranborne Chase, Blackmore Vale and the Dorset Downs.

The major coast resorts, - Weymouth, Poole and Bournemouth - offer a wide range of activities, combined with some beautiful scenery, and yet more of historic interest. The best example of the latter is probably Corfe Castle, which sits on the Isle of Purbeck. The keep was built by the Normans, and the whole thing was completed by 1300. Unfortunately for future generations, the castle was ruined during a Civil War siege.

ABBOTSBURY

ABBOTSBURY SWANNERY
New Barn Rd DT3 4JG (9m from Weymouth on
the B3157 coastal road to Bridport)
☎ 01305 871684 & 871858
🖹 01305 871092

Abbotsbury is the breeding ground of the only
managed colonial herd of mute swans. The
swans can be seen safely at close quarters, and
the site is also home or stopping point for many
wild birds. The highlight of the year is the cygnet
season, end of May to the end of June, when
there may be over 100 nests on site with an
average of six eggs per nest. Please ring for
details of special events.
Times: Open Etr-Oct, daily 10-6, last admission 5pm
Fee: *£4.80 (ch 5-16 £2.50 & pen £4). Family ticket £13.
🅿 🍴 ✗ (wheelchair loan, herb garden for
blind) toilets for disabled shop ✈ 🍵

ATHELHAMPTON

ATHELHAMPTON HOUSE & GARDENS
DT2 7LG (on A35 1m E of Puddletown)
☎ 01305 848363 🖹 01305 848135

Athelhampton, one of the finest 15th-century
houses in England, contains magnificently
furnished rooms including The Great Hall of 1485
and the library. The glorious Grade I gardens
contain the world-famous topiary pyramids,
fountains, and collections of tulips, magnolias,
roses, clematis and lilies in season.
Times: Open Mar-Nov, daily 10.30-5. Also Sundays in Winter.
(Closed Sat).
Fee: *House & Garden £4.80 (ch £1.50, pen £4.50). Garden
only £3 (ch free). Family £10. Party.
🅿 🍴 ✗ licensed ♿ toilets for disabled shop ✈ ex
assistance dogs 🍵

BEAMINSTER

PARNHAM
DT8 3NA (1m S on A3066)
☎ 01308 862204 🖹 01308 863444

This fine Tudor mansion is most famous as the
home of John Makepeace and his furniture-
making workshop. The workshop is open to
visitors, and completed pieces are shown in the
house. There are also continuous exhibitions by
living designers and craftsmen. Surrounding the
house are 14 acres of restored gardens, formal
terraces and woodlands. Ring for details of
special events.
Times: Open Apr-Oct: Sun, Tue-Thu & BH's 10-5.
Fee: *£5 (ch £2, under 5 free)
🅿 ✗ licensed ♿ toilets for disabled shop

BLANDFORD FORUM

ROYAL SIGNALS MUSEUM
Blandford Camp DT11 8RH (signposted off the
B3082 Blandford/Wimborne road)
☎ 01258 482248 🖹 01258 482084

The Royal Signals Museum depicts the history of
military communications, science and technology
from the Crimea to the Gulf. As well as displays

on all major conflicts involving British forces,
there are the stories of the ATS, the Long Range
Desert Group, Air Support, Airborne, Paras and
SAS Signals.
Times: Open Mon-Fri 10-5, Sat-Sun 10-4 (May-Oct). Closed
10 days over Xmas & New Year
Fee: *£4 (ch 5-16 £2, pen £3). Family £9
🅿 🍴 ♿ (ramps & chair lift) toilets for disabled shop ✈

BOVINGTON CAMP

CLOUDS HILL
BH20 7NQ (4m SW of Bere Regis)
☎ 01929 405616

T E Lawrence ('Lawrence of Arabia') bought this
cottage in 1925 when he was a private in the
Tank Corps at Bovington. He would escape here
to play records and entertain friends to feasts of
baked beans and China tea. Lawrence's sleeping
bag, together with other memorabilia. Three
rooms only are on show.
Times: Open 28 Mar-31 Oct, Wed-Fri & Sun, also BH Mon,
12-5, or dusk if earlier.
Fee: *£2.30.
(Braille guide) ✈ 🚲 🦌

THE TANK MUSEUM
BH20 6JG (off A352, follow brown tank signs
from Bovington and Wool)
☎ 01929 405096 🖹 01929 405360

The Tank Musem houses the world's finest
international collection of Armoured Fighting
Vehicles. Tanks in Action displays are held every
Thursday at noon during July-September and
every Friday in August. Armoured vehicle rides
are available throughout the summer, and
various special events take place - please
telephone for details.
Times: Open all year, daily 10-5 (Closed from 23 Dec-4 Jan).
Fee: *£6 (ch £4, under 5 free, pen £5). Family ticket £15.
🅿 ✗ licensed ♿ (wheelchairs available, Braille & audio tours)
toilets for disabled shop ✈ (ex guide dogs) 🍵

BROWNSEA ISLAND

BROWNSEA ISLAND
BH15 7EE (located in Poole Harbour)
☎ 01202 707744 🖹 01202 701635

Visitors to this 250-acre nature reserve managed
by the Dorset Trust for Nature Conservation can
take advantage of a guided tour. The island is
most famous as the site of the first scout camp,
held by Lord Baden-Powell in 1907. Scouts and
Guides are still the only people allowed to stay
here overnight. The island is also famous for its
dragonflies, moths and butterflies, and birds.
Times: Open 27 Mar-3 Oct, daily 10-5 (10-6 Jul-Aug); check
for time of last boat.
Fee: *£2.50 (ch £1.30). Family ticket £6.30
🍴 ✗ ♿ (Braille guide, 2 selfdrive vehicles- booking
advisable) toilets for disabled shop ✈ 🦌

🏛 CANFORD CLIFFS
COMPTON ACRES GARDENS
Canford Cliffs Rd BH13 7ES (on B3065)
☎ 01202 700778 🖷 01202 707537

The nine and a half acres of Compton Acres incorporate Japanese, Roman and Italian gardens, rock and water gardens, and heather gardens. There are fine views over Poole Harbour and the Purbeck Hills, and a collection of bronze and marble statuary.
Times: Open Mar-Oct, daily 10-6 (last entry 5.15)
🅿 ♨ ✗ licensed ⅗ (level paths and ramps into shops and cafe) toilets for disabled shop garden centre ✘ (ex guide & hearing dogs) *Details not confirmed for 2000* 🐾
See advert under Poole.

🏛 CHETTLE
CHETTLE HOUSE
DT11 8DB (6m NE of Blandford Forum off A354)
☎ 01258 830209 🖷 01258 830380

This small country house was designed by Thomas Archer, and is a fine example of the English Baroque. Around the house there are beautifully laid-out gardens. There is an exhibition area and a vineyard.
Times: Open Etr-3 Oct, daily 11-5. (Closed Tue & Sat).
Fee: *£2 (ch free).
🅿 ♨ ⅗ (access to house with assistance) ✘ (ex guide dogs)

🏛 CHRISTCHURCH
CHRISTCHURCH CASTLE & NORMAN HOUSE
(near Christchurch Priory)

All that remain of the castle buildings are a ruined keep and an interesting, well preserved Norman house, believed to have been the home of the castle constable.
Times: Open any reasonable time.
⌗

RED HOUSE MUSEUM & GARDENS
Quay Rd BH23 1BU
☎ 01202 482860 🖷 01202 481924

A museum with plenty of variety, featuring local history, archaeology, and natural history, displayed in this Georgian house. There's an excellent costume collection, and gardens, with a woodland walk and herb garden. Temporary exhibitions include contemporary art and change regularly.
Times: Open all year, Tue-Sat 10-5.30, Sun 2-5.30 (Closed Mon ex BH).
Fee: *£1 (ch & pen 60p). Family ticket £2.60.
🅿 (200yds) ♨ ⅗ shop ✘

🏛 CORFE CASTLE
CORFE CASTLE
BH20 5EZ (on A351)
☎ 01929 481294

Built in Norman times, the castle was added to by King John. It was defended during the Civil War by Lady Bankes, who surrendered after a stout resistance. Parliament ordered the demolition of the castle, and today it is one of the most impressive ruins in England. Ring for details of special events.
Times: Open daily (closed 25, 26 Dec & 2 days end of Jan; 1-27 Mar & 25-31 Oct 10-4.30. 28 Mar-24 Oct 10-5.30. 1 Nov-4 Mar 2000 11-3.30.
Fee: *£4 (ch £2). Family ticket £6-£10. Party 15+ by arrangement.
🅿 (charged) ♨ ✗ licensed (Braille guide & menu) shop 🐾

🏛 DORCHESTER
DORSET COUNTY MUSEUM
High West St DT1 1XA
☎ 01305 262735 🖷 01305 257180

Displays cover prehistoric and Roman times, including sites such as Maiden Castle, and there's a gallery on Dorset writers with sections on the poet William Barnes, Thomas Hardy (with a reconstruction of his study), and twentieth century writers. Exhibition for the millenium - 2000 Years of the Church in Wessex.
Times: Open daily 10-5. (Closed Sun Sep-Jun, Good Fri, 25 Dec).
Fee: *£3 (students, UB40 & pen £2, ch £1.50) . Family ticket £7.50. Party 15+.
🅿 (150 yds) ⅗ shop ✘ (ex guide dogs)

HARDY'S COTTAGE
Higher Bockhampton DT2 8QJ (3m NE of Dorchester, 0.5m S of A35)
☎ 01305 262366

Thomas Hardy was born in this thatched house in 1840. It was built by his great-grandfather and has not changed much in appearance since. The inside can only be seen by appointment with the tenant.
Times: Open 28 Mar-31 Oct daily execpt Fri & Sat, 11-5 or dusk if earlier. Open Good Friday.
Fee: *£2.60. Interior by appointment.
🅿 ⅗ (car parking by arrangement with custodian) ✘ 🐾

MAIDEN CASTLE
DT1 9PR (2m S, access off A354, N of bypass)

This Iron Age fort ranks among the finest in Britain. It covers 47 acres, and has daunting earthworks, with a complicated defensive system around the entrances. One of its main purposes may well have been to protect grain from

DORCHESTER

The county town of Dorset was Durnovaria to the Romans and the model for Casterbridge in the novels of Thomas Hardy. Hardy was born just two miles from Dorchester at Higher Bockhampton and spent much of his life in the town, where he is honoured with a statue in High West Street.

The walls of the Roman town were replaced by 18th-century tree-lined walks, such as Bowling Alley Walk, Colliton Walk and West Walk, and the architecture of the town's centre is mainly 17th century and Georgian. Dorchester is the centre of an agricultural community, and one of its busiest days is market day on Wednesday.

marauding bands. The first single-rampart fort dates from around around 700BC and by 100BC the earthworks covered the whole plateau. It was finally overrun by Roman troops in AD43.

Times: Open any reasonable time.

🅿 ✿

THE MILITARY MUSEUM OF DEVON & DORSET

The Keep, Bridport Rd DT1 1RN (situated near the top of High West St)

☎ 01305 264066   🗎 01305 250373

Three hundred years of military history, with displays on the Devon Regiment, Dorset Regiment, Dorset Militia and Volunteers, the Queen's Own Dorset Yeomanry, and Devonshire and Dorset Regiment (from 1958). The Museum uses modern technology and creative displays to tell the stories of the Infantry, Cavalry and Artillerymen.

Times: Open all year, Mon-Sat 9-5 (Jul & Aug Sun 10-4).

Fee: *£2.50, (ch, student & pen £1.50). Family ticket £7

🅿 ♿ (lift avalible) toilets for disabled shop ✕

⌂ POOLE

POOLE POTTERY

The Quay BH15 1RF

☎ 01202 666200   🗎 01202 682894

Founded in 1873, this well-known company has

contd.

been producing its distinctive Poole Pottery since 1921. There is a display of past and present pottery manufacture, factory tour and shop.

Times: Open all year, daily 10-4. (Closed 22 Dec-2 Jan).
Fee: *Factory tours £3.50 (ch £2.50, pen & students £3). Party 10+.
P (500 yds) ■✖ licensed & (wheelchairs available) toilets for disabled shop ✖ ➤

WATERFRONT MUSEUM & SCAPLEN'S COURT

4 High St BH15 1BW (off Poole quay)
☎ 01202 683138 🖹 01202 660896

The museum tells the story of Poole's seafaring past. Learn of the Roman occupation, hear the smuggler tell his tale and see material raised from the Studland Bay wreck. Scaplen's Court, just a few yards from the museum, is a beautifully restored domestic building dating from the medieval period. There is a Victorian school room, a kitchen and scullery in which cooking demonstrations take place from time to time, a children's room and other displays.

Times: Museum: open Apr-Oct, Mon-Sat 10-5, Sun noon-5; Nov-Mar, Mon-Sat 10-3, Sun noon-3. Scaplen's Court: Aug, Mon-Sat 10-5, Sun noon-5.
Fee: *Museum: £2-£4 (ch £1.35-2.85, pen & student £1.70-£3.40). Family Ticket £6.30-£11.50.
P (250meters) & (ex Town Cellars & Scaplen's Court) toilets for disabled ✖ (ex guide dogs) ➤

⛪ PORTLAND

PORTLAND CASTLE

Castle Town DT5 1AZ (overlooking Portland harbour)
☎ 01305 820539

One of the best preserved of Henry VIII's coastal forts, built of white Portland stone and originally intended to thwart attack by the Spanish and French. The castle was much fought over in the Civil War.

Times: Open Apr-1 Nov, daily 10-6 (or dusk if earlier in Oct).
Fee: £2.50 (ch £1.30).
P & shop ✖ ⌗

PORTLAND MUSEUM

217 Wakeham DT5 1HS (A354,through Fortuneswell to Portland Heights Hotel, then English Heritage signs)
☎ 01305 821804 🖹 01305 761654

Avice's cottage in Thomas Hardy's book `The Well-Beloved', this building is now a museum of local and historical interest, with varied displays. Regular temporary exhibitions are held. The adjoining Marie Stopes cottage houses the shop and a display of maritime history.

Times: Open: Etr-Oct 10.30-5 (Closed 1-1.30 & all day Wed-Thu), Nov-Etr.
Fee: *£1.70 (ch & students free, pen 95p).
P & (talking tapes for blind & partially sighted) shop

⛪ SHERBORNE

SHERBORNE CASTLE

☎ 01935 813182 🖹 01935 816727

This 16th-century house, built by Sir Walter Raleigh, has been the home of the Digby family since 1617. Built beside the ruins of the old castle, the house contains fine furniture, paintings and porcelain; and the grounds were designed by `Capability' Brown in the 18th century. Ring for details of special events.

Times: Open Apr-Oct. House open Tue, Thu, Sat, Sun & BH Mon 12.30-5. Grounds open Tue, Thu, Fri 12.30-5.
Fee: *£4.80 (ch £2.40, pen £4). Family ticket £12. Grounds only £2.40 (ch £1.20). Party 25+.
P ■ shop ✖ (ex in grounds)

SHERBORNE MUSEUM

Abbey Gate House, Church Ln DT9 3BP
☎ 01935 812252

The museum features a model of Sherborne's original Norman castle, as well as a fine Victorian doll's house and other domestic and agricultural bygones. There are also items of local geological, natural history and archeological interest, including Roman material.

Times: Open Apr-Oct, Tue-Sat 10.30-4.30, Sun 2.30-4.30; BH Mon 2.30-4.30
Fee: *£1 (ch & students free)
P (400yds) & toilets for disabled shop ✖ (ex guide dogs)

SHERBORNE OLD CASTLE

D19 5NR (half a mile E off B3145)
☎ 01935 812730

The 12th-century castle was built by Roger, Bishop of Salisbury. In Elizabethan times it belonged to Sir Walter Raleigh, but was largely destroyed by Cromwell in the Civil War. The ruined Norman buildings remain.

Times: Open Apr-1 Nov, daily 10-6 (or dusk if earlier in Oct); 2 Nov-Mar, Wed-Sun 10-4, (closed 1-2pm). Grounds only open.
Fee: £1.60 (80p).
P & ✖ ⌗

⛪ SWANAGE

SWANAGE RAILWAY

Station House BH19 1HB (Park & Ride Station at Norden, signposted from A351)
☎ 01929 425800 🖹 01929 426680

The railway from Swanage to Wareham was closed in 1972, and in 1976 the Swanage Railway took possession and have gradually restored the line, which now runs for 6 miles, passing the ruins of Corfe Castle. Ring for details of special events.

Times: Open every weekend throughout the year, daily 1 Apr-31 Oct.

Fee: *Swanage-Corfe £5.50 return, £3 single. Swanage-Norden £6 return, £3.60 single. (ch 5-15 & pen 50% reduction in price). Family ticket £17. Day Rover £10 (ch & pen £5).

P ⬛ ✖ licensed ♿ (special disabled persons coach) toilets for disabled shop (shop at Swanage Station) 🔻

⛪ TOLPUDDLE
Tolpuddle Martyrs Museum
DT2 7EH (on A35, 7m E of Dorchester, 4.5m W of Bere Regis)
☎ 01305 848237   📄 01305 848237

Tolpuddle was made famous by the agricultural workers from the village who united to improve their wages and conditions of employment. They were arrested and transported in 1834 and became known as the Tolpuddle Martyrs. In the 1930s the TUC built a museum and six cottages named after them. The museum tells the story of the martyrs, and the Tolpuddle Martyrs Rally is held on the third Sunday of July each year, 12.30-4pm.

Times: Open all year, Apr-Oct, Tue-Sat 10-5.30, Sun 11-5.30; Nov-Mar, Tue-Sat 10-4, Sun 11-4. Open BH Mon. (Closed 24 Dec-1 Jan).

Fee: Free.

P (outside museum) ♿ toilets for disabled shop ✖

⛪ WEST LULWORTH
Lulworth Cove Heritage Centre
Lulworth Cove BH20 5RQ (From A352 go to Wool, then onto B3071 and follow brown signs)
☎ 01929 400587

The centre traces the history of Lulworth from prehistoric through to modern times. Displays include coastal and other local wildlife, flora, geology and fossils. The centre is at Lulworth Cove with access to spectacular coastal walks.

Times: Open daily Nov-Mar 10-4; Apr-Oct 10-6 (Closed 25 Dec)

P (charged) ♿ toilets for disabled shop ✖ *Details not confirmed for 2000* 🔻

⛪ WEYMOUTH
RSPB Nature Reserve Radipole Lake
The Swannery Car Park DT4 7TZ (in the town, close to seafront & railway station)
☎ 01305 778313   📄 01305 773519

Covering 222 acres, the Reserve offers firm paths, hides and a visitor centre. Several types of warblers, mute swans, gadwalls, teals and great crested grebes may be seen, and the visitor centre has viewing windows overlooking the lake. Phone for details of special events.

Times: Open daily 9-5

P (charged) ♿ shop *Details not confirmed for 2000* 🔻

⛪ WIMBORNE
Kingston Lacy House, Garden & Park
BH21 4EA (1.5m W of Wimbourne B3082)
☎ 01202 883402   📄 01202 882402

Kingston Lacy House was the home of the Bankes family for over 300 years. The original house is 17th century, but in the 1830s was given a stone façade. The Italian marble staircase, Venetian ceiling, treasures from Spain and an Egyptian obelisk were also added. There are outstanding pictures by Titian, Rubens, Velasquez, Reynolds and Van Dyck. Please ring for details of special events. No photography is allowed in the house.

Times: Garden & Park; 27 Mar-Oct daily ex 9,10 Jul & 6 Aug 11-6. Nov & Dec open Fri-Sun 11-4. House; 27 Mar-Oct daily ex Thur & Fri 12-5.30. Last admission 4.30pm. Closed 9 & 10 Jul & 6 Aug.

Fee: *£6 (ch £3). Park & Gardens only: £2.50 (ch £1.25).Party.

P ✖ licensed ♿ (parking by arrangement) toilets for disabled shop ✖ (ex on leads in park & wood) 🦮

County Durham

The Durham Dales lie between the Northumberland National Park and the Yorkshire Dales, and form around a third of the county's area. This huge expanse of waterfalls, meadows, heath and river valleys contains some beautiful scenery.

Top: Durham Castle

There are two record-breaking geographic features in the area, which should make an afternoon's ramble more interesting. One is the road from Killhope to Nenthead in Cumbria, which rises to over 2,000 feet, making it the highest classified road in England. The other is the waterfall at High Force, where the River Tees falls 70 feet onto rocks, making it the highest waterfall in England.

The history of the area is as rich as the scenery. In the middle ages the Prince Bishops ruled the County Palatine with a unique blend of political and ecclesiastic power. This power extended into Northumberland and Yorkshire, and provided the first line of defence against the marauding Scots. These unusual figures maintained their own armies, had their own courts and nobility, and minted their own coins. Essentially they were the rulers of virtually independant states. The best expression of this dual worldly and heavenly power is Durham's own cathedral, once described as "Half Church of God, half Castle 'gainst the Scot."

In the 19th century the area around Weardale was the centre of the world lead-mining industry. The industry has long since disappeared, and the 34-foot waterwheel and mine at the Killhope Lead Mining Centre are among the few reminders that this massive undertaking ever took place.

BARNARD CASTLE
BARNARD CASTLE
☎ 01833 38212

The town's name comes from Bernard Baliol, who built the castle in 1125. The impressive ruins cling to the steep banks of the River Tees.
Times: Open all year, Apr-1 Nov, daily 10-6 (or dusk if earlier); 2 Nov-Mar, Wed-Sun 10-4.
Fee: £2.30 (ch £1.20).
P & shop ✪ Details not confirmed for 2000

THE BOWES MUSEUM
DL12 8NP (4m from the village of Bowes on the A66, Scotch Corner-Penrith)
☎ 01833 690606 ▤ 01833 637163

This splendid château-style mansion was built in 1869 by John Bowes, who made his fortune in Durham coal and married a French actress. They amassed an outstanding collection of works of art, and built the flamboyant château to house them. The museum contains paintings by El Greco, Goya and Canaletto among others; porcelain and silver, furniture, ceramics and tapestries. There is a local history section, and a formal garden. Temporary exhibitions are held.
Times: Open daily 11-5.
Fee: *£3.90 (concessions £2.90). Family ticket £12.
P ◖ & (lift, ramped entrance, reserved parking) toilets for disabled shop ✖ (ex guide dogs) ◆

EGGLESTONE ABBEY
DL12 8QN (1m S on minor road off B6277)

The remains of this Premonstratensian abbey make a picturesque sight on the bank of the River Tees. A large part of the church can be seen, as can remnants of monastic buildings.
Times: Open any reasonable time.
P & ✪

BEAMISH
NORTH OF ENGLAND OPEN-AIR MUSEUM
DH9 0RG (off A693 & A6076 signposted off A1(M) J63)
☎ 01207 231811 ▤ 01207 290933

Set in 200 acres of beautiful countryside, Beamish vividly recreates life in the north of England early this century. Stroll along the cobbled streets of The Town, with fully stocked shops, dentist's surgery, working pub, and sweet factory. Guided tours of a real 'drift' mine, and a row of miner's cottages, show how pitmen and their families lived. There is a Methodist chapel and a village school, and traditional breeds of animals fill the farmyard at Home Farm. At The Railway Station, complete with goods yard, signal box and weighbridge house, locomotives and rolling stock are on display.

Times: Open all year: Summer, 27 Mar-Oct, daily from 10am. Winter visits centred on The Town & tramway, other areas closed, Nov-Mar from 10am but closed Mon & Fri. Closing times vary according to season it is advisable to check. Also check for Christmas times.
Fee: Summer £10 (ch £6, pen £7). Winter £3 (ch £3, pen £3).
P ◖ & toilets for disabled shop ◆

BOWES
BOWES CASTLE
DL12 9LD (on A66)

Built inside the earthworks of the Roman fort of 'Lavatrae', the castle dates from the 12th century and its great ruined Norman keep still stands to a height of three storeys.
Times: Open any reasonable time.
⚓ ✪

COWSHILL
KILLHOPE LEAD MINING CENTRE
DL13 1AR (beside A689 midway between Stanhope & Alston)
☎ 01388 537505 ▤ 01388 537617

Equipped with hard hats and lamps, you can descend into the depths of the earth and explore the working conditions of lead miners. The lead mine and 19th-century crushing mill have been restored to look as they would have done in the 1870s, and the 34ft water wheel has been restored to working order. There's also a visitor centre and exhibition based on the life of miners and their families.
Times: Open Apr-Oct, daily 10.30-5. Last entry 4.30pm. Nov, Sun 10.30-4.
Fee: *£3.40 (ch, disabled, & UB40 £1.70, pen £2.40). Additional charge for mine visit £1.60(ch, disabled, UB40 80p)
P ◖ & toilets for disabled shop ◆

DURHAM

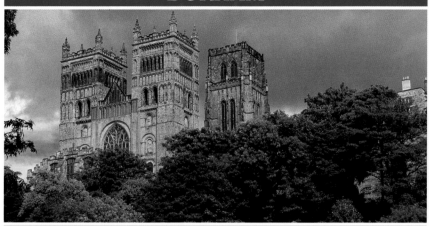

Durham was founded in 995 when a Saxon church was built on the rock in the River Wear's hairpin bend, where less than a century later, Bishop William of Calais began building Durham Cathedral. Like the Saxon church before it, was originally built to house the shrine of St Cuthbert, one-time prior of Lindisfarne, whose remains were believed to work miracles. The Venerable Bede is also buried there.

The castle was built by William the Conqueror, and the entrance to its main hall is the most extravagant piece of Norman work remaining in Britain. Much of the castle was renewed at a later date, and is now used by the university.

▥ DARLINGTON
DARLINGTON RAILWAY CENTRE & MUSEUM
North Rd Station DL3 6ST (0.75m N off A167)
☎ 01325 460532

Housed in the carefully restored North Road Station, this museum's prize exhibit is *Locomotion*, which pulled the first passenger train and was built by Robert Stephenson & Co in 1825. Several other steam locomotives are also shown, together with models and other exhibits relating to the Stockton and Darlington and the North Eastern Railway companies. Live steam days throughout the year.
Times: Open daily 10-5 (closed Jan); Last admission 4.30pm. May be subject to amendment.
Fee: *£2.10 (ch £1.05, OAP £1.50). Parties 10+.
🅿 ▣ ⚹ (guide tape for visually handicapped) toilets for disabled shop ✖ (ex guide dogs)

▥ DURHAM
DURHAM CATHEDRAL
DH1 3EH (A1(M) to Durham turn off at A690 into city take turning into the market place & follow signs)
☎ 0191 386 4266 ▤ 0191 386 4267

Founded in 1093 as a shrine to St Cuthbert, whose bones still rest in the Feretory. The cathedral is a remarkable example of Norman architecture, set in an impressive position high above the River Wear. A full programme of concerts throughout the year. St Cuthbert's Day Procession (phone for details).
Times: Open all year, daily, Sep-Apr 7.15-6, May-Aug 7.15-8.
🅿 (in city centre) ▣ ✖ licensed ⚹ (braille guide touch & hearing centre) toilets for disabled shop ✖ *Details not confirmed for 2000*

DURHAM LIGHT INFANTRY MUSEUM & DURHAM ART GALLERY
Aykley Heads DH1 5TU (0.5m NW, turn right off A691)
☎ 0191 384 2214 ▤ 0191 386 1770

The history of the Regiment is told in displays of artefacts, medals, uniforms and vehicles. The Art Gallery has a continuous programme of temporary exhibitions, and holds regular lectures and concerts.
Times: Open all year, Tue-Sat 10-4.30 & Sun 2-4.30 (Closed Mon, ex BHs).
Fee: *£2 (£1 concessions).
🅿 ▣ ⚹ (wheelchair available, lift, ramps) toilets for disabled shop ✖ ▰

FINCHALE PRIORY
(3m NE)
☎ 0191 386 3828

This lovely setting was the refuge chosen by St Godric in 1110 for his years of solitary meditation, and the priory, used by monks from

Durham Cathedral, was founded in 1180.
Remains of the 13th-century church can be seen.
Times: Open Apr-Sep, daily 10-6, Oct 10-5.
Fee: £1.30 (ch 70p).
🅿 (charged) ♿ ✕ ♨

⛪ HARTLEPOOL
HARTLEPOOL HISTORIC QUAY
Maritime Av TS24 0XZ (from A19 take A179 and
follow signs for marina then historic quay)
☎ 01429 860077   📄 01429 867332

Britain's maritime heritage is brought to life, with
the sights, sounds and smells of an 1800's
quayside. Learn about the birth of the Royal
Navy, and visit the Quayside shops, gaol,
admiral's house and the Hartness market. There's
a full programme of events, including re-
enactments by naval and military groups, craft
fairs, musical events, Christmas and Easter
themed events, phone for details.
Times: Open daily 10-5 (10-7 in summer). Closed 25 Dec &
1 Jan.
🅿 💻 ✕ licensed ♿ (all areas ramped or lift access) toilets
for disabled shop ✕ *Details not confirmed for 2000* 🛎

HMS TRINCOMALEE TRUST
Jackson Dock TS24 0SQ (follow brown heritage
signs)
☎ 01429 223193   📄 01429 864385

HMS *Trincomalee*, launched in 1817, is the oldest
British warship afloat, and is undergoing
restoration.
Times: Open all year, Mon-Fri 10.30-3.30, wknds & BH 10.30-
4.30. (Closed Xmas & New Year (inc Boxing day)).
Fee: *£2.50 (£1.50 concessions) Family ticket £6.50.
🅿 ♿ ✕

MUSEUM OF HARTLEPOOL
Marina Way, Jackson Dock TS24 0XZ
☎ 01429 222255   📄 01429 523477

Telling the story of Hartlepool from prehistory to
the present day and includes many original
artefacts, models, computer interactives and
hands-on exhibits. See how iron and steel ships
were built and climb aboard the fishing coble *The
Three Brothers Grant*. The Humber ferry *Wingfield
Castle*, a paddle steamer built in Hartlepool in
1934 is moored alongside the museum and
houses further displays and a café. Traditional
fishing and pilot cobles are moored in the dock.
Times: Open all year, daily (closed 25-26 Dec & 1 Jan).
🅿 💻 ♿ toilets for disabled shop ✕ (ex guide dogs) *Details
not confirmed for 2000*

⛪ STAINDROP
RABY CASTLE
P O Box 50 DL2 3AY (1m N, off A688)
☎ 01833 660202   📄 01833 660169

The castle was built during Saxon times but is
substantially 14th century, with many later
additions. It has an impressive gateway; nine
towers; a vast medieval hall; and a Victorian
octagonal drawing-room. The castle contains
fine pictures, interesting furniture and ceramics,
and a carriage collection. There are gardens, and
a 200-acre park with both red and fallow deer.
Ring for details of special events.
Times: Open May-Jun, Wed & Sun; Jul-Sep, Sun-Fri; BH
weekends, Sat-Wed (incl Etr). Castle open 1-5. Park & gardens
11-5.30, (last admission 4.30pm).
Fee: *Castle, Gardens & Carriage Collection £4 (ch £1.50, pen
£3). Family ticket £10. Park, Gardens & Carriage Collection
£1.50 (ch & pen £1). Party25+.
🅿 💻 ♿ toilets for disabled shop ✕ (ex in Park) 🛎

⛪ TANFIELD
TANFIELD RAILWAY
Old Marley Hill NE16 5ET (on A6076 1m S of
Sunniside)
☎ 0191 388 7545   📄 0191 387 4784

A 3-mile working steam railway and the oldest
existing railway in the world. The Causey Arch,
the first large railway bridge of its era, is the
centrepiece of a deep wooded valley, with
picturesque walks. You can ride in carriages that
first saw use in Victorian times, and visit Marley
Hill shed, the home of 35 engines; inside the
shed you can see the stationary steam engine at
work driving some of the vintage machine tools.
The blacksmith is also often at work forging new
parts for the restoration work. Special events are
held throughout the year, please telephone for
details.
Times: Open all year, summer daily 10-5; winter daily 10-4.
Trains: Sun & Summer BH's weekends; also Thu & Sat mid Jul-
Aug. Santa's Specials Sat & Sun in Dec (booking essential).
Mince pie specials Boxing Day.
Fee: *Admission free. Train travel £3.50 (ch & pen £2) Family
discount tickets avalible £9.
🅿 💻 ♿ (all trains carry ramps for wheelchair access) toilets
for disabled shop

Essex

Essex and its inhabitants have for some time been the butt of jokes that imply financial acuity but a lack of taste, discernment and sophistication. This might be due to the county's proximity to London, which has led to the development of commuter towns and changed the nature of an area once rural to something suburban.

However, moving northeast into East Anglia there are some fine country towns and villages, and, approaching the Suffolk border, all the scenic delights of Constable country around the Stour Valley.

The big resorts of Southend and Clacton are the best known on the Essex coast, but by contrast there are pretty places on the Tendring Peninsula, the sailing centres of Burnham-on-Crouch and Maldon, the marshy headland of the Naze, and the birdlife of Maplin Sands.

From medieval times to the 18th century, Saffron Walden was the centre of the saffron crocus industry. It was saffron wealth that bought the town the largest parish church in Essex, and the streets around the church reflect this historic prosperity.

Colchester lays claim to being England's oldest town, and is a fascinating place to visit. There is evidence of a settlement from the fifth century BC, and the town was King Cymbeline's capital in the first century AD. The Romans also made it their capital in 43 AD and the town prospered despite being burnt by Boudicca/Boadicea in 60 AD. The Roman walls are largely intact, and there are the remains of the Norman castle to be seen.

Top: Middle Street, Clavering

⚑ AUDLEY END
AUDLEY END HOUSE
CB11 4JF (1m W of Saffron Walden on B1383)
☎ 01799 522399

Built on a grandiose scale by Thomas Howard, Earl of Suffolk, to entertain King James I, Audley End House was gradually reduced in size over the next century, but what we see today is still impressive in scale and the 30 rooms open to the public display a stunning collection of art, as well as period furnishings. Gardens and a landscaped park surround the mansion.
Times: Open Apr-Oct, Wed-Sun & BH's 11-6 (or dusk if earlier). Park and gardens open from 10am. Last admissions 5pm.
🅿 (charged) 💷 ⅙ shop ✖ ✪ *Details not confirmed for 2000*

⚑ CASTLE HEDINGHAM
HEDINGHAM CASTLE
CO9 3DJ (on B1058, 1m off A604)
☎ 01787 460261   ▤ 01787 461473

This impressive Norman castle was built in 1140. It was besieged by King John, and visited by Henry VII, Henry VIII and Elizabeth I, and was home to the de Veres, Earls of Oxford, for over 500 years. Please telephone for details of special events.
Times: Open wk before Etr-Oct, daily 10-5.
Fee: *£3.50 (ch £2.50). Family ticket £10.50.
🅿 💷 shop 🖙

⚑ COGGESHALL
PAYCOCKE'S
West St CO6 1NS
☎ 01376 561305

This timber-framed house is a fine example of a medieval merchant's home. It was completed in about 1505 and has interesting carvings on the outside timbers, including the Paycocke trade sign. Inside there are further elaborate carvings and linenfold panelling. Behind the house is a pretty garden.
Times: Open 29 Mar-11 Oct Tue, Thu, Sun & BH Mon 2-5.30. (Closed Good Fri). Last admission 5pm.
🅿 (400yds) ⅙ ✖ 🚲 ❧ *Details not confirmed for 2000*

⚑ COLCHESTER
BETH CHATTO GARDENS
Elmstead Market CO7 7DB (5m E of Colchester on the A133)
☎ 01206 822007   ▤ 01206 825933

Begun almost 40 years ago, when Beth Chatto and her husband began working on four acres of wasteland. Today the wasteland has become a garden of three distinctive areas. The south-west facing dry garden is on gravel, and has plants which can cope with drought, such as yucca and pineapple broom. It faces a group of oaks which shade the second area, with woodland and other shade-loving plants, including some chosen for their fine foliage. Lastly, there is the wetland garden, with five large pools filled with fish and surrounded by swathes of exotic and native bog plants. The former grass car park has been transformed into a new gravel garden for plants adapted to drought, and the nursery has over 2000 different plants.
Times: Open all year, Mar-Oct, Mon-Sat 9-5; Nov-Feb, Mon-Fri 9-4. (Closed BHs & Sun.
Fee: *£3 (accompanied ch free)
🅿 ⅙ (access to parts of garden may be difficult) toilets for disabled garden centre ✖ 🖙

COLCHESTER CASTLE MUSEUM
Castle Park, High St CO1 1TJ (at eastern end of the High St)
☎ 01206 282931 & 282932
▤ 01206 282925

The largest Norman castle keep in Europe - built over the remains of the magnificent Roman Temple of Claudius which was destroyed by Boudicca in AD60. Colchester was the first capital of Roman Britain, and the archaeological collections are among the finest in the country. Please telephone for details of a range of events held in the school holidays.
Times: Open all year, Mon-Sat 10-5, Sun (Mar-Nov) 1-5.
Fee: *£3.70 (concessions £2.40)
🅿 (town centre) ⅙ (ramps to all areas & lift) toilets for disabled shop ✖ 🖙

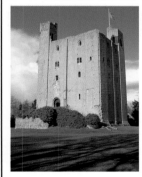

⛫ HADLEIGH
HADLEIGH CASTLE
(0.75m S of A13)
☎ 01536 402840

The subject of several of Constable's paintings, the castle has fine views of the Thames estuary. It is defended by ditches on three sides, and the north-east and south-east towers are still impressive.

Times: Open any reasonable time.
♯

⛫ LAYER MARNEY
LAYER MARNEY TOWER
CO5 9US (off B1022 Colchester to Maldon road, signposted)
☎ 01206 330784 ▤ 01206 330784

The the tallest Tudor gatehouse in the country, intended to be the entrance to a courtyard which would have rivalled Hampton Court Palace. The death of Henry, 1st Lord Marney in 1523, and of his son in 1525, meant that the building work ceased before completion. The parish church of St Mary the Virgin in the grounds contains fine Italianate terracotta. Terracotta is also used on the Tower itself and adjoining wings. The Tower may be climbed, and there are stunning views of the surrounding countryside. Special events are planned, including craft fairs, plays, and the church fete. Please telephone for details.

Times: Open Apr-Sep, Mon-Fri 12-5, Sun 12-5 & BHs 11-5.
Fee: *£3.25 (ch £1.75). Family ticket £9. Guided tour £4.50. Party 20+.
🅿 ➐ ♿ (ramps in garden and farm) toilets for disabled shop ✖ (ex guide dogs)

⛫ MISTLEY
MISTLEY TOWERS
CO11 1NJ (on B1352, 1.5m E of A137 at Lawford)

All that remains of the grand hall and church, designed by Robert Adam, are the lodges built in 1782 for the hall, and two square towers, topped with drums and domes which came from an earlier church.

Times: Open all reasonable times. Key available from Mistley Quay Workshops & Teashop.
♿ (exterior only) ✖ (in certain areas) ♯

⛫ TILBURY
TILBURY FORT
RM18 7NR (0.5m off A126)
☎ 01375 858489

The largest English example of 17th-century military engineering, the fort originally dates from the earlier Tudor period, and is most famous for Queen Elizabeth I's review of her troops before the defeat of the Spanish Armada. It defended the country again in the 17th century against the Dutch and the French; ironically, it

MALDON

Maldon is an ancient and attractive town, and when you stand by the 7th-century Chapel of St Cedd on its remote peninsula it's hard to believe that you're less than fifty miles from the centre of London. Maldon is an attractive mix of old and new. Promenade Park was opened in 1895, and includes a children's adventure playground and tennis courts in a landscape setting beside the River Blackwater. Other places worth visiting are the 15th-century Moot Hall, the 13th-century All Saints Church, where George Washington's great grandfather is buried, Northey Island (a managed National Trust nature reserve) and Hythe Quay, home to a number of Thames Sailing Barges.

had been redesigned by a Dutch engineer in the French style. There is a good site museum, and much to explore and enjoy.

Times: Open all year, Apr-Oct, daily 10-6 (or dusk if earlier); Nov-Mar, Wed-Sun 10-4. Closed 24-26 Dec & 1 Jan.
Fee: £2.50 (ch £1.30).
 ⟁ shop ✖ (in certain areas) ♯♯

▥ WALTHAM ABBEY
LEE VALLEY PARK FARMS
Stubbings Hall Ln, Crooked Mile EN9 2EG (off B194)
☎ 01992 892781 & 892291
🖹 01992 893113

Two different views of farming methods. Hayes Hill Farm has a traditional-style farmyard and

you can also look round Holyfield Hall Farm, a working commercial dairy and arable farm of some 600 acres. There are 140 Friesian cows, and milking takes place at 2.45pm every day. Booked guided tours are available. Various events take place, please telephone for details.

Times: Open all year, Mon-Fri 10-4.30, wknds & BH 10-5.30pm.
Fee: *£2.95 (concessions £1.95).
🅿 ▣ ⟁ (graded concrete paths, signed routes) toilets for disabled shop ⊲

WALTHAM ABBEY GATEHOUSE, BRIDGE & ENTRANCE TO CLOISTERS

Beside the great Norman church at Waltham are the slight remains of the abbey buildings - bridge, gatehouse and part of the north cloister. The bridge is named after King Harold, founder of the abbey.

Times: Open any reasonable time.
♯♯ *Details not confirmed for 2000*

Gloucestershire

EVENTS & FESTIVALS

February
4th-6th Cheltenham
Millennium Folk Festival

March
14th-16th National Hunt
Festival Meeting, Cheltenham

April
27th-30th (provisional)
Cheltenham Jazz Festival

May
4th-7th The Badminton
Horse Trials
29th Annual Wool/Sack
Races & Street Fair, Tetbury

June
15th 900th Anniversary
Rededication of
Gloucester
Cathedral

July
1st-16th:
Cheltenham
International
Festival of
Music & Fringe
22nd-23rd RAF
Fairford Air Tattoo
tbc Cheltenham Cricket
Festival, Cheltenham

August
4th-6th Flower Festival,
Gloucester Cathedral

September
23rd-24th Cotswold Country
Fair, Cirencester Park

October
6th-22nd Cheltenham
Festival of Literature

Top: Gloucester Cathedral

Most of the Cotswolds lie in the county of Gloucestershire; limestone hills dotted with picturesque villages built from the local stone, varying in hue from honey gold to silver grey. The large churches and substantial manor houses are a legacy from the wealth of the medieval wool trade.

The bits of Gloucestershire outside the Cotswolds include the county town of Gloucester, the Regency spa town of Cheltenham and the countryside around the Severn estuary, the site of the Slimbridge wildfowl reserve. The county's other major natural feature is the Forest of Dean, a mining area from Roman times until the 20th century.

In redbrick Gloucester there is plenty to see and do. The Victorian docks have been redeveloped to provide offices, shops, cafés and museums, while the canal, opened in 1827 in an attempt to reverse the decline of trade via the Severn, is busy now with pleasure craft.

Nearby Cheltenham is rather more upmarket with its elegant Regency architecture and exclusive boutiques. The mineral spring was discovered there in 1715 through the observation of pigeons coming and going. Pigeons are incorporated into the town's crest to this day, though Cheltenham is probably better known for its horse-racing.

South of Cheltenham is the charmingly old-fashioned and rather less self-conscious Cirencester, the 'capital of the Cotswolds'. It was once an immensely powerful town known as Corinium by the Romans, and in those days second only to Londinium. However, little of its Roman heritage remains.

🏛 BARNSLEY
BARNSLEY HOUSE GARDEN
GL7 5EE (3m NE of Cirencester on B4425
Barnsley House is on right on entering village
from Cirencester)
☎ 01285 740281 🖹 01285 740281

A lovely garden, with herbs and a knot garden,
and a vegetable garden planted as a French
'potager orné', with small paths forming a
chequerboard around fruit trees trained as
pyramids, ornamental brassicas and other
decorative kitchen plants. Other features include
a laburnum walk (good in early June) and a lime
walk. Two 18th-century summerhouses complete
the picture.
Times: Open all year Mon, Wed, Thu & Sat 10-6; Parties &
guided tours by appointment only. House not open.
🅿 ᕆ shop garden centre ✖ *Details not confirmed for 2000*

🏛 BERKELEY
BERKELEY CASTLE
GL13 9BQ (on B4509 1.5m W of A38)
☎ 01453 810332

Home of the Berkeleys for almost 850 years, the
castle is a rambling great place surrounded by
14ft thick walls, with a Norman keep, a great
hall, medieval kitchens, and the dungeon where
Edward II was gruesomely murdered. Outside
there are Elizabethan terraced gardens and an
extensive park.
Times: Open: Tue-Sun, 1-5 Apr-May. Tue-Sat 11-5, Sun 1-5,
Jun & Sep. Mon-Sat 11-5, Sun 1-5 Jul & Aug. Sun only 1-5 Oct.
BH Mon 11-5.
Fee: *Castle & Gardens: £5.20 (ch £2.70, pen £4.20). Gardens
only £1.85 (ch 90p). Party 25+
🅿 💷 shop ✖ 🍴

JENNER MUSEUM
Church Ln, High St GL13 9BH (follow tourist
signs from A38 to town centre, turn left into
High St & left again into Church Ln)
☎ 01453 810631 🖹 01453 811690

This beautiful Georgian house was the home of
Edward Jenner, the discoverer of vaccination
against smallpox. The house and the garden,
with its Temple of Vaccinia, are much as they
were in Jenner's day. The displays record Jenner's
life as an 18th-century country doctor, his work
on vaccination and his interest in natural history.
Times: Open Apr-Sep, Tue-Sat 12.30-5.30, Sun 1-5.30. Oct,
Sun 1-5.30. (Closed Mon, ex BH Mon 12.30-5.30).
Fee: *£2.20 (ch £1, students & pen £1.50). Family ticket £5.50.
Party 20+
🅿 ᕆ (level wide access, hand rails) toilets for disabled shop
✖ (ex guide dogs)

🏛 CHEDWORTH
CHEDWORTH ROMAN VILLA
Yanworth GL54 3LJ (3m NW of Fossebridge
on A429)
☎ 01242 890256 🖹 01242 890544

The remains of a Romano-British villa, excavated
1864-66. Set in a beautiful wooded combe, there
are fine 4th-century mosaics, two bath houses,
and a temple with spring. The museum houses
the smaller finds and there is a 9-minute video
programme. Telephone for further details of
special events.
Times: Open Mar-2 Nov, Tue-Sun & BH Mon 10-5; 4-30 Nov,
Tue-Sun 10-4 also 6 & 7 Dec.
🅿 ᕆ (wheelchair available) toilets for disabled shop ✖ 🐾
Details not confirmed for 2000

🏛 CHELTENHAM
ART GALLERY & MUSEUM
Clarence St GL50 3JT (close to town centre and
bus station)
☎ 01242 237431 🖹 01242 262334

The museum has an outstanding collection
relating to the Arts and Crafts Movement,
including fine furniture and exquisite metalwork.
The Art Gallery contains Dutch and British
paintings from the 17th century to the present
day. The Oriental Gallery features pottery,
costumes and treasures from the Ming Dynasty
to the reign of the last Chinese Emperor. There is
also a display about Edward Wilson, one of
Cheltenham's famous sons, who journeyed with
Captain Scott on the ill-fated Antarctic Expedition
of 1911-12. There is a continuous programme of
contd.

special exhibitions throughout the year. Telephone for details.

Times: Open all year, Mon-Sat 10-5.20. (Closed BHs).
Fee: Free.
P ⊙ & (handling tables; speech reinforcement system) toilets for disabled shop ✖ (ex guide dogs)

HOLST BIRTHPLACE MUSEUM
4 Clarence Rd, Pittville GL52 3JE (just off Evesham Rd)
☎ 01242 524846 ▤ 01242 262334

Gustav Holst, composer of *The Planets* was born at this Regency house in 1874. The museum contains unique displays on Holst's life, including his original piano. The rooms of the house have been carefully restored, each area evoking a different period in the history of the house from Regency to Edwardian times.

Times: Open Tue-Sat 10-4.20 (Closed Mon & BHs). From Apr 2000, please telephone for opening details.
Fee: *£2.25 (concessions 75p)
P (100 yds) shop ✖ (ex guide dogs)

PITTVILLE PUMP ROOM & MUSEUM
Pittville Park GL52 3JE (at N end of town, close to Cheltenham racecourse)
☎ 01242 523852 ▤ 01242 526563

Built in Greek Revival style in the 19th century, the Pump Room has a colonnaded façade and a pillared and balconied hall. It replaced a much humbler building, a thatched shelter over a spring where pigeons had been noticed pecking at salt crystals.

Times: Ring for opening times.
Fee: *Pump room free.
P & shop ✖

⌂ CIRENCESTER
CORINIUM MUSEUM
Park St GL7 2BX
☎ 01285 655611 ▤ 01285 643286

Cirencester was the second largest town in Roman Britain and the Corinium Museum brings the period to life with full-scale reconstructions. There's a Cotswold Prehistory gallery, a Medieval Cotswolds gallery, and galleries on Roman military history, the Roman town of Corinium, and the Civil War in the Cotswolds. Ring for details of exhibitions.

Times: Open all year, Apr-Oct, Mon-Sat 10-5, Sun 2-5; Nov-Mar, Tue-Sat 10-5, Sun 2-5. Also open BHs. (Closed Xmas).
P (440yds town centre) & (Braille guide for exhibits) toilets for disabled shop *Details not confirmed for 2000*

⌂ CLEARWELL
CLEARWELL CAVES ANCIENT IRON MINES
GL16 8JR (1.5m S of Coleford town centre, off B4228)
☎ 01594 832535 ▤ 01594 833362

The mines were worked during the Iron Age, 2,500 years ago, and the industry grew under the Romans. Over half a million tons of ore were extracted in the 19th century, and mining continues today. Nine large caverns can be explored, with deeper trips for the more adventurous. There are engine rooms, a blacksmith's shop, and exhibits of local mining and geology from the Forest of Dean.

Times: Open Mar-Oct daily 10-5. Sat-Sun in Jan, Feb & Nov. Christmas Fantasy 1-24 Dec, 10am-5pm daily. 27 Dec-1 Jan
Fee: *£3.50 (ch £2.20, concessions £3)
P ⊙ & ("Hands-on" exhibits, contact in advance) toilets for disabled shop ✖ (ex guide dogs) ⬤

⌂ CRANHAM
PRINKNASH ABBEY AND POTTERY
GL4 8EX (on A46)
☎ 01452 812066 ▤ 01452 812529

Set in a large park, the old abbey building is a 12th-to 16th-century house, used by Benedictine monks and guests of Gloucester Abbey until 1539. It became an abbey for Benedictine monks from Caldey in 1928. Rich beds of clay were discovered when foundations were being dug for a new building, and so the pottery was established, employing local craftspeople.

Times: Open all year. Abbey Church: daily 5am-8pm. Pottery: Mon-Sat 11-4.30 (Sun pm). Pottery shop & tearoom 9-5.30. (Closed Good Fri, 25 & 26 Dec).
P ⊙ & toilets for disabled shop *Details not confirmed for 2000* ⬤

⌂ DEERHURST
ODDA'S CHAPEL
(off B4213 near River Severn at Abbots Court SW of parish church)

This rare Saxon chapel was built by Earl Odda and dedicated in 1056. When it was discovered, it had been incorporated into a farmhouse. It has now been carefully restored.

Times: Open any reasonable time.
⌗

⌂ DYRHAM
DYRHAM PARK
SN14 8ER (8m N of Bath)
☎ 0117 937 2501

Dyrham Park is a splendid William and Mary house, with interiors which have hardly altered since the late 17th century. It has contemporary Dutch-style furnishings, Dutch pictures and blue-and-white Delft ware. Around the house is an

GLOUCESTER

Lying in the lush Severn Valley and overlooked by the Cotswolds, Gloucester was destroyed by the Saxons in the 6th century when they routed the Christian communities of Wales and the West. Ironically, the most prominent feature of the city is its Norman Cathedral, completed in 1160. It was remodelled by London masons in the 14th century after Edward II was buried there. The east window is one of the largest in Britain. Gloucester is Britain's most inland port, and the warehouses built during the 19th century were once the centre of the city's trade. A restoration programme has restored much of the bustle by turning many of the warehouses into a shopping centre.

ancient park with fallow deer, and a Jazz Festival takes place in July.

Times: Open - House) 27 Mar-Oct; daily ex Wed & Thu, 12-5.30 or dusk if earlier. Garden open same as house except 11-5.30. Park open all year daily 12-5.30 or dusk if earlier. (Closed 2-3 Jul for concerts).

Fee: *£5.50 (ch £2.70) Family £13.50. Garden & park only £2.50 (ch £1.20) Family £6.50. Park only ticket on days when house & gardens closed: £1.80 (ch 90p).

🅿 ➧ ✖ licensed ᕕ (Braille & audio guides to house, Braille menu) toilets for disabled shop ✖ (ex in dog walk area). 🐾

🏛 GLOUCESTER
CITY MUSEUM & ART GALLERY
Brunswick Rd GL1 1HP
☎ 01452 524131   📠 01452 410898

This museum contains a range of exhibits showing the early life and natural history of the city. These include dinosaur displays, unusual Roman remains and the amazing Birdlip mirror. Artists on display at the gallery include Turner and Gainsborough.

Times: Open all year, Mon-Sat 10-5. (Also Jul-Sep, Sun 10-4).
Fee: *£2 (concessions £1). Free for Gloucester City residents and under 18's.
🅿 (adjacent) ᕕ (lift suitable only for manual wheelchairs) toilets for disabled shop ✖

FOLK MUSEUM
99-103 Westgate St GL1 2PG
☎ 01452 526467   📠 01452 330495

A group of Tudor and Jacobean half-timbered houses illustrate the local history, domestic life and rural crafts of the city and county. Displays include Civil War armour, Victorian toys and games, farming, shoemaker's workshop, and a school room c1900. There is a pin factory on the top floor with an 18th-century forge in situ. Regular special exhibitions are held throughout the year - telephone for details.

Times: Open all year, Mon-Sat 10-5. (Also Jul-Sep, Sun 10-4). Open BH Mon.
Fee: *£2 (concessions £1). Free to under 18's, free to Gloucester city residents.
🅿 (200yds) ᕕ (parking on request, ramps) shop ✖ (ex guide dogs) ➧

NATIONAL WATERWAYS MUSEUM
Llanthony Warehouse, The Docks GL1 2EH
(follow signs for historic docks off M5 and also within the city, situated to the south of the city)
☎ 01452 318054   📠 01452 318066

Based in Gloucester Docks, this museum takes up three floors of a seven-storey Victorian warehouse, and documents the 200-year history of Britain's water-based transport. The emphasis is on hands-on experience, including working models and engines, interactive displays, actual

contd.

craft, and the chance to have a go at blacksmithing or tug driving.
Times: Open all year, daily 10-5 (Closed 25 Dec).
Fee: *£4.75 (ch & pen £3.75). Family tickets £11-£13.
P (charged) (wheelchair, lifts, limited access to floating exhibits) toilets for disabled shop (ex guide dogs)

Nature in Art
Wallsworth Hall, Tewkesbury Rd, Twigworth GL2 9PA (on A38, from village follow tourist signs)
☎ 01452 731422 01452 730937

Nature, in any art medium, from any period and from all over the world, is the theme at this gallery, and there are many outstanding exhibits including sculpture (both indoor and outdoor), tapestries and ceramics. There is a comprehensive 'artist in residence' programme for ten months of the year, and events include regular monthly talks, film showings and a full programme of temporary exhibitions and art courses.
Times: Open all year, Tue-Sun & BH's 10-5. Mon by arrangement. (Closed 24-26 Dec).
Fee: *£3.10 (ch, pen & students £2.40, ch under 8 free). Family ticket £9.50. Party 15+
P (lift & ramps at entrance) toilets for disabled shop (ex guide dogs)

Robert Opie Collection-Museum of Advertising & Packaging
Albert Warehouse, Gloucester Docks GL1 2EH (On entering Gloucester head for 'Historic Docks')
☎ 01452 302309 01452 308507

Robert Opie has been collecting old and new advertisements, packs, comics, newspapers, games, toys and other artefacts of our everyday life for the past 35 years, and is still adding to this remarkable collection almost on a daily basis. It forms the country's only Museum of Advertising and Packaging.
Times: Open all year, daily, 10-6; winter Tue-Fri 10-5, Sat & Sun 10-6. (Closed 25-26 Dec).
Fee: *£3.50 (ch £1.25, pen & students £2.30). Party 10+.
P (charged) shop (ex guide dogs)

GREAT WITCOMBE
Witcombe Roman Villa
(off A417, 0.5m S of reservoir in Witcombe Park)

Several mosaic pavements and evidence of a hypocaust have been preserved in the remains of this large Roman villa.
Times: Open any reasonable time. Guided tours may be available contact 0117 9750700
P #

HAILES
Hailes Abbey
(2m NE of Winchcobme off B4632)
☎ 01242 602398

This Cistercian abbey was, in the Middle Ages, one of the main centres of pilgrimage in England because it possessed a phial reputed to contain some of Christ's blood. Good medieval sculpture and floor tiles are displayed in the museum.
Times: Open Apr-Oct, daily 10-6 (or dusk if earlier in Oct); wknds in winter 10-4, (closed 1-2). Closed 24-26 Dec, 1 Jan.
Fee: £2.60 (ch £1.30).
P shop #

LITTLEDEAN
Littledean Hall
GL14 3NR
☎ 01594 824213 01594 824213

The largest known Roman temple in rural Britain was unearthed here in 1984 and the manor itself is Norman. The house has always been lived in, and has been relatively untouched since the 19th century. Inside there are interpretive displays and the grounds offer beautiful walks. There are fish pools in the walled garden, and, of course, the Roman excavations.
Times: Open - House, Grounds & Archaeological site, Apr-Oct, daily 11-5.
Fee: *£3.50 (ch £1.50, pen £2.50)
P (ex in grounds)

MICKLETON
Hidcote Manor Garden
Chipping Campden GL55 6LR (1m E of B4632)
☎ 01386 438333 01386 438817

One of the most delightful gardens in England, created by the horticulturist Major Laurence Johnston and comprising a series of small gardens within the whole, separated by walls and hedges of different species. The gardens are famous for rare shrubs, trees, herbaceous borders, 'old' roses and interesting plant species. Telephone for details of special events.
Times: Open, Gardens only 1 Apr-Sep, daily (ex Tue & Fri) 11-7; also open Tue in Jun & July only 11-7; Oct-1 Nov, daily (ex Tue & Fri) 11-6. Last admission 1hr before closing.
P licensed (limited due to stone paths) toilets for disabled shop garden centre *Details not confirmed for 2000*

⛫ MORETON-IN-MARSH
Bᴀᴛsғᴏʀᴅ Aʀʙᴏʀᴇᴛᴜᴍ
GL56 9QF (1.5m NW, off A44 from Moreton-in-Marsh)
☎ **01608 650722**   ▤ **01608 650290**

One of the largest private collections of woody plants in Great Britain. Of particular note are the oaks, maples, magnolias and cherries. Many other rare and unusual trees, shrubs and bamboos also feature. Spring is a procession of colour with masses of naturalised bulbs, particularly daffodils and narcissi, followed by magnolias and cherries. Autumn is equally impressive, with the fiery oranges and reds of the Japanese maples.

Times: Open Feb-mid Nov daily 10-5.
Fee: *£3.50 (ch under 16 free, pen £3). Party 12+.
▣ ▄ ♿ (some steep & slippery paths not suited to wheelchairs) toilets for disabled shop garden centre

⛫ NORTHLEACH
Cᴏᴛsᴡᴏʟᴅ Hᴇʀɪᴛᴀɢᴇ Cᴇɴᴛʀᴇ
Fosseway GL54 3JH (12m E of Cheltenham on A429)
☎ **01451 860715**   ▤ **01451 860091**

The story of everyday rural life in the Cotswolds is told here, in the remaining buildings of the Northleach House of Correction. There's a unique collection of Gloucestershire harvest-wagons; a 'below stairs' gallery showing a dairy, kitchen and laundry; and the work of local craftsmen and artists is promoted through exhibitions, workshops and demonstrations.
Times: Open Apr-Oct, Mon-Sat 10-5, Sun 2-5 & BHs. Open at other times by prior arrangement.
Fee: *£2.50 (ch 80p, pen £2 & student £1). Family ticket £5. Party.
▣ ▄ ♿ (wheelchair available, parking at entrance) toilets for disabled shop ☜

⛫ OWLPEN
Oᴡʟᴘᴇɴ Mᴀɴᴏʀ
GL11 5BZ (3m E of Dursley off B4066, follow brown tourist signs)
☎ **01453 860261**   ▤ **01453 860819**

A romantic Tudor manor house, with unique 17th-century painted cloth wallhangings, furniture, pictures and textiles. The house is set in formal terraced gardens, and is part of a picturesque Cotswold manorial group including a Jacobean Court House, a Victorian church and medieval tithe barn.
Times: Open Apr-Oct, Tue-Sun & BH Mon, 2-5.
▣ ▄ ✖ licensed ✱ *Details not confirmed for 2000* ☜

⛫ PAINSWICK
Pᴀɪɴsᴡɪᴄᴋ Rᴏᴄᴏᴄᴏ Gᴀʀᴅᴇɴ
GL6 6TH (on B4073 0.5m NW of Painswick)
☎ **01452 813204**   ▤ **01452 813204**

This beautiful Rococo garden (a compromise between formality and informality) is the only one of its period to survive complete. There are ponds, woodland walks, a kitchen garden and herbacious borders, all set in a Cotswold valley famous for snowdrops in the early spring. Ring for details of special events.

Times: Open Jan-Nov, Wed-Sun, 11-5. (Daily in Jul & Aug)
▣ ▄ ✖ ♿ toilets for disabled shop *Details not confirmed for 2000* ☜

⛫ SLIMBRIDGE
WWT Sʟɪᴍʙʀɪᴅɢᴇ
GL2 7BT (off A38, signed from M5 J13 & 14)
☎ **01453 890333 & 890065**
▤ **01453 890827**

Slimbridge is home to the world's largest collection of exotic wildfowl - and the only place in Europe where all six types of flamingo can be seen. Up to 8,000 wild birds winter on the 800-acre reserve of flat fields, marsh and mudflats on the River Severn. There is a packed programme of events and activities throughout the year including evening talks and guided walks. Ring for details.
Times: Open all year, daily from 9.30-5.30 (winter 4pm). (Closed 25 Dec).
▣ ▄ ✖ licensed ♿ (wheelchairs, tapes for blind) toilets for disabled shop ✱ *Details not confirmed for 2000* ☜

⛫ SNOWSHILL
Sɴᴏᴡsʜɪʟʟ Mᴀɴᴏʀ
WR12 7JU (3m SW of Broadway)
☎ **01386 852410**   ▤ **01386 852410**

A Cotswold Tudor manor house, best known for Charles Paget Wade's collections of craftmanship and design, including musical instruments, clocks,

contd.

toys, bicycles, weavers' and spinners' tools, and Japanese armour. Special Interest days include craft demonstrations, collector's days, and music in the garden. Please telephone for details.
Times: Open Apr-Nov, daily (ex Tue & Good Friday) 1-5. Grounds & visitor facilities open May-Sep, noon-5.30. Last admission to manor 45 mins before closing.
P ✕ shop ✕ ✺ *Details not confirmed for 2000* ✺

▥ SOUDLEY
DEAN HERITAGE CENTRE
Camp Mill GL14 2UB (on B4227)
☎ 01594 822170 ▤ 01594 823711

The Centre tells the story of this unique area with museum displays which include a reconstucted cottage, coal mine and waterwheel. There are also nature trails (one of which is level), and picnic areas. Charcoal burning takes place twice a year.
Times: Open all year, daily, Apr-Sep 10-6, Oct-Mar 10-4. (Closed 24-26 Dec).
Fee: *£3.30 (ch £2, pen & concessions £2.80). Family ticket £9.50. Under 5's free.
P ▣ & toilets for disabled shop ✕ (ex guide dogs)

▥ ULEY
ULEY TUMULUS
(3.5m NE of Dusrley on B4066)

This 180ft Neolithic long barrow is popularly known as Hetty Pegler's Tump. The mound, surrounded by a wall, is about 85ft wide. It contains a stone central passage, and three burial chambers.
Times: Open any reasonable time.
⌘

▥ WESTBURY-ON-SEVERN
WESTBURY COURT GARDEN
GL14 1PD (9m SW of Gloucester on A48)
☎ 01452 760461

This formal water garden with canals and yew hedges was laid out between 1696 and 1705. It is the earliest of its kind remaining in England and was restored in 1971 and planted with species dated pre-1700, including apple, pear and plum trees.
Times: Open Apr-Nov, Wed-Sun & BH Mon 11-6. (Closed Good Fri). Other months by appointment only.
P & (braille guide, wheelchair available) toilets for disabled
✕ ✺ *Details not confirmed for 2000*

▥ WESTONBIRT
WESTONBIRT ARBORETUM
GL8 8QS (3m S Tetbury on A433)
☎ 01666 880220 ▤ 01666 880559

Begun in 1829, this arboretum contains one of the finest and most important collections of trees and shrubs in the world. There are 18,000 of them, planted from 1829 to the present day, covering 600 acres of landscaped Cotswold countryside. Magnificent displays of rhododendrons, azaleas, magnolias and the wild flowers of Silkwood can be seen in spring. There is a concert with fireworks in July, please ring for details.
Times: Open all year, daily 10-8 or sunset. Visitor centre & shop all year. (Closed Xmas & New Year)
Fee: £4 (ch £1, pen £3).
P ▣ & (electric & manual wheelchair for loan) toilets for disabled shop garden centre ✺

▥ WINCHCOMBE
SUDELEY CASTLE & GARDENS
GL54 5JD (B4632 to Winchcombe, Castle is signposted from town)
☎ 01242 603197 & 602308
▤ 01242 602959

Sudeley Castle was home to Katherine Parr, who is buried in the Chapel. Henry VIII, Anne Boleyn, Lady Jane Grey and Elizabeth I all stayed here; and it was the headquarters of Prince Rupert during the Civil War. The Queens Garden is famous for its rose collection, and there is a wildfowl sanctuary, exhibition centre, and children's adventure playground. Special events are held throughout the year, please telephone for details.
Times: Open daily: Apr-Oct, Gardens, exhibition, shop & plant centre 10.30-5.30. Apr-Oct, Castle apartments & Church 11-5.
Fee: *Castle & Gardens £6 (ch £3 & pen £5). Gardens only £4.50 (ch £2.25 & pen £3.50). Family ticket £17.
P ✕ licensed & (some parts unaccessible to disabled) shop garden centre ✕ (by request on arrival)

Greater Manchester

An urban conurbation in the northwest of England, Greater Manchester incorporates the towns of Bolton, Oldham, Rochdale, Salford, Stockport and Wigan, with the city of Manchester as its administrative headquarters.

Manchester was founded in Roman times, and developed during the 17th century as a textile town, becoming the centre of the English cotton industry. Magnificent Victorian Gothic public buildings are reminders of Manchester's prosperous heyday. These include the town hall designed by Alfred Waterhouse which takes up one side of Albert Square. Other gems to look out for are the newly restored Royal Exchange, - which was damaged in the Manchester bombing of 1996 - the Athenaeum, The Theatre Royal, and the Free Trade Hall. The Castlefield area, 15 minutes' walk southwest of the town hall, has been redeveloped in recent times to include a reconstruction of the Roman fort that once stood on the site.

Another impressive feature is the Manchester Ship Canal, completed in 1894, linking with the Mersey and the sea, bringing ocean-going vessels into Manchester and enabling the city to compete with its major rival, Liverpool.

The city of Manchester is alive with a vibrant youth culture (it has England's largest student population), a flourishing club scene, and a whole range of multi-cultural festivals and events. To take in the atmosphere, take a stroll around Britain's biggest Chinatown (between Charlotte Street and Princess Street), or wander down to Rusholme to take in the tempting aromas of the curry houses, and browse among the sari shops, Asian grocers, and Indian sweet shops.

EVENTS & FESTIVALS

February
6th Chinese New Year Celebrations, parade from Town Hall to Chinatown

May/June
Manchester Jazz Festival
e-mail: info@manchesterjazz.com
web site: www.manchesterjazz.com

June
10th Lord Mayor's Parade, Manchester
tbc Manchester Jazz Festival

July
15th-16th (provisional) Caribbean Carnival, Manchester

August
25th-28th Mardi Gras, Manchester

September
10th (provisional) Castlefield Carnival, Manchester

Top: Dobcross

MANCHESTER

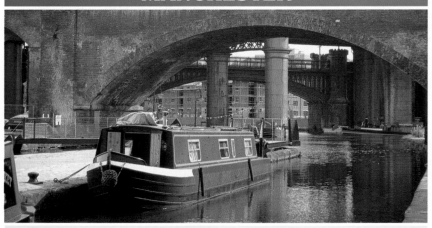

In the 19th century, visitors went to Manchester to gaze in wonder at a noisy, cramped, dirty city of atrocious slums and factory chimneys belching smoke. Manchester has moved away from this image, and is one of the most influential cities in Britain. Manchester United FC ride high in the Premiership, while Man City lay claim to a more fanatical local following, if not similar success.

Manchester also has many clubs and venues that are the place to hear dynamic live music, as well as some of Britain's most innovative DJs. TV fans can visit the set of Coronation St at Granada Studios.

🏛 ALTRINCHAM
DUNHAM MASSEY HALL
WA14 4SJ (3m SW of Altrincham (off A56), J19 off M6 or J7 off M56, then follow brown signs)
☎ 0161 941 1025 📠 0161 929 7508

A fine 18th-century house and park, home of the Earls of Stamford until 1976. It contains fine furniture and silverware, and some thirty rooms, including the library, billiard room, fully-equipped kitchen, butler's pantry and laundry. The garden is on an ancient site with mature trees and fine lawns. Ring for details of special events.
Times: Open: 27 Mar-29 Sep, Sat-Wed 12-5 (11-5 BH Sun & Mon). Oct, Sat-Sun 12-4 (Mon-Wed 12-4 open to pre-booked groups). Garden Open 27 Mar-31 Oct, 11-5.30 (closes 4.30 in Oct).
Fee: *House & Garden £5 (ch £2.50). House only £3 (ch £1.50). Garden only £3 (ch £1.50). Family ticket £12.50. Park only, £3 per car.
🅿 (charged) ✕ licensed ♿ (batricar & wheelchairs for loan, lift to restaurant) toilets for disabled shop ✖ (ex on lead in Park) 🐾 ⛴

🏛 ASHTON-UNDER-LYNE
MUSEUM OF THE MANCHESTERS
Market Place OL6 6DL (situated in the town centre, follow signs for the museum)
☎ 0161 342 3078 📠 0161 343 2869

The social and regimental history of the Manchesters is explored at this museum, tracing the story back to its origins in the 18th century. The Manchesters fought in both World Wars, the Boer War, and the Crimea.
Times: Open all year, Mon-Sat, 10-4. (Closed Sun).
Fee: Free.
🅿 (50yds) (pay & display) ♿ toilets for disabled shop ✖ (ex guide dogs)

🏛 MANCHESTER
CITY ART GALLERY
Mosley St/Princess St M2 3JL
☎ 0161 236 5244 📠 0161 236 7369

The Mosley Street Galleries have permanent displays of European art, ceramics and silver, displayed with furniture in an elaborate decorative scheme. There's a superb collection of Victorian art, including some major Pre-Raphaelite paintings. Decorative and applied arts, including porcelain, furniture and sculpture can also be seen.
Times: Whole gallery closed until 2001 for major expansion scheme.

GALLERY OF COSTUME
Platt Hall, Rusholme M14 5LL (situated in Platt Fields Park, access from Wilmslow Rd. 2m S of city centre)
☎ 0161 224 5217 📠 0161 256 3278

With one of the most comprehensive costume collections in Great Britain, this gallery makes captivating viewing. Housed in a fine Georgian mansion, the displays focus on the changing styles of everyday fashion and accessories over the last 400 years. Contemporary fashion is also illustrated. Because of the vast amount of material in the collection, no one period is permanently illustrated.

Times: Open all year, daily 10-5.30 (Nov-Feb 10-4).
Fee: Free.
🅿 & shop ✗ (ex guide dogs)

GRANADA STUDIOS TOUR
Water St M60 9EA
☎ 0161 832 9090 & 0161 833 0880
🖹 0161 834 3684

Walk down Coronation Street, and visit the Giant Room, from the children's programme Return of the Antelope, where chairs loom overhead. Explore the history of cinema at Projections, experience Motion Master where the seats move with the action, and see arms apparently severed in the gory make up show! You should allow a possible five hours for your visit.

Times: Open all year, daily summer 9.45-7 (last entry 4); winter 9.45-5.30 weekdays (last entry 3), 9.45-6.30 weekends & BH's (last entry 4). Closed Mon & Tue first half of Feb, Mar, Apr (except Etr), first half of Oct, Nov & Dec (except 28 & 29 Dec). Closed Mon May-Sep (except BH's). Closed 19-25 Dec. Open 1 & 2 Jan and weekends only.
🅿 (charged) 💻 ✗ licensed & (ramps & lift throughout) toilets for disabled shop ✗ *Details not confirmed for 2000*

JOHN RYLANDS LIBRARY
150 Deansgate M3 3EH
☎ 0161 834 5343 🖹 0161 834 5574

Founded as a memorial to Manchester cotton-magnate and millionaire John Rylands, this is the Special Collections Division of the John Rylands University Library of Manchester. Internationally renowned, it extends to two million books, manuscripts and archival items representing some fifty cultures and ranging in date from the third millennium BC to the present day.

Times: Open all year, Mon-Fri 10-5.30, Sat 10-1. (Closed BH & Xmas-New Year).
Fee: *Free. Guided tours Wed at noon £1.
🅿 (400yds) shop ✗ (ex guide dogs by arrangement)

MANCHESTER UNITED MUSEUM & TOUR CENTRE
Sir Matt Busby Way, Old Trafford M16 0RA (2m from city centre, off A56)
☎ 0161 877 4002 🖹 0161 876 5800

This Museum was opened in 1986 and is the first purpose-built British football museum. It covers the history of Manchester United in words, pictures, sound and vision, from its inception in 1878 to the present day. Stadium tour available. The new part of the museum was opened in April 1998 by Pelé.

Times: Open daily 9.30-5. (Closed 25 Dec)
Fee: *Stadium tour & Museum: £7.50 (ch & pen £5) Family ticket £20. Museum only: £4.50 (ch & pen £3) Family ticket £12.
🅿 💻 ✗ & toilets for disabled shop ✗ 🍴

THE MUSEUM OF SCIENCE AND INDUSTRY IN MANCHESTER
Liverpool Rd, Castlefield M3 4FP (follow brown tourist signs from city centre)
☎ 0161 832 2244 0161 832 1830
🖹 0161 833 2184

Located in the buildings of the world's oldest passenger railway station, there's plenty to do at this excellent museum. You can walk through a reconstructed Victorian sewer - complete with sounds and smells, or try the Super X flight simulator. Fibres, Fabrics & Fashion follows the story of Manchester's cotton industry, and Futures, a new gallery about communications, incorporates a Digital Access Centre where you can surf the Internet.

Times: Open all year, daily 10-5. Last admission 4.30. (Closed 24-26 Dec).
Fee: *£6.50 (ch 5-18 free ex £2 admission to certain exhibitions, concessions £3.50) group rates & season tickets available.
🅿 (charged) 💻 & (lifts, hearing system) toilets for disabled shop ✗ (ex guide dogs) 🍴

WHITWORTH ART GALLERY
University of Manchester, Oxford Rd M15 6ER (follow brown tourist signs)
☎ 0161 275 7450 🖹 0161 275 7451

The gallery houses an impressive range of modern and historic drawings, prints, paintings

contd.

and sculpture, as well as the largest collection of textiles and wallpapers outside London and an internationally famous collection of British watercolours. A programme of temporary exhibitions runs throughout the year, those for 2000 include: Treasures of the North (24 Feb-9 Apr), The Times of Our Lives - a 3 part exhibition, (Part 1 - Etr-mid Jun, Part 2 - Jul-end Sep, Part 3 - Oct-Dec), Ana Maria Pacheco (late Jul-mid Oct).

Times: Open Mon-Sat 10-5, Sun 2-5. (Closed Good Fri & Xmas-New Year).

Fee: Free.

P ✗ licensed ৬ (wheelchair available, induction loop, Braille lift buttons) toilets for disabled shop ✖ (ex guide dogs)

🏛 SALFORD

LANCASHIRE MINING MUSEUM
Buile Hill Park, Eccles Old Rd M6 8GL (signposted off A576)
☎ 0161 736 1832   🖹 0161 736 8581

Two reproduction coal mines, a gallery to illustrate the history and development of coal mining, and exhibitions of mining art are housed in this listed Georgian building.

Times: Open all year, Mon-Fri 10-12.30 & 1.30-5, Sun 2-5. (Closed Sat, Good Fri, Etr Sun, 24-26 Dec & 1 Jan).

Fee: Free.

P shop ✖ (ex guide dogs) 🖚

SALFORD MUSEUM & ART GALLERY
Peel Park, Crescent M5 4WU (on A6)
☎ 0161 736 2649   🖹 0161 745 9490

The pride of this gallery is its collection of L S Lowry's works which are displayed in the art gallery together with Victorian paintings and decorative arts. The small museum features a reconstructed street scene from the turn of the century.

Times: Open all year, Mon-Fri 10-4.45, Sat & Sun 1-5. (Closed Good Fri, Etr Sat, 25 & 26 Dec, 1 Jan).

Fee: Free.

P 🖚৬ (Braille labelling & large print information) toilets for disabled shop ✖ (guide dogs) 🖚

🏛 UPPERMILL

SADDLEWORTH MUSEUM & ART GALLERY
High St OL3 6HS (on A670)
☎ 01457 874093 & 870336

Based in an old mill building next to the Huddersfield canal, the museum brings to life the history of the Saddleworth area - a piece of Yorkshire stranded on the Lancashire side of the Pennines. Woollen weaving is the traditional industry, displayed in the 18th century Weaver's Cottage and the Victoria Mill Gallery. The textile machinery is run regularly by arrangement. In the Art Gallery, exhibitions change monthly.

Times: Open all year, Nov-late Mar, daily 1-4; late Mar-Oct, Mon-Sat 10-5, Sun 12-5.

Fee: £1.25 (concessions 65p) Family ticket £3.15.

P (charged) ৬ (stairlift, ramps, braille & large print guides, wheelchair) toilets for disabled shop ✖ (ex guide dogs)

🏛 WIGAN

WIGAN PIER
Wallgate WN3 4EU (Follow brown & white tourist signs from major motorway networks)
☎ 01942 323666   🖹 01942 322031

Part museum, part theatre, Wigan Pier is a mixture of entertainment and education. The professional actors of the Wigan Pier Theatre Company bring the past to life with themed plays, Victorian music hall shows and the infamous schoolroom. Please telephone for details of special events.

Times: Open all year, Mon-Thu 10-5; Sat & Sun 11-5. Closed 25-1 Jan & Fri (ex Good Fri).

Fee: *£6.95 (£5.25 concessions) Family £19.50 (all day passes).

P 🖚 ✗ licensed ৬ toilets for disabled shop ✖ (ex guide dogs) 🖚

Hampshire

Hampshire is mainly rural with a gentle landscape and coastal cities - Portsmouth and Southampton - enjoy a proud maritime history.

Portsmouth has been an important naval base since the 12th century, and Southampton has long been associated with the romance of the ocean liner. Both cities were badly bombed in World War II, though areas of interest remain for the visitor to see.

A more attractive destination is the charming town of Lyndhurst at the heart of the glorious New Forest. Recently celebrating its 900th anniversary, the Forest is a huge expanse of woodland, heath and hills set aside as a royal hunting ground by William the Conqueror in 1079, and spreads across some 93,000 acres. Now millions visit every year. 'Forest' can seem a bit of a misnomer as large areas are quite open and covered only by heather and gorse. In 1992 it was given the protection of National Park status. Wildlife flourishes in this huge expanse, and walkers can see red, fallow, roe and muntjac deer, as well as badgers, adders, and the well-known ponies. Lyndhurst itself was home to Alice Hargreaves, (née Liddell) who was the inspiration for Alice in Lewis Carroll's world-famous books. She is buried in the graveyard of St Michael and All Angels Church.

Hampshire has many small and picturesque villages. Alresford is home to the Watercress Line, Silchester has nearby Roman remains including an amphitheatre, and Old Basing has the delightful River Loddon and the remains of Basing House.

EVENTS & FESTIVALS

February
tbc Wiinchester Children's Festival, Winchester

April
29th-1st May Alton Millennium Heritage Festival
12-6th Tall Ships Race 2000, Southampton
tbc Winchester Folk Festival

June
4th Seawings 2000 Airshow, Southampton
30th-2nd July Winchester Hat Fair

July
7th-16th Winchester Festival
25th-27th New Forest Show, Brockenhurst
28th-30th Festival of the Ocean, Southampton
tbc Power in the Park, pop festival

August
4th-6th Portsmouth & Southsea Show
26th-28th International Kite Festival, Southsea Common

September
2nd Alresford Agricultural Show
15th-24th Southampton International Boat Show

November
tbc Winchester Firework Display

Top: Near Lyndhurst

ALDERSHOT

AIRBORNE FORCES MUSEUM

Browning Barracks, Queens Av GU11 2BU
(from motorway take A325 to Aldershot then
take next left)

☎ 01252 349619   🖹 01252 349203

The museum tells the story of the creation and
operation of the parachute forces from 1940
onwards. There are aircraft models and briefing
models for World War II operations, and a post-
war display includes captured enemy arms,
vehicles, parachutes, equipment and many scale
models. Telephone for details of special events.
Times: Open all year, daily 10-4.30 (last admission 3.45pm)
(Closed Xmas).
Fee: *£2.50 (ch, students, pen and ex-servicemen £1)
🅿 ♿ Wheelchair ramps shop ✸ (ex guide dogs) 🦮

ALDERSHOT MILITARY MUSEUM

Evelyn Woods Rd, Queens Av GU11 2LG (follow
brown signs to museum)

☎ 01252 314598   🖹 01252 342942

A look behind the scenes at the daily life of
soldiers and civilians as Aldershot and
Farnborough grew up around the military camps
to become the home of the British Army.
Times: Open Mar-Oct, daily 10-5; Nov-Feb, daily 10-4.30.
Fee: *£2 (ch/pen/UB40 £1)
🅿 ♿ shop

ALRESFORD

WATERCRESS LINE

The Railway Station SO24 9JG (stations at Alton
& Alresford signposted off A31)

☎ 01962 733810   🖹 01962 735448

The Watercress Line runs through ten miles of
rolling scenic countryside between Alton and
Alresford. All four stations are 'dressed' in period
style, and there's a locomotive yard and picnic
area at Ropley. Please telephone for details of
special events.
Times: Open weekends throughout the year except for Nov &
Jan, also some weekdays over Xmas, Easter school half term
holidays and Jun-Aug. Alresford station shop & buffet open
daily ex 25 Dec.
Fee: *Unlimited travel for the day, £8 (ch £5, pen £6). Family
ticket £24.
🅿 (charged) 🍽 ✸ licensed ♿ (ramp access to trains)
toilets for disabled shop 🦮

AMPFIELD

SIR HAROLD HILLIER GARDENS & ARBORETUM

Jermyns Ln SO51 OQA (signposted off A3090
& B3057)

☎ 01794 368787   🖹 01794 368027

The largest collection of trees and shrubs of its
kind in the British Isles, set in 180 acres of
attractive landscape, with all-year interest -
superb colour in spring and autumn in particular.
Special events, include early opening (gates open

5.30am, breakfast at 7am), exhibitions and
festivals, please telephone for details.
Times: Open all year, Apr-Oct weekdays 10.30-6, weekends &
Bank Holidays 9.30-6. Nov-Mar daily 10.30-5 or dusk if earlier
(closed Xmas).
Fee: *Apr-Oct: £4.25 (ch £1, pen £3.75). Nov-Mar: £3.25 (ch
£1, pen £2.75)
🅿 ✸ licensed ♿ (all ability path) toilets for disabled garden
centre ✸ (ex guide dogs)

ASHURST

LONGDOWN DAIRY FARM

Longdown SO40 4UH (off A35 between
Lyndhurst & Southampton)

☎ 023 80293326   🖹 023 80293376

A wonderful opportunity to get close to lots of
friendly farm animals - piglets, ducklings, goats,
cows, and many more. You can touch and feed
many of the residents, watch the afternoon
milking from the viewing gallery and learn about
modern farming methods. Also home to the
National Dairy Council Museum Collection.
Times: Open daily, Etr-Oct
Fee: *£4.30 (ch 3-14 £3, pen £3.50). Saver ticket £14 (2 adults
+ 2 children) £9.75 (1 adult + 2 children).
🅿 ♿ toilets for disabled shop ✸ (kennels provided) 🦮

BASINGSTOKE

MILESTONES

Leisure Park RG21 6YR

☎ 01256 845384 & 01962 846315
🖹 01962 869836

When open, Milestones will bring Hampshire's
recent past to life through stunning period street
scenes and exciting interactive areas, all under
one roof. Nationally important collections of
transport, technology and everyday life are
presented in an entertaining way.
Times: Open summer 2000. Contact for opening times
Fee: Admission payable.
🅿 🍽 ✸ ♿ toilets for disabled shop ✸ (ex guide dogs)

BEAULIEU

BEAULIEU : NATIONAL MOTOR MUSEUM

SO42 7ZN (M27 Westbound J2, A326, B3054,
then follow tourist signs)

☎ 01590 612345   🖹 01590 612624

This 16th-century house is worth seeing just for
its lovely setting, but it has become most famous

as the home of the National Motor Museum, one of the world's largest collections of vehicles and motoring memorabilia. Other attractions are a high-level monorail through the grounds, veteran bus rides and a replica of a 1930s country garage. Please ring for details of special events.

Times: Open all year - Palace House & Gardens, National Motor Museum, Beaulieu Abbey & Exhibition of Monastic Life, May-Sep 10-6; Oct-Apr 10-5. (Closed 25 Dec & 1 Jan)
Fee: *£9 (ch £6.50, pen £7.75). Family £29 Party.
🅿 🚙 ♿ (ramp access to most areas) toilets for disabled shop 🍴

🏛 BISHOP'S WALTHAM
BISHOP'S WALTHAM PALACE
SO3 1AH (on A333)
☎ 01489 892460

Bishop's Waltham Palace was once among the greatest stately homes of the medieval period. Although mostly destroyed in the Civil War, remains are still impressive.
Times: Open Apr-Oct, daily 10-6 (or dusk if earlier).
Fee: £2 (ch £1).
🅿 ♿ ✈ (in certain areas) ⌗

🏛 BUCKLER'S HARD
BUCKLER'S HARD VILLAGE & MARITIME MUSEUM
SO42 7XB (M27 Westbound J2, A326, B3054 then follow tourist signs)
☎ 01590 616203 📠 01590 612624

Wooden warships, including some of Nelson's fleet, were built here, using New Forest oak, and the wide main street was used for rolling great logs to the 'hard' where the ships were built. The 18th-century homes of a shipwright and labourer, and a master shipbuilder's office can be seen. The Bucklers Hard Village Festival is held on the last Sunday in July, with people in period costume to recapture the atmosphere of the village féte.
Times: Open all year, Etr-Spring BH 10-6; Spring BH-Aug 10-9; Sep-Etr 10-4.30. (Closed 25 Dec).
🅿 🚙 ✗ licensed ♿ shop *Details not confirmed for 2000* 🍴

🏛 BURGHCLERE
SANDHAM MEMORIAL CHAPEL
RG20 9JT (4m S Newbury off A34)
☎ 01635 278394 📄 01635 278394

Stanley Spencer, one of the most original artists of his generation, painted the murals covering the walls of the Chapel between 1927 and 1932. Celebrating the daily routine of the common soldier during the Great War, they present a symbolic narrative which Spencer described as 'a mixture of real and spiritual fact'. The initial impact is quite overwhelming and leaves a deep and lasting impression.
Times: Open Apr-Oct, Wed-Sun 11.30-5. Nov & Mar, Sat & Sun 11.30-4. Also open BH Mons, (but closed the Wed after). Dec-Feb by appointment only.
Fee: *£2 (ch £1).
🅿 ♿ ✈ (ex on leads in grounds) 🐾

🏛 CHAWTON
JANE AUSTEN'S HOUSE
GU34 1SD (1m SW of Alton, in centre of village)
☎ 01420 83262 📄 01420 83262

Jane Austen lived and wrote here from 1809 to 1817. Restored to look as it would have done in the early 1800s, with items such as the author's donkey cart and writing table to be seen. Please telephone for details of special events.
Times: Open daily Mar-1 Jan, also Feb half term. Jan & Feb wknds only. (Closed 25 & 26 Dec).
Fee: *£2.50 (ch 8, 85p, pen & students £2) party 15+.
🅿 (300yds) ♿ (wheelchair ramp) toilets for disabled shop ✈ (ex guide dogs)

See advert on page 91

🏛 EXBURY
EXBURY GARDENS
Exbury Estate Office SO45 1AZ (3m from Beaulieu, off B3054)
☎ 023 80891203 📄 023 80899940

A 200-acre landscaped woodland garden on the East bank of the Beaulieu River, with one of the finest collections of rhododendrons, azaleas, camellias and magnolias in the world - as well as many rare and beautiful shrubs and trees. A labyrinth of tracks and paths enable you to explore the intricate plantings, cascades and ponds, a rose garden, rock garden, heather garden and iris garden, daffodil meadow and river walk. Ring for details of special events.
Times: Open daily 27 Feb-31 Oct 10-5.30 or dusk if earlier.
Fee: *27th Feb-mid Mar £3.50 (ch 10-15 £2.50, OAP £3). Mid Mar-mid Jun £5 (ch £4, OAP £4.50. Mid Jun-Oct £3.50 (ch £2.50, OAP £3)
🅿 ♿ (wheelchair access, impaired mobility routes within gardens) toilets for disabled shop garden centre

🏛 GOSPORT
ROYAL NAVY SUBMARINE MUSEUM & HMS ALLIANCE
Haslar Jetty Rd PO12 2AS (M27 J11, follow signs for HMS Dolphin/RNH Haslar & Submarine Museum)
☎ 023 92529217 & 92510354
📄 023 92511349

The great attraction of this museum is the chance to see inside a submarine, and there are guided tours of *HMS Alliance*, as well as displays exploring the development of submarines. Two periscopes from *HMS Conqueror* can be seen in the reconstruction of a nuclear submarine control room, giving panoramic views of Portsmouth Harbour. A new gallery shows the development of submarine weapons from the tiny torpedo to the huge polaris nuclear missile.
Times: Open all year, Apr-Oct 10-5.30; Nov-Mar 10-4.30. (Closed 24 Dec-1 Jan). Allow 3 hrs for visit. Last tour 1 hour before closing.
Fee: *£3.50 (ch & pen £2.50). Family ticket (2 adults & 4 ch) £10. Party 12+. Joint ticket with Fort Nelson & Royal Armouries now available. Discounted entry scheme "Follow the Drum", in association with Southern Military Museums.
🅿 ♿ (information in Braille) toilets for disabled shop ✈ 🍴

🏛 HARTLEY WINTNEY
WEST GREEN HOUSE GARDENS
West Green RG27 8JB (off A30, at Phoenix Green take sign to West Green, along Thackhams Lane. House last left)
☎ 01252 844611 📄 01252 844611

The gardens surrounding this Queen Anne house date back three hundred years and have been closed for the past three years for major repairs and replanting. When restoration is complete there will be ten acres of garden and pleasure grounds - four walled gardens, a lake, follies, green theatre, nymphaeum, mixed border and potager. Ring for details of lecture days.
Times: Open May-Aug, Weds-Sun 11am-4pm.
Fee: *£3 (ch 7 free).
🅿 ♿ (most areas accessible) toilets for disabled ✈ (ex guide dogs)

🏛 HIGHCLERE
HIGHCLERE CASTLE & GARDENS
RG20 9RN (4.5m S of Newbury, off A34)
☎ 01635 253210 📄 01635 255315

This splendid early Victorian mansion stands in beautiful parkland. It has sumptuous interiors and numerous Old Master pictures. Also shown are early finds by the 5th Earl of Carnarvon, one of the discoverers of Tutankhamun's tomb. Ring for details of special events, which include car shows, theatre and concerts.
Times: Open 01 Jul-05 Sept (closed 17/18 July) Mon-Fri & Sun 11-5 (last admission 4pm). Sat 11-3.30 (last admission 2.30pm).
Fee: *£6 (ch £3, pen £4.75). Grounds & gardens only £3 (ch £1.50). Party.
🅿 ✕ licensed ♿ (wheelchair available) toilets for disabled shop ✈ (ex guide dogs) 🍴

🏛 HINTON AMPNER
HINTON AMPNER
So24 0LA (off A272, 1m W of Bramdean)
☎ 01962 771305 📠 01962 771305

Set in superb Hampshire countryside, this delightful garden combines formality of design with informality of planting. Full of scent and colour, the walks open up into unexpected vistas. The house, restored after a fire in 1960, displays a fine collection of Regency furniture and Italian paintings.
Times: Open Garden: 21 & 28 Mar then 3 Apr-Sep, Sat, Sun, BH Mon, Tue & Wed 1.30-5.30. Last admission 5pm. House: 3 Apr-end Sept Tue & Wed only, Sat & Sun in Aug 1.30-5.30.
Fee: *House and Garden £4, garden only £3.20.
🅿 💺 & (Braille guides, special parking) toilets for disabled 🐾 ♨

🏛 HURST CASTLE
HURST CASTLE
(on Pebble Spit S of Keyhaven)
☎ 01590 642344

Built by Henry VIII, Hurst Castle was the pride of Tudor England's coastal defences. Crouched menacingly on a shingle spit, the castle has a fascinating history, including involvement in the smuggling trade in the 17th and 18th centuries.
Times: Open Apr-Jun & Sep-Oct, 10-5.30 (last admission 4.30) Jul-Aug, daily 10-6 (last admission 5.15pm).
💺 🐾 (in certain areas) ⛴

🏛 LIPHOOK
HOLLYCOMBE STEAM COLLECTION
Iron Hill, Midhurst Rd GU30 7LP (1.5m SE on unclass rd)
☎ 01428 724900

An all-encompassing collection of steam-driven equipment, including a Bioscope showing old films, fairground organs, steam-driven roundabouts, big wheel, steam yacht, razzle dazzle, a steam farm and paddle steamer engine. There are demonstrations of threshing and steam rolling, and traction engine rides. Three steam-hauled trains run through a woodland setting with spectacular views of the South Downs. Please telephone for details of special events.
Times: Open Good Friday, BH & Sun until 11 Oct, daily 20-24 Jul & 16-31 Aug
🅿 💺 & shop 🐾 (guide dogs on request) *Details not confirmed for 2000* 🔔

🏛 LYNDHURST
NEW FOREST MUSEUM & VISITOR CENTRE
Main Car Park, High St SO43 7NY
☎ 023 80283914 📠 023 80284236

The story of the New Forest - history, traditions, character and wildlife, told through an audio-visual show and exhibition displays. With life-size models of Forest characters, and the famous New Forest embroidery.
Times: Open all year, daily from 10am (Closed 25 Dec)
Fee: *£2.75 (ch £1.75 pen £2.25) Family ticket £7.50. Party 10+.
🅿 & toilets for disabled shop 🔔

🏛 MARWELL
MARWELL ZOOLOGICAL PARK
Colden Common SO21 1JH (on B2177)
☎ 01962 777406 & 777407
📠 01962 777511

Devoted to the conservation and breeding of rare wild animals, Marwell has a worldwide reputation. The animals are housed in spacious enclosures or can be seen grazing in paddocks, and there is an enclosure where animals can be approached and stroked by children. Covering 100 acres of parkland, the collection includes over 1000 animals, and some of the species here no longer exist in the wild. New animals are being added constantly. There are many attractions for younger children, including a children's farmyard, Tropical World, Penguin World and road trains. Numerous events are held throughout the year, including a Christmas `Winter Wonderland'.
Times: Open all year, daily (ex 25 Dec), 10-6 (or dusk). Last admission 4.30pm or 1 hour before dusk (whichever is earliest).
🅿 💺 🐾 licensed & (special tours for visually impaired by arrangement) toilets for disabled shop 🐾 (incl guide dogs) *Details not confirmed for 2000* 🔔

🏛 MIDDLE WALLOP
MUSEUM OF ARMY FLYING
SO20 8DY (on A343, between Andover & Salisbury)
☎ 01980 674421 📠 01264 781694

One of the country's finest historical collections of military kites, gliders, aeroplanes and helicopters. Imaginative dioramas and displays trace the development of Army flying from before the First World War to more recent conflicts in Ireland, the Falklands and the Gulf. Sit at the controls of a real Scout helicopter and test your skills at 'hand and eye' co-ordination on the helicopter flight simulator - which is not as easy as it might look. Please telephone for details of special events.
Times: Open all year, daily 10-4.30. Closed week prior to Xmas. Evening visits by special arrangement.
Fee: *£4.50 (ch £3, OAP/student £3.50) Family £12.50. Party 10+.
🅿 🐾 licensed & (lifts to upper levels) toilets for disabled shop 🐾 (ex guide dogs or in grounds) 🔔

🏛 MINSTEAD
FURZEY GARDENS
SO43 7GL (1m S of JA31/M3 Cadnam off A31 or A337 near Lyndhurst)
☎ 023 80812464 & 80812297
▤ 023 80812297

A cottage dating from 1560 is the venue for refreshments and displays of local arts and crafts, and the eight acres of peaceful glades which surround it include winter and summer heathers, rare flowering trees and shrubs and a mass of spring bulbs. There is a lake, and the nursery, run by the Minstead Training Project for Young People with Learning Disabilities, sells a wide range of produce.
Times: Open daily 10-5 (or dusk if earlier). (Closed Xmas).
Fee: *Mar-Oct: £3 (ch £1.50, OAP £2.50) Family £8. Nov-Feb: £1.50 (ch 50p, OAP £1) Family £3. Party 10+.
🅿 ᜑ (gardens accessible for wheelchair visitors with assistance) shop garden centre ✖ (guide dogs)

🏛 MOTTISFONT
MOTTISFONT ABBEY GARDEN
SO51 0LP (4.5m NW Romsey, on the A3057)
☎ 01794 340757 ▤ 01794 341492

In a picturesque setting by the River Test, Mottisfont Abbey is an 18th-century house adapted from a 12th-century priory. The north front shows its medieval church origins quite clearly, and the garden has splendid old trees and a walled garden planted with the national collection of old-fashioned roses. The estate includes Mottisfont village and surrounding farmland and woods.
Times: Open 27 Mar-Oct, Sat-Wed 12-6 (or dusk if earlier). 12-27 June special opening daily from 11-8.30. Last admission- to grounds 1hr before closing, to house at 4.30pm.
Fee: *£4.50 (ch £2.25) Family ticket £11.
🅿 ✖ licensed ᜑ (Braille guide, wheelchair available, volunteer driven buggy) toilets for disabled shop garden centre ✖ ⚘

🏛 NETLEY
NETLEY ABBEY
(4m SE of Southampton, facing Southampton Water)
☎ 023 80453076

A romantic ruin, set among green lawns and trees, this 13th-century Cistercian abbey was founded by Peter des Roches, tutor to Henry III. Nearby is the 19th-century-Gothic Netley Castle.
Times: Open Apr-Sep, daily, 10-6; Oct-Mar, daily, 10-4.
🅿 ᜑ ✖ ⚏

🏛 NEW MILTON
SAMMY MILLER MOTORCYCLE MUSEUM
Bashley Cross Rd BH25 5SZ (signposted off A35)
☎ 01425 620777 ▤ 01425 619696

With machines dating back to 1900, some the only surviving examples of their type. The Racing collection features World Record breaking bikes and their history, including the first bike to lap a Grand Prix Course at over 100 miles per hour.

Special events include Triumph Day, Velocette & Brough Day, etc, please telephone for details.
Times: Open all year, daily 10-4.30.
Fee: *£3.50 (ch £1.50)
🅿 🖭 ᜑ toilets for disabled shop ✖ ⬤

🏛 OLD BASING
BASING HOUSE
Redbridge Ln RG24 7HB (signed from Basingstoke Ring Road)
☎ 01256 467294 ▤ 01256 326283

The largest house of Tudor England, almost entirely destroyed by Parliament during a two-year siege ending in 1645. Built on the site of a Norman castle in 1530, the ruins include a 300ft long tunnel. There is a re-creation of a garden of 1600 and exhibitions showing the history of the house. A fine 16th-century tithe barn stands nearby.
Times: Open Apr-Sep, Wed-Sun & BH 2-6.
Fee: *£1.50 (ch & pen 70p). Registered disabled free.
🅿 ᜑ (disabled parking by prior arrangement) toilets for disabled shop

🏛 PORTCHESTER
PORTCHESTER CASTLE
PO16 9QW (off A27)
☎ 023 92378291

Built on the site of a Roman fort, the castle has witnessed many famous events of English history. From here Henry V embarked for France and the Battle of Agincourt; here Henry VIII courted Anne Boleyn, and later still the castle was 'home' to prisoners during the Napoleonic wars. Remains of the church and other medieval buildings can also be seen.
Times: Open all year, Apr-Oct, daily 10-6 (or dusk if earlier); Nov-Mar, daily 10-4. Closed 24-26 Dec & 1 Jan.
Fee: £2.70 (ch £1.40).
🅿 ᜑ shop ✖ (in certain areas) ⚏

🏛 PORTSMOUTH & SOUTHSEA
CHARLES DICKENS' BIRTHPLACE MUSEUM
393 Old Commercial Rd PO1 4QL
☎ 023 92827261 ▤ 023 92875276

Built in 1805, this is the birthplace and early home of the famous novelist. Now restored, and furnished to illustrate middle-class taste of the early 19th century, the museum displays items pertaining to Dickens' work, portraits of the family, and the couch on which he died. There are Dickens readings at 3pm on the first Sunday of each month, also at 11am during the Christmas opening period.

Times: Open Mar-Oct, daily 10-5.30 (last admission 5pm). Also 25 Nov-19 Dec 10-4.00 (last admission 3.30pm).

Fee: *£2 (ch & student £1.20, accompanied ch 13 free, pen £1.50p). Family ticket £5.20.

🅿 (150mtrs) shop ✖ (ex guide & helper dogs) ➷

CITY MUSEUM & RECORDS OFFICE

Museum Rd PO1 2LJ (M27/M275 into Portsmouth, follow museum symbol on signposts)
☎ 023 92827261   📄 023 92875276

Dedicated to local history and decorative and fine art. 'The Story of Portsmouth' displays room settings showing life here from the 17th century to the 1950s. The 'Portsmouth at Play' exhibition features leisure pursuits from the Victorian period to the 1970's. Temporary exhibitions are also held.

Times: Open all year, Apr-Oct daily 10-5.30; Nov-Mar daily 10-4. Closed 24-26 Dec and Record Office closed on public holidays.

Fee: Free.

🅿 💺 ♿ (induction loops, lift & wheelchair available) toilets for disabled shop ✖ (ex guide dogs)

D-DAY MUSEUM & OVERLORD EMBROIDERY

Clarence Esplanade PO5 3NT (M27/M275 into Portsmouth follow D Day Museum signposts)
☎ 023 92827261   📄 023 92875276

Portsmouth's D-Day Museum tells the dramatic story of the Allied landings in Normandy in 1944. The centrepiece is the magnificent 'Overlord Embroidery', 80 metres long with 34 individual panels. Military equipment, vehicles, landing craft and personal memories complete this special story.

Times: Open all year, Apr-Oct daily 10-5.30. Nov-Mar Mon pm only 1-5. Tue-Sun 10-4. Closed 24-26 Dec.

Fee: *£4.75 (ch £2.85, pen £3.60). Family ticket £12.35.

🅿 (charged) 💺 ♿ (induction loops sound aids for blind wheelchairs available) toilets for disabled shop ✖ (ex guide & helper dogs) ➷

HMS VICTORY

HM Naval Base PO1 3PZ (follow Flagship Portsmouth signs)
☎ 023 92839766   📄 023 92819604

Still in commission and manned by regular serving officers and men, Lord Nelson's famous flagship is an outstanding example of maritime restoration. A tour around her decks gives some idea of the sailors' way of life in Nelson's day, and visitors can see where the Admiral received his fatal wound, and the surgery below decks where he eventually died.

Times: Open Mar-Oct, daily 10-5.30; Nov-Feb, daily 10.00-5. (Closed 25 Dec).

Fee: *£5.95 (ch £4.45, pen £5.20). Prices include Royal Naval Museum. Combination tickets with other Flagship Portsmouth attractions avalible.

🅿 (charged) ♿ (lower gun deck tour) toilets for disabled shop ✖ ➷

HMS WARRIOR 1860

Victory Gate, HM Naval Base PO1 3QX (follow 'Historic Ship' signs)
☎ 023 92291379   📄 023 92821283

Originally launched in 1860, *HMS Warrior* was the world's first iron-hulled armoured warship. Restored with painstaking attention to detail, visitors can wander through four vast decks, and see the rich furnishings and excellent craftmanship. Victorian Navy Days take place in the summer - please telephone for details.

Times: Open all year, Mar-Oct 10-5.30; Nov-Feb 10-5. (Last admission 1 hr before closing). Closed 24-25 Dec.

Fee: *£5.95 (ch £4.45 & pen £5.20). Combination tickets with other Flagship Portsmouth attractions avalible.

🅿 (charged) 💺 ✖ ♿ (stairlift to main gun deck) toilets for disabled shop ✖

THE MARY ROSE MUSEUM

HM Naval Base PO1 3LX (enter Portsmouth via M275 & follow signs for Portsmouth Historic Ships)
☎ 023 92750521   📄 023 92870588

Remarkably preserved in the Solent silts for 437 years, Henry VIII's warship was a Tudor time-capsule, complete with the everyday possessions, tools and weapons of her 700 men. The great oak hull can be seen in a special dry-dock workshop, and there's a themed display of many of the 20,000 artefacts recovered, including cannon, gaming boards, a shaving bowl - even the contents of the barber-surgeon's chest, with syringes and jars of ointment. Please ring for details of special events.

Times: Open all year, daily from 10am. (Closed 24 & 25 Dec).

Fee: *£5.95 (ch & students £4.45, pen £5.20). Combination tickets to other Flagship Portsmouth attractions avalible.

🅿 (charged) 💺 ✖ licensed ♿ (hands-on exhibits & audio guide for visually impaired) toilets for disabled shop ✖ (ex guide dogs) ➷

NATURAL HISTORY MUSEUM & BUTTERFLY HOUSE

Cumberland House, Eastern Pde PO4 9RF
☎ 023 92827261   📄 023 92875276

Focussing on the natural history and geology of the area, with wildlife dioramas including a riverbank scene with fresh water aquarium. During the summer British and European butterflies fly free in the Butterfly House.

Times: Open daily, Apr-Oct 10-4.00, Nov-Mar 10-4.30. (Closed 24-26 Dec).

Fee: *£2 (ch £1.40, accompanied ch under 13 free & pen £1.60). Family ticket £5.40; Oct-Mar £1.50 (ch 90p & pen £1.10) Family ticket £3.90

🅿 (200mtrs) shop ✖ (guide & helper dogs) ➷

THE ROYAL MARINES MUSEUM

PO4 9PX (signposted from seafront)
☎ 023 92819385   ▤ 01705 838420

Telling the story of the 330 year history of the Marines through dramatic displays, exciting films and videos, state of the art interactives and even a live snake and scorpion! There's also a world famous medal collection, portraits and silverware. Ring for details of special events.
Times: Open all year, Spring BH-Aug daily 10-5; Sep-May daily 10-4.30. (Closed 3 days Xmas)
Fee: *£3.75 (ch £2, pen £2.75) Family ticket £10.
🅿 ▉ ✘ licensed ⅗ (access for disabled and toilets from Etr 97) toilets for disabled shop ✈ (ex guide dogs or in grounds) ➷

ROYAL NAVAL MUSEUM

HM Naval Base PO1 3NH (M275 into Portsmouth then follow signs)
☎ 023 92727562   ▤ 023 92727575

A multi-million pound redevelopment programme at the museum means three new galleries - 'Horatio Nelson - The Hero and the Man' charts the story of Nelson's private and public life. 'The Sailing Navy' looks at life on board through the ages, and 'The Victory Gallery' features 'The Battle of Trafalgar Experience'. Please telephone for details of special events.
Times: Open all year, daily 10-5. (Closed 25-26 Dec).
Fee: *£3.50 (ch £2 & pen £3). Combined ticket available with HMS Victory and other Flagship Portsmouth attractions.
🅿 (charged) ▉ ✘ ⅗ (loop system) toilets for disabled shop ✈ (ex small dogs if carried)

SOUTHSEA CASTLE

Clarence Esp PO5 3PA
☎ 023 92827261   ▤ 023 92875276

Part of Henry VIII's national coastal defences, this fort was built in 1545 and contains displays illustrating Portsmouth's development as a military fortress, including an audio-visual show, underground tunnels, and panoramic views of the Solent and Isle of Wight. Home of Fort

Cumberland Guard. Please ring for details of special events.
Times: Open all year, Apr-Oct, daily 10-5.30. Nov-Mar, Sat & Sun 10-4, and school holidays. (Closed 24-26 Dec).
Fee: *£2 (ch & students £1.20, ch accompanied 13 free, pen £1.50). Family ticket £5.20.
🅿 (charged) ▉ ⅗ (wheelchair available) shop ✈ ➷

SPITBANK FORT
☎ 01329 664286

Built in the 1860s as part of the coastal defences against the French, this massive granite and iron fortress stands a mile out to sea, with magnificent views across the Solent. The interior is a maze of passages connecting over 50 rooms on two levels.
Times: Open May-Sep, Tue-Sun. (Weather permitting).
Fee: *£6.50 (ch £5) includes ferry charge. Boat ride takes approx 20 mins, visitors should allow 2hr to view. Ferries depart HM Naval Base Portsmouth.
🅿 ▉

⛰ RINGWOOD

MOORS VALLEY COUNTRY PARK

Horton Rd, Ashley Heath BH24 2ET (1.5m from Ashley Heath roundabout on A31 near Three Legged Cross)
☎ 01425 470721   ▤ 01425 471656

Fifteen hundred acres of forest, woodland, heathland, lakes, river and meadows provide a home for a wide variety of plants and animals, and there's a Visitor Centre, Adventure Playground, picnic area, Moors Valley Railway, and Tree Top Trail.
Times: Open all year (ex 25 Dec), 8-dusk. Visitor centre open 9.30-4.30 (later in summer).
Fee: *No admission charge but parking up to £3.50 per day.
🅿 (charged) ▉ ⅗ (visitor centre & most of park accessible) toilets for disabled shop ✈ (ex in park on lead)

⛰ ROCKBOURNE

ROMAN VILLA

SP6 3PG (from Salisbury, take A354 to Blandford, follow signs from the side of Coombe Bissett.)
☎ 01725 518541

Discovered in 1942, the site features the remains of a 40 room Roman villa and is the largest in the

area. Displays include mosaics and a very rare hypocaust system. The museum displays the many artifacts found on the site during excavations. Roman re-enactments are performed - please ring for details.

Times: Open Apr-Oct, Mon-Fri noon-6, Sat, Sun & BH 10.30-6; Jul & Aug daily 10.30-6. Last admission 5.30pm.

Fee: *£1.75 (concessions 95p).

P 🖥 ♿ (ramps in/out of museum) toilets for disabled shop ✖

🏛 SELBORNE

Gilbert White's House & The Oates Museum

The Wakes, High St GU34 3JH (on village High St)
☎ 01420 511275   📠 01420 511040

Charming 18th-century house, home of famous naturalist, the Rev. Gilbert White, author of *The Natural History and Antiquities of Selborne*. There are also exhibitions on two famous members of the Oates family - Captain Oates who accompanied Scott to the South Pole, and Frank Oates, a Victorian explorer. Special events include an Unusual Plants Fair in June - please ring for details.

Times: Open daily 1 Jan-24 Dec, 11-5.

Fee: *£4 (ch £1, pen £3.50).

P (200yds) 🖥 ♿ shop ✖ 🍴

🏛 SHERBORNE ST JOHN

The Vyne

RG24 9HL (4m N of Basingstoke, off A340, signposted)
☎ 01256 881337   📠 01256 881720

Much of the exterior of the house is 16th-century, with several major alterations and additions, including the earliest classical portico to be added to an English country house. The chapel has original 16th-century stained glass, and the Oak Gallery has superb linenfold panelling. The house is set in a pleasant garden with a lake. Telephone for details of special events.

Times: Open House 24 Mar-end Oct daily except Mon & Tue 1.30-5.30. Grounds 24 Mar-end Oct daily except Mon & Tue 12.30-5.30. Also open Good Fri & BH Mon.

Fee: *House & Grounds £5. Family ticket £12.50. Grounds only £2.50 (ch half price for each ticket).

P 🖥 ✖ licensed ♿ (Braille guide) shop ✖ (ex guide & hearing dogs) 🐾

🏛 SILCHESTER

Calleva Museum

Bramley Rd RG7 2LU

Little remains of the Roman town of Calleva Atrebatum except the 1.5 miles of city wall, still an impressive sight, and the ampitheatre. This small museum shows what life may have been like in a Roman town, while the main artefacts from the site can be seen in the Silchester Gallery at Reading Museum. Guides to the site are on sale at the Calleva Arms in the village. July & August should see an archaeological dig in progress.

Times: Open daily 9am-sunset. Closed 25 Dec.

Fee: Free.

P

🏛 SOUTHAMPTON

Southampton City Art Gallery

Civic Centre, Commercial Rd SO14 7LP (situated on the Watts Park side of the Civic Centre, a short walk from the station)
☎ 023 80632601   📠 023 80832153

The largest gallery in the south of England, with the finest collection of contemporary art in the country outside London. Varied displays of landscapes, portrait paintings or recent British art are always available, as well as a special display, selected by members of the public.

Times: Open all year, Tue, Wed & Fri 10-5, Thu 10-5, Sat 10-5, Sun 1-4. (Closed 25-27 & 31 Dec).

Fee: Free.

P (250yds) 🖥 ♿ toilets for disabled shop ✖

Southampton Hall of Aviation

Albert Rd South SO1 1FR
☎ 023 80635830

Inspired by the development of the Spitfire at the nearby Supermarine Aviation Works at Woolston, where it evolved from aircraft built for the Schneider Trophy air races. The company won the Trophy in 1931 with the Supermarine 6B, and there's a Supermarine S6A on display as well as one of the last Spitfires produced, the Mark 24, and other aircraft of local interest. The museum is built around a huge Sandringham flying-boat which visitors can board.

Times: Open all year, Tue-Sat 10-5, Sun 12-5. Also BH Mon & School Holidays. (Closed Xmas).

Fee: *£3 (ch 5-16 £2, pen & students £2.50). Family ticket available. Party.

P (150 yds) (roadside parking on meter) ♿ (lift to all levels) toilets for disabled shop ✖

Southampton Maritime Museum

The Wool House, Town Quay SO1 1LX
☎ 023 80223941 & 80635904
📠 023 80339601

The Wool House was built in the 14th century as a warehouse for wool, and now houses a maritime museum, with models and displays telling the history of the Victorian and modern port of Southampton.

Times: Open all year, Tue-Fri 10-12 & 1-5, Sat 10-12 & 1-4, Sun 2-5. (Closed BHs).

P (400 yds) (metered parking adjacent) ♿ shop ✖ *Details not confirmed for 2000*

⛪ STRATFIELD SAYE

STRATFIELD SAYE HOUSE

RG7 2BZ (off A33 between Reading &
Basingstoke)
☎ 01256 882882   📠 01256 882882

Given by the nation to the first Duke of
Wellington in 1817, after his victory over
Napoleon at the Battle of Waterloo. Stratfield
Saye remains the home of the Duke of
Wellington and contains many mementoes of the
lst Duke, including his magnificent funeral
carriage. Please telephone for details of special
events.
Times: Open Sat & Sun in May and BH Mon; Daily ex Fri Jun-
Aug; Sat & Sun in Sep. Groups by prior booking during week.
Fee: *£5 (ch £2.50). Party 20+.
🅿 ✕ licensed ♿ toilets for disabled shop ✖ (ex in grounds)

⛪ TITCHFIELD

TITCHFIELD ABBEY

(half a mile N off A27)
☎ 023 92527667

Also known as `Palace House', in Tudor times
this was the seat of the Earl of Southampton,
built on the site of the abbey founded in 1232. He
incorporated the gatehouse and the nave of the
church into his house.
Times: Open Apr-Sep, daily, 10-6; Oct-Mar, daily, 10-4.
🅿 ♿ ✖ ♨

⛪ WINCHESTER

GURKHA MUSEUM

Peninsula Barracks, Romsey Rd SO23 8TS (off
B3040)
☎ 01962 842832   📠 01962 877597

This museum tells the fascinating story of the
Gurkha's involvement with the British Army.
Travel from Nepal to the North-West Frontier and
beyond, with the help of life-sized dioramas,
interactive exhibits and sound displays. Special
attractions are held at half term, Easter, summer
and before Christmas. Please ring for deatils.
Times: Open all year, BH Mon, Tue-Sat 10-5, Sun 12-4.
Telephone for Xmas opening times. (Closed 25-26 Dec, 1 Jan
and Tue following BH Mon)
Fee: *£1.50 (pen 75p). Party 15+.
🅿 ♿ (lift & stair lift) toilets for disabled shop ✖

HOSPITAL OF ST CROSS

SO23 9SD (1.5m S of city, on A3335)
☎ 01962 851375   📠 01962 878221

Founded in 1132 for the benefit of 13 poor men,
and still functioning as an almshouse.
Throughout the Middle Ages the hospital handed
out the Dole - bread and beer - to travellers, and
this is still done. The Church of St Cross,

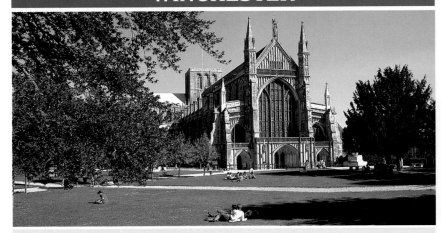

WINCHESTER

*Winchester is a deeply historic, and also very attractive city, offering some lovely parks,
fine old buildings and great shopping in a picturesque setting. Through the centuries
Winchester has played a major role. The Domesday Book was compiled here, King
Alfred united England under Wessex with Winchester as his capital, Henry III was born
at the castle, Mary Tudor married Philip of Spain here, and some believe that the city
was the fabled Camelot. Winchester still has a vibrant cultural life, as can be seen in its
folk festival, the Hat Fair, Winchester Festival, Cross Street Fete and Christmas concerts.
Motorists be warned that the central one-way system can be tricky to negotiate!*

Brethrens Hall and medieval kitchen, and the walled Master's Garden are all worthy of note.
Times: Open all year, Apr-Oct, Mon-Sat 9.30-5; Nov-Mar 10.30-3.30. (Closed Sun, Good Fri & 25 Dec).
Fee: *£2 (ch 50p, students & pen £1.25).
P (200 yds) (2 hrs) 🍽 ♿ (A resident Brother can act as guide and assistant) toilets for disabled shop ✻ (ex guide dogs)

ROYAL HAMPSHIRE REGIMENT MUSEUM & MEMORIAL GARDEN
Serle's House, Southgate St SO23 9EG
☎ 01962 863658   📄 01962 888302

This fine 18th-century house contains an excellent collection of militaria from the history of the Royal Hampshire Regiment 1702 - 1992. The gardens are a memorial to the Regimental dead.
Times: Open all year(ex 2 weeks Xmas & New Year), Mon-Fri 10-12.30 & 2-4; Apr-Oct wknds & BH noon-4.
Fee: Free.
P (800mtrs) ♿ shop ✻ (ex guide dogs)

ROYAL HUSSARS (PWO) REGIMENTAL MUSEUM
Peninsula Barracks, Romsey Rd SO23 8TS
☎ 01962 828539   📄 01962 828538

The Royal Hussars were formed by the amalgamation of two regiments raised at the time of the Jacobite Rebellion in 1715. Visitors to the museum will learn the story of the Royal Hussars from its founding to the present day.
Times: Open 5 Jan-18 Dec, Tue-Fri 10-4, Sat, Sun & BH's 12-4.
Fee: Free.
P ♿ (lift to first floor) toilets for disabled shop ✻

THE GREAT HALL
Castle Av SO23 8PJ
☎ 01962 846476

The only surviving part of Winchester Castle, once home to the Domesday Book, this 13th century hall was the centre of court and government life. The round table, closely associated with the legendary King Arthur, has hung here for over 600 years.
Times: Open all year, Mar-Oct daily 10-5; Nov-Feb, daily 10-5, weekends 10-4. Closed Xmas.
Fee: *Donations welcome.
P (200yds) ♿ toilets for disabled shop garden centre ✻ (ex guide dogs) 🐾

WINCHESTER CATHEDRAL
SO23 9LS (in city centre - follow city heritage signs)
☎ 01962 857200 & 866854
📄 01962 857201

The longest medieval church in Europe, founded in 1079 on a site where Christian worship had already been offered for over 400 years. Among its treasures are the 12th-century illuminated Winchester Bible, the font, medieval wall paintings and Triforium Gallery Museum.
Times: Open all year, daily 8.30-6.30. Access may be restricted during services.
Fee: *Recommended donations.
P 🍽 ✗ licensed ♿ (chair lift to east end of Cathedral, touch & hearing model) toilets for disabled shop ✻

WINCHESTER CITY MILL
Bridge St SO23 8EJ (by the city bridge between King Alfred's statue & Chesil St)
☎ 01962 870057   📄 01962 870057

Built over the fastflowing River Itchen in 1744, the mill has a delightful small island garden and an impressive millrace.
Times: Open Apr-Oct, Wed-Sun & BH Mons 11-4.45; Mar wknds only. Last admission 15 mins before closing.
Fee: Free.
P (200 yds) shop ♻ 🐾

WINCHESTER COLLEGE
77 Kingsgate St SO23 9NA (S of Cathedral Close)
☎ 01962 621209   📄 01962 621215

Founded in 1382, Winchester College is one of the oldest schools in England. The college has greatly expanded over the years but the original buildings remain intact. The chapel and (during term time) the cloisters and Fromond's Chantry are open to the public. Also open is the War Cloister, which contains memorials to Wykhamists killed in World War I and conflicts since.
Times: Open for unbooked guided tours Mar-Sep daily (ex Sun am) 11, 2 & 3.15. Booked tour (parties of 10+) all year.
Fee: *£2.50 (pen & students 18 £2)
P (250 yards) (Most streets have permit parking) ♿ toilets for disabled shop ✻

Herefordshire

Herefordshire is split in two by the River Wye which meanders through the county on its way to the Severn and the sea. The entire county is largely rural, with Hereford, Leominster and Ross-on-Wye the only towns or cities of any size.

The countryside and ancient villages of Herefordshire are probably the county's major asset, and visitors can take advantage of a number of trails which will guide them through much of interest. These are set out on leaflets available from Tourist Information Centres. Those especially interested in villages should try the Black and White Village Trail, which takes the motorist on a 35-mile drive around timber-framed villages in the northwest of the county from Leominster to Weobley, (established in the 7th century and known as a centre of witchcraft in the 18th), Kinnersley Castle, Eardisley (where the Church of St Mary Magdalene boasts a early 12th-century carved font), Great Oak, Kington (one of the five market towns of Herefordshire), Pembridge, and others.

Other trails include the Mortimer Trail - a 30 mile walk through unspoilt countryside between Ludlow and Kington; the Hop Trail - which goes from Bromyard to Ledbury through surrounding fields which display the varying stages of hop growing - and the Hidden Highway, which begins at Ross-on-Wye and ends in Chester, taking in much of the area's dramatic countryside and secret places on the way.

Top: Abbey Dore

🏛 ASHTON

BERRINGTON HALL

Berrington HR6 0DW (3m N of Leominster)
☎ 01568 615721   🖨 01568 613263

An elegant neo-classical house of the late 18th century, designed by Henry Holland and set in a park landscape by 'Capability' Brown. There is a restored bedroom suite, a nursery, a Victorian laundry and a tiled Georgian dairy. Special events throughout the year, please telephone for details.
Times: Open 27 Mar-Oct daily (ex Thur-Fri) 1.30-5.30 (4.30pm in Oct). Last admission 30min before closing. Garden open 12.30-6 (5.30pm in Oct). Park walk open July-Oct, same times as house.
Fee: *£4.20 (ch £2.10) Family ticket £10. Garden only £2.
🅿 ✕ licensed shop ✖ (ex guide dogs) 🐾 🍽

🏛 BROCKHAMPTON

LOWER BROCKHAMPTON

WR6 5UH (2m E of Bromyard on A44)
☎ 01885 488099

A late 14th-century moated manor house, with an attractive half-timbered 15th-century gatehouse, a rare example of this type of structure, and the ruins of a 12th-century chapel. It is part of a larger National Trust property covering over 1700 acres of Herefordshire countryside with various walks including a Sculpture Trail. Phone for details of special events.
Times: Open: Medieval hall, Parlour, Minstrel gallery, Information room, gatehouse & chapel 29 Mar-Sept, Wed-Sun & BH Mon 10-5 (closed Good Fri). Oct, Wed, Wed-Sun 10-4.
🅿 ♿ (special parking for disabled) ✖ 🐾 *Details not confirmed for 2000*

🏛 CROFT

CROFT CASTLE

HR6 9PW (off B4362)
☎ 01568 780246

Home of the Croft family since Domesday (with a break of 170 years from 1750); walls and towers date from the 14th and 15th centuries; the interior is mainly 18th century. There is a splendid avenue of 350-year-old Spanish chestnuts, and an Iron Age Fort (Croft Ambrey) may be reached by footpath. Please ring for details of special events.
Times: Open Etr Sat & Sun. Apr Sat, Sun & BH Mon 1.30-4.30. Oct-1 Nov Sat & Sun 1.30-4.30. May-Sep, Wed-Sun & BH Mon 1.30-5.30. Last admission to house half hour before closing. Parkland open all year. Closed Good Fri.
🅿 (charged) ♿ (parking available, braille guide) ✖ (ex in parkland) 🐾 *Details not confirmed for 2000*

🏛 DINMORE

DINMORE MANOR

HR4 8EE (off A49, signposted)
☎ 01432 830322   🖨 01432 830503

The manor is set in a spectacular hillside location, with outstanding views of the surrounding countryside. The chapel dates back to the 12th century, and is in a unique setting beside the rock garden, pools, the collection of old acers, and the 1200-year-old yew tree. There's a collection of 1930s stained glass, an 18th-century chamber organ, and Victorian aeolian pipe organ.
Times: Open all year, daily 10-5.30
🅿 ♿ shop (plant centre) ✖ (ex guide dogs) *Details not confirmed for 2000*

🏛 GOODRICH

GOODRICH CASTLE

HR9 6HY (5m S of Ross-on-Wye, off A40)
☎ 01600 890538

Goodrich Castle dominates an ancient crossing of the River Wye. Its huge towers, graceful arches and chapel are well worth the visit, and there is a maze of rooms, passages and a gloomy dungeon to be explored. It was besieged in the Civil War, and the locally made cannon used to bombard it, and nicknamed 'Roaring Meg', is on display in Hereford Cathedral.
Times: Open all year, Apr-Oct, daily 10-6 (or dusk if earlier in Oct); Nov-Mar 10-4. Closed 24-26 Dec & 1 Jan.
🅿 ✖ ♿ *Details not confirmed for 2000*

🏛 HEREFORD

CHURCHILL HOUSE MUSEUM & HATTON ART GALLERY

3 Venn's Ln HR1 1DE
☎ 01432 267409 & 260693
🖨 01432 342492

The museum is laid out in a Regency house with fine grounds, and has 18th-and early 19th-century rooms, displays of costume, and a gallery devoted to works by the local artist Brian Hatton.
Times: Open 2-5 Apr-Sep, Wed-Sun, inc BH Mons.
Fee: Free.
🅿 ♿ (access guide & tape, braille guides & plans) shop ✖

CIDER MUSEUM & KING OFFA DISTILLERY

21 Ryelands St HR4 OLW (off A438 Hereford to Brecon road)
☎ 01432 354207

Explore the fascinating history of cider making - old cidermaking equipment, the cooper's workshop and Vat house with hydraulic presses and bottling machinery. Various events take place throughout the year, including

contd.

LEOMINSTER

Leominster, - remember it's pronounced 'Lemster', and avoid alienating the locals - lies at the heart of the Herefordshire Marches, in a valley at the junction of the River Lugg and Pinsley Brook. The town dates from the 7th century, and its name may derive from Lady Godiva's husband and Earl of Hereford, Leofric. In its long and colourful history, Leominster has been a centre for wool and cattle trade, and a strategic centre in battles involving the Welsh, the Danes and the Saxons. Half-timbered Tudor buildings and medieval buildings are still common in Leominster, and the town's historic past carries on into the present via its importance as a centre of the antique trade.

demonstrations and exhibitions - please ring for details.
Times: Open all year, Apr-Oct, daily 10-5.30; Nov-Mar, Tue-Sun 11-3. Pre-booked groups at any time.
Fee: *£2.30 (concessions £1.80). Party 15+.
P 🅿 ♿ shop ✈ (ex guide dogs)

HEREFORD CATHEDRAL
Broad St HR1 2NG (signed from city inner ring roads)
☎ 01432 359880 📄 01432 355929

The first bishop was appointed to the See of Hereford in 676AD. The cathedral is mainly Norman with a 13th-century Lady Chapel. Hereford's two outstanding treasures are exhibited together in the museum building at the West front. The Mappa Mundi - drawn in 1289, and the famous Chained Library - containing over 1400 chained books and 227 manuscripts dating from the 8th century.
Times: Cathedral open daily for visitors 9.30-5; Mappa Mundi & Chained Library Exhibition Mon-Sat 11-4.15 (last admission), Sun 12-3.15.
Fee: *Cathedral admission free (donation invited). Mappa Mundi & Chained Library Exhibition £4 (concessions £3). Family £10. Party 10+.
P 🅿 (0.25m) 🍴 ♿ (touch facility for blind & partially sighted) shop ✈ (ex guide dogs) 🏷

🏛 KINGTON
HERGEST CROFT GARDENS
HR5 3EG (0.25m W off A44)
☎ 01544 230160 📄 01544 230160

From spring bulbs to autumn colour, this is a garden for all seasons. A fine collection of trees and shrubs surrounds the Edwardian house. There's an old fashioned kitchen garden with spring and summer borders, and Park Wood, a hidden valley with splendid rhododendrons.
Times: Open Apr-Oct, 1.30-6.00.
Fee: *£3.50 (ch under 16 free). Party 20+
P 🅿 ♿ toilets for disabled shop garden centre 🏷

🏛 LEDBURY
EASTNOR CASTLE
Eastnor HR8 1RL (the castle is 2.5m E of Ledbury on the A438 Tewkesbury road)
☎ 01531 633160 📄 01531 631776

A magnificent Georgian castle in a lovely setting, with a deer park, arboretum and lake. Inside are tapestries, fine art and armour, and the Italianate and Gothic interiors have been beautifully restored. There's an adventure playground, nature trails and lakeside walks. Please phone for details of special events which take place throughout the summer.

Times: Open Etr-end Sep Sun & Bh Mon, Jul & Aug Sun-Fri 11-5 last admission 4.30pm.
Fee: *Castle & grounds £4.75 (ch £2.50) Family £12. Grounds £2.75 (ch £1.50).
🅿 💺 ✕ ♿ shop garden centre 🐕

🏛 SWAINSHILL
THE WEIR GARDENS
HR4 7QF (5m W of Hereford, on A438)
☎ **01684 850051**

A delightful riverside garden which is at its best in spring when there are lovely displays of naturalised bulbs set in woodland and grassland walks. Cliff garden walks can be taken here, with fine views of the River Wye and the Welsh hills.
Times: Open 14 Feb-1 Nov, Wed-Sun 11-6. Also open Good Frand BH Mon.
🅿 ✕ 🚲 🦌 *Details not confirmed for 2000*

Hertfordshire

This southeastern county is close to London, making its county town of Hertford and the towns of Hemel Hempstead, Watford and Harpenden a haven for commuters to the capital.

EVENTS & FESTIVALS

April
Easter Sunday & Monday
Gamekeeper & Countryman
Fair, Hertford Showground,
Exit 9 M1

May
13th-14th Herts Garden
Show, Knebworth House
27th-28th May Herts County
Show

June
tbc Hertford
Carnival

July
1st
(provisional)
Ware
Carnival
1st-23rd St
Albans
Festival
11th
Fireworks &
Laser
Concert,
Knebworth
House

September
9th Hoddeson Carnival

St Albans, less than 19 miles (30km) from London, has retained its distinctive character, along with many historic remains. The Roman city of Verulamiun is situated in a nearby park, and excavations have revealed an amphitheatre, a temple, parts of the city walls and the foundations of houses. Some spectacular mosaic pavements are displayed in the Verulamiun Museum.

The abbey church at St Albans is built on the site where St Alban, the first British Christian martyr, was executed in the 4th century. The abbey was founded in 793, and contains his shrine, made of Purbeck marble. Lost for years, it was discovered in the 19th century, broken in peices, and restored by Sir Giles Gilbert Scott. Rebuilt by the Normans, the abbey contains some wonderful medieval wall paintings.

Nicholas Breakspear was born in St Albans, the son of an abbey tenant. In 1154 he took the name Adrian IV, and became the first, and so far only, English pope.

Another famous historic son of Hertfordshire was Sir Francis Bacon, Elizabethan scholar and Lord High Chancellor, who some believe was the real author of Shakespeare's plays. He was born at Gorhambury House near Hemel Hempstead in 1561.

In the market town of Hitchin lavender is grown and distilled in the time honoured way. The practice was introduced from Naples in the 16th century.

Top: Grand Union Canal, Berkhampstead

GARDEN CITIES OF HERTFORDSHIRE

Letchworth was founded in 1903 as the first garden city in England by Ebenezer Howard (1850-1928), a town planner and founder of the Garden City Association. His ideal of a garden city - a town built in a rural area designed to combine all the best of town and country life - is outlined in his book Tomorrow *published in 1898 (republished in 1902 as* Garden Cities of Tomorrow*).*

Welwyn Garden City was founded by Howard in 1919-20. Some of his ideas were taken up in the New Towns Act, 1946, and Stevenage was the first place chosen to be developed as a new town. Welwyn Garden City was designated a new town in 1948.

AYOT ST LAWRENCE
SHAW'S CORNER
AL6 9BX (at SW end of village)
☎ 01438 820307

George Bernard Shaw lived here from 1906 until his death in 1950. He gave the house to the National Trust in 1946, and the contents are much as they were in his time. Among the displays are his hats, including a soft homburg he wore for 60 years, his exercise machine, fountain pen, spectacles and several pictures.
Times: Open Apr-1 Nov. Wed-Sun & BH Mon 1-5. Last admission 4.30pm. (Closed Good Fri)
🅿 ♿ ✈ ♨ *Details not confirmed for 2000*

BERKHAMSTED
BERKHAMSTED CASTLE
HP4 1HF
☎ 01536 402840

Roads and a railway have cut into the castle site, but its huge banks and ditches remain impressive. The original motte-and-bailey was built after the Norman Conquest, and there is a later stone keep, owned by the Black Prince, eldest son of King Edward III, where King John of France was imprisoned.
Times: Open all year daily 10-4.
🅿 ♿ ♿

HATFIELD
HATFIELD HOUSE
AL9 5NQ (2m from jct 4 A1(M) on A1000, 7m from M25 jct 23)
☎ 01707 262823   🖷 01707 275719

Robert Cecil built this great Jacobean mansion in 1607-11, replacing the palace where Elizabeth I spent much of her childhood. There are portraits of the queen, and historic possessions such as her silk stockings. The great park and gardens include a parterre planted with yews and roses, a scented garden and a knot garden. Hatfield is still the home of the Cecils, who once had a private

contd.

waiting room at the nearby railway station. Please ring for details of special events.

Times: Open 25 Mar-4 Oct. (Closed Good Fri). House: weekdays 12-4, Sun 1-4.30. (Closed Mon ex BH 11-4.30). Gardens: daily 11-6.

🅿 ✗ licensed ♿ toilets for disabled shop garden centre 🐾 (ex park) *Details not confirmed for 2000*

⛫ KNEBWORTH
KNEBWORTH HOUSE, GARDENS & COUNTRY PARK
SG3 6PY (direct access J7 A1(M) at Stevenage)
☎ 01438 812661   🖷 01438 811908

The original Tudor manor was transformed in 1843 by the spectacular high Gothic decoration of Victorian novelist Sir Edward Bulwer Lytton. Outside, the formal gardens, laid out by Lutyens in 1908, include a Jekyll herb garden, a maze, and wilderness walks. The 250-acre park includes a miniature railway, an adventure playground, and a deer park. Many special events and activities take place here, including craft fairs, Medieval jousting, and classic car shows. Ring for details.

Times: Open - Park, Playground & Gardens: 4 Apr-20 Apr & 23 May-7 Sep. Weekends & BHs 25 Apr-17 May, also weekends only 12-27 Sep, 11-5.30. House: as Park (ex closed Mon but open bank holidays), 12-5.

🅿 🚌 ♿ (with prior notice visitors can be driven to front door) toilets for disabled shop 🐾 (ex in park) *Details not confirmed for 2000*

⛫ LETCHWORTH
FIRST GARDEN CITY HERITAGE MUSEUM
296 Norton Way South SG6 1SU
☎ 01462 482710   🖷 01462 486056

The museum tells the history of the world's first Garden City from its foundation in 1903 up to the present. The museum provides a insight into this unique architectural and social concept which set a precedent in town planning.

Times: Open all year, Mon-Sat 10-5. (Closed 25-26 Dec).

🅿 (150 yds) ♿ (parking by prior arrangement) shop 🐾 *Details not confirmed for 2000*

MUSEUM & ART GALLERY
Broadway SG6 3PF (Museum is situated next door to the Public Library)
☎ 01462 685647   🖷 01462 481879

The museum features local archaeology and natural history, with a regular programme of changing exhibitions held in the Art Gallery. Ring for further details.

Times: Open all year Mon-Sat 10-5. (Closed most BHs).

Fee: Free.

🅿 (100 yds) ♿ (special provisions on request) shop 🐾 (ex guide dogs)

🏛 LONDON COLNEY
DE HAVILLAND AIRCRAFT HERITAGE
Salisbury Hall AL2 1EX (signposted from J22 of M25)
☎ 01727 822051 & 826400
📄 01727 826400

The oldest aircraft museum in Britain, opened in 1959 to preserve the de Havilland Mosquito prototype on the site of its conception. The collection includes photographs, memorabilia and aero-engine displays, as well as aircraft: Mosquitoes, Venoms, a Tiger Moth, a Dove and a Horsa among others. You can visit the workshops, and there's an Annual Flying Weekend in June; please ring for details.
Times: Open Mar-Oct, Sun & BH Mons 10.30-5.30, Tue, Thu & Sat 2-5.30.
Fee: *£4 (ch & pen £2) Family ticket £10.
🅿 ♿ (wheelchairs available) toilets for disabled shop ✖ (ex on lead & under control) 🐾

🏛 ST ALBANS
GARDENS OF THE ROSE (ROYAL NATIONAL ROSE SOCIETY)
Chiswell Green AL2 3NR (2m S off B4630 Watford Rd in Chiswell Green Ln)
☎ 01727 850461   📄 01727 850360

The gardens of the Royal National Rose Society, which include the International Trial Ground for new roses. The gardens contain over 30,000 plants in 1,650 different varieties. These include old-fashioned roses, modern roses and the roses of the future. The National Miniature Rose Show

takes place on 20-30 July and entry is free to visitors to the gardens.
Times: Open 23 Apr-4 Jun (Sun & BH Mon only) 10-4. 10 Jun-24 Sep, Mon-Sat 9-5 (Sun & BH Mon 10-6).
Fee: *Spring season: £2.50 (ch 6-16 £1, pen & UB40 £2) Party 20+. Summer season: £4 (ch £6-16 £1.50, pen & UB40 £3.50) Party 20+.
🅿 🍴 ♿ (ramps where necessary) toilets for disabled shop 🐾

GORHAMBURY
AL3 6AH (entry via lodge gates on A414)
☎ 01727 855000   📄 01727 843675

This house was built by Sir Robert Taylor between 1774 and 1784 to house an extensive picture collection of 17th-century portraits of the Grimston and Bacon families and their contemporaries. Also of note is the 16th-century enamelled glass collection and an early English pile carpet.
Times: Open May-Sep, Thu 2-5.
Fee: *£4 (ch £2.50, pen £2). Party.
🅿 shop ✖

MUSEUM OF ST ALBANS
Hatfield Rd AL1 3RR (situated in City Centre on A1057 Hatfield road)
☎ 01727 819340   📄 01727 837472

Exhibits include the Salaman collection of craft tools, and reconstructed workshops. The history of St Albans is traced from the departure of the Romans up to the present day. Please ring for details.
Times: Open all year, daily 10-5, Sun 2-5. Closed 25 & 26 Dec.
Fee: Free.
🅿 ♿ toilets for disabled shop ✖ (ex guide dogs) 🐾

ROMAN THEATRE OF VERULAMIUM
St Michaels AL3 6AH (off A4147)
☎ 01727 835035   📄 01727 843675

The theatre was discovered in 1847 and excavated in 1935. It is unique in England. First constructed around AD160, it is semi-circular in shape, 180ft across and could hold 1,600 spectators.
Times: Open all year, daily 10-5 (4 in winter).
Fee: *£1.50 (ch 50p, students & OAPs £1). Ch under 5yrs free.
🅿 ♿ shop

ST ALBANS CATHEDRAL
Sumpter Yard AL1 1BY (in the centre of St Albans)
☎ 01727 860780   📄 01727 850944

An imposing Norman abbey church built on the site of the execution of St Alban, Britain's first martyr (c250AD). The cathedral is constructed from recycled Roman brick taken from nearby Verulamium.
Times: Open daily, 9-5.45
Fee: Free.
🅿 (200mtrs) ✖ licensed ♿ (touch & hearing centre, braille guides) toilets for disabled shop 🐾 (ex guide dogs)

VERULAMIUM MUSEUM

St Michaels AL3 4SW (follow signs for St Albans, museum signposted)

☎ 01727 866100 🖹 01727 859919

Verulamium was one of the largest and most important Roman towns in Britain - by the lst century AD it was declared a `municipium', giving its inhabitants the rights of Roman citizenship, the only British city granted this honour. A mosaic and underfloor heating system can be seen in situ, and the museum has wall paintings, jewellery, pottery and other domestic items. Regular talks and demonstrations at weekends. On the second weekend of every month legionaries occupy the galleries and describe the tactics and equipment of the Roman Imperial Army and the life of a legionary.

Times: Open all year weekdays 10-5.30, Sun 2-5.30.
Fee: *£3 (ch, pen & students £1.70). Family ticket £7.50.
🅿 (charged) ♿ (ramp access to main entrance) toilets for disabled shop 🐕 (ex guide dogs) 💳

⅏ TRING

THE WALTER ROTHSCHILD ZOOLOGICAL MUSEUM

Akeman St HP23 6AP (signposted from A41)

☎ 01442 824181 🖹 01442 890693

An unusual museum, founded in the 1890s by Lionel Walter, 2nd Baron Rothschild, scientist, eccentric and natural history enthusiast. Famous for its magnificent collection of thousands of mammals and birds, it also has displays of reptiles, fish, insects and domestic dogs, to say nothing of the remarkable exhibition of dressed fleas. Exhibitions are organised throughout the year (details on request).

Times: Open all year, Mon-Sat 10-5, Sun 2-5. (Closed 24-26 Dec).
Fee: *£3 (concessions £1.50, Ch 16 and under free).
🅿 ♿ toilets for disabled shop 🐕

Kent

Often called the 'garden of England', Kent is renowned for its fruit production in the agricultural area of the Weald, and its hop growing for the brewing industry. Hops were picked by itinerant workers, many from London, who moved in for the season.

For many years, Londoners have flocked to the seaside resorts of the Isle of Thanet, Margate, Broadstairs and Ramsgate. Of these, Broadstairs retains a quiet charm, and is probably best known as Charles Dickens' resort of choice, where he lived overlooking the bay, in a rather forbidding residence since known as Bleak House. More popular yet with visitors from all over the world is the ancient city of Canterbury, the metropolis of the Anglican church since Augustine's mission to England in 597, and site of the magnificent cathedral.

The Channel Tunnel and the Channel ports of Dover, Folkestone and Ramsgate ensure good transport links into the county. The administrative centre is Maidstone, and other main towns are Chatham, home of the historic Royal Naval Dockyard; Rochester with its lovely cathedral; and the elegant spa town of Royal Tunbridge Wells.

Kent is blessed with some fine castles, houses and gardens. Chief among these are Leeds Castle, east of Maidstone; Hever Castle, birthplace of Anne Boleyn; Knole, southeast of Sevenoaks, England's largest house with 365 rooms; Churchill's house, Chartwell, near Westerham; Penshurst Place, a 14th-century house with a splendid hall and long gallery; and the inspirational Sissinghurst Garden created by Vita Sackville-West.

EVENTS & FESTIVALS

April
22nd-24th Easter Family Fun at Leeds Castle

May
13th-14th Festival of English Food & Wine, Leeds Castle
21st Tonbridge Carnival
27th-29th May Sellindge Steam Festival, Ashford
28th-29th Finchcocks Spring Garden Fair, Goudhurst, Cranbrook
28th-29th Kent Garden Show, Kent & County Showground

June
17th-24th Broadstairs Dickens Festival

July
13th-15th Kent County Show, Maidstone

August
6th Margate Summer Carnival
9th Broadstairs Water Gala

September
9th-10th The Great Leeds Castle Balloon & Vintage Car Weekend

November
18th Tonbridge Philharmonic Society Choral Concert

December
9th Christmas Craft Fair, Sandwich

Top: Whitstable Harbour

🏛 AYLESFORD
AYLESFORD PRIORY
The Friars ME20 7BX (M20 J6 then signed)
☎ 01622 717272   🖨 01622 715575

Built in the 13th and 14th centuries, the priory has been restored and is now a house of prayer, guesthouse, conference centre and a place of pilgrimage and retreat. It has fine cloisters, and displays sculpture and ceramics by modern artists.
Times: Open all year, daily 9-dusk. Gift & book shop May-Sep, 10-5; Oct-Apr, 10-4 (Sun 11am). Guided tours of the priory by arrangement.
Fee: *Donations. £2 for annual fund-raising day.
🅿 (charged) ☕ 🕭 (wheelchairs available, ramps) toilets for disabled shop ✖

🏛 BELTRING
HOP FARM & COUNTRY PARK
TN12 6PY (on A228)
☎ 01622 872068   🖨 01622 872630

The largest group of Victorian oast houses and galleried barns in the country, with features including the Hop Story Exhibition, Shire Horse Centre, birds of prey including daily owl-flying displays, rural museum and pottery workshop. Please ring for details of special events.
Times: Open all year, Summer 10-6 (last admission 5). Winter 10-4, (Closed 25-26 & 31 Dec)
🅿 ☕ ✖ licensed 🕭 toilets for disabled shop *Details not confirmed for 2000* 🍴

🏛 BRASTED
EMMETTS GARDEN
Ide Hill TN14 6AY (1m S of A25, Sundridge-Ide Hill road)
☎ 01732 868381 (Chartwell office)
🖨 01732 868193

Emmetts is a charming hillside shrub garden, with bluebells, azaleas and rhododendrons in spring and fine autumn colours. It has magnificent views over Bough Beech Reservoir and the Weald. Emmetts Concert in August. Telephone 01892 891001 for details.
Times: Open Apr & May, Wed-Sun; Jun-Oct, Wed & wknds 11-5.30 (last admission 4.30pm). Special arrangement for pre-booked parties at other times.
Fee: *£3 (ch £1.50). Family ticket £7.50. Party.
🅿 ☕ 🕭 (buggy service from car park to garden) toilets for disabled shop 🐾

🏛 BROADSTAIRS
BLEAK HOUSE DICKENS MARITIME & SMUGGLING MUSEUM
Fort Rd CT10 1EY (off Eastern Esplanade, near Viking Bay)
☎ 01843 862224

The house was a favourite seaside residence of Charles Dickens, and he wrote the greater part of *David Copperfield* and other works here, and drafted the idea for *Bleak House*. There are also

exhibitions of relics salvaged from the Goodwin Sands.
Times: Open Etr-Jun & Oct-Nov 10-6, Jul-mid Sep 10-6.
Fee: *£3 (ch 12 £1.80, pen £2.50, students £2). Party 10+.
🅿 (100 yds) 🕭 (provisions made for blind) shop

DICKENS HOUSE MUSEUM
Victoria Pde CT10 1QS (on the seafront)
☎ 01843 862853

The house was immortalised by Charles Dickens in *David Copperfield* as the home of the hero's aunt, Betsy Trotwood. Dickens' letters and possessions are shown, with local and Dickensian prints, costumes and general Victoriana. The Broadstairs Dickens Festival takes place in June.
Times: Open Apr-mid Oct, daily 2-5.
Fee: *£1.50 (ch 50p).
🅿 (400yds) shop 🍴 (ex guide dogs)

🏛 CANTERBURY
CANTERBURY HERITAGE MUSEUM
Stour St CT1 2RA (in the Medieval Poor Priest's Hospital, just off Saint Margaret's St)
☎ 01227 452747   🖨 01227 455047

An award-winning museum in a lovely medieval building beside the river. The tour starts in Roman times and continues up to the present day. Some of the most exciting of the city's treasures are shown - the Canterbury Cross, Anglo-Saxon gold, and Viking finds. The displays include a reconstruction of Becket's tomb; a medieval street with a pilgrim badge shop; the city in the Civil War; and Stephenson's locomotive `Invicta'. There is a Rupert Bear Gallery and a collection of Joseph Conrad memorabilia.
Times: Open all year, Mon-Sat 10.30-5 & Sun (Jun-Oct) 1.30-5 (last admission 4pm). (Closed Good Fri & Xmas period).
Fee: *£2.30 (ch 5-18 & disabled £1.15, pen & students £1.50). Family ticket £5.15. Party 10+
🅿 🕭 shop 🍴

CANTERBURY ROMAN MUSEUM
Butchery Ln, Longmarket CT1 2RA
☎ 01227 785575   🖨 01227 455047

Underground, at the level of the Roman town, you will find this famous Roman house with its mosaic floors. There is a fascinating reconstruction of some Roman buildings, including a market place with stallholders' wares. Displays reveal a wealth of Roman artefacts. A computer-generated reconstruction video guides you on the tour.
Times: Open all year, Mon-Sat 10-5 & Sun (Jun-Oct) 1.30-5. Last admission 4pm. (Closed Good Fri & Xmas period).
Fee: *£2.30 (ch 5-18 & disabled £1.15, pen & students £1.50). Family ticket £5.15.
🅿 (500mtrs) 🕭 (lift) toilets for disabled shop 🍴

CANTERBURY

Canterbury is one of England's most charming cities, probably best known for its cathedral, and the series of tales written by Chaucer in the 14th century. These were inspired by pilgrimages made to the city by the faithful who believed that the tomb of the martyr, St Thomas á Becket, had miraculous powers. The city is currently the focus of the worldwide Anglican Communion.

Canterbury was called Durovernum by the Romans, and Cantwarabyrig by the Saxons. It retains some of the flavour of a medieval walled city, even though much of it was destroyed in WWII, and then rebuilt in the 'brutalist' modern architectural style.

CANTERBURY TALES VISITOR ATTRACTION

Saint Margaret's St CT1 2TG

☎ 01227 479227   📄 01227 765584

Step back in time to join Chaucer's famous band of pilgrims on their journey to the shrine of St Thomas Becket in Canterbury Cathedral. Hear their tales of love, greed, chivalry and intrigue and experience life in the 14th century, complete with authentic sights, sounds and smells!

Commentaries are available in English, Dutch, French, German, Italian, Japanese and Spanish.

Times: Open all year, Mar-Jun & Sep-Oct daily 9.30-5.30; Jul-Aug daily 9-5.30, Nov-Feb, Sun-Fri 10-4.30, Sat 9.30-5.30.

Fee: *£5.25 (ch £4.25, students & pen £4.50). Family ticket £16.50.

P (200 mtrs) 💳 ♿ (notice required for wheelchairs) toilets for disabled shop ✗ 🍴

CANTERBURY WEST GATE MUSEUM

Saint Peter's St (at the end of the main street beside the river, the entrance is under the main arch)

☎ 01227 452747   📄 01227 455047

The last of the city's fortified gatehouses sits astride the London road with the river as a moat. Rebuilt in around 1380 by Archbishop Sudbury, it was used as a prison for many years. The battlements give a splendid panoramic view of the city and are a good vantage point for photographs. Arms and armour can be seen in the guardroom, and there are cells in the towers.

Times: Open all year (ex Good Fri & Xmas period), Mon-Sat; 11-12.30 & 1.30-3.30. Last admission 15 mins before closure

Fee: *£1 (ch & disabled 50p, pen, students & UB40 65p). Family ticket £2.30. Party 10+.

P (100 yds) shop ✗

Druidstone Wildlife Park

Honey Hill, Blean CT2 9JP (3m NW on A290)
☎ 01227 765168 🖹 01227 768860

Enjoy the company of the animals and birds in a relaxing country setting. Experience a taste of the South American plains with the rhea, mara and peccary. Make friends with the animals in the farmyard, meet the parrots, walk through the gardens which are home to the owls and wallaby, or along the woodland trail where you can see a surprising variety of wildlife and white fallow deer.

Times: Open Mar & Nov, wknds only; Etr-Oct, daily 10-5.30.
Fee: *£3.50 (ch £2 & pen £2.50). Family £9
🅿 💻 ♿ toilets for disabled shop ✖

St Augustine's Abbey

Longport CT1 1PF (off A28)
☎ 01227 767345

The abbey, founded by St Augustine in 598, when he brought Christianity from Rome to England, is one of the oldest monastic sites in the country. Its long and fascinating history can be traced in the ruins.
Times: Open all year, Apr-Oct, daily 10-6 (or dusk if earlier); Nov-Mar, daily 10-4. Closed 24-26 Dec & 1 Jan.
Fee: £2.50 (ch £1.30).
🅿 ♿ shop ♯

🏛 CHARTWELL

Chartwell

TN16 1PS (2m S of Westerham, off B2026)
☎ 01732 866368 (info line) & 868381
🖹 01732 868193

The former home of Sir Winston Churchill is filled with reminders of the great statesman, from his hats and uniforms to gifts presented by Stalin and Roosevelt. There are paintings of Churchill and other works by notable artists, and also many paintings by Churchill himself. Telephone 01892 891001 for details of events.
Times: Open Apr-1 Nov, house, garden & studio, Wed-Sun & Bh Mon) 11-5. Open BH Mons & Tue in Jul/Aug. Last admission 4.15pm.
Fee: *House, Garden & studio £5.50 (ch £2.75). Gardens and studio only £2.60 (ch £1.30). Family ticket £13.75.Entrance by timed ticket in summer to avoid congestion, waiting time can be spent in garden.
🅿 ✖ licensed ♿ (two steps to lift, grounds partially accessible) toilets for disabled shop ✖ (ex garden) 🐾 ⬤

🏛 CHATHAM

Fort Amherst

Dock Rd ME4 4UB (adjacent to the A231 dock road, 0.5m from Chatham Dockyard)
☎ 01634 847747 🖹 01634 847747

A fine Georgian fortress set in over 15 acres of attractive parkland. A fascinating collection of caves, tunnels, gun-batteries and barracks gives visitors an insight into the life of the Napoleonic soldier. Please telephone for details of special events, including historic re-enactments.
Times: Open daily 10.30-last entry 4pm
Fee: *£4 (ch, pen & students £2) Family tickets £10.
🅿 💻 ♿ (wheelchair provided, road access up to fort) toilets for disabled shop ✖ (ex guide dogs) ⬤

World Naval Base

The Historic Dockyard ME4 4TZ (signposted from M25)
☎ 01634 823800 🖹 01634 823801

A Royal dockyard until 1984, now an 80-acre working museum with 47 Scheduled Ancient Monuments, forming the most complete Georgian/early Victorian dockyard in the world. Eight museum galleries cover 400 years of shipbuilding history, with real ships and a submarine to explore.
Times: Open Apr-Oct, daily 10-5; Feb, Mar & Nov, Wed, Sat & Sun 10-4.
Fee: *£8.50 (ch 5-16 £5.50, student & pen £6.30). Family ticket £22.50 Party
🅿 💻 ✖ licensed ♿ (wheelchair available, Braille guides) toilets for disabled shop ⬤

🏛 DEAL

Deal Castle

Victoria Rd CT14 7BA (SW of Deal town centre)
☎ 01304 372762

This huge, austere structure, shaped like a Tudor rose, was an important part of the coastal defences built by Henry VIII. Its unrelenting walls are rounded to deflect cannon shot and inside, the dark passages tell the reality of garrison life.
Times: Open all year, Apr-Oct, daily 10-6 (or dusk if earlier); Nov-Mar, Wed-Sun 10-4. Closed 24-26 Dec & 1 Jan.
Fee: £3 (ch £1.50).
♿ shop ♯

Walmer Castle
Walmer, Kingsdown Rd CT14 7LJ (1m S on coast, off A258)
☎ 01304 364288

Of similar design to Deal Castle, Walmer was also part of the defences of Tudor England. It is the official residence of the Lord Warden of the Cinque Ports (Dover, Sandwich, Hythe, Romney and Hastings were the original five) an honorary post held by the Duke of Wellington in his day, by Sir Winston Churchill after World War II and now by Queen Elizabeth the Queen Mother. The castle gardens are delightful.
Times: Open all year, Apr-Oct, daily 10-6 (or dusk if earlier in Oct); Nov-Mar, Wed-Sun 10-4. Closed 24-26 Dec, 1 Jan & when Lord Warden in residence.
Fee: £4.50 (ch £2.30).
P ♿ shop (in certain areas)

DOVER
Crabble Corn Mill
Lower Rd, River CT17 0UY (follow signs to River from A258)
☎ 01304 823292 01304 826040

Visit this beautifully restored working Kentish water mill dating from 1812. Regular milling demonstrations take place, producing stoneground wholemeal flour from Kentish organic wheat. Flour for sale, also home-baked produce in café. Exhibition space displays work of local artists and craftspeople.
Times: Open all year, Etr-Jun & Sep, Sat & Sun 11-5; Jul-Aug, Wed-Sun 11-5; Winter Sun 11-5.
P licensed ♿ shop *Details not confirmed for 2000*

Dover Castle and Hellfire Corner
CT16 1HU
☎ 01304 201628

A giant among England's castles, set high on the famous white cliffs, Dover Castle traces its history back to the Iron Age, and many relics of its different periods remain. The underground tunnel system, nicknamed Hellfire Corner, was originally built in medieval times and was also a command centre and military hospital during the Second World War.
Times: Open all year, Apr-Oct, daily 10-6 (or dusk if earlier); Nov-Mar, daily 10-4. Closed 24-26 Dec & 1 Jan.
Fee: £6.90 (ch £3.50).
P ♿ shop (in certain areas)

Roman Painted House
New St CT17 9AJ
☎ 01304 203279

Visit five rooms of a Roman hotel built 1800 years ago, famous for its unique, well-preserved Bacchic frescos. The Roman underfloor heating system and part of a late-Roman defensive wall are also on view. There are extensive displays on Roman Dover, and special events are held throughout the year.
Times: Open Apr-Sep, Tue-Sun 10-5, also BH Mon & Mon Jul & Aug.
Fee: *£2 (ch & pen 80p)
P ♿ (touch table, glass panels on gallery for wheelchairs) shop

The White Cliffs Experience
Market Sq CT16 1PB (signposting on entering town centre from A2 and M20/A20, follow signs)
☎ 01304 214566 & 210101
01304 212057

This award-winning attraction provides an entertaining and exciting encounter with life in Roman Britain and during World War II. A wide range of special events takes place throughout the year - experience wartime rationing or Roman food and drink. Please ring for details. The new Dover Bronze Age Boat Gallery contains what is believed to be the world's oldest sea-going boat.
Times: Open all year daily, Apr-Oct 10-5. Nov-Mar 10-3. Closed 1hr after last admissions.
Fee: *£5.75 (ch 4-14 £3.95, pen & students £4.60) Family ticket £17.95.
P (150 yds) ♿ (lifts, ramped access, wheelchair & seat sticks) toilets for disabled shop (ex guide dogs/hearing dogs)

DUNGENESS
RSPB Nature Reserve
TN29 9PN (off Lydd to Dungeness rd, 1m SE of Lydd)
☎ 01797 320588 01797 321962

This coastal reserve comprises 2106 acres of shingle beach and flooded pits. An excellent place to watch breeding terns, gulls and other water birds. Wheatears, great crested and little grebes also nest here, and outside the breeding

contd.

season there are large flocks of teals, shovelers, and goldeneyes, goosanders, smews and both Slavonian and red-necked grebes. Dungeness is famous for migrants including many rarities. Phone for details of special events.

Times: Open daily except Tue 9am-9pm (or sunset if earlier). Visitor Centre daily except Tue 9-5 summer, 9-4 winter. (Closed 25 & 26 Dec).

🅿 ♿ shop ✖ *Details not confirmed for 2000* 🏴

🏛 DYMCHURCH
MARTELLO TOWER
(access from High St not seafront)

One of the many artillery towers built around the coast, which formed part of a chain of strongholds intended to resist an invasion by Napoleon. It is fully restored, with an original 24-pounder gun on the roof.

Times: Open 10-13 Apr, 2-4 May, 9 May-11 Jul (wknds & BHs), 18 Jul-Aug, Sep (wknds), 2-5.30.

✖ ♿

🏛 EYNSFORD
EYNSFORD CASTLE
(off A225)

The walls of this Norman castle, still 30ft high, come as a surprise in the pretty little village. Its founder, William de Eynsford, ended his days as a monk.

Times: Open all year, Apr-Sep, daily 10-6; Oct-Mar, daily 10-4. (Closed 24-26 Dec & 1 Jan).

🅿 ♿ ♿

LULLINGSTONE ROMAN VILLA
(half mile SW off A225)
☎ 01322 863467

The excavation of this Roman villa in 1949 uncovered one of the most exciting archaeological finds of that century. These are the most remarkable villa remains in Britain, including wonderful mosaic floors, wall paintings and one of the earliest Christian chapels.

Times: Open all year, Apr-Oct, daily 10-6 (or dusk if earlier); Nov-Mar, daily 10-4. Closed 24-26 Dec & 1 Jan.

Fee: £2.60 (ch £1.30).

🅿 ✖ ♿

🏛 GILLINGHAM
ROYAL ENGINEERS MUSEUM
Prince Arthur Rd ME4 4UG (follow brown signs from Gillingham & Chatham town centres)
☎ 01634 406397   📧 01634 822371

The museum covers the diverse and sometimes surprising work of the Royal Engineers. Learn about the first military divers, photographers, aviators and surveyors; see memorabilia relating to General Gordon and Field Marshal Lord Kitchener, Wellington's battle map from Waterloo and a Harrier jump-jet. From October 1999 until

summer 2002, a changing exhibition will mark the centenary of the Anglo-Boer War.

Times: Open all year, Mon-Thu 10-5, Sat-Sun & BH Mon 11.30-5. (Closed Good Fri, 25-26 Dec & 1 Jan). Friday by appointment only.

Fee: *£3 (ch, pen & UB40s £1.50). Family ticket £6.50. Guided tour £4. Party 15+.

🅿 ♿ (help available if required) toilets for disabled shop ✖ (guide dogs)

🏛 HAWKINGE
KENT BATTLE OF BRITAIN MUSEUM
Aerodrome Rd CT18 7AG (Hawkinge off A260, 1m along Aerodrome road)
☎ 01303 893140

Once a Battle of Britain Station, today it houses the largest collection of relics and related memorabilia of British and German aircraft involved in the fighting. Also shown full-size replicas of the Hurricane, Spitfire and Me 109 used in Battle of Britain films. The year 2000 is 60th anniversary of the Battle of Britain and a new memorial will be unveiled.

Times: Open Etr-Sep, daily 10-5; Oct, daily 11-4. Closed Nov-Etr. Last admission 1 hour before closing.

Fee: *£3 (ch £1.50, pen £2.50). Group 20+.

🅿 ♿ shop ✖ (ex guide dogs)

🏛 HEVER
HEVER CASTLE & GARDENS
TN8 7NG (M25 J5 or 6, 3m SE of Edenbridge, off B2026)
☎ 01732 865224   📧 01732 866796

This enchanting, double-moated, 13th-century castle was the childhood home of Anne Boleyn. Restored by the American millionaire William Waldorf Astor at the beginning of the 20th century, it shows superb Edwardian craftsmanship. Astor also transformed the grounds, creating a lake, a spectacular Italian garden filled with antique sculptures; and a maze. Recent additions to the gardens include a 110 metre herbaceous border and a 'splashing' water maze on the Sixteen Acre Island. Special events include jousting and longbow demonstrations, please ring for details

Times: Open 1 Mar-Nov, daily. Castle 12-6, Gardens 11-6. Last admission 5pm. (Closes 4pm Mar & Nov).

Fee: *Castle & Gardens £7.30 (ch 5-16 £4, pen £6.20). Family ticket £18.60. Gardens only £5.80 (ch 5-16 £3.80, pen £4.90). Family ticket £15.40. Party 15+.

🅿 🍴 ✖ licensed ♿ (wheelchairs available, book in advance) toilets for disabled shop garden centre ✖ (ex on leads in grounds) 🏴

🏛 HYTHE
ROMNEY, HYTHE & DYMCHURCH RAILWAY
TN28 8PL (off M20 J11, off A259 signed New Romney)
☎ 01797 362353 & 363256
📧 01797 363591

The world's smallest public railway has its headquarters here. The concept of two enthusiasts coincided with Southern Railway's plans for expansion, and so the thirteen-and-a-half mile stretch of 15 inch gauge railway came into being, running from Hythe through New Romney and Dymchurch to Dungeness Lighthouse. Please ring for details of special events.

Times: Open daily Etr-Sep, also wknds in Mar & Oct. For times apply to: The Manager, RH & DR., New Romney, Kent.
Fee: *Charged according to journey.
🅿 (charged) 🍽 ⛫ (stairlift to Toy & Model Museum) toilets for disabled shop 🍴

🏛 IGHTHAM

IGHTHAM MOTE

TN15 0NT (2.5m S off A227, 6m E of Sevenoaks)
☎ 01732 810378 & 811145 (info line)
🖹 01732 811029

This beautiful moated manor house is a splendid example of medieval architecture. Extensively remodelled through the centuries, notable features include the drawing room with its Jacobean fireplace and frieze, Palladian window and hand-painted Chinese wallpaper. Special events include concerts - ring 01892 891001.
Times: Open Apr-1 Nov, daily ex Tue & Sat, 11-5.30. Pre-booked parties wkday am only. Open Good Fri. Last admission 4.30pm.
Fee: *£5 (ch £2.50). Family ticket £12.50.
🅿 🍽 ⛫ (wheelchairs available,special parking ask at ticket office) toilets for disabled shop 🍴 🌿 🛍

🏛 LAMBERHURST

BAYHAM OLD ABBEY

TN3 8BG (off B2169, 2m W in East Sussex)
☎ 01892 890381

Set in the wooded Teise valley, these ruins date back to the 13th century and include parts of the old church, cloisters and gatehouse.
Times: Open Apr-Oct, daily 10-6 (or dusk if earlier). Winter wknds 10-4.
Fee: £2.10 (ch £1.10).
🅿 ⛫ ⛩ *Details not confirmed for 2000*

OWL HOUSE GARDENS
TN3 8LY (1m NE off A21)
☎ 01892 890230   🖷 01892 891290

A small, timber-framed 16th-century house, surrounded by 14 acres of gardens, offering romantic walks with spring flowers, azaleas, rhododendrons, roses, shrubs and ornamental fruit trees. The sweeping lawns lead to lovely woodlands of oak and birch, and informal sunken water gardens.
Times: Open all year, daily 11-6. (Closed 25-26 Dec & 1 Jan).
Fee: *£4 (ch £1).
🅿 ₤ shop (must be on lead)

SCOTNEY CASTLE GARDEN
TN3 8JN (1m S of Lamberhurst on A21)
☎ 01892 891081   🖷 01892 890110

The beautiful gardens at Scotney were planned in the 19th century around the remains of the old, moated Scotney Castle. There is something to see at every time of year, with spring flowers followed by rhododendrons, azaleas and a mass of roses, and then superb autumn colours. Open-air opera performances are given - ring 01892 891001 for details.
Times: Open Garden: 27 Mar-Oct. Old Castle open May-12 Sep Wed-Fri 11-6, Sat & Sun 2-6 or sunset if earlier. BH Sun & Mon 12-6 (Closed Good Fri. Last admission 1hr before closing.
Fee: *£4 (ch £2). Family ticket £10.
🅿 ₤ (wheelchair available) shop ✖ ❄

🏛 MAIDSTONE
LEEDS CASTLE
ME17 1PL (4m E of Maidstone at J8 of M20/A20)
☎ 01622 765400   🖷 01622 735616

The site of a manor of the Saxon royal family in the 9th century, Leeds has been described as 'the loveliest castle in the world'. Built on two islands in the middle of a lake and set in 500 acres of landscaped parkland, it was converted into a royal palace by Henry VIII. Beautifully restored and furnished; it has some beautiful pictures and other treasures, and, more unusual, a museum of medieval dog collars. Outside are the 14th-century barbican and mill, a maze and grotto, and water and woodland gardens. The Fairfax Hall, a 17th-century tithe barn, is the venue for 'Kentish Evenings' most Saturday nights (except during August). There are also many special events throughout the year.
Times: Open all year daily, Mar-Oct 10-5 (Castle 11-5.30). Nov-Feb 10-3 (Castle from 10.15pm).
Fee: *Castle, Park & Gardens £9.30 (ch 5-15 £6, students & pen £7.30); Park & gardens £7.30 (ch 5-15 £4.50, students & pen £5.80). Family ticket £25, Park & gardens only £20. Party 15+.
🅿 🖵 ✖ licensed ₤ (Braille information, induction loops & wheelchair, lift) toilets for disabled shop garden centre ✖ (ex guide dogs) ◥

MAIDSTONE MUSEUM & ART GALLERY
St Faith's St ME14 1LH (close to County Hall)
☎ 01622 754497   🖷 01622 602193

Set in an Elizabethan manor house which has been much extended over the years, this museum houses an outstanding collection of fine and applied arts, including watercolours, furniture, ceramics, and a collection of Japanese art and artefacts. The museum of the Queen's Own Royal West Kent Regiment is also housed here. Please apply for details of temporary exhibitions, workshops etc.
Times: Open all year, Mon-Sat 10-5.15, Sun 11-4 & BH Mon 11-4. (Closed 25-26 Dec).
Fee: Free.
🅿 (100 yds) 🖵 ₤ shop ✖

MUSEUM OF KENT LIFE
Lock Ln, Sandling ME14 3AU (From A229, follow signs for Aylesford. From M20 J6 onto A229 Maidstone road)
☎ 01622 763936   🖷 01622 662024

Kent's award-winning open air museum is home to an outstanding collection of historic buildings which house exhibitions on life in Kent 100 years ago. The UK's last traditionally working oasthouse, plus barn granary and hoppers' huts,

along with an 18th century farmhouse can all be explored. Please ring for details of special events.

Times: Open Etr-Oct, daily 10-5.30.
🅿 💺 ✖ licensed ♿ (wheelchairs available, ramps) toilets or disabled shop *Details not confirmed for 2000*

TYRWHITT DRAKE MUSEUM OF CARRIAGES

The Archbishop's Stables, Mill St ME15 6YE (close to River Medway & Archbishop's Palace)
☎ 01622 754497   🖷 01622 682451

A wide array of horse-drawn carriages and vehicles is displayed in these late-medieval stables, which are interesting in themselves. The exhibits include state, official and private carriages, and some are on loan from royal collections.

Times: Open all year, Apr-Oct daily 10.30-5.30; Nov-Mar noon-4.30. Last admission 4pm. (Closed 25-26 Dec).
Fee: *£1.50 (ch & pen £1).
🅿 (100 yds) ♿ shop ✖

🏛 MINSTER-IN-THANET

MINSTER ABBEY
CT12 4HF
☎ 01843 821254

One of the first nunneries in England was built on this site in the 7th century. Rebuilt in later centuries, it is still a religious community, run by Benedictine nuns. The ruins of the old abbey and the cloisters are open to the public. One wing dates back to 1027, and there is a 12th century carving of Christ. Garden fete first Saturday in August.

Times: Open all year, May-Sep, Mon-Fri 11-12 & 2-4.30, Sat 11-12; Oct-Apr, Mon-Sat 11-12.
🅿 ♿ shop *Details not confirmed for 2000*

🏛 PENSHURST

PENSHURST PLACE & GARDENS
TN11 8DG (from M25 J5 take A21 Hastings rd to Tonbridge North exit then follow signs)
☎ 01892 870307   🖷 01892 870866

Built between 1340 and 1345, the original house is perfectly preserved. Enlarged by successive

contd.

owners during the 15th, 16th and 17th centuries, the great variety of architectural styles creates a dramatic backdrop for the extensive collections of English, French and Italian furniture, tapestries and paintings. The chestnut-beamed Baron's Hall is the oldest and finest in the country, and the house is set in magnificent formal gardens. The leisure area includes an adventure playground and nature trail. Special events take place, please telephone for details.

Times: Open: House 27 Mar-Oct daily. Gardens, Grounds & venture playground open 11-6 and also wknds from 27 Feb. **Fee:** *House & Grounds £5.70 (ch £3.20 pen, students & UB40 £5.30). Grounds, Toy Museum & Venture playground £4.20 (ch £2.80, pen, students & UB40 £3.70). Party 20+. Garden season ticket £20.
🅿 ✕ licensed ♿ (ramp into Barons Hall, Braille room guides) toilets for disabled shop garden centre ✖ (ex guide dogs) ▆

⛫ RECULVER
RECULVER TOWERS & ROMAN FORT
CT6 6SU (3m E of Herne Bay)
☎ 012273 66444

Regulbium was one of the forts built during the 3rd century AD by the Romans to defend the Saxon Shore. It suffered some damage in the 18th century when erosion of the cliff on which it stands caused part of its walls to collapse. The towers are the remains of a Norman church, built on the site of a 7th-century Anglo-Saxon church.
Times: Open Apr-Sep, daily, 10-6; Oct-Mar, daily, 10-4.
🅿 ♿ ✖ ✇

⛫ RICHBOROUGH
RICHBOROUGH CASTLE
CT13 9JW (one and a half miles N of Sandwich off A257)
☎ 01304 612013

Now landlocked in the Kent countryside, Richborough Castle once stood on the coast, the bridgehead from which the Romans launched their invasion of Britain in AD43. The foundations of the great monumental archway can still be seen, and the remains of the massive wall and defensive ditches vividly convey the power of the ancient Roman empire.
Times: Open Apr-Oct, daily 10-6 (or dusk if earlier); Nov-Mar, 10-4 Wed-Sun. Wknds only Dec-Feb.
🅿 ♿ ✖ (in certain areas) ✇ *Details not confirmed for 2000*

⛫ ROCHESTER
CHARLES DICKENS CENTRE
Eastgate House, High St ME1 1EW
☎ 01634 844176   📄 01634 827980

A fine late Tudor building with an early 20th century extension, which houses a series of themed displays relating to the life and works of Charles Dickens. In the garden is Dicken's Swiss chalet study from Gads Hill Place. Eastgate House appeared as Westgate House in *The Pickwick Papers* and The Nun's House in *Edwin Drood*.
Times: Open all year, daily 10-5.30. (Closed Xmas). Last admission 4.45pm.
🅿 (250 yds) shop ✖ *Details not confirmed for 2000* ▆

GUILDHALL MUSEUM
High St ME1 1PY
☎ 01634 848717   📄 01634 832919

Housed in two adjacent buildings, one dating from 1687 and the other from 1909. The collections are arranged chronologically from prehistory to the Victorian and Edwardian periods. They cover local history and archaeology, fine and decorative art. There is a gallery devoted to the prison hulks of the River Medway.
Times: Open all year, daily 10-5.30. (Closed Xmas).
Fee: *Donations box.
🅿 (250 yds) ♿ shop ✖

ROCHESTER CASTLE
ME1 1SX (by Rochester Bridge, A2, J1 M2, J2 M25)
☎ 01634 402276

This great Norman castle is one of the largest and best-preserved in England, with walls 100 feet high and 12 feet thick. Inside, the splendid great hall with its gallery is a 'must' and a climb to the battlements is rewarded with superb views.
Times: Open all year, Apr-Oct, daily 10-6; Nov-Mar, daily 10-4. Closed 24-27 Dec & 1 Jan.
shop ✇

⛫ ROLVENDEN
C M BOOTH COLLECTION OF HISTORIC VEHICLES
Falstaff Antiques, 63 High St TN17 4LP (on A28)
☎ 01580 241234

Not just vehicles, but various other items of interest connected with transport. There is a unique collection of three-wheel Morgan cars, dating from 1913, and the only known Humber tri-car of 1904, as well as a 1929 Morris van, a 1936 Bampton caravan, motorcycles and bicycles. There is also a toy and model car display.

Times: Open all year, Mon-Sat 10-6. (Closed 25-26 Dec).

Fee: *£1.50 (ch 75p)

P (roadside) unrestricted shop

SEVENOAKS

KNOLE

TN15 0RP (S end of Sevenoaks, E of A225)

☎ 01732 462100 & 450608 (info line)

📄 01732 465528

In the 15th century Thomas Bourchier, Archbishop of Canterbury, transformed Knole from a simple medieval manor house into a palace. A century later Henry VIII extended it to even grander proportions. In the middle of the 16th century Elizabeth I gave it to Thomas Sackville and the Sackvilles kept the house for ten generations. The State rooms are rich in architectural detail with fine portraits and outstanding furniture. Outside, there are 26 acres of gardens.

Times: Open 27 Mar-Oct, Wed-Sat 12-4 (last admission 3.30pm); Sun, BH Mon & Good Fri 11-5 (last admission 4pm), Garden 1st Wed in month, May-Sep 11-4.

Fee: *£5 (ch £2.50). Garden £1 (ch 50p). Deer Park free to pedestrians. Family ticket £12.50. Parking £2.50 per car.

P (charged) 💷 ✕ ৬ toilets for disabled shop 🐕 (ex in grounds) ♨

SISSINGHURST

SISSINGHURST CASTLE GARDEN

TN17 2AB (1m E of village)

☎ 01580 715330   📄 01580 713911

The Tudor mansion of Sissinghurst Castle was bought in a neglected state in 1930 by Sir Harold Nicolson and his wife, the writer Vita Sackville-West. They set about restoring house and gardens and the gardens now rank among the most attractive and popular in England.

Times: Open: Gardens Apr-15 Oct, Tue-Fri 1-6.30; Sat, Sun & Good Fri 10-5.30 (last admission 30mins before close. Closed Mon incl BH Mon). Due to limited capacity timed tickets are in operation so visitors may have to wait for admission, also the garden may be closed when its capacity has been reached. Garden is least crowded in Apr, Sep & Oct.

Fee: *£6

P ✕ licensed ৬ (Admission restricted to 2 wheelchairs at any one time) toilets for disabled shop 🐕 (ex guide dogs) ♨

SITTINGBOURNE

DOLPHIN SAILING BARGE MUSEUM

Crown Quay Ln ME10 3SN (N on A2, signed)

☎ 01795 423215

The museum presents the history of the Thames spritsail sailing barge, many of which were built along the banks of Milton Creek. Tools of the trade, photographs and associated artefacts can be seen at the barge yard along with the sailing barge Cambria. Privately owned barges are repaired - there's a forge, shipwright's shop and sail loft.

Times: Open Etr-Oct, Sun & BHs 11-5. Other times by arrangement.

Fee: *£1.50 (ch, pen & UB40 75p).

P ৬ toilets for disabled shop

SMALLHYTHE

SMALLHYTHE PLACE

TN30 7NG (2m S of Tenterden, on E side of the Rye Road on the B2082)

☎ 01580 762334   📄 01580 762334

Once a Tudor harbour master's house, this half-timbered, 16th-century building was Dame Ellen Terry's last home, and is now a museum of Ellen Terry memorabilia. The barn is now a theatre and is open most days courtesy of the Barn Theatre Company.

Times: Open Apr-Oct, Sat-Wed 1.30-6 or dusk if earlier, also Good Fri. Last admission 30 mins before closing. The Barn Theatre may be closed some days at short notice.

Fee: *£3 (ch £1.50). Family ticket £7.50.

P 🐕 ♨

🏛 TUNBRIDGE WELLS
A Day at the Wells
The Corn Exchange, The Pantiles TN2 5QJ
☎ 01892 546545   📄 01892 513857

The legacy of the Georgians surrounds the visitor to Royal Tunbridge Wells and 'A Day at the Wells' is a journey to discover the essence of life in this most English of Georgian towns. Experience the sights, sounds and smells of a summer's day on the Pantiles in the 1740s.
Times: Open daily, Apr-Oct 10-5, Nov-Mar 10-4. Closed 25 Dec.
Fee: *£4.95 (ch & pen/student £3.95).
🅿 (charged) 🍽 ✕ licensed ♿ (specially designed flat route) toilets for disabled shop 🐕 (ex guide dogs) 🔊

🏛 UPNOR
Upnor Castle
ME2 4XG (on unclass road off A228)
☎ 01634 718742

This attractive turreted castle stands on the banks of the River Medway, with a backdrop of wooded hills. It saw action in the 17th century in the Civil War, and in more recent times was used a s a gunpowder store.
Times: Open Apr-Sep, daily 10-6.
🅿 ♿ 🐕 (in certain areas) ⌗

🏛 WESTERHAM
Quebec House
TN16 1TD (at E end of village on N side of A25 facing junct with B2026 Edenbridge Road.)
☎ 01892 890651   📄 01892 890110

Westerham was the birthplace of General Wolfe, who spent his childhood in this multi-gabled, square brick house, now renamed Quebec House. The house probably dates from the 16th century and was extended and altered in the 17th century. It contains a Wolfe museum and an exhibition on Wolfe and the Quebec campaign.
Times: Open 28 Mar-26 Oct, Tue & Sun only 2-6 (last admission 5.30pm). Parties by written arrangement.
Fee: *£2.50 (ch £1.25).
🅿 (150m) ♿ 🐕 🐾

Squerryes Court Manor House & Gardens
TN16 1SJ (0.5m W of town centre, signed off A25)
☎ 01959 562345 & 563118
📄 01959 565949

This beautiful manor house, built in 1681, has been the home of the Wardes since 1731. It contains a fine collection of pictures, furniture, porcelain and tapestries. The lovely garden was landscaped in the 18th century and has a lake, restored formal garden, and woodland walks.
Times: Open Apr-Sep, Wed, Sat & Sun, also BH Mon. Garden noon-5.30, House 1.30-5.30. (last entry 5pm).
Fee: *House & grounds £4 (ch 14 £2.30 & pen £3.60). Grounds £2.40 (ch 14 £1.40 & pen £2.10)
🅿 🍽 (part of grounds only, very limited) shop 🐕 (ex on lead in grounds)

🏛 WEST MALLING
St Leonard's Tower
(on unclass road W of A228)

The fine early Norman tower, dating from the 11th century, is all that remains of a castle or fortified manor house built by Gundulf, Bishop of Rochester.
Times: Open Apr-Sep, daily, 10-6; Oct-Mar, daily, 10-4.
♿ ⌗

Lancashire

Lancashire was at the centre of the British cotton industry in the 19th century, which lead to the urbanisation of great tracts of the area. The cotton boom came and went, but the industrial profile remains.

These days Preston is the county's administrative headquarters, and is part of the Central Lancashire New Town, along with Fulwood, Bamber Bridge, Leyland and Chorley. The former county town, Lancaster, boasts a castle incorporating Roman building and one of the younger English universities dating from 1964. Other towns, built up to accommodate the mill-workers with back-to-back terraced houses, are Burnley, Blackburn, Rochdale and Accrington.

Lancashire's resorts, Blackpool, Southport and Morecambe Bay, were developed to meet the leisure needs of the cotton mill town workers. Blackpool is the biggest and brashest, celebrated for its tower, miles of promenade, and the colourful 'illuminations'. Amusements are taken very seriously here, day and night, though sadly the beach has suffered some pollution in recent times.

To get out of town, you can head for the Pennines, the 'backbone of England', a series of hills stretching from the Peak District National Park to the Scottish borders. To the north of the county is the Forest of Bowland, which despite its name, is fairly open high country, with magnificent views.

EVENTS & FESTIVALS

March
2nd Lancashire Food Festival, Accrington Town Hall
12th Brass Band Championships, Blackpool

May
tbc May Day Festival, Burnley
19th-21st Lancashire Clog Dancing Festival, Accrington
tbc Rossfest Festival of the Arts, Rossendale

June
tbc Rossfest Festival of the Arts, Rossendale
2nd-4th June (provisional) Great Days of Folk Festival, Clitheroe
10th (provisional) King Cotton Carnival, Burnley

July
2th-29th Royal Lancashire Show, Astley Park, Chorley

August
tbc Colne Street Festival, Colne

September
1st-3rd (provisional) Autumn Gold Garden Festival, Whalley Abbey, Clitheroe

October
tbc Autumn Steam Weekend, East Lancs Railway

Top: Morecambe Pier

BLACKPOOL

Looking at Blackpool today, with its Golden Mile, Pleasure Beach and world-famous illuminations, it's hard to believe that up until the 18th century the town was little more than a cluster of cottages. The mid-19th century saw a boom in the town, and over the years facilities dedicated to holidaymakers grew and grew.

The town is dominated by the 518ft high Blackpool Tower, which was built in 1894. The Blackpool Illuminations are an amazing sight and constitute one of England's most colourful free entertainments. Things have moved on considerably since 1879, when holidaymakers were awed at the switching on of eight electric arc lamps!

🏛 CHARNOCK RICHARD
CAMELOT THEME PARK
PR7 5LP (from M6 J27/28, or M61 J8)
☎ 01257 453044   📄 01257 452320

Based on the legend of King Arthur, this theme park offers jousting tournaments and the Sooty Show, as well as a wide variety of stomach-churning rides, including the Tower of Terror, and an indoor entertainment centre. Please ring for details of special events.
Times: Open Apr-Oct. Telephone for further details.
Fee: *£7.99 (ch over 1 metre £7.99, under 1metre free, pen/disabled £6.50)
🅿 🖭 ✗ ♿ toilets for disabled shop ✖ (ex guide dogs) 🗢

🏛 CHORLEY
ASTLEY HALL MUSEUM & ART GALLERY
Astley Park PR7 1NP (2m W off A581 Southport rd)
☎ 01257 515555   📄 01257 515556

A charming Tudor/Stuart building set in beautiful parkland, this lovely Hall retains a comfortable 'lived-in' atmosphere. There are pictures and pottery to see, as well as fine furniture and rare plasterwork ceilings. Series of special events and temporary exhibitions all year.
Times: Open Apr-Oct, Tue-Sun 12-5. Nov-Mar Sat-Sun 12-4.
Fee: *£2.80 (concessions £1.80). Family ticket £6.50. Party 10+.
🅿 (200 yds) ♿ (video of upper floors, large print/Braille guide) shop ✖ (ex guide dogs) 🗢

🏛 CLITHEROE
CLITHEROE CASTLE MUSEUM
BB7 1BA (in town centre)
☎ 01200 424635   📄 01200 426339

The museum has a good collection of carboniferous fossils, and items of local interest. Displays include local history and the industrial archaeology of the Ribble Valley, while special features include the restored Hacking ferry boat, printer's and clogger's shops. The grounds have magnificent views of the Ribble Valley.
Times: Open from Feb, 11-4.30, mid Apr-Sep 11-5, Oct-20 Dec 11-4.30.
Fee: *£1.45 (ch 25p, pen 65p). Family ticket £3.10
🅿 (500yds) (disabled only parking at establishment) ♿ shop ✖ (ex guide dogs)

🏛 LANCASTER
CITY MUSEUM (ALSO 15 CASTLE HILL)
Market Sq LA1 1HT
☎ 01524 64637 📄 01524 841692

The fine Georgian town hall is the setting for the museum, which explores the history and archaeology of the city from prehistoric and Roman times onwards. Also housed here is the museum of the King's Own Royal Lancaster Regiment. The Cottage Museum, furnished in the style of an artisan's house of around 1820, faces Lancaster Castle.
Times: Open all year, Mon-Sat 10-5, (Closed 25 Dec-1Jan). 15 Castle Hill, Etr-Sep, daily 2-5.
Fee: *City Museum free. 15 Castle Hill 75p (concessions 25p)
P (5 mins walk) & (ramp to entrance/ground floor, stairlifts)) shop ✖ (ex guide dogs)

MARITIME MUSEUM
St George's Quay LA1 1RB (from A6 follow signs to Lancaster town centre)
☎ 01524 64637 📄 01524 841692

Graceful Ionic columns adorn the front of the Custom House, built in 1764. Inside, the histories of the 18th century transatlantic maritime trade of Lancaster, the Lancaster Canal and the fishing industry of Morecambe Bay are well illustrated. An extension to the building houses preserved boats, audio-visual shows and reconstructions.
Times: Open all year, daily, Etr-Oct 11am-5pm; Nov-Etr 12.30-4pm.
Fee: *£2 (concessions £1).
P ■ & toilets for disabled shop ✖ (ex guide dogs)

SHIRE HALL
Lancaster Castle, Castle Pde LA1 1YJ
☎ 01524 64998

Founded on the site of three Roman forts, Lancaster Castle dominates Castle Hill, above the River Lune. The Norman keep was built in about 1170 and King John added a curtain wall and Hadrian's Tower. The Shire Hall, noted for its Gothic revival design, contains a splendid display of heraldry, with the coats of arms of all the sovereigns from Richard I. The Crown Court (still sited here) was notorious as having handed out the greatest number of death sentences of any court in the land.
Times: Open 15 Mar19 Dec, daily 10.30 (1st tour)-4 (last tour). Court sittings permitting -it is advisable to telephone before visiting except in August or at weekends.
Fee: £3.50 (ch, pen & students £2). Part tour when Court in session £2.50 (ch & pen & students £1.50).
P (100m) (voucher system) & shop ✖ (ex guide dogs)

🏛 LEYLAND
BRITISH COMMERCIAL VEHICLE MUSEUM
King St PR5 1LE (0.75m from J28 M6)
☎ 01772 451011 📄 01772 623404

A unique line-up of historic commercial vehicles and buses spanning a century of truck and bus building. There are more than 50 exhibits on permanent display.
Times: Open 2 Apr-Sep, Sun, Tue & BH (Oct Sun only).
Fee: *£4 (ch & pen £2). Family ticket £10 (2 adults + 3 children)
P ■ & (ramps to decked viewing area) toilets for disabled shop ✖ (ex guide dogs)

🏛 MARTIN MERE
WWT MARTIN MERE
L40 0TA (6m from Ormskirk, off A59)
☎ 01704 895181 📄 01704 892343

One of Britain's most important wetland sites, where you can get really close to a variety of ducks, geese and swans from all over the world as well as two flocks of flamingos. Thousands of wildfowl, including pink-footed geese, Bewick's and Whooper swans, winter here. Other features include a children's adventure playground, exhibition gallery, craft area and an educational centre. Facilities for disabled people include free wheelchair loan, purpose built toilets and braille notices around the grounds. There is a packed programme of events and activities throughout the year.
Times: Open all year, daily 9.30-5.30 (4pm in winter). (Closed 25 Dec).
P ■ & (wheelchair loan, Braille trail, heated hide) toilets for disabled shop ✖ *Details not confirmed for 2000* 🐦

LANCASTER CASTLE
Owned by HM The Queen in right of her Duchy of Lancaster

Used as a Court and a Prison – see
- where the Lancashire Witches were tried, convicted and condemned to die
- the Shire Hall, with its display of heraldic shields
- the dungeons, 'Drop Room' and 'Hanging Corner'
- the court from which convicts were transported to Australia
- the Grand Jury Room where Queen Victoria dined

Open daily mid-March to mid-December
Tours every half-hour from 10.30am-4pm (Court sittings permitting)
Check by telephoning (01524) 64998
http://www.lancashire.com/lcc/res/ps/castle/index/html
Email: lynette.morrissey@dpshq.lancscc.gov.uk

Lancashire County Council

🏛 PADIHAM
GAWTHORPE HALL
BB12 8UA (off A671)
☎ 01282 771004　📄 01282 770178

An early 17th-century manor house, built around Britain's most southerly pele tower, restored in 1850. A collection of portraits from the National Portrait Gallery and the Kay Shuttleworth Collections of costume, embroidery and lace are on show. Exhibitions during high season. Ring for details.
Times: Open 27 Mar-7 Nov, Garden: daily 10-6. Hall: Tue-Thu, Sat & Sun 1-5. Also open BH Mon & Good Friday. (Last admission 4.15pm).
Fee: *House: £2.90 (ch £1.30). Family ticket £8. Garden free. Party 15+.
🅿 🖭 ♿ toilets for disabled shop ✙ ❧ ➴

🏛 PRESTON
HARRIS MUSEUM & ART GALLERY
Market Square PR1 2PP (in town centre)
☎ 01772 258248　📄 01772 886764

An impressive Greek Revival building containing extensive collections of fine and decorative art including a gallery of Clothes and Fashion. The Story of Preston covers the town's history and the lively exhibition programmes of contemporary art and social history are accompanied by events and activities all year.
Times: Open all year, Mon-Sat 10-5. (Closed Sun & BHs).
Fee: Free.
🅿 (5 mins walk) (orange badge disabled parking only) 🖭 ♿ (Wheelchair available. Chair lift mezzanine galleries) toilets for disabled shop ✙ (ex guide/assistance dogs)

🏛 RUFFORD
RUFFORD OLD HALL
L40 1SG (off A59, 7m North of Ormskirk)
☎ 01704 821254　📄 01704 821254

There is a story that William Shakespeare performed here for the owner Sir Thomas Hesketh in the magnificent Great Hall. Built in 1530, it was the Hesketh family seat for the next 250 years. The Carolean Wing, altered in 1821, features fine collections of 16th and 17th century oak furniture, arms, armour and tapestries.
Times: Open Apr-Oct, Sat-Wed, Hall 1-5 (Last admission 4.30pm); Garden & shop 12-5.30.
Fee: *£3.80 (ch £1.90). Family ticket £9.50. Garden only £2.
🅿 ✗ ♿ (braille guide, wheelchairs, adapted cutlery etc) shop ✙ (ex in grounds) ❧

🏛 SAMLESBURY
SAMLESBURY HALL
Preston New Rd PR5 0UP (M6 J31, A677 for 3m)
☎ 01254 812010 & 812229
📄 01254 812174

Restored half-timbered manor house, built during the 14th and 15th centuries, and set in 5 acres of beautiful grounds. Sales of antiques and collector's items, craft shows and exhibitions are held all year. Please ring for details.
Times: Open all year ex last wk Dec & 1st 2 wks Jan, Tue-Sun 11-4.30.
Fee: *£2.50 (ch 4-16 £1).
🅿 ✗ licensed ♿ toilets for disabled ✙ ♿

🏛 SILVERDALE
RSPB NATURE RESERVE
Mayers Farm LA5 0SW (nr Silverdale stn)
☎ 01524 701601

A large reed swamp with meres with willow and alder scrub in a valley with woodland on its limestone slopes. The reserve covers 321 acres, and is home to Britain's largest concentration of bitterns, together with bearded tits, reed, sedge and grasshopper warblers, shovelers, pochards, tufted ducks and marsh harriers. Black terns and ospreys pass through in spring and greenshanks and various sandpipers in the autumn. Wintering wildfowl include mallards, teals, wigeons, and shovelers. Otters can sometimes be seen from the hides, as can roe and red deer. Phone for details of special events.
Times: Open daily 9am-9pm (or sunset if earlier). Visitor Centre daily 10-5. (closed Xmas Day).
🅿 🖭 ♿ (chair lift to 1st floor, ramp access to 4 hides) toilets for disabled shop ✙ *Details not confirmed for 2000* ➴

🏛 TURTON BOTTOMS
TURTON TOWER
BL7 0HG (on B6391, off A666 or A676)
☎ 01204 852203　📄 01204 853759

A historic house incorporating a 15th-century tower house and Elizabethan half-timbered buildings, and displaying a major collection of carved wood furniture. During the 19th century, the house became associated with the Gothic revival and later typified the idealism of the Arts and Crafts movement. The gardens are being restored in late-Victorian style.
Times: Open May-Sep, Mon-Thu 10-12 & 1-5. Wknds 1-5; Mar, Apr & Oct Sat-Wed, 1-4; Nov & Feb, Sun 1-4. Other times by prior arrangement.
Fee: *£2 (ch & pen £1). Family ticket £5. Guided tour with supper/lunch , prices vary.
🅿 🖭 ♿ toilets for disabled shop ✙ (ex in grounds)

🏛 WHALLEY
WHALLEY ABBEY
BB7 9SS
☎ 01254 822268　📄 01254 824227

The ruins of a 13th-century Cistercian abbey, set in the delightful gardens of the Blackburn Diocesan Retreat and Conference House, a 17th-century manor house with gardens reaching down to the River Calder. The remains include two gateways, a chapter house and the abbot's lodgings and kitchen. Special events for 2000 include: Flower Festival 11-13 August, Autumn Gold Festival 1-3 Sept, Second Hand & Antiquarian Book Fayre 9 Dec.
Times: Grounds open all year; coffee shop, shop & exhibition area, Jan-Dec daily 11-5 (closed Xmas & New Year).
Fee: *£1.50 (ch 25p, pen £1).
🅿 🖭 ✗ licensed ♿ (chair lifts, ramps) shop ✙ (ex guide dogs)

Leicestershire

Leicestershire is divided between the large country estates of its eastern side and the industrial towns of the East Midlands to its west.

Coal mining was an important part of the county's industrial development in the 19th and early 20th centuries, and this is reflected in its heritage, including a reclaimed mine near Coalville, now divided between a nature reserve and Snibston Discovery Park.

Agricultural areas focus around the pleasant market towns of Market Harborough and Market Bosworth. The latter was the site of the Battle of Bosworth Field, the final engagement of the War of the Roses in 1485, where Richard III, the Yorkist king was defeated and killed by Henry of Richmond, who was crowned Henry VII.

The administrative centre is the city of Leicester, and other major towns are Loughborough, which includes bell-founding among its many industries, and Melton Mowbray, home of Stilton cheese and a particularly English item, the pork pie.

Around Melton Mowbray is serious fox-hunting country for the Belvoir, Cottesmore and Quorn hunts. Northeast of Melton Mowbray is the lovely Vale of Belvoir, beneath which are large deposits of coal.

Charnwood Forest, with fewer trees than one would expect, provides a wild and rugged landscape conveniently situated for escape from the city. It lies to the northwest of Leicester extending to Loughborough and Coalville, and is dissected by the M1.

EVENTS & FESTIVALS

February
11th-20th Comedy Festival, Leicester

May
tbc Historic Transport Pageant, Leicester

June
16th-25th Leicester International Music Festival
tbc Belgrave Mela Carnival

August
tbc Castle Park Week, Leicester
5th Caribbean Carnival, Leicester
12th Abbey Park Festival, Leicester

October/November
tbc Diwali Celebrations

Top: Beacon Hill

ASHBY-DE-LA-ZOUCH
ASHBY-DE-LA-ZOUCH CASTLE
☎ 01530 413343

The most striking feature of these impressive ruins is the splendid 15th-century Hastings Tower, named after Edward, Lord Hastings who also built the chapel. During the Civil War, the castle was slighted by Cromwell, and the remains include the tower, walls, underground passage and large kitchen. A torch is recommended for exploring the passage.

Times: Open Apr-Oct, daily 10-6 (or dusk if earlier); Nov-Mar, Wed-Sun 10-4.

Fee: £2.50 (ch £1.30).

🅿 ♿ ✈ ♨

BELVOIR
BELVOIR CASTLE
NG32 1PD (between A52 & A607)
☎ 01476 870262   📠 01476 870443

Although Belvoir Castle has been the home of the Dukes of Rutland for many centuries, the turrets, battlements, towers and pinnacles of the house are a 19th-century fantasy. Amongst the many treasures to be seen inside are paintings by Van Dyck, Murillo, Holbein and other famous artists. Also here is the museum of the Queens Royal Lancers. The castle's lovely terraced gardens are adorned with sculptures. Please ring for details of forthcoming events.

Times: Open Apr-Sep, Tue-Thu, Sat-Sun & BH Mon 11-5.

🅿 🍽 ✕ licensed ♿ toilets for disabled shop ✈ *Details not confirmed for 2000*

CASTLE DONINGTON
DONINGTON PARK GRAND PRIX COLLECTION
Donington Park DE74 2RP (adjacent to Donington Park Motor Racing Circuit)
☎ 01332 811027   📠 01332 812829

A journey through motor sport history. Five halls of exhibits include the largest collection of McLaren Racing Cars in the world and cars driven by many of the famous drivers of the past. Most of the exhibits are in full working order and regularly appear at motor sport events including the Goodwood Festival of Speed.

Times: Open daily 10-5 (last admission 4pm). Open later on race days. Closed 25-26 Dec & 1 Jan - telephone to confirm additional closing dates over Xmas period.

Fee: *£7 (ch6-16 £2.50 pen £5). Family ticket £14. Party.

🅿 🍽 ✕ licensed ♿ shop ✈ (ex guide dogs) 🍵

KIRBY MUXLOE
KIRBY MUXLOE CASTLE
(off B5380)
☎ 01533 386886

When Lord Hastings drew up designs for his castle in the late 15th century, he first had to obtain 'licence to crenellate', but his moated, fortified manor was never completed, as he was executed only a few years after the work was begun. It stands as a ruin in his memory.

Times: Open Apr-Nov, wknds & BH's 12-5.

Fee: £1.85 (ch 90p).

🅿 ♿ ♨

LEICESTER
BELGRAVE HALL
Church Rd, off Thurcaston Rd, Belgrave LE4 5PE (off Belgrave/Loughborough road, 1 mile from the city centre)
☎ 0116 266 6590   📠 0116 261 3063

A delightful three-storey Queen Anne house dating from 1709 with beautiful period and botanic gardens. Authentic room settings contrast Edwardian elegance with Victorian cosiness and include the kitchen, drawing room, music room and nursery.

Times: Open all year, Apr-Oct, Mon-Sat 10-5, Sun 2-5; Nov-Mar, Mon-Sat 10-4.30, Sun 2-4.30. Closed 24-26 Dec/New Year.

Fee: *Admission free - donations welcome. Small charge for some events.

🅿 ♿ (loan of wheelchair) toilets for disabled shop garden centre ✈

LEICESTERSHIRE MUSEUM & ART GALLERY
53 New Walk LE1 7EA
☎ 0116 255 4100   📠 0116 247 3005

This major regional venue houses local and national collections. There's an internationally famous collection of German Expressionism and other displays include the Rutland Dinosaur and thousands of butterflies. There are lots of 'hands on' exhibits and a changing programme of temporary exhibitions, as well as lunchtime concerts and special events.

Times: Open all year, Apr-Oct, Mon-Sat 10-5, Sun 2-5. Nov-Mar, Mon-Sat 10-4.30, Sun 2-4.30. Closed 24-26 Dec/New Year.

Fee: *Admission free - donations welcome. Small charge for some events.

🅿 ♿ (wheelchair for loan) toilets for disabled shop ✈ (ex guide dog)

LEICESTERSHIRE RECORD OFFICE
Long St, Wigston Magna LE18 2AH
☎ 0116 257 1080   📠 0116 257 1120

Housed in a converted 19th-century school in Wigston, the Record Office holds photographs, electoral registers and archive film, files of local newspapers, history tapes and sound recordings, all of which can be studied. Please telephone for details of special events.

Times: Open all year, Mon, Tue & Thu 9.15-5, Wed 9.15-7.30, Fri 9.15-4.45, Sat 9.15-12.15. (Closed Sun & BH wknds Sat-Tue).

Fee: Free.

🅿 ♿ toilets for disabled ✈ 🚗

LEICESTERSHIRE'S CHEESES

Leicester cheese is one of the mildest of English cheeses with a delightful crumbly texture. Its distinctive orange hue comes from the addition of the colouring anatto. The quality of Leicester cheese has always been protected. The town crier of Leicester was employed to call out dire warnings of fines and punishments for those caught spoiling or adulterating the cheese. Stilton, a fine blue cheese, dates from the 17th century. Its origin is something of a mystery. Some say it was invented by Mrs Paulet, the housekeeper at Quenby Hall, who also supplied her brother-in-law, the landlord of the Bell Inn in Stilton. Others say its creator was Mrs Orton of Little Dalby, nr Melton Mowbray.

UNIVERSITY OF LEICESTER BOTANIC GARDENS

Beaumont Hall, Stoughton Dr South, Oadby LE2 2NA (3m SE A6)
☎ 0116 271 7725

The grounds of four houses, now used as student residences and not open to the public, make up this 16-acre garden. A great variety of plants in different settings provide a delightful place to walk, including rock, water and sunken gardens, trees, borders, heathers and glasshouses.
Times: Open all year, Mon-Fri 9-3.30. (Closed BHs).
Fee: Free.
🅿 ♿ ✈

🏛 LOUGHBOROUGH
GREAT CENTRAL RAILWAY

Great Central Rd LE11 1RW (signposted from A6)
☎ 01509 230726   📠 01509 239791

This private steam railway runs over eight miles from Loughborough Central to Leicester North, with all trains calling at Quorn & Woodhouse and Rothley. The locomotive depot and museum are at Loughborough Central. A buffet car runs on most trains.
Times: Open Sat, Sun & BH Mon & midweek May-Sep.
🅿 ♨ ✕ licensed ♿ (Disabled coach available on most trains, check beforehand) toilets for disabled shop *Details not confirmed for 2000* ➰

🏛 MARKET BOSWORTH
BATTLEFIELD STEAM RAILWAY LINE

CV13 6NW (from A444/A447 take B585 to Market Bosworth and follow signs for Congerstone/Shackerstone.)
☎ 01827 880754

Together with a regular railway service (mainly steam) from Shackerstone to Shenton, there is an extensive railway museum featuring a collection of rolling stock and many other relics from the age of steam. There is a dining train, the Tudor Rose, which offers Sunday lunches on certain dates. Ring for details of special events.
Times: Open all year, Station & Museum, Sat & Sun, 10.30-5.30. Passenger steam train service operates Etr-Oct, Sat, Sun & BH Mon. Diesel trains operate Jun-Sep, Wed & Sat only.
🅿 ♨ ✕ ♿ shop *Details not confirmed for 2000* ➰

BOSWORTH BATTLEFIELD VISITOR CENTRE & COUNTRY PARK

Ambion Hill, Sutton Cheney CV13 0AD (follow brown tourist signs from A447, A444 & A5)
☎ 01455 290429   📠 01455 292841

The Battle of Bosworth Field was fought in 1485 between the armies of Richard III and the future Henry VII. The visitor centre offers a comprehensive interpretation of the battle, with exhibitions, models and a film theatre. Special

contd.

medieval attractions are held in the summer months. Ring for details of special events.

Bosworth Battlefield Visitor Centre & Country Park

Times: Open all year - Country Park & Battle trails all year during daylight hours. Visitor Centre Apr-Oct, Mon-Fri 1-5, (from 11am Jul & Aug), wknds, BH Mon & Good Fri 11-6. Parties all year by arrangement.
Fee: *Visitor Centre £2.80 (ch, pen & UB40 £1.80). Family ticket £7.40. Special charges apply on event days.
🅿 (charged) 🍺 ♿ (wheelchair on request, trail accessible with helper) toilets for disabled shop

⬛ MOIRA
HEART OF THE NATIONAL FOREST VISITOR CENTRE
Bath Ln DE12 6BD (located on B5003)
☎ 01283 213731 & 216633
🖷 01283 229496

The vision of the patrons of this Leicestershire Forest Park was to create a wonderful new wooded parkland to celebrate the new millennium and would be the means of restoring great tracts of derelict land laid waste by the old Leicestershire coalfields. In area it will ultimately span 1000 acres and at present 200 square miles are being forested by the planting of 30 million trees. The Visitor Centre is at the heart of this woodland creation and includes a fascinating exhibition of British trees, woodland trails, craft workshops and an adventure playground.
Times: Open daily, summer 10-6, winter 10-4.30. Closed Jan-Feb except wkends & Xmas/New Year.
Fee: *£2.95 (ch 5-15 £1.95, pen & concessions £2). Ch under 5 yrs free. Family ticket £8.
🅿 🍺 ✕ licensed ♿ toilets for disabled shop garden centre
✈ (ex guide dogs)

⬛ SWINFORD
STANFORD HALL
LE17 6DH (7.5m NE of Rugby)
☎ 01788 860250   🖷 01788 860870

A beautiful William and Mary house, built in 1697 by Sir Roger Cave, ancestor of the present owner. The house contains antique furniture, paintings (including the Stuart Collection) and family costumes. Outdoor pursuits include fishing and a nature trail, and special events include car and motorcycle owners' club rallies, Music & Firework Spectacular in August, and a craft fair in October. Please telephone for further details.
Times: Open Etr Sat-end Sep, Sat, Sun, BH Mon & Tue following 2.30-5.30; noon on BH & Event Days (House 2.30). Last admission 5pm.
Fee: *House & Grounds £4 (ch £2); Grounds only £2.20 (ch £1); Motorcycle Museum £1 (ch 35p). Party 20+.
🅿 🍺 ♿ (museum also accessible) toilets for disabled shop
✈ (ex guide dogs & in park)

⬛ TWYCROSS
TWYCROSS ZOO PARK
CV9 3PX (1.5m NW off A444)
☎ 01827 880250   🖷 01827 880700

Set up during the 1960s, Twycross specialises in primates, and has collections of gibbons, gorillas, orang-utangs and chimpanzees, as well as tiny tamarind, spider monkeys and howler monkeys. There are also various other animals such as lions, tigers, elephants and giraffes, and a pets' corner for younger children. Other attractions include a Penguin Pool with underwater viewing and a Children's Adventure Playground.
Times: Open all year, daily 10-6 (4pm in winter). (Closed 25 Dec).
Fee: *£6 (ch £4, pen £4.50)
🅿 🍺 ♿ toilets for disabled shop ✈ (ex guide dogs)

Lincolnshire

Lincolnshire is an east coast county with an agricultural economy, attractive seaside resorts, some lovely countryside, and quintessentially English market towns.

Much of the fenland around the Wash has been drained of its marshes and reclaimed as highly productive farmland. Further north, the coastline, with its sandy beaches, has been developed to accommodate the holiday industry, with caravans, campsites and the usual seaside paraphernalia. The main resorts are Skegness, Mablethorpe, Cleethorpes and Ingoldmells. Inland, the chalky margin of the Lincolnshire Wolds offers an undulating landscape of hills and valleys, designated as an Area of Outstanding Natural Beauty.

Lincoln, the county town, is dominated from its hilltop position by the magnificent cathedral. Most of interest in the city is in the uphill area, Steep Hill, ascending from the River Witham; the Bailgate spanned by the Newport Arch, and the Minster Yard with its medieval and Georgian architecture.

Boston, on the banks of the River Witham, was England's second biggest seaport in the 13th and 14th centuries, when the wool trade was at its height. The town is distinguished by the Boston Stump, the 272-ft (83m) tower on the church of St Boltoph, which can be seen for miles around.

There are market towns all over the county still holding weekly markets, including Barton-upon-Humber, Boston, Bourne, Brigg, Crowland, Gainsborough, Grantham, Great Grimsby, Holbeach, Horncastle, Long Sutton, Louth, Market Rasen, Scunthorpe, Sleaford, Spalding (the centre of the flower industry), and the elegant Edwardian spa resort of Woodhall Spa.

EVENTS & FESTIVALS

April
29th-1st May South Holland Church Flower Festival
28th-30th Beer Festival, Cleethorpes
28th-1st May Folk Festival, Lincoln
29th-1st May Spalding Flower Festival

May
tbc Grand May Day Carnival, Spilsby
tbc Steam & Vintage Rally, Carrington
29th April-1st Spalding Flower Festival

June
3rd-4th Deeping Agricultural Show & Country Fayre
21st-22nd Lincolnshire Show

July
17th-29th Mystery Plays, Lincoln Cathedral
24th-25th July International Air Show, RAF Waddington

August
31st-3rd September Burghley Horse Trials

September
22nd-26th International Clowns Festival

Top: Surfleet on the River Glen

BELTON
BELTON HOUSE PARK & GARDENS
NG32 2LS (3m NE Grantham on A607)
☎ 01476 566116 ▤ 01476 579071

The ground floor of the house has a succession of state rooms, with the Marble Hall as its centrepiece. Splendid furnishings and decorations throughout the house include tapestries and hangings, family portraits, porcelain and fine furniture. Outside are rolling grounds and gardens. Ring for details of special events.
Times: Open 28 Mar-1 Nov, Wed-Sun & BH Mon (Closed Good Fri). House open 1-5.30 (last admission 5pm). Grounds open 11-5.30.
▣ ✗ licensed ⌖ (braille guide, hearing scheme) toilets for disabled shop ✖ (ex in grounds) ✿ *Details not confirmed for 2000* ◥

CONINGSBY
BATTLE OF BRITAIN MEMORIAL FLIGHT VISITOR CENTRE
LN4 4SY (on A153)
☎ 01526 344041

View the aircraft of the Battle of Britain Memorial Flight, comprising the only flying Lancaster in Europe, four Spitfires, one Hurricane, a Dakota and a Chipmunk. Because of operational commitments, specific aircraft may not be available. Ring to check before planning a visit.
Times: Open all year, Mon-Fri, conducted tours 10-3.30. (Closed BH's & 2 wks Xmas). (phone prior to visiting to check security situation)
▣ ⌖ (electric wheelchairs not allowed in hangars) shop ✖
Details not confirmed for 2000

EPWORTH
OLD RECTORY
1 Rectory St DN9 1HX (on A161, 3m S of M180 J2)
☎ 01427 872268

John and Charles Wesley were brought up in this handsome rectory, built in 1709. Maintained by the World Methodist Council as 'The Home of the Wesleys' rather than as a museum, the house displays items which belonged to John and Charles Wesley and their parents.
Times: Open daily Mar-Oct, Mon-Sat 10-12 & 2-4, Sun 2-4 (only in Mar, Apr & Oct) May-Sept Mon-Sat 10-4.30. Sun 2-4.30. Other times by prior arrangement.
Fee: *£2.50 (ch & student £1, OAP £2) Family £6.
▣ ▆ ✗ ⌖ shop ✖ (ex guide dogs) ◥

GAINSBOROUGH
OLD HALL
Parnell St DN21 2NB
☎ 01427 612669 ▤ 01427 612779

A complete medieval manor house dating back to 1460-80 with a remarkable Great Hall and original kitchen. Richard III, Henry VIII, the Mayflower Pilgrims and John Wesley all visited the Old Hall. Special events include craft fairs

and Living History weekends - please ring for details.
Times: Open all year, Mon-Sat 10-5; Etr-Oct, Sun 2-5.30. Closed 25-26 Dec, 1 Jan & Good Fri.
Fee: *£2.50 (ch £1, 60+ £1.50)
Ⓟ (100 yds) (unrestricted parking 100yds from Hall) ▆ ⌖ (audio tour, induction loop) shop ✖ (ex guide dogs)

GRIMSBY
NATIONAL FISHING HERITAGE CENTRE
Alexandra Dock DN31 1UZ (follow signs off M180)
☎ 01472 323345 ▤ 01472 323555

Sign on as a crew member for a journey of discovery, and experience the harsh reality of life on board a deep sea trawler built inside the Centre. Through interactive games and displays, your challenge is to navigate the icy waters of the Arctic in search of the catch.
Times: Open all year, Sat-Thu, telephone for opening times. (Closed 25-26 Dec & 1 Jan).
Fee: *£4.95 (concessions £3.85). Family ticket £16.50.
▣ ▆ ⌖ (easy access route) toilets for disabled shop ✖ ◥

GRIMSTHORPE
GRIMSTHORPE CASTLE
PE10 0NB (on A151, 8m E of Colsterworth rbt on A1)
☎ 01778 591205 ▤ 01778 591259

Seat of the Willoughby de Eresby family since 1516, the castle has a medieval tower and a Tudor quadrangular house with a Baroque north front by Vanbrugh. There is an important collection of furniture, pictures and tapestries. There are formal gardens, parkland and a lake. Various special events are held, ring for details.
Times: Open 12 Apr-27 Sep, Sun, Thu & BH's. Daily in Aug ex Fri & Sat. Park & Gardens 11-6, Castle 2-6 (last admission 5pm).
▣ ▆ ✗ licensed ⌖ toilets for disabled shop *Details not confirmed for 2000*

LINCOLN
LINCOLN CATHEDRAL
LN2 1PZ
☎ 01522 544544

'The most precious piece of architecture in the British Isles' (John Ruskin).
Times: Open all year, summer 7.15-8 (6pm winter).
Ⓟ ▆ ⌖ toilets for disabled shop *Details not confirmed for 2000*

LINCOLN

Even though it remains one of England's most unspoilt cathedral cities, Lincoln has seen its share of change and upheaval (including a literal one in 1185, when it was hit by an earthquake!). The first settlement began here c. 8000BC, and the Romans, the Vikings, the Normans, the Black Death, the Civil War and the Industrial Revolution have all played important roles in the city's past. This history is still very much in evidence, as a stroll around the city or a visit to the cathedral or castle demonstrate. Lincoln also offers cruises on the River Witham, plenty of green spaces, Hartsholme Country Park, and all the modern amenities you could want from a charming and historic city.

MUSEUM OF LINCOLNSHIRE LIFE

Burton Rd LN1 3LY (5m walk from Lincoln Castle)
☎ 01522 528448   🖷 01522 521264

A large and varied social history museum, where two centuries of Lincolnshire life are illustrated by displays of domestic implements, industrial machinery, agricultural tools and a collection of horse-drawn vehicles. The Royal Lincolnshire Regiment museum is also housed here. A full list of events and temporary exhibitions is available.
Times: Open all year, May-Sep, daily 10-5.30; Oct-Apr, Mon-Sat 10-5.30, Sun 2-5.30.
Fee: *£2 (ch 60p).
P 🍽 ᵶ (wheelchair available, parking space) toilets for disabled shop ✈

USHER GALLERY

Lindum Rd LN2 1NN (in city centre, signed)
☎ 01522 527980   🖷 01522 560165

Built as the result of a bequest by Lincoln jeweller James Ward Usher, the Gallery houses his magnificent collection of watches, porcelain and miniatures, as well as topographical works, watercolours by Peter de Wint, Tennyson memorabilia and coins. The Gallery also has an active exhibitions and 'outreach' programme.

Times: Open all year, Mon-Sat 10-5.30, Sun 2.30-5. (Closed Good Fri, Xmas & 1 Jan).
Fee: *£2 (ch & students 50p).
P (150yds) 🍽 ᵶ (large print exhibition guides) toilets for disabled shop ✈ (ex guide dogs) 💳

🏛 SCUNTHORPE

NORMANBY HALL COUNTRY PARK

Normanby DN15 9HU (5m N off B1430)
☎ 01724 720588   🖷 01724 721248

A whole host of activities and attractions are offered in the 350 acres of grounds that surround this, including golf, riding, nature trails and a farming museum. Inside, Regency mansion rooms are decorated and furnished in period style. Ring for details of special events.

contd.

Times: Open, Park all year, daily 9am-dusk. Walled garden: daily 11-5 (4pm winter). Hall & Farming Museum: Apr-Sep daily 1-5.
Fee: *Apr-Sep £2.50 (concessions £1.50) Family ticket £6.50. Oct-Mar £2 per car.
P (charged) ◼✕ licensed ♿ (audio tour & sensory bed in walled garden) toilets for disabled shop garden centre (ex guide dogs)

SKEGNESS
CHURCH FARM MUSEUM
Church Rd South PE25 2HF (follow brown Museum signs on entering Skegness)
☎ **01754 766658** ▤ **01754 766658**

A farmhouse and outbuildings, restored to show the way of life on a Lincolnshire farm at the end of the 19th century, with farm implements and machinery plus household equipment on display. Temporary exhibitions are held in the barn, and craftsmen give demonstrations on summer weekends. There are also school activity days. Special events are held - please ring for details.
Times: Open Apr-Oct, daily 10.30-5.30
Fee: *£1 (ch 50p).
P ◼ ♿ (wheelchair available) toilets for disabled shop ✕ (ex guide dogs)

SPALDING
SPALDING TROPICAL FOREST
Glenside North PE11 3SD
☎ **01775 710822** ▤ **01775 710882**

Spalding Tropical Forest is the largest of its kind in the British Isles. There are four zones: oriental, temperate, tropical and dry tropics. Cascading waterfalls and lush, colourful tropical plants. There is also a Water Garden Centre and a Plant House where unusual specimens are for sale.
Times: Open daily summer 10-5.30, winter 10-4. Closed 25-26 Dec & New Years day.
Fee: *£2.45 (ch5-16 £1.40, pen £1.99). Family ticket £6 (2 adults 2 ch) then £1 for each extra child.
P ◼ ♿ (disabled parking close to establishment) toilets for disabled shop garden centre ◥

SPRINGFIELDS GARDENS
Camelgate PE12 6ET (1m E on A151, signposted from the Spalding by-pass)
☎ **01775 724843 / 713253**
▤ **01755 711209**

The 25-acre gardens provide an amazing spectacle in the spring when thousands of bulbs are blooming among the lawns and lakes.
Times: Open 19 Mar-9 May, daily 10-6 (last admission 5pm)
Fee: *£3 (accompanied ch free, pen £2.70). Prices vary for special events.
P ◼✕ licensed ♿ (free wheelchair hire) toilets for disabled shop garden centre ✕ (guide dogs)

STAMFORD
BURGHLEY HOUSE TRUST LIMITED
PE9 3JY (1.5m off A1 at Stamford)
☎ **01780 752451** ▤ **01780 480125**

This great Elizabethan palace, built by William Cecil, has all the hallmarks of that ostentatious period. The vast house is three storeys high and the roof is a riot of pinnacles, cupolas and paired chimneys in classic Tudor style. However, the interior was restyled in the 17th century, and the state rooms are now Baroque, with silver fireplaces, elaborate plasterwork and painted ceilings. These were painted by Antonio Verrio, whose Heaven Room is quite awe-inspiring. The Burghley Horse Trials are held here (early Sep), and there are fireworks and laser concerts in the summer (ring 01625 560000 for details).
Times: Open 1 Apr-3 Oct, daily, 11-4.30. (Closed 4 Sep).
Fee: *Please telephone for admission charges.
P ◼✕ licensed ♿ (chairlift access to restaurant and staterooms) toilets for disabled shop ✕ (guide dogs) ◥

STAMFORD SHAKESPEARE COMPANY
Rutland Open Air Theatre, Tolethorpe Hall, Little Casterton PE9 4BH (off A6121, follow heritage signs to Tolethorpe Hall)
☎ **01780 54381** ▤ **01780 481954**

An Elizabethan manor house set in seven acres of grounds. It was acquired by the nationally renowned amateur Shakespeare Company in a near derelict state in 1977 and since restored. A 600 seat open-air theatre with a covered auditorium in the grounds is the venue for the Stamford Shakespeare Company's annual season, attracting more than 30,000 people. Phone or write for details.
Times: Open daily 10-4, May-Sep. Rutland Open Air Theatre performances 1 Jun-29 Aug.
P ◼ ♿ toilets for disabled shop ✕ *Details not confirmed for 2000*

TATTERSHALL
TATTERSHALL CASTLE
LN4 4LR (S of A153)
☎ **01526 342543**

This large fortified house was built in 1440 by Ralph Cromwell, Treasurer of England, and has a keep 100ft high. On each of the four storeys is a fine heraldic chimneypiece: these were sold at one point, but were rescued from export in 1911. There is also a museum in the guardhouse.
Times: Open Apr-1 Nov, Sat-Wed & BH Mons (closed Good Fri) 10.30-5.30. Nov-20 Dec, Sat & Sun only 12-4pm.
P ♿ toilets for disabled shop ✕ ♨ *Details not confirmed for 2000* ◥

WOOLSTHORPE
WOOLSTHORPE MANOR
23 Newton Way NG33 5NR (7m S of Grantham, 1m W of A1)
☎ **01476 860338**

A fine stone-built, 17th-century farmhouse, birthplace of scientist and philosopher Sir Isaac Newton. He also lived at the house from 1665-66 during the Plague. An early edition of his *Principia Mathematica* (1687) is in the house.
Times: Open Apr-1 Nov, Wed-Sun & BH Mon 1-5.30. (closed Good Fri).
P ✕ ♨ *Details not confirmed for 2000*

London

The capital of England and the United Kingdom, London is the largest city in Europe with a population of nearly seven million people.

Londinium was established in 43 AD, at the lowest crossing point of the River Thames. In the second century the city walls were built, but London soon grew beyond them to merge with Westminster and, by the 11th century, was the main city in England and the home of William the Conqueror.

London continued to flourish until the plague of 1665 and the Great Fire of London in 1666. Much of the city was rebuilt at this time under the direction of Sir Christopher Wren. During WWII the Blitz did immense damage to the city, razing whole streets and destroying domestic and public buildings alike. Post-war architecture introduced modern structures of concrete and glass. Ancient sights include the Tower of London, built by William the Conqueror on a Roman site; the 15th-century Guildhall; and the Monument, designed by Wren to commemorate the Great Fire. Most of the public buildings are 18th-century or Victorian.

London's role as a port has declined, with most activity now outside the metropolitan area. The East End docks have been redeveloped to provide housing, offices, factories and the Docklands Railway. London is a major financial centre, and the focus of the national media, including film and publishing.

London has been a cosmopolitan city for centuries, and much of the excitement of the city's life is derived from its cultural diversity. The foods, dress, languages, art and music of every continent can be experienced on its streets.

EVENTS & FESTIVALS

January
7th-16th International Boat Show, Earls Court

February
6th Chinese New Year Celebrations

March
Head of the River Race, Mortlake to Putney

April
18th-29th World Piano Competition, South Bank

May
23rd-26th Chelsea Flower Show
26th-4th June (provisional) Maritime Festival, Docklands

June
18th-25th Flower Festival, Covent Garden

July
Greenwich International Festival

August
26th-27th Notting Hill Carnival, Notting Hill

September
6th-30th Creating Sparks - Science & Arts Festival, South Kensington
12th-16th, Son et Lumiere, Royal Hospital, Chelsea
17th Thames Festival

November
11th Lord Mayor's Show, City of London

Top: Law courts building

🏛 LONDON

EC2
BANK OF ENGLAND MUSEUM
Threadneedle St EC2R 8AH (the museum is housed in the Bank of London, the entrance is in Bartholomew Lane)
☎ 020 7601 5545 📄 020 7601 5808

Housed within the Bank of England itself, at the heart of the City of London, the museum traces the history of the Bank from its foundation by Royal Charter in 1694. There are gold bars from ancient times to the modern market bar, coins and a unique collection of banknotes, as well as the pikes and muskets once used to defend the Bank. Interactive systems allow you to look behind the doors of The Bank or observe the intricacies of banknote design.

Times: Open all year, Mon-Fri 10-5. (Closed wknds & BH's).
Fee: Free.
ℙ (10 mins walk) . ♿ (advance notice helpful) toilets for disabled shop

SW1
BANQUETING HOUSE AT WHITEHALL PALACE
Whitehall SW1A 2ER (Underground - Westminster, Charing Cross or Embankment)
☎ 020 7930 4179 📄 020 7930 8268

Designed by Inigo Jones, this is the only surviving building of the vast Whitehall Palace, destroyed by fire 300 years ago. The Palace has seen many significant royal events, including the execution of Charles I in 1649. The Banqueting House is a welcome retreat, away from the bustle of the city; its Rubens ceiling paintings are stunning examples of the larger works of the Flemish Master and its classical Palladian style set the fashion for much of London's later architecture. Banqueting House will take part in the 'String of Pearls' event for the Millennium.

Times: Open all year, Mon-Sat 10-5. (Closed Good Fri, 24 Dec-1 Jan & BH's). Liable to close at short notice for Government functions.
Fee: *£3.60 (ch 16 £2.30 (under 5 free) students & pen £2.80).
ℙ (no parking in Whitehall) ♿ toilets for disabled shop ✈ (ex guide dogs) 🔊

SE1
BRAMAH TEA & COFFEE MUSEUM
The Clove Building, Butler's Wharf SE1 2NQ (Underground - London Bridge & Tower Hill)
☎ 020 7378 0222 📄 020 7378 0219

The museum tells the fascinating history of the tea and coffee trade, carried on in this area for 350 years. A collection of over 1,000 teapots and coffee makers illustrate the many ways that tea and coffee have been made and served. Other displays include expresso machines from the 1950s, 'tetsubin' tea kettles and a 'Raku' tea master bowl, used in the elaborate Japanese Tea Ceremony.

Times: Open all year, daily 10-6. (Closed 25 & 26 Dec).
ℙ (100yds) 🔌 ♿ toilets for disabled shop ✈ *Details not confirmed for 2000* 🔊

WC1
BRITISH MUSEUM
Great Russell St WC1B 3DG (Underground - Russell Sq,Tottenham Court Rd)
☎ 020 7580 1788 (recorded information) 📄 020 7323 8614

Behind its imposing Neo-Classical facade the British Museum displays the rich and varied treasures which make it one of the great museums of the world. Founded in 1753, displays cover the works of humanity from pre-historic to modern times. The galleries are the responsibility of ten departments, which include Egyptian, Greek and Roman, Japanese, Medieval and later, Prints and Drawings, and Ethnography. Among the treasures to be seen are the Egyptian mummies, the sculptures from the Parthenon, the Anglo-Saxon treasure from the Sutton Hoo ship burial and the Vindolanda Tablets from Hadrian's Wall. There is a regular programme of gallery talks, guided tours and lectures, and young visitors can enjoy special children's trails.

Times: Open all year, Mon-Sat 10-5, Sun 12-6 (Closed Good Fri, Christmas & 1 Jan).
Fee: Free.
ℙ (5 mins walk) 🔌 ✗ licensed ♿ (parking by arrangement; tours for visual/hearing impaired) toilets for disabled shop ✈ (ex guide/companion dogs)

W1
BROADCASTING HOUSE TOUR & EXHIBITION
Broadcasting House W1A 1AA (Underground - Oxford Circus, Great Portland St)
☎ 0870 6030304

A day in the life of Broadcasting House - explore the corporation's heritage through a series of interactive displays which allow visitors to try out a range of broadcasting activities including the chance to 'Present the Weather' 'Direct Eastenders', 'Commentate on a Sports Event' and 'Create a Radio Play'.

Times: Open all year, daily 9.30-5.30 (last tour commences). Closed 25 Dec.
ℙ 🔌 ♿ toilets for disabled shop *Details not confirmed for 2000* 🔊

SW1
BUCKINGHAM PALACE
Buckingham Palace Rd (Underground - Victoria, Green Park)
☎ 020 7839 1377 📄 020 7930 9625

The official London residence of Her Majesty The Queen, whose personal standard flies when Her Majesty is in residence. Each August and September the State Rooms are open to visitors. These principle rooms, which form the backdrop to the pageantry of court ceremonial and official entertaining, occupy the main west front overlooking the garden and are all opulently decorated with the finest pictures and works of art from the Royal Collection.

Times: Open 10 Aug- 30 Sep 9.30-4.30 (provisional dates)
ℙ (200yds) ♿ (except gardens, pre booking essential) toilets for disabled shop ✈ *Details not confirmed for 2000* 🔊

WC2
CABARET MECHANICAL THEATRE
33/34 The Market, Covent Garden WC2E 8RE
(Underground - Covent Garden)
☎ 020 7379 7961 ▯ 020 7497 5445

The exhibition museum offers entertainment for
the whole family with its impressive collection of
Automata. Buy a ticket in the foyer area, get it
stamped by the mechanical stamping man and
enter the magical world of Cabaret, where at the
touch of a button or the insertion of a coin,
machines are set in motion. The collection
includes work by Paul Spooner, Ron Fuller and
Tim Hunkin.
Times: Open all year, Mon-Sat 10-6.30, Sun 11-6.30, school
holiday open until 7pm. (Closed 25 & 26 Dec & 1 Jan).
Fee: *£1.95 (ch, students, pen & UB40's £1.20). Family ticket
£4.95.
shop ✕ ☜

SW1
CABINET WAR ROOMS
Clive Steps, King Charles St SW1A 2AQ
(Underground - Westminster)
☎ 020 7930 6961 ▯ 020 7839 5897

The underground emergency accommodation
used to protect the Prime Minister, Winston
Churchill, his War Cabinet and the Chiefs of Staff
during the Second World War provides a
fascinating insight into those tense days and
nights. Among the 21 rooms are the Cabinet
Room, the Map Room (where information about
operations on all fronts was collected) and the
Prime Minister's room, all carefully preserved
since the end of the war. 'Churchill - The War
Years' is a changing exhibition of documents
devoted to the life and achievements of Winston
Churchill during the War.
Times: Open all year, daily 9.30-6. (10-6 Oct-Mar) last
admission 5.15 (Closed 24-26 Dec).
Fee: *£4.80 (ch under 16 free, students & pen £3.50).
Party 10+.
▣ (10 mins walk) ☖ toilets for disabled shop ✕ ☜

SW3
CARLYLE'S HOUSE
24 Cheyne Row SW3 5HL (Underground - Sloane
Square)
☎ 020 7352 7087

'The Sage of Chelsea' - distinguished essayist and
writer of historical works, Thomas Carlyle - lived
in this 18th-century town house from 1834 until
his death in 1881. His soundproofed study and
the kitchen, where such literary notables as
Tennyson, Thackeray and Browning were
entertained have been preserved exactly as the
Carlyles knew them.
Times: Open Apr-1 Nov, Wed-Sun & BH Mons 11-5. Last
admission 4.30. (Closed Good Fri)
▣ (street metered) ✕ ♿ ✖ *Details not confirmed for
2000*

SW3
CHELSEA PHYSIC GARDEN
66 Royal Hospital Rd, (entrance in Swan Walk)
SW3 4HS (Underground - Sloane Square)
☎ 020 7352 5646 ▯ 020 7376 3910

Begun in 1673 for the study of plants used by the
Society of Apothecaries, the garden is still used
for botanical and medicinal research, and offers
displays of many fascinating plants in lovely
surroundings. There will be an exhibition for the
year 2000 on "Timely Cures" - a photographic
exhibition of pharmaceutical plants with the
launch of a pharmaceutical garden.
Times: Open Apr-Oct, Wed 12-5, Sun 2-6. Additional opening
during Chelsea Flower Show week, 24-28 May & Chelsea
Festival week Jun, 21-25. Groups at other times by
appointment.
Fee: *£4 (ch 5-15, students & unemployed £2).
▣ (0.5m) (west end of Battersea Park) ☖ & (disabled
parking) toilets for disabled shop garden centre ✕ (ex guide
dogs) ☜

W8
COMMONWEALTH INSTITUTE
Kensington High St W8 6NQ (Underground -
High Street Kensington)
☎ 020 7603 4535 ▯ 020 7602 7374

When the Commonwealth Institute reopens it
will launch an Australia Season for the second
half of the year 2000. Please ring for details.
Times: Commonwealth Institute is being redeveloped please
ring 0171 603 4535 for details.
Fee: *not confirmed
▣ (500yds) ☖ & (lift from car park, intercom at Holland
Park gate) toilets for disabled shop ✕ ☜

WC2
COURTAULD GALLERY
Somerset House, Strand WC2R 0RN
(Underground - Temple, Embankment)
☎ 020 7873 2526 ▯ 020 7873 2589

The Galleries contain the superb collection of
paintings begun by Samuel Courtauld in the
1920s and 1930s and presented to the University
of London in memory of his wife. This is the
most important collection of Impressionist and
post-Impressionist works in Britain and includes
paintings by Monet, Renoir, Degas, Cézanne, Van

contd.

Gogh and Gauguin. There are also works by Michelangelo, Rubens, Goya, and other notable Masters, as well as early Italian paintings. British and French 20th-century works given to the University by Roger Fry are also displayed here. Exhibitions are changed regularly.

Times: Open Mon-Sat 10-6, Sun 2-6. The Gallery will be closed to visitors for refurbishment from 31 August 1997 to autumn 1998.

P (NCP Drury Lane) 🅿 ♿ (parking arranged, lift) toilets for disabled shop ✖ *Details not confirmed for 2000*

SE17
CUMING MUSEUM
155-157 Walworth Rd SE17 1RS (Underground - Elephant & Castle, North line exit follow signs for the shopping centre)
☎ 020 7701 1342 ▤ 020 7703 7415

The museum of Southwark's history - the collections of the Cuming family and the local history of Southwark, from Roman times through the days of Chaucer, Shakespeare and Dickens to the present day. Special exhibitions and lectures on local themes, please telephone for details.

Times: Open all year, Tue-Sat 10-5. (Closed BH's & Sat of BH wknd).

Fee: Free.

P (20 yds) (on street pay & display meters) shop ✖ (ex guide dogs)

SE1
DESIGN MUSEUM
Butler's Wharf, 28 Shad Thames SE1 2YD (Underground - London Bridge & Tower Hill)
☎ 020 7403 6933 ▤ 020 7378 6540

The Design Museum is dedicated to the study of 20th-century design. Housed within a converted 1950s warehouse, the Museum's highly acclaimed programme of exhibitions strives to capture the excitement of design evolution, ingenuity and inspiration.

Times: Open all year: Daily 11.30-6 (last entry 5.30) closed 25-26 Dec only.

Fee: *£5.50 (concessions £4) Family £12.

P (3 mins walk) 🅿 ✖ licensed ♿ (ramped entrance, wheelchair & lift, Audio guides.) toilets for disabled shop ✖ (ex guide dogs) 🔊

WC1
DICKENS HOUSE
48 Doughty St WC1N 2LF (Underground - Russell Square)
☎ 020 7405 2127 ▤ 020 7831 5175

Charles Dickens lived in Doughty Street in his twenties and it was here he worked on his first full-length novel, *The Pickwick Papers*, and later *Oliver Twist* and *Nicholas Nickelby*. Pages of the original manuscripts are on display, together with valuable first editions, his marriage licence and many other personal mementoes.

Times: Open all year, Mon-Fri 9.45-5.30, Sat 10-5 (Closed Sun & some public hols).

Fee: *£3.50 (ch under 16 £1.50, pen & students £2.50). Family ticket £7.

P (in street) (metered, 2 hrs max) ♿ shop ✖ 🔊

EC4
DR JOHNSON'S HOUSE
17 Gough Square EC4A 3DE (Underground - Temple, Blackfriars)
☎ 020 7353 3745 ▤ 020 7353 3745

The celebrated literary figure, Dr Samuel Johnson, lived here between 1748 and 1759. He wrote his English Dictionary here, and a facsimile first edition is on display at the house. The dictionary took eight and a half years to complete and contained 40,000 words. Johnson then undertook the formidable task of editing the complete works of Shakespeare. The house is a handsome example of early 18th-century architecture, and exhibits include a fine collection of prints, letters and other Johnson memorabilia.

Times: Open all year, May-Sep, daily 11-5.30; Oct-Apr 11-5. (Closed Sun, BH's, Good Fri & 24 Dec).

Fee: *£3 (ch £1, under 10 free, students & pen £2). Party. shop ✖

SE1
FLORENCE NIGHTINGALE MUSEUM
2 Lambeth Palace Rd SE1 7EW (Underground - Westminster, Waterloo . On the site of St Thomas' Hospital)
☎ 020 7620 0374 ▤ 020 7620 0374

Florence Nightingale needs no introduction, but this museum shows clearly that she was more than 'The Lady with the Lamp'. Beautifully designed, the museum creates a personal setting in which are displayed some of Florence's possessions, a lamp from the Crimean War, and nursing artefacts.

Times: Open all year, Tue-Sun 10-4 (last admission). (Closed Xmas, 1 Jan, Good Fri & Etr Sun).

P (charged) ♿ toilets for disabled shop ✖ *Details not confirmed for 2000* 🔊

WC2
GILBERT COLLECTION
Somerset House, Strand WC2R 0RN
(Underground - Temple, Embankment)
☎ 020 7240 5782   📠 020 7240 8704

The Gilbert Collection of decorative arts is one of
the most important bequests ever made to the
Britsh nation and will be on view in a new
museum in central London from May 2000. The
collection comprises some 800 works of art and
is the gift of Arthur Gilbert who was born in
London in 1913 and moved to California in 1949.
Magnificent European silver, spectacular gold
snuff boxes and remarkable Italian mosaics will
occupy the South Building of Somerset House,
which is undergoing major restoration and
renovation.
Times: Opening May 2000, Mon-Sat 10-6, Sun & BHs noon-
6pm. Last admission 5.15pm.
Fee: £4 (pen £2, under 18, students, unemployed free). Joint
ticket with Courtauld Gallery £7 (pen £5).
💻 ♿ shop ✖

SE1
GOLDEN HINDE EDUCATIONAL MUSEUM
St Mary Overie Dock, Cathedral St SE1 9DE (On
the Thames path between Southwark Cathedral
and the new Globe Theatre)
☎ 020 7403 0123   📠 020 7407 5908

A full size replica of Sir Francis Drake's famous
16th century galleon. Just like the original, this
Golden Hinde has circumnavigated the globe.
You can explore the five decks, and costumed
crew add to the atmosphere. Please telephone for
details of special events, which include Living
History re-enactments. There are holiday
workshops for children and the ship is also
available for private hire.
Times: Open all year, Summer daily 10-6, Winter daily 10-5.
Visitors are advised to check opening times as they may vary
due to closures for functions.
Fee: *£2.30 (ch 5 £1.50, under 5yrs free, concessions £1.90)
P (on street parking) 💻 shop (ex guide dogs) 🍴

EC2
THE GUILDHALL
Gresham St EC2V 5AE (Underground - Bank,
St Paul's)
☎ 020 7606 3030   📠 020 7260 1119

The Court of Common Council (presided over by
the Lord Mayor) administers the City of London
and meets in the Guildhall. Dating from 1411, the
building was badly damaged in the Great Fire
and again in the Blitz. The great hall, traditionally
used for the Lord Mayor's Banquet and other
important civic functions, is impressively
decorated with the banners and shields of the
livery companies, of which there are more than
90. The Clock Museum, which has a collection of
700 exhibits, charts the history of 500 years of
time-keeping.
Times: Open all year, May-Sep, daily 10-5; Oct-Apr, Mon-Sat
10-5. (Closed Xmas, New Year, Good Fri, Etr Mon &
infrequently for Civic occasions).
♿ shop ✖ *Details not confirmed for 2000*

SE1
HMS BELFAST
Morgans Ln, Tooley St SE1 2JH (Underground -
London Bridge/Tower Hill/Monument. Rail -
London Bridge)
☎ 020 7940 6300   📠 020 7403 0719

Europe's last surviving big gun, armoured
warship from World War II, *HMS Belfast* was
launched in 1938 and served in the North
Atlantic and Arctic with the Home Fleet. She led
the Allied naval bombardment of German
positions on D-Day, and was saved for the nation
in 1971. A tour of the ship will take you from the
Captain's Bridge all the way down through nine
decks to the massive Boiler and Engine Rooms,
well below the ship's waterline. You can see
inside the triple six-inch gun turrets; operate the
light anti-aircraft guns; and visit the cramped
Messdecks, Officers' Cabins, Galley, Sick Bay,
Dentist and Laundry. Special events run throughout the year, please telephone 020 7940 6320.
Times: Open all year, daily. Mar-Oct 10-6, last admission 5.15;
Nov-28 Feb 10-5, last admission 4.15. (Closed 24-26 Dec).
Fee: *£4.70 (ch £2.40, students & pen £3.60). Group rates
avalible. Children under 16 free from Apr 99.
P (150yds) 💻 ♿ (wheelchair lift for access on board)
toilets for disabled shop ✖ (ex guide dogs) 🍴

SE1

IMPERIAL WAR MUSEUM

Lambeth Rd SE1 6HZ (Underground - Lambeth
North, Elephant & Castle or Waterloo)
☎ 020 7416 5000   ▤ 020 7416 5374

Founded in 1917, this museum illustrates and
records all aspects of the two World Wars and
other military operations involving Britain and
the Commonwealth since 1914. A thoroughly
modern museum, it employs all the latest
technology to make its exhibitions more vital and
atmospheric for the visitor. There are always
special exhibitions and the programme of events
includes film shows and lectures. The museum
has a wealth of military reference material,
although some reference departments are open
to the public by appointment only. A major
exhibition until the end of May 2000 is "From the
Bomb to the Beatles", telling the story of social
and cultural change, 1945 to 1965.
Times: Open all year, daily 10-6. (Closed 24-26 Dec).
Fee: *£5.20 (ch free, concessions £4.20). Free admission after
4.30 daily.
P (metered) ▆ & (disabled parking sometimes available,
wheelchair access) toilets for disabled shop ✖ (ex guide dogs
▬

See advert on page 137.

NW1

THE JEWISH MUSEUM

Raymond Burton House, 129-131 Albert St,
Camden Town NW1 7NB (Underground -
Camden Town)
☎ 020 7284 1997   ▤ 020 7267 9008

The Jewish Museum opens a window onto the
history and religious life of the Jewish community
in Britain and beyond. The attractive premises in
an elegant Victorian building in Camden Town
include a History Gallery tracing the history of the
Jewish community in Britain from the Norman
Conquest until recent times, and a Ceremonial
Art Gallery illustrates Jewish religious life with an
outstanding collection of rare and beautiful
objects. There are changing exhibitions, and

audio visual programmes are available. Guided
walks of Jewish London can be arranged.
Times: Open Sun-Thu, 10-4. Closed Jewish Festivals & public
holidays.
Fee: *£3 (ch, students & UB40 £1.50) Family ticket £7.50.
P & (induction loop in lecture room linked to audio-visual
unit) toilets for disabled shop ✖ (ex guide dogs)

W8

KENSINGTON PALACE STATE APARTMENTS & ROYAL CEREMONIAL DRESS COLLECTION

Kensington Gardens W8 4PX (Underground -
High Street Kensington or Notting Hill Gate)
☎ 020 7937 9561   ▤ 020 7376 0198

Highlights of a visit to Kensington include the
recently restored Kings Apartments with a fine
collection of Old Masters; Tintoretto and Van
Dyke amongst them. The Royal Ceremonial Dress
Collection includes a selection of HM The
Queen's dresses, representations of tailor's and
dressmaker's workshops, and Queen Mary's
Wedding Dress.
Times: Open 10-4, from Mar-Winter season daily 10-5, Open
Wed-Sun 10-4 during Winter.
Fee: *£8.50 (ch £6.10, concessions £6.70) Family ticket £26.10.
P (500yds) ▆ & (cafeteria has wheelchair access ramp)
toilets for disabled shop ✖ (ex guide dogs) ▬

W14

LEIGHTON HOUSE MUSEUM & ART GALLERY

12 Holland Park Rd W14 8LZ (Underground -
High Street Kensington)
☎ 020 7602 3316   ▤ 020 7371 2467

A opulent and exotic example of High Victorian
taste, Leighton House was built for the President
of the Royal Academy, Frederic Lord Leighton.
The main body of the house was built in 1866 but
the fabulous Arab Hall, an arresting `Arabian
Nights' creation, was not completed until 13
years later. The hall is decorated with gilt,
ancient tiles from the Middle East and a fountain.
Ring for details of a changing exhibition
programme.
Times: Open all year, daily 11-5.30. Garden open Apr-Sep 11-
5. (Closed Sun & BH).
✖ *Details not confirmed for 2000*

W8
Linley Sambourne House
18 Stafford Ter W8 7BH (Underground - High
Street Kensington)
☎ 020 7937 0663 📄 020 7995 4895

The home of Linley Sambourne (1844-1910),
chief political cartoonist at *Punch* magazine, has
had its magnificent artistic interior preserved,
almost unchanged, since the late 19th century.
Also displayed are many of Sambourne's own
drawings and photographs.
Times: Open Mar-Oct, Wed 10-4, Sun 2-5. At other times by
appointment only.
P (metered parking) shop ✖ *Details not confirmed for 2000*

SE1
London Aquarium
County Hall, Riverside Building, Westminster
Bridge Rd SE1 7PB (Underground-Waterloo &
Westminster. On south bank next to
Westminster Bridge)
☎ 020 7967 8000 📄 020 7967 8029

One of Europe's largest displays of global aquatic
life. Explore the waters of the world and witness
breathtakingly beautiful and dramatic
underwater scenes, featuring thousands of living
specimens from rivers, oceans and seas across
our planet. Please ring for details of special
events.
Times: Open all year, daily 10-6. Last admission 1hr before
closing. Closed 25 Dec.
Fee: *£8 (ch 3-14 £5, pen, students & unemployed £6.50, ch
under 3yrs free). Family ticket £22.
P (600m) ♿ (free entry for wheelchair users, wheelchairs
available) toilets for disabled shop ✖

SE1
London Dungeon
28-34 Tooley St SE1 2SZ (Underground - London
Bridge)
☎ 020 7403 7221 📄 020 7378 1529

A modest entrance off a street near London
Bridge station will lead you through a series of
vaults where the seamy side of life in past
centuries is re-created. Viewing takes about 2
hours; this attraction is not recommended for the
faint-hearted. Entry includes the `Jack the Ripper'
show, which presents a 15 minute tour through
Victorian Whitechapel.
Times: Open all year, daily, Apr-Sep 10-5.30; Oct-Mar 10.30-
4.30.
Fee: *£9.50 (ch 14 & pen £6.50, students £7.95).
P (NCP 200yds) 🅿 ♿ toilets for disabled shop ✖ (ex
guide dogs)

NW1
London Planetarium
Marylebone Rd NW1 5LR (Underground - Baker
Street)
☎ 020 7935 6861 📄 020 7465 0923

A visit to the Planetarium consists of two
interactive Space Zone areas plus a half hour star
show under the famous green dome. The
'Planetary Quest' takes visitors on an

intergalactic journey of discovery and is both
educational and entertaining. Star shows every
40 minutes daily from 12:20pm. Shows start
earlier at 10.20am during school holidays, on
Bank Holidays and at weekends. Not
recommended for under 5s.
Times: Open daily (ex 25 Dec), star shows from 12.20, every
40 mins (10.20am wknds & holidays).
P (200 mtrs) ♿ toilets for disabled shop ✖ *Details not
confirmed for 2000*

WC2
London Transport Museum
The Piazza, Covent Garden WC2E 7BB
(Underground - Covent Garden, Leicester Sq)
☎ 020 7379 6344 & 0171 565 7299
📄 020 7565 7250

Covent Garden's original Victorian flower market
is home to this excellent museum which explores
the colourful story of London and its famous
transport system from 1800 to the present day.
There are buses, trams, tube trains, and posters,
as well as touch-screen displays, videos and
working models to bring the story to life. Special
exhibitions, guided tours, film shows, children's
craft workshops and gallery talks mean there's
something for everyone.
Times: Open all year, daily 10-6, Fridays 11-6. Last admission
5.15pm. (Closed 24/26/31 Dec & 1 Jan)
Fee: *£4.95 (concessions £2.95, under 5 free). Family ticket
£12.85. Family season ticket £24.95. Party.)
P (5 mins walk) (parking meters) 🅿 ♿ (lift & ramps) toilets
for disabled shop ✖ (ex guide dogs)

NW1
Madame Tussaud's
Marylebone Rd NW1 5LR (Underground - Baker
Street)
☎ 020 7935 6861 📄 020 7465 0923

Madame Tussaud's world-famous waxwork
collection was founded in Paris in 1770. It moved
to England in 1802 and found a permanent home
in London's Marylebone Road in 1884. Mingle
with the famous and infamous, meeting such
diverse characters as Naomi Campbell, Eric
Cantona, the Queen and Marilyn Monroe all in
one afternoon. The Spirit of London takes you
back in time through 400 years of London's
history.
Times: Open all year 10-5.30 (9.30am wknds, 9am summer).
(Closed 25 Dec).
P (200 mtrs) 🅿 ♿ (except Spirit of London ride) toilets for
disabled shop ✖ *Details not confirmed for 2000*

SW1
Mall Galleries
The Mall SW1Y 5BD (Underground - Charing
Cross)
☎ 020 7930 6844 📄 020 7839 7830

The venue for the annual open exhibitions of
eight national art societies. There is also a wide
range of individual and group shows. During
2000, the Royal Society of Portrait Painters will
exhibit 'People's Portraits', portraits of ordinary

contd.

people, and the Pastel Society celebrate their centenary with a major retrospective.
Times: Open all year, daily 10-5.
Fee: *£2.50 Depending on exhibition (ch & pen £1).
P (50 yds) (no parking at the Mall) & (chairlit to galleries)
✕ ▼

EC4
MIDDLE TEMPLE HALL
The Temple EC4Y 9AT (Underground - Temple, Blackfriars)
☎ 020 7427 4800 ▯ 020 7427 4801

Between Fleet Street and the Thames are the Middle and Inner Temples, separate Inns of Court, so named because of the Knights Templar who occupied the site from about 1160. Middle Temple Hall is a fine example of Tudor architecture and was completed in about 1570. The hall has a double hammerbeam roof and beautiful stained glass. The 29ft-long high table was made from a single oak tree from Windsor Forest. Sir Francis Drake was a visitor to and friend of the Middle Temple, and a table made from timbers from the *Golden Hind* - the ship in which he sailed around the world - is shown.
Times: Open all year, Mon-Fri 10-12 & 3-4 (Closed BH & legal vacations).
& ✕ ⚐ *Details not confirmed for 2000*

EC3
THE MONUMENT
Monument St EC3R 8AH (Underground - Monument)
☎ 020 7626 2717 ▯ 020 7796 2621

Designed by Wren and Hooke and erected in 1671-7, the Monument commemorates the Great Fire of 1666 which is reputed to have started in nearby Pudding Lane. The fire destroyed nearly 90 churches and about 13,000 houses. This fluted Doric column stands 202ft high (Pudding Lane is exactly 202ft from its base) and you can climb the 311 steps to a platform at the summit. The views over the City and beyond are splendid. Be warned - there is no lift or escalator.
Times: Visitors are advised to check the opening dates before making a visit.
✕ *Details not confirmed for 2000*

W1
MUSEUM OF MANKIND
6 Burlington Gardens W1X 2EX (Underground - Piccadilly Circus)
☎ 020 7323 8043 ▯ 020 7323 8013

The ethnographical department of the British Museum was re-housed in 1970 at Burlington Gardens to form the Museum of Mankind. Its vast collections embrace the art and material culture of tribal, village and pre-industrial societies from most areas of the world other than Western Europe. It also houses archaeological collections from the Americas and Africa. The museum's policy is to mount a number of fascinating temporary exhibitions (usually lasting for at least a year) rather than have permanent

displays on show, although there are a number of outstanding exhibits on permanent display. The reserve collection is stored in Shoreditch and can be made available for serious study. Film shows and educational services are provided.
Times: Open all year, Mon-Sat 10-5, Sun 2.30-6. (Closed Good Fri, May Day, Xmas & 1 Jan).
P (NCP 50yds) ▣ & (parking available tel 020 7323 8047) toilets for disabled shop ✕ *Details not confirmed for 2000*

WC2
MUSEUMS OF THE ROYAL COLLEGE OF SURGEONS
35-43 Lincolns Inn Fields WC2A 3PN (Underground - Holborn)
☎ 020 7973 2190 ▯ 020 7405 4438

Two museums are housed here - the Hunterian Museum contains the anatomical and pathological specimens collected by John Hunter FRS (1728-1793), a renowned surgeon and teacher of anatomy, and displays relating to the work of Sir Joseph Lister, pioneer of antiseptic surgery. The Odontological Museum contains an extensive collection of human and animal skulls and teeth as well as dental instruments.
Times: Open Mon-Fri 10-5. Closed wkends, BHs & Xmas/New Year.
Fee: Free.
& (prior notice required) shop ✕ (ex guide dogs)

SW3
NATIONAL ARMY MUSEUM
Royal Hospital Rd, Chelsea SW3 4HT (Underground - Sloane Square)
☎ 020 7730 0717 ▯ 020 7823 6573

The museum offers a unique insight into the lives of Britain's soldiers, with displays including weapons, paintings, equipment, models, medals, and uniforms. An exhibition for 2000 marks the centenary of the Boer War.
Times: Open all year, daily 10-5.30. (Closed Good Fri, May Day, 24-26 Dec & 1 Jan).
Fee: Free.
P ▣ & (wheelchair lift to access lower ground floor) toilets for disabled shop ✕ (ex guide dogs) ▼

WC2
NATIONAL GALLERY
Trafalgar Square WC2N 5DN (Underground - Charing Cross, Leicester Square, Embankment & Piccadilly. Rail: Charing Cross)
☎ 020 7747 2885 ▯ 020 7747 2423

All the great periods of Western European painting from 1260-1900 are represented here, although most of the national collection of British works is housed at the Tate. The gallery's particular treasures include Velazquez's *Toilet of Venus*, Leonardo da Vinci's cartoon (*The Virgin and Child with Saints Anne and John the Baptist*), Rembrandt's *Belshazzar's Feast*, Van Gogh's *Sunflowers*, and Titian's *Bacchus and Ariadne*. The British paintings include Gainsborough's *Mr and*

Mrs Andrews and Constable's *Haywain*. Lectures, guided tours and children's quizzes are available.
Times: Open all year, daily 10-6, (Wed until 9pm). Special major charging exhibitions open normal gallery times (ex Wed until 10pm) Closed Good Fri, 24-26 Dec & 1 Jan.
Fee: *Free. Admission charged for some major exhibitions.
P (100yds) 💷 ✕ licensed ♿ (wheelchairs available, induction loop, lifts) toilets for disabled shop 🐕 (ex guide dogs) ⬛

WC2
NATIONAL PORTRAIT GALLERY
2 St Martin's Place WC2H 0HE (Underground - Charing Cross, Leicester Square)
☎ 020 7306 0055 🖷 020 7306 0058

The aim of the gallery is to illustrate British history through a collection of portraits of famous, and infamous, men and women. The portraits are arranged in chronological order from the top floor, and as well as paintings, there are sculptures, miniatures, engravings, photographs and cartoons among the displays. The new wing opens to the public in spring 2000 and will include new galleries. Exhibitions for 1999/2000 include Faces of the Century (16 Oct 1999-30 Jan 2000) and Snowden: photographs (25 Feb-June 2000).
Times: Open all year 10-6, Sat 10-6 & Sun 12-6. (Closed Good Fri, May Day, 24-26 Dec & 1 Jan).
P (200yds) 💷 ♿ (direct access, stair climber, touch tours) toilets for disabled shop 🐕

SW7
THE NATURAL HISTORY MUSEUM
Cromwell Rd SW7 5BD (Underground - South Kensington)
☎ 020 7938 9123 🖷 020 7938 9066

This vast and elaborate Romanesque-style building, with its terracotta facing showing relief mouldings of animals, birds and fishes, covers an area of four acres. A multitude of fascinating galleries cover every aspect of natural history. A major permanent exhibition on dinosaurs includes new skeletons, recreated robotic models, and displays on how dinosaurs lived, why they became extinct, and how they were dug up and studied by scientists. Recently opened exhibitions From The Beginning, Earth's Treasury and Earth Today and Tomorrow, join

with Visions of Earth, The Power Within and Restless Surface to tell the Earth's dramatic story from the "big bang" to its inevitable end. There is a continuing programme of events workshops, lectures and videos throughout the year, but especially at weekends and school holidays.
Times: Open all year, Mon-Sat 10-5.50, Sun 11-5.50 (Closed 23-26 Dec).
Fee: *£6.50 (ch under 16 free, concessions £3.50).
P (metered 180yds) 💷 ✕ licensed ♿ (ex top floor & one gallery, wheelchairs available) toilets for disabled shop 🐕 (ex guide dogs) ⬛

SW1
THE QUEEN'S GALLERY
Buckingham Palace, Buckingham Palace Rd SW1A 1AA (Underground - Victoria)
☎ 020 7799 2331 (24hr info line) 🖷 020 7930 9625

The Queen's Gallery at Buckingham Palace was first opened to the public in 1962 to display paintings, drawings, furniture and other works of art in the Royal Collection.
Times: Open all year daily 9.30-4.30 (ex for short periods between exhibitions). Telephone 0171-799 2331 for detailed information.
P (200yds) shop 🐕 (ex guide dogs) *Details not confirmed for 2000* ⬛

W1
ROYAL ACADEMY OF ARTS
Burlington House, Piccadilly W1V 0DS (Underground - Piccadilly Circus)
☎ 020 7300 8000 & 0171 439 4996/7 🖷 020 7300 8001

Known principally for its exhibitions, the Royal Academy of Arts was founded in 1768 and is Britain's oldest Fine Arts institution. Two of its founding principles were to provide a free school and to mount 'an annual exhibition open to all artists of distinguished merit', now known as the Summer Exhibition. Both continue today. The Royal Academy's most prized possession, Michelangelo's tondo, *The Virgin and Child with the Infant St John*, one of only four marble sculptures by the artist outside Italy, is on permanent display in the Sackler Wing.
Times: Open all year, daily 10-6. (Closed 25 Dec & Good Fri).
💷 ✕ licensed ♿ toilets for disabled shop 🐕 ⛟ *Details not confirmed for 2000* ⬛

SW1
THE ROYAL MEWS
Buckingham Palace, Buckingham Palace Rd SW1W 0QH (Underground - Victoria)
☎ 020 7799 2331 (info line)
🖷 020 7930 9625

Designed by John Nash and completed in 1825, the Royal Mews houses the State Coaches. These include the Gold State Coach, made in 1762, with panels painted by the Florentine artist Cipriani. It has been used for every coronation since that date. As one of the finest working stables in existence, the Royal Mews provides a unique

contd.

opportunity for you to see a working department of the Royal Household.

Times: Open 1 Jan-23 Mar & 2 Oct-31 Dec Wed only, 24 Mar-2 Aug Tue-Thu only 12-4 (last admission 3.30pm). 3 Aug-1 Oct Mon-Thu 10.30-4.30 (last admission 4pm).

P (200yds) & toilets for disabled shop ✖ (ex guide dogs) *Details not confirmed for 2000* ◄

SW7
SCIENCE MUSEUM
Exhibition Rd, South Kensington SW7 2DD (Underground - South Kensington)
☎ 020 7938 8000

Of all the Exhibition Road museums, the Science Museum is the most attractive to children (and often adults too). Among the displays are many working models with knobs to press, handles to turn and buttons to push to various different effects: exhibits are set in motion, light up, rotate and make noises. The collections cover the application of science to technology and illustrate the development of engineering and industry through the ages; there are galleries dealing with printing, chemistry, nuclear physics, navigation, photography, electricity, communications and medicine. Please telephone for details of special events.

Times: Open all year, daily 10-6. (Closed 24-26 Dec).
💻 & toilets for disabled shop ✖ *Details not confirmed for 2000* ◄

SE1
SHAKESPEARE'S GLOBE EXHIBITION
New Globe Walk, Bankside SE1 9DT (Underground - London Bridge, walk along Bankside. Mansion House, walk across Southwark Bridge)
☎ 020 7902 1500   ▤ 020 7902 1515

Guides help to bring England's theatrical heritage to life at the 'unparallel'd and astonishing' recreation of this famous theatre. Discover what an Elizabethan audience would have been like, find out about the rivalry between the bankside theatres, the bear baiting and the stews, hear about the penny stinkards and find out what a bodger is. A new exhibition for 2000 is dedicated to Shakespeare and his workplace.

Times: Open all year; Sep-May, daily 10-5 (ex 24-25 Dec). May-Sep (theatre season), opening times restricted, phone for details.
Fee: *£6 (ch £4, pen & students £5). Family ticket £16.
P (10 mins walk) 💻 ✖ licensed & toilets for disabled shop ✖ (ex guide dogs) ◄

WC2
SIR JOHN SOANE'S MUSEUM
13 Lincoln's Inn Fields WC2A 3BP (Underground - Holborn)
☎ 020 7405 2107 & 020 7430 0175 (Inf ▤ 020 7831 3957

Sir John Soane was responsible for some of the most splendid architecture in London, and his house, built in 1812, contains his collections of antiquities, sculpture, paintings, drawings and books. Amongst his treasures are the *Rake's*

Progess and *Election* series of paintings by Hogarth.

Times: Open all year, Tue-Sat 10-5. Also first Tue of month 6-9pm. (Closed BH). Lecture tour Sat 2.30 (limited no of tickets sold from 2pm)
Fee: Free.
P (200yds) (metered parking) & (wheelchair available, phone for details of accessibility) shop ✖ (ex guide dogs)

SW1
TATE GALLERY
Millbank SW1P 4RG (Underground - Pimlico)
☎ 020 7887 8000 & rec info
020 7887 8008   ▤ 020 7887 8007

In 1892 Sir Henry Tate, sugar magnate and prominent collector of contemporary British painting and sculpture, offered to finance the building of a new and permanent home for his growing collection of British Art. Officially opened to the public in 1897, a number of extensions to the building have followed, the most recent being the Clore Gallery in 1987 which houses the Turner Bequest. A series of new developments will transform the gallery for the new millenium, with a new gallery for British art at the current site, and modern international art at the converted Bankside Power Station in Southwark.

Times: Open daily 10-5.50. (closed 24-26 Dec.)
Fee: *Free. Charge for major loan exhibitions.
P 💻 ✖ licensed & (wheelchairs on request, parking by prior arrangement) toilets for disabled shop ✖ (ex guide & hearing dogs) ◄

WC2
THEATRE MUSEUM
Russell St, Covent Garden WC2E 7PA (Underground - Covent Garden, Leicester Sq)
☎ 020 7836 7891   ▤ 020 7836 5148

Major developments, events and personalities from the performing arts, including stage models, costumes, prints, drawings, posters, puppets, props and a variety of other theatre memorabilia. There are guided tours, costume workshops, and demonstrations on the art of stage make-up, you can dress up in costumes from National Theatre companies; and watch unique recordings of live performances from London and regional productions. Groups are advised to book in advance.

Times: Open all year, Tue-Sun 10-7. (closed 25 Dec & other public hols)
Fee: *£4.50 (concessions £2.50, ch under 16 free)
P (meters, NCP 250yds) & toilets for disabled shop ✖ ◄

SE1
THE TOWER BRIDGE EXPERIENCE
SE1 2UP (Underground - Tower Hill or London Bridge)
☎ 020 7378 1928   ▤ 020 7357 7935

One of the capital's most famous landmarks, its glass-covered walkways stand 142ft above the Thames, affording panoramic views of the river. Much of the original machinery for working the bridge can be seen in the engine rooms. The exhibition, The Tower Bridge Experience, uses state-of-the-art effects to present the story of the bridge in a dramatic and exciting fashion. Ring for details of special events.

Times: Open all year, Apr-Oct, 10-6.30; Nov-Mar 9.30-6 (last ticket sold 75 mins before closing). (Closed 24-25 Dec, 19 Jan).
Fee: *£6.15 (ch 5+, Pen, Student £4.15) Family ticket £15.50. Party 10+.
P (100yds) & (lifts to all levels, ramp for clear view from walkways) toilets for disabled shop ✕ 🍽

EC3
TOWER OF LONDON
Tower Hill EC3N 4AB (Underground - Tower Hill)
☎ 020 7709 0765

Perhaps the most famous castle in the world, the Tower of London has played a central part in British history. The White Tower, built by William the Conqueror as a show of strength to the people of London, remains one of the most outstanding examples of Norman military architecture in Europe. For hundreds of years the Tower was used, among other things, as the State Prison. It was here that Henry VIII had two of his wives executed, here that Lady Jane Grey died and here that Sir Walter Raleigh was imprisoned. The Yeoman Warders, or 'Beefeaters' play an important role in the protection of the Tower - home of the Crown Jewels - and are informative and entertaining. Look out for the ravens, whose continued residence is said to

ensure that the Kingdom does not fail. The Crowns and Diamonds exhibition features a number of crowns never displayed to the public before and more than 12,000 rough and polished diamonds.

Times: Open all year, Mar-Oct, Mon-Sat 9-6, Sun 10-6 (last admission 5pm); Nov-Feb, Tue-Sat 9-5, Sun 10-5 (last admssion 4pm). (Closed 24-26 Dec & 1 Jan).
Fee: *£10.90 (ch £6.90, concessions £7.90).Family ticket £31.
P (100yds) (NCP Lower Thames St) 🅿& (access guide can be obtained in advance call 0171 488 5694) toilets for disabled shop (x4) ✕ 🍽

SW7
VICTORIA & ALBERT MUSEUM
Cromwell Rd SW7 2RL (Underground - South Kensington)
☎ 020 7938 8500 🖹 020 7938 8341

The world's finest museum of the decorative arts, with collections spanning 2000 years, and comprising sculpture, furniture, fashion and textiles, paintings, silver, glass, ceramics, jewellery, books, prints, and photographs from Britain and all over the world. Highlights include the national collection of watercolours; the Dress Court showing fashion from 1500 to the present day; a superb Asian collection; the Jewellery Gallery including the Russian Crown Jewels; and the 20th Century Gallery, devoted to comtemporary art and design. Special exhibitions for 2000 are: A Grand Design - the art of the Victoria and Albert (14 Oct 1999-16 Jan 2000); Designing in the Digital Age (23 June 1999-3 Jan 2000); Art Nouveau (6 Apr-30 Jul 2000) and Brand New (19 Oct-14 Jan 2001).

Times: Open all year, Mon-Sun 10-5.50. (Closed 24-26 Dec). Tel for BH openings. British Galleries closed for redevelopment. Wed late view (seasonal) 6.30-9.30.
Fee: *£5 (senior citizens £3) ES40, disabled with carer, students & under 18 free.
P (500yds) ✕ licensed & (braille guide, tour tape. for further info, please phone) toilets for disabled shop ✕ 🍽

SE1
Vinopolis, City of Wine
1 Bank End SE1 9BU (Underground - London Bridge)
☎ 020 7645 3700 🖷 020 7403 7093

Spread over two acres of Bankside between the Globe Theatre and London Bridge, the vast arched vaults of Vinopolis house the Wine Odyssey, which takes the visitor on a multimedia tour of the world's wine cultures, grand tasting halls, and an art gallery housing one of the world's largest private contemporary collections.
Times: Open all year, daily 10-5.30. Closed 25 Dec.
Fee: *£10 including entry, personal audioguide, five wine tastings plus entry into art gallery.
P licensed toilets for disabled shop (ex guide dogs)

W1
Wallace Collection
Hertford House, Manchester Square W1M 6BN (Underground - Bond Street, Baker Street)
☎ 020 7935 0687 🖷 020 7224 2155

An elegant 18th-century town house is an appropriate gallery for this outstanding collection of art. Founded by the 1st Marquis of Hertford, it was bequeathed to the nation in 1897 and came on public display three years later. As well as an unrivalled representation of 18th-century French art with paintings by Boucher, Watteau and Fragonard, Hertford House is the home of Frans Hals' *Laughing Cavalier* and of paintings by Gainsborough, Rubens, Delacroix and Titian. It also houses the largest collection of arms and armour outside the Tower of London.
Times: Open all year, Mon-Sat 10-5, Sun 2-5. Apr-Sep, Sun 11-5 (Closed Good Fri, May Day, 24-26 Dec & 1 Jan).
P (NCP & meters) (ramp wheelchair available upon request) shop *Details not confirmed for 2000*

W1
Wellington Museum
Apsley House, 149 Piccadilly, (Hyde Park Corner) WIV 9FA (Underground - Hyde Park Corner)
☎ 020 7499 5676 🖷 020 7493 6576

Number One, London, is the popular name for one of the Capital's finest private residences, 19th-century home of the first Duke of Wellington. Built in the 1770's, its rich interiors have been returned to their former glory, and house the Duke's magnificent collection of paintings, silver, porcelain, sculpture and furniture.
Times: Open Tue-Sun 11-5. (Closed Mon ex BH Mon, Good Fri, May Day BH, 24-26 Dec & 1 Jan). Last admission 4.30pm.
Fee: *£4.50 (ch under 18 free, pen, disabled, UB40 £3). Includes the use of a soundguide.
P (NCP 10mins walk) (lift all parts accessible with help) shop (ex guide dogs)

EC1
Wesley's Chapel, House & Museum of Methodism
49 City Rd EC1Y 1AU (Underground - Old Street)
☎ 020 7253 2262 🖷 020 7608 3825

Wesley's Chapel has been the Mother Church of World Methodism since its construction in 1778. The crypt houses a museum which traces the development of Methodism from the 18th century to the present day. Wesley's house - built by him in 1779 - was his home when not touring and preaching. Special events are held on May 24 (the anniversary of Wesley's conversion), and November 1st (the anniversary of the Chapel's opening).
Times: Open all year, Mon-Sat & BH 10-4 (Closed 25 & 26 Dec). Main service 11am Sun followed by an opportunity to tour the museum and house.
Fee: *House & museum £4 (ch, students, UB40's & pen £2) Party 20+ 10% discount.
P (lift to the crypt of the chapel) toilets for disabled shop (ex guide dogs)

SW1
Westminster Abbey
SW1P 3PA
☎ 020 7222 5152 🖷 020 7233 2072

At the heart of English history for nearly a thousand years, the Abbey has been the setting for every coronation since 1066. The Abbey is a 'Royal Peculiar' and unlike other churches is under the jurisdiction of a Dean and Chapter subject only to the Sovereign. The beautiful Gothic nave is the tallest in Britain and the Chapter House is one of the largest in England. The Norman Undercroft houses a museum with Coronation regalia and Royal effigies. Many famous people are buried here, including the

Kings and Queens of England, and in Poets' Corner are memorials to poets from Chaucer to the present time.

Times: Open all year. Abbey: Mon-Fri 9.30-4.45, Sat 9-2.45. Last admission 60 mins before closing. Cloister daily 8-6. No tourist visiting on Sundays, however visitors are welcome at services. The Abbey may at short notice be closed for special services & other events.

Fee: *Royal Chapels £5 (ch 16 £2, pen & students £3). Family ticket £10.

🍺 ♿ (areas accessible induction loop) shop ✖

SW1
WESTMINSTER CATHEDRAL
Victoria St SW1P 1QW (300 yards from Victoria Station)
☎ 020 7798 9055 🖹 020 7798 9090

Westminster Cathedral is a fascinating example of Victorian architecture. Designed in the Early Christian Byzantine style by John Francis Bentley, its strongly oriental appearance makes it very distinctive. The foundation stone was laid in 1895 but the interior was never completed. The interior is stunning, with fine marble work and mosaics. The Campanile Bell Tower is 273ft high and has a four-sided viewing gallery with magnificent views over London. The lift is open daily 9am-5pm Mar-Nov but shut Mon-Wed from Dec-Feb.

Times: Open all year, daily 7-7.
Fee: Free.

Ⓟ (0.25m) (2hr metered parking) 🍺 ♿ (all parts accessible except side chapels) shop ✖

SW1
WESTMINSTER HALL
Westminster SW1A 0AA (Underground - Westminster Hall)
☎ 020 7219 4272

The great Westminster Hall, where Charles I was tried in 1649, has survived virtually intact since it was remodelled at the end of the 14th century. It escaped the fire in 1834 which destroyed much of the medieval Palace of Westminster, and the magnificent hammerbeam roof is the earliest surviving example of its kind.

Times: Westminster Hall can only be viewed by those on a tour of the Houses of Parliament, which must be arranged by an MP or Peer.
Fee: *Free although guides require payment if employed.
♿ toilets for disabled shop ✖

SE1
WINSTON CHURCHILL'S BRITAIN AT WAR EXPERIENCE
64/66 Tooley St SE1 2TF
☎ 020 7403 3171 🖹 020 7403 5104

How did it feel to be a British citizen during World War II? Journey back in time and take the lift to the London Underground and shelter from the air raids. Crouch in an Anderson Shelter and hear enemy aircraft overhead. The special effects recreate the sights, sounds and smells of the London Blitz. Special activities for children in all school holidays, phone for details.

Times: Open all year, Apr-Sep 10-5.30pm; Oct-Mar 10-4.30. (Closed 24-26 Dec)
Fee: *£5.95 (ch 16 £2.95, student, pen & UB40 £3.95). Family ticket £14.
Ⓟ (100mtrs) ♿ shop ✖ (ex guide dogs) 🍴

AA Hotel Booking Service

The AA Hotel Booking Service - Now you have a free, simple way to reserve a place to stay for a week, weekend, or a one-night stopover.

Do you want to book somewhere in the Lake District that has leisure facilities; a city-centre hotel in Glasgow with parking facilities, or do you need accommodation near Dover which is handy for the Eurotunnel?

The AA Booking Service can take the hassle out of booking the right place for you.

And if you are touring round the UK or Ireland, simply give the AA Hotel Booking Service your list of overnight stops, and from one phone call all your accommodation can be booked for you.

Telephone 0870 5050505

Office hours
Monday-Friday 9am-6pm
Saturday 9am-1pm
Not available Sundays or Bank Holidays

Full listings of AA recognised accommodation available through the Hotel Booking Service can be found and booked at the AA's Internet Site:

http://www.theaa.co.uk/hotels

⛰ BEXLEY
HALL PLACE
Bourne Rd DA5 1PQ (near jct of A2 & A233)
☎ 01322 526574 📠 01322 522921

Hall Place is an attractive Grade I listed mansion of chequered flint and brick, with wonderful gardens. There is topiary in the form of the `Queen's Beasts'; rose, rock, peat and water gardens; and a herb garden with a fascinating range of plants (labelled in braille) for medicine and cooking. There is also a conservatory, a local studies centre and museum. Please telephone for details of the programme of temporary exhibitions, lectures and concerts in the museum and Great Hall.
Times: Open all year, House: Mon-Sat 10-5, Sun & BHs 2-6 (summer); Mon-Sat 10-4.15 (winter). Gardens: Mon-Fri 7.30-dusk, Sat & Sun 9-dusk.
Fee: Free.
🅿 💺 ✕ licensed ♿ toilets for disabled shop ✖ (ex guide/hearing dogs)

⛰ BLACKHEATH (SE3)
RANGERS HOUSE
Chesterfield Walk
☎ 020 8853 0035

This beautiful villa, built around 1700 on the edge of Greenwich Park, houses two important collections: one of Jacobean and Stuart portraits, the second of musical instruments. The house has a busy programme of chamber concerts, poetry readings, holiday projects and workshops.
Times: Apr-Sep 10-6; Oct 10-5; Nov-Mar, Wed-Sun 10-4. Closed 24-26 Dec & 1 Jan.
Fee: £2.50 (ch £1.30).
🅿 ♿ (ground floor only) toilets for disabled ⌗

⛰ BRENTFORD
KEW BRIDGE STEAM MUSEUM
Green Dragon Ln TW8 0EN (Underground - Kew Gardens, district line then 391 bus. Museum 100yds from the N side of Kew Bridge)
☎ 020 8568 4757 📠 020 8569 9978

This Victorian pumping station has steam engines and six beam engines, of which five are working and one is the largest in the world. A forge, diesel house, waterwheel and old workshops can also be seen along with London's only steam narrow-gauge railway which operates on the second and last weekend of each month (Mar-Nov). The Water for Life Gallery tells the story of London's water supply from Pre-Roman times. Please ring for details of special events.
Times: Open all year, daily 11-5. In steam wknds & BHs. (Closed Good Fri & Xmas wk).
Fee: *Weekdays: £2.80 (ch 5-15 £1, OAP/students £1.50) Family ticket £7. Weekends: £3.80 (ch £2, OAP/students £2.50) Family ticket £10.50.
🅿 💺 ♿ (tours for partially sighted by arrangement) shop ✖

⛰ CHISLEHURST
CHISLEHURST CAVES
Old Hill BR7 5NB (off A222)
☎ 020 8467 3264

Miles of mysterious caverns and passages hewn out of the chalk over some 4,000 years can be explored with experienced guides to tell the history and legends of the caves.
Times: Open all year, daily during school hols (incl half terms). All other times Wed-Sun, 10-4. Closed 24-25 Dec.
Fee: *£3 (ch & pen £1.50); longer tours: Sun & BH's only £5 (ch & pen £2.50).
🅿 💺 ♿ (ramps) toilets for disabled shop ✖ guide dogs

⛰ CHISWICK (W4)
CHISWICK HOUSE
Burlington Ln, Chiswick W4 2RP (Underground - Gunnersbury)
☎ 020 8995 0508

Built by Lord Burlington in the 1720s, Chiswick House is inspired by the architecture of ancient Rome. The interior has a fine collection of art and the Italianate gardens delight visitors with their statues, temples, urns and obelisks.
Times: Open all year, Apr-Oct, daily 10-6 (or dusk if earlier); Nov-Mar, Wed-Sun 10-4. Closed 24-26 Dec & 4-17 Jan 1999
Fee: £3 (ch £1.50).
🅿 ♿ shop ✖ (in certain areas) ⌗

COLINDALE (NW9)
ROYAL AIR FORCE MUSEUM
Grahame Park Way, Hendon NW9 5LL
(Underground - Colindale)
☎ 020 8205 2266 & 020 8200 1763
🖥 020 8205 8044

Seventy full-size original aeroplanes and other
exhibits, all under cover, tell the story of flight
through the ages. Extensive galleries show the
political and historical impact of flight - including
the `Battle of Britain Experience', the story of
history's most famous air battle. There's a
Tornado flight simulator, guided tours, and the
new `touch and try' Jet Provost - climb in the
cockpit and try out the controls for yourself.
Times: Open daily 10-6. (Closed 24-26 & 31 Dec-1 Jan).
Fee: *£6.50 (pen £4.90, ch & concessions £3.25). Family ticket
£16.60. (2+2) Party 10+.
🅿 💻 ✕ licensed & (lifts, ramps & wheelchairs available)
toilets for disabled shop ✖ ➥

CRAYFORD
WORLD OF SILK
Bourne Rd DA1 4BP (on A223, signposted from
A2 Black Price Interchange. 10mins from J2 on
the M25)
☎ 01322 559401 🖥 01322 556420

Established in 1843 on the banks of the River
Cray, David Evans are the last of the old London
silk printers. Pre-book a guided tour of the
printshop and museum and learn about the
traditional methods of printing silk, as well as
seeing today's craftsmen at work. Please ring for
details of special events.
Times: Open all year, Mon-Sat 9.30-5 (4pm Sat). (Closed Sun
& BH).
Fee: *Museum only: £2 (pen & student £1.50). Guided Tour
of Craft Centre & Mill by appointment £3 (pen & student
£2.50). Family ticket £10.
🅿 💻 & toilets for disabled shop ✖ (ex guide dogs) ➥

DOWNE
DARWIN MUSEUM, DOWN HOUSE
Luxted Rd BR6 7JT (Off A233, signposted)
☎ 01689 859119

The home of Charles Darwin for forty years. The
drawing room and Old Study are furnished as
they were when he was working on his famous
book *On the Origin of Species by means of Natural
Selection*. The Museum includes memorabilia
from his voyage on HMS *Beagle*. The garden is
also maintained, including the famous Sand Walk
or thinking path, along which he took his daily
walk.
Times: Open all year, Wed-Sun 1-6 (last admission 5.30).
Also BH Mon. (Closed 14 Dec-1 Jan & Feb).
🅿 & shop ✖ *Details not confirmed for 2000*

DULWICH (SE21)
DULWICH PICTURE GALLERY
College Rd SE21 7AD (N of South Circular A205
follow signs to Dulwich village)
☎ 020 8693 5254 🖥 020 8693 0923

Closed for refurbishment until May 2000, this is
the oldest public picture gallery in England,
housing a magnificent collection of Old Masters,
including works by Poussin, Claude, Rubens,
Murillo, Van Dyck, Rembrandt, Watteau and
Gainsborough. Temporary exhibitions are held
throughout the year.
Times: Dulwich Picture Gallery is closed for refurbishment
until May 2000. Open all year, Tue-Fri 10-5, Sat 11-5, Sun 2-5.
(Closed Mon). Guided tours Sat & Sun 3pm.
Fee: *£3 (pen, students £1.50, UB40, disabled & ch free)
🅿 & (wheelchair available) shop ✖ ➥

ELTHAM (SE9)
ELTHAM PALACE HOUSE & GARDENS
☎ 020 8859 2112

Eltham Palace is noted for its great hall with a
15th-century hammerbeam roof and one of its
most charming features is the old bridge,
spanning the moat.
Times: Apr-Sep, Wed-Fri, Sun & BH, 10-6; Oct 10-5; Nov-Mar
10-4. Closed 24-26 Dec & 1 Jan.
Fee: £5.50 (ch £2.75).
⌗

ENFIELD
FORTY HALL MUSEUM
Forty Hill EN2 9HA (M25 J25 onto A10, turn right
into Bullsmoor Lane)
☎ 020 8363 8196 & 020 8363 4046
🖥 020 8367 9098

Built in 1629 for Sir Nicholas Raynton, Lord
Mayor of London, and altered in the 18th century.
The house has fine plaster ceilings and
collections of furniture, paintings, ceramics and
glass, as well as local history displays and
temporary exhibitions.
Times: Open all year, Thu-Sun 11-5 & BH's.
Fee: Free.
🅿 💻 & (Disabled parking in main car park & 3 near house)
toilets for disabled shop ✖ (ex guide dogs)

ESHER
CLAREMONT LANDSCAPE GARDEN
Portsmouth Rd KT10 9JG (E of A307)
☎ 01372 467806 & 469421
🖥 01372 464394

Laid out by Vanbrugh and Bridgeman before
1720, extended and naturalised by Kent, this is
the earliest surviving example of an English
landscape garden. Its 50 acres include a lake
with an island pavilion, a grotto and a turf

amphitheatre. Telephone 01372 451596 for details of events.

Times: Open all year, Jan-Mar, Tue-Sun 10-5 or sunset if earlier, Apr-Oct Mon-Fri 10-6, Sat-Sun & BH Mon 10-7 (closed all day 14 Jul-18 Jul, closes 2pm); Nov-Mar Tue-Sun 10-5 or sunset if earlier. Closed 25 Dec and 1 Jan. Last admission 30 mins before closing.

Fee: *£3 (ch £1.50). Family ticket £7.50.

P **💷** **⑂** (wheelchairs available, Braille guide) toilets for disabled shop **✳** (ex on leads, Nov-Mar only) **🐾** **🔊**

⛰ FOREST HILL (SE23)
HORNIMAN MUSEUM & GARDEN
London Rd, Forest Hill SE23 3PQ (on the A205)
☎ 020 8699 2339 (rec info)
020 8699 1872 🖥 020 8291 5506

Founder Frederick Horniman, a tea merchant, gave the museum to the people of London in 1901. The collection has grown considerably since then, and the galleries cover Natural History - including World Culture displays; African Worlds - a new exhibition which celebrates the diversity of African culture; and The Music Room, containing more than 1,500 instruments from around the world. There are 16 acres of gardens, and the museum hosts a variety of workshops and activities for adults and children.

Times: Open all year, Mon-Sat 10.30-5.30, Sun 2-5.30 (Closed 24-26 Dec). Gardens close at sunset.

Fee: Free.

P (opposite museum) **💷** **⑂** (chair lift to parts of upper floor) toilets for disabled shop **✳** (ex guide dogs or in gardens)

⛰ GREENWICH (SE10)
CUTTY SARK CLIPPER SHIP
King William Walk, Greenwich SE10 9HT (situated in dry dock beside Greenwich Pier)
☎ 020 8858 3445 & 020 8858 2698
🖥 020 8853 3589

The fastest tea clipper ever, built in 1869, she once sailed 363 miles in a single day. Preserved in dry dock since 1957, her graceful lines dominate the riverside at Greenwich. Exhibitions and a video presentation the story of the ship, and restoration work can be seen.

Times: Open all year, daily 10-5 (Closed 24-26 Dec). Last ticket 30 mins before closing.

Fee: *£3.50 (concessions £2.50). Family ticket £8.50. Party 10+ 20% reduction.

P (100 yds metered) **⑂** shop **✳** **🔊**

MILLENNIUM DOME
Drawdock Rd, Greenwich SE10 0BB
☎ 0171 808 8200 🖥 0171 808 8240

Discover more about who we are, what we do and where we live by visiting themed zones, each covering a fascinating and diverse view of human experience. A Millennium Show three times daily offers a live carnival from ground to roof level. The attraction will close on 31 Dec 2000.

Times: Open all year 10-6.

Fee: £20 (ch 5-15 & student £16.50, pen £18). Ch under 5 free. Family ticket £57. Party 15+.

P (car parking linked to public transport) **💷** **✗** **⑂** toilets for disabled shop **✳** (ex guide dogs) **🔊**

NATIONAL MARITIME MUSEUM
Romney Rd SE10 9NF (central Greenwich)
☎ 020 8858 4422 & 8312 6565 info line
🖥 020 8312 6632

Britain's seafaring history displayed in an impressive modern museum. Themes include exploration and discovery, Nelson, 20th-century seapower, trade and empire, passenger shipping and luxury liners, maritime London, costume, art and the sea, the future of the sea and the global garden. There are interactive displays for children.

Times: Open all year, daily 10-5. (Closed 24-26 Dec & 1 Jan)

Fee: *Ticket to National Maritime Museum £7.50 (ch 5-16 free, students & pen £6).

P (50 yds) (parking in Greenwich limited in 2000) **✗** licensed **⑂** (wheelchairs, advisory service for hearing/sight impaired) toilets for disabled shop **✳** **🔊**

OLD ROYAL OBSERVATORY
Greenwich Park, Greenwich SE10 9NF (off A2)
☎ 020 8858 4422 & 8312 6565
recording 🖥 020 8312 6632

Charles II founded the Royal Observatory in 1675 'for perfecting navigation and astronomy'. It stands at zero meridian longitude and is the original home of Greenwich Mean Time. It houses an extensive collection of historic timekeeping, astronomical and navigational instruments. Planetarium shows throughout the year. Events are planned for the school holidays.

Times: Open all year, daily 10-5 (Closed 24-26 Dec & 1 Jan)

Fee: *Royal Observatory £5 (ch 5-16 free, students & pen £4).

P **⑂** toilets for disabled shop **✳** **🔊**

THE QUEENS HOUSE
Romney Rd SE10 9NF (central Greenwich)
☎ 020 8858 4422 & 8312 6565 info line
🖥 020 8312 6632

The first Palladian-style villa in England, designed by Inigo Jones for Anne of Denmark and completed for Queen Henrietta Maria, wife of Charles I. Restoration means that the housecan be seen as it appeared when new, with bright silks and furnishings. The Great Hall, the State Rooms and a Loggia overlooking Greenwich Park are notable features.

Times: Open from 1 Dec - 24 Sep.

Fee: *Prices not confirmed

P (50 yds) (parking in Greenwich limited in 2000) **✗** licensed **⑂** (Blind kit/stairclimber/wheelchairs) toilets for disabled shop **✳** **🔊**

Royal Naval College

Greenwich SE10 9NN
☎ 020 8858 2256 📠 020 8858 7854

With the Queen's House as its focal point, the Old Royal Naval College occupies one of the masterpieces of English architecture; the grand sequence of buildings, was planned by Sir Christopher Wren as a hospital and refuge for disabled or veteran seamen of the Royal Navy. Additions were subsequently made by such notables as Vanbrugh, Hawksmoor and Ripley.

Times: Open all year (Painted Hall and Chapel only), daily 12-5 (last admission 4.30).

Fee: *Free except for special exhibitions.

P (200m) (all local streets: yellow line roads) (can be given access if prior notice given) shop

HAM

Ham House

TW10 7RS (W of A307, between Kingston & Richmond)
☎ 020 8940 1950 📠 020 8332 6903

This lovely house was built in 1610 and redecorated by the Duke and Duchess of Lauderdale in the 1670s. There are secret servants' passages and stories of a ghostly Duchess. Special events include Spring Plant Fair, garden and ghost tours, childrens activities in school holidays and summer proms concert. Ring for further details.

Times: Open gardens: all year, Sat-Wed 10.30-6 or dusk if earlier. (Closed 25-26 Dec & 1 Jan). House: 27 Mar-Oct, Sat-Wed 1-5. Last admission 4.30.

Fee: *House £5 (ch £2.50). Family ticket £12.50. Garden only £1.50 (ch 75p).

P (500 yds) ♿ (Braille guide, wheelchairs & stairclimber available) toilets for disabled shop (ex guide/hearing dogs)

HAMPSTEAD (NW3)

Fenton House

Windmill Hill NW3 6SP (Underground - Hampstead)
☎ 020 7435 3471 📠 020 7435 3471

A William and Mary mansion built about 1693 and set in a walled garden. It contains a display of furniture and some notable pieces of Oriental and European porcelain as well as the Benton Fletcher collection of early keyboard instruments, including a harpsichord once played by Handel. Summer concerts are arranged.

Times: Open 1-22 Mar, Sat & Sun only 2-5; Apr-1 Nov, Sat-Sun & BH Mon 11-5pm, Wed-Fri 2-5pm. Last admission 30mins before closing.

♿ *Details not confirmed for 2000*

Freud Museum

20 Maresfield Gardens, Hampstead NW3 5SX (Underground - Finchley Road)
☎ 020 7435 2002 & 7435 5167
📠 020 7431 5452

In 1938, Sigmund Freud left Vienna as a refugee from the Nazi occupation and chose exile in England, transferring his entire domestic and working environment to this house. He worked here until his death a year later. His extraordinary collection of Egyptian, Greek, Roman and Oriental antiquities, his working library and papers, and his fine furniture including the famous desk and couch are all here.

Times: Open all year, Wed-Sun 12-5 (Closed BH's, telephone for Xmas Holiday times).

Fee: *£4 (ch 12-18, students, UB40 & pen £2, ch under 12 free).

P ♿ (personal tours can be arranged if booked in advance) shop

Kenwood

Hampstead Ln NW3 7JR (Underground - Hampstead)
☎ 020 8348 1286 📠 020 8348 7325

Forming part of Hampstead Heath, the wooded grounds of Kenwood were laid out in the 18th century by the first Earl of Mansfield. He engaged Robert Adam to enlarge and transform the existing house, and the 'Great Room' is rated as one of his finest achievements. House, contents and grounds were bequeathed to the nation in the 1920s by Lord Iveagh. The house contains a notable collection of paintings, and musical evenings and other events are held in its grounds in summer.

Times: Open all year, Apr-Oct daily 10-6 (or dusk if earlier in Oct); Nov-Mar daily 10-4. (Closed 24-26 Dec & 1 Jan).

P licensed ♿ toilets for disabled shop (ex grounds) #

HAMPTON COURT

Hampton Court Palace

KT8 9AU (on A308, close to A3, M3 & M25 exits)
☎ 020 8781 9500 & 8781 9501
📠 020 8781 5362

Presented to Henry VIII by his Lord Chancellor, Cardinal Wolsey, as a placatory gesture when he fell out of favour with the King. Henry expanded the palace, and later monarchs (and Cromwell) left their own mark: Elizabeth I added plants from the New World, William and Mary commissioned Wren to remodel part of the building. There are handsome gardens, and special attractions are the Tudor Kitchens, the Orangery, the Great Vine, and the maze, laid out in the time of William III. Events and activities take place throughout the year, during school holidays. Please ring for details.

Times: Open all year, mid Mar-Oct, Mon 10.15-6, Tue-Sun 9.30-6 (4.30pm Nov-mid Mar). (Closed 24-26 Dec).

Fee: *£10 (ch 5-16 £6.60, pen, students £7.60). Family £29.90.

P (charged) licensed ♿ (lifts, buggies for gardens, wheelchairs, wardens to assist) toilets for disabled shop 4 shops on site (ex in gardens)

⛏ HIGHGATE (N6)
HIGHGATE CEMETERY
Swains Ln N6 6PJ (Underground - Archway)
☎ 020 8340 1834

Highgate Cemetery is the most impressive of a series of large, formally arranged and landscaped cemeteries which were established around the perimeter of London in the mid-19th century. There's a wealth of fine sculpture and architecture amongst the tombstones, monuments and mausoleums as well as the graves of such notables as the Rossetti family, George Eliot, Michael Faraday and Karl Marx.
Times: Open all year. Eastern Cemetery: daily 10 (11 wknds)-5 (4 in winter). Western Cemetery by guided tour only: Sat & Sun 11-4 (3 in winter); midweek tours 12, 2 & 4 (12, 2 & 3 in winter). No weekday tours in Dec, Jan & Feb. Special tours by arrangement. (Closed 25-26 Dec & during funerals).
Fee: *East cemetery £1. Tour of West cemetery £3 (ch 8-16 £1, no ch under 8 on tours). Donations encouraged to assist restoration. Camera permits for private use £2 (no video or flash).
🅿 shop ✖

⛏ ISLEWORTH
SYON HOUSE
TW8 8JF (Approach via A310 Twickenham road into Park Rd)
☎ 020 8560 0881   ✆ 020 8568 0936

Set in 200 acres of parkland, Syon House is the London home of the Duke of Northumberland, whose family have lived here since the late 16th century. During the second half of the 18th century the first Duke of Northumberland engaged Robert Adam to remodel the interior and 'Capability' Brown to landscape the grounds. Adam was also responsible for the furniture and decorations, and the result is particularly spectacular in the superbly coloured Ante-Room and Long Gallery. Ring for details of special events.
Times: Open Apr-Oct, Wed-Sun & BH 11-5 (last ticket 4.15pm). Fri-Sat closes 3.30pm.
🅿 ⛟ ⛨ toilets for disabled shop garden centre ✖ *Details not confirmed for 2000* 🥽

SYON PARK
TW8 8JF (A310 Twickenham road into Park Rd)
☎ 020 8560 0881   ✆ 020 8568 0936

Contained within the 55 acres that make up Syon Park is one of the inspirations for the Crystal Palace at the Great Exhibition of 1851: a vast crescent of metal and glass, the first construction of its kind in the world and known as the Great Conservatory. Although the horticultural reputation of Syon Park goes back to the 16th century - when the use of trees purely as ornaments was looked upon as unique - its beauty today is thanks to the master of landscape design, 'Capability' Brown. A

miniature steam railway runs through the gardens (weekends Apr-Oct and BHs).
Times: Open all year, daily 10-6 or dusk. (Closed 25 & 26 Dec).
🅿 ⛟ ⛨ toilets for disabled shop garden centre ✖ *Details not confirmed for 2000* 🥽

⛏ ISLINGTON (N1)
THE LONDON CANAL MUSEUM
12/13 New Wharf Rd N1 9RT (Underground - Kings Cross)
☎ 020 7713 0836

The museum covers the development of London's canals (particularly Regent's Canal), canal vessels and trade, and the way of life of the canal people. Housed in a former ice warehouse and stables, it also illustrates horse transport and the unusual trade of importing ice from Norway; there are two large ice wells under the floor. Facilities include temporary moorings, so you can arrive by boat if you want. There are regular special exhibitions.
Times: Open all year, Tue-Sun & BH Mon 10-4.30 (last admission 4). Closed 24-26 & 31 Dec.
Fee: *£2.50 (ch, students, pen & UB40s £1.25, under 8's free). Groups 10+
🅿 (250yds) (metered parking Mon-Fri before 6pm) ⛨ shop ✖ (ex guide dogs) 🥽

⛏ KEW
KEW GARDENS (ROYAL BOTANIC GARDENS)
TW9 3AB (Underground - Kew Gdns)
☎ 020 8940 1171   ✆ 020 8332 5197

The world-famous gardens at Kew began with George III's mother, Princess Augusta, in 1759. The 19th-century botanist, Sir Joseph Banks, and head gardener, William Aiton (later curator), were largely responsible for laying the foundations of the great collection of plants, shrubs and trees which exist here today; a collection which forms part of the world's foremost botanical research centre. The west of the gardens is largely woodland and arboretum, while the formal gardens, with their lawns and neatly manicured beds are in the eastern half. The elegant Palm House is an early example of a glass and wrought iron building, completed in 1848. But the most famous landmark at Kew is the Chinese Pagoda, standing 163ft high. Ring for details of special events.
Times: Open all year, Gardens daily 9.30-between 4 & 6.30pm on weekdays, between 4-7.30pm Suns & BH's, depending on the time of sunset.(Closed 25 Dec & 1 Jan)
Fee: *£5 (concessions £3.50, ch 5-16 £2.50). Family ticket £13.
🅿 (charged) ⛟ ✖ licensed ⛨ (16 seat bus tour: enquiries ring 0181-332 5623) toilets for disabled shop ✖ 🥽

KEW PALACE
Royal Botanic Gardens TW9 3AB (Underground - Kew Bridge)
☎ 020 8781 9540

A favourite country residence during the reign of the first three Hanoverian Kings, Kew was the site of several royal houses. A fairly modest red-

contd.

brick building, built in the Dutch style with gables, Kew Palace was built in 1631 and used for nearly a century until 1818 when Queen Charlotte died. It remains much as it was in George III's time, reflecting the quiet country life his family enjoyed here. Family paintings and personal relics, furniture and tapestries are on display, and a charming 17th-century garden has been recreated.

Times: Closed for refurbishment. Ring for information.

PUBLIC RECORD OFFICE MUSEUM

Ruskin Av TW9 4DU (Underground - Kew Gardens)

☎ 020 8876 3444   ▤ 020 8392 5266

The Public Record Office houses one of the finest, most complete archives in Europe, comprising the records of the central government and law courts from the Norman Conquest to the present century. It is a mine of information and some of the most interesting material including Domesday Book is on display from Spring 2000.

Times: Museum due to reopen Spring 2000. Please telephone for details.

Fee: Free.

🅿 ➰ ✖ ♿ shop ✖

QUEEN CHARLOTTE'S COTTAGE

Royal Botanic Gardens TW9 3AB (Underground - Kew Bridge)

☎ 020 8332 5189

Typical of the fashionable rustic style popular with the gentry in the 18th century, the cottage was built for George III and Queen Charlotte as a home for their menagerie of exotic pets, as well as a picnic spot and summer house.

Times: Open weekends only between May & Sep.

Fee: *Free with entry to Botanical Gardens.

shop ✖

⌂ OSTERLEY

OSTERLEY PARK HOUSE

TW7 4RB (Underground - Osterley)

☎ 020 8560 3918   ▤ 020 8758 2116

This Elizabethan mansion has been transformed into an 18th-century villa, its elegant interior decoration designed in neo-classical style by

Robert Adam. The State Apartments include a Gobelin tapestry ante-room and a dressing-room decorated in the Etruscan style.

Times: Open all year: Park & pleasure grounds, daily 9-7.30 or sunset if earlier. House: Apr-1 Nov, Wed-Sun 2-5, BH Sun & Mon 1-5. Last admission 4.30. (Closed Good Fri & 25-26 Dec). 🅿 (charged) ➰ ♿ toilets for disabled shop ✖ ✿ *Details not confirmed for 2000*

⌂ REGENT'S PARK (NW1)

LONDON ZOO

Regents Park NW1 4RY (Underground - Camden Town or Regents Park)

☎ 020 7722 3333   ▤ 020 7586 5743

London Zoo is home to over 12,000 animals, insects, reptiles and fish. First opened in 1828, the Zoo can claim the world's first aquarium, insect and reptile house. Daily events such as Animals in Action, feeding times and Animal Encounters give an insight into animal behaviour. Exhibits include the Aquarium, Reptile House, and the Moonlight World where day and night are reversed. The 'Web of Life' exhibition introduces the amazing range of life forms found in Earth's major habitats, through live animal exhibits and interactive displays.

Times: Open all year, daily from 10am. (Closed 25 Dec).

Fee: *£9 (ch 4-14 £7, concessions £8). Saver ticket £28. Group 20+

🅿 (charged) ➰ ♿ (wheelchairs & booster scooter available) toilets for disabled shop ✖ 🛒

⌂ ST JOHNS WOOD (NW8)

THE M.C.C. MUSEUM & TOUR OF LORD'S

Lord's Ground NW8 8QN (Underground - St John's Wood)

☎ 020 7432 1033   ▤ 020 7289 9100

Established in 1787, Lord's is the home of the MCC and cricket. Guided tours take you behind the scenes, and highlights include the Long Room and the MCC Museum, where the Ashes and a large collection of paintings and memorabilia are displayed. The Museum is open on match days for spectators.

Times: Open all year, Oct-Mar tours at 12 & 2pm. Apr-Sep 10am, 12 & 2pm (restrictions on some match days). Telephone for details & bookings.

Fee: *Guided tour £5.80 (ch, students & pen £4.20). Family ticket (2 adults & 2 ch) £18. Party 25+. Museum only £2 (concessions £1) plus ground admission (match days only). ▣ ✗ licensed ♿ (by arrangement) toilets for disabled shop ✖ (ex guide dogs)

🏛 SHOREDITCH (E2)
GEFFRYE MUSEUM
Kingsland Rd E2 8EA (Underground - Old Street or Liverpool Street
☎ 020 7739 9893 ▤ 020 7729 5647

The only museum in the UK to specialise in the domestic interiors and furniture of the urban middle classes. Displays span the 400 years from 1600 to the present day, forming a sequence of period rooms which capture the nature of English interior style. Set in the Grade I listed 18th-century almshouses of the Ironmongers' Company, the museum and its delightful gardens are brought to life through a programme of seminars, workshops, drama and music. Special exhibitions throughout the year explore a wide variety of themes - a traditional favourite is the annual Christmas Past exhibition, when the period rooms are festively decorated to reflect 400 years of Christmas traditions in English homes.

Times: Open all year, Tue-Sat 10-5, Sun & BH Mons 12-5 (Closed Mon, Good Friday, Xmas & New year).

Fee: *Free. Prices for special lectures on request. ▣ (150yds) (on street parking) ✗ ♿ (wheelchair available) toilets for disabled shop ✖ (ex guide dogs)

🏛 TWICKENHAM
MARBLE HILL HOUSE
Richmond Rd TW1 2NL
☎ 020 8892 5115

An example of the English Palladian school of architecture, Marble Hill House was built in the 18th century for a mistress of George II. The perfectly proportioned villa contains a notable collection of paintings and furniture, as well as the Lazenby Chinoiserie Bequest.

Times: Open all year, daily, Apr-Oct, 10-6 (or dusk if earlier); Nov-Mar, Wed-Sun 10-4. (Closed 24-25 Dec & 4-7 Jan).

Fee: £3 (ch £1.50). ▣ 💺 ✗ licensed ♿ toilets for disabled shop ✖ (ex in grounds) ⚏

MUSEUM OF RUGBY & TOUR
Rugby Football Union, Rugby Rd TW1 1DZ (M3 into London, A316 follow signs to museum)
☎ 020 8892 8877 ▤ 020 8892 2817

Located beneath the East Stand of the Twickenham Stadium, home of the England team and headquarters of the Rugby Football Union, the museum uses interactive displays, period set pieces and video footage to bring the history of the game to life. The tour includes a visit to the England dressing room, and magnificent views of

the stadium from the top of the north stand. Please ring for details of special events.

Times: Museum: open Tue-Sat 10.30-5, Sun 2-5. Last admission 4.30pm. Tours: 10.30am, noon, 1.30pm, & 3pm; Sun 2pm & 2.30pm. No tours on match days or for ch under 5yrs. Museum open on match days for ticket holders only. Ground closed Mon (ex BH), 24-26 Dec, Good Fri & the Sunday after a match.

Fee: *Museum: £3 (ch, pen, student £2). Twickenham Experience Tour: £3 (ch, pen, students £2). Joint ticket for Museum and Tour £5 (ch, pen, students £3). Family ticket £15. ▣ 💺 ✗ licensed ♿ (special tours and lifts to all floors) toilets for disabled shop ✖ 💺

ORLEANS HOUSE GALLERY
Riverside TW1 3DJ (off A305, along Orleans Rd to Riverside)
☎ 020 8892 0221 ▤ 020 8744 0501

Stroll beside the Thames and through the woodland gardens of Orleans House, where you will find stunning 18th century interior design and an excellent public art gallery. Visitors of all ages can try out their own artistic talents in pre-booked workshops, and wide-ranging temporary exhibitions are held throughout the year - please telephone for details.

Times: Open all year, Tue-Sat 1-5.30 (4.30pm Oct-Mar), Sun & BH 2-5.30 (Oct-Mar 2-4.30). (Closed 24-25 Dec). Woodland Gardens daily, 9-dusk.

Fee: Free. ▣ ♿ (handling objects & large print labels for some exhibitions) toilets for disabled shop ✖ (ex guide dogs) 💺

🏛 WALTHAMSTOW (E17)
WILLIAM MORRIS GALLERY
Lloyd Park, Forest Rd E17 4PP (Underground - Walthamstow Central)
☎ 020 8527 3782 ▤ 020 8527 7070

Victorian artist, craftsman, poet and free thinker William Morris lived here from 1848 to 1856, and the house has been devoted to his life and work and that of his followers, contemporaries, and the Morris Company. Displays include fabrics, stained glass, wallpaper and furniture, as well as Pre-Raphaelite paintings, sculpture by Rodin, ceramics and a collection of pictures by Frank Brangwyn, who worked briefly for Morris. A varied programme of events is run by the museum throughout the year.

Times: Open all year, Tue-Sat and 1st Sun in each month 10-1 & 2-5. (Closed Mon & BH's). Telephone for Xmas/New Year opening times.

Fee: Free. ▣ ♿ shop ✖

🏛 WEMBLEY
WEMBLEY STADIUM TOURS
Empire Way HA9 0DW (Underground - Wembley Park)
☎ 020 8902 8833 ▤ 020 8903 5733

A fascinating tour of this world famous stadium, including behind-the-scenes areas the public don't normally see - the event control rooms, TV studio, cinema, hospital, England changing room

contd.

and the player's tunnel. You can walk up the famous steps to receive the cup to the roar of the crowd and sit in the Royal Box.

Times: Open all year, daily summer 10-4, winter 10-3 (Closed on major event days & 25-26 Dec). The Stadium is scheduled to be re-developed in Spring 2000. Please telephone for opening details.

Fee: *£7.45 (ch & pen £5.25, students £5.95). Party 20+.
🅿 💻 ♿ (limited tour by arrangement) toilets for disabled shop ✕ (ex guide dogs) 🏳

🏛 WIMBLEDON (SW19)
WIMBLEDON LAWN TENNIS MUSEUM
All England Lawn Tennis &, Croquet Club, Church Rd SW19 5AE (Underground - Southfields)
☎ 020 8946 6131   🖷 020 8944 6497

Trophies, pictures, displays and memorabilia trace the development of the game over the last century. See the world famous Centre Court, and the Championships' trophies, as well as film and video footage of great players in action from the 1920s to the present day.

Times: Open daily all year, 10.30-5. (Closed Fri-Sun before the Championships, middle Sun of Championships, Mon immediately following the Championships, 24-26 Dec & 1 Jan).

Fee: *£4 (concessions £3). Party 20+.
🅿 💻 ♿ (lift) toilets for disabled shop ✕ (ex guide dogs) 🏳

🏛 WOOLWICH (SE18)
MUSEUM OF ARTILLERY IN THE ROTUNDA
Repository Rd, Woolwich SE18 4BQ
☎ 020 8781 3127   🖷 020 8316 5402

The guns, muskets, rifles and edged weapons that form the collections in this museum are contained in the rotunda designed by John Nash that once stood in St James's Park. The collection tells the story of the gun from its beginning in the 13th-century to the present day, in an unrivalled display of ordnance, including some ammunition.

Times: Open all year, Mon-Fri 1-4. (Closed Sat, Sun & all BH Mons)
Fee: Free.
🅿 ♿ shop ✕ (ex guide dogs)

THAMES BARRIER VISITORS CENTRE
Unity Way SE18 5NJ
☎ 020 8305 4188   🖷 020 8855 2146

Spanning a third of a mile, the Thames Barrier is the world's largest movable flood barrier. The visitors' centre and exhibition on the South Bank explains the flood threat and the construction of this £480 million project, now valued at £1 billion. Each month a test closure of all ten gates, lasting over 2 hours, is carried out and the annual full day closure of all ten gates takes place in the autumn.

Times: Open all year, Mon-Fri 10-5, Sat & Sun 10.30-5.30. (Closed Xmas - telephone for details). Evening openings by special arrangements for groups - telephone for details.
Fee: *£3.40 (ch & pen £2). Car park £1. Coach park Free. Family ticket £7.50. Party.
🅿 (charged) 💻 ✕ licensed ♿ (lift from river pier approach) toilets for disabled shop ✕ 🏳

Merseyside

Northwestern metropolitan county on the River Mersey, with Liverpool as its administrative centre, Merseyside incorporates the towns of Bootle, Birkenhead, St Helens, Wallasey, and Southport.

The fortunes of the area have declined since the 19th century when Liverpool was England's second greatest port, and the area has been dogged by urban deprivation and unemployment. The area is now on the upturn, due in part to the indomitable Scouse spirit.

When the port of Chester silted up in medieval times, Liverpool took up the slack. The first dock was built in 1715 and the port came to prominence with the slave trade. Following abolition, the port grew to a seven-mile stretch of docks, busy with freight cargoes of cotton, tobacco and sugar and the huge wave of emigration from Europe to the New World in the 19th and early 20th centuries. In its turn, immigration brought an influx of people to Merseyside to join its expanding population, including many from Ireland fleeing the potato famine of 1845.

In the second half of the 20th century, accessible air travel brought to an end the era of the ocean-going liners. At the same time, trade with Europe was picked up by the southeastern ports. Merseyside waned and its population dwindled.

Liverpool's shipping heritage is part of its attraction today, in the museums and galleries of the redeveloped Albert Dock, and in the impressive architecture reflecting the city's civic pride. Look out for the Royal Liver Building and the Cunard Building on the waterfront, and the architecture around St George's Hall, Dale Street, Water Street and William Brown Street.

EVENTS & FESTIVALS

September 1999
24th Sep 1999-9th Jan 2000 Exhibition 21, Walker Art Gallery, Liverpool

October 1999
2nd Oct 1999-2nd Jan 2000 The Art of the Harley, Liverpool Museum, Liverpool (Customising Harley Davidson motorcycles)

February
4th-2nd Apr, Adrian Henri exhibition, (Four decades of art from the Liverpool painter/poet)

March
27th Mar 1999-1st Mar 2000, Violent Incident (exhibition of challenging contemporary art), Liverpool

April
6th-8th Grand National, Aintree, Liverpool

May
1st May 1999-1 Mar 2000, Victor Pasmore exhibition, Tate Gallery, Liverpool (tribute to British abstract artist)

March
tbc Annual Festival of Contemporary Dance, Liverpool

August
17th-19th, Southport Flower Show, Southport

Top: The Liver Building overlooking the Mersey

₥ BIRKENHEAD
HMS PLYMOUTH & HMS ONYX
East Float, Dock Rd L41 1DJ (end of M53 all docks turn off follow tourist signs.)
☎ 0151 650 1573 ▤ 0151 650 1473

HMS Onyx served in the Falklands and is the only submarine afloat in the UK that visitors can explore. HMS Plymouth, an anti-submarine frigate also served in the Falklands. The U534 is the only WWII German U-Boat to be raised from the sea bed. Pre-booking required, adults only admitted to U-Boat.

Times: Open all year, Sep-Mar daily 10-4, Apr-Aug daily 10-5. (Closed 24-26 Dec).
Fee: *£5 (ch £3, pen £4). Family ticket £14. Combined ships & U-Boat £13 (adults only). U-Boat £10.
P ◧ shop ✗

₥ LIVERPOOL
THE BEATLES STORY
Britannia Pavilion, Albert Dock L3 4AA
☎ 0151 709 1963 ▤ 0151 708 0039

Relive the story of the four lads from Liverpool who took the world by storm and changed the face of popular music for ever.

Times: Open Apr-Oct daily 10-6, Nov-Mar daily 10-5 (last admission always 1hr before close).
Fee: *£6.45 (concessions £4.75). Family ticket £16. Groups.
P & toilets for disabled shop ✗ (ex guide dogs) ➥

CROXTETH HALL & COUNTRY PARK
Muirhead Av East L12 0HB (5m NE of city centre, near J4 M57)
☎ 0151 228 5311 ▤ 0151 228 2817

Step back in time and join an Edwardian house party - the Edwardian rooms are furnished with period pieces and character figures. The grounds contain a Victorian walled garden, a collection of rare breed animals, a miniature railway and an adventure playground.

Times: Open, all facilities daily 11-5 in season (phone for details); Some facilities remain open through winter, hours on request.
Fee: *Hall £1.80; Farm £1.80; Walled Garden £1.05 Concessions. All inclusive ticket £3.60 (ch & pen £1.80). Family Saver (2 adults 2 ch) £9.
P ◧ & (permit parking next to the Hall) toilets for disabled shop ✗ (ex in park & grounds)

HM CUSTOMS & EXCISE NATIONAL MUSEUM
Merseyside Maritime Museum, Albert Dock L3 4AQ
☎ 0151 478 4499 ▤ 0151 478 4590

A chance to experience the activities of customs officers today through interactive displays. Try to detect concealed goods or spot the smugglers among a group of suspicious characters. There are a wide range of confiscated goods on display as well as sniffer dog demonstrations and a new exhibition on 18th-century smuggling.

Times: Open all year, daily 10-5. Last admission 4. (Closed 23-26 Dec & 1 Jan)
Fee: *£3 (ch free, concessions £1.50). Family ticket £7.50. Party 20+.
P ◧ ✗ licensed & (restricted wheelchair access, no access to basement) toilets for disabled shop ✗ (ex guide dogs) ➥

LIVERPOOL FOOTBALL CLUB VISITORS CENTRE TOUR
Anfield Rd L4 0TH
☎ 0151 260 6677 ▤ 0151 261 1695

See all the first team kit set out for a match day, listen to a recorded 'team talk' from Gerard Houllier, and then touch the famous 'This is Anfield' sign to the sound of 45,000 cheering fans - a marvellous experience for any Liverpool fan!

Times: Open: Museum daily 10-5 last admission 4pm. (Closed 25-26 Dec). Match days 9am until last admission- 1hr before kick off. Museum & Tour - tours are run subject to daily demand. Advance booking is essential to avoid disappointment.
Fee: *Museum only £5 (ch 5-16 £3, pen £3) Family £14. Museum & Tour £8 (ch 5-16 £5, pen £5) Family £22.
P & (lifts to all areas for wheelchairs) toilets for disabled shop ✗ ➥

MERSEYSIDE MARITIME MUSEUM
Albert Dock L3 4AA
☎ 0151 478 4499   ▤ 0151 478 4590

A large museum in restored 19th-century docklands, which includes a Cooperage and the Albert Dock Warehouse, containing varied displays about the Port of Liverpool. There are floating craft, outdoor exhibits and demonstrations.
Times: Open all year, daily 10-5 (Closed 23-26 Dec & 1 Jan).
Fee: *Details not confirmed
🅿 ▣ ⅏ (lifts, wheelchairs, ramps, ex pilot boat & basement) toilets for disabled shop ✻ (ex guide dogs) ➘

METROPOLITAN CATHEDRAL OF CHRIST THE KING
Mount Pleasant L3 5TQ
☎ 0151 709 9222   ▤ 0151 708 7274

A modern Roman Catholic cathedral which provides a focal point on the Liverpool skyline. The imposing structure of curving concrete ribs and stained glass was designed by Sir Frederick Gibberd and consecrated in 1967.
Times: Open daily 8-6 (Sun 5pm in winter).
Fee: Free.
🅿 ▣ ⅏ (lift, loop system, no access to Crypt) toilets for disabled shop ✻ (ex guide dogs) ➘

MUSEUM OF LIVERPOOL LIFE
Pier Head L3 4AA (follow signs for Albert Dock, museum is on Pier Head side)
☎ 0151 478 4080   ▤ 0151 478 4090

This museum explores the history of Liverpool, its people and their contribution to national life. Displays focus on three main themes: Mersey Culture, Making a Living and Demanding a Voice.
Times: Open all year, daily 10-5. (Closed 23-26 Dec & 1 Jan).
Fee: *£3 (ch free, concessions £1.50). Party 20+.
🅿 (charged) ⅏ (wheelchairs available) toilets for disabled shop ✻ (ex guide dogs) ➘

TATE GALLERY LIVERPOOL
Albert Dock L3 4BB
☎ 0151 709 3223 & 0151 709 0507 (info)   ▤ 0151 709 3122

A converted Victorian warehouse with stunning views across the River Mersey, Tate Gallery Liverpool displays the best of the National

Collection of 20th-Century Art. A changing programme of exhibitions draws on works from public and private collections across the world. Please contact the Gallery for exhibition details.
Times: Open Tue-Sun 10-6. (Closed Mon ex BH Mon, 24-26 Dec & 1 Jan).
Fee: *Admission free. Fee for Special exhibitions, phone for details.
🅿 ▣ ⅏ (wheelchairs available) toilets for disabled shop ✻ ➘

WALKER ART GALLERY
William Brown St L3 8EL (follow brown and white signs)
☎ 0151 478 4199   ▤ 0151 478 4199

An outstanding collection of European paintings and sculpture. Especially notable are the Italian, Netherlands, and Pre-Raphaelite and Victorian paintings. There is an award-winning sculpture gallery and temporary exhibitions are held throughout the year. Please telephone for details.
Times: Open all year, Mon-Sat 10-5, Sun 12-5. (Closed 23-26 Dec & 1 Jan).
Fee: *£3 (ch free, concessions £1.50).
🅿 (charged) ▣ ⅏ (prior notice appreciated, wheelchair on request) toilets for disabled shop ✻ (ex guide dogs)

▥ PORT SUNLIGHT
PORT SUNLIGHT HERITAGE CENTRE
95 Greendale Rd L62 4XE (junc 4 of M53 on B5137)
☎ 0151 644 6466   ▤ 0151 645 8973

This picturesque garden village was built by William Hesketh Lever for the workers in his soap factory. The Heritage Centre tells the story of the village, the factory and its workers and a village trail incorporates the varied architecture, beautiful open spaces and the Lady Lever Art Gallery with its world-famous collection of pre-Raphaelite paintings and Wedgewood.
Times: Open all year. Apr-Oct, daily 10-4. Nov-Etr, Mon-Fri 10-4.
🅿 (on road 1hr limit) ⅏ shop ✻ *Details not confirmed for 2000*

▥ SOUTHPORT
ATKINSON ART GALLERY
Lord St PR8 1DH
☎ 01704 533133 ext 2110
▤ 0151 934 2110

The gallery specialises in 19th-and 20th-century oil paintings, watercolours, drawings and prints, as well as 20th-century sculpture.
Times: Open all year, Mon-Wed & Fri 10-5, Thu & Sat 10-1. (Closed 25-26 Dec & 1 Jan).
Fee: Free.
🅿 (pay & display) ⅏ shop ✻

SOUTHPORT

Southport has been described as one of England's most elegant seaside resorts. This is reflected in its architecture, public parks and splendid Promenade. Attractions include the Model Village and Garden Railway; Pleasureland; the Marine Lake; and Southport Zoo, which houses snow leopards, penguins, monkeys and reptiles among others.

Southport's most notable claim to fame is its position as 'Floral Capital of England's North West.' The town is home to the internationally famous Southport Flower Show, second only to the Chelsea Flower Show. The town also hosts a major airshow, and a rally of model aircraft and full-size bikes, cars and military vehicles.

⛫ SPEKE

SPEKE HALL

The Walk L24 1XD (follow signs for Liverpool Airport)

☎ 0151 427 7231   ▤ 0151 427 9860

A remarkable timber-framed manor house set in tranquil gardens and grounds. The house has a Tudor Great Hall, Stuart plasterwork, and William Morris wallpapers. Outside are varied grounds, including a rose garden, bluebell woods, and woodland walks. Special events, including Open Air Shakespeare, are held, please ring for details. **Times:** House open: Apr-Oct, daily (ex Mon but open BH Mon) 1-5.30; Nov-17 Dec, Sat & Sun 12-4.30. Garden open daily (ex Mon & closed 24-26 Dec, 31 Dec, 1 Jan & Good Fri). **Fee:** *Hall & Gardens: £4.10 (ch £2.05). Gardens only: £1.50 (ch 80p). Family ticket £10.30.

🅿 🖭 ♿ (Wheelchairs & Electric car) toilets for disabled shop ✕ ✕ 🗢

Norfolk

A fertile agricultural county in the east of the country, sparsely populated, with plenty of fresh air and wide open spaces.

Norfolk is the northern bit of East Anglia, en route to nowhere, and too far from London to be colonised. Its coastline encompasses fenland round the Wash, the wonderfully unspoilt seaside towns of the north coast, and two of the country's most important nature reserves at Blakeney Point and the Cley marshes. Common features of the countryside are windmills and attractive houses built of Norfolk flint with Dutch gables, a relic of the area's historical trade links with the Low Countries.

The Norfolk Broads are the county's main tourist attraction. The 'broads' are waterways set in marshy fenland, which came about from extensive peat cutting and subsequent flooding in the 13th and 14th centuries. Reed cutting for local thatching helped to keep the waterways clear. The Broads now has National Park status, to help protect the important wetland site from the demands of tourism and agriculture. The best way to see the Broads is to hire a boat, and there is plenty of opportunity for this at boatyards in Wroxham and Hoveton.

The county town is the city of Norwich, the largest in East Anglia, with a fine cathedral, a huge market place and an attractive medieval centre. Norwich came to prominence in the 17th century as a focus for the textile industry. Today it is most famously associated with Coleman's, the mustard company.

EVENTS & FESTIVALS

April
Primrose Weeks, Fairhaven Garden

May
13th-14th Food Fair, Norwich
Primrose Weeks, Fairhaven Garden

June
4th Wymondham Carnival
28th-29th Royal Norfolk Show, Dereham Road, Norwich

July
1st Raft Race on Diss Mere
1st-8th Wymondham Music week, Wymondham Abbey & other venues
7th-9th Lord Mayor's Weekend Celebration, Norwich

August
18th-19th Firework & Laser Symphony Concert, Blickling Hall, Norwich
tbc Norfolk & Norwich Festival

October
tbc Norfolk & Norwich Festival
tbc Real ale Festival, Norwich

November
4th (provisional) Firework Spectacular, Earlham park, Norwich

Top: Berney Arms wind-pump beside River Yare

BACONSTHORPE

BACONSTHORPE CASTLE
NR25 6LN (three quarters of a mile N off unclass road)

The 'castle' is really a moated and semi-fortified house, built by the Heydon family in the 15th century. Gatehouses, curtain walls and towers still remain.

Times: Open all year daily 10-4.

BLICKLING

BLICKLING HALL
NR11 6NF (signposted off A140 Norwich to Cromer road)
☎ 01263 738030 ▤ 01263 731660

Flanked by dark yew hedges and topped by pinnacles, the warm red brick front of Blickling is a memorable sight. The grounds include woodland and a lake, a formal parterre, and a dry moat filled with roses, camellias and other plants. In June, Blickling holds an annual 'Last Night of the Proms' concert, and in August a laser symphony concert with fireworks.

Times: Open: 27 Mar-Oct, Wed-Sun 1-4.30. Garden open same days as Hall 10.30-5.30 (daily in Aug).

Fee: *£6.20 (ch £3.10).

P ⬛ ✕ licensed ♿ (wheelchairs & batricars, Braille guide, lift, parking) toilets for disabled shop garden centre ✕ (ex guide dogs) ✦ ☕

BRESSINGHAM

BRESSINGHAM STEAM MUSEUM & GARDENS
IP22 2AB (on A1066 2.5 miles W of Diss)
☎ 01379 687382 & 687386
▤ 01379 688085

Alan Bloom is an internationally recognised nurseryman and a steam enthusiast, and has combined his interests to great effect at Bressingham. There are three miniature steam-hauled trains, including a 15in gauge running through two and a half miles of the wooded Waveney Valley. The Dell Garden has 5000 species of perennials and alpines; Foggy Bottom has wide vistas, pathways, trees, shrubs, conifers and winter colour (restricted opening). A steam roundabout is another attraction, and the Norfolk fire museum is housed here. Various events are held, including Friends of Thomas the Tank Engine, please telephone for details.

Times: Open - Steam Museum & Dell Garden - Apr-Oct, daily 10.30-5.30. Telephone to confirm details.

P ✕ licensed ♿ (wheelchair can be taken onto Nursery Line Railway) toilets for disabled shop garden centre ✕ *Details not confirmed for 2000* ☕

BURGH CASTLE

BERNEY ARMS WINDMILL
NR30 1SB
☎ 01493 700605

Access is by boat from Great Yarmouth or by rail to Berney Arms station: the road is unsuitable for cars. The seven-storey landmark was built in the 19th century to grind clinker for cement and then to help drain the marshes.

Times: Open Apr-Sep, daily 9-5.

✕ ☕

THE CASTLE
NR31 9PZ (off A143)

Burgh Castle was built in the third century AD by the Romans, as one of a chain of forts along the Saxon Shore - the coast where Saxon invaders landed. Sections of the massive walls still stand.

Times: Open any reasonable time.

☕

CAISTER-ON-SEA

ROMAN TOWN

The name Caister has Roman origins, and this was in fact a Roman naval base. The remains include the south gateway, a town wall built of flint with brick courses and part of what may have been a seamen's hostel.

Times: Open any reasonable time.

☕

CASTLE ACRE

CASTLE ACRE PRIORY
☎ 01760 755394

The priory was built for the Cluniac order in the Norman period. After the Dissolution under Henry VIII, the priory fell into ruin, but its extensive remains are dominated by the glorious, arcaded west front of the priory church, a reminder of past splendour. The chapel and 15th-century gatehouse also remain, and there are impressive ruins of a great castle which also stood nearby.

Times: Open all year, Apr-Oct, daily 10-6 (or dusk if earlier in Oct); Nov-Mar, Wed-Sun 10-4.

Fee: £3.10 (ch £1.60).

P ♿ shop ✕ (in certain areas) ☕

CASTLE RISING

CASTLE RISING CASTLE
PE31 6AH (off A149)
☎ 01553 631330

The fine Norman keep was built around 1140 by Henry Albini to celebrate his marriage to the widow of Henry I. The walls still stand to their full height, towering above the 12 acres of impressive man-made earthworks.

Times: Open all year, Apr-Sep, daily 10-6; Oct, 10-4; Nov-Mar, Wed-Sun 10-4.

P ♿ (exterior only) toilets for disabled shop ✕ ☕

CROMER

CROMER MUSEUM
East Cottages, Tucker St NR27 9HB
☎ 01263 513543 ▤ 01263 511651

The museum is housed in five 19th-century fishermen's cottages, one of which has period furnishings. There are pictures and exhibits from Victorian Cromer, with collections illustrating

local natural history, archaeology, social history and geology.
Times: Open all year, Mon-Sat 10-5, Sun 2-5. Closed Mon 1-2. (Closed Good Fri, Xmas period & 1 Jan).
P (200yds) shop ✖ *Details not confirmed for 2000*

HENRY BLOGG MUSEUM
No 2 Boathouse, The Promenade NR27 9HE
☎ 01263 511294   ▤ 01263 513018

A lifeboat has been stationed at the Lifeboat Station on the pier since 1804, and the museum in No 2 boat house at the bottom of The Gangway covers local lifeboat history and the RNLI in general.
Times: Open May-Oct daily 10-4. Or by appointment with the Curator.
Fee: *Donations welcome.
P & shop

⊞ FAKENHAM
PENSTHORPE WATERFOWL PARK & NATURE RESERVE
Pensthorpe NR21 0LN (signed off A1067 Norwich to Fakenham road)
☎ 01328 851465   ▤ 01328 855905

Covering 200 acres of beautiful Norfolk countryside, with five lakes which are home to the largest collection of waterfowl and waders in Europe. Spacious walk-through enclosures and a network of hardsurfaced pathways ensures close contact with birds at the water's edge. Various events and exhibitions take place, please contact for details.
Times: Open all year, daily 10-5 mid Mar-end of year.
Fee: *£4.80 (ch £2.25, pen £4.20)
P ✖ licensed & (network of hard surfaced pathways ensures access to shore) toilets for disabled shop ✖ (ex guide dogs) ⬗

⊞ FELBRIGG
FELBRIGG HALL
NR11 8PR (off B1436)
☎ 01263 837444   ▤ 01263 837032

Felbrigg is a 17th-century house built on the site of an existing medieval hall. It contains a superb collection of 18th-century furniture and pictures and an outstanding library. A 550 acre wood shelters the house from the North Sea. Please phone for details of special events.
Times: Open: House 28 Mar-1 Nov, Sat-Wed 1-5. BH Sun & Mon 11-5. Garden opens 11am. Park walks daily dawn-dusk.
P ▣ ✖ licensed & (battery operated vehicle for garden, braille guide) toilets for disabled shop ✖ (ex park) ✖ *Details not confirmed for 2000* ⬗

⊞ GREAT YARMOUTH
MARITIME MUSEUM FOR EAST ANGLIA
Marine Pde NR30 2EN
☎ 01493 842267

The sea and the fishing industry have played an enormous part in East Anglia's history and this museum has exhibits on the herring fishery, the wherry, life-saving and the most recent industry - oil and gas in the North Sea.
Times: Open Etr fortnight, Mon-Fri 10-5, Sun 2-5 (closed Good Fri); Sun before Whitsun-end Sep, Sun-Fri 10-5. Under review.
P shop ✖ *Details not confirmed for 2000*

OLD MERCHANT'S HOUSE
Row 111 (follow signs to dock and south quay)
☎ 01493 857900

Two 17th-century Row Houses, a type of building unique to Great Yarmouth, contain original fixtures and display items salvaged from the bombing raids of WWII. Nearby are the remains of a Franciscan friary, with a rare vaulted cloister, discovered during bomb-damage repairs.
Times: Open Apr-Sep 10-6. Tours start from Row 111 houses at 10am, 11am, noon, 2pm, 3pm & 4pm.
Fee: £1.85 (ch 90p).
✖ ⬗

⊞ GRESSENHALL
NORFOLK RURAL LIFE MUSEUM & UNION FARM
Beech House NR20 4DR (A47, B1110 through East Dereham towards Holt, B1146 to Fakenham, 1.5m on right)
☎ 01362 860563   ▤ 01362 860385

Housed in a former workhouse, the museum reflects the rural history of the county over the past 200 years. Displays include Cherry Tree Cottage and garden, a typical farm labourer's home of the early 20th century, as well as reconstructed craftsmen's workshops. Union Farm is a working farm, which is worked with heavy horses and stocked with rare breeds of sheep, cattle, pigs and poultry. Farm trail, woodland and riverside walk, osier beds. Special events and demonstrations throughout the season.
Times: Open 5 Apr-1 Nov, Mon-Sat 10-5, Sun 12-5.30. Also BH Mons 10-5.
P ▣ & (sound guide & wheelchair loan) toilets for disabled shop ✖ *Details not confirmed for 2000* ⬗

⊞ GRIMES GRAVES
GRIMES GRAVES
(7m NW of Thetford off A134)
☎ 01842 810656

Grimes Graves is the largest known group of Neolithic flint mines in Britain. It consists of a network of hundreds of pits, the oldest dating from about 3000BC. Vertical shafts lead through the flint seams to galleries. Flints would have been prised out with antler picks and wooden levers. Visitors can climb down a shaft, and there are regular demonstrations of the craft of flint-knapping.
Times: Open all year, Apr-Oct, daily 10-6 (or dusk if earlier); Nov-Mar, Wed-Sun 10-4. Last visit to pit 20 minutes before closing).
Fee: £1.85 (ch 90p).
P & (exhibition area, grounds only; access track rough) shop ✖ (in certain areas) ⬗

⚏ HEACHAM

NORFOLK LAVENDER

Caley Mill PE31 7JE (on A149 at junc with B1454)
☎ 01485 570384 ▤ 01485 571176

This is the largest lavender-growing and distilling
operation in Britain. Different coloured lavenders
are grown in strips and harvested in July and
August. There are also rose and herb gardens
and a fragrant Plant Centre, and guided tours of
the distillery and gardens.

Times: Open all year, daily 10-5. (Closed 25-26 Dec & 1 Jan).
Fee: *Admission to grounds Free. Guided tours £1.50 (May-
Sep). Trip to Lavender Field £3.95, mid Jun-mid Aug.
🅿 ▣ ⚹ (wheelchairs for loan) toilets for disabled shop
garden centre ➹

⚏ HOLKHAM

HOLKHAM HALL & BYGONES MUSEUM

NR23 1AB (off A149, 2m W of Wells-next-the-Sea)
☎ 01328 710227 ▤ 01328 711707

This classic Palladian mansion was built between
1734 and 1764 by Thomas Coke, 1st Earl of
Leicester, and is home to his descendants. It has
a magnificent alabaster entrance hall and the
sumptuous state rooms house Greek and Roman
statues, fine furniture and paintings by Rubens,
Van Dyck, Gainsborough and others. The park is
equally fine, with deer, geese on the lake, and an
impressive collection of trees, especially ilexes.
The Bygones Museum, housed in the stable
block, has over 5,000 items on display - from
gramophones to fire engines.

Times: Open 28 May-28 Sep Sun-Thu, 1-5. Etr, May, Spring &
Summer BHs Sun & Mon 11.30-5.
Fee: *Hall £4 (ch £2). Bygones £4 (ch £2). Combined ticket
Hall & Bygones: £6 (ch £3)
🅿 ▣ ⚹ (wheelchair ramps at all entrances) toilets for
disabled shop garden centre ✚ (ex guide dogs & in park)

⚏ HORSEY

HORSEY WINDPUMP

NR29 4EF
☎ 01493 393904

The windpump mill was built 200 years ago to
drain the area, and then rebuilt in 1912 by Dan
England, a noted Norfolk millwright. It has been
restored since being struck by lightning in 1943,
and overlooks Horsey Mere and marshes, noted
for their wild birds and insects.

Times: Open 28 Mar-Sep, daily 11-5. (Closed Good Fri).
🅿 (charged) ▣ shop ✚ ⚘ *Details not confirmed for 2000*
➹

⚏ KING'S LYNN

AFRICAN VIOLET CENTRE

Terrington St Clement PE34 4PL (4m W of Kings
Lynn, on A17)
☎ 01553 828374 ▤ 01553 827520

A mecca for African violet lovers, the centre has
won 10 Chelsea Gold Medals. Visitors may
explore a half-acre of greenhouses.

Times: Open daily 10-5. (Closed Xmas & New Year).
Fee: Free.
🅿 ▣ ⚹ toilets for disabled shop garden centre ✚ (ex
guide dogs) ➹

ST GEORGE'S GUILDHALL

27 Kings St
☎ 01553 773578 ▤ 01553 770591

Although it has been used for many purposes,
the theatrical associations of this 15th-century
Guildhall are strongest: Shakespeare himself is
said to have performed here. The annual King's
Lynn Festival takes place towards the end of July.
Ring for details.

Times: When not in use as a theatre or cinema open Mon-Fri
10-4, Sat 10-1 & 2-3.30. (Closed Good Fri, Aug BH Mon, 25-26
Dec & 1 Jan).
🅿 (100yds) (pay & display) ▣ ✗ licensed ✚ ⚘ *Details not
confirmed for 2000*

NORWICH

Constructed around a magnificent Norman cathedral, with an imposing 315 ft high spire, central Norwich is perhaps the most complete medieval city in England. The cathedral was begun in 1094 and completed by 1145, the spire being added in the 15th century. Inside are over 1,000 sculptured roof bosses, the largest concentration of medieval art in Europe. The city also has many other ancient churches. Norwich Castle towers over all of this, and is one of Britain's great treasure houses; home to a museum of local history, a collection of works by the 19th-century Norwich School of painters, and the biggest teapot collection in the world.

NORTH CREAKE

Creake Abbey

NR21 9LF (1m N off B1355)

Church ruin with crossing and eastern arm belonging to a house of Augustinian canons founded in 1206.

Times: Open any reasonable time.

#

NORWICH

Norwich Castle Museum

Castle Meadow NR1 3JU

☎ 01603 223624 🖷 01603 765651

The Castle keep was built in the 12th century, and the museum houses displays of art, archaeology, natural history, Lowestoft porcelain, Norwich silver, a large collection of paintings (with special emphasis on the Norwich School of Painters) and British ceramic teapots. There are also guided tours of the dungeons and battlements. A programme of exhibitions, children's events, gallery and evening talks takes place throughout the year. Please ring for details.

Times: Open all year, Mon-Sat 10-5, Sun 2-5. (Closed Good Fri, Xmas period & New Year).

P (200mtrs) ☕ ♿ (lift to first floor, special parking by prior arrangement) toilets for disabled shop 🐕 *Details not confirmed for 2000*

Norwich Cathedral

The Close NR1 4DH (A47, A11 to city centre, inner ring rd to Barrack St rdbt, take rd towards city centre to Tombland)

☎ 01603 764385 & 767617 (weekends)

🖷 01603 766032

Originally a Benedictine foundation, the cathedral possesses the largest monastic cloisters in England and is of great architectural and artistic interest. Of particular note are the Saxon bishop's throne, nave bosses depicting Biblical scenes, and the 14th-century Despenser reredos. Services take place several times every day, and there is a regular programme of concerts, recitals and exhibitions, details on request.

Times: Open daily, 7.30-7 (6pm mid Sep-mid May).

Fee: *Donations welcomed.

P (440yds) (parking at Cathedral for services only) ☕ ♿ (parking on site touch & hearing centre) toilets for disabled shop 🐕 (ex guide dogs)

Royal Norfolk Regimental Museum

Shirehall, Market Av NR1 3JQ (adjacent to Norwich Castle Museum)

☎ 01603 223649 🖷 01603 765651

Museum displays deal with the social as well as military history of the county regiment from 1685, including the daily life of a soldier. Audio-visual displays and graphics complement the

contd.

collection and there's a programme of temporary exhibitions.

Times: Open all year, Mon-Sat 10-5, Sun 2-5. (Closed Good Fri, Xmas period & 1 Jan).

Fee: *£1.80 (ch 90p, concessions £1.30). Joint ticket with Castle Museum available.

P (400yds) & (stair lift available, ring for details) shop ✖

SAINSBURY CENTRE FOR VISUAL ARTS

University of East Anglia NR4 7TJ
☎ 01603 456060 & 593199
▤ 01603 259401

The collection of Sir Robert and Lady Sainsbury was given to the University in 1973. European art of the 19th and 20th centuries is on display together with ethnographical art. You can see African tribal sculpture and Oceanic works along with North American and Pre-Colombian art. There's a regularly changing programme of temporary exhibitions, as well as children's workshops and talks, please ring for details.

Times: Open Tue-Sun 11-5. (Closed Mon & University closure at Xmas).

Fee: *Collection & exhibition £2 (concessions £1).

P ▆ ✖ licensed & (parking at main entrance, wheelchair available on loan) toilets for disabled shop ✖ (guide dogs by arrangement) ▄

▥ OXBOROUGH

OXBURGH HALL

PE33 9PS
☎ 01366 328258 ▤ 01366 328066

The outstanding feature of this 15th-century moated building is the 80ft high gatehouse which was spared from the extensive alterations made in Victorian times. Henry VII lodged in the King's Room in 1487. A parterre garden of French design stands outside the moat, and there are woodland walks.

Times: Open House, Garden & Estate Walks 29 Mar-2 Nov, Sat-Wed 1-5. (Garden 11-5.30). BH Mons 11-5. (Closed Good Fri).

P ✖ licensed & (braille guide & wheelchairs available) toilets for disabled shop ✖ ♨ *Details not confirmed for 2000* ▄

▥ ST OLAVES

ST OLAVES PRIORY

(5.5m SW of Great Yarmouth on A143)

The fine brick undercroft in the cloister is one of the most notable features of the ruin of this small 13th-century Augustinian priory.

Times: Open any reasonable time.
⌗

▥ SANDRINGHAM

SANDRINGHAM HOUSE, GROUNDS, MUSEUM & COUNTRY PARK

PE35 6EN (off A148)
☎ 01553 772675 ▤ 01485 541571

The private country retreat of Her Majesty The Queen, this neo-Jacobean house was built in 1870 for King Edward VII. The main rooms used by the Royal Family when in residence are all open to the public. Sixty acres of glorious grounds surround the House and offer beauty and colour throughout the season. Sandringham Museum contains fascinating displays of Royal memorabilia.

Times: Open Apr-3 Oct, daily (House closed 21 Jul-4 Aug inc; Museum & Grounds closed 25 Jul-4 Aug inc). House 11-4.45. Museum 11-5. Grounds 10.30-5.

Fee: *House, Museum & Grounds: £5 (ch £3, pen £4). Family ticket £13. Grounds & Museum £4 (ch £2.50, pen £3.50). Family ticket £10.50.

P ▆ ✖ licensed & (loan of wheelchairs, free transport in grounds) toilets for disabled shop ✖ (ex guide dogs) ▄

▥ SAXTHORPE

MANNINGTON GARDENS & COUNTRYSIDE

Mannington Hall NR11 7BB (2.25m NE)
☎ 01263 584175 ▤ 01263 761214

The moated manor house, built in 1460 and still a family home, forms a centre-piece for the pretty gardens which surround it. Enjoy the roses, the chief feature of the gardens, and lovely countryside walks. Special events take place throughout the season, including theatre events

and Nature Discovery Days for children. Please phone for details.
Times: Open: Gardens Jun-Aug, Wed-Fri 11-5; also Sun noon-5 May-Sep. Walks open every day from 9am. Hall open by prior appointment only.
Fee: *Garden £3 (accompanied ch 16 free, students & pen £2.50). Walks free (car park for walkers £1).
🅿 ⬛ ♿ (boardwalk across meadow, wheelchair ramps) toilets for disabled shop garden centre ✖ (ex guide dogs)

SHERINGHAM
NORTH NORFOLK RAILWAY
Sheringham Station, Station Approach NR26 8RA
☎ 01263 822045 📠 01263 823794

A steam railway with trains operating on most days (Apr-Sep), with extra days as the season progresses and a daily service in the summer. On Sundays, lunch is served on the train. At Weybourne station is a collection of steam locomotives and rolling stock, some of which are undergoing or awaiting restoration. There is also a museum of railway memorabilia.
Times: Open Apr-Sep; daily during summer season; Dec (Santa specials). Telephone for details of other running days.
Fee: *Return £6.50 (ch £3.50, pen £5.50). Family ticket £17.50.
🅿 (adjacent) ⬛ ♿ (ramps to trains) shop ▼

SOUTH WALSHAM
FAIRHAVEN GARDEN TRUST
School Rd NR13 6DZ (9m NE of Norwich on B1140)
☎ 01603 270449 📠 01603 270449

These delightful woodland and water gardens, with a private inner broad, offer a combination of cultivated and wild flowers. In spring there are masses of primroses and bluebells, with azaleas and rhododendrons in several areas. Candelabra primulas and some unusual plants grow near the waterways, and in summer the wild flowers come into their own, providing a habitat for butterflies, bees and dragonflies. There is a separate wildlife sanctuary for bird watchers. Riverboats run from the gardens around the two South Walsham Broads, or to St Benets Abbey

ruins. Special events are planned, please telephone for details.
Times: Open daily 10-5, extended opening until 9pm Wed & Thu, May-Aug. (Closed 25 Dec).
Fee: *£3 (ch £1, under 5 free, pen £2.70). Season tickets £10. Family season ticket £25.
🅿 ⬛ ♿ (ramp, grab rail) toilets for disabled shop garden centre (on leads) ▼

THETFORD
THETFORD PRIORY
(on W side of Thetford near station)

Extensive remains of the Cluniac monastery founded in 1103 include the 14th-century gatehouse and complete ground plan of the cloisters.
Times: Open any reasonable time.
✖ ⌗

WARREN LODGE
(2m NW, on B1107)

The remains of a two-storey hunting lodge, built in 15th-century of flint with stone dressings.
Times: Open any reasonable time.
⌗

TITCHWELL
RSPB NATURE RESERVE
PE31 8BB (6m E of Hunstanton on A149)
☎ 01485 210779

A firm path takes you to three hides and on to the beach where a platform overlooking the sea is suitable for wheelchairs. A colony of avocets nest on the enclosed marsh with gadwalls, tufted ducks, shovelers and black-headed gulls. Bearded tits, water rails, bitterns and marsh harriers are found on the reedbeds. During the season many migrants visit the marsh including wigeon, black-tailed godwits, curlews, and sandpipers. Phone for details of special events.
Times: Open at all times. Visitor Centre daily 10-5 (4pm Nov-Mar)
🅿 (charged) ⬛ ♿ toilets for disabled ✖ *Details not confirmed for 2000* ▼

WEETING
WEETING CASTLE
IP27 0RQ (2m N of Brandon off B1106)

This ruined 11th-century fortified manor house stands in a moated enclosure. There are interesting but slight remains of a three-storey cross-wing.
Times: Open any reasonable time.
⌗

🏛 WELNEY
WWT WELNEY
Pintail House, Hundred Foot Bank PE14 9TN (off A1101, N of Ely)
☎ 01353 860711 📄 01353 860711

This important wetland site on the beautiful Ouse Washes is famed for the breathtaking spectacle of wild ducks, geese and swans which spend the winter here. Impressive observation facilities, including hides, towers and an observatory, offer outstanding views of the huge numbers of wildfowl which include Bewick's and whooper swans, wigeon, teal and shoveler. Floodlit evening swan feeds take place between November and February. There are two hides for wheelchair users.

Times: Open all year, daily 10-5. (Closed 25 Dec).
🅿 ☕ ♿ (wheelchair access to major parts of reserve) toilets for disabled shop ✈ *Details not confirmed for 2000* 🐟

🏛 WEYBOURNE
THE MUCKLEBURGH COLLECTION
Weybourne Military Camp NR25 7EG (on A149, coast road, 3m W of Sheringham)
☎ 01263 588210 & 588608
📄 01263 588425

The largest privately-owned military collection of its kind in the country, which incorporates the Museum of the Suffolk and Norfolk Yeomanry. Exhibits include restored and working tanks, armoured cars, trucks and artillery of World War II, and equipment and weapons from the Falklands and the Gulf War. Live tank demonstrations are run daily during school holidays, or take a ride in a Gama Goat - a six-wheeled personnel carrier.

Times: Open 13 Feb-29 Oct, 10-5 daily.
Fee: *£4 (ch £2 & pen £3). Family ticket £10.50.
🅿 ☕ ✗ licensed ♿ (ramped access, wheelchairs available) toilets for disabled shop ✈ (ex guide dogs) 🐟

Northamptonshire

Northamptonshire is a mainly rural county of gentle beauty, with farmland, forest and great country estates. Rivers, canals and watermeadows are all part of the tranquil scene, providing a haven for wildlife.

Northamptonshire is ideal country for touring, walking and exploring lovely villages of stone and thatch, and visiting some particularly impressive churches. Among the most interesting of these are the Saxon churches at Brixworth and Earls Barton.

In the main square of the pretty village of Geddington stands one of the three surviving Eleanor Crosses. Edward I, grief-stricken with the death of his queen, erected a series of these crosses to mark the resting place of his wife's body, each night, on its journey south from Leicestershire to London. Another such cross can be seen on the southern outskirts of Northampton at Hardingstone. In recent times, Althorp, home of the Spencer family and last resting place of Diana Princess of Wales, has put the county firmly on the tourist map, in quite a similar way.

Northampton is the county town, and along with Kettering, has long been associated with the production of footwear. Kettering was the second largest town until it was overtaken by the rapid development of Corby as a major centre of the steel industry. With the decline of the steel industry, Corby, as an enterprise zone, has fought back to provide a home for a variety of modern industries.

EVENTS & FESTIVALS

January
18th-22nd Millennium Extravaganza, The Castle, Wellingborough

May
27th-29th British Waterways Boat Show, Crick

June
tbc Music & Arts Festival, Northampton
Sunday afternoon & evening brass band concerts in Abington Park, Northampton, at the Victorian band stand

July
1st-23rd Oundle International Festival, Oundle
1st-2nd Hollowell Steam & Heavy Horse Show, Hollowell, nr Northampton
tbc British Grand Prix, Silverstone Circuit, nr Towester
21st-23rd Northampton Town Show
Sunday afternoon & evening brass band concerts in Abington Park, Northampton at the Victorian band stand (ex Sunday of Town Show)

August
18th-20th Northampton Balloon Festival
Sunday afternoon & evening brass band concerts in Abington Park, Northampton

Top: Church of St Mary Magdalen, Ecton

CANONS ASHBY
CANONS ASHBY HOUSE
NN11 3SD
☎ 01327 860044 ▤ 01327 860168

Home of the Dryden family since the 16th century, this is an exceptional small manor house, with Elizabethan wall paintings and Jacobean plasterwork. It has restored gardens, a small park and a church - part of the original 13th-century Augustinian priory.

Times: Open 11 Apr-1 Nov, Sat-Wed & BH Mon (closed Good Fri) 1-5.30 or dusk if earlier. Last admission 5pm.

🅿 ■ & (hearing scheme taped guide wheelchair available) toilets for disabled shop ✖ (ex on lead in home paddock) ❧ *Details not confirmed for 2000* ➥

DEENE
DEENE PARK
NN17 3EW (0.5m off A43, between Kettering & Stamford)
☎ 01780 450223 & 450278
▤ 01780 450282

A mainly 16th-century house of great architectural importance, and home of the Brudenell family since 1514 (including the 7th Earl of Cardigan who led the Charge of the Light Brigade). There's a large lake and park, and extensive gardens with old-fashioned roses, rare trees and shrubs. Phone for details of antiques fairs and garden openings.

Times: Open BH's (Sun & Mon) Etr, May, Spring & Aug; Jun-Aug, Sun 2-5. Party 20+ by prior arrangement with House Keeper.

Fee: *House & Gardens: £4.50 (ch 10-14 £2). Gardens only: £2.50 (ch £1.25). Children under 10 free admission with accompanying adult.

🅿 ■ & (ramps to Old Kitchen and gardens) toilets for disabled shop ✖ (ex guide dogs in garden only)

KIRBY HALL
NN17 3EN (on unclass road off A43, 4m NE of Corby)
☎ 01536 203230

A beautiful Elizabethan manor house boasting an unusual richness and variety of architectural detail in the Renaissance style. The extensive gardens were among the finest in England at their peak during the 17th century.

Times: Open all year, Apr-Oct, daily 10-6 (or dusk if earlier); Nov-Mar, wknds 10-4. Closed 24-26 Dec & 1 Jan.

Fee: £2.50 (ch £1.50).

🅿 & shop ✖ (in certain areas) ✪

HOLDENBY
HOLDENBY HOUSE, GARDENS & FALCONRY CENTRE
NN6 8DJ (7m NW of Northampton, off A5199 or A428)
☎ 01604 770074 ▤ 01604 770962

Once the largest house in England, Holdenby was built to impress Elizabeth I. Subsequently the palace and prison of Charles I, it was destroyed by a Parliamentarian but restored in 1870 by the current owner's great-great-grandmother. Ring for details of special events.

Times: Open; Gardens & Falconry Centre Etr-Sep, Sun-Fri 2-6, (Closed Sat). House open BH Mon 1-6 ex May 3rd.

Fee: *Gardens & Falconry Centre £3 (ch £1.75, pen £2.50). House, Gardens & Falconry Centre £4 (ch £2).

🅿 ■ & (gravel paths with ramps) toilets for disabled shop (on leads)

KETTERING
ALFRED EAST GALLERY
Sheep St NN16 OAN
☎ 01536 534274 ▤ 01536 534370

National, regional and local art, craft and photography are displayed in frequently changing exhibition. A collection of paintings by Sir Alfred East RA and Thomas Cooper Gotch are on view by appointment, when not on display. There will also be a series of lunchtime concerts and talks on selected Fridays throughout the year. Ring for brochure.

Times: Open all year, Mon-Sat 9.30-5 (ex Wed closed until 10am & closed BHs)

Fee: Free.

🅿 (300yds) & shop ✖ (ex guide dogs)

LYVEDEN NEW BIELD
LYVEDEN NEW BIELD
PE8 5AT (4m SW Oundle via A427)
☎ 01832 205358

The 'New Bield', or 'new building', is an unfinished shell of a garden lodge dating from around 1600. It was designed by Sir Thomas Tresham to symbolise the Passion. The shape is a Greek cross, on which a frieze shows the cross, crown of thorns and other 'emblems of the Passion'. Even the building's dimensions are symbolic.

Times: Open daily. Party by arrangement with the custodian.

� ❧ *Details not confirmed for 2000*

NASSINGTON
PREBENDAL MANOR HOUSE
PE8 6QG
☎ 01780 782575

Dating from the early 13th century, this is the oldest manor in Northamptonshire. There's a 15th century dovecote and tithe barn museum, and the largest re-created medieval garden in Europe, boasting fishponds, herbers, arbours, turf seats, trellised herbers, medieval vegetable garden and vineyard.

Times: Open May-Jun & Sep Sun & Wed 2-5.30; Jul & Aug Sun, Wed & Thu 1-5.30. BH Mon (Closed Xmas)

Fee: *£3.80 (ch £1.20) Party 20+

🅿 ■ & (ramps) ✖ (guide dogs)

NORTHAMPTON

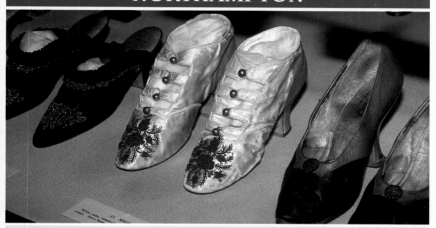

Northampton is in an attractive setting on the River Nene, and is one of the biggest market towns in England. It has a remarkable number of fine churches, notably the rare round church of the Holy Sepulchre, dating from 1110. Sadly, much of the town's architectural heritage was destroyed in the fire of 1675, and most of what is seen today is modern, but still of some interest. The town has a long association with the footwear industry. Shoe-makers in Northampton shod Cromwell's army in the Civil War, and during the Napoleonic Wars the population of the town tripled with the influx of workers set to making army boots.

NORTHAMPTON
CENTRAL MUSEUM & ART GALLERY
Guildhall Rd NN1 1DP (situated in the town centre)

☎ 01604 238548   📠 01604 238720

Reflecting Northampton's proud standing as Britain's boot and shoe capital, the museum houses a collection of boots and shoes which is considered one of the finest in the world. Other displays include the History of Northampton, Decorative Arts, the Art Gallery, and special temporary exhibitions.

Times: Open all year, Mon-Sat 10-5, Sun 2-5. (Closed 24 Dec from 12pm then 25, 26, 31 of Dec also 1 & 2 of Jan).

Fee: Free.

P (200 yds) & (wheelchairs available, large print catalogues) toilets for disabled shop ✶ (ex guide/assistance dogs)

ROCKINGHAM
ROCKINGHAM CASTLE
LE16 8TH (2m N of Corby, on A6003. Vehicle entrance S of junction A6003/A6116)

☎ 01536 770240

Set on a hill overlooking three counties, the castle was built by William the Conqueror. The site of the original keep is now a rose garden, but the outline of the curtain wall remains as do the foundations of the Norman hall, and the twin

towers of the gatehouse. A royal residence for 450 years, the castle was granted to Edward Watson in the 16th century, and the Watson family have lived there ever since.

Times: Open Etr Sun-18 Oct, Thu, Sun, BH Mon & following Tue (also Tues in Aug) 1-5. Grounds open at 11.30 am on Sun & BH Mon.

P ◖ & (may alight at entrance, ramped) shop *Details not confirmed for 2000*

RUSHTON
TRIANGULAR LODGE
NN14 1RP

☎ 01536 710761

Almost every detail of the lodge built by Sir Thomas Tresham in 1593 has a meaning. The building was designed as an expression of his staunch Roman Catholic faith; intriguing symbols of the Trinity and the Mass abound.

Times: Open Apr-1 Nov, daily 10-6 (or dusk if earlier).

Fee: £1.40 (ch 70p).

& ✶ ✿ *Details not confirmed for 2000*

🏛 STOKE BRUERNE

CANAL MUSEUM
NN12 7SE (4m S junc 15 M1)
☎ 01604 862229 🖂 01604 862229

The three storeys of a former corn mill have been converted to hold a marvellous collection of bygones from over two centuries of the canals. Among the hundreds of exhibits is the reconstructed interior of a traditional narrow boat, complete with furniture, crockery, brassware and traditional art. There are working narrowboats on show and the opportunity for a boat trip through the mile-long Blisworth Tunnel nearby.

Times: Open Nov-Etr, Tue-Sun 10-4; Etr-Oct daily 10-6. (Closed Xmas).

🅿 (charged) ♿ (ramps radar key) toilets for disabled shop ✖
Details not confirmed for 2000

🏛 SULGRAVE

SULGRAVE MANOR
Manor Rd OX17 2SD (off the B4525)
☎ 01295 760205 🖂 01295 768056

Home to George Washington's ancestors until 1656 when his great grandfather, John, emigrated to Virginia. Inside the house there are many relics of George Washington. Though much of the house is a 20th-century restoration, original parts include the porch (with a carving of the original American flag), a screens passage, the great hall and the great Chamber. There is a new set of courtyard buildings funded by the Lottery Heritage Fund and including a traditionally timbered, galleried hall. Phone for details of special events.

Times: Open Apr-Oct, Mon-Fri (ex Wed) 2-5.30, Sat, Sun & BH 10.30-1 & 2-5.30; Mar, Nov & Dec, Sat & Sun only 10.30-1 & 2-4.30; Other times by appointment. (Closed 25-26 Dec & Jan also Apr 8-9).

Fee: *£3.75 (ch £2). Party 12+. Special event days £4.50 (ch £2.25). Family ticket £12. Party 12+.

🅿 ☕ ✖ licensed ♿ (induction loop available in shop or ticket office) toilets for disabled shop garden centre ✖ (ex guide & outside on leads)

Northumberland

Northumberland is a county of wide open spaces taking in the Northumberland National Park to the northwest, with miles of moorland around Hadrian's Wall rising to the Cheviot Hills on the Scottish border, and incorporating great swathes of Forestry Commission planted conifers.

The Pennine Way walking trail runs through the park from Hadrian's Wall to The Cheviot, the National Park's highest peak at 2,674 feet/(815 metres), and crosses the border into Scotland. Towards the east, the park changes character in the gentle valleys of the rivers Coquet, Redesdale and North Tyne.

Hadrian's Wall, the Romans' astonishing feat of engineering and an enduring legacy, runs for 73 miles across northern England, and there are several well preserved forts, including Housestead's, one of the most popular sites on the wall.

The long, low lying coastline of Northumberland, designated an Area of Outstanding Natural Beauty, is dotted with a series of magnificent castles, Warworth, Alnwick, Bamburgh, plus the remains of the 12th-century castle at Berwick-upon-Tweed and the impressive Elizabethan ramparts. Berwick is England's northernmost town, held alternately by the Scottish and English over centuries of bitter struggle.

The county town is Morpeth, which is the administrative centre, though this is disputed to some extent by Alnwick, the seat of the Duke of Northumberland. The attractive market town of Hexham warrants some exploration, with its Abbey, Moot Hall and other medieval remains, and also makes a good base for visiting Hadrian's Wall.

EVENTS & FESTIVALS

May
1st Riding the Bounds, Berwick-upon-Tweed
21st (provisional) Border Marches, Berwick-upon-Tweed (walks along the Tweed Valley)

June
tbc Hexham Jazz Festival
tbc North Pennines Festival, various locations

August
5th-12th International Music & Dance Festival

October
7th-22nd Northumberland Traditional Music Festival, events all over the county

September
2nd-3rd Military Tattoo, Barracks, Berwick-upon-Tweed, (evening shows)

NORTHUMBERLAND NATIONAL PARK

Top: Hadrian's Wall

ALNWICK
ALNWICK CASTLE
NE66 1NQ
☎ 01665 510777 & 603942 wknds
🖳 01665 510876

Described by the Victorians as 'The Windsor of the North', Alnwick Castle is the main seat of the Duke of Northumberland whose family, the Percys, have lived here since 1309. The stern, medieval exterior belies the treasure house within, furnished in palatial Renaissance style, with paintings by Titian, Van Dyck and Canaletto, fine furniture and an exquisite collection of Meissen china. The Regiment Museum of Royal Northumberland Fusiliers is housed in the Abbot's Tower of the Castle. Other attractions include the Percy State Coach, the dungeon, the gun terrace and the grounds, which offer peaceful walks and superb views over the surrounding countryside. Please ring for details of special events.

Times: Open Etr-Sep, daily ex Fri, 11-5 (House noon-5). Last admission 4.15. Open BH's incl Good Fri.

🅿 🍴 ♿ (Castle lift for those able to walk a little) toilets for disabled shop ✖ *Details not confirmed for 2000* 🦜

BAMBURGH
BAMBURGH CASTLE
NE69 7DF (A1 Belford by-pass, E on B1342 to Bamburgh)
☎ 01668 214515 & 214208
🖳 01668 214060

Rising dramatically from a rocky outcrop, Bamburgh Castle is a huge, square Norman castle. Restored in the 19th century, it has an impressive hall and an armoury with a large collection of armour from the Tower of London. Guide services are available.

Times: Open Apr-Oct, daily 11-5 (last admission 4.30pm). Other times by prior arrangement.

Fee: *£4 (ch £1.50 & pen £3). Party 15+.

🅿 (charged) 🍴 ♿ shop ✖

BARDON MILL
VINDOLANDA (CHESTERHOLM)
Vindolanda Trust NE47 7JN (signposted from A69 or B6318)
☎ 01434 344277 🖳 01434 344060

Vindolanda was a Roman fort and frontier town. It was started well before Hadrian's Wall, and became a base for 500 soldiers. The civilian settlement lay just west of the fort and has been excavated. The excellent museum in the country house of Chesterholm nearby has displays and reconstructions. There are also formal gardens, and an open-air museum with Roman Temple, shop, house and Northumbrian croft has opened.

Times: Open daily from 10am, all facilities mid Feb-mid Nov.

Fee: *£3.50 (ch £2.50, student & pen £2.90, free admission for disabled). Party.

🅿 🍴 ♿ toilets for disabled shop ✖ (ex guide dogs) 🦜

BELSAY
BELSAY HALL, CASTLE AND GARDENS
NE20 0DX (on A696)
☎ 01661 881636

Belsay Castle, with its splendid turrets and battlements, dates from 1370 and was the home of the Middleton family, until they built the Jacobean manor house beside it, and then the magnificent Grecian-style Hall. There are also wonderful gardens.

Times: Open all year, daily Apr-Oct 10-6 (or dusk if earlier); Nov-Mar, daily 10-4 (or dusk if earlier). Closed 24-26 Dec & 1 Jan.

Fee: £3.80 (ch £1.90).

🅿 ✖ ♿ toilets for disabled shop ✖ (in certain areas) ⬚

BERWICK-UPON-TWEED
BERWICK BARRACKS, MUSEUM & ART GALLERY
(on the Parade, off Church St, Berwick town centre)
☎ 01289 304493

Enclosed by its Elizabethan ramparts, Berwick is an outstanding example of a fortified town, and the barracks have changed little since 1721. The museum covers 200 years of military and regimental history, and the Art Gallery houses the important Burrell collection.

Times: Open all year, Apr-Oct daily 10-6 (or dusk if earlier); Nov-Mar Wed-Sun 10-4, closed 1-2pm.

Fee: £2.60 (ch £1.30).

🅿 ♿ shop ✖ ⬚

PAXTON HOUSE
TD15 1SZ (3m from A1 Berwick-upon-Tweed bypass on B6461 Kelso road)
☎ 01289 386291 🖳 01289 386660

Built in 1758 for the Laird of Wedderburn, the house is a fine example of neo-Palladian architecture. Much of the house is furnished by Chippendale and there is a large picture gallery. The house is set in 80 acres beside the River Tweed, and the grounds include an adventure playground. Please phone for details of special events.

Times: Open daily from Apr-Oct, House & gallery 11-5 (last tour of house 4.15pm). Grounds 10-sunset.

Fee: *House &.Grounds £4.50 (adult concessions £4.25). Family ticket £12.

🅿 ✖ licensed ♿ (lifts to main areas of house, parking close to reception) toilets for disabled shop garden centre ✖ (ex guide dogs) 🦜

CAMBO
WALLINGTON HOUSE WALLED GARDEN & GROUNDS
NE61 4AR (6m NW of Belsay)
☎ 01670 774283

The house is set in a great moorland estate of over 12,000 acres. It features delicate plasterwork, Capability Brown gardens and William Bell Scott murals. In the 19th century Ruskin and other writers and artists came here as guests. Please contact for details of special events, which will include open air concerts and theatre productions.

Times: Open: House Apr-Sep, daily (ex Tue) 1-5.30, Oct daily (ex Tue) 1-4.30. Last admission half hour before closing. Walled garden Apr-Oct, daily 10-7 or dusk; Nov-Mar, 10-4 or dusk if earlier. Grounds open all year.

Fee: *House, walled garden & grounds: £5.20, family ticket £13. Walled gardens & grounds only: £3.80. Party.

🅿 ✖ ♿ (Vessa Ventura scooter, braille guide) toilets for disabled shop garden centre ✈ (ex on lead in grounds) ♨

⛫ CARRAWBROUGH
ROMAN WALL (MITHRAIC TEMPLE)
(on B6318)

This fascinating Mithraic temple was uncovered by a farmer in 1949. Its three altars to the war god, Mithras, date from the third century AD, and are now in the Museum of Antiquities in Newcastle, but there are copies on site.

Times: Open any reasonable time.

🅿 ⌗

⛫ CHILLINGHAM
CHILLINGHAM CASTLE
NE66 5NJ (signposted from A1 & A697)
☎ 01668 215359 & 215390
🗎 01668 215463

This remarkable castle with its alarming dungeons and torture chamber is now undergoing restoration. Romantic grounds laid out by Sir Jeffry Wyatville command views over the Cheviots and include topiary gardens and woodland walks. Weddings, private functions and meals can be arranged, and fishing is available. Please ring for details of special events.

Times: Open Etr wknd & May-Sep, daily (ex closed Tue in May, Jun & Sep) 12-5 (Last admission 5.30pm). Other times by prior arrangement.

Fee: *£4.80 (ch free with paying adult max 5, pen £3.80). Party 10+.

🅿 🍺 ✖ licensed ♿ shop ✈

⛫ CORBRIDGE
CORBRIDGE ROMAN STATION
(0.5m NW on minor road - signposted)
☎ 01434 632349

The remains of Roman 'Corstopitum', built around AD210, include granaries, portico

columns and the probable site of legionary headquarters.

Times: Open all year, Apr-Oct, daily 10-6 (or dusk if earlier in Oct); Nov-Mar, Wed-Sun 10-4 (or dusk if earlier, closed 1-2pm). (Closed 24-26 Dec & 1 Jan).

Fee: £2.80 (ch £1.40).

🅿 ♿ ✈ (in certain areas) ⌗

⛫ EMBLETON
DUNSTANBURGH CASTLE
NE66 3XF (1.5m E on footpaths from Craster or Embleton)
☎ 01665 576231

The skeletal ruins of the huge castle, partly built by John of Gaunt, stand on cliffs 100ft above the North Sea. Already a ruin by Tudor times, its setting has inspired many paintings, including three by Turner.

Times: Open all year, Apr-Oct, daily 10-6 (or dusk if earlier); 10-4; Nov-Mar, Wed-Sun 10-4 (or dusk if earlier). Closed 24-26 Dec & 1 Jan.

Fee: £1.80 (ch 90p).

🅿 (charged) ⌗

⛫ FORD
HEATHERSLAW CORN MILL
TD12 4TJ (signposted from A697 & A1 from Berwick-upon-Tweed)
☎ 01890 820338 🗎 01890 820384

This beautifully restored 19th-century water-powered double corn mill is in daily use, and you can see local wheat milled by traditional methods using the original machinery. Everything is visible, from the huge wooden water wheel to the slowly grinding burr stone.

Times: Open Mar-Sep 10-6; Oct-Nov 10-5. Winter by arrangement.

🅿 🍺 ♿ (Braille guide plus tactile facility) shop ✈ *Details not confirmed for 2000*

LADY WATERFORD HALL
(signposted from A697, N of Worcester & A1 Berwick-upon-Tweed)
☎ 01890 820224 🗎 01890 820384

Commissioned as a school in 1860 by Louisa Anne, Marchioness of Waterford, this beautiful Victorian building was decorated with murals of favourite Bible stories. Lady Waterford spent 21

contd.

THE ISLANDS OF NORTHUMBERLAND

The rocky Farne islands are now owned by the National Trust, and provide a sanctuary for many species of seabirds and grey seals. Points of interest are the chapel on the site of the hermitage at St Cuthbert on Inner Farne, and the Longstone lighthouse where Grace Darling made her dramatic rescue of shipwrecked sailors on 7 September 1838.

Holy Island, or Lindisfarne, north of the Farnes, is connected to the mainland by a causeway exposed only at low tide. St Aiden founded a monastery here in 635 as a centre for the Celtic Church. The monks were driven from the island by Vikings in 875, but they returned in 1082, rebuilt the priory, and christened it 'Holy Island'.

years painting these outstanding murals, choosing the children of the village and their parents as models, many of her smaller works are also displayed in the gallery.
Times: Open Mar-Nov, daily 10.30-12.30 & 1.30-5.30. Open by appointment in winter.
Fee: £1.50 (ch 12 50p, pen £1), Party 11+.
P & shop

﹏ HOUSESTEADS
HOUSESTEADS ROMAN FORT
Bardon Mills (2.5m NE of Bardon Mill on B6318)
☎ 01434 344363

Housesteads was the Roman fort of *Vercovicium*. It has a spectacular site on Hadrian's Wall, and is also one of the best preserved Roman forts. It covers five acres, including the only known Roman hospital in Britain, and a 24-seater latrine with a flushing tank.
Times: Open all year, Apr-Oct, daily 10-6; Nov-Mar, daily 10-4. (Closed 24-26 Dec & 1 Jan).
Fee: £2.80 (ch £1.40)
P (0.25m from fort) shop ✖ ♯ ⚘

﹏ LONGFRAMLINGTON
BRINKBURN PRIORY
NE65 8AS (off B6344)
☎ 01665 570628

The priory was founded in 1135 for Augustinian canons, and stands on a bend of the River

Coquet. After the Dissolution of the Monasteries it fell into disrepair, but was restored in 1858.
Times: Open Apr-Oct, daily 10-6.
Fee: £1.60 (ch 80p).
P ✖ (in certain areas) ♯

﹏ NORHAM
CASTLE
TD15 2JY
☎ 01289 382329

One of the strongest Border fortresses, this castle has a fine Norman keep and overlooks the River Tweed.
Times: Open Apr-Oct, 10-6 (or dusk if earlier).
Fee: £1.80 (ch 90p).
P & ✖ ♯

﹏ PRUDHOE
PRUDHOE CASTLE
NE42 6NA (on minor road off A695)
☎ 01661 833459

Standing on the River Tyne, this medieval castle was the stronghold of the d'Umfravelles and Percys. The keep stands in the inner bailey and a notable gatehouse guards the outer bailey. Access is to the Pele Yard only.
Times: Open Apr-Oct, daily 10-6 (or dusk if earlier).
Fee: £1.80 (ch 90p).
P shop ✖ (in certain areas) ♯

⛏ ROTHBURY
CRAGSIDE HOUSE, GARDEN & GROUNDS
(1m N of Rothbury, off A697 & B6341)
☎ 01669 620333 & 620150

This splendid Victorian masterpiece was designed by the architect Richard Norman Shaw. The huge drawing room has a curved glass roof and 10-ton marble-lined inglenook. This was the first house to be lit by electricity generated by water-power. The grounds were planted with seven million trees, streams were diverted and lakes created.

Times: Open, Grounds:Apr-Oct, daily ex Mon 10.30-7; Weekends & selected days in Nov & Dec 10.30-4. House: daily (ex Mon, open BH Mon's) 1-5.30, last admission 4.45pm. Gardens Apr-Oct, daily ex Mon 10.30-6.30. Weekends & selected days in Nov & Dec. The Grounds, Visitor Centre & Garden will be open Mons in June, but the house will be closed.

Fee: *House, Garden & Grounds & Visitor Centre £6.20 Garden, Grounds & Visitor Centre only £3.95. Family ticket for House, Garden & Grounds £15.50. Family ticket for Garden & Grounds £9.85. Party.

🅿 💺 ✗ licensed ♿ fishing pier braille guide toilets for disabled shop ✖ (ex in grounds on lead) ♨

⛏ WALWICK
CHESTERS ROMAN FORT & MUSEUM
(0.5m W of Chollerford on B6318)
☎ 01434 681379

One of the Roman forts on Hadrian's Wall is now in the park of Chesters, an 18th-century mansion. The fort named *Cilurnum* housed 500 soldiers and covered nearly 6 acres. Excavations have shown that it was destroyed and rebuilt three times. Evidence of an aqueduct and substantial remains of a bath house show that the standard of living was high.

Times: Open all year, Apr-Sep, daily 9.30-6; Oct, daily 10-dusk; Nov-Mar, daily 10-4 (or dusk if earlier). Closed 24-26 Dec & 1 Jan.

Fee: £2.80 (ch £1.40).

🅿 💺 ♿ shop ✖ (in certain areas) ⚏

⛏ WARKWORTH
WARKWORTH CASTLE
NE66 OUJ
☎ 01665 711423

The castle dominates Warkworth from its site on the bands of the River Coquet. It makes a splendid ruin, with its keep and curtain wall. Once home of the turbulent Percy family, one of whose members, Sir Henry Percy (Harry Hotspur) was immortalised by Shakespeare in *Henry IV*. Nearby is the 14th-century bridge over the river, now only open to pedestrians.

Times: Open all year, Apr-Oct, daily 10-6 (or dusk if earlier); Nov-Mar, daily 10-4 (or dusk if earlier, closed 1-2pm). Closed 24-26 Dec & 1 Jan.

Fee: £2.40 (ch £1.20).

🅿 ♿ ✖ (in certain areas) ⚏

WARKWORTH HERMITAGE
☎ 01665 711423

Upstream from Warkworth Castle is the Hermitage, a refuge dug into the rockface by a 14th-century hermit. It consists of a chapel and two living chambers. Nearby is Coquet Island, which was also the home of hermit monks.

Times: Open Apr-Sep, Wed, Sun & BH's 11-5.

🅿 ♿ ✖ ⚏ *Details not confirmed for 2000*

Nottinghamshire

The inland county of Nottinghamshire in eastern England is strongly associated with the legend of Robin Hood, though Robin's territory, the former royal hunting ground of Sherwood Forest, has been somewhat tamed since his outlaw days.

The county is divided between the old coalfields north of the Nottingham, the commuter belt of the Wolds to the south, and the area of most interest, that of Sherwood Forest and the great country estates known as the 'Dukeries'. One of these, Clumber Park is now owned by the National Trust.

The traditional industry of Nottinghamshire, alongside agriculture, was coal mining, though this has declined in recent years. It is also an oil producing area, and during World War II produced the only oil out of reach of the U-Boats.

D H Lawrence was a Nottinghamshire man, the son of a miner and former schoolteacher. He grew up in poverty, and his book *Sons and Lovers* reflects the experiences of his early years. There is a D H Lawrence commemorative walk from his home at Eastwood to Old Brinsley Colliery.

Other towns of note are the river port and market town of Newark, which hosts a major antiques fair six times a year, and Southwell, known for its medieval minster with its exquisite carving depicting the foliage of Sherwood Forest.

EVENTS & FESTIVALS

December 99
29th-31st: Millennium Festival
31st-3rd Jan: Sound & Light Festival

January
1st-3rd (provisional): Millennium Festival, Nottingham

May
1st or 8th: May Day, Brewhouse Yard
13th: Lord Mayor's Day

June
18th: A Time to Sing, Nottingham
19th-24th: Nottingham Open 2000

July
1st: Wollaton Community Festival, Nottingham

August
5th-6th: Riverside Festival, Nottingham
19th-20th: Carnival 2000, Nottingham

September
17th: Royal British Legion Celebrations, Nottingham

October
5th-7th: Goose Fair 2000, Nottingham
26th-29th: Robin Hood Pageant, Nottingham Castle

Nov
NOW2000 Dance to the Music of Time Festival

Top: Sherwood Forest

EASTWOOD

Durban House Heritage Centre

Mansfield Rd NG16 3DZ (signed on A610)
☎ 01773 717353 📠 01773 713509

Tread in the footsteps of D H Lawrence and go on a fascinating journey through the development of his hometown - Eastwood - exploring the landscape, people and their influence on the writer in an exciting interactive exhibition.

Times: Open all year, Apr-Oct, daily 10-5; Nov-Mar, daily 10-4. Closed 24 Dec-1 Jan.
Fee: *£1.75 (concessions £1)
(lift to exhibition) toilets for disabled shop (ex guide dogs)

EDWINSTOWE

Sherwood Forest Country Park & Visitor Centre

NG21 9HN (on B6034 N of village between A6075 and A616)
☎ 01623 823202 & 824490
📠 01623 823202

At the heart of the Robin Hood legend is Sherwood Forest, scene of many an outlaw tale. Today it is a country park and visitor centre with 450 acres of ancient oaks and shimmering silver birches. Waymarked pathways guide you through the forest. A year round programme of events and activities, including the spectacular Robin Hood Festival, bring the natural beauty and colourful history of the forest to life.

Times: Country Park: open daily dawn to dusk. Visitor Centre: open daily 10.30-5 (4.30pm Nov-Mar)
Fee: *Admission free but car parking charges apply at wknds & BHs Easter-Dec, daily during summer school holidays.
toilets for disabled shop

FARNSFIELD

White Post Modern Farm Centre

NG22 8HL (1m W)
☎ 01623 882977 & 882026
📠 01623 883499

This award-winning working farm gives an introduction to a variety of modern farming methods. It explains how farms work, with exhibits such as llamas, deer, pigs, cows, snails, quails, snakes and fish. There's lots to see indoors, including the owl houses, incubator room, mousetown and a reptile house.

Times: Open all year, Mon-Fri 10-5. Wknds & BH's 10-6.
Fee: *£4.50 (ch 4-16 £3.50, under 4 free, pen & people with special needs £3.50). Party 10+.
(sign language, free hire wheelchairs, book if more than 6) toilets for disabled shop (ex guide dogs)

NEWARK-ON-TRENT

Newark Air Museum

The Airfield, Winthorpe NG24 2NY (easy access from A1, A46, A17 & Newark relief road, follow tourism signs)
☎ 01636 707170 📠 01636 707170

A diverse collection of transport, training and reconnaisance aircraft, jet fighters, bombers and helicopters, now numbering more than forty. An Undercover Aircraft Display Hall and an Engine Hall make the museum an all-weather attraction. Everything is displayed around a WWII airfield. Various special events are planned, please ring for details.

Times: Open all year, Mar-Sep, Mon-Fri 10-5, Sat & Sun 10-6; Oct-Feb, daily 10-4. (Closed 24-26 Dec). Other times by appointment.
Fee: *£3.75 (ch £2.25, pen £3). Family ticket £10. Party 10+.
toilets for disabled shop

NOTTINGHAM

Nottingham is situated on the River Trent, and although Saxons, Danes and Normans have held sway here, it was the industrial revolution that made it a flourishing centre of commerce and one of England's biggest cities. Many traditional products are still made, such as cigarettes, bicycles and lace. Nottingham Castle, which features so prominently in tales of Robin Hood's adventures, is alas no more. Falling from grace following the Civil War, it was replaced in the 17th century by the Duke of Newcastle's palace, which in turn was gutted by Reform Bill rioters in 1831. (The Duke was opposed to parliamentary reform.) These days the castle houses a museum and art gallery.

NEWSTEAD

NEWSTEAD ABBEY

NG15 8GE (off A60)

☎ 01623 455900 ▤ 01623 455904

This beautiful house is best known as the home of poet Lord Byron. Visitors can see Byron's own rooms, mementoes of the poet and other splendidly decorated rooms. The grounds of over 300 acres include waterfalls, ponds, water gardens and Japanese gardens. Special events include outdoor theatre and opera, Christmas events and Ghost Tours. Please phone for details.

Times: Open: Grounds all year, daily 9-dusk (ex last Fri in Nov); House Apr-Sep, daily 12-5. Last admission 4pm

Fee: *House & Grounds £4 (ch £1.50, concessions £2). Grounds only £2 (concessions £1.50). Subject to change.

🅿 ⬛✖ licensed ♿ (audio tour for visually impaired, mobility car for loan) toilets for disabled shop ✖ (ex guide dogs or in garden)

NOTTINGHAM

BREWHOUSE YARD MUSEUM

Castle Boulevard NG7 1FB

☎ 0115 915 3600 & 0115 915 3640

▤ 0115 915 3601

Housed in 17th-century cottages, the museum depicts everyday life in Nottingham over the past 300 years. Locally made or used objects are shown in a mixture of period rooms, re-created shops and displays. Caves behind the houses are also part of the museum.

Times: Open all year 10-4. (Closed Fridays Nov-Mar & 25-26 Dec).

Fee: *Free Mon-Fri but donations appreciated. Weekends & BH's £1.50 (concessions 80p). Family ticket £3.80.

🅿 (100yds) ♿ (mobility car from Castle, wheelchairs available) toilets for disabled shop ✖ ▥

CASTLE MUSEUM

NG1 6EL

☎ 0115 915 3700 ▤ 0115 915 3653

This 17th-century building is both museum and art gallery, with major temporary exhibitions as well as the permanent collections. There is a 'Story of Nottingham' exhibition, and a guided tour of the underground passages most afternoons.

Times: Open all year, daily 10-5. (ex Fri Nov-Feb 12-5) Grounds 8-dusk. (Closed 25 & 26 Dec).

Fee: *Mon-Fri free, wknds & BH's £2 (ch & concessions £1). Family ticket £5.

🅿 (400yds) ⬛✖ licensed ♿ (chair lift, mobility car available) toilets for disabled shop ✖

THE GALLERIES OF JUSTICE
The Shire Hall, High Pavement, Lace Market
NG1 1HN
☎ 0115 952 0555 ▤ 0115 952 0557

There are two 19th-century prisons, complete
with cells and bath house, a transportation
gallery, and exercise yard. Costumed interpreters
help bring the scene to life. Visitors can attend a
modern crime scene and assess the evidence
through the use of forensic science and state-of-
the-art computers.

Times: Open Tue-Sun & BH Mon's 10-5. Last admission one
hour before closing. (Closed 24-26 Dec & 1 Jan).
Fee: *£7.95 (ch £4.95, concesssions £6.95). Family ticket
£23.95. Ticket vaild for one visit to three exhibitions for 12
months from date of purchase.
🅿 ✖ licensed & (two lifts with braille control, induction
loop) toilets for disabled shop ✖ (ex guide dogs) ▼

THE LACE CENTRE
Severns Building, Castle Rd NG1 6AA (follow
signs for the Castle, situated opposite the Robin
Hood statue on Castle road)
☎ 0115 941 3539

Exquisite Nottingham lace fills this small
building, with panels also hanging from the
beamed ceiling. There are weekly
demonstrations of lace-making on Thursday

afternoons from Easter to October. Telephone for
details.

Times: Open all year, Jan-Mar, daily 10-4; Apr-Nov, 10-5.
Every Sun 11am-4pm. (Closed Xmas & New Year)
Fee: Free.
🅿 (100yds) (metered street parking) & shop

MUSEUM OF COSTUME & TEXTILES
43-51 Castle Gate NG1 6AF
☎ 0115 915 3500 ▤ 0115 915 3653

Costume from 1730 to 1960 is displayed in
appropriate room settings. Other rooms contain
embroidery, dress accessories, the Lord
Middleton collection and map tapestries. Knitted,
woven and printed textiles are also on show,
together with embroidery from Europe and Asia.
Times: Open all year, Wed-Sun & BHs 10-4.
Fee: Free.
🅿 (200yds) & shop ✖

MUSEUM OF NOTTINGHAM LACE
3-5 High Pavement, The Lace Market NG1 1HF
(Follow signs for Lace Market Parking from the
city centre)
☎ 0115 989 7365 ▤ 0115 989 7301

The atmospheric lace market is the setting for
this fascinating museum, which has working
machinery and audio tours. From April to June

contd.

2000 there will be an exhibition of CDs decorated by international lacemakers.
Times: Open daily 10-5 (Closed 25-26 Dec & New Year's Day). Last admission 4pm.
Fee: *£2.95 (ch 5-16 £1.95, concessions £2.50) Party 12+. Lace Market Audio Tour £1.95 (deposit required for equipment)
P (100yds) 🅿 ♿ (counters at lower level, lift to upper floor) shop ✖ (ex guide dogs) 🐟

NATURAL HISTORY MUSEUM
Wollaton Hall, Wollaton NG8 2AE (3m W, off A52 & A6514)
☎ 0115 915 3911   🖹 0115 915 3932

Standing in a large deer park, this imposing Elizabethan mansion houses a wide variety of displays, including birds, mammals, fossils and minerals.
Times: Open all year, daily 11-4 (Closed Fri Nov-Mar & 25-26 Dec).
Fee: *Weekdays free, wknds & BH £1.50 (concessions 80p) Family £3.80.
P (charged) ♿ (special handling exhibition) toilets for disabled shop ✖

NOTTINGHAM INDUSTRIAL MUSEUM
Courtyard Buildings, Wollaton Park NG8 2AE (3m W off A609 Ilkeston Rd)
☎ 0115 915 3910   🖹 0115 915 3941

Nottingham's industrial history is on display in this 18th-century stable block. Lace, hosiery, pharmaceuticals (Nottingham was the home of the founder of Boots the Chemists), tobacco and much else are among the exhibits. There are a beam and other steam engines, regularly in steam. Please contact the museum for programmes of events.
Times: Open all year, Apr-Sep, Mon-Sat 10-4.30, Sun 1-4.30; Oct-Mar, Thu-Sat 10-4.30, Sun 1.30-4.30.
P (charged) ♿ (hand & powered wheelchairs available) toilets for disabled shop ✖ *Details not confirmed for 2000*

TALES OF ROBIN HOOD
30-38 Maid Marian Way NG1 6GF
☎ 0115 948 3284   🖹 0115 950 1536

Special effects and adventure cars transport the visitor back to medieval Nottingham and Sherwood Forest, legendary home of Robin Hood. There is commentary in seven languages via portable CD players. Medieval banquets and other events take place throughout the year.
Times: Open all year, daily 10-6 (last admission 4.30pm). (Closed 25-26 Dec).
Fee: *£4.75 (ch £3.75, pen & students £4.25). Party.
P (NCP 200 yds) 🅿 ♿ (specially adapted 'car') toilets for disabled shop ✖ 🐟

🏛 OLLERTON
RUFFORD ABBEY AND COUNTRY PARK
NG22 9DF (2m S of Ollerton, adjacent to A614)
☎ 01623 822944

At the heart of the wooded country park stand the remains of a 12th-century Cistercian Abbey, housing an exhibition on the life of a monk at Rufford. Many species of wildlife can be seen on the lake, and there are lovely formal gardens, with sculpture and Britain's first centre for studio ceramics.
Times: Open all year, Abbey and Orangery, Etr-Sep daily 10.30-5; Oct-Etr daily 11-4. Craft centre, gallery & ceramics centre, Mar-Dec daily 10.30-5; Jan-Feb daily 11-4.
Fee: *Parking charge Etr-Oct wknds & BH's, daily (school summer holidays) £1.50. Coaches, minibuses (with more than 12 seats), disabled badge holders free.
P (charged) 🅿 ✖ licensed ♿ (lift to craft centre) toilets for disabled shop garden centre ✖ (ex park)
See advert under Nottingham.

🏛 SUTTON-CUM-LOUND
WETLANDS WATERFOWL RESERVE & EXOTIC BIRD PARK
Off Loundlow Rd DN22 8SB (Signposted on Retford to Bawtry Road A638)
☎ 01777 818099

The Reserve is a 32-acre site for both wild and exotic waterfowl. Visitors can see a collection of birds of prey, parrots, geese, ducks, and wigeon among others. There are also many small mammals and farm and wild animals, including llamas, wallabies and emus.
Times: Open all year, daily 10-5.30 (or dusk whichever is earlier). (Closed 25 Dec).
Fee: *£2 (ch & pen £1.25).
P 🅿 ♿ (wheelchair available) shop ✖ (ex guide dogs)

🏛 WORKSOP
CLUMBER PARK
The Estate Office, Clumber Park S80 3AZ (4.5m SE of Worksop, signposted from A1)
☎ 01909 476653   🖹 01909 500721

An impressive, landscaped park, laid out by 'Capability' Brown. An outstanding feature is the lake running through the park, a haven for wildfowl, covering an area of 80 acres. The park is a mixture of woodland, open grass and heathland. Please telephone for details of events.
Times: Open all year, daily during daylight hours. Walled Garden, Victorian Apiary, Fig House, Vineries & Garden Tools exhibition Apr-Sep Sat, Sun & BH Mon 10-5. last admission 4.30pm. Conservation centre Apr-27 Sep Sat, Sun & BH Mon 1-5. Telephone for Chapel opening times)
P (charged) 🅿 ✖ licensed ♿ (powered self-drive vehicle available if booked) toilets for disabled shop garden centre 🐾
Details not confirmed for 2000

Oxfordshire

The city of Oxford, situated on the River Thames (known locally as the Isis), is renowned for its ancient buildings and 'dreaming spires'. It is home to Britain's oldest university, established during the 12th century, with a collegiate system dating from the 13th.

Other well-known towns include Banbury, though the Banbury Cross of nursery rhyme fame was destroyed in 1602 by the Puritans, to be replaced in 1858. Henley-on-Thames is home to the Royal Regatta, an amateur rowing competition of world renown and a highlight of the social calendar. Witney is a blanket-making town, using two important local resources, wool, and power from the River Windrush.

The Cotswold Hills extend over the border from Gloucestershire into the east of Oxfordshire, dotted with pretty towns and villages built of mellow Cotswold stone hewn from the hillsides. These settlements prospered from the sheep who grazed the hills, producing wool for the flourishing medieval wool trade. Great churches are a feature of the area, an enduring symbol of medieval wool wealth.

To the southeast of the county are the Chiltern Hills, chalk downlands excellent for walking. The Chilterns range from the Berkshire Downs to the East Anglian Ridge, passing through Oxfordshire and reaching their highest point at Coombe Hill, near Wendover in Buckinghamshire, at 852 ft (260m).

Southwest of Oxford is the Vale of the White Horse, a prehistoric figure, 374 ft (114m) long, carved into the chalk, some 18 miles (29km) from the city.

EVENTS & FESTIVALS

March
tbc Poohsticks World Championships, Little Wittenham

April
29th-1st May Blenheim Craft Fair, Woodstock

May
29th April-1st Blenheim Craft Fair, Woodstock
1st May Morning Choir, Magdalen College, Oxford
12th-14th Oxford Balloon Fiesta
tbc Lord Mayor's Parade

June
28th-2nd July Henley Regatta, Henley-on-Thames

July
28th June-2nd Henley Regatta, Henley-on-Thames
tbc Banbury Carnival
17th-21st Swan Upping, River Thames (Sunbury-Abingdon)

September
4th-5th St Giles Fair, Oxford
7th-10th Blenheim International Horse Trials
9th (provisional) Florence Park Open Day
21st Thame Agricultural Show

October
tbc Abingdon Fair

Top: Clifton Hampton on the River Thames

⚓ BURFORD
COTSWOLD WILDLIFE PARK
OX18 4JW (2m S of Burford on the A361)
☎ 01993 823006 ▯ 01993 823807

This 180-acre landscaped zoological park, surrounding a listed Gothic-style manor house, has a varied collection of animals from all over the world. There's lots to do, with an adventure playground, a children's farmyard, and train rides during the summer. Also during the summer there are Snake Days and bird of prey demonstrations (weekends & BHs). Penguin feeding times 11am and 4pm daily (except Fridays). Car Rallies & Snake Awareness Days, please phone for details.

Times: Open all year, daily (ex 25 Dec) from 10am, last admission 5pm or dusk if earlier.

Fee: *£5.80 (ch 3-16 & pen £3.80). Party 20+

🅿 ☕ ✗ licensed ♿ (parking, free hire of wheelchairs) toilets for disabled shop 🛍

⚓ BUSCOT
BUSCOT PARK
SN7 8BU (off A417)
☎ 01367 240786 ▯ 01367 241794

A highlight of this 18th century house is the Faringdon Collection which includes work by Reynolds, Gainsborough, Rembrandt, Murillo, several of the Pre-Raphaelites, and some 20th-century artists. The charming formal water gardens were laid out by Harold Peto in the early 20th century. There is also an attractively planted kitchen garden, with unusual concentric walls.

Times: House & grounds Apr-Sep (incl Good Fri, Etr Sat & Sun) Wed-Fri 2-6. Also every 2nd & 4th wknd in each month 2-6 (last admission to house 5.30pm). Grounds as House but also Mon & Tue 2-6 (ex BH Mon)

🅿 ☕ ✗ 🐾 *Details not confirmed for 2000*

⚓ DEDDINGTON
DEDDINGTON CASTLE
OX5 4TE (S of B4031 on E side of Deddington)

The large earthworks of the outer and inner baileys can be seen; the remains of 12th-century castle buildings have been excavated, but they are not now visible.

Times: Open any reasonable time.
⌗

⚓ DIDCOT
DIDCOT RAILWAY CENTRE
OX11 7NJ (on A4130 at Didcot Parkway Station)
☎ 01235 817200 ▯ 01235 510621

The biggest collection anywhere of Great Western Railway stock is housed in the GWR engine shed, including 20 steam locomotives, a diesel railcar, and a large amount of passenger and freight rolling stock. A typical GWR station has been re-created and a section of Brunel's original broad gauge track has been relaid. Phone for details of special events.

Times: Open all year Apr-1 Oct, daily 10-5; Nov-Feb Sat & Sun 10-4. Steam days first & last Sun of each month from Mar, BH's & Wed Jul-Aug.

Fee: *£4-£8 depending on event (ch £3-£6.50, over 60's £3.50-£5.50).

🅿 (100yds) ☕ ♿ (advance notice recommended) toilets for disabled shop 🛍

⚓ GREAT COXWELL
GREAT COXWELL BARN
(2m SW of Faringdon between A420 & B4019)
☎ 01793 762209

William Morris said that the barn was `as noble as a cathedral'. It is a 13th-century stone-built tithe barn, 152ft long and 44ft wide, with a beautifully crafted framework of timbers supporting the lofty stone roof. The barn was built for the Cistercians.

Times: Open all reasonable times. For details please contact Estate Office.

🅿 🐾 *Details not confirmed for 2000*

⛪ HENLEY-ON-THAMES
GREYS COURT
Rotherfield Greys RG9 4PG (3m W)
☎ 01491 628529

This appealing house has evolved over hundreds
of years. The present gabled building has a pre-
medieval kitchen but dates mainly from the 16th
century. Additions were made in the 18th century
and there are some fine decorations and
furniture. Also of great interest is the wheelhouse
with its huge wheel, once turned by a donkey to
bring water up from the well.
Times: Open: House (part of ground floor only) Apr-Sep,
Mon, Wed & Fri 2-6. (Closed Good Fri). Garden daily except
Thu & Sun 2-6. Last admission 5.30pm. (Closed Good Fri).
🅿 💺 ✖ 🐾 *Details not confirmed for 2000*

RIVER & ROWING MUSEUM
Mill Meadows RG9 1BF (off A4130, signposted to
Mill Meadows)
☎ 01491 415600 ▤ 01491 415601

Your visit will take you on a spectacular journey
through over 250,000 years of life on the river.
Discover the river's role in feeding the nation, its
wildlife, nature, and transformation from a major
trade route to a recreational paradise. Meet the
people who shape Britain's oldest amateur sport,
from innovative boatbuilders to athletes who
strive for Olympic glory.
Times: Open Apr-Oct, Mon-Sat 10-6.30, Sun 11-6.30; Nov-
Mar, Mon-Sat 10-5.30, Sun 11-5.30. (Closed 24-25 Dec).
Fee: *£4.95 (concessions £3.75). Family ticket £13.25. Party 10+.
🅿 💺 ✖ licensed ⅋ toilets for disabled shop ✖ 🌀

⛪ MAPLEDURHAM
MAPLEDURHAM HOUSE & WATERMILL
RG4 7TR (off A4074, follow tourist signs)
☎ 0118 972 3350 ▤ 0118 972 4016

The small community at Mapledurham includes
the house, a watermill and a church. The fine
Elizabethan mansion, surrounded by quiet
parkland which runs down to the River Thames,
was built by the Blount family in the 16th
century. The estate has literary connections with
the poet Alexander Pope, with Galsworthy's
Forsyte Saga and Kenneth Graham's *Wind in the*

Willows, and was the setting for the the the film *The
Eagle has Landed*.
Times: Open Etr-Sep, Sat, Sun & BH's 2-5.30 Picnic area 2-
5.30. Last admission 5pm. Group visits midweek by
arrangement.
Fee: *Combined house, watermill & grounds £5 (ch £2.50).
House & grounds £4 (ch £2). Watermill & grounds £3 (ch
£1.50).
🅿 💺 ⅋ shop ✖ (ex park area)

MAPLEDURHAM WATERMILL
RG4 7TR (off A4074)
☎ 0118 972 3350 ▤ 0118 972 4016

Close to Mapledurham House (above) stands the
last working corn and grist mill on the Thames,
still using traditional wooden machinery and
producing flour for local bakers and shops. The
watermill's products can be purchased in the
shop. When Mapledurham house is open (details
from estate office), the mill can be reached by
river launch.
Times: Open Easter-Sep, Sat, Sun & BHs 2-5.30. Picnic area 2-
5.30. Last admission 5. Groups midweek by arrangement.
Fee: *Watermill & grounds £3 (ch £1.50)
🅿 💺 ⅋ shop ✖ (ex in country park)

⛪ MINSTER LOVELL
MINSTER LOVELL HALL & DOVECOT
(adjacent to Minster Lovell church, 3m W of
Witney off A40)
☎ 01993 775315

Home of the ill-fated Lovell family, the ruins of
the 15th-century house are steeped in history
and legend. One of the main features of the
estate is the medieval dovecote.
Times: Open any reasonable time.
🅿 (ex Dovecot) ✖ ⚏

⛪ NORTH LEIGH
NORTH LEIGH ROMAN VILLA
(2m N)

Excavations show that the villa was occupied
from the second to fourth centuries AD. A
tessellated pavement and a 2-3ft high wall span,
are on show.
Times: Open, grounds all year. No access to mosaic.
Pedestrian access only from the main road - 600 yds.
✖ ⚏

⛪ OXFORD
ASHMOLEAN MUSEUM OF ART &
ARCHAEOLOGY
Beaumont St OX1 2PH (opposite The Randolph
Hotel)
☎ 01865 278000 ▤ 01865 278018

First opened in 1683 and the oldest museum in
the country, the Ashmolean Museum was re-
housed in C R Cockerell's building of 1845.
Archaeological exhibits, coins, medals, paintings,
drawings, porcelain, pottery and metalwork from
all over the globe are among the exhibits.

contd.

OXFORD

Oxford is commonly regarded, along with Cambridge, as being among the world's most important centres of learning. Its first school was University College, founded in 1249. Other colleges have been added over the centuries, and the most recent date from the Second World War. A good way to get a look at these colleges, as well as other Oxford landmarks, is by going on a guided walking tour. After getting a look at the city from the road and pavement, it's a pleasant idea to spend some time in a punt on the Thames or Cherwell, and get a relaxing look at things from the river. Nightlife with a cultural edge includes theatres, art centres and music venues.

Temporary exhibitions are held please phone for details.
Times: Open all year, Tue-Sat 10-5, Sun 2-5. (Closed Etr & during St.Giles Fair in early Sep, Xmas & 1 Jan).
Fee: *Free. Guided tours by arrangement.
P (100-200metres) ⬛ & (entry ramp from Beaumont St) toilets for disabled shop ✖ ⬛

MUSEUM OF OXFORD
St Aldate's OX1 1DZ
☎ 01865 252761   ▤ 01865 252254

Permanent displays depict the archaeology and history of the city through the ages. There are temporary exhibitions, facilities for school parties and groups, and an audio tour. `Dynamic Toys' is

an exhibition running from December until Easter 2000, illustrating the forces of nature and basic mechanics as observed through traditional and contemporary toys from all over the world. Please telephone for details of special events.
Times: Open all year, Tue-Fri 10-4, Sat 10-5 & Sun 12-4. (Closed 25-26 Dec, Good Fri & Etr Sun).
Fee: *£3 (ch 5-17 & concessions £1.50). Family ticket £7 shop ✖ ⬛

MUSEUM OF THE HISTORY OF SCIENCE
Old Ashmolean Building, Broad St OX1 3AZ
☎ 01865 277280   ▤ 01865 277288

The first purpose-built museum building in Britain, containing the world's finest collection of

early scientific instruments - astronomy, navigation, surveying, sundials, microscopes, telescopes, physics and chemistry.
Times: Closed for major building work and gallery refurbishment. Open second half 2000.
Fee: Free.
P (in street,limited) & toilets for disabled shop ✈ (ex guide dogs)

THE OXFORD STORY
6 Broad St OX1 3AJ
☎ 01865 728822 ▤ 01865 791716

Capturing the essence of Oxford University's fascinating history, which is brought to life with sights, sounds - and smells - from the past. Includes a look at the famous alumni of Oxford who have made an impact on the world in sport, medicine, literature and politics.

Times: Open all year, Apr-Jun & Sep-Oct daily 9.30-5, Jul-Aug 9-6 & Nov-Mar daily 10-4.30.
Fee: *£5.50 (concessions £4.50). Family ticket £16.50.
P (Park & Ride all round city) & (advisable to phone in advance) toilets for disabled shop ✈ (ex guide dogs) ▱

UNIVERSITY OF OXFORD BOTANIC GARDEN
High St OX1 4AX
☎ 01865 276920 ▤ 01865 276920

Founded in 1621, these botanic gardens are the oldest in the country and are of great interest. There is a collection of over 8000 species of plants from all over the world.
Times: Open all year, daily 9-5 (9-4.30 Oct-Mar), Greenhouses, daily 2-4. (Closed Good Fri & 25 Dec).
Fee: *Apr-Aug £2. otherwise free.
P (0.5 mile) & toilets for disabled ✈ (ex guide dogs)

⛫ ROUSHAM
ROUSHAM HOUSE
OX6 3QX (1m E of A4260. 0.5m S of B4030)
☎ 01869 347110

This attractive mansion was built by Sir Robert Dormer in 1635. During the Civil War it was a Royalist garrison. The house contains over 150 portraits and other pictures, and also much fine contemporary furniture. The gardens are a masterpiece by William Kent, and are his only work to survive unspoiled.
Times: Open all year, garden only, daily 10-4.30. House, Apr-Sep, Wed, Sun & BH Mon 2-4.30 (last entry).
Fee: *House £3, Garden £3. Groups by arrangement. No children under 15.
P & ✈

⛫ RYCOTE
RYCOTE CHAPEL
OX9 2PE (off B4013)

This small private chapel was founded in 1449 by Richard Quatremayne. It has its original font, and a particularly fine 17th-century interior. The chapel was visited by both Elizabeth I and Charles I.
Times: Open Apr-Sep, Fri-Sun & BH's 2-6.
Fee: £1.60 (ch 80p).
P & (if assisted) ✈ ⌗

⛫ STONOR
STONOR HOUSE & PARK
RG9 6HF (on B480).
☎ 01491 638587 ▤ 01491 638587

The house dates back to 1190 but features a Tudor façade. It has a medieval Catholic chapel which is still in use today, and shows some of the earliest domestic architecture in Oxfordshire. Its treasures include rare furniture, paintings, sculptures and tapestries from Britain, Europe and America. The house is set in beautiful gardens commanding views of the surrounding deer park.
Times: Open Apr-Sep, Sun 2-5.30; Jul & Aug, Wed 2-5.30; BH Mons, Sat 29 May & 28 Aug only 2-5.30. Parties by appointment.
Fee: *£4.50 (ch 14 accompanied free). Gardens only £2.50. Party 12+
P ▆ & shop ✈ (ex in grounds on lead)

⛫ UFFINGTON
CASTLE, WHITE HORSE & DRAGON HILL
(S of B4507)

An Iron Age fort on the ancient Ridgeway Path. It covers about eight acres and has only one gateway. On the hill below the fort is the White Horse, a 375ft prehistoric figure carved in the chalky hillside and thought to be about 2000 years old. The B4508 gives a good view.
Times: Open - accessible any reasonable time.
P ⌗

⛫ WATERPERRY
WATERPERRY GARDENS
OX33 1JZ (2.50m from A40, turn off at Wheatley)
☎ 01844 339226 & 339254
▤ 01844 339883

The manor of Waterperry is mentioned in the Domesday Book. The present house (not open) was rebuilt by Sir John Curson in 1713. The peaceful gardens and nurseries which surround the house were the home of a celebrated horticultural school between 1932 and 1971, and have fine herbaceous borders, a rock garden,

contd.

riverside walk, shrub borders, lawns and trees. Please phone for details of special events.

Times: Open all year, Gardens (ex Xmas & New Year & during "Art in Action" 15-18 Jul). Apr-Oct 9-5.30, Nov-Mar 9-5 daily.

Fee: *Apr-Oct, £3.25 (ch 10-16 £1.75, ch under 10 free, pen £2.75). Nov-Mar £1.50 Party 20+.

🅿 💻 ✕ licensed ♿ (grounds mostly accessible) shop garden centre ✖ (ex on leads) 🦮

🏛 WITNEY

COGGES MANOR FARM MUSEUM

Church Ln, Cogges OX8 6LA (0.5m SE off A4022)

☎ 01993 772602   🖹 01993 703056

The museum includes the Manor, dairy and walled garden, and has breeds of animals typical of the Victorian period. The first floor of the manor contains period rooms. Special events take place through the season.

Times: Open Apr-Oct, Tue-Fri & BH Mon 10.30-5.30, Sat & Sun 12-5.30. Early closing Oct. (Closed Good Fri).

Fee: *£3.50 (ch £1.75, pen, students & UB40 £2.25). Family ticket £10.

🅿 💻 ♿ (wheelchair available) toilets for disabled shop 🦮

🏛 WOODSTOCK

BLENHEIM PALACE

OX20 1PX (M40 J9, follow signs to Blenheim, on A44 8m N of Oxford)

☎ 01993 811091 & 811325 (information line)   🖹 01993 813527

The Royal Manor of Woodstock and the sum of £240,000 to build the Palace were given to the Duke of Marlborough by Queen Anne as a reward for his military victory over the French at the Battle of Blenheim in 1704. The Palace was designed by Sir John Vanbrugh. It is set in a 2100 acre park landscaped by 'Capability' Brown who created a lake spanned by a 390 foot bridge. Sir Winston Churchill was born in the Palace in 1874 and he is buried nearby. Events are held in the park during the year, please phone for details.

Times: Open: Palace & Gardens mid Mar-Oct, daily 10.30-5.30 (last admission 4.45pm). Park all year.

Fee: *£8.50 (pen, 16-17 year olds & students £6.50). Family ticket £23. Group rates.

🅿 💻 ✕ licensed ♿ (ramps, disabled parking) toilets for disabled shop ✖ (ex in park on leads) 🦮

Rutland

A mere twenty miles across, the county of Rutland was reinstated in 1997 due to public demand from Rutlanders who had fiercely maintained their identity through twenty years as part of Leicestershire. The county motto is "Multum in Parvo", which is Latin for 'much in little'.

Oakham is the only town of any size in the county, and as Rutland only has a population of around 35,000 it's not hard to imagine what kind of size that is! Those who don't live there inhabit one of the fifty or so villages, or the other two towns, Uppingham and Stamford.

Many of these villages have their own little oddities which are so tantalising to students of eccentric England. For example, Wing has a strange ancient turf maze, the story of the fools who tried to fence a cuckoo in, and the Wise Woman of Wing.

Some famous connections with Rutland are John Clare, the 18th-century pastoral poet; the Gunpowder Plotters (who are said to have met at Stoke Dry); Thomas Barker, a pioneer of modern weather forecasting, and more recently the TV production of George Eliot's 'Middlemarch', which was filmed at Stamford.

Apart from its small attractions, Rutland also has a large one. Rutland Water is, at 5,000 acres, the largest man-made reservoir in Europe. As well as a mass of wildlife and water pursuits such as windsurfing and sailing, Rutland Water has its own church, Normanton Church, which sits on an outcrop that juts out onto the Water itself.

EVENTS & FESTIVALS

May
28th Rutland Agricultural Show
29th Exton Street Market

August
18th-20th British Birdwatching Fair, Egleton Nature Reserve

Top: Normanton Church at Rutland Water

OAKHAM

Oakham, the county town of Rutland, has all the hallmarks of a fine old English settlement including a castle, L-shaped market place, octagonal butter cross, and the town's historic stocks and pump. Market days, when the town is at its liveliest, are Wednesdays and Saturdays.

Notable buildings include the exclusive Oakham School, founded in the 16th century, All Saints Church, dating from the 13th century, and Flore's House, a late 14th-century building, where you will now find the Tourist Information Centre.

⛪ LYDDINGTON
BEDE HOUSE
☎ 01572 822438

Built in the late 15th century as the episcopal residence of the Bishops of Lincoln, Bede House was the administrative centre of their vast diocese. Later it became an almshouse. Beautiful wooden ceilings, painted glass and a grand fireplace bear witness to its former life as a palace.
Times: Open Apr-1 Nov, daily 10-6 (or dusk if earlier).
& ✈ ♨

⛪ OAKHAM
OAKHAM CASTLE
off Market Place
☎ 01572 723654 📠 01572 757576

An exceptionally fine Norman Great Hall of a 12th-century fortified manor house. Earthworks, walls and remains of an earlier motte can be seen along with medieval sculptures and unique presentation horseshoes forfeited by peers of the realm and royalty to the Lord of the Manor. Please enquire for details of any events in connection with Oakham Festival in June.
Times: Open all year. Grounds daily 10-5.30 (4pm late Oct-late Mar). Great Hall Tue-Sat & BH Mon 10-1 & 2-5.30, Sun 2-5.30 (4pm late Oct-late Mar).Closed Mon, Good Fri & Xmas.
P (400 yds) (disabled parking only by notificatin) & shop ✈
Details not confirmed for 2000

RUTLAND COUNTY MUSEUM
Catmos St LE15 6HW (on A6003)
☎ 01572 723654 📠 01572 757576

The Museum of Rutland Life has displays of farming equipment, machinery and wagons, rural tradesmen's tools, domestic collections and local archaeology, all housed in a splendid late 18th-century cavalry riding school. There is a special gallery on the Volunteer Soldier in Leicestershire and Rutland. A programme of temporary exhibitions takes place - please enquire for details.
Times: Open all year, Mon-Sat 10-5. Sun 2-5 (Apr-Oct, 2-4 Nov-Mar). (Closed Good Fri & Xmas)
P (adjacent) ☕ & toilets for disabled shop ✈ *Details not confirmed for 2000*

Shropshire

Shropshire is a mainly agricultural county in the west of England, on the Welsh border. Home to beautiful rivers and lakes, as well as spectacular walking opportunities, the county is sparsely populated and has some fine market towns.

Britain's longest river, the Severn, flows from northwest to southeast, and other natural features are the 'Shropshire Lakes' at Ellesmere in the northwest, and the Clee Hills in the south, between Ludlow and Kidderminster, rising to 1,800 ft (610m). Brown Clee is the highest coalfield in Britain. The two ridges, Wenlock Edge and the Long Mynd, running either side of Church Stretton, are much favoured by walkers. This lovely part of the country was immortalised in A E Houseman's nostalgic collection of verses, *A Shropshire Lad*, published in 1896.

The two largest centres of population in a generally sparsely populated county are Shrewsbury, the county town, situated on a hilly site in a loop of the River Severn, and Telford New Town, named after the famous engineer, Thomas Telford. In the 5th century, Shrewsbury was the capital of the kingdom of Powys, with the name Pengwern (later part of Mercia). A rich legacy of half-timbered Tudor buildings and red brick Georgian buildings remains, along with the castle, which has Norman origins.

There are some fine market towns, well worth a visit. Chief among these are Ludlow, capital of the Marches, and widely held to be one of the most beautiful of British towns, with its intricately decorated black and white buildings; Bishop's Castle, retaining much of its medieval character, and the dramatically located hilltop town of Bridgnorth.

EVENTS & FESTIVALS

April
15th-16th FIM World Championship Motorcycle Trials 2000, Hawkstone Park
28th-1st May Shrewsbury Children's Book Festival

May
1st Shropshire Game Fair, Newport
19th-20th Shropshire & West Midlands Agricultural Show, Shrewsbury Showground

June
18th (provisional) Shrewsbury Carnival
20th-25th Much Wenlock Festival
23rd-29th International Music Festival, Shrewsbury

July
8th-9th Real Ale Festival, Bishop's Castle
22nd-5th August Church Stretton & South Shropshire Arts Festival
24th June-9th Ludlow Festival

August
11th-12th Shrewsbury Flower Show
tbc County of Salop Steam Rally
25th-27th Bridgnorth Folk Festival, Bridgnorth

September
10th-11th Shrewsbury Real Ale Festival

Top: Telford, the River Severn

ACTON BURNELL
ACTON BURNELL CASTLE
SY5 7PE (on unclass road 8m S of Shrewsbury)

Now ruined, this fortified manor house was built in the late 13th century by Robert Burnell, the Chancellor of the time.
Times: Open at all reasonable times.
&. ✠

ACTON SCOTT
ACTON SCOTT HISTORIC WORKING FARM
Wenlock Lodge SY6 6QN (follow tourist signs off A49)
☎ 01694 781306 & 781307
🖹 01694 781569

Acton Scott Historic Working Farm is a microcosm of an upland farm at the turn of the century. Throughout the farming season visitors can see ploughing, sowing, reaping and harvesting of both corn and root crops, and demonstrations by blacksmiths, farriers, wheelwrights, and woodland craftsman. Domestic life is reacreated in the bailiff's cottage.
Times: Open 28 Mar-29 Oct, Tue-Sun 10-5; BH Mon 10-5.
Fee: *£3.50 (ch £1.50, under 5 free, pen £3).
P 🖥 & (Braille guide, wheelchairs available) toilets for disabled shop ✕ (ex guide dogs)

ATCHAM
ATTINGHAM PARK
SY4 4TP (4m SE of Shrewsbury on B4380)
☎ 01743 708123   🖹 01743 708175

Though Attingham was constructed around an earlier building, most of what one sees today dates from the 18th and early 19th centuries. This even applies to the garden, where the planting remains very much as advised by Humphry Repton in 1797-8. The picture gallery was designed by Nash, who made early use of curved cast iron and glass for the ceiling.
Times: House open 26 Mar-Oct, Fri-Tue 1.30-5, BH Mon 11-5. Pre-booked parties allowed daily ex Wed & Thu. Last admission 4.30pm. Grounds open all year, daily (ex 25 Dec), 8-8 (Nov-Feb 8-5).
Fee: *£4 (ch £2). Family ticket £10. Park & Grounds £1.80 (ch 90p).
P 🖥 & (2 electric self drive buggies) toilets for disabled shop ✕ (ex guide & hearing dogs) ✿

BENTHALL
BENTHALL HALL
TF12 5RX (on B4375)
☎ 01952 882159

The exact date of the house is not known, but it seems to have been started in the 1530s and then altered in the 1580s. It is an attractive sandstone building with mullioned windows, fine oak panelling and a splendid carved staircase.
Times: Open Apr-Sep, Wed, Sun & BH Mon 1.30-5.30. Last admission 5pm. Other days by appointment only.
Fee: *House £3 (ch £1). Garden only £2.
P & ✕ ✿ ✒

BOSCOBEL
BOSCOBEL HOUSE AND THE ROYAL OAK
(on unclass road between A41 and A5)
☎ 01902 850244

The house was built around 1600 by John Giffard, a Roman Catholic, and includes a number of secret hiding places, used by Charles II after his defeat at the Battle of Worcester in 1651.
Times: Open all year, Apr-Oct, daily 10-6 (or dusk if earlier); Nov-Mar, Wed-Sun 10-4, last admission 3.30pm. Entry to house by guided tour only. Closed 24-26 Dec & all Jan.
Fee: £4 (ch £2).
P 🖥 & shop ✕ ✠

WHITELADIES PRIORY (ST LEONARDS PRIORY)

Only the ruins are left of this Augustinian nunnery, which dates from 1158 and was destroyed in the Civil War. After the Battle of Worcester Charles II hid here and in the nearby woods before going on to Boscobel House.
Times: Open any reasonable time.
✠

BUILDWAS
BUILDWAS ABBEY
TF8 7BW (on S bank of River Severn on B4378)
☎ 01743 701101

The beautiful, ruined, Cistercian abbey was founded in 1135, and stands in a picturesque setting. The church with its stout round pillars is roofless but otherwise complete.
Times: Open Apr-Oct, daily 10-6 (or dusk if earlier). Please telephone for further details.
Fee: £1.85 (30p).
& ✠ *Details not confirmed for 2000*

BURFORD
BURFORD HOUSE GARDENS
WR15 8HQ (off A456)
☎ 01584 810777   🖹 01584 810673

The beauty of Burford House Gardens is a tribute to the late John Treasure who, since the early 1950's, transformed the setting of this early Georgian house into a garden of quiet serenity and fascination. Harmonising combinations of colour have been achieved, and especial use has been made of clematis - the garden, now boasting over 150 varieties, is home to the National Collection. The garden is famous for its range of unusual plants, many of which are sold in Treasures Plant Centre adjacent, who specialise in clematis, herbaceous, shrubs, trees and climbers. Also on site is the Burford House Gallery, Burford Buttery, Craft Shop and Craft Workshops. Special events this year: 4th Annual Botanical Exhibition and 2 contemporary art shows (April-October), Christmas Fair (early Nov-24 Dec). Ring for further details.
Times: Open all year 10-5. dusk if earlier.
P 🖥 ✕ licensed & (ramp into gardens, sloping paths) toilets for disabled shop garden centre ✕ (ex in Plant Centre)
Details not confirmed for 2000 ✒

⛫ COSFORD
ROYAL AIRFORCE MUSEUM
TF11 8UP (on A41, 1m S of Jct 3 on M54)
☎ 01902 376200   🖹 01902 376211

This is one of the largest aviation collections in the UK. Exhibits include the Victor and Vulcan bombers, the Hastings, York and British Airways airliners, the Belfast freighter and the last airworthy Britannia. The research and development collection includes the notable TSR2, Fairey Delta, Bristol 188 and many more important aircraft.
Times: Open all year daily, 10-6 (last admission 4pm). Closed 24-26 Dec & 1 Jan).
Fee: *£5 (ch £3 & pen £4). Family ticket £13. Party 20+.
🅿 ✕ ♿ (limited amount of wheelchairs on request) toilets for disabled shop ✕ ♨

⛫ HAUGHMOND ABBEY
HAUGHMOND ABBEY
(off B5062)
☎ 01743 709661

The ruined abbey was founded for Augustinian canons around 1135, and partly converted into a house during the Dissolution. The chapter house has a fine Norman doorway, and the abbot's lodging and the kitchens are well preserved.
Times: Open Apr-Oct, daily 10-6 (or dusk if earlier)
Fee: £1.85 (ch 90p).
🅿 ♿ ✕ ⚏

⛫ IRONBRIDGE
IRONBRIDGE GORGE MUSEUMS
TF8 7AW (M54 junc 4, signposted)
☎ 01952 433522, 432166 or 0800 590258   🖹 01952 432204

Ironbridge is the site of the world's first iron bridge, it was cast and built here in 1779, to span a narrow gorge over the River Severn. Now Ironbridge is the site of a remarkable series of museums relating the story of the bridge, recreating life in Victorian times and featuring ceramics and social history displays. An introduction to the Ironbridge Gorge is given at the Ironbridge Visitor Centre.
Times: Open all year, 10-5. Some small sites closed Nov-Mar. Telephone or write for exact winter details.
Fee: *£9.50 (ch £5.50, pen £8.50). Family £29. Passport to all sites, until all have been visited, on different days if necessary.
🅿 💺 ✕ licensed ♿ (wheelchairs,potters wheel,braille guide,lifts,hearing loop) toilets for disabled shop ✕ (ex Blists Hill & guide dogs) ♨

IRONBRIDGE GORGE

The famous iron bridge, built by Abraham Darby III was opened on New Year's Day 1781, and is a symbol of the Industrial Revolution. The area was a centre of iron-smelting and transport, powered by the River Severn, and has been developed to offer nine museums spread over six square miles of what is now designated a World Heritage Site. The museums comprise the Iron Bridge itself and its Tollhouse, the Coalport China Museum, The Tar Tunnel with its spring of natural bitumen, the Jackfield Tile Museum, the Coalbrookedale Museum of Iron, the Darby Ironmaster Houses, Blists Hill Victorian Town, the Ironbridge Visitor Centre, and Broseley Clay Tobacco Pipe Museum.

🏛 LILLESHALL
LILLESHALL ABBEY
TF10 9HW (1.5m SW off A518 on unclass road)

In the beautiful grounds of Lilleshall Hall, ruined Lilleshall Abbey was founded shortly before the middle of the 12th century and from the high west front visitors can look down the entire 228ft length of the abbey church.

Times: Open Apr-Nov, wknds & BHs only, 12-5.

🅿 ✈ ♻

🏛 LUDLOW
LUDLOW CASTLE
Castle Square SY8 1AY
☎ 01584 873355

Ludlow Castle dates from about 1086. In 1473, Edward IV sent the Prince of Wales and his brother - later to become the Princes in the Tower - to live here and Ludlow Castle became a seat of government. John Milton's *Comus* was first performed at Ludlow Castle in 1634; now contemporary performances of Shakespeare's plays, together with concerts, are put on in the castle grounds during the Ludlow Festival (2 weeks, end June-early July).

Times: Open Jan Sat-Sun 10-4; Feb-Apr daily 10-4; May-Jul daily 10-5; Aug daily 10-7; Sep daily 10-5; Oct-Dec daily 10-4 (last admission 30 minutes before closing).

Fee: *£3 (ch under 6 free, ch 6+ £1.50, pen £2.50). Family ticket £8.50.

🅿 (100 yds) ♿ toilets for disabled shop ◀

🏛 MORETON CORBET
CASTLE

A small 13th-century keep and the ruins of an impressive Elizabethan house are all that remain: the house was destroyed in the Civil War.

Times: Open all reasonable times.

🅿 ♿ ♻

🏛 MUCH WENLOCK
MUCH WENLOCK PRIORY
☎ 01952 727466

The original priory, founded here as a convent in the 7th century, was destroyed by the Danes but was rebuilt and the ruins date from the 11th century and later periods.

Times: Open all year, Apr-Oct, daily 10-6; Nov-Mar, Wed-Sun 10-4. Closed 24-26 Dec & 1 Jan.

🅿 ♻

🏛 OSWESTRY
OLD OSWESTRY HILL FORT
(1m N, accessible from unclass road off A483)

This Iron Age hill-fort covers 68 acres, has five ramparts and an elaborate western portal. Part of the prehistoric Wat's Dyke abuts the site.

Times: Open any reasonable time.

♻

⛫ QUATT
DUDMASTON
WV15 6QN (4m SE of Bridgnorth on A442)
☎ 01746 780866   🖷 01746 780744

The 17th-century flower paintings which belonged to Francis Darby of Coalbrookdale are exhibited in this house of the same period, with modern works, botanical art and fine furniture. The house stands in an extensive parkland garden and there are dingle and lakeside walks. Please phone for details of special events.
Times: Open Apr-Sep, Wed & Sun & BH Mons, 2-5.30. Garden noon-6. Closed Good Fri.
Fee: *House & Garden £3.50. Garden only £2.50. Family ticket £8. Parties 15+
🅿 ➍ ⅃ (Braille guides, taped tours) toilets for disabled shop ✖ (ex in grounds) ⌕ ⌁

⛫ SHREWSBURY
SHREWSBURY CASTLE AND SHROPSHIRE REGIMENTAL MUSEUM
The Castle, Castle St SY1 2AT
☎ 01743 358516   🖷 01743 354811

The museum of The King's Shropshire Light Infantry and The Shropshire Yeomanry is housed in the main surviving building of Shrewsbury Castle which once dominated the town. The grounds contain the medieval 'motte' and the romantic 'Laura's Tower'. Telephone for details of special events.
Times: Open Tue-Sat 10-4.30, also Sun from Etr-Sep & BH Mon. Castle grounds open Mon also. Closed Dec/Jan.
🅿 (3 mins NCP) (on street parking by voucher only) ⅃ toilets for disabled shop ✖ Details not confirmed for 2000

SHREWSBURY QUEST
193 Abbey Foregate SY2 6AH (opposite Shrewsbury Abbey)
☎ 01743 243324   🖷 01743 244342

An opportunity to experience the sights, sounds and smells of medieval England. The Quest is based on 12th-century England in general and monastic life in particular. It provides a full 'hands-on' experience for visitors, who are encouraged to create their own illuminated manuscript, try their hand at medieval cloister games and interact with the historical characters in this 12th-century world.
Times: Open Apr-Oct 10-5 (last admission); Nov-Mar 10-4 (last admission).
Fee: *£4.25 (ch £2.95, concessions £3.60). Family £13.
🅿 (charged) ✖ licensed ⅃ (Braille maps, induction loop, lift) toilets for disabled shop ✖ (ex assistance dogs) ⌁

⛫ STOKESAY
STOKESAY CASTLE
SY7 9AH (1m S of Craven Arms off A49)
☎ 01588 672544

Well-preserved and little altered, this 13th-century manor house has a romantic setting. It has a fine timber-framed Jacobean gatehouse, a great hall and a solar with 17th-century panelling.
Times: Open all year, Apr-Oct, daily 10-6 (or dusk if earlier in Oct); Nov-Mar, Wed-Sun 10-4, closed 1-2pm Nov-Mar.
🅿 ⅃ (tape tour for visually handicapped, ramp for wheelchairs) toilets for disabled ✖ ⌗

⛫ WESTON-UNDER-REDCASTLE
HAWKSTONE HISTORIC PARK & FOLLIES
SY4 5UY (3m from Hodnet off A53)
☎ 01939 200300   🖷 01939 200311

After almost one hundred years of neglect, Hawkestone, created by the Hill family in the 18th century, has now been restored and designated a Grade I historic park. Visitors can once again experience a magical world of intricate pathways, arches and bridges, towering cliffs and follies. The Grand Valley has wild flowers and tidy lawns, centuries-old oaks, wild rhododendrons and lofty monkey puzzles. The Park covers nearly 100 acres of hilly terrain and visitors are advised to wear sensible shoes and clothing. Allow 3-4 hours for the tour, which is well signposted. The setting for BBC TV series 'The Chronicles of Narnia' and 'One Foot in the Past', the park is believed by some to be the last hiding place of the Holy Grail. Deer have been

contd.

reintroduced into the park after an absence of 150 years. There is generally a special event each month, please ring for details.

Times: Open 28 Mar-1 Nov, daily 10-6; Dec wknds only for Father Christmas visits.

🅿 ☕ shop *Details not confirmed for 2000* 🐟

🏛 WROXETER

Roman Town
(5m E of Shrewsbury, 1m S of A5)
☎ **01743 761330**

These excavated remains of the Roman town of Virconium probably date from AD140 - 150. There is an interesting museum with educational facilities.

Times: Open all year, Apr-Oct, daily 10-6 (or dusk if earlier); Nov-Mar, Wed-Sun 10-4 (closed 1-2pm). Closed 24-26 Dec & 1 Jan.

Fee: £3.10 (ch £1.60).

🅿 ♿ shop ✈ ♯

Somerset

Somerset is rich with history and legend, as well as having some beautiful coastline and countryside. The name of the county comes from the Saxon, and literally translated means 'Land of the Summer People.'

One of the county's most famous landmarks is Glastonbury Tor, which once gave refuge to the ancient Britons. Legend has it that Joseph of Arimathea came to Glastonbury in a bid to convert the English. It is also the place where King Arthur and Gwynevere are said to be buried. Those interested in Arthurian legend should also visit South Cadbury, an Iron Age hill fort reputed to be the site of Camelot.

At the other end of the county lies the timeless, rugged beauty of Exmoor, most of which is now a National Park. R D Blackmore's novel *Lorna Doone* is set here. There is also a mystery on Exmoor. No one knows when the Tarr Steps were built across the Barle, but they may be prehistoric.

The seaside resorts of Minehead, Burnham-on-Sea and Weston-super-Mare are great places to enjoy a family holiday. Dunster is further inland and walking through it is a little like taking a time machine through 900 years of history. The town is overshadowed by the Norman splendour of Dunster Castle, owned by the National Trust.

In the heart of Somerset lies Wells, the smallest city in England, whose cathedral is decorated with stone figures. The city also boasts Vicar's Close, often described as the most complete medieval street in Europe.

EVENTS & FESTIVALS

February
25th-5th March Bath Literature Festival

April
28th-30th Custom & Classic Bike Show, Shepton Mallett
29th-1st May Bath Flower Show, Royal Victoria Park, Bath

May
31st-3rd June The Royal Bath & West Show

June
9th-11th Crook Peak Festival 2000, Axbridge
23rd-25th (provisional) Glastonbury Festival of Performing Arts

July
28th-30th Glastonbury Children's Festival

September
1st-3rd National Amateur Gardening Show, Bath

October
21st-28th Bach Festival, Bath

November
3rd-12th or 10th-19th Mozartfest, Bath

December
13th-15th Carols by Candlelight, City of Bath Choir, Bath

Top: Stogursey Castle gatehouse

BATH

Bath is an elegant spa resort set in the Avon valley. Its Georgian terraces, crescents and squares are arranged around spacious landscaped parks, and the source of the city's prosperity still bubbles, at a steady 46.5°C, into cisterns and baths built by the Romans nearly 2,000 years ago. In the 18th century, Beau Nash and other high society visitors made Bath the sophisticated social centre it is still known as today. The city is built around the River Avon, and there can be few pastimes more relaxing than taking a punt out from the Victorian Boating Station. The Kennet and Avon Canal also provides an ideal opportunity for relaxation, and stretches out five miles to Limpley Stoke Valley.

AXBRIDGE
KING JOHN'S HUNTING LODGE
The Square BS26 2AP
☎ 01934 732012

Nothing to do with King John or with hunting, this jettied and timber-framed house was built around 1500. It gives a good indication of the wealth of the merchants of that time and is now a museum of local history, with old photographs, paintings and items such as the town stocks and constables' staves.

Times: Open Etr-Sep, daily 2-5. Write for details of tours.
✄ *Details not confirmed for 2000*

BARRINGTON
BARRINGTON COURT GARDEN
TA19 0NQ (5m NE of Ilminster on B3168)
☎ 01460 241938

The house dates from the 17th century, but the gardens were created in the 1920s, with the help (through the post) of Gertrude Jekyll. They are laid out in 'rooms' and there is a large walled kitchen garden supplying fresh fruit and vegetables to the restaurant.

Times: Open: Garden & Court House 1 Apr-31 Oct, daily ex Fri, 11-5.30, last admission 5pm.
🅿 ✗ licensed & (batricars available, braille guides) ✈ ✄
Details not confirmed for 2000

BATH
AMERICAN MUSEUM
Claverton Manor BA2 7BD (2.5m SE)
☎ 01225 460503   ▤ 01225 480726

Claverton Manor is two miles south east of Bath, in a beautiful setting above the River Avon. The house was built in 1820 by Sir Jeffrey Wyatville, and is now a museum of American decorative arts. The gardens are well worth seeing, and include an American arboretum and a replica of George Washington's garden at Mount Vernon. The Folk Art Gallery and the New Gallery are among the many exhibits in the grounds along with seasonal exhibitions.

Times: Open 20 Mar-7 Nov, Tue-Sun 2-5. Gardens 1-6. BH Sun & Mon 11-5.
Fee: *£5 (ch £3, pen £4.50).
🅿 ■ & toilets for disabled shop ✈ (on leads only) ◥

BATH ABBEY
BA1 1LY
☎ 01225 422462   ▤ 01225 429990

The 15th-century abbey church was built on the site of the Saxon abbey where King Edgar was crowned in 973. The church is Perpendicular style with Norman arches and superb fan-vaulting. The famous West Front carvings

represent the founder-bishop's dream of angels ascending and descending from heaven.
Times: Open all year, Mar-Oct 9-6, Oct-Mar 9-4. Closed for sightseeing Sun and other times when services are taking place.
Fee: *Visitors invited to give at least £2 each.
P & toilets for disabled shop ✈

BATH INDUSTRIAL HERITAGE CENTRE
Camden Works, Julian Rd BA1 2RH
☎ 01225 318348   🖹 01225 318348

The centre houses the Bowler collection, and the entire stock-in-trade of various Victorian craftsmen. Also here is `The Story of Bath Stone', with a replica of a mine face before mechanisation, and a Bath cabinet-maker's workshop. There will be a series of lectures throughout the year.
Times: Open all year, Etr-1 Nov, daily 10-5; Nov-Etr, wknds 10-5. (Closed 25-26 Dec).
Fee: *£3.50 (ch, pen & students £2.50). Family ticket £10.
P 💻 shop ✈

THE BUILDING OF BATH MUSEUM
Countess of Huntingdon's Chapel, The Vineyards, The Paragon BA1 5NA (M4 J18 A46 towards city centre. Take A4, 2nd exit at mini rdbt. Along road on right)
☎ 01225 333895   🖹 01225 445473

This new museum relates the fascinating story of how Georgian Bath was created. 17th Century Bath was a medieval market town but in the space of 100 years it was transformed into one of the most beautiful and glamorous cities in Europe. The exhibition depicts elegant society life in 'Beau' Nash's spa resort and explains how the houses were constructed. After a visit, the street scene outside seems like an extension of the exhibition. Ring for details of special events such as concerts and lectures.
Times: Open 15 Feb-1 Dec, Tue-Sun & BH's 10.30-5.
Fee: *£3.50 (ch £1.50 & concessions £2.50). Party 10+.
P (500m) & shop ✈ (ex guide dogs)

HOLBURNE MUSEUM & CRAFT STUDY CENTRE
Great Pulteney St BA2 4DB
☎ 01225 466669   🖹 01225 333121

This elegant building shows 17th-and 18th-century collections of fine and decorative art, notably silver, porcelain, glass, furniture and Old Master paintings. There are also displays of 20th-century crafts, embracing ceramic, textiles and furniture. There is an annual programme of events.
Times: Open mid Feb-mid Dec, Mon-Sat & BHs 11-5, Sun 2.30-5.30 (Closed Mon Nov-Etr).
Fee: *£3.50 (ch £1.50, UB40 & student £2, other concessions £3). Family ticket £7.
P 💻 & (lift to all floors) toilets for disabled shop ✈

MUSEUM OF COSTUME
Bennett St BA1 2QH
☎ 01225 477789   477785
🖹 01225 444793 & 477743

The Museum of Costume is a prestigious collection of fashionable dress covering the period from the late 16th century to the present day. It is housed in Bath's famous 18th century Assembly Rooms designed by John Wood the Younger in 1771. 'Catwalk Classics', an exhibition of modern fashion, runs until November 2000. Entrance to the Assembly Rooms is free.
Times: Open all year, Mon-Sat 10-5, Sun 11-5. (Closed 25 & 26 Dec).
P (park & ride recommended) & (audio guides available) toilets for disabled shop ✈ 🍴

No 1 ROYAL CRESCENT
BA1 2LR
☎ 01225 428126   🖹 01225 481850

Bath is very much a Georgian city, but most of its houses have naturally altered over the years to suit changing tastes and lifestyles. Built in 1768 by John Wood the Elder, No 1 Royal Crescent has been restored to look as it would have done some 200 years ago. Note the first-floor windows, which are the original (shorter) length.
Times: Open 9 Feb-Oct, Tue-Sun 10.30-5; 2-28 Nov, Tue-Sun 10.30-4. Open BH Mon. (Closed Good Fri). Last admission 30 mins before closing.
Fee: *£4 (ch, students & pen £3). Family ticket £8.Party.
P shop ✈ (ex guide dogs)

ROMAN BATHS & PUMP ROOM
Abbey Church Yard BA1 1LZ
☎ 01225 477785   🖹 01225 477743

The remains of the Roman baths give a vivid impression of life nearly 2000 years ago. Built next to Britain's only hot spring, the baths served the sick and the pilgrims visiting the adjacent Temple of Sulis Minerva. Above the Temple Courtyard, the Pump Room became a popular meeting place in the 18th century. No visit is complete without a taste of the famous hot spa

contd.

water, renowned for 2000 years for its curative properties.

Roman Baths & Pump Room

Times: Open all year, Apr-Jul & Sep, daily 9-6; Aug daily 9-9.30; Oct-Mar, daily 9.30-5. Disabled visitors free admission to ground floor areas.
Fee: *£6.70 (ch £4). Family ticket £17. Combined ticket with Museum of Costume £8.70 (ch £5.20)
P (500yds) (park & ride recommended) ✗ licensed 🕭 (sign language & audio tours) toilets for disabled shop ✈ ➴

ROYAL PHOTOGRAPHIC SOCIETY
The Octagon, Milsom St BA1 1DN
☎ 01225 462841   ▤ 01225 448688

The Octagon was built in 1796 as a chapel, but is now the headquarters of the world's oldest photographic society. A huge collection of cameras, the first photograph, and other classics are displayed. Temporary exhibitions often include top contemporary work. A variety of workshops, seminars and talks will be held throughout the year.
Times: Open all year, daily 9.30-5.30, last admission 4.45pm. (Closed 25-26 Dec).
P (5 mins walk) ➴ ✗ licensed 🕭 (chair lift to all floors) toilets for disabled shop ✈ *Details not confirmed for 2000*

SALLY LUNN'S REFRESHMENT HOUSE & MUSEUM
4 North Pde Passage BA1 1NX
☎ 01225 461634   ▤ 01225 447090

This Tudor building is Bath's oldest house and was a popular 18th-century meeting place. The traditional 'Sally Lunn' is similar to a brioche, and it is popularly believed to carry the name of its first maker who came to Bath in 1680. The bun is still served in the restaurant, and the original oven, Georgian cooking range and a collection of baking utensils are displayed in the museum.
Times: Open all year, Museum - Mon-Fri 10-6, Sat 10-6, Sun 12-6. (Closed 25-26 Dec & 1 Jan).
Fee: *30p (concessions free)
P ➴ ✗ licensed (braille menu for the blind) shop ✈ (ex guide dogs) ⛬ ➴

▥ CASTLE CARY
HADSPEN GARDEN & NURSERY
Hadspen House BA7 7NG (2m SE off A371)
☎ 01749 813707   ▤ 01749 813707

Situated within a 17th-century curved wall, this five acre garden has borders planted with roses and herbaceous plants, many of which have been developed here. Plants grown in the garden are available in the adjoining nursery.
Times: Open Mar-1 Oct, Thu-Sun & BHs 10-5.
Fee: *£2.50 (ch 50p). Free admission for wheelchair users.
P ✗ 🕭 toilets for disabled garden centre ✈ (ex guide dogs)

▥ CLEVEDON
CLEVEDON COURT
Tickenham Rd BS21 6QU (off B3130 1.5m E)
☎ 01275 872257

Clevedon Court is a remarkably complete manor house of around 1320AD. Additions have been made in each century, so it is a pleasing variety of styles, with an 18th-century terraced garden.
Times: Open 28 Mar-Sep, Wed-Thu, Sun & BH Mon 2-5.
Fee: *£4.10 (ch £2). Party 20+ by arrangement.
P ➴ (ground floor accessible via 4 steps) ✈ ⛬

▥ CRANMORE
EAST SOMERSET RAILWAY
Cranmore Railway Station BA4 4QP (on A361 between Frome & Shepton Mallet)
☎ 01749 880417   ▤ 01749 880764

Five steam locomotives and rolling stock can be seen at Cranmore station, which has an engine shed and workshops. The art gallery displays David Shepherd's work. Telephone for details of events and a timetable for Steam Days.
Times: Open daily Mar-24 Dec from 10am. For days when steam trains are operating phone 01749 880417.
P ➴ ✗ licensed 🕭 (ramp from road to platform) toilets for disabled shop *Details not confirmed for 2000* ➴

▥ DUNSTER
DUNSTER CASTLE
TA24 6SL (3m SE of Minehead, approach from A39)
☎ 01643 821314

The castle's picturesque appearance is largely due to 19th century work, but older features can also be seen, the superb 17th century oak staircase for example. Sub-tropical plants flourish in the 28-acre park and the terraced gardens are noted for exotica such as a giant lemon tree, yuccas, mimosa and palms.
Times: Open: Garden & park, daily 11-4 (10-5 Apr-Sep). Last admission 30 mins before closing. Castle, 30 Mar-Sept, Sat-Wed 11-5; 3 Oct-1 Nov, Sat-Wed 11-4. Closed 25 Dec.
P 🕭 (Braille guide, Batricar for grounds) toilets for disabled shop ⛬ *Details not confirmed for 2000*

🏛 EAST HUNTSPILL
SECRET WORLD-BADGER & WILDLIFE RESERVE CENTRE
New Rd TA9 3PZ (Signposted from A38)
☎ 01278 783250 🖹 01278 793109

This wildlife rescue centre enables visitors to see foxes, badgers, owls and other animals in natural surroundings. The 17th-century farmhouse is now a tearoom, serving meals throughout the day. There are farm demonstrations and talks as well.
Times: Open Mar-Nov, daily 10-6. Nov-Dec, daily 10-5. Feb-Mar, daily 10-5.
🅿 ⬛ ✕ ♿ toilets for disabled shop garden centre *Details not confirmed for 2000* ☜

🏛 EAST LAMBROOK
EAST LAMBROOK MANOR GARDEN
TA13 5HL (signed off A303, at South Petherton roundabout)
☎ 01460 240328 🖹 01460 242344

Walter and Margery Fish created the cottage-style garden after buying the 15th-century manor in 1937. Margery Fish's book *We Made a Garden* described the work, and aroused so much interest that she started a nursery to sell the types of plants she used. Plants are still sold. The garden is now Grade I listed and has been fully restored. NCCPG National Geranium Collection. Please ring for special events.
Times: Open Tue-Thu, Sat & BHs 10-5.
Fee: *£2.50 (ch 50p & pen £2). Party.
🅿 shop garden centre ✈

🏛 FARLEIGH HUNGERFORD
FARLEIGH HUNGERFORD CASTLE
BA3 6RS (3.5m W of Trowbridge on A366)
☎ 01225 754026

The ruined 14th-century castle has a chapel containing wall paintings, stained glass and the fine tomb of Sir Thomas Hungerford who built the castle. His powerful family and the castle are linked with various grim tales.
Times: Open all year, Apr-Oct, daily 10-6 (or dusk if earlier); Nov-Mar, Wed-Sun 10-4 (closed 1-2pm). Closed 24-26 Dec & 1 Jan.
🅿 ♿ ✈ ⌗ *Details not confirmed for 2000*

🏛 GLASTONBURY
GLASTONBURY ABBEY
Magdalene St BA6 9EL (on A361 between Frome & Taunton)
☎ 01458 832267 🖹 01458 832267

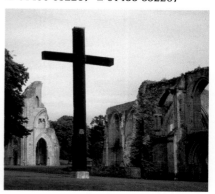

Few places in Britain are as rich in myth and legend as Glastonbury. Tradition maintains that the impressive ruins mark the birth place of Christianity in Britain. Joseph of Arimathea is said to have founded a chapel here in AD61, planting his staff in the ground where it flowered both at Christmas and Easter. Later, it is said, King Arthur and Guinevere were buried here, and the abbey has been a place of pilgrimage since the Middle Ages. The present abbey ruins date mostly from the 12th and 13th centuries, and the
contd.

Abbey fell into decay after the Dissolution. The display area contains artefacts and a model of the Abbey as it might have been in 1539. Please telephone for details of special events, which include Miracle Plays and concerts.

Times: Open all year, daily, Jun-Aug 9-6; Sep-May 9.30-6pm or dusk, whichever is the earliest. Dec-Feb open at 10am. (Closed 25 Dec).

Fee: £3 (ch 5-16 £1, pen & students £2.50). Family ticket £6.50.

🅿 (charged) 🖵 ♿ (all areas except Lady Chapel) toilets for disabled shop

KINGSDON
LYTES CARY MANOR
TA11 7HU (off A303)
☎ 01985 843600

Much of the present house was built in the 16th century although the oldest part, the chapel, dates from 1343. The Great Hall was a 15th-century addition. Unfortunately the gardens did not survive, but the present formal gardens are being restocked with plants that were commonly grown at the time of building.

Times: Open Apr-Oct, Mon, Wed & Sat 2-6 or dusk if earlier. Last admission 5.30.

🅿 ♿ ✱ 🌺 *Details not confirmed for 2000*

MONKSILVER
COMBE SYDENHAM COUNTRY PARK
TA4 4JG
☎ 01984 656284   ▤ 01984 656273

The 16th-century house was the home of Sir Francis Drake's second wife, Elizabeth, and is currently being restored. The only part of the house that visitors can see is the Court Room, which has been restored using, wherever possible, the materials of the period, and guides are on hand to answer questions from visitors. There are an Elizabethan-style garden, woodland walks, a medieval corn mill, picnic site, and a children's play area. There is also a fish farm with coarse fishing available.

Times: Open Apr-Sep. Country Park: daily 9-5. Other attractions open by guided tour, Spring BH-Sep, Mon, Thu & Fri at 2pm.

Fee: *Country Park: £3 per vehicle. Guided Tour: £5 (ch £2.50)

🅿 (charged) ♿ ✱ (ex in park)

MONTACUTE
MONTACUTE HOUSE
TA15 6XP (off A3088)
☎ 01935 823289

Set amidst formal gardens, Montacute House was built by Sir Edward Phelips. He was a successful lawyer, and became Speaker of the House of Commons in 1604. Inside there are decorated ceilings, ornate fireplaces, heraldic glass and fine wood panelling. The Long Gallery displays a permanent collection of Tudor and

Jacobean portraits from the National Portrait Gallery in London.

Times: Open, Garden & Park: Apr-1 Nov daily (ex Tue) 11.30-5.30 or dusk if earlier. 4 Nov-Mar Wed-Sun 11.30-4. House: Apr-1 Nov, daily (ex Tue) 12-5.30. Last admission 5pm.

🅿 ✗ licensed ♿ (Braille guide) toilets for disabled shop garden centre ✱ (ex park) 🌺 *Details not confirmed for 2000*

MUCHELNEY
MUCHELNEY ABBEY
TA10 0DQ
☎ 01458 250664

Encircled by marshes, Muchelney seemed a suitably remote spot in the 8th century for a Benedictine Abbey. The ruins that remain date from the 15th and 16th centuries, however, and there is also a 14th-century priest's house nearby. Exhibitions include Stuart furnishings and examples of the work of the modern potter, John Leach, whose pottery is nearby.

Times: Open Apr-Sep, daily 10-6; Oct 10-5.

Fee: £1.70 (ch 90p).

🅿 ♿ ✱ ♯

NETHER STOWEY
COLERIDGE COTTAGE
TA5 1NQ (off A39)
☎ 01278 732662

It was in this small cottage that Coleridge was most inspired as a poet and here that he wrote *The Ancient Mariner*. The Coleridge family moved to Nether Stowey in 1796 and became friendly with the Wordsworths who lived nearby.

Times: Open Apr-1 Oct, Tue-Thu & Sun 2-5 (Parlour & Reading room only). In winter by written application to custodian.

🅿 ✱ 🌺 *Details not confirmed for 2000*

NUNNEY
NUNNEY CASTLE
(3.5m SW of Frome, off A361)

Built in 1373, and supposedly modelled on France's Bastille, this crenellated manor house has one of the deepest moats in England. It was ruined by Parliamentarian forces in the Civil War.

Times: Open any reasonable time.

♿ ♯

SPARKFORD
HAYNES MOTOR MUSEUM
BA22 7LH (from A303 follow A359 road towards Castle Cary, the museum is clearly signposted)
☎ 01963 440804   ▤ 01963 441004

Spectacular collection of historic cars, motorcycles and motoring memorabilia. Vehicles range from a 1903 Oldsmobile to sports cars of the 50s and 60s and modern day classics. Also at the Museum is a 70 seat video cinema, the Hall of Motorsports, a millenium hall and a picnic area and children's adventure playground. Please phone for details of special driving-related events.

Times: Open all year, Mar-Oct , daily 9.30-5.30; Nov-Feb, 10-4.30. Etr-summer hols open to 6.30pm. (Closed 25 Dec & 1 Jan).

Fee: *£4.95 (ch 5 £2.95, concessions £3.95)

🅿 💻 ♿ (ramps & loan wheelchairs available) toilets for disabled shop 🐕 (ex in grounds) 🍴

🏛 STOKE ST GREGORY
WILLOW & WETLANDS VISITOR CENTRE
Meare Green Court TA3 6HY (between North Curry & Stoke St Gregory)
☎ 01823 490249 ▤ 01823 490814

This centre gives a fascinating insight into the levels and moors of Somerset, which are the most important remaining 'wetland' areas in Britain. There are informative sections on local flora and fauna. Also of note is the guided tour, covering all aspects of the withy growing and processing industry and offering visitors the chance to see basket weaving in progress. There is also a basket museum.

Times: Open all year, Mon-Fri 9-5 (guided tours 10-4), Sat (no tours) 9-5. Closed Sun.

Fee: *£2.50 (ch £1.25, pen £2). Party. Credit cards only accepted if total admission price exceeds £10.

🅿 ♿ shop 🍴

🏛 STREET
THE SHOE MUSEUM
C & J Clark Ltd, High St BA16 0YA
☎ 01458 443131 ▤ 01458 843110

The museum is in the oldest part of the shoe factory set up by Cyrus and James Clark in 1825. It contains shoes from Roman times to the present, buckles, engravings, fashion plates, machinery, hand tools and advertising material. One section illustrates the early history of the shoe firm and its role in the town.

Times: Open all year.

Fee: Free.

🅿 (charged) 💻 ✗ ♿ toilets for disabled shop 🐕

🏛 TAUNTON
HESTERCOMBE GARDENS
Cheddon Fitzpaine TA2 8LG (3m N, off A361 near Cheddon Fitzpaine).
☎ 01823 413923 ▤ 01823 413727

There are three period gardens to enjoy at Hestercombe: the 40-acre Georgian pleasure grounds with woodland walks, temples, Witch House and Great Cascade; the Victorian terrace with its newly restored fountain; and the Edwardian gardens, where the work of Gertrude Jekyll and architect Edwin Lutyens are shown off to full effect. Contact the Gardens Office for details of special events.

Times: Open every day, 10-6 (last admission 5).

Fee: *£3.50 (ch5-15 £1).

🅿 💻 ♿ toilets for disabled shop garden centre (Apr-Oct) 🐕 (ex on lead)

🏛 TINTINHULL
TINTINHULL HOUSE GARDEN
BA22 9PZ (.5m S off A303)
☎ 01935 822545

An attractive, mainly 17th-century farmhouse with a Queen Anne façade, it stands in four acres of beautiful formal gardens and orchard. The gardens were largely created by Mrs Reiss, who gave the property to the National Trust in 1953.

Times: Open Apr-Sep, Wed-Sun & BH Mons 12-6 (last admission 5.30pm).

🅿 🐕 ♨ *Details not confirmed for 2000*

🏛 WASHFORD
CLEEVE ABBEY
TA23 0PS (0.25m S of A39)
☎ 01984 40377

The now ruined Cistercian abbey was founded at the end of the 12th century. Little remains of the church, but the gatehouse, dormitory and refectory are in good condition, with traceried windows, a fine timbered roof and wall paintings to be seen.

Times: Open all year, Apr-Oct, daily 10-6 (or dusk if earlier); Nov-Mar, Wed-Sun 10-4 (closed 1-2pm). Closed 24-26 Dec & 1 Jan.

Fee: £2.60 (ch £1).

🅿 ♿ shop 🐕 (in certain areas) ♯

⚑ WELLS
THE BISHOP'S PALACE
Henderson Rooms BA5 2PD (next to cathedral off the Market Sq)
☎ 01749 678691 📄 01749 678691

Close to the cathedral is the moated bishop's palace. The early part of the palace, the bishop's chapel and the ruins of the banqueting hall date from the 13th century; the undercroft remains virtually unchanged from this time. There are several state rooms and a long gallery which houses portraits of former Bishops. Events include a Sealed Knot battle re-enactment (August). Please telephone for details.
Times: Open Apr-Oct, Tue-Fri & BH's; daily in Aug 10.30-6 Sun 2-6. Gates close at exactly 6pm.
Fee: *£3 (ch 12 accompanied free, UB40's £1.50, pen £2, disabled £1.50). Party 10+.
📶 🍴 ✕ licensed ♿ (free use of electric wheelchair)

⚑ WESTON-SUPER-MARE
THE HELICOPTER MUSEUM
Weston Airport, Locking Moor Rd BS22 8PL (outskirts of town on A371)
☎ 01934 635227 📄 01934 822400

The world's largest rotary-wing collection and the only helicopter museum in Britain. More than 50 helicopters and autogyros are on display - including examples from Farance, Germany, Poland, Russia and the United States, from 1935 to the present day - with displays of models, engines and other components explaining the history and development of the rotocraft. Special events include `Open Cockpit Days', when visitors can try out the pilot's seat of a helicopter, and learn from the museum guides how it really flies. On Restoration Open Days, tours of the restoration hangar show work in progress, and Weston Super Helidays take place on the seafront and include flying and static displays of up to 50 helicopters.
Times: Open all year, Nov-Mar Wed-Sun 10-4. Apr-Oct daily 10-6. (closed 24-26 Dec & 1 Jan)
Fee: *£3.50 (ch under 5 free, ch 5-16 £2.50, pen £3). Family ticket £10. Party 10+.
📶 🍴 ♿ toilets for disabled shop 💳

⚑ WOOKEY HOLE
WOOKEY HOLE CAVES & PAPERMILL
BA5 1BB
☎ 01749 672243 📄 01749 677749

A half-mile guided tour leads visitors through this amazing complex of caves, with stalagmites, stalactites and other interesting geological features. There is also a Victorian papermill, and fairground attractions such as a mirror maze and penny arcade.
Times: Open all year, Mar-Oct 10-5; Nov-Feb 10.30-4.30. (Closed 17-25 Dec).
Fee: *£7 (ch £3.50)
📶 ✕ licensed ♿ (Papermill only) toilets for disabled shop ✖ (ex guide dogs) 💳

⚑ YEOVILTON
FLEET AIR ARM MUSEUM
Royal Naval Air Station BA22 8HT (on B3151)
☎ 01935 841524 📄 01935 840181

A collection of over 50 historic aircraft, several unique, are on display here. Special exhibitions using modern audio visual aids and displays put the exhibits in their original context. In addition, you can climb aboard and walk through Concorde 002, the British prototype. The Ultimate Aircraft Carrier Experience offers all the sights, sounds, smells and action of a real aircraft carrier.
Times: Open all year, daily (ex 24-26 Dec) 10-5.30 (4.30pm Nov-Mar).
Fee: *phone for price details.
📶 🍴 ✕ licensed ♿ (wheelchairs available) toilets for disabled shop ✖ (ex guide dogs) 💳

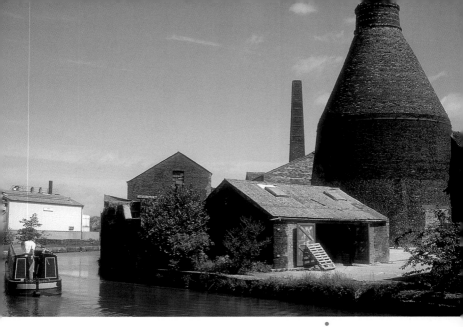

Staffordshire

For many, the main attractions of Staffordshire are the rollercoaster entertainment of Alton Towers or the precision craftsmanship of the world-famous potteries of Stoke-on-Trent. Yet the county also has some beautiful countryside and historic sites.

Part of the Peak District National Park forms the top right-hand corner of the county, and contains landscape ideal for hiking or pony trekking, as well as more adventurous pastimes such as rock climbing or hang-gliding.

Toward the south lies Cannock Chase, 30,000 acres of forest and heathland that was once a royal hunting preserve, and where a large herd of fallow deer still run free. The Chase is also home to cemeteries of fallen servicemen, including 5,000 Germans who died in Britain during two World Wars.

The Vale of Trent is known for its gentle beauty, and provides a welcome contrast to the craggy splendour of the moorland. Miles of rural canals (more than any other county) are also a welcoming sight.

Staffordshire has many historic attractions, including Lichfield's three-spired cathedral which contains the 7th-century Gospels of St Chad. The town was also the birthplace of Dr Samuel Johnson, who was born in a bookshop, and each year there are celebrations to commemorate the man who gave us the first Dictionary of the English Language.

Burton-upon-Trent is the 'Brewing Capital of England', and the Bass Museum Visitors Centre will surely provide a certain something that will banish the thirst.

EVENTS & FESTIVALS

March
18th Stafford Half Marathon

April
15th-16th Classic Bike Show, Stafford

May
31st-1st June Staffordshire County Show, Stafford
tbc Medieval Heritage Fun, Stafford Castle

June
tbc Staffordshire County Show, Bingley Hall

July
tbc Stafford Festival
tbc Goose Fair, Shugborough
22nd Firework & Laser Symphony Concert, Shugborough Hall

September
tbc Heavy Horse & Harvest, Shugborough

Top: Pottery Factory

⚏ ALTON
ALTON TOWERS
ST10 4DB (signposted from M1 junc 23A, M6 junc 15, M1 junc 28 or M6 junc 16)
☎ 0990 204060 🖷 01538 704097

Alton Towers offers rides, shows and attractions guaranteed to suit every member of the family. There are enchanting children's areas and the theme park has more thrill rides than any other in Europe. The Alton Towers Hotel displays a weird and wonderful array of artefacts and memorabilia from a bygone age. On top of all this, there are 200 acres of landscaped gardens and the majestic ruins of the Towers themselves.

Times: Open mid Mar-early Nov 9.30 until 1 hr after attractions close. Attractions 10-5, 6, 7 as shown daily at main entrance gate.

Fee: *£19.50 (ch £15.50, under 4's free, pen £10). Prices subject to change.

🅿 💺 ✕ licensed ♿ (disabled guest guide books) toilets for disabled shop ✈ (ex guide dogs) 🍽

⚏ BIDDULPH
BIDDULPH GRANGE GARDEN
Grange Rd ST8 7SD (off A527, 0.5m N of Biddulph)
☎ 01782 517999 🖷 01782 510624

This rare survival of a high Victorian garden has undergone extensive restoration. Conceived by James Bateman, the fifteen acres are divided into a number of smaller gardens which were

designed to house specimens from his extensive plant collection.

Times: Open 27 Mar-31 Oct, Wed-Fri 12-6. Sat-Sun & BH Mon 11-6 (last admission 5.30 or dusk if earlier); 6 Nov-19 Dec, Sat-Sun 12-4.

Fee: *Mar-Oct; £4.20 (ch £2.10). Family ticket £10.50. Nov-Dec; £2 (ch £1). Family ticket £5.

🅿 💺 shop ✈ 🐾

⚏ BURTON-UPON-TRENT
THE BASS MUSEUM
PO Box 220, Horninglow St DE14 1YQ (from N junc 28 M1, A38, A511; from S junc 24 A564, A38)
☎ 01283 511000 🖷 01283 513509

The museum is housed in the Engineers' Department and Company's Joiner's Shop, built in 1866. Three floors of entertaining and interesting exhibits trace the history of the brewing industry. Other attractions include a model of Burton as it was in 1921, stables with Shire horses, and a steam locomotive. There is a fine collection of drinking glasses and of course, the beer. Phone for details of special events.

Times: Open all year, Mon-Fri 10-5, Sat & Sun 11-5. Last admission 4pm. (Closed 25-26 Dec & 1 Jan).

Fee: *£4.50 (ch £2, pen £3). Family ticket £12.50. Brewery tours by arrangement only, at extra charge (inc free glass of beer/lager/soft drink)

🅿 ✕ licensed ♿ (lift to all floors) toilets for disabled shop ✈ (ex guide dogs) 🍽

🏛 CHEDDLETON
CHEDDLETON FLINT MILL
Beside Caldon Canal, Leek Rd ST13 7HL (3m S of Leek on A520)
☎ 01782 502907

Two water mills complete with wheels are preserved here, and both are in running order. The 17th-century south mill was used to grind corn, but the 18th-century north mill was built to grind flint for the pottery industry. The restored buildings have displays on aspects of the pottery industry. Exhibits include examples of motive power, such as a Robey steam engine, and of transport, such as the restored 70ft horse-drawn narrow boat 'Vienna', which is moored on the Caldon Canal. There is also a haystack boiler of around 1770.
Times: Open all year, Sat & Sun 2-5, Mon-Fri 10-5.
Fee: *Donations.
P &

🏛 LICHFIELD
ERASMUS DARWIN CENTRE
Beacon St WS13 7AD (signposted Lichfield Cathedral. Access by foot through the cathedral close)
☎ 01543 306260   📠 01543 306109

The Centre is dedicated to Erasmus Darwin, Charles Darwin's grandfather, a talented doctor, inventor, philosopher and poet, who resided in Lichfield for more than 20 years. It is contained in a beautiful 18th century house complete with a delightful period garden. Period rooms, audio-visual and interactive displays re-create the story of Erasmus' life, ideas and inventions.
Times: Open Tue-Sat 10-4.30, Sun noon-4.30, BH Mons 10-4.30.
Fee: *£2 (concessions £1.50). Family ticket £5.
P (200mtrs) & toilets for disabled shop garden centre ✈ (ex guide dogs)

LICHFIELD CATHEDRAL
WS13 7LD (signposted from all major roads and within city)
☎ 01543 306240   📠 01543 306109

The three spires, known as the Ladies of the Vale, dominate the landscape. The first cathedral here was founded in AD700 to house the shrine of St Chad. The present building, with its elaborate carvings, has been much restored since it was attacked during the Civil War. Among its treasures is an 8th-century illuminated manuscript, the Lichfield Gospels. Musical events are held, please ring for details.
Times: Open daily 7.45-6.
Fee: *Suggested donation of £3 for each adult visitor.
P (200mtrs) 🍽 ✗ licensed & (Touch & hearing centre for blind) toilets for disabled shop ✈ (ex guide dogs)

LICHFIELD HERITAGE CENTRE
Market Square WS13 6LG
☎ 01543 256611   📠 01543 414749

Fine silver in the Treasury and lively presentations on the Civil War are featured here. The displays tell the story of the city and include photographs and memorabilia. The City's ancient charters and archives can be seen in the Muniment room. Phone for details of events.
Times: Open all year, daily 10-5. Last admission 4.14pm. (Closed Xmas, New Year & Spring BH Mon).
Fee: *£2 (ch, students & pen £1.50. Family ticket £6. (Joint ticket with Samuel Johnson Birthplace Museum £3.20, concessions £1). Viewing platform £1 (80p concessions) School parties by arrangement. Prices are under review.
P (200yds) 🍽 & (lift) toilets for disabled shop ✈

SAMUEL JOHNSON BIRTHPLACE MUSEUM
Breadmarket St WS13 6LG
☎ 01543 264972   📠 01543 258441

A statue of Dr Johnson sits at one end of Market Square facing his birthplace on the corner of Breadmarket Street. The house, where Samuel's father had a bookshop, is now a museum containing many of Johnson's personal relics. His favourite armchair and walking stick are among the collection. Johnson Birthday celebrations take place in September.
Times: Open daily 10.30-4.30. (Closed Xmas, New Year & Sun Nov-Jan).
Fee: *£2 (ch & pen £1.10). Joint ticket with Lichfield Heritage Centre £3.20 (ch & pen £2.20). Family ticket £5.40.
P (500yds) shop ✈

🏛 MOSELEY
MOSELEY OLD HALL
V10 7HY (4m N of Wolverhampton, off A460)
☎ 01902 782808   📠 01902 782808

Charles II sheltered in Moseley Old Hall after the Battle of Worcester in 1651. There are numerous pictures and other reminders of the king. The house itself is an Elizabethan timber-framed building which was encased in brick in the 19th century. The small garden has a nut walk, period herbs and plants, and a formal knot garden. For details of special events please send a 9" x 4" envelope.
Times: Open 20 Mar-19 Dec; Mar-May Wed, Sat-Sun, BH Mon and Tues 1.30-5.30 (BH 11-5). June-Oct Wed & Sat-Sun, BH Mon and Tue; also Tue in July & Aug 1.30-5.30 (BH Mon 11-5); Nov & Dec: Sun 1.30-4.30 (guided tour only, last tour at 4pm).
Fee: *£3.90 (ch £1.95). Family ticket £9.75. Party 15+.
P 🍽 ✗ licensed & (braille & large print, 1 wheelchair) toilets for disabled shop ✈ (ex guide dogs) 🐾 🛍

STOKE-ON-TRENT

Stoke-on-Trent is the heart of one of Britain's oldest industrial conurbations, known as The Potteries. For many years a thick pall of smoke from the pottery furnaces hung over the six towns which now make up modern Stoke-on-Trent. Today, pottery production continues but the industrial grime has all but disappeared. The potteries run visitor centres, factory shops and museums, while the city is turning into something of a cultural centre complete with new theatres and a concert hall. Famous folk from The Potteries include novelist Arnold Bennett, Spitfire designer Reginald Mitchell, footballing legend Sir Stanley Matthews, and Bourne and Clowes, Primitive Methodists.

SHUGBOROUGH
SHUGBOROUGH ESTATE
ST17 OXB (6m E of Stafford off A513, signposted from M6 J13)
☎ **01889 881388** 🖹 **01889 881323**

Set on the edge of Cannock Chase, Shugborough is the magnificent 900-acre seat of the Earls of Lichfield. The 18th-century mansion contains fine collections of ceramics, silver, paintings and French furniture, and part of the house is still lived in by the Lichfield family. Visitors can enjoy the Grade I listed historic garden and a unique collection of neo-classical monuments. Other attractions include the museum and the original servants quarters, the laundry, kitchens, brewhouse and coachhouses which have all been restored and costumed guides show you how the servants lived and worked over 100 years ago. Shugborough Park Farm is a Georgian farmstead that has an agricultural museum, working corn mill and rare breeds centre. Please telephone for details of special events.
Times: Open 27 Mar-27 Sep, daily 11-5. Sun only Oct. Site open all year to pre-booked parties.
🅿 (charged) 🍽 ✕ licensed & (step climber for wheelchairs, 2 Batricars) toilets for disabled shop ✖ (ex in parkland) ✿ *Details not confirmed for 2000* 🍽

STAFFORD
SHIRE HALL GALLERY
Market Square ST16 2LD
☎ **01785 278345** 🖹 **01785 278327**

A fine gallery housed in the 18th-century Shire Hall - one of Staffordshire's most magnificent buildings. It holds exhibitions of contemporary arts, contains historic courtrooms and a Crafts Council selected craft shop.
Times: Open all year, Mon-Fri 10-5, Sat 10-5. Gallery closes for exhibition changes, please telephone for information.
Fee: Free.
🅿 (200yds) 🍽 & toilets for disabled shop ✖ (ex guide dogs) 🍽

STOKE-ON-TRENT
CERAMICA
Burslem Old Town Hall, Market Place, Burslem ST6 4AR
☎ **01782 832001** 🖹 **01782 832001**

An entertaining and educational experience on the theme of the potteries industry. Key exhibits include the Arnold Bennett study room, Bizzareland for children, Magic Carpet Ride and pavillions illustrating pottery manufacturing (past, present and future).
Times: Open daily 10-5 (Sun 10-4).
Fee: £3 (concessions £2, ch under 3 free)
🅿 (charged) & toilets for disabled shop ✖ (ex guide dogs)

ETRURIA INDUSTRIAL MUSEUM

Lower Bedford St, Etruria ST4 7AF (M6 J16, A500 onto Stoke Rd (A5006))

☎ 01782 233144   ▤ 01782 233145

The Etruscan Bone and Flint Mill was built in 1857 to grind materials for the agricultural and pottery industries, and is Britain's sole surviving, steam-powered potters' mill. There is a working blacksmiths forge on site and regular demonstrations of steam machinery from April to December (phone for details). A Canal Festival takes place on 3-4 June 2000.

Times: Open all year, Wed-Sun 10-4. (Closed Xmas & New Year).
Fee: *£1.50 (concessions £1). Family ticket £4.
🅿 💻 ౬ toilets for disabled shop 🐾 (ex guide dogs)

GLADSTONE POTTERY MUSEUM

Uttoxeter Rd, Longton ST3 1PQ (on A50, signposted from A500 link with M6)

☎ 01782 319232   ▤ 01782 598640

The last complete Victorian pottery factory from the days of bottle kilns. Tour the factory and see the pottery making skills of the craftsmen and craftswomen. You can perhaps throw a pot or make a bone china flower. With its cobbled yard and giant bottle kilns, Gladstone perfectly captures the City's atmospheric past. The head clerk of 1910 will talk about life in the factory at that time. There is a new `family-sized' potters' wheel where all the family can have a go at throwing a pot.

Times: Open all year, daily 10-5 (last admission 4pm). Limited opening Xmas & New Year.
Fee: *£3.95 (ch £2.50, students & pen £2.95). Family ticket £10.
🅿 💻 ✕ licensed ౬ toilets for disabled shop 🐾 (ex guide dogs)

THE POTTERIES MUSEUM & ART GALLERY

Bethesda St, Hanley ST1 3DE

☎ 01782 232323   ▤ 01782 232500

The history of the Potteries under one roof, including a dazzling display of the world's finest collection of Staffordshire ceramics. Other displays introduce natural, social and archaeological history from in and around The Potteries, and a Mark 16 Spitfire commemorating its locally born designer - Reginald Mitchell. Phone for details of special events.

Times: Open all year, Mon-Sat 10-5, Sun 2-5. (Closed Xmas-New Year).
Fee: Free.
🅿 (500mtrs) 💻 ౬ (lift, induction loop, 2 wheelchairs available) toilets for disabled shop 🐾 (ex guide/helping dogs)

ROYAL DOULTON VISITOR CENTRE

Nile St, Burslem ST6 2AJ (follow Brown tourist signs)

☎ 01782 292434   ▤ 01782 292424

The Centre houses over 1,500 Royal Doulton figures including many rare models. The Sir Henry Doulton Gallery combines magnificent treasures from the varied Royal Doulton past. Factory tours can be booked from Monday to Friday. A full promotional calendar is available on request.

Times: Open all year, Mon-Sat 9.30-5, Sun 10.30-4.30. Factory tours by advance booking Mon-Fri 10.30-2 (1.30 Fri). (Closed Xmas week). No tours during factory holidays.
Fee: *Visitor Centre only £3 (concessions £2.25); Factory Tour & Visitor Centre £6.50 (concessions £5). Parties 12+
🅿 💻 ✕ ౬ (Visitor Centre fully accessible) toilets for disabled shop 🐾 (ex guide dogs)

SPODE

Church St ST4 1BX (A500, then one-way-system to Elenora St, entrance on right. Do not follow city centre signs)

☎ 01782 744011   ▤ 01782 747612

Spode (established 1770) is the oldest English pottery company still on its original site, and is where Josiah Spode first perfected the formula for fine bone china. The Spode site houses a restaurant, factory shop outlets, and a visitors centre with exhibits on the history and heritage of the ceramics industry. Factory tours are available.

Times: Visitor Centre, Museum & Site factory shops. Mon-Sat 9-5, Sun 10-4. Factory Tours by prior appointment weekdays only, not available during factory closures-ring for details.
Fee: *Visitor Centre & Museum £2.75 (ch over 5 & concessions £2.25). Standard factory tours £4.75 (ch over 12 & concessions £3.75). Connoisseur tour £7 & £6. Tours by appointment only.
🅿 (charged) ✕ ౬ (limited access for the disabled) toilets for disabled shop (parking fee refundable on purchases) 🐾 (ex guide dogs)

WEDGWOOD VISITOR CENTRE

Barlaston ST12 9ES (5m S)

☎ 01782 204141 & 204218
▤ 01782 204402

The complex includes an art gallery with works by Reynolds, Stubbs and Romney, and a reconstruction of Wedgwood's original 18th-century Etruria workshops, as well as a museum with a large collection of Wedgwood ware.

contd.

Traditional pottery skills are regularly demonstrated.

Times: Open all year, Mon-Fri 9-5, Sat & Sun 10-5; (Closed Xmas & 1 Jan).

P ✕ licensed ♿ toilets for disabled shop ✈ *Details not confirmed for 2000*

TAMWORTH

Drayton Manor Theme Park & Zoo

B78 3TW (on A4091)

☎ 01827 287979 📠 01827 288916

A family theme park set in 250 acres of parkland and lakes with a zoo and zoo farm. There are over 100 rides and attractions for all age groups, including the UK's first stand-up roller coaster, Splash Canyon Raft Ride, Pirate Adventure, Dinosaur Land, Jungle Cruise, Victorian Carousel, Looping Roller Coaster, and Log Flume. End of season firework display, usually held last weekend in Oct. Ring for details.

Times: Park & Zoo open Etr-30 Oct, daily 10.30-6. Park (rides) 10.30-5, 6 or 7 (depending on season).

Fee: *£3 (ch 4-15 & pen £2). Wristband for unlimited rides £11 (junior-under 13yrs £8). Wheelchair and helper £5 each.

P ☕ ✕ licensed ♿ toilets for disabled shop garden centre ✈ (ex in park) 💳

Tamworth Castle

The Holloway B79 7LR (from M42 J10 & M6 J12, access via A5)

☎ 01827 63563 & 709626 📠 01827 56567 or 709630

Tamworth is a dramatic Norman motte and bailey castle set in an attractive town centre park with floral terraces. 15 authentically furnished rooms are open to the public, including the Great Hall, the Dungeon, and the Haunted Bedroom. There are also 'Living Images' of Baron Marmion, the Black Lady ghost, and a Victorian prisoner. "The Tamworth Story" exhibition tells the history of the town from Roman times to the present day, while "Tamworth on the Move" explores the evolution of transport in the area since the Norman conquest.

Times: Open all year, Mon-Sat 10-5.30; Sun 2-5.30. Last admission 4.30.(Closed 24-26 Dec).

Fee: *£4 (ch £2, pens £3). Family £11. Prices subject to change

P (100yds & 400yds) ♿ (one wheelchair for use inside the castle) shop ✈ (ex guide dogs & hearing dogs)

WALL

Wall Roman Site

Watling St (off A5)

☎ 01543 480768

Wall was originally the Roman fort of Letocetum, standing at the crossroads of Watling Street and Rykneild Street. It was an important military base

from about AD50. Excavations have revealed the most complete bath house ever found in Britain.
Times: Open Apr-Nov, daily 10-6 (or dusk if earlier)
Fee: £2.25 (ch £1.10).
✦ ✿ ♨

⌂ WHITTINGTON
STAFFORDSHIRE REGIMENT MUSEUM, WHITTINGTON BARRACKS
WS14 9PY (on A51 between Lichfield/Tamworth)
☎ 0121 311 3240/3229
🖹 0121 311 3205

Located next to Whittington Barracks, the museum tells the story of the soldiers of the Staffordshire Regiment and its predecessors. Exhibits include vehicles, uniforms, weapons, medals and memorabilia relating to three hundred years of regimental history, including distinguished service in the First and Second World Wars and the Gulf War.
Times: Open all year, Tue-Fri 10-4.30 (Last admission 4), weekends and BH 1-5 (closed Xmas-New Year). Parties at other times by arrangement.
Fee: *£1.50 (concessions £1). Regimental Association Members & Serving Soldiers free.
🅿 ♿ (ramps) toilets for disabled shop ✦ (outside only ex guide dogs)

⌂ WILLOUGHBRIDGE
THE DOROTHY CLIVE GARDEN
TF9 4EU (on A51 between Nantwich & Stone)
☎ 01630 647237 🖹 01630 647902

This 200-year-old gravel quarry has been converted into a delightful woodland garden. The quarry is at the top of a small hill and the garden has fine views of the countryside and adjoining counties. There is a variety of rare trees and shrubs. The garden provides colour and interest throughout the seasons from spring to glowing autumn tints.
Times: Open Apr-Oct daily 10-5.30.
Fee: *£3 (ch up to 11 yrs free, ch 11-16: £1, pen £2.50). Party 20+.
🅿 🚾 ♿ (wheelchairs for use, special route) toilets for disabled ✦ (ex on leads)

Suffolk

Britain's most easterly county has plenty to offer to visitors, aside from the enviable fact that it has the driest regional climate in England.

Suffolk was once part of the kingdom of East Anglia. Back then the kingdom was protected by almost impenetrable boundaries; sea to the north and east, the undrained Fens to the west, and a barrier of oak forest to the south. However, these natural defences didn't stop invasion from Romans, Angles, Vikings, and Saxons, all of whom have left their mark on the area. In later years Icelandic fisherfolk settled in the coastal towns, and Flemish weavers helped the wool towns boom and also took part in the brewing industry.

Lavenham has some marvellous medieval timber houses as well as a church with a massive tower. John Constable, world-famous painter of 'The Haywain', went to school here and was born in nearby East Bergholt. Thomas Gainsborough was another artistic son of Suffolk, born in Sudbury, where a statue of him stands in the village square. Sudbury also features as 'Eatanswill' in Dickens' *The Pickwick Papers*.

Known collectively as the Sunrise Coast, the resorts of Lowestoft, Kessingland and Southwold have won awards for the cleanliness and safety of their sandy beaches. Lowestoft is Britain's most easterly town and sits between sandy beaches on one side and beautiful broadland on the other. Sparrow's Nest Park is located just below the lighthouse and the town also features a maritime museum, a War Memorial Museum and the Royal Naval Patrol Museum.

EVENTS & FESTIVALS

February
19th-27th Primrose & Spring Plant Festival, Ipswich

April
6th-8th Bury St Edmunds Beer Festival

May
1st Woodbridge Horse Show, Suffolk Showground, Ipswich
tbc Felixstowe Drama Festival

June
tbc Felixstowe Drama Festival
9th-25th Aldeburgh Festival of Music & Arts
31st May-1st June, Suffolk Show, Suffolk Show Showground, Ipswich
tbc Great Annual Recreation of Tudor Life, Kentwell Hall, Long Melford

July
tbc Great Annual Recreation of Tudor Life, Kentwell Hall, Long Melford

August
Snape Proms, Snape, nr Aldeburgh (all through month)
tbc Exhibition & Sale of Guild of Weavers, Spinners & Dyers, Southwold
tbc Felixstowe Carnival, Fair & Fireworks

September
tbc Ipswich Beer Festival

Top: Moot Hall, Aldeburgh

BUNGAY

OTTER TRUST

Earsham NR35 2AF (off A143)
☎ 01986 893470 📠 01986 892461

Otters are a rare sight in the wild nowadays, but at the Otter Trust it is possible to see these beautiful creatures at close quarters. One of the Trust's main aims is to breed this endangered species in captivity in sufficient numbers so that it can re-introduce young otters into the wild every year wherever suitable habitat remains to reinforce the vanishing wild population. The Trust has introduced captive-bred otters into the wild in Norfolk, Suffolk, Dorset, Hampshire, Essex, Wiltshire and Hertfordshire and subsequent scientific monitoring has shown that all these animals are breeding successfully. The Otter Trust covers 23 acres on the banks of the River Waveney. As well as the otter pens there are three lakes with a large collection of European waterfowl, lovely riverside walks and picnic areas.
Times: Open Apr (or Good Fri if earlier)-Sept, daily 10.30-6.
P 💷 よ toilets for disabled shop ✖ *Details not confirmed for 2000*

BURY ST EDMUNDS

ABBEY VISITOR CENTRE

Abbey Precinct, Abbey Gardens IP33 1RS
☎ 01284 763110

Local history museum housed in 11th century Norman house. Temporary exhibitions all year as well as resident collections which include 'Murder in the Red Barn' relics. Visitor centre with 'hands-on' activities and interpretation of medieval life in Bury St Edmunds.
Times: Open Etr Sat-Oct, daily 10-5.
P (200yds) よ shop ✖ *Details not confirmed for 2000*

MOYSE'S HALL MUSEUM

Cornhill IP33 1DX (in town centre)
☎ 01284 757488 📠 01284 757079

Moyse's Hall is a 12th-century Norman house built of flint and stone which now serves as a local history museum, and among the fascinating exhibits are memorabilia of the notorious William

Corder 'Murder in the Red Barn'. Telephone for details of events and acitivities for children.
Times: Open all year Mon-Sat 10-5, Sun 2-5. (Closed 25-26 Dec & Good Fri).
Fee: *£1.60 (concessions £1). Residents free.
P (200yds) よ shop ✖ (ex guide dogs)

CAVENDISH

THE SUE RYDER FOUNDATION MUSEUM

Sue Ryder Home & Headquarters CO10 8AY (on A1092 Long Melford to Clare road)
☎ 01787 280252 📠 01787 280548

The museum shows the work and history of the small but effective international foundation which cares for the sick and disabled. The Home's garden and chapel are also open.
Times: Open all year, daily 10-5.30. (Closed 25 Dec).
P ✖ よ toilets for disabled shop ✖ *Details not confirmed for 2000*

EUSTON

EUSTON HALL

IP24 2QP (on A1088, 3m S of Thetford)
☎ 01842 766366 📠 01842 766764

Home of the Duke and Duchess of Grafton, this 18th-century house is notable for its fine collection of pictures, by Stubbs, Lely, Van Dyck and other Masters. The grounds were laid out by John Evelyn, William Kent and `Capability' Brown, and include a 17th-century church in the style of Wren.
Times: Open 3 Jun-30 Sep, Thu only & Suns 27 Jun & 5 Sep 2.30-5.
Fee: *£3 (ch 50p, pen £2.50). Party 12+.
P 💷 よ shop ✖ (guide dogs by permission)

FLIXTON

EAST ANGLIA'S AVIATION HERITAGE CENTRE

The Street NR35 1NZ (off A143, take B1062)
☎ 01986 896644

Situated in the picturesque Waveney Valley, the museum has over 24 historic aircraft. There is also a Bloodhound surface-to-air missile, the 446th Bomb Group Museum, RAF Bomber Command Museum, and the Royal Observer

contd.

Corps Museum. Among the displays are Decoy Sites and Wartime Deception, and Fallen Eagles - Wartime Luftwaffe Crashes.

Times: Open Apr-Oct Sun-Thu 10-5 (last admission 4); Nov-Mar 10-4 (last admission 3) Tue, Wed, Sun. New year closed 2 weeks either side.

Fee: Free.

P & (ramp) toilets for disabled shop ✈

⛪ FRAMLINGHAM

FRAMLINGHAM CASTLE

IP13 9BP (on B1116)

☎ 01728 724189

Built by Hugh Bigod between 1177 and 1215, the castle has fine curtain walls, 13 towers and an array of Tudor chimneys. In the 17th century the castle was bequeathed to Pembroke College, Cambridge, which built almshouses inside the walls.

Times: Open all year, Apr-Oct, daily 10-6 (or dusk if earlier); Nov-Mar, daily 10-4. Closed 24-26 Dec & 1 Jan.

Fee: £3.10 (ch £1.60).

P & shop ✈ ⌗

⛪ HORRINGER

ICKWORTH HOUSE, PARK & GARDENS

The Rotunda IP29 5QE (2.5m S of Bury St Edmunds).

☎ 01284 735270   🖷 01284 735175

The eccentric Earl of Bristol created this equally eccentric house, begun in 1795, to display his collection of European art. The Georgian Silver Collection is considered the finest in private hands. Capability Brown designed the parkland, and also featured are a deer enclosure, waymarked walks and an adventure playground. Special events take place all year round, please phone for details.

Times: Open: House & Garden 23 Mar-3 Nov Tue, Wed, Fri, Sat & BH Mons 1-5; Garden all year daily 23 Mar-3 Nov 10-5. 4 Nov-Mar 10-4; Park daily 7am-7pm.

P ✗ licensed & (braille guide batricars stairlift to shop & restaurant) toilets for disabled shop ✈ (ex in park) 🐾 *Details not confirmed for 2000*

⛪ IPSWICH

CHRISTCHURCH MANSION

Soane St IP4 2BE (South side of Christchurch Park)

☎ 01473 253246 & 213761

🖷 01473 210328

The house was built in 1548 on the site of an Augustinian priory. Set in a beautiful park, it displays period rooms and an art gallery which has changing exhibitions. The Suffolk Artists' Gallery has a collection of paintings by Constable and Gainsborough.

Times: Open all year, Tue-Sat 10-5 (dusk in winter), Sun 2.30-4.30 (dusk in winter). (Closed Good Fri & 24-26 Dec & 1-2 Jan). Open BH mon.

P & (tape guide for partially sighted) shop ✈ *Details not confirmed for 2000*

IPSWICH MUSEUM

High St IP1 3QH

☎ 01473 213761 & 263550   🖷 01473 281274

The Museum has sections on Victorian Natural History, Suffolk wildlife, Suffolk geology, Roman Suffolk, and Peoples of the World. There is also one of the best bird collections in the country. Please ring for further information.

Times: Open all year, Tue-Sat 10-5. (Closed Sun, BH's, 24-26 Dec & 1 Jan).

Fee: Free.

P & shop ✈ (ex guide dogs)

⛪ LAVENHAM

LAVENHAM GUILDHALL

Market Place CO10 9QZ

☎ 01787 247646

Although it has been much restored, there are still many of the original Tudor features left in this picturesque timber-framed building. The hall and its small museum are a testament to the time when East Anglia had a flourishing woollen industry. There is a walled garden with a 19th-century lock-up and mortuary.

Times: Open 28 Mar-1 Nov, daily 11-5. (Closed Good Fri).

P (adjacent) ☕ shop ✈ 🐾 *Details not confirmed for 2000*

🏛 LEISTON
LEISTON ABBEY
(1m N off B1069)

For hundreds of years this 14th-century abbey was used as a farm and its church became a barn. A Georgian house, now used as a retreat house, was built into its fabric and remains of the choir, the church transepts and parts of the cloisters still stand.
Times: Open any reasonable time.
🅿 ♿ ⚘

🏛 LINDSEY
ST JAMES'S CHAPEL
Rose Green

Built mainly in the 13th century, this small thatched, flint-and-stone chapel incorporates some earlier work.
Times: Open all year.
♿ ⚘

🏛 LONG MELFORD
KENTWELL HALL
CO10 9BA (signposted off A134)
☎ 01787 310207 📄 01787 379318

Best known for its authentic re-creations of Tudor life, when participants carry on daily activities as they would have been done in Tudor times, this E-shaped Tudor mansion has preserved much of its original character. It has a brick-paved rose maze and exceptionally fine gardens. There is also a farm of rare breeds. Telephone for information about the events.
Times: Open 8 Mar-7 June Sun only; 14 Jun-5 Jul, Sat & Sun for Re-Creation; 8 Jul-6 Sep, daily, 6 Sept-25 Oct Wed, Thur, Sun, 12-5 (11-5 Re-Creations, 11-6 for BH weekends). Open BH weekends from Etr-Aug, Sat-Mon.
🅿 ✗ ♿ toilets for disabled shop ✗ Details not confirmed for 2000 🍴

MELFORD HALL
CO10 9AA (off A134, 3miles N of Sudbury)
☎ 01787 880286

Queen Elizabeth I was a guest at this turreted, brick-built Tudor house in 1578. It features an 18th-century drawing room, a Regency library and a Victorian bedroom. There is also a large collection of Chinese porcelain, and a display on Beatrix Potter, who was related to the owners and often stayed here. The garden has a Tudor pavilion, which may have been built as a guardhouse.
Times: Open Apr, wknds & BH Mon 2-5.30; May-Sep, Wed-Sun & BH Mon 2-5.30; Oct, wknds 2-5.30. Last admission 5pm
🅿 ♿ (stairlift) toilets for disabled ✗ (ex in park) 🌳 Details not confirmed for 2000

🏛 LOWESTOFT
EAST ANGLIA TRANSPORT MUSEUM
Chapel Rd, Carlton Colville NR33 8BL (3m SW of Lowestoft, on B1384. Follow brown signs from A12 & A146)
☎ 01502 518459 📄 01502 518459

A particular attraction of this museum is the reconstructed 1930s street scene which is used as a setting for working vehicles: you can ride by tram, trolley bus and narrow gauge railway. Other motor, steam and electrical vehicles are exhibited. There is also a woodland picnic area served by trams. Ring for details of special events.
Times: Open Good Fri & Etr Sat 2-4, Etr Sun-Etr Mon 11-5.30. May-Sep, Sun & BH's 11-5.30; Jun-Sep, Wed & Sat 2-5 (last entry 1 hour before closing).
Fee: *£4 (ch 5-15 & pen £2). Price includes rides. Party.
🅿 🍴 ♿ toilets for disabled shop

MARITIME MUSEUM
Sparrow Nest Gardens, Whapload Rd NR32 1XG (on A12)
☎ 01502 561963 & 511260

Models of ancient and modern fishing and commercial boats, fishing gear and shipwrights' tools are among the exhibits. There is also an art gallery.
Times: Open May-Sep, daily 10-5. Etr, Fri-Mon.
Fee: *50p (ch, students & pen 25p)
🅿 ♿ shop ✗ (ex guide & small dogs)

SOUTHWOLD

Suffolk's most attractive coastal town, overlooking Sole Bay, Southwold was once an important fishing port, though the industry has declined to a just a few boats these days, with catches of herring, sprats and cod in season. The town was devastated by fire in 1659, and Dutch and Flemish influences are apparent in the buildings that followed: flint, brick and colour-washed cottages set around a series of greens, some overlooking the sea. The towns main sights are the lighthouse, the Saxon church and Adnams, the town's brewery. Southwold was once known for its raw amber, and amber jewellery is available for sale in the town.

🏛 NEWMARKET
NATIONAL HORSERACING MUSEUM AND TOURS
99 High St CB8 8JL
☎ 01638 667333 🖹 01638 665600

A chance to meet the horses and stable staff at close quarters, watch the horses on the historic gallops and see them in the equine swimming pool. Retired jockeys will answer questions and let you ride the horse simulator at up to 40mph. Another attraction lets you record your own racing commentary. Ring for details of special tours. For 2000 there is an exhibition celebrating two thousand years of people and horses.
Times: Open Etr-Oct, Tue-Sat (also BH Mons & Mon in Jul & Aug) 10-5.
Fee: *£3.50 (ch £1.50, pen £2.50). Party 20+. Equine tours Tue-Sat when museum is open.
🅿 (300yds) 🍽 ✕ licensed ♿ toilets for disabled shop ✖ (ex guide dogs) ➷

🏛 ORFORD
ORFORD CASTLE
(on B1084)
☎ 01394 450472

Built by Henry II circa 1165, the castle's magnificent keep survives almost intact with three immense towers reaching to 90 feet. Inside there are many rooms to explore.
Times: Open all year, Apr-Oct, daily 10-6; Nov-Mar, Wed-Sun, 10-4. Closed 24-26 Dec & 1 Jan.
Fee: £2.50 (ch £1.30).
🅿 ✖ ✠

🏛 SAXTEAD GREEN
SAXTEAD GREEN POST MILL
(2.5m NW of Framlingham on A1120)
☎ 01728 685789

Dating from 1854, this is one of the finest examples of a traditional Suffolk post-mill. Machinery and millstones are in perfect order.
Times: Open Apr-Oct, Mon-Sat 10-6 (or dusk if earlier). Closed 1-2pm.
Fee: £2 (ch £1).
(exterior only) ✖ ✠

🏛 STOWMARKET
MUSEUM OF EAST ANGLIAN LIFE
IP14 1DL (signposted from A14 and B1115)
☎ 01449 612229 🖹 01449 672307

The extensive, 70-acre, all-weather museum is set in an attractive river-valley site. There are reconstructed buildings, including a water mill, a smithy and a wind pump, and the Boby Building houses craft workshops. Displays on Victorian domestic life, gypsies, farming and industry include working steam traction engines, the only surviving pair of Burrell ploughing engines of 1879, and a working Suffolk Punch horse. Other attractions include a charcoal burner at work and an adventure playground. Various events are held throughout the year, please phone for details.
Times: Open Apr-Oct.
🅿 (adjacent) 🍽 ♿ (wheelchairs available, special parking facilities) toilets for disabled shop *Details not confirmed for 2000* ➷

🏛 SUDBURY

GAINSBOROUGH'S HOUSE

46 Gainsborough St CO10 2EU

☎ 01787 372958 📠 01787 376991

The birthplace of Thomas Gainsborough RA (1727-88). The Georgian-fronted town house, with an attractive walled garden, displays more of the artist's work than any other gallery, together with 18th-century furniture and memorabilia. There's a varied programme of exhibitions throughout the year including fine art, craft, photography, printmaking and sculpture.

Times: Open all year - House Tue-Sat 10-5, Sun & BH Mons 2-5; (4pm Nov-Mar). (closed Good Fri & Xmas-New Year).

Fee: *£3 (ch, students & disabled £1.50 pen £2.20). Party rates available.

P (300 yds) & toilets for disabled shop ✈ 🍴

🏛 WESTLETON

RSPB NATURE RESERVE MINSMERE

IP17 3BY (signposted from A12 & Westleton)

☎ 01728 648281 📠 01728 648770

One of the RSPB's most popular sites, famous for its nesting avocets, marsh harriers and bitterns. Ideal for families and birdwatchers alike, there are countryside walks of varying lengths and eight hides. A Visitor Centre featuring interpretation, shop and tearoom is now open. Education programmes for school groups are also available. Full calender of events and activities available from the reserve.

Times: Open Wed-Mon 9am-9pm (or sunset if earlier). Visitor centre, shop & tearoom Apr-Oct 9-5, Nov-Mar 9-4.

P 🖵 & toilets for disabled shop ✈ *Details not confirmed for 2000* 🍴

🏛 WEST STOW

WEST STOW ANGLO SAXON VILLAGE

West Stow Country Park IP28 6HG (off A1101, follow brown tourist signs)

☎ 01284 728718 📠 01284 728277

The village is a reconstruction of a pagan Anglo-Saxon settlement dated 420-650 AD. Six buildings have been reconstructed on the site of the excavated settlement. There is a Visitors' Centre and a children's play area. Special events take place throughout the year, especially at Easter and in summer. Phone for details.

Times: Open all year, daily 10-5. Last entry 4.15pm

Fee: *£4.50 (ch £3.50) family ticket £13.

P 🖵 & (ramp, audio guides) toilets for disabled shop ✈ (ex guide dogs) 🍴

Surrey

Surrey is profoundly affected by its proximity to London, and much of the county has been developed to accommodate affluent commuters to the capital. Despite this, it has the reputation of being Britain's most wooded county, and it has some lovely countryside.

Particularly attractive are the areas around Haslemere and Shere. High points are the North Downs west of Guildford rising to a peak at Box Hill near Dorking, and Leith Hill which is 970 ft (294m) tall, making it the highest point in the southeast of England.

There are a number of attractions located within the area bounded by the M25 motorway. These include Sandown Park and Epsom racecourses, and the south's two huge theme parks, Thorpe Park and Chessington World of Adventures, where you can enjoy all the thrills and spills of white knuckle rides and a variety of themed areas to appeal to all age groups.

Kingston-upon-Thames is the county's administrative headquarters. Other main towns are Woking, Dorking and Guildford. The latter has a modern cathedral, consecrated in 1961, and the keep of the Norman Castle. The castle was frequented by King John, who signed the Magna Carta at Runnymede, a meadow on the south bank of the Thames, in 1215. The castle at Farnham is still in one piece, it dates from 1160 and was occupied until 1927. Farnham is a pleasant town with some graceful Georgian buildings, particularly in Castle Street.

Top: St Mary's Church, Chiddingfold

🏛 ASH VALE

ARMY MEDICAL SERVICES MUSEUM

Keogh Barracks GU12 5RQ (off M3 J4 on A331 to
Mytchett then follow tourist signs)
☎ 01252 340212 📄 01252 340224

The museum traces the history of Army
medicine, nursing and dentistry from 1660 until
the present day. Displays including uniforms and
medals are complemented by medical equipment
and ambulances. There is also a small veterinary
display.
Times: Open all year, Mon-Thu 9-3.30, Fri 9-3. (Closed Xmas,
New Year & BH). Wknds & BH by appointment only.
Fee: Free.
🅿 ♿ toilets for disabled shop ✖

🏛 EAST CLANDON

HATCHLANDS

GU4 7RT (E off A246)
☎ 01483 222482 📄 01483 223176

Robert Adam's first commission was to decorate
the interior of this 18th-century house. A
collection including instruments played by
Chopin, Mahler and Elgar is housed here. The
garden, by Gertrude Jekyll, has been restored and
new walks opened in the Repton park. Concerts
are held in the house and gardens. Please
contact Regional Box Office for details (01372)
451596.
Times: Open Apr-Oct, Tue-Thu, Sun & BH Mon 2-5.30. Last
admission 5pm. (Closed Good Fri). Also open Fri in Aug.
Gardens open as house. Park walks daily during open season
11.30-6.
Fee: *£4.30 (ch £2.15). Joint ticket with Clandon Park £6.20.
Grounds and Park walks £1.75. Family ticket £10.75.
🅿 ✖ licensed ♿ (wheelchair available & special parking)
toilets for disabled shop ✖ (ex guide dogs) 🐾

🏛 FARNHAM

BIRDWORLD & UNDERWATERWORLD

Holt Pound GU10 4LD (3m S on A325)
☎ 01420 22140 📄 01420 23715

Eighteen acres of garden and parkland are home
to a wide variety of birds, from the tiny tanager
to the great ostrich, and there is also an
aquarium with tropical, freshwater and marine
fish. During the breeding season there are lots of
rare baby birds to be seen in the Incubation
Research Station. A children's farm and play
area complete the scene. Telephone for details of
events.
Times: Open all year, daily from 9.30. (Closed 25 Dec).
🅿 💭 ♿ (wheelchairs available) toilets for disabled shop ✖
Details not confirmed for 2000 🔖

FARNHAM CASTLE KEEP

(half mile N on A287)
☎ 01252 713393

Built by an 11th-century bishop of Winchester,
the castle made a convenient resting place on
the journey to London. His tower, standing on a
mound, was later encircled by high walls.
Times: Open Apr-Oct, daily 10-6 (or dusk if earlier)
Fee: £2 (ch £1).
🅿 ✖ ♯

🏛 GREAT BOOKHAM

POLESDEN LACEY

RH5 6BD (2m S off A246 from village of
Bookham)
☎ 01372 452048 📄 01372 452023

King George VI and Queen Elizabeth (the Queen
Mother) spent part of their honeymoon here, and
photographs of other notable guests can be seen.
The house is handsomely furnished and full of
charm, and it is set in spacious grounds. There is
also a summer festival, where concerts and plays
are performed. Please phone 01372 451596 for
details of special events.
Times: Open all year. Grounds, Garden & Landscape walks:
daily 11-6. House: 27 Mar-Oct, Wed-Sun 1.30-5.30. Also BH
Mon 11-5.30. (last admission 30mins before closing)
Fee: *Ground, Garden & Landscape walks: £3; House: £3.
Family £7.50. Garden & House £5. Party 15+.
🅿 💭 ✖ licensed ♿ (braille guide & disabled parking by
arrangement) toilets for disabled shop ✖ (ex guide dogs or
grounds) 🐾

🏛 GUILDFORD

DAPDUNE WHARF

Wharf Rd GU1 4RR (off Woodbridge Road to rear
of Surrey County Cricket Ground)
☎ 01483 561389 📄 01483 531667

The Wey is one of the earliest historic waterways
in Britain dating from 1653. A series of
exhibitions, models and displays tells the story of
the Waterway, the people who lived and worked
on it and the barges built there. A restored Wey
barge, the 'Reliance', can be explored. A hurdle-
making day is planned for 18th June 2000.
Times: Open 27 Mar-Oct, Thu, wknds & BHs 12-5.
Fee: *£2.50 (ch £1). Family ticket £6
🅿 💭 ♿ (braille guide) toilets for disabled ✖ (ex on lead) 🐾

GUILDFORD CASTLE

GU1 3TU
☎ 01483 444702 📄 01483 444444

The three-storey ruined castle keep dates from
the 12th century and gives fine views; the castle
ditch has been transformed into a colourful
garden. Concerts and open-air theatre
performances are sometimes given in summer.
Times: Open: Grounds daily 8-dusk (Closed 25 Dec); Keep
Apr-Sep 10.30-6.
Fee: *85p (ch 40p).
🅿 (50yds) ♿

GUILDFORD HOUSE GALLERY

155 High St GU1 3AJ (N side of High St, opposite
Sainsbury's)
☎ 01483 444740 📄 01483 444742

An impressive building in its own right, Guildford
House dates from 1660 and has been Guildford's
art gallery since 1959. A changing selection from
the Borough's Art Collection is on display,
including pastel portraits by John Russell,
topographical paintings and contemporary
craftwork, as well as temporary exhibitions.
Times: Open Tue-Sat 10-4.45.
Fee: Free.
🅿 (100yds) 💭 ♿ shop ✖ 🔖

GUILDFORD

A single three-storey keep is all that remains of the castle built by William the Conqueror, and frequented by Edward I and his queen, Eleanor. The Guildhall in the city's High Street has ornate frontage and a gilded projecting clock which has kept time since 1683. The city also has a connection with the Reverend Charles Dodgson, aka Lewis Carroll. Dodgson rented a house here for his six unmarried sisters, and it was during his visits that he created many of the characters for 'Alice in Wonderland' and 'Alice's Adventures through the Looking-Glass.' Dodgson is buried in the Mount Cemetery and statues commemorating his characters can be seen around the city.

LOSELEY PARK
GU3 1HS (2m SW of Guildford, off A3 onto B3000)
☎ 01483 304440 & 505501
🖹 01483 302036

Sir William More built this house over four hundred years ago with stone from the ruins of Waverley Abbey, and the house is a fine example of Elizabethan architecture, set in magnificent parkland. The Walled Gardens include a Herb Garden, which illustrates the culinary, medicinal, dyeing and cosmetic uses of herbs.
Times: Walled Garden open 3 May-25 Sep, Wed-Sat & BH 11-5. House open 31 May-30 Aug, Wed-Sat & BH 2-5 (last tour 4pm). Estate trailer tour 31 May-30 Aug, Sat only 12-4.
Fee: *House & Gardens £5 (ch £3, ch under 3 free, concessions £4). Gardens only £2.50 (ch £1.50, concessions £2). Estate trailer tours £3 (ch £1.50, concessions £2.50).
🅿 💺 ♿ (wheelchair available, parking outside house) toilets for disabled shop ✈ (ex guide dogs)

⬛ HASCOMBE
WINKWORTH ARBORETUM
Hascombe Rd GU8 4AD (2m NW on B2130, follow brown tourist signs from Godalming)
☎ 01483 208477

This lovely woodland covers a hillside of nearly 100 acres, with fine views over the North Downs. The best times to visit are April and May, for the

azaleas, bluebells and other flowers, and October for the autumn colours.
Times: Open all year, daily during daylight hours. (could close when weather is bad)
Fee: *£2.70 (ch £1.35). Family ticket £6.75.
🅿 💺 ♿ toilets for disabled shop (Apr-Sep, Wed-Sun 11-5.30 & BH Mon) ✈ (ex on leads) ⬛

⬛ PAINSHILL PARK
PAINSHILL LANDSCAPE GARDEN
KT11 1JE (W of Cobham, on A245)
☎ 01932 868113   🖹 01932 868001

Painshill Landscape Garden is a fascinating 18th-century landscape created by the Hon Charles Hamilton. The huge lake, filled by a massive water wheel, meanders through the garden, giving a perfect setting for a Gothic temple, ruined abbey, and a Turkish tent.
Times: Open Apr-Oct, Tue-Sun & BH, 10.30-4.30. (gates close 6pm). Nov-Mar, Tue-Thu, wknds & BH 11-4 (gates close 4pm).
Fee: *£3.80 (ch over 5 £1.50, concessions £3.30). Party 10+.
🅿 💺 ♿ (wheelchairs & buggies available - prebooked)) toilets for disabled shop ✈ (ex guide dogs) ◀

⬛ WEST CLANDON
CLANDON PARK
GU4 7RQ (on A247)
☎ 01483 222482   🖹 01483 223479

An 18th-century house displaying a collection of Meissen Italian comedy figures and the Gubbay collection of porcelain, furniture and needlework.

This is also home to The Queens Royal Surrey regimental museum. There is a garden with parterre, grotto and Maori House. Concerts are held in the Marble Hall, please contact Regional Box Office for details - 01372 451596.

Times: Open 28 Mar-Oct, Tue, Wed, Thu, Sun & Good Fri, Etr Sat & BH Mons, 11.30-4.30. Last admission 4pm. Garden open daily 9-dusk. Museum open as House, 12-5.

Fee: *House & Garden £4.30 (ch £2.15). Family ticket £10.75. Combined ticket with Hatchlands £6.20.

🅿 💷 ✗ licensed ♿ (wheelchairs, braille guide & disabled parking) toilets for disabled shop ✖ (ex guide dogs) 🐾 🍽

⌂ WEYBRIDGE
BROOKLANDS MUSEUM
Brooklands Rd KT13 0QN (exit M25 at J10/11, museum off B374)
☎ 01932 857381   🖨 01932 855465

Brooklands racing circuit was the birthplace of British motorsport and aviation. From 1907 to 1987 it was a world-renowned centre of engineering excellence. The Museum features old banked track and the 1-in-4 Test Hill. Many of the original buildings have been restored including the Clubhouse, the Shell and BP Petrol Pagodas, and the Malcolm Campbell Sheds in the Motoring Village. Many motorcycles, cars and aircraft are on display. Ring for details of special events.

Times: Open Tue-Sun & BHs 10-5 (4pm in winter). Closed Good Friday & 23-31 Dec.

🅿 💷 ♿ toilets for disabled shop ✖ *Details not confirmed for 2000*

⌂ WISLEY
RHS GARDEN
GU23 6QB (on A3, close to M25 J10)
☎ 01483 224234   🖨 01483 211750

These experimental gardens of the Royal Horticultural Society were established in 1904. The property now covers over 240 acres, half of which is devoted to garden. The gardens have a wide variety of trees, shrubs and plants, many of which are unusual in Britain. There are also greenhouses and specialist gardens. Please telephone for details of special events.

Times: Open all year, Mon-Fri 10-6 or dusk (4.30pm Jan, Nov & Dec), opens 9am Sat. Sun members only 9-6 (4.30 Nov-Jan). (Closed 25 Dec). Glasshouses close at 4.15 or sunset Mon-Fri.

Fee: *£5 (ch 6-16 £2). Garden entry card £3.50. Party 10+.

🅿 💷 ✗ licensed ♿ (free wheelchairs) toilets for disabled shop garden centre ✖ (ex guide dogs) 🍽

East Sussex

Natural features of East Sussex include Beachy Head, the highest headland on the South Coast at 590 feet (180m), and the South Downs, the great chalky ridge that once connected England and the Continent, which stretches from Beachy Head into Hampshire.

The heathlands of Ashdown Forest are Winnie the Pooh country, including the bridge where Poohsticks was first played and a monument to A A Milne on Gill's Lap, the Enchanted Place of the much loved Pooh Bear stories.

The coastline is almost entirely built up, and major resorts are Brighton, Hastings and Eastbourne, with Newhaven as the cross channel port. Eastbourne enjoys the reputation of being one of Britain's sunniest seaside destinations, consistently at the top of the sunshine league tables. It is the most respectable of 19th-century resorts with a shingle beach and a fine Victorian pier. Hastings has a fading grandeur, but the Old Town is the most interesting quarter, which can be reached by the West Hill Cliff funicular railway.

Lewes, the county town, is set either side of the River Ouse, where it cuts through the South Downs and provides some dramatic vistas. Attractive streets and lanes known as 'twittens' are overlooked by the Norman castle.

There are castles in abundance in East Sussex: Hastings, Herstmonceux, Pevensey and Bodiam. The town of Battle, six miles (10km) from Hastings, is the site of the famous Battle of Hastings, where the Normans, led by William I, defeated Wessex, led by Harold II, on 14 October 1066.

EVENTS & FESTIVALS

January
31st December-1st Brighton New Year's Eve Street Party Celebrations

Feb
5th-6th Majik Glimpses Psychic Fair, Hove Town Hall

April
15th-16th Art Deco Fair, Hove Town Hall
Last week April & first week May (provisional) Lewes Festival
29th-30th & 1st May Festival of Motoring, Bexhill

May
6th-28th Brighton Festival
11th-14th International Street Theatre Weekend, Brighton

July
1st-14th Battle Festival

August
5th-3rd September, David Hockney Exhibition, Hove Museum
Bank Holiday weekend, Herstmonceux Castle Medieval Weekend

November
5th London-Brighton Veteran Car Run
25th Torchlit Blacksmiths' Procession (evening), Mayfield

Top: Seven Sisters, Seaford

🏛 ALFRISTON

ALFRISTON CLERGY HOUSE

The Tye BN26 5TL (4m NE of Seaford, E of
B2108, next to church in village)
☎ 01323 870001   ▤ 01323 871318

The thatched and timber-framed parish priests'
house was built in about 1350 and had not
changed very much by 1896, when it was
acquired by the National Trust (the first building
to be taken over by the Trust). Now carefully and
sensitively restored, it gives a vivid idea of
medieval living conditions. Outside the house is
a pretty cottage garden.
Times: Open 27 Mar-Oct, Sat-Mon, Wed & Thu 10-5(last
entrance 4.30 or sunset if earlier).
Fee: *£2.50.(ch £1.25). Family ticket £6.25.
P ((0.25 mile) (braille guide) shop ✖ (ex guide dogs) ♨

DRUSILLAS PARK

BN26 5QS (off A27)
☎ 01323 870234 & 870656
▤ 01323 870846

Drusillas presents animals in interesting and
naturalistic settings. There's lots to do and see,
including a penguin pool with underwater
viewing, and animal encounter sessions where
you can get close to anything from hamsters to
leopard geckos. There's an adventure playland,
face-painting, and a train ride. Special events
include Easter Egg Hunts, Clown's Day and Bird
of Prey displays. Please ring for details.

Times: Open all year, daily 10-5 (winter 10-4). Closed 24-26
Dec.
Fee: *£6.95 (ch 3-12 £5.75, pen/concessions £5.25). Ch under
3 free. Party 15+.
P 🍽 ✖ licensed ⅙ (rear carriage on train, sensory trail)
toilets for disabled shop ✖ (ex guide dogs) ⬛

🏛 BATTLE

BATTLE ABBEY

High St TN33 0AD (leave A21 onto A2100, abbey
at end of Battle High St)
☎ 01424 773792

Built by William the Conqueror, to atone for the
terrible slaughter of the Battle of Hastings in
1066, the Abbey's high altar stood on the spot
where Harold fell, and is still marked by a
memorial stone. The mile-long Battlefield Walk
takes you round the full perimeter of the
battlefield itself.
Times: Open all year, Apr-Oct, daily 10-6 (dusk if earlier in
Oct); Nov-Mar, Wed-Sun 10-4 . Closed 24-26 Dec & 1 Jan.
Fee: £4 (ch £2).
P (charged) ⅙ shop ✖ (allowed in certain areas) ▦

BATTLE & DISTRICT HISTORICAL SOCIETY MUSEUM (OPPOSITE ABBEY GREEN CAR PARK)

Memorial Hall, High St TN33 0AQ
☎ 01424 775955

The focal point of this museum is a diorama of
the Battle of Hastings and a reproduction of the
Bayeux Tapestry. There are also local history
exhibits. A Summer Arts Festival is held, and the
Battle Festival takes place in June/July. Special
displays of old photographs, toys etc are
arranged throughout the season.
Times: Open Etr-Sep, daily 10.30-4.30 (Sun 2-5).
Fee: *£1 (ch 20p, ch accompanied free).
P (20yds) shop ✖ (ex guide dogs)

🏛 BODIAM

BODIAM CASTLE

TN32 5UA (2m E of A21 Hurst Green)
☎ 01580 830436   ▤ 01580 830398

With its tall round drum towers at each corner,
Bodiam is something of a fairytale castle. It was
built in 1386 by Sir Edward Dalnygrigge, for
comfort and defence. The walls measure some
6ft 6in thick, and the great gatehouse was
defended by gun loops and three portcullises.
Telephone for details of special events.
Times: Open 14 Feb-1 Nov, daily 10-6 or dusk if earlier; 3
Nov-2 Jan, Tue-Sun 10-4 or dusk. (Closed 24-26 Dec).
Fee: *£3.50 (ch £1.75). Family ticket £8.75. Car £1.
P (charged) 🍽 ✖ ⅙ (Braille guides, special parking on
request) toilets for disabled shop ✖ (ex in grounds on a lead)
♨ ⬛

🏛 BRIGHTON

MUSEUM & ART GALLERY

Church St BN1 1UE
☎ 01273 290900   ▤ 01273 292841

The museum houses an exciting range of
collections of local and national importance.
Highlights include Art Nouveau and Art Deco
furniture, glass and ceramics, fashion from the
18th century and 'My Brighton' - local history via
touch screen computer. Special exhibitions are
staged all year. Ring for details.
Times: Open all year, Mon, Tue, Thu, Fri, & Sat 10-5. Sun 2-5.
(Closed Wed, Good Fri, 25 & 26 Dec & 1 Jan). A major
redevelopment is continuing until mid-2000. The musem will
remain open throughout with staggered closure of galleries.
Fee: Free.
P (NCP/street parking, fee payable) 🍽 ⅙ shop ✖

Preston Manor
Preston Drove BN1 6SD (off A23)
☎ 01273 290900 & 292770
🖷 01273 292871

This charming Edwardian manor house is beautifully furnished with notable collections of silver, furniture and paintings and presents a unique opportunity to see an Edwardian home both `upstairs' and `downstairs'. The servants' quarters can also be seen, featuring kitchen, butler's pantry and boot hall. The house is set in beautiful gardens, which include a pet cemetery and the 13th-century parish church of St Peter.
Times: Open all year, Tue-Sat 10-5, Sun 2-5, Mon 1-5 (BH Mons 10-5). (Closed Good Fri & 25-26 Dec).
Fee: *£3.10 (ch 5-15 £1.95, pen, students & UB40 £2.60). Family ticket £5.05-£8.15. Party 20+. Joint ticket with Royal Pavilion £6.50.
P ♿ 🐕

Royal Pavilion
BN1 1EE
☎ 01273 290900 🖷 01273 292871

Justifiably termed 'the most extraordinary palace in Europe', this former seaside residence of the Prince Regent, later King George IV, with its myriad domes and minarets and opulent interiors is a building no visitor to Brighton should miss. It is set in stunning Regency gardens and group tours are available by arrangement. Ring for details of special events.
Times: Open all year, Jun-Sep, daily 10-6; Oct-May, daily 10-5. (Closed 25-26 Dec).
Fee: *£4.50 (ch £2.75, concessions £3.25) Family ticket £7.25-£11.75. Joint ticket with Preston Manor £6.50. Groups 20+.
P (NCP & on street) ☕ ♿ (tours for the blind by arrangement, wheelchairs) toilets for disabled shop 🐕

BURWASH
Bateman's
TN19 7DS (0.5m SW off A265)
☎ 01435 882302 🖷 01435 882811

Rudyard Kipling lived for over 34 years in this 17th-century manor house, and it remains much the same as it was during his lifetime. His 1928 Rolls Royce Phantom is on display, and the watermill at the bottom of the garden grinds corn into flour on a Saturday afternoon.
Times: Open 27 Mar-Oct, Sat-Wed 11-5.30, also open Good Fri, (last admission 4.30pm). House closes at 5pm.
Fee: *£5 (ch £2.50). Family ticket £12.50.
P ☕ ✕ licensed ♿ toilets for disabled shop 🐕 (dog creche in car park) 🌿 💳

EASTBOURNE
Redoubt Fortress and Museum
Royal Pde BN22 7AQ
☎ 01323 410300 🖷 01323 732240

This huge fortification was built in 1804 in case of invasion by Napoleon, and has places for 11 guns. It is now the home of the Sussex Combined Services Museum (The Royal Sussex Regiment and the Queen's Royal Irish Hussars) and the National Collection of the British Model Soldier Society. There are over 50,000 exhibits covering 300 years of conflict on land, sea and air. Phone for details of special events.
Times: Open Etr-5 Nov, 9.30-5.30.
Fee: *£2.10 (ch 16 & pen £1.05). Party 10+.
P (200yds) ☕ shop 💳

FIRLE
Firle Place
BN8 6LP (off A27, Eastbourne to Brighton road)
☎ 01273 858335 & 858188
🖷 01273 858188

Home of the Gage family for over 500 years, the house has a Tudor core but was remodelled in the 18th century. Its treasures include important European and English Old Master paintings, fine English and French furniture, and porcelain, including notable examples from Sèvres and English factories. There are family monuments and brasses in the church at West Firle.
Times: Open Jun-Sep, Sun, Wed & Thu; also Etr, Spring, May & Aug BH Sun & Mon 2-4.30. Party 25+.
Fee: *£4 (ch £2). Groups 25+. Connoisseurs Day £4.85. Private viewing 25+ by appointment only.
P ✕ licensed ♿ toilets for disabled shop 🐕 (ex in garden)

FLIMWELL
Bedgebury National Pinetum
TN17 2SL (1.5m N off A21 onto B2079)
☎ 01580 211044 🖷 01580 212423

The national collection of hardy conifers. Some 320 species are currently on show, landscaped around three lakes and two streams. Rhododendron species and hybrids add to the collection's beauty and wildflowers are also plentiful. Visitors can walk in most areas, although two waymarked walks with information are included. There are areas of steep ground so it is advisable to wear stout shoes.
Times: Visitor Centre open Mar-Xmas & wknds Jan/Feb. Pinetum daily all year.
P ☕ shop *Details not confirmed for 2000* 💳

GLYNDE
Glynde Place
Lewes BN8 6SX (off A27 between Lewes & Eastbourne)
☎ 01273 858224 🖷 01273 858224

A lovely Elizabethan manor with 18th-century additions, in a beautiful downland setting. It is still a family home, lived in by descendants of the original owner.
Times: Open Jun & Sep, Wed & Sun 2-5, Jul & Aug Wed, Thu & Sun, also BH's & Suns in May. Garden open Suns in Apr.
Fee: *£4 (ch £2).
P ☕ 🐕

⛰ GROOMBRIDGE
Groombridge Place Gardens & Enchanted Forest
TN3 9QG (off A264 4m SW of Tunbridge Wells on B2100)
☎ 01892 863999 & 861444
▤ 01892 863996

Surrounded by acres of breathtaking parkland, Groombridge Place has an intriguing history stretching back to medieval times. The beautiful formal gardens are flanked by a medieval moat, with a classical 17th-century manor as a backdrop. Hidden from view, high above the gardens and vineyard, secret mysterious gardens to challenge and delight are found in The Enchanted Forest.
Times: Open Apr-Oct daily 9-6.(to be confirmed).
Fee: *£6.50 (ch & pen £5.50).
🅿 ✗ licensed ㅊ (Enchanted Forest not accessible) toilets for disabled shop garden centre ✹ (ex guide dogs) ➴
See advert under Tunbridge Wells.

⛰ HAILSHAM
Michelham Priory
Upper Dicker BN27 3QS (2m N off A27)
☎ 01323 844224 ▤ 01323 844030

Set on a tranquil moated island surrounded by spacious gardens, Michelham Priory is one of the most beautiful historic houses in Sussex. Founded in 1229 for Augustinian canons, the Priory is approached through a 14th-century gatehouse spanning the longest medieval moat in the country. Most of the original buildings were demolished during the Dissolution, but the remains were incorporated into a Tudor farm that became a splendid country house, now containing a fascinating array of exhibits. Outside, the picturesque gardens are enhanced by a working watermill, physic garden, smithy, rope museum and the dramatic Elizabethan Great Barn. Facilities include licensed restaurant and tearooms, picnic and play area and a Sussex crafts shop. Please telephone for details of special events.
Times: Open 15 Mar-Oct, Wed-Sun (daily in Aug & BH Mons). Mar & Oct 11-4, Apr-Jul & Sep 10.30-5, Aug 10.30-5.30.
🅿 ➴ ✗ licensed ㅊ (wheelchairs & braille guide available) toilets for disabled shop ✹ (ex in car park) *Details not confirmed for 2000* ➴

⛰ HASTINGS
Hastings Embroidery
White Rock Theatre, White Rock TN34 1JX (situated on the A259 Seafront road opposite the pier)
☎ 01424 781010 ▤ 01424 781170

The 80yd embroidery illustrates great events in British history from 1066 to modern times. It was sewn by the Royal School of Needlework, using threads, cords, metals, lace, jewels and appropriate cloths.
Times: Open Apr-Feb Tue-Sun 11-4 (last entry 3.30).
Fee: *£2 (concessions £1).
🅿 (charged) ✗ ㅊ toilets for disabled shop ✹ ➴

1066 Story in Hastings Castle
Castle Hill Rd, West Hill TN34 3RG
☎ 01424 781111 ▤ 01424 781133

The ruins of the Norman castle stand on the cliffs, close to the site of William the Conqueror's first motte-and-bailey castle in England. It was excavated in 1825 and 1968, and old dungeons were discovered in 1894. An unusual approach to the castle can be made via the West Hill Cliff Railway which is located in George Street precinct.
Times: Open Mar-Sep 10-5 (5.30 school holidays). Oct-Feb 11-3.30 (Closed 4 Jan for 5 days).
Fee: *£2.90 (ch £1.90, pen & students £2.30). Family ticket £8.75.
🅿 ㅊ shop ✹

⛰ HERSTMONCEUX
The Truggery
Coopers Croft BN27 1QL (from A22 at Hailsham, Boship roundabout, take A271 in direction of Bexhill for 4m)
☎ 01323 832314 ▤ 01323 832314

The art of Sussex trug making can be seen through all the work processes including preparing timber, use of the draw knife and assembly of trug.
Times: Open May-Sep 10-5. Closed Sun & Mon ex BHs. Oct-Apr opening times may vary.
🅿 shop ➴ ➴

RYE

Rye is set on a hill-top just a couple of miles from the sea, and is most people's idea of what a medieval town should look like. In the middle ages Rye was heavily fortified against the French, who all but destroyed it in 1377. The bay silted up during the 16th century, after which Rye became something of a smuggling centre. The town has an important literary connection in the shape of Henry James, the American author of The Bostonians, *and* Portrait of a Lady *who lived in Lamb House from 1898 until his death in 1916. Other literary connections include E.F.Benson, author of the Mapp and Lucia series, and Radcliffe Hall, author of* The Well of Loneliness.

⚏ LEWES

ANNE OF CLEVES HOUSE MUSEUM
52 Southover High St BN7 1JA
☎ 01273 474610   📠 01273 486990

This 16th-century town house was given to Anne of Cleves by her ex-husband, Henry VIII as part of her divorce settlement, though she never lived in the house. It is now devoted to Sussex arts and crafts, agricultural, industrial and domestic life, with a notable collection of Sussex ironwork including early gun-founding material. There is a medieval herb garden outside. In the summer guided tours take place to nearby Lewes Priory.
Times: Open 25 Mar-8 Nov, daily 10-5.30 (Sun 12-5.30); 9 Nov-24 Mar, Tue, Thu & Sat 10-5.30.
📵 (25yds) (on street-2 hr restriction) shop ✖ *Details not confirmed for 2000*

⚏ NORTHIAM

GREAT DIXTER
TN31 6PH (off A28)
☎ 01797 252878   📠 01797 252879

Birthplace and home of Christopher Lloyd, gardening writer, Great Dixter was built in 1460 and boasts one of the largest timber-framed buildings in the country. Lutyens was employed to restore both the house and gardens in 1910. The gardens are now a combination of meadows, ponds, topiary and notably the Long Border and Exotic Garden.
Times: Open Apr-Oct, Tue-Sun & BH Mon, 2-5; Gardens only open from 11am on Sun & Mon BH wknds only.
Fee: *House & Gardens £5 (ch £1.50). Gardens only £4 (ch £1). Party 25+.
📵 ♿ toilets for disabled shop garden centre ✖ (ex guide dogs) 🍴

⚏ PEVENSEY

PEVENSEY CASTLE
BN24 5LG (off A259)
☎ 01323 762604

Witness to seventeen centuries of conflict, from its origins as a Roman fortress to its use as a coastal base during the Second World War, this powerful castle has never been taken by force.
Times: Open all year, Apr-Oct, daily 10-6 (or dusk if earlier in Oct); Nov-Mar, Wed-Sun 10-4 (closed 1-2pm). Closed 24-26 Dec & 1 Jan.
Fee: £2.50 (ch £1.30).
📵 (charged) 🍴 ♿ ✖ (in certain areas) ♨

⚏ RYE

LAMB HOUSE
West St TN31 7ES
☎ 01892 890651   📠 01892 890110

This 18th-century house was the home of novelist Henry James from 1898 until his death in 1916, and was later occupied by the writer, E F

Benson. Some of James' personal posessions can be seen. There is also a charming walled garden.

Times: Open 27 Mar-30 Oct; Wed & Sat 2-6, (last admission 5.30pm).

Fee: *£2.50 (ch £1.25).

P (200m) ✖ 🚲 ♿

RYE CASTLE MUSEUM
3 East St TN31 7JY
☎ 01797 226728

Part of the museum is housed in a stone tower built as a fortification in 1249. The museum's collection of ironwork, medieval pots and smuggling items are on display here, while the East Street site contains the rest of the collection, including pottery made in Rye, military uniforms, fashions and an eighteenth-century fire engine.

Times: Open Jan-Mar wknds only 10.30-4.30; Apr-Oct daily 10.30-5.30. (last entry 5pm).

Fee: *Entrance to both sites: £3 (ch 7-16 £1, concessions £2). Family ticket £6. Ypres Tower only: £2 (ch 7-16) 75p, concessions £1.50). Family ticket £4. Party 8+

P (30yds) (street limited to 2hrs) ♿ toilets for disabled shop ✖

⛫ SHEFFIELD PARK
SHEFFIELD PARK GARDEN
TN22 3QX (5m E of Haywards Heath off A275)
☎ 01825 790231 📠 01825 791264

Sheffield Park was originally landscaped by `Capability' Brown, in about 1775 to create a beautiful park with four lakes and a cascade. Further extensive planting was done at the beginning of the 20th century, to give emphasis to autumn colour among the trees. In May and

June masses of azaleas and rhododendrons bloom and later there are magnificent waterlilies on the lakes.

Times: Open Jan-Feb Sat-Sun 10.30-4; Mar Tue-Sun 10.30-4; Apr-Nov Tue-Sun (open BH Mons) 10.30-6; Nov-Dec Tue-Sun 10.30-4 (Last admission 1 hour before closing).

Fee: *£4.20 (ch £2.10). Family ticket £10.50.

P 🍴 ♿ (powered self drive cars & wheelchairs available) toilets for disabled shop ✖ (ex guide/hearing dogs) 🚲 🍽

⛫ SHEFFIELD PARK STATION
BLUEBELL RAILWAY
Sheffield Park Station TN22 3QL (4.5m E of Haywards Heath, off A275)
☎ 01825 723777, 722370 & 722008
📠 01825 724139 or 724084

The Bluebell Railway runs historic steam trains through nine miles of pretty Sussex countryside. Please note that there is NO PARKING at Kingscote Station. If you wish to board the train here, catch the bus (service 473) which connects Kingscote and East Grinstead. A luxurious Pullman dining train runs on Saturday evenings and Sunday lunchtimes and may be hired for private parties. Special events take place throughout the year, please ring for further details.

Times: Open all year, Sat & Sun, daily May-Sep & during school holidays. Santa Specials run Dec. For timetable and information regarding trains contact above.

Fee: *3rd class return fare £7.40 (ch £3.70). Family ticket £19.90. Admission to Sheffield Park Station only £1.60 (ch 80p). Other tickets available on request.

P 🍴 ✖ licensed ♿ (contact for details) toilets for disabled shop 🍽

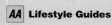

West Sussex

West Sussex is a county of weald and downland, once dominated by the forest that stretched through The Weald from Kent into Hampshire. The oaks of the forest were used to smelt the local iron ore, and though the forest is now somewhat diminished, the country remains green and lush.

The county town of Chichester, the only city in Sussex, is a gem in its own right. South of the city is the headland of Selsey. Selsey was originally an island and is still almost encircled by water, it offers a number of beaches of different character, including the Witterings and Pagham Harbour which is notable for its birdlife. Pre-Norman Selsey, with its cathedral, was lost to the sea long ago.

Further east, the county's main seaside resorts are Bognor Regis, Littlehampton and Worthing. Bognor Regis was one of the first bathing resorts in the late 18th century, and Queen Victoria was particularly fond of the place.

Outside Worthing, at Highdown Hill, there is a Bronze Age settlement beneath an Iron Age hill fort, where the Saxons later buried their dead.

The main towns are Horsham, Haywards Heath, and Crawley. The third of these is the only new town south of London, and is close to Gatwick Airport. Despite its new town status it has several buildings dating back to the 15th century. Arundel is a particularly handsome town, at a crossing point on the River Arun, dominated by the sprawling, much restored castle and the Roman Catholic Cathedral.

EVENTS & FESTIVALS

May
tbc Bluebell Time, Handcross
tbc Rhododendron & Azalea Weekend, Haywards Heath
tbc Craft Fair, Petworth
tbc Steyning Street Fair

June
tbc Heavy Horse Spectacular, Weald & Downland Open Air Museum, Singleton
8th-10th South of England Show, Ardingly Show Ground

July
7th-23rd (provisional) Chichester Festivities
8th-9th Horsham Festival
28th Torchlight Procession & Fireworks, Worthing
29th (provisional) Bognor Carnival

August
1st-5th Goodwood Week, Goodwood Racecourse, nr Chichester
5th-6th International Festival of the Arts, Crawley
25th-3rd September (provisional) Arundel Festival

September
3rd Birdman Rally, human flight off Bognor Pier
9th Sheep Fair, Findon

November
5th London-Brighton Veteran Car Run, George Hotel, Crawley

Top: The Causeway, Horsham

ARDINGLY
WAKEHURST PLACE GARDEN
RH17 6TN (1.5m NW, on B2028)
☎ 01444 894066 ▤ 01444 894069

Woodland and lakes linked by a pretty watercourse make this large garden a beautiful place to walk, and it also has an amazing variety of interesting trees and shrubs, a Winter Garden, and a Rock Walk. It is administered and maintained by the Royal Botanic Gardens at Kew.
Times: Open all year, Nov-Jan 10-4; Feb & Oct 10-5; Mar 10-6; Apr-Sep 10-7. (Closed 25 Dec & 1 Jan). Last admission 30 mins before closing. Mansion closes one hour before garden.
Fee: *£5 (ch £2.50, students, UB40 & pen £3.50). NT members and ch under 5 free.
P ▄ ✗ licensed ♿ (wheelchair available) toilets for disabled shop garden centre ✖ (ex guide dogs) ♨ �

ARUNDEL
ARUNDEL CASTLE
BN18 9AB
☎ 01903 882173 ▤ 01903 884581

This great castle, home of the Dukes of Norfolk, dates from the Norman Conquest. Containing a very fine collection of furniture and paintings, it is still a family home reflecting the changes of nearly a thousand years.
Times: Open Apr-last Fri in Oct, Sun-Fri 12-5. Last admission 4pm (Closed Sat & Good Fri).
Fee: *£6.70 (ch 5-15 £4.20, pen £5.70). Family ticket £18. Party 20+
P ▄ shop ✖ (ex guide dogs) ▥

WWT ARUNDEL
Mill Rd BN18 9PB (signposted from A27 & A29)
☎ 01903 883355 ▤ 01903 884834

More than a thousand ducks, geese and swans from all over the world can be found here, many of which are so friendly that they will even feed from your hand. The wild reserve attracts a variety of wild birds and includes a reedbed habitat considered so vital to the wetland wildlife it shelters that it has been designated a Site of Special Scientific Interest. Visitors can walk on a specially designed boardwalk, right through this reedbed without getting their feet wet. Other features include four activity stations around the grounds where visitors of all ages can find out more about wetlands and their wildlife (opening times vary), a large viewing gallery and several comfortable hides from which to observe wild birds. Facilities for disabled people include free wheelchair loan, and purpose-built toilets. There is a packed programme of events and activities throughout the year.
Times: Open all year, daily. Summer 9.30-5.30; Winter 9.30-4.30. Last admission Summer 5pm; Winter 4pm. (Closed 25 Dec).
P ✗ licensed ♿ (level paths, free wheelchair loan) toilets for disabled shop ✖ *Details not confirmed for 2000* ▥

BIGNOR
BIGNOR ROMAN VILLA & MUSEUM
RH20 1PH (between A29 & A285)
☎ 01798 869259 ▤ 01798 869478

Rediscovered in 1811, this Roman house was built on a grand scale. It is one of the largest known, and has spectacular mosaics. The heating system can also be seen, and various finds from excavations are on show. The longest mosaic in Britain (82ft) is on display here in its original position.
Times: Open Mar-May & Oct 10-5 (Closed Mon ex BHs). Jun-Sep daily 10-6.
Fee: *£3.35 (ch 16 £1.45, pen £2.35). Party 10+. Guided tours by arrangement.
P ▄ ♿ shop ✖ (ex guide dogs)

BRAMBER
BRAMBER CASTLE
BN4 3FB (on W side of village off A283)

A former home of the Dukes of Norfolk, this ruined Norman stronghold lies on a ridge of the South Downs and gives wonderful views.
Times: Open any reasonable time.
P ♨ *Details not confirmed for 2000*

CHICHESTER
CHICHESTER CATHEDRAL
West St PO19 1PX
☎ 01243 782595 ▤ 01243 536190

The beauty of the 900-year-old cathedral, site of the shrine of St Richard, is enhanced by many art treasures, ancient and modern.
Times: Open daily, Etr-mid-Sep 7.30-7, mid Sep-Etr 7.30-5. Visiting restricted during services and concerts.
Fee: *Donations invited.
P (within city walls) ▄ ✗ ♿ toilets for disabled shop ✖

PALLANT HOUSE GALLERY
9 North Pallant PO19 1TJ
☎ 01243 774557 ▤ 01243 536038

The gallery is housed in a restored Queen Anne townhouse. The rooms contain fine furniture, and there is a Victorian kitchen. Permanent collections on display include the Modern British Art of the Hussey and Kearley bequests; the Geoffrey Freeman collection of Bow porcelain. There is a programme of temporary exhibitions. Ring for details of special events.
Times: Open all year, Tue-Sat 10-5, Sun & BHs 12.30-5.
Fee: *£4 (ch & W Sussex students free, other students £2.50, concessions £3).
P ▄ ♿ shop ✖ (ex guide dogs)

EAST GRINSTEAD
STANDEN
RH19 4NE (2m S of East Grinstead, signposted from B2110)
☎ 01342 323029 ▤ 01342 316424

Standen is a showpiece of the 19th-century Arts and Crafts movement. It was designed by Philip Webb for the Beale family, and was always

contd.

CHICHESTER & GOODWOOD

The county town of West Sussex, with ancient city walls, a medieval cathedral and fine Georgian streets, Chichester has much to commend it to the visitor. Originally a Roman settlement, the Roman criss-cross layout is still evident in the street plan, which centres on the splendid 16th-century butter cross. To the southwest of the town is Chichester Harbour, a great yachting centre. Goodwood racecourse, north of the city, is the venue for one of racing's premier events, Goodwood Week in late July, a highlight of the social calendar. "Glorious Goodwood" enjoys a lovely setting on a hill overlooking the city with the South Downs in the background.

meant to be decorated with William Morris wallpapers and fabrics. The interior has been carefully preserved. Webb also designed some of the furniture and details. There is a beautiful hillside garden. For events please contact the Regional Box Office 01372 451596.

Times: Open 24 Mar-7 Nov, Wed-Sun (inc Good Fri) also BH Mon. House 12.30-4, Shop: 12.30-5, Garden: 12.30-6. 12 Nov-19 Dec, Garden & shop open, Fri-Sun, 1-4.Entry may be delayed at peak times.

Fee: *House & garden £5. Garden only £3 (#2 in Nov-Dec). Children half price. Family ticket £12.50.Joint ticket which includes same day entry to Nymans garden #7, available Wed-Fri.

🅿 ✗ licensed ♿ (braille guide) shop ✖ (ex guide dogs/Woodland Walk) 🐾

🏛 FISHBOURNE
FISHBORNE ROMAN PALACE
Salthill Rd PO19 3QR (N of A259 in Fishbourne)
☎ 01243 785859 🖨 01243 539266

This is the largest known Roman residence in Britain, but the reason for building such a magnificent house here is not known. It was occupied from the 1st to the 3rd centuries AD, when its 100 or so rooms must have been a wonderful sight with their mosaic floors and painted walls; 25 of these mosaic floors can still be seen in varying states of completeness, including others rescued from elsewhere in the area. Outside, the northern part of the palace garden has been replanted to its original 1st-

century plan. The museum gives an account of the history of the palace, and shows a full-size reconstruction of a Roman dining room. There are also an audio-visual theatre, mosaic-making area for children, a museum of Roman gardening and a reconstructed Roman garden.

Times: Open all year, daily 8 Feb-13 Dec. Feb, Nov-Dec 10-4; Mar-Jul & Sep-Oct 10-5; Aug 10-6. Sun only 14 Dec-7 Feb 10-4.

🅿 💻 ♿ (self guiding tapes & tactile objects for the blind) toilets for disabled shop garden centre ✖ *Details not confirmed for 2000* 🔊

🏛 FONTWELL
DENMANS GARDEN
BN18 0SU (5m E of Chichester on A27)
☎ 01243 542808 🖨 01243 544064

This garden has been created from land which was part of an estate owned by Lord Denman in the 19th century. The present three-and-a-half-acre garden was begun in the 1940s and has gradually developed over the last 50 years. There is a Walled Garden and a Gravel Stream with grasses, bamboo and a pond. The South Garden has fine maples and cherry trees, and many mature, rare trees. A school of Garden Design is housed in the Clock House.

Times: Open Mar-Oct daily 9-5.

Fee: *£2.80 (ch £1.50, ch under 4 free, pen £2.50). Party 15+.

🅿 💻 ♿ shop garden centre ✖ (ex guide dogs)

🏛 GOODWOOD
GOODWOOD HOUSE
PO18 0PX (3m NE of Chichester)
☎ 01243 755000   📠 01243 755005

Ancestral home of the Dukes of Richmond for 300 years. Following refurbishment the State Apartments have taken on new life. Goodwood was the country home of the scandalous and glamorous Lennox sisters, immortalised in the BBC TV production of 'Aristocrats'. Unrivalled as an English ancestral collection, the paintings include works by Van Dyck, Reynolds, Stubbs and Canaletto. Phone for details of special events.
Times: Open Sun from 21 Feb. Etr Sun-27 Sep, house open Sun-Mon, Sun-Thu in Aug, 1-5. (Closed 18-19 Apr, 9-10 May, Jun & 19 Sep).
Fee: *£6 (ch & disabled £3). Groups 20+.
🅿 🍴 ♿ (ramp at front of house, disabled parking area) toilets for disabled shop 🐾

🏛 HANDCROSS
NYMANS GARDEN
RH17 6EB (on B2114)
☎ 01444 400321 & 400777
📠 01444 400253

Set in the Sussex Weald, Nymans has flowering shrubs and roses, a flower garden in the old walled orchard, and a secret sunken garden. There are some fine and rare trees. Summer events are held in the garden. For details please call regional box office (01372) 451596.
Times: Open Mar-Oct, daily (ex Mon & Tue) but open BH Mon 11-6 or sunset if earlier. Last admission 1 hour before closing. Winter wknds 11-4, restricted according to ground conditions. Phone for more information.
Fee: *£5. Family ticket £12.50, joint ticket which includes same day entry to Standen £7, available Wed-Fri.
🅿 🍴 ♿ (wheelchair route, wheelchair available, braille guide) toilets for disabled shop 🐾 (ex guide dogs & hearing dogs) 🐾

🏛 HAYWARDS HEATH
BORDE HILL GARDEN
Balcombe Rd RH16 1XP (1.5m N of Hayward Heath on Balcombe Road)
☎ 01444 450326   📠 01444 440427

Borde Hill set in 200 acres of spectacular Sussex parkland boasts fine displays of rhododendrons, camellias, magnolias and azaleas during the spring. Extensive planting with a new rose and herbaceous garden for the summer. There are woodland walks, nature trails and a hundred `champion' trees. Attractions include coarse fishing, childrens' trout fishing aand an adventure playground. Phone for details of special events.
Times: Open all year, 10-6 (or dusk).
Fee: *£4 (ch 3-15 £1.50). Family ticket £10.
🅿 🍴 ✕ licensed ♿ (wheelchairs available) toilets for disabled shop garden centre (on leads) 🔔

🏛 LOWER BEEDING
LEONARDSLEE GARDENS
RH13 6PP (4m SW from Handcross,at J of B2110/A281)
☎ 01403 891212   📠 01403 891305

This Grade I listed garden is set in a peaceful valley with walks around seven beautiful lakes. It is a paradise in spring, with banks of rhododendrons and azaleas along paths lined with bluebells. The Rock Garden is a kaleidoscope of colour in May. There is a fascinating Bonsai exhibition, and an Alpine House with 400 plants in a rocky landscape. There are several animals and a collection of Victorian Motor Cars.
Times: Open Apr-Oct, daily 9.30-6 (May 9.30-8).
Fee: *Apr & Jun-Oct £4, May £5, (ch £2.50).
🅿 🍴 ✕ licensed shop garden centre 🐾

🏛 PETWORTH
PETWORTH HOUSE & PARK
GU28 0AE (in centre of Petworth, A272/283)
☎ 01798 342207 & 343929
📠 01798 342963

Petworth was rebuilt by the Duke of Somerset in the 17th century, and all that remains of the 13th-century building is the chapel. The state rooms and galleries contain one of the finest art collections in England, including works by Turner, Gainsborough, Rembrandt and Van Dyck. Six rooms in the servants' block have been opened, including the old kitchen. Please telephone for details of special events.
Times: Open 27 Mar-Oct, Sat-Wed (open Good Fri). House 1-5.30, last admission 4.30. Park open daily 8-sunset (ex 25-27 Jun). Extra rooms shown on weekdays but not BH
Fee: *£5.50 (ch £2.50). Family ticket £13.50. Party 15+.
🅿 (charged) 🍴 ✕ licensed ♿ (wheelchairs available, braille guide) toilets for disabled shop 🐾 (ex guide dogs) 🐾 🔔

🏛 PULBOROUGH
PARHAM HOUSE & GARDENS
Parham Park RH20 4HS (3m SE off A283,between Pulborough & Storrington)
☎ 01903 744888 (info line)
📠 01903 746557

Surrounded by a deer park, fine gardens and 18th-century Pleasure Grounds in a beautiful downland setting, this Elizabethan family home contains an important collection of paintings, furniture, carpets and rare needlework. A brick and turf maze has been created in the grounds - designed with children in mind, it is called `Veronica's Maze'. A special Garden Weekend is held on 18-19 July 1998. Steam Rally (13-14 Jun), Craft Show (21-23 Aug), Country Show (12-13 Sep).
Times: Open 1 Apr-29 Oct, Wed, Thu, Sun & BH. Gardens 12-6; House 2-6 (last entry 5). Guided tours on Wed & Thu mornings and Mon, Tue & Fri afternoons by special arrangement.
🅿 🍴 ♿ (wheelchairs available by arrangement/tape tour) shop garden centre 🐾 (ex in grounds) *Details not confirmed for 2000* 🔔

RSPB NATURE RESERVE
Uppertons Barns Visitor Centre, Wigginholt
RH20 2EL (on A283,1m S of Pulborough & 1m N
of Storrington)
☎ 01798 875851   ▤ 01798 873716

Set in the scenic Arun Valley and easily reached
via the visitor centre on the A283 at Wigginholt,
this is an excellent reserve for year-round family
visits. A nature trail winds through hedgerow-
lined lanes to viewing hides overlooking watermeadows. Breeding summer birds include
nightingales and warblers, ducks and wading
birds, and nightjars and hobbies on nearby
heathland. In winter, thousands of colourful
ducks, geese, swans and waders are joined by
barn owl, peregrine falcon and the occasional
hen harrier. Unusual waders and hedgerow birds
regularly pass through on spring and autumn
migration. Other wildlife includes many butterfly
and dragonfly species in the summer, with deer
and smaller animals all year round. This years
events include: Seasonal guided walks/activities
for all ages, backgrounds and abilities. Contact
Visitor Centre for an events leaflet.
Times: Open daily, 9-9, (or sunset if earlier). Visitor centre
daily, 10-5. Reserve closed 25 Dec, visitor centre closed 25-26
Dec.
🅿 ▣ ✕ licensed ♿ (ramps at some hides/batricar
bookable/easy gradient trail) toilets for disabled shop ✖
Details not confirmed for 2000 ➤

⛪ SINGLETON
WEALD & DOWNLAND OPEN AIR MUSEUM
PO18 0EU (6m N of Chichester on A286)
☎ 01243 811348   ▤ 01243 811475

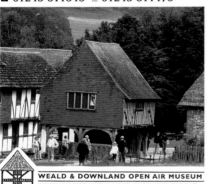

WEALD & DOWNLAND OPEN AIR MUSEUM
SINGLETON, CHICHESTER, SUSSEX PO18 0EU TEL: (01243) 811346 FAX: (01243) 811475

A showcase of English architectural heritage,
where the main exhibits, historic buildings, have
been rescued from destruction and rebuilt in a
beautiful parkland setting. Vividly demonstrating
the evolution of building techniques and use of
local materials, these homes and workplaces
include a furnished medieval farmstead,
complete with gardens, fields and animals, a
Victorian school, and working watermill. There

are demonstrations of traditional rural skills and
a hands-on building gallery.
Times: Open all year, Mar-Oct, daily 10.30-6 (last admission
5); Nov-Feb, Wed, Sat & Sun 10.30-4, also 26 Dec-4 Jan,
10.30-4.
Fee: *£5.20 (ch & students £2.50). Family ticket £14. Party.
🅿 ▣ ♿ toilets for disabled shop ✖ (ex on leads) ➤

⛪ SOUTH HARTING
UPPARK
GU31 5QR (1.5m S on B2146)
☎ 01730 825415   01730 825857
▤ 01730 825873

On 30th August 1989 this late 17th-century house
was partially destroyed by fire. The attic and the
first floor were completely gutted, but virtually all
of the 18th-century contents were saved.
Following an ambitious restoration project,
Uppark has been restored to its state `the day
before the fire'. The garden, landscaped by
Repton, and its magnificent views, can also be
enjoyed.
Times: Open Apr-29 Oct, Sun-Thu. House 1-5. Car park,
woodland walk, garden & Exhibition 11.30-5.30. Last admission
to house 4pm. Timed tickets will be in operation.
Fee: *House, garden & exhibition £5.50. Family ticket £13.75.
🅿 ▣ ♿ (ramps,lift,stair to exhibition) toilets for disabled
shop ✖ (ex woodland walk & car park) 🐾

⛪ TANGMERE
TANGMERE MILITARY AVIATION MUSEUM TRUST
PO20 6ES (off A27)
☎ 01243 775223   ▤ 01243 789490

Based at an airfield which played an important
role during the World Wars, this museum spans
80 years of military aviation. There are
photographs, documents, aircraft and aircraft
parts on display along with a Hurricane replica,
Spitfire replica and cockpit simulator. A hangar
houses a Supermarine Swift and the record-
breaking aircraft Meteor and Hunter. Phone for
details of special events.
Times: Open Mar-Oct, daily 10-5.30; Feb & Nov, daily 10-4.30.
Fee: *£3 (ch £1.50 & pen £2.50).
🅿 ▣ ♿ (wheelchairs available) toilets for disabled shop ✖
(ex guide dogs)

⚏ WEST DEAN

WEST DEAN GARDENS

Estate Office PO18 0QZ (on A286, 6m N of Chichester)

☎ 01243 818210 & 811301

🖹 01243 811342

A historic garden of 35 acres in a tranquil downland setting. Noted for its 300ft long Harold Peto pergola, mixed and herbaceous borders, rustic summerhouses, water garden and specimen trees. The Visitors Centre provides a high level of facilities with a beautiful prospect of the River Lavant and West Dean Park. Events take place through the summer, please phone for details.

Times: Open Mar-Oct, daily 11-5. Last ticket 4.30pm.

Fee: *£4 (ch £2, pen £3.50). Party+.

🅿 ✗ licensed ♿ (reserved parking) toilets for disabled shop ✈ (ex guide dogs) ⛟

Tyne & Wear

Tyne & Wear is a metropolitan county, created by local government reorganisation in 1974. It includes the towns of Newcastle-upon-Tyne, Gateshead, South Shields and Sunderland. It is cut through by the two rivers the Tyne and the Wear, and includes a section of Hadrian's Wall.

EVENTS & FESTIVALS

April
15th-16th Gateshead Spring Flower show

May
27th-29th Window on the World International Music Festival, Fish Quay, North Shields

July
7th-9th International Jazz Festival, Park Hotel, Tynemouth
tbc North of England Motorshow, Links, Whitley Bay

November
tbc Newcastle Comedy Festival

The area grew prosperous on coal and shipbuilding, and buildings of Victorian grandeur reflect its heyday. George Stephenson established an ironworks here in 1826, and the first engine on the Stockton and Darlington railway was made in Newcastle. Industrial decline has hit hard, but the Geordie spirit survives and brings immense vitality to the place.

Newcastle's 'new castle' is believed to date from the 11th century, though the present keep dates from the 12th. Other ancient buildings include the 14th-century cathedral, and the 17th-century Guildhall. Contemporary constructions include the Metro, which links Newcastle to Gateshead (along with several bridges), and the Metro Centre in Gateshead, Britain's largest shopping centre. The most famous of the bridges are High Level Bridge, a road and rail bridge, built by Robert Stephenson in 1849, and the Tyne Bridge dating from 1929.

Jarrow, five miles east of Newcastle, is mainly remembered for the Jarrow Crusade of 1936, when 200 men marched to London to bring attention to the plight of unemployed shipbuilders. The town was also the home of monk-scholar, the Venerable Bede, whose 8th-century work, *Historia Ecclesiastica Gentis Anglorum*, was the first important history book written about the English. He was buried at Jarrow, and his bones remained there until the 11th century when they were moved to Durham.

Top: Tyne Bridge

⛬ JARROW
BEDES WORLD & ST PAUL'S CHURCH
Church Bank NE32 3DY (off A185 nr South end of Tyne tunnel)
☎ 0191 489 2106 ▤ 0191 428 2361

The Venerable Bede was one of early Britain's greatest scholars, and was the author of the "Historia Ecclesiastica Gentis Anglorum", the definitive history of the early medieval period. As well as exhibits detailing Bede's monastic life and work, the museum demonstrates Anglo-Saxon farming and living history re-enactments.
Times: Open all year, Apr-Oct, Tue-Sat & BH Mons 10-5.30, Sun noon-5.30; Nov-Mar, Tue-Sat 10-4.30 & Sun; Xmas-New Year opening times vary. Church open Mon-Sat 10-4 & Sun 2.30-4, unless service being held.
Fee: *£3 (ch & concessions £1.50). Family ticket £7.20. UB40 family ticket £4.
🅿 🖭 ♿ (electric wheelchair on request) toilets for disabled shop ✖ (ex guide dogs) 🥤

⛬ NEWCASTLE UPON TYNE
HANCOCK MUSEUM
Barras Bridge NE2 4PT
☎ 0191 222 7418 ▤ 0191 222 6753

The museum houses geological exhibits and John Hancock's magnificent collection of birds. Land of the Pharaohs explores life and death in Ancient Eygpt. The Earth galleries explore the cosmic and geological processes that have shaped the earth, and investigate the history of life on our planet.
Times: Open all year, Mon-Sat, 10-5, Sun 2-5. Closed 25/26 Dec & 1 Jan.
🅿 🖭 ♿ (Lift,audio guides,braille guides) toilets for disabled shop ✖ *Details not confirmed for 2000* 🥤

MUSEUM OF ANTIQUITIES
The University NE1 7RU
☎ 0191 222 7849 ▤ 0191 222 8561

Artefacts from north east England from prehistoric times to AD 1600 are on display here. The principal museum for Hadrian's Wall, this collection includes models of the wall, life-size Roman soldiers and a recently refurbished reconstruction of the Temple of Mithras. There is also a museum book shop.
Times: Open all year, daily (ex Sun), 10-5 (Closed Good Fri, 24-26 Dec & 1 Jan).
🅿 (400yds) ♿ (Large print guide) shop ✖ *Details not confirmed for 2000* 🥤

⛬ ROWLANDS GILL
GIBSIDE
NE16 6BG (6m SW of Gateshead, on B6314)
☎ 01207 542255

The important early 18th-century landscaped park contains a chapel - an outstanding example of Palladian architecture, built to a design by James Paine as the mausoleum for members of the Bowes family. It stands at one end of the Great Walk of Turkey oaks, looking towards the column of British Liberty.
Times: Open Apr-31 Oct daily (ex Mon),11-5. Open BH Mon. Last admission 4.30. Grounds only 7 Nov-end Mar, Sun 10-4.
Fee: *£3. (Winter opening £2). Party.
🅿 🖭 ♿ (braille guide, wheelchair) shop ✖ (ex on leads) 🐾 🥤

⛬ SOUTH SHIELDS
ARBEIA ROMAN FORT & MUSEUM
Baring St NE33 2BB
☎ 0191 456 1369 454 4093
▤ 0191 427 6862

In South Shields town are the extensive remains of Arbeia, a 2nd-century Roman fort. It was the supply base for the Roman army's campaign against Scotland. On the site of the west gate is a full-scale simulation of a Roman gateway with interior scenes of life at the fort. Archaeological excavations are in progress throughout the summer. Market Day in June - telephone for details.
Times: Open all year, Apr-Sep, Mon-Sat 10-5.30, Sun 1-5; Oct-Mar, Mon-Sat 10-4. Closed 25-26 Dec, 1 Jan & Good Friday.
Fee: *Fort & Museum free of charge ex for 'Timequest'Archaeological Interpretation Gallery £1.50 (ch & concessions 80p).
🅿 ♿ (Minicom system) toilets for disabled shop

⛬ TYNEMOUTH
TYNEMOUTH CASTLE & PRIORY
NE30 4BZ (near North Pier)
☎ 0191 257 1090

The castle and priory are a testament to the strategic importance of the site and its great religious significance. The soaring arches of the presbytery are an eloquent reminder of the priory's former wealth, and the Percy Chantry is still almost complete.
Times: Open all year, Apr-Oct, daily 10-6 (or dusk if earlier); Nov-Mar, Wed-Sun 10-4 (or dusk if earlier, closed 1-2pm). Closed 24-26 Dec & 1 Jan.
Fee: £1.80 (ch 90p).
♿ shop ✖ ⚏

⛬ WASHINGTON
WASHINGTON OLD HALL
(follow signs for District 4 Washington New Town)
☎ 0191 416 6879

The home of George Washington's ancestors from 1183 to 1613, the Old Hall was originally an early medieval manor, but was rebuilt in the 17th century. The house has been restored and filled with period furniture. The property was given to the National Trust in 1956. There will be celebrations to mark American Independence Day in July.
Times: Open 2 Apr-31 Oct, Sun-Wed; open Good Fri,11-5. Last admission 4.30.
Fee: *£2.80. Party.
🅿 🖭 shop ✖ 🐾 🥤

TYNEMOUTH

Tynemouth is both a port and a resort set on a promontory between the river and the sea. Long Sands, overlooked by the usual seaside amusements, is thought to be one of the finest beaches in the country. The ruins of Tynemouth Priory and Castle are set on the clifftop above the North Tyne Pier.

The first volunteer life brigade was established in Tynemouth in 1869 and its noble history is recorded in the Tynemouth Volunteer Life Brigade Museum.

WWT WASHINGTON
NE38 8LE (signposted off A195 & A1231)
☎ 0191 416 5454   ▤ 0191 416 5801

Set in a busy industrial area, on the north bank of the River Wear, WWT Washington is the home of a wonderful collection of exotic wildfowl from all over the world. There is also a heronry where visitors can watch a colony of wild Grey Herons on closed circuit television. The 100-acre site includes an area for wintering wildfowl which can be observed from hides, and a flock of Chilean Flamingos. Other features include a discovery centre with activities for children, waterfowl nursery, large picture windows and a viewing gallery from which to observe the birds. Facilities for the disabled include free wheelchair loan, and purpose-built toilets. There is a packed programme of events and activities available throughout the year.
Times: Open all year, daily 9.30-5 or dusk if earlier. (Closed 25 Dec).
🅿 ▣ ♿ (lowered windows in certain hides) toilets for disabled shop ✖ *Details not confirmed for 2000* 🥤

▥ WHITBURN
SOUTER LIGHTHOUSE
(coast road 2m S from South Shields)
☎ 0191 529 3161

This 150ft-high lighthouse was opened by Trinity House in 1871 and contains a bi-optic light, still in its original condition, which was the first reliable electrically powered lighthouse light. The Engine and Battery Rooms are all in working order and are included in the guided tour, along with the light tower, museum cottage and video. Ring for details of special events.
Times: Open Apr-Oct daily ex Fri,(open Good Fri),11-5. Last admission 4.30.
Fee: *£2.50. Party £2.
🅿 ✖ ♿ toilets for disabled shop ✖ 🐾 🥤

Warwickshire

The countryside of south Warwickshire, located in the Heart of England, was beloved of William Shakespeare. The bard is forever associated with the town of Stratford-upon-Avon, the place of his birth and death, which now has two theatres built in his honour.

These days, the small market town he knew as home is packed with tourists - the most visited British tourist destination outside London. North of the county, around Coventry, which is itself officially part of the West Midlands, the scene is much more industrial/urban and seems a world away from this mainly rural area.

Warwickshire has some fine towns, including Warwick itself, the county town, which boasts one of the greatest English castles. The castle is medieval, though it was comprehensively restored in the 19th century, and its enormous bulk dominates the town. The centre of Warwick is mainly Georgian, built following a fire in 1694 that destroyed the earlier medieval buildings, though some do remain on the periphery. The county's other great castle is Kenilworth, a Norman fortress built of sandstone standing to the west of Kenilworth town.

Leamington Spa came to prominence when the fashion for 'taking the waters' was at its height in the late 18th and early 19th century. Rugby, however, is best known as the home of one of England's most elevated public schools, immortalised in Thomas Hughes' *Tom Brown's Schooldays*. The school was also the home of the ballgame that bears its name.

EVENTS & FESTIVALS

February
19th-27th February Frolics, Hatton Garden World

March
25th-26th Craft Fair, Ragley Hall

April
23rd Easter Egg Trail, Baddesley Clinton

May
13th-14th Amateur Spring Gardening Show, NAC Stoneleigh

June
17th-18th 30 Years of the Range Rover, Heritage Motor Centre

July
3rd-6th The Royal Show, NAC Stoneleigh
29th-30th Newfoundland Dog Trials, Ragley Hall
30th Neptune Coastline Campaign, Baddesley Clinton

August
5th Fireworks & Laser Show, Ragley Hall

Top: Long Compton

⏛ ALCESTER

RAGLEY HALL

B49 5NJ (1.5m SW, off A435)
☎ 01789 762090 ▯ 01789 764791

Ragley Hall is set in four hundred acres of parkland and gardens. The Great Hall contains some of England's finest Baroque plasterwork designed by James Gibbs. Graham Rust's mural The Temptation can be seen on the south staircase. Ample picnic areas beside the lake, as well as an adventure playground, maze and woodland walks.

Times: Open 2 Apr-4 Oct, Thu-Sun & BH Mon; Jul-Aug park & garden open everyday. House 11-5, park & gardens 10-6.
🅿 ◨ ♿ (lift to first floor) toilets for disabled shop (ex in park & gardens) *Details not confirmed for 2000*

⏛ BADDESLEY CLINTON

BADDESLEY CLINTON HALL

B93 0DQ (0.75m W off A4141, 7.5m NW of Warwick)
☎ 01564 783294 ▯ 01564 782706

A romantically-sited medieval moated house, dating from the 14th century, that has changed very little since 1634. With family portraits, priest holes, chapel, garden, ponds, nature trail and lake walk. There is a Midsummer opera on the lawn, and 'Murder on the Menu' evening functions. An autumn lecture programme is planned, along with other events, please telephone for details.

Times: House open 3 Mar-31 Oct, Wed-Sun & BH Mon (closed Good Fri). Mar-Apr 1.30-5, May-Sept 1.30-5.30, Oct-31 Oct 1.30-5. (last admissions 30 mins before closing). Grounds open 14 Feb-12 Dec, Wed-Sun & BH Mon (closed Good Fri). Feb Nov-12 Dec 12-4.30, Mar-Apr, Oct 12-5, May-Sep 12-5.30.
Fee: *£5. Family ticket £12.50. Grounds,restaurant & shop only £2.50.
🅿 ✗ licensed ♿ (wheelchairs available, hearing scheme, braille guides) toilets for disabled shop ✈ (ex guide dogs) ♨ ◥

⏛ CHARLECOTE

CHARLECOTE PARK

CV35 9ER (5m E of Stratford, 1m W of Wellesbourne on B4086)
☎ 01789 470277 ▯ 01789 470544

Built in the 1550s and later visited by Queen Elizabeth I, Charlecote Park was landscaped by 'Capability' Brown and has a herd of red and fallow deer, reputedly poached by Shakespeare, and a flock of Jacob sheep first introduced in 1756. The principal rooms are decorated in Elizabethan Revival style.

Times: Open 3 Apr-1 Nov; Fri-Tue 12-5. (closed Good Fri)
🅿 ✗ licensed ♿ (Braille guides & hearing scheme available) toilets for disabled shop ✈ ♨ *Details not confirmed for 2000*

⏛ COUGHTON

COUGHTON COURT

B49 5JA (2m N of Alcester on E side of A435)
☎ 01789 762435 ▯ 01789 765544

During the Civil War this formerly moated and mainly Elizabethan house was attacked by both Parliamentary and Royalist forces. There are exhibitions on the Gunpowder Plot and Children's Clothes. Outdoor concert with fireworks in July. Please telephone for details of concerts and other events.

Times: Open 13 Mar-end Mar, Sat-Sun. 3 Apr-Sep daily (ex Mon & Tue). Also 6 Apr, Tue 1 Jun and all Tue in Aug (closed Good Fri and first Sat in Jun, Jul). Oct, Fri & Sat. Open 11.30-5 (BH Mon 11-5).
Fee: *£6.25. Family ticket £19. Grounds only £4.50. Family ticket £14.
🅿 ✗ licensed ♿ (braille guide, wheelchair available) toilets for disabled shop ✈ ♨ ◥

⏛ FARNBOROUGH

FARNBOROUGH HALL

OX17 1DU (6m N of Banbury,0.5m W of A423)
☎ 01295 690202

A classical mid 18th-century stone house with notable plasterwork; the entrance hall, staircase and two principal rooms are shown. The grounds contain charming 18th-century temples, a 1/4-mile terrace walk and an obelisk.

Times: House, grounds & terrace walk open Apr-Sep, Wed & Sat, 3/4 May 2-6pm. Terrace walk Thu & Fri only, 2-6. Last admission 5.30pm.
🅿 ♿ ✈ ♨ *Details not confirmed for 2000*

⏛ GAYDON

HERITAGE MOTOR CENTRE

Banbury Rd CV35 0BJ (Exit M40 at junc 12 and take B4100)
☎ 01926 641188 ▯ 01926 641555

Home to the largest collection of historic British cars anywhere in the world. Other attractions on the 65-acre site include a children's playground, nature trail, Land Rover shuttle ride, four-wheel-drive demonstration circuit, Childrens' Hands-on Road Safety and a quad bike circuit for all the family. There are special activities for families and children at weekends and during school holidays.

Times: Open all year, Apr-Oct, daily 10-6; Nov-Mar. daily 10-4.30. (check fo Christmas opening. Closed 24-26, 31 Dec & 1 Jan).
Fee: *£6 (ch 5-16 £4, under 5 free, & senior £5). Family ticket £17.
🅿 ◨ ✗ licensed ♿ (lifts, wide doors, graded ramps & pathways) toilets for disabled shop ✈ (ex guide dogs & hearing dogs) ◥

⏛ KENILWORTH

KENILWORTH CASTLE

☎ 01926 52078

Kenilworth is the largest castle ruin in England, its massive walls towering over the countryside. Originally founded in the 11th century, it was already ancient when Queen Elizabeth I visited her favourite, Robert Dudley, Earl of Leicester, here in 1575; he built a new wing for her use.

Times: Open all year, Apr-Oct, daily 10-6 (or dusk if earlier); Nov-Mar, daily 10-4. Closed 24-26 Dec & 1 Jan.
Fee: £3.50 (ch £1.80).
🅿 ♿ shop ✈ ⌗

🏛 MIDDLETON

Ash End House Farm "The Childrens Farm"

Middleton Ln, Middleton B78 2BL (signposted from A4091)

☎ 0121 329 3240   📄 0121 329 3240

Ash End House is a children's farm, specifically set up with children in mind. Guided tours give them an opportunity to get close to friendly farm animals. A host of animals from the gigantic shire-horse, through to hatching tiny chicks and fluffy ducklings can be seen daily. There are also rare breeds such as Bagot goats, Saddleback pigs and Soay sheep. Special events are held during the year.

Times: Open daily 10-5 or dusk in winter. (Closed 25-27 Dec & 1 Jan).

🅿 💺 ♿ toilets for disabled shop ✖
See advert on page 208.

Middleton Hall

B78 2AE (on A4091 midway between Belfry & Drayton Manor)

☎ 01827 283095   📄 01827 285717

Once the home of two great 17th-century naturalists, Francis Willoughby and John Ray, the Hall shows several architectural styles, from c1300 to a Georgian west wing. The grounds include a nature reserve, lake, meadow, orchard and woodland, all Sites of Special Scientific Interest. Events take place throughout the year; a programme is available on application to the secretary.

Times: Open 4 Apr-3 Oct, Sun 2-5, BH 11-5.
Fee: *£1.50 (ch free, pen 70p)
🅿 💺 ♿ (lightweight wheelchair available) toilets for disabled shop ⛿

🏛 NUNEATON

Arbury Hall

CV10 7PT (2m SW of Nuneaton, off B4102 Meriden road)

☎ 024 76382804   📄 024 76641147

The 16th-century Elizabethan house, Gothicised in the 18th century, has been the home of the Newdegate family for over 450 years. It is the finest complete example of Gothic revival architecture in existence, and contains pictures, furniture, and beautiful plasterwork ceilings. The 17th-century stable block, with a central doorway by Wren, houses the tearooms and a large collection of veteran bicycles.

Times: Open Etr-Sep 2-5.30 (last admission 5pm). Hall & gardens: Sun & Mon of BH weekends. For other opening days & times, contact the Administrator.
Fee: *£4.50 (ch £2.50) gardens only £3. (ch £2.)
🅿 💺 ♿ shop ✖ (ex in grounds, on leads only)

🏛 PACKWOOD HOUSE

Packwood House

B94 6AT (on unclass road off A34)

☎ 01564 782024

Dating from the 16th century, Packwood House has been extended and much changed over the

years. An important collection of tapestries and textiles is displayed. Equally important are the stunning gardens with renowned herbaceous borders, attracting many visitors, and the almost surreal topiary garden based on the Sermon on the Mount.

Times: Open Etr-wknd-Sep, Wed-Sun, BH Mon, 1.30-6 (House 2-6); Oct, Wed-Sun, 12-4.30. Closed Good Fri. Last admission 30mins before closing time.
🅿 (charged) ♿ (wheelchairs available) toilets for disabled shop ✖ (ex guide dogs) 🐾 *Details not confirmed for 2000*
▬

🏛 RUGBY

The James Gilbert Rugby Football Museum

5 Saint Matthew's St CV21 3BY

☎ 01788 333888   📄 01788 540795

An intriguing collection of Rugby football memorabilia is housed in the shop in which Gilbert's have made their world famous Rugby balls since 1842. From Monday-Friday 10am-5pm and Saturday 10am-2pm, watch a craftsman at work, hand-stitching the footballs. Situated near to Rugby School and its famous playing field.

Times: Open all year, Mon-Fri 9-5, Sat 9-4. Phone for holiday opening times.
Fee: Free.
🅿 (500 yds) ♿ shop ✖ ▬

🏛 RYTON-ON-DUNSMORE

Ryton Organic Gardens

CV8 3LG (5m SE of Coventry signposted off the A45, on the road to the village of Wolston)

☎ 024 76303517   📄 024 76639229

The gardens are the home of the Henry Doubleday Research Association, which studies organic gardening. Visitors can stroll around the herb garden, the bee garden, fruit beds, vegetable gardens, shrub borders and many other attractions. There is an Education Centre with exhibitions, courses and special events, for details telephone 01203 308211.

Times: Open all year 9-5. (Closed Xmas).
Fee: *£2.50 (ch £1.25, students, pen, disabled & UB40 £2).Party 14+ 20% discount.
🅿 ✖ licensed ♿ (wheelchairs available) toilets for disabled shop garden centre ✖ (ex guide dogs) ▬

🏛 SHOTTERY

Anne Hathaway's Cottage

☎ 01789 292100

Before her marriage to William Shakespeare, Anne Hathaway lived in this substantial 12-roomed thatched Tudor farmhouse with her prosperous yeoman family. The house now shows many aspects of domestic life in 16th-century England, and has a lovely traditional cottage garden and Shakespeare tree garden.

Times: Open all year, 20 Mar-19 Oct Mon-Sat 9-5, Sun 9.30-4; Jan-19 Mar & 20 Oct-Dec Mon-Sat 9.30-4, Sun 10-4. (Closed 23-26 Dec).
🅿 (charged) 💺 ✖ licensed shop garden centre ✖ *Details not confirmed for 2000*

STRATFORD-UPON-AVON

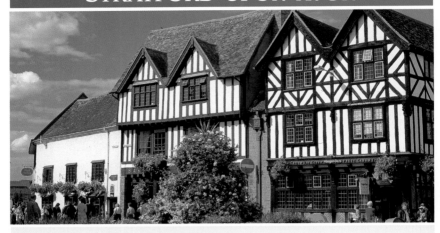

Stratford-upon-Avon is an undeniably attractive town, with its half-timbered buildings and a pleasant location on the River Avon, and William Shakespeare is undeniably one of the most important writers of all time, so it is not perhaps surprising that the town is overwhelmed by visitors interested in his heritage. The town's main attractions are the five Shakespeare Birthplace Trust properties: Anne Hathaway's Cottage, Mary Arden's House, Shakespeare's Birthplace, Hall's Croft, home to Shakespeare's daughter Susanna and son-in-law Dr John Hall, and the site of New Place, where Shakespeare died, which is now marked by an Elizabethan-style knot garden.

STRATFORD-UPON-AVON

COX'S YARD
Bridgefoot CV37 6YY (opposite Bancroft Gardens)
☎ **01789 404600** 🖷 **01789 404633**

Beautifully situated on the banks of the River Avon in Stratford town centre, Cox's Yard is the town's newest attraction. Formerly the site of a historic timber yard and mill, it incorporates a micro-brewery showing visitors traditional methods in the brewing of 'Jester Ale' and 'The Stratford Tales' attraction where one can embark on a time travel journey through Stratford from the 16th century to the present day, by means of models and audio-visual presentations, meeting people whose stories of local life you can share. A camera obscura puts the present residents of Straford centre-stage by means of an electronically operated camera on top of a 20 metre high chimney.
Times: Open all year, daily from 9am.
Fee: *Free entry to Cox's Yard, admission to The Stratford Tales £3.95 (ch £2.50, pen £3.25).
🅿 🍽 ✗ licensed ♿ (lift to all levels, parking on site) toilets for disabled shop 🥢

ROYAL SHAKESPEARE COMPANY COLLECTION
Royal Shakespeare Theatre, Waterside CV37 6BB
☎ **01789 296655** 🖷 **01789 294810**

The RSC gallery is housed in the original Victorian building which was part of Charles Flower's Shakespeare Memorial, opened in 1879, comprising Theatre, Paintings and Sculpture Gallery, Library and Reading Room, the latter were not destroyed when the Theatre was burnt down in 1926. Temporary exhibitions include the work of the current artist(s) in residence.
Times: Open all year, Mon-Sat 9.15-end evening interval, Sun 12-4.30 (Nov-Mar Sun 11-3.30).(Closed 24 & 25 Dec).Theatre tours usually Mon-Fri (ex matinee days), 1.30 & 5.30, Sun 12, 1, 2 & 3.
Fee: *Exhibition £2 (ch, pen & students £1.50). Family ticket £4. Theatre Tours £4 (ch, pen & students £3) - advisable to book in advance.
🅿 (charged) 🍽 ✗ licensed ♿ toilets for disabled shop 🥢

SHAKESPEARE'S BIRTHPLACE
Henley St CV37 6QW
☎ **01789 204016** 🖷 **01789 296083**

Shakespeare was born in the timber-framed house in 1564. It contains numerous exhibits of the Elizabethan period and Shakespeare memorabilia, and the acclaimed exhibition, Shakespeare; His Life and Background.
Times: Open all year, 20 Mar-19 Oct Mon-Sat 9-5, Sun 9.30-5; 20 Oct-19 Mar Mon-Sat 9.30-4, Sun 10-4. (Closed 23-26 Dec). Last admission 1 hour before closing time.
🅿 (100 yds) (no parking outside Birthplace) ♿ toilets for disabled shop 🥢 *Details not confirmed for 2000* 🥢

THE TEDDY BEAR MUSEUM
19 Greenhill St CV37 6LF
☎ 01789 293160

Ten settings in a house which dates from Shakespeare's time, are devoted to bears of all shapes and sizes. Many old bears are displayed and there are also mechanical and musical bears. Some of the bears belong to famous people, for example, Jeffrey Archer and Prince Philip, or are famous in their own right, such as the original Sooty and Fozzie bear.

Times: Open all year, daily 9.30-6, Jan-Feb 9.30-5. Closed 25 & 26 Dec.

Fee: *£2.25 (ch £1). Family ticket £5.95.Party 20+.

Ⓟ (30yds & 200yds) (access to ground floor shop only) shop ✖ ⬳

⛪ UPTON HOUSE
UPTON HOUSE
OX15 6HT (on A422, 7m NW of Banbury,12M SE of Stratford)
☎ 01295 670266

The house, built of mellow local stone, dates from 1695, but the outstanding collections it contains are the chief attraction. They include paintings by English and Continental Old Masters, Brussels tapestries, Sèvres porcelain, Chelsea figures and 18th-century furniture. The garden is also of great interest. Please telephone for details of events.

Times: Open 4 Apr-1 Nov, Sat-Wed & BH Mon 2-6; Closed Thu-Fri & Good Fri. Last admissions 5.30pm (Oct/Nov 5pm) Ⓟ ⬳ ♿ (Braille guide,parking nr house,buggy for lower garden) toilets for disabled shop ✖ ⬳ *Details not confirmed for 2000* ⬳

⛪ WARWICK
LORD LEYCESTER HOSPITAL
High St CV34 4BH
☎ 01926 492797

These lovely half-timbered buildings were built in the late 14th century and adapted into almshouses by the Earl of Leycester in 1571. The Hospital is still a home for ex-servicemen and their wives. Originally it was built as a Guildhouse and the old Guildhall, Great Hall, Chapel and courtyard remain. The buildings also

contd.

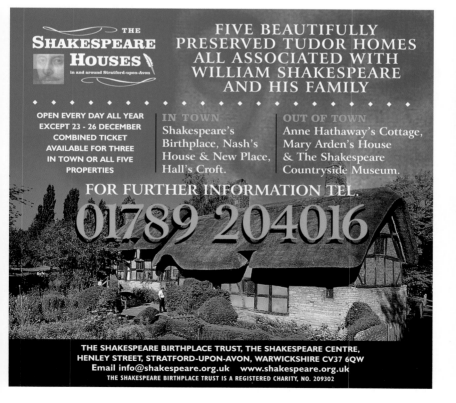

house the Regimental Museum of the Queen's Own Hussars.
Times: Open all year, Tue-Sun & BH's 10-5 (4pm in winter). (Closed Good Fri & 25 Dec).
P ✕ & shop *Details not confirmed for 2000*

WARWICK CASTLE
CV34 4QU (2m from M40 exit 15)
☎ 01926 406600   ▤ 01926 401692

From the days of William the Conqueror to the reign of Queen Victoria, Warwick Castle has provided a backdrop for many turbulent times. Attractions include the gloomy Dungeon and Torture Chamber, the grand State Rooms, the Great Hall, and a reconstruction of the Royal Weekend Party of 1898, where "Daisy", Countess of Warwick held sway. Throughout the year there are regular special events including falconry, jousting and medieval festivals.
Times: Open daily 10-6 (5pm Nov-Mar). Closed 25 Dec.
Fee: *£9.50 (ch 4-16 £5.80, pen £6.85). Family ticket £27. Jun-Aug £10.50 (ch 6.25, pen £7.50). Family ticket £28.
P (charged) ▆ ✕ licensed & (Free admission to wheelchair bound visitors) toilets for disabled shop ✖ (ex assistance dogs) ◥

WARWICKSHIRE YEOMANRY MUSEUM
The Court House Vaults, Jury St CV34 4EW
☎ 01926 492212   ▤ 01926 494837

The vaults of the court house display militaria from the county Yeomanry, dating from 1794 to 1945. It includes regimental silver, paintings, uniforms and weapons. A small room in the cellars is devoted to Warwick Town Museum.
Times: Open Good Fri-Sep, Fri-Sun & BHs 10-1 & 2-4. Other times by prior arrangement.
Fee: *Donations
P (300yds) shop ✖

West Midlands

At the centre of England, the West Midlands is a metropolitan county with a mainly industrial base. Birmingham is the administrative centre and the other main towns are Coventry, Dudley, Smethick, Walsall, West Bromwich and Wolverhampton.

The area was badly affected by the decline in British manufacturing, but has fought back by diversification into the service sector, with impressive conference and exhibition facilities offered in Birmingham, in the form of the International Convention Centre and National Exhibition Centre, home to many of the country's biggest trade fairs. Industrial heritage museums have blossomed, including the Black Country Museum at Dudley, and Cadbury World, which tells the story of chocolate, and the chocolate factory established at Bournville by the renowned Quaker family.

Birmingham, AKA 'Brum', is Britain's second largest city, its position at the hub of things emphasised by the miles of canals criss-crossing the city and its amazing tangle of flyovers. There are some splendid public buildings, notably the Town Hall and the City Museum and Art Gallery. Modern developments include the infamous 60s-designed Bull Ring shopping centre.

The West Midlands' multi-racial population gives a buzz to its cultural life, which offers a feast of arts, products, foods and festivals from around the world. The artistic life of the community is rich, with the world class Birmingham Symphony Orchestra and the Birmingham Royal Ballet in residence, plus a wide range of visual art in a variety of galleries.

EVENTS & FESTIVALS

January
19th-23rd Antiques & Fine Art Fair, NEC, Birmingham

February
Chinese New Year Celebrations, Birmingham

March
9th-12th Crufts 2000, NEC, Birmingham

April
27th-1st May BBC Good Homes Show, NEC
tbc BBC Match of the Day

May
tbc International Classic Motor Show, Birmingham
tbc Lord Mayor's Festival & Parade, Birmingham

June
3rd-11th Godiva Festival, Coventry.
21st-24th International Church Music Festival, Coventry Cathedral

July
7th-16th International Jazz Festival, Birmingham

August
24th-28th Coventry Jazz Festival

October
tbc Diwali Celebrations, Birmingham

November
9th-19th International Motorcycle Show, Birmingham
tbc Festival of Lights, Coventry

Top: Gas Street Canal Basin, Birmingham

COVENTRY

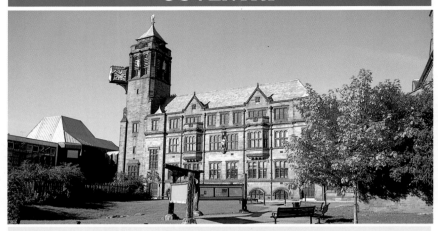

Surrounded by the rich farmland of the West Midlands and Warwickshire, Coventry has been an important city since the 14th century, but one of its most famous characters dates from the 11th. A nunnery destroyed by the Danes was replaced by a Benedictine monastery founded by Leofric, Earl of Mercia. It was his wife, Godiva, who is said to have ridden naked through the streets of the city in protest against the oppression of the people by her husband. In more recent times Coventry suffered massive bombardment by the Luftwaffe during World War II. Coventry's blackest night was November 14, 1940 when 40 acres of the city, including most of the fine cathedral were destroyed.

🏛 BIRMINGHAM

BIRMINGHAM BOTANICAL GARDENS & GLASSHOUSES

Westbourne Rd, Edgbaston B15 3TR (2m W of city centre,follow signs for Edgbaston,then brown tourist signs)

☎ 0121 454 1860 📠 0121 454 7835

Originally opened in 1832, the gardens include the Tropical House, which has a 24ft-wide lily pool and lush vegetation. The Orangery features a wide variety of citrus fruits and the Cactus House gives a desert scene with its giant agaves and opuntias. Outside, a tour of the gardens includes rhododendrons and azalea borders and a collection of over 200 trees. Bands play every

Sunday afternoon in the summer. Please telephone for details of events and flower shows.
Times: Open daily all year, wkdays 9-7 or dusk, Sun 10-8 or dusk whichever is earlier. (Closed 25 Dec).
Fee: *£4.20 (£4.50 summer Sun, concessions £2.30)
🅿 ☕ ✕ licensed ♿ (3 wheelchairs + 2 electric scooters available free) toilets for disabled shop garden centre ✈

BIRMINGHAM MUSEUM & ART GALLERY

Chamberlain Sq B3 3DH

☎ 0121 303 2834 📠 0121 303 1394

One of the world's best collections of Pre-Raphaelite paintings can be seen here, including important works by Burne-Jones, a native of Birmingham. Also on display are fine silver, ceramics and glass. The archaeology section has prehistoric Egyptian, Greek and Roman antiquities, and also objects from the Near East, Mexico and Peru.
Times: Open all year Mon, Thu & Sat 10-5, Fri 10.30-5 and Sun 12.30-5.
Fee: *Museum & Art Gallery free, admission charged for Gas Hall Exhibitions tel: 0121-303 1966 for details.
☕ ✕ licensed ♿ (lift) toilets for disabled shop ✈ 🍴

BIRMINGHAM RAILWAY MUSEUM

670 Warwick Rd, Tyseley B11 2HL (3m S, A41 Warwick Rd)

☎ 0121 707 4696 📠 0121 765 4645

This is a working railway museum with a fully equipped workshop. There are numerous steam locomotives and historic carriages, wagons and

other vehicles. Steam-hauled train rides can be taken when available. Steam locomotive driving courses on an Express Passenger Steam and Tank Loco are also available. Various special events are planned, please telephone for details.
Times: Open weekends and BH summer, 10-5 and winter 10-4.
Fee: *£2.50 (ch, pen & UB40s £1.25). Family Ticket £6.20
[P] ⬛ ✕ & (ramps to platforms) shop ✖ (ex guide dogs)

SELLY MANOR MUSEUM
Maple Rd, Bournville B30 2AE (off A38)
☎ 0121 472 0199 ◈ 0121 471 4101

These two timber-framed manor houses date from the 13th and early 14th centuries, and have been re-erected in the 'garden suburb' of Bournville. There is a herb garden and regular exhibitions and events are held all year. A charity Christmas card fair takes place in November and December.
Times: Open mid Jan-mid Dec, Tue-Fri & BH 10-5 (Apr-Sep, Sat-Sun 2-5), phone for details.
Fee: *£1.50 (ch 50p)
[P] & toilets for disabled shop

🏛 COVENTRY
COVENTRY CATHEDRAL & VISITOR CENTRE
7 Priory Row CV1 5ES (signposted on all approaches to the city)
☎ 024 76227597 ◈ 024 76227597

Coventry's old cathedral was bombed during an air raid of November 1940 which devastated the city. The remains have been carefully preserved. The new cathedral was designed by Sir Basil Spence and consecrated in May 1962. It contains outstanding modern works of art, including a huge tapestry designed by Graham Sutherland, the west screen (a wall of glass engraved by John Hutton with saints and angels), bronzes by Epstein, and the great baptistry window by John Piper. There is also an opportunity to enjoy an audio-visual display in the visitors' centre. International Church Music Festival (21-24 Jun); Coventry Mystery Plays (July); Tightrope walk between towers of Holy Trinity and Cathedral (31 Dec 1999).
Times: Open all year, daily, Etr-Sep 9.30-6; Oct-Etr 9.30-4.30. Visitor centre open Oct-Apr 11am-3pm, Apr-Oct 10-4.
Fee: *Visitor centre £1.25 (ch 6 free, ch 6-16, students & pen 75p).Party 10+. Cathedral £2 donation. Camera charge £1. Video charge £3.
[P] (250 yds) ⬛ & (lift, touch and hearing centre, paved wheelchair access) toilets for disabled shop ✖

HERBERT ART GALLERY & MUSEUM
Jordan Well CV1 5QP
☎ 024 76832381 ◈ 024 76832410

'Godiva City', tells Coventry's story over 1,000 years, through interactive exhibits, objects, pictures and words. Changing displays of art, craft, social and industrial history. Full activity

programme throughout the year, please telephone for details.
Times: Open all year, Mon-Sat 10-5.30, Sun 12-5. (Closed 24-3 Jan).
Fee: Free.
[P] (500yds) ⬛ & (parking for disabled, automatic doors, access to tea rooms) toilets for disabled shop ✖

LUNT ROMAN FORT
Coventry Rd, Baginton CV8 3AJ (S side of city, off Stonebridge highway, A45)
☎ 024 76832381 ◈ 024 76832410

The turf and timber Roman fort from around the end of the 1st century has been faithfully reconstructed. An Interpretation Centre is housed in the granary.
Times: 3 Apr-Oct 10-5, 29 May-6 Jun, daily 10-5. 24 Jul-12 Sep, Thu-Tue 10-5.
Fee: *£1.80 (concessions 80p). Audio tour 80p.
[P] & (ramp to Granary Interpretation Centre) toilets for disabled shop

MUSEUM OF BRITISH ROAD TRANSPORT
St Agnes Ln, Hales St CV1 1PN (just off junc 1 ring road, Tower Street)
☎ 024 76832425 ◈ 024 76832465

The museum illustrates the role of Coventry and the West Midlands in the development of transport throughout the world. There are over 400 exhibits, in displays of motor cars, commercial vehicles, motor cycles and associated items including die-cast models.
Times: Open all year, daily 10-5. Closed 24-26 Dec.
Fee: Free.
[P] (adjacent) ⬛ & (audio tour, tactile floor & models) toilets for disabled shop ✖ 🍴

🏛 DUDLEY
BLACK COUNTRY LIVING MUSEUM
Tipton Rd DY1 4SQ (on A4037, opposite Dudley Guest Hospital)
☎ 0121 557 9643 & 0121 520 8054
◈ 0121 557 4242

The museum is really a recreation of a Black Country village, complete with cottages, a chapel, chemist, baker and a pub serving real ale. One of the buildings is a chainmaker's house with a brewhouse, and demonstrations of chainmaking and glass cutting are given in traditional workshops. There is also a canal boat dock with a range of narrowboats, and boats set off daily for canal trips into the Dudley Tunnel, an eerie underground ride. Transport around the village is provided by an electric tramway. You can go underground in an 1850s mine, and see a replica of the world's first steam engine, venture into a pit-pulled cottage (affected by subsidence due to mining). Costumed guides and demonstrations bring the buildings to life and regular `Theme' weekends are held throughout the summer. Recent additions include a pair of unique cast iron houses, a fully working 1930s Fish and Chip shop, and a 1925 charabanc bus

contd.

which transports visitors around the site. Please contact for details of special events

Times: Open all year, Mar-Oct daily 10-5; Nov-Feb, Wed-Sun 10-4. (telephone for Christmas closing)

Fee: *£7.50 (ch 5-17 £4.50, pen £6.50). Family ticket £20. Party 10+(rates available on application)

🅿 ▣ ⚿ (ramps available) toilets for disabled shop ✕ ➤

MUSEUM & ART GALLERY

St James's Rd DY1 1HU

☎ 01384 815575 ▤ 01384 815576

The museum houses the Brooke Robinson collection of 17th, 18th and 19th century European painting, furniture, ceramics and enamels. A fine geological gallery, 'The Time Trail' has spectacular displays of fossils from the local Wenlock limestone and coal measures, and a wide variety of temporary exhibitions are staged throughout the year.

Times: Open all year, Mon-Sat 10-5. (Closed some BHs).

🅿 (25mtrs) ⚿ shop ✕ *Details not confirmed for 2000* ➤

⚒ KINGSWINFORD

BROADFIELD HOUSE GLASS MUSEUM

Barnett Ln DY6 9QA

☎ 01384 273011

This magnificent collection of 19th-and 20th-century glass focuses on the cut, etched, engraved and coloured glass made in nearby Stourbridge during the last century. Highlights include cameo glass by Alphonse Lechevrel and George Woodall, and rock crystal engraving by William Fritsche. Also on display are the Michael Parkington collection of 18th-, 19th-and 20th-century British glass, the Hulbert of Dudley collection, and the Notley/Lerpiniere collection of Carnival Glass.

Times: Open all year, Tue-Fri & Sun 2-5, Sat 10-1 & 2-5. BH's 2-5.

🅿 ⚿ shop ✕ *Details not confirmed for 2000*

⚒ SOLIHULL

NATIONAL MOTORCYCLE MUSEUM

Coventry Rd, Bickenhill B92 0EJ (nr junc 6, of M42, off A45 nr NEC)

☎ 01675 443311 ▤ 0121 711 3153

Five exhibition halls showing British motorcycles built during the Golden Age of motorcycling.

Spanning 90 years, the immaculately restored machines are the products of around 150 different factories. Over 650 machines are on show, most are owned by the museum, others are from collections or private owners. Restoration work is carried out by enthusiasts, and new motorcycles are acquired from all over the world. All the machines are made in Britain from the 1898 20mph Beeston 'Trike' to the 1992 TT winning 191mph Nortons, the museum is the legacy of almost a century of world-beating motorcycling and a glorious celebration of speed.

Times: Open all year, daily 10-6. (Closed 24-26 Dec).

Fee: *£4.50 (ch 12 & pen £3.50). Party 20+.

🅿 ✕ licensed ⚿ toilets for disabled shop ✕ ➤

⚒ WALSALL

WALSALL LEATHER MUSEUM

Littleton St WS2 8EQ (On Walsall ring-road on North side of town)

☎ 01922 721153 ▤ 01922 725827

Award winning working museum in the saddlery and leathergoods 'capital' of Britain. Watch skilled craftsmen and women at work in this beautifully restored Victorian leather factory. Displays tell the story of Walsall's leatherworkers past and present. Regular special exhibitions; collection of contemporary leather design. Large shop stocks range of Walsall-made leathergoods, many at bargain prices. Saddle Room Cafe serves delicious home-cooked cakes and light lunches.

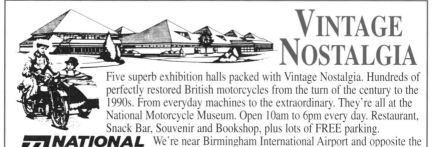

Attractive gardens with picnic seats. Groups very welcome, guided tours available.
Times: Open all year, Tue-Sat 10-5 (Nov-Mar 4pm), Sun noon-5. Open BH Mon. Closed 24-26 Dec, 1 Jan & Etr Sun.
Fee: Free.
P (10metres) 💻 �& (satff with sign language training) toilets for disabled shop ✈ (ex guide dogs) ➷

⛫ WOLVERHAMPTON
WIGHTWICK MANOR
WV6 8EE (3m W, beside Mermaid Inn)
☎ 01902 761400 📄 01902 764663

This house was begun in 1887 and in its style of decoration is one of the finest examples of the achievements of the late 19th-century. All aspects of William Morris's talents are shown in this house - wallpapers, textiles, carpets, tiles, embroidery and even books. The garden reflects late Victorian and Edwardian design.
Times: Open Mar-Dec, Thu, Sat & BH Sun & Mon 2.30-5.30.
Fee: *£5.40 (accompanied ch & students £2.70). Gardens only £2.20.
P 💻 �& shop ⚘

⛫ WORDSLEY
STUART CRYSTAL
Red House Glassworks DY8 4AA (1m from Stourbridge on the main A491 Stourbridge to Wolverhampton Road)
☎ 01384 828282 & 261777
📄 01384 70463

Fine glass has been made in the area since the beginning of the 17th century when French glass makers arrived in the area. The 200 year old Redhouse Glass Cone and associated building have recently been restored in the first stage of creating a museum. On the site there is also a fctory shop, a chip repair service and glass sculpture. At the Red House factory the focal point is the Redhouse Cone. The tour of the factory shows the complete glassmaking process from glass-blowing to cutting and decorating.
Times: Open all year, daily. (Closed 25-26 Dec & 1 Jan). Tours:Mon-Thu on the hour 10-4(not 12),Fri 10,11 & 1; Shop open Mon-Sat, 9-5, Sun 10-4; Glass Blowing: Wed-Sat.
Fee: Free.
P 💻 �& (Cone/Museum accessible- factory tours are not) shop ✈ (ex guide dogs) ➷

Isle of Wight

EVENTS & FESTIVALS

April
April-October A Century of Sea & Sail, Shanklin

May
13th-14th Isle of Wight Flower Show

June
3rd-4th June (provisional) Yarmouth Maritime Festival (incorporating the Old Gaffers)
9th-12th Isle of Wight Heavy Horse & Rural Life Festival, Binstead
10th Island Sailing Club Hoya Round the Island Yacht Race, Cowes
tbc Brading 10km Open Road Race

July
1st-8th July East Cowes Victorian Festival
22nd-23rd Royal Isle of Wight Agricultural Society County Show at Northwood Showground
29th-5th August Cowes Week International Yacht Racing Regatta

August
29th July-5th Cowes Week International Yacht Racing Regatta
19th-20th Isle of Wight Garlic Festival, Fighting Cocks Cross Roads, Newport Road

Top: Freshwater Bay

Despite its size, - less than 23 miles (39km) across at its widest point - the Isle of Wight offers plenty of scenic variety, and is popular as a holiday destination because of its lovely countryside, pleasant resorts and mild climate.

There's lots to see and do, with an abundance of museums, children's activity parks, and leisure facilities including watersports, riding, cycling, paragliding, golf, and sea and freshwater fishing. Local specialities are freshly caught crab and lobster, which can be enjoyed with a glass of wine from one of the island's five vineyards.

A chalk ridge runs east to west of the island, popular with walkers for the fine views afforded from its vantage points. The interesting coastline takes in the chalky pinnacles of The Needles, some splendid cliffs, and the curious multi-coloured sand at Alum Bay, which can be bought bottled in colourful layers from local souvenir shops. Coastal paths follow the shoreline from Totland to St Lawrence on the south coast, and Yarmouth to Cowes on the north coast.

The east coast has the most developed seaside resorts, with Ryde, Sandown, Shanklin and Ventnor, and their sandy beaches. Newport, the island's capital, is the only inland town and is a good shopping centre.

In addition to its natural features, the island has some fine castles and historic houses. Chief among these are medieval Carisbrooke Castle outside Newport, Osborne House at East Cowes, Brading Roman Villa, and lovely manor houses at Arreton, Barton, Haseley, Nunwell, Appuldurcombe and Morton.

🏛 ALUM BAY

THE NEEDLES OLD BATTERY

West High Down PO39 0JH (0.75m SW)
☎ **01983 754772**

This former Palmerston fort, built in 1862, has recently been restored. A tunnel leads to a look-out position with spectacular views of the Needles chalk stacks and lighthouse, and across the bay to Dorset. In the fort are two of the original 12-ton gun barrels. The powder house has an exhibition of the history of the Needles headland.

Times: Open 21 Mar-28 Oct, Sun-Thu; also open Etr wknd & daily in Jul & Aug 10.30-5. (last admission 4.30).
Fee: *£2.50 (ch £1.20). Family ticket £6.
P (0.75m) 🍽 shop ♿

🏛 ARRETON

HASELEY MANOR

PO30 3AN (on Sandown to Newport rd)
☎ **01983 865420**   📄 **01983 867547**

This is the oldest and largest manor open to the public on the Island. Parts of the south wing have some of the original building, c1300, but the rest of the house is a mixture of styles including Georgian and Victorian. The manor fell into disuse and was derelict by the 1970s but has since been carefully restored and now 20 rooms can be viewed, furnished in period style. Tableaux of figures in costume appear in many of the rooms. Outside, there is a re-constructed 18th-century farm complete with animals, and a well-stocked herb garden. There is also a children's play area with a tree house, and a small lake with an island castle. Visitors can also see pottery demonstrations, and children can make and take away a mouse. 1999 saw the opening of the Isle of Wight Museum of the Countryside.

Times: Open Etr-Oct, 10-5.30 Mon-Fri (closed Sat & Sun)
Fee: *£4.75 (ch £3.15, pen £4) Family £4.60. Party.
P 🍽 ✗ licensed ♿ (wheelchair ramps) toilets for disabled shop 🛒

🏛 BEMBRIDGE

BEMBRIDGE WINDMILL

PO30 4EB (0.5m S of Bembridge on B3395)
☎ **01983 873945**

The only windmill on the island to survive, Bembridge mill was built about 1700 and was in use until 1913. The stone-built tower with its wooden cap and machinery have been restored since it was given to the National Trust in 1961.

Times: Open Apr-30 Oct, daily (ex Sat) & Etr Sat & Jul-Aug, daily 10-5. Last admission 4.45.
Fee: *£1.40 (ch 70p)
P shop 🛒 ♿ 🛒

🏛 BRADING

MORTON MANOR

PO36 0EP (off A3055 in Brading, well signposted)
☎ **01983 406168**

The manor dates back to 1249, but was rebuilt in 1680 with further changes during the Georgian period. The house contains furniture of both the 18th and 19th centuries, but its main attraction lies in the beautiful gardens and the vineyard. The garden is landscaped into terraces, with ornamental ponds, a sunken garden and a traditional Elizabethan turf maze. In recent years vine-growing for wine has become popular on the island, and Morton Manor is one of the places to have an established vineyard and winery. A museum of winemaking relics has been set up, and has some unusual exhibits, including a modern working winery and video.

Times: Open Apr-Oct, daily 10-5.30 (Closed Sat).
Fee: *£3.50,ch £1.50 & pen £3.25). Party 15+.
P ✗ licensed ♿ shop garden centre (ex house)

NUNWELL HOUSE & GARDENS

Coach Ln PO36 0JQ (Off Ryde-Sandown Rd, A3055)
☎ **01983 407240**

Set in beautiful gardens, Nunwell is an impressive, lived-in and much loved house where King Charles I spent his last night of freedom. It has fine furniture and interesting collections of family militaria.In summer, concerts are occasionally held in the music room. Phone for details.

Times: Open House & Gardens: 30-31 May then 28 Jun-8 Sep, Mon-Wed 1-5. Groups welcome when house open & at other times by appointment.
Fee: *£4 inc guide book, (concessions)
P shop 🛪 (ex guide dogs)

🏛 CARISBROOKE

CARISBROOKE CASTLE

PO30 1XY (one and quarter miles SW of Newport, off B3401)
☎ **01983 522107**

This is the only medieval castle on the island and its most famous resident was King Charles I who was imprisoned here. There are two medieval wells: the one in the keep can be reached by climbing down 71 steps; the one in the courtyard had winding gear traditionally driven by a donkey, and displays of it working are still given.

Times: Open all year, Apr-Oct, daily 10-6 (or dusk if earlier in Oct); Nov-Mar, daily 10-4. Closed 24-26 Dec & 1 Jan.
Fee: £4.50 (ch £2.30).
P 🍽 ♿ shop ♯ 0

COWES

Cowes is a busy harbour all year round. It is a centre for yachting and boating of all kinds, and many national and international events are held here, both for sailing and power boats. The best known of these is Cowes Week, the internationally renowned sailing regatta held at the beginning of August.

The Isle of Wight was beloved of Queen Victoria, and Osborne House in East Cowes was her favourite holiday home. It was designed for her by Prince Albert, with magnificent terraced gardens overlooking Osborne Bay. After Albert's death, she made the house her permanent home.

FRESHWATER
DIMBOLA LODGE
Terrace Ln, Freshwater Bay PO40 9QE (off A3054)
☎ 01983 756814 ▤ 01983 755578

Home of Julia Margaret Cameron, the pioneer Victorian portrait photographer. The house has the largest permanent collection of Cameron prints on display in the UK, as well as galleries exhibiting work by young, up and coming, and acclaimed modern photographers; and a large display of cameras and accessories. Please ring for details of special events.
Times: Open all year 10-5 (Closed 5 days at Xmas).
Fee: *£2.50 (ch 16 free, concessions £1).
🅿 ✕ ♿ shop ✖

HAVENSTREET
ISLE OF WIGHT STEAM RAILWAY
The Railway Station PO33 4DS
☎ 01983 882204 ▤ 01983 884515

When the Newport to Ryde railway was closed, Haven Street Station was taken over by a private company, the Isle of Wight Steam Railway. A number of volunteers restored the station, locomotives and rolling stock, and steam trains now run the five miles from Wootton, via Haven Street to Smallbrook Junction where there is a direct interchange with the BR Ryde-Shanklin line. Locomotives in operation include former LSWR tank engine *Calbourne*, built in 1891, and LSBCR/Freshwater, Yarmouth & Newport Railway locomotive *Freshwater,* built in 1875. The rolling stock includes 70/80-year-old LBSCR/SECR carriages, plus vintage goods wagons. At Haven Street, the old gas works houses a display of Island railway memorabilia.
Times: Open Mar 21/25/28. Apr 1-11,15,18,22,25,28-29. May Wed, Thu, Sun & Bank Holidays. Jun-Aug daily. Sep daily till 26th then 30th. Oct Sun & Thu & 26-27)
Fee: *Return Fares £6.50 (ch 4-15 £4). Family ticket £19.
🅿 💻 ♿ (with assistance) toilets for disabled shop

🏛 NEWPORT
ROMAN VILLA
Cypress Rd PO30 1EX (S of
Newport,signposted'Roman Villa')
☎ 01983 529720 📄 01983 823841

Archaeologists have uncovered this 3rd-century
Roman villa where visitors can now see the well-
preserved baths and re-constructed rooms in
which the family once lived. The site museum
houses some of the finds from the excavation.
Recent refurbishment has provided new displays
in reconstructed rooms, a renewed artefact
gallery and a Roman garden.

Times: Open Etr-Oct, daily 10-4.30. Other times by
appointment.

Fee: *£2 (ch 90p. concessions £1.20)

P (100 yds) & shop ✈

🏛 NEWTOWN
OLD TOWN HALL
Town Ln PO30 4PA (1m N of A3054 between
Yarmouth & Newport)
☎ 01983 531785

This unusual town hall stands alone, surrounded
by grass and a few houses, not in a crowded high
street. Newtown was once the island's capital,
returning two members to Parliament. It was
badly burned in 1377 and never fully recovered.
In 1699 the town hall was rebuilt and has been
further restored recently. An exhibition depicts
the exploits of the anonymous group of National
Trust benefactors known as 'Ferguson's Gang'.

Times: Open 29 Mar-28 Oct, Mon, Wed & Sun 2-5 (also open
Good Fri, Etr Sat & Tue & Thu in Jul-Aug). Last admission
4.45pm.

Fee: *£1.30 (ch 65p)

P (Braille guide books available) ✈ 🌿

🏛 OSBORNE HOUSE
OSBORNE HOUSE
PO32 6JY (1m SE of East Cowes)
☎ 01983 200022

Designed by Prince Albert and Thomas Cubitt in
the mid 19th century, Osborne was Queen
Victoria's favourite home, especially after the
death of Prince Albert. She died here in 1901. The
interior of the house is largely unchanged since
Victorian times, and is a fascinating insight into
the private life of the Royal family of that day.
The lovely grounds are full of interest, and
include a Swiss-style cottage used by Queen
Victoria's children.

Times: House open Apr-Oct, daily 10-5(last admission
4.30pm). Grounds 10-6 (last admission 5); Oct 10-5 or dusk if
earlier.

Fee: £6.90 (ch £3.50).

P 🅿 & shop ✈ ⚏

🏛 SHANKLIN
SHANKLIN CHINE
12 Ponona Rd PO37 6PF
☎ 01983 866432 📄 01983 874215

Shanklin Chine is a natural gorge of great scenic
beauty with a spectacular 45ft waterfall. A path
winds down through the gorge, overhanging
trees, ferns and other flora that cover its steep
sides. The Heritage Centre features details of
nature trails, rare flora and life in Victorian
Shanklin. Features of historic interest include
sections of PLUTO (pipeline under the ocean),
which carried petrol to the Allied troops in
Normandy. There is a memorial to 40
Commando, Royal Marines. Pictorial History of
Shanklin & Isle of Wight Exhibition, featuring
"Poets and the Island - a celebration" in the
Heritage Centre.

Times: Open 3 Apr-18 May 10-5, 19 May-17 Sept 10-10
(illuminated at night), 18 Sept-29 Oct 10-5, (opening period
may be extended depending on weather conditions)

Fee: £2.50 (ch £1, pen & students £1.50, disabled £1). Family
ticket £6.50-£7.25

P (450 yds) 🅿 shop ✈ (ex on lead at all times)

🏛 VENTNOR
MUSEUM OF THE HISTORY OF
SMUGGLING
Botanic Gardens PO38 1UL (on A3055, 1m W of
Ventnor)
☎ 01983 853677

Situated underground in extensive vaults, this
unique museum shows methods of smuggling
used over a 700-year period right up to the

contd.

present day. There is an adventure playground in the Botanic Gardens.

Times: Open Etr-Sep, daily 10-5.30.

Ⓟ (charged) 🍽 ✕ licensed shop garden centre *Details not confirmed for 2000*

VENTNOR BOTANIC GARDEN
Undercliff Dr PO38 1UL
☎ 01983 855397 📠 01983 856154

Many rare and tender plants from all over the world can be found in the 22 acres of the Ventnor Botanic Garden, one of the Island's largest gardens. The temperate house features special displays which may be seen for a small charge. Facilities for the disabled include a garden of raised beds with highly scented plants. Guided tours by prior arrangement with the curator. There are two gift shops, a picnic area, and a children's playground which is suitable for children of all abilities, including those in wheelchairs, pushchairs, and the visually impaired.

Times: Open all year - Garden; Temperate House 8 Mar-1 Nov, daily 10-5.30 O8 Nov-Mar 1999, Sun 11-4.

Ⓟ (charged) ✕ licensed ♿ toilets for disabled shop ✈ (ex in garden) *Details not confirmed for 2000* 🍽

🏛 WROXALL
APPULDURCOMBE HOUSE
PO38 3EW (off B3327, half a mile W)
☎ 01983 852484

The manor began life as a priory in 1100, but when it came into the hands of the Worsley family they demolished it and built this Palladian house on the site. Now ruined, it stands in beautiful grounds, landscaped in the 18th century by Capability Brown.

Times: Open Apr-Nov, daily 10-6 (or dusk if earlier). Last admission 30 mins before closing.

Ⓟ ♿ ⌗

🏛 YARMOUTH
YARMOUTH CASTLE
Quay St PO41 0PB (adjacent to car ferry terminal)
☎ 01983 760678

Modern buildings surround this well preserved castle which dates from the Tudor period. Fine views of the harbour can be obtained from the gun platform.

Times: Open Apr-Oct, daily 10-6 (or dusk if earlier), closed 1-2pm.

Ⓟ (200yds) ♿ ✈ ⌗

Wiltshire

To many visiting the county, Wiltshire has three attractions: Salisbury, Stonehenge and Longleat. While these are all worthwhile, (indeed Stonehenge could be rightly called one of the wonders of the world) there is still plenty more to be discovered in the county.

After seeing Stonehenge, those interested in prehistoric sites should visit Avebury, where the stones are more approachable. Even though there is a lot of tourist activity in the village, the area remains relatively untouched, mostly given over to farmland and moor. This is also a good area for encountering crop circles.

Stonehenge and the Avebury circles seem to be part of a larger complex which still baffles investigators, and includes nearby features such as Windmill Hill with the remains of an earthwork camp some 5,500 years old; Silbury Hill, a man-made mound of earth which covers five and a half acres; West Kennet Long Barrow, a burial mound; and possibly the chalk-carved White Horses on surrounding hillsides.

Miss Matilda Talbot left the village of Lacock to the National Trust in the 1940s. Another Talbot, William Henry Fox, produced the first-ever photographic negative here in 1831. The village was also used for the recent BBC production of Jane Austen's *Pride & Predjudice*.

Malmesbury in Northern Wiltshire, is the oldest borough in England and is home to a partially ruined 12th-century abbey, notable for a very impressive porch carving of the Apostles.

EVENTS & FESTIVALS

April
23rd-24th (Easter Sun & Mon), Easter Bunny Trail, Woodland Park, Westbury
22nd Downton Cuckoo Fair, Downton, Salisbury

May
26th-29th Chippenham Folk Festival
tbc Salisbury Festival
tbc Steam & Vintage Rally, Castle Combe

June
tbc Dickens Festival, Pickwick, Corsham
7th-25th Devizes Festival

July
tbc Festival of Music & Arts/International Jazz Festival, Marlborough
tbc Bradford-on-Avon Town Festival
19th-25th Royal International Air Tattoo Tel 01285 713000
22nd-23rd Salisbury Country & Garden Show, Hudson's Field, Salisbury

September
1st-3rd City of Birmingham Dog Show, Perry Park
23rd Pewsey Illuminated Carnival (at night)

Top: Avebury

🏛 AVEBURY

AVEBURY MANOR
SN8 1RF (6m W of Marlborough, from A4 take
A4361/B4003)
☎ 01672 539250

Avebury Manor has a monastic origin, and has
been much altered since then. The present
buildings date from the early 16th century, with
notable Queen Anne alterations and Edwardian
renovation. The flower gardens contain medieval
walls, and there are examples of topiary.
Times: Open: Garden Apr-1 Nov, daily ex Mon & Thur, open
BH Mon 11am-5.30pm.(last admission 5pm). House Apr-28
Oct Tue,Wed, Sun & BH Mon 2-5.30, (last admission 5pm).
🅿 🚻 shop ✈ ☙ *Details not confirmed for 2000*

AVEBURY MUSEUM
(Alexander Keiller Museum)
☎ 01672 539250

This is one of the most important prehistoric
sites in Europe, and was built before Stonehenge.
An avenue of great stones leads to the site,
which must have been a place of great religious
significance. The small museum has recently
been refurbished and contains many new
exhibits.
Times: Open all year, Apr-Oct, daily 10-6; Nov-Mar, 10-4.
Closed 24-26 Dec & 1 Jan.
🅿 🚻 shop ✈ ⚏ ☙ *Details not confirmed for 2000*

🏛 BRADFORD-ON-AVON

GREAT CHALFIELD MANOR
SN12 8NJ (3m SW of Melksham)
☎ 01985 843600

Built during the Wars of the Roses, the manor is
a beautiful, mellow, moated house which still has
its great hall. It was restored in the 1920s. There
is a small 13th-century church next to the house.
Times: Open Apr-29 Oct, Tue-Thu. Tours starting at 12.15,
2.15, 3, 3.45, 4.30.
🅿 ✈ ☙ *Details not confirmed for 2000*

TITHE BARN

This impressive tithe barn, over 160ft long by 30ft
wide, once belonged to Shaftesbury Abbey. The
roof is of stone slates, supported outside by
buttresses and inside by massive beams and a
network of rafters.
Times: Open Apr-Oct, daily 10.30-5; Nov-Mar, daily 10.30-4.
🅿 🚻 ✈ ⚏

🏛 CORSHAM

CORSHAM COURT
SN13 0BZ (4m W of Chippenham off the A4)
☎ 01249 701610   ▤ 01249 701610

The Elizabethan manor was built in 1582, and
then bought by the Methuen family in the 18th
century to house their collections of paintings
and statues. 'Capability' Brown made additions to
the house and laid out the park, and later John
Nash made further changes. There is furniture by
Chippendale, Adam, Cobb and Johnson inside, as
well as the Methuen collection of Old Master
paintings. The garden has flowering shrubs,
herbaceous borders, a Georgian bath house and
peacocks.
Times: Open Summer: 20 Mar-30 Sep daily ex Mon but incl
BH's 11-5.30 last admission 5pm. Winter: 1 Oct-19 Mar open
weekends only 2-4.30pm last admission 4pm. (Closed
December). Open throughout year by appointment for
groups 15 +.
Fee: *House & Gardens: £4.50 (ch £2.50, pen £3.50).
Gardens only £2 (ch £1 & pen £1.50). Party 15+
🅿 🍽 🚻 shop ✈

🏛 HOLT

THE COURTS
BA14 6RR (3m N of Trowbridge, on B3107)
☎ 01225 782340

Weavers came to The Courts to have their
disputes settled until the end of the 18th century.
The house is not open, but it makes an attractive
backdrop to the gardens - a network of stone

CORSHAM COURT HOME OF THE METHUEN FAMILY

Corsham Court is one of England's finest Stately Homes. It was a Royal Manor in the days of the Saxon
Kings, and the present building is based upon an Elizabethan Manor dating from 1582. Magnificent
Georgian State Rooms were added in 1760. It houses one of the oldest and most distinguished collections of Old Masters and Furniture in the country, and with its 'Capability' Brown gardens and arboretum, and architecture by John
Nash and Thomas Bellamy,
Corsham Court provides the visitor
with a wonderful opportunity to
enjoy the many delights of the historic and beautiful Stately Home.

Tel/Fax:
01249 701610

For opening times see gazetteer entry.

paths, yew hedges, pools and borders with a strange, almost magical atmosphere.

Times: Open Apr-1 Nov, daily (ex Sat) 1.30-5.30. Out of season by appointment.

    Details not confirmed for 2000

LACOCK

LACKHAM COUNTRY ATTRACTIONS

SN15 2NY (3m S of Chippenham, on A350)

☎ 01249 443111   📠 01249 444474

Various visitor attractions are situated within the 210-hectare estate of Lackham College. Thatched and refurbished farm buildings accommodate the farm museum and the grounds feature a walled garden, glasshouses, rhododendron glades, riverside and woodland walks, a children's adventure playground and farm park. There is a major collection of historical roses in the Italian Garden. For children, Rupert Bear and his friends (models only) are in their new Nutwood.

Times: Open Apr, May, Sept & Oct, weekends and Bank Hols. June, July & Aug, daily. 10am-5pm. Last entry 4pm.

P 💷 ✗ & (wheelchair available) toilets for disabled shop *Details not confirmed for 2000*

LACOCK & LACOCK ABBEY

SN15 2LG (3m S of Chippenham, E of A350)

☎ 01249 730227

The beautifully preserved National Trust village of Lacock, with its fascinating old houses and streets, is the setting for Lacock Abbey, an interesting manor whose history is bound up with the development of photography. William Henry Fox Talbot made a series of innovative experiments here in the 19th century. The abbey was founded in the 13th century. At the Dissolution it was sold to William Sherrington, who destroyed the church and turned the nuns' quarters into a grand home. A museum devoted to Fox Talbot (one of Sherrington's descendants) is housed in an old barn.

Times: Museum,Cloisters & Grounds, Mar-1 Nov,daily 11-5.30. Closed Good Fri. Abbey, 1 Apr-1 Nov daily, ex Tue, 1-5.30. Last admissions 5pm..

P & (taped guides) toilets for disabled shop ✱ *Details not confirmed for 2000*

LONGLEAT

LONGLEAT

The Estate Office BA12 7NW (Entrance on Warminster-Frome road A362).

☎ 01985 844400   📠 01985 844885

The late Marquess of Bath was the first peer to open his house to the public on a regular basis, a trend which many would follow. The Longleat estate has now grown to offer the visitor a safari park (home to hundreds of wild animals, including Britain's only white tiger); an exciting Adventure Castle; a maze; safari boats; narrow-gauge railway and a multitude of exhibitions and other attractions. The centrepiece of all this tourist activity is the majestic Elizabethan house,

built by Sir John Thynne in 1580 and decorated in the Italian Renaissance style in the late-19th century. It contains a mixture of furnishings and artefacts reflecting the tastes and interests of the Thynne family through the centuries, and the fully restored Victorian kitchens offer an interesting glimpse of life `below stairs'. The magnificent grounds, laid out by 'Capability' Brown, offer many lovely walks. Heaven's Gate is particularly spectacular when the rhododendrons are flowering.

Times: Open all year. House daily, 10-6 (Nov-Etr 10-4). Safari park, 13 Mar-31 Oct 10-6, last car admitted 5.30pm or sunset if earlier.

Fee: *House: £5 (ch £4, pen £4) Safari Park: £6 (ch £4.50 pen £4.50). Passport ticket for all attractions: £13 (ch & pen £10).

P 💷 ✗ licensed & toilets for disabled shop ✱ (in Safari park-free kennels) ⬤

LUDGERSHALL

LUDGERSHALL CASTLE

SP11 9QR (7m NW of Andover on A342)

Although a ruin since the 16th century, this was once a royal castle and hunting palace. The visitor can see large earthworks of the Norman motte-and-bailey castle and the flint walls of the later hunting palace. The stump of a medieval cross stands in the village street.

Times: Open all reasonable times.

P & ♯

LYDIARD PARK

LYDIARD PARK

Lydiard Tregoze SN5 9PA (from M4 exit 16. Follow brown Tourist Information signs)

☎ 01793 770401   📠 01793 877909

Set in beautiful country parkland, this fine Georgian house belonged to the St John family (the Bolingbrokes) for 500 years up until 1943 when the house and parkland were purchased by the Swindon Corporation. Since then the sadly dilapidated house has been restored and much of the original furnishings returned, together with the large St John family portrait collection dating from Elizabethan to Victorian times. Exceptional plasterwork, early wallpaper, a rare painted glass window, and a room devoted to the talented 18th-century amateur artist, Lady Diana Spencer, can also be seen. Adjacent, the church of St Marys has many fine and unusual memorials to the St John family. The grounds offer a variety of pleasant woodland walks, spacious lawns, lakes and children's adventure playground.

Times: Open all year, House: Mon-Fri 10-1 & 2-5, Sat 10-5, Sun 2-5.30. Winter closing 4pm (Nov-Feb). Park: all year, daily closing at dusk each day.

Fee: *£1.20 (ch 60p). Car parking 60p for 2 hours, £1 for day.

P (charged) 💷 & (Easiriders may be booked at visitors centre Tel:771419) toilets for disabled shop ✱ (ex park/guide dogs in house)

SALISBURY & MARLBOROUGH

The medieval city of Salisbury is known particularly for its magnificent cathedral, with its soaring 405 foot (123 metre) spire - the tallest in England. The beautifully preserved cathedral close - the largest in England - has several fine buildings dating from the 14th to the 18th century.

The historic town of Marlborough, on the River Kennet with high downs to the north and south, is believed to have the widest High Street in Europe, lined with handsome Georgian buildings. The town is also known for its famous public school.

MARLBOROUGH

CROFTON BEAM ENGINES

Crofton Pumping Station, Crofton SN8 3DW (6m SE of Marlborough, signposted from A338/A346/B3087 at Burbage also 6m SW of Hungerford on A4)

☎ 01672 870300

The oldest working beam engine in the world still in its original building and still doing its original job, the Boulton and Watt 1812, is to be found in this rural spot. Its companion is a Harvey's of Hayle of 1845. Both are steam driven, from a hand-stoked, coal-fired boiler, and pump water into the summit level of the Kennet and Avon Canal with a lift of 40ft. Telephone Marlborough (01672) 870300 for information. The surrounding countryside is pleasant, and walks can be taken along the canal towpath and to a working windmill nearby.

Times: Open daily 2 Apr-31 Oct. Steaming weekends 3-5 Apr, 1-3 May, 29-31 May, 26-27 Jun, 24-25 Jul, 28-30 Aug, 25-26 Sep.

Fee: *Steaming weekend: £3.50 (ch £1, under 5 free & pen £2.50). Family ticket £7. Non-steaming days £2 (ch 50p, pen £1.50).

🅿 ▣ ♿ (phone warden in advance, sighted guides provided) shop ✈ (not inside)

MIDDLE WOODFORD

HEALE GARDENS, PLANT CENTRE & SHOP

SP4 6NT (4m N of Salisbury, between A360 & A345)

☎ 01722 782504

Heale House and its eight acres of beautiful garden lie beside the River Avon at Middle Woodford. Much of the house is unchanged since King Charles II sheltered here after the Battle of Worcester in 1651. The garden provides a wonderfully varied collection of plants, shrubs, and musk and other roses, growing in the formal setting of clipped hedges and mellow stonework, which are at their best in June and July. In January great drifts of snowdrops and aconites bring early colour and a promise of spring. Particularly lovely in spring and autumn is the water garden, planted with magnificent magnolia and acers, surrounding the authentic Japanese Tea House and Nikko Bridge which makes an exciting focus in this part of the garden. National Gardens Day 1st Sunday in August. Specialist plant centre.

Times: Open all year, daily 10-5.

Fee: *£3 (ch under 14 accompanied, free). Party 20+.

🅿 ♿ shop garden centre 🍽

🏛 SALISBURY

MOMPESSON HOUSE
Chorister's Green, Cathedral Close SP1 2EL
☎ 01722 335659

With its high wrought-iron railings and perfect proportions this Queen Anne house makes an impressive addition to the elegant Cathedral Close in Salisbury. Inside there are stucco ceilings, a carved oak staircase and period furniture plus an important collection of 18th-century glasses, china and some outstanding paintings.
Times: Open Apr-1 Nov, daily (ex Thu & Fri) 12-5.30. Last admission 5pm.
P 🖭 & shop ✈ ❦ *Details not confirmed for 2000*

OLD SARUM
(2m N on A345)
☎ 01722 335398

Impressive remains of an Iron-Age camp surround what was the original site of Salisbury cathedral and its thriving community. It was abandoned in medieval times, and the bishop and his flock moved to found a new cathedral where the present city stands. However, for many hundreds of years after its desertion, until the Reform Bill of 1832, ten voters continued to return two MPs to parliament at Westminster.
Times: Open all year, Apr-Oct, daily 10-6 (or dusk if earlier); Nov-Mar, daily 10-4. Closed 24-26 Dec & 1 Jan.
Fee: £2 (ch £1).
P & ✿

ROYAL GLOUCESTERSHIRE, BERKSHIRE & WILTSHIRE REGIMENT MUSEUM
The Wardrobe, 58 The Close SP1 2EX
☎ 01722 414536

An interesting and historic building in Cathedral Close displaying mementoes, relics, uniforms and weapons. Riverside Garden also now open to the public.
Times: Open Apr-Oct, daily 10-4.30; Feb, Mar & Nov, Mon-Fri 10-4.30. (Closed Dec & Jan).
P 🖭 & shop ✈ *Details not confirmed for 2000*

SALISBURY CATHEDRAL
33 The Close SP1 2EJ
☎ 01722 555120, 555124 & 555121
🖹 01722 555116

Built in one phase between 1220 and 1258, the Cathedral is probably Britain's finest piece of medieval architecture. The spire is 123 metres tall, making it the highest in England. The Chapter House houses a frieze of Genesis and the finest surviving Magna Carta. Around 750 years ago the choir began performing at daily services and continue to do so to this day, accompanied by Europe's finest romantic church organ. The surrounding Cathedral Close contains two museums and two small stately homes.

© Steve Day, Photographer

Times: Open all year, 5 Sep-25 Apr 7-6.15, 26 Apr-4 Sep 7-8.15.
Fee: *£3 (ch £1, pen & students £2). Family £6.
P (charged) 🖭 & (loop system, interpretive model for blind, wheelchairs) toilets for disabled shop

SALISBURY & SOUTH WILTSHIRE MUSEUM
The King's House, 65 The Close SP1 2EN (in Cathedral Close)
☎ 01722 332151 🖹 01722 325611

One of the most outstanding of the beautiful buildings in Cathedral Close houses this local museum. Galleries include Stonehenge, History of Salisbury, the Pitt Rivers collection, ceramics and pictures and the Wedgwood room, a reconstruction of a pre-NHS surgery, and a costume, lace and embroidery gallery. Exhibitions for 2000 include 'the 20th Century Community Show', showing changes in the last hundred years through memories and souvenirs of local people, also 'Textiles 2000' a celebration of all textile arts.
Times: Open all year Mon-Sat 10-5; also Suns Jul & Aug, 2-5. (Closed Xmas).
Fee: *£3 (under 5's free, ch 75p, pen, students & UB40s £2). Party. Five-visit saver tickets available.
P ✗ & (parking by prior arrangement) toilets for disabled shop ✈ (ex guide dogs) 🥢

🏛 STONEHENGE

STONEHENGE
(2m W of Amesbury on junc A303 and A344/A360)
☎ 01980 624715

One of the most famous prehistoric monuments in Europe, the henge was started about 5,000 years ago, but redesigned several times during the following 1,500 years. The earliest part is the ditch and bank, and later 80 huge Blue Stones, each weighing about 2 tons, were somehow transported from south-west Wales. Enormous sarsens, each weighing more than 50 tons, were dragged from the Marlborough Downs, and all were then worked into the design we see today -
contd.

an outer ring of upright stones with lintels, and an inner horseshoe of five pairs of uprights, also with lintels. The axis of the horseshoe points towards the midsummer sunrise. Little is known about the Bronze Age society that organised the monument, but there was no connection with the Druids.

Times: Open all year, Apr-Sep; Oct 9.30-5; Nov-Mar 9.30-4. Closed 24-26 Dec & 1 Jan. There is an audio tour available in six languages.

Fee: £4 (ch £2).

🅿 💺 ♿ shop ✖ ♯

🏛 STOURHEAD
STOURHEAD HOUSE & GARDEN
BA12 6QH (off B3092)
☎ 01747 841152

The Palladian house was built in 1720. What makes Stourhead especially memorable is the superb gardens, laid out in 1741. They feature a grotto and a temple to Flora around two springs and a large triangular lake. There are many varieties of oak, elm, willow and exotic trees. For details of events phone 0891 335203.

Times: Open - House 28 Mar-1 Nov, Sat-Wed 12-5.30 or dusk if earlier. Last admission 5pm. Garden daily all year 9-7 or dusk if earlier (ex 23-25 Jul when garden closes at 5pm). King Alfreds Tower, 28 Mar-1 Nov, Good Fri & BH's Tue-Fri 2-5.30, wknds 11.30-5.30 or dusk if earlier.

🅿 💺 ✖ licensed ♿ toilets for disabled shop ✖ (ex in gardens Nov-Feb only) ✿ *Details not confirmed for 2000*

🏛 STOURTON
STOURTON HOUSE FLOWER GARDEN
Stourton House BA12 6QF (3m NW of Mere, on A303)
☎ 01747 840417

Set in the attractive village of Stourton, the house has more than four acres of beautifully maintained flower gardens. Many grass paths lead through varied and colourful shrubs, trees and plants; and Stourton House also specialises in unusual plants, and dried flowers, many of which are for sale. It is also well-known for its

collections of daffodils, delphiniums, and 270 different hydrangeas.

Times: Open Apr-end Nov, Wed, Thu, Sun & BH Mon 11-6 (or dusk if earlier).Also open Dec-Mar for plant/dried flower sales.

Fee: *£2.50 (ch 50p)

🅿 💺 ♿ (wheelchairs available) toilets for disabled shop (plants for sale) garden centre ✖ (ex by arrangement)

🏛 SWINDON
GREAT WESTERN RAILWAY MUSEUM
Faringdon Rd SN1 5BJ (in Swindon town centre)
☎ 01793 466555   📄 01793 484073

Swindon was once one of the busiest railway towns in Britain, and the museum has a fascinating collection of locomotives and other exhibits relating to the GWR. Plans are underway for a new, enlarged museum Steam - the Museum of the Great Western Railway on the Swindon GWR Works Site. Funding for a new museum was granted in early 1997, and the new museum will open in Spring 2000.

Times: Open all year, Mon-Sat 10-5, Sun 2-5. (Closed Good Fri, 24-26 Dec & 1 Jan).

Fee: *£2.40 (ch £1.20, under 5 free). (Charge includes admission to the Railway Village museum).

🅿 (100 yds) ♿ shop ✖

🏛 TISBURY
OLD WARDOUR CASTLE
SP3 6RP (2m SW)
☎ 01747 870487

Substantial remains of this hexagonal 14th-century castle are still standing, with walls 60ft high. It was twice besieged, and finally ruined during the Civil War.

Times: Open all year, Apr-Oct, daily 10-6 (or dusk if earlier); Nov-Mar Wed-Sun 10-4, (closed 1-2pm) . Closed 24-26 Dec & 1 Jan.

Fee: £1.90 (ch 90p).

🅿 ♿ ♯

🏛 WESTWOOD
WESTWOOD MANOR
BA15 2AF (1.5m SW of Bradford on Avon, off B3109)
☎ 01225 863374

This late 15th-century stone manor house has some particularly fine Jacobean plasterwork. The house, which is situated by the parish church, was altered in 1610 but still retains its late Gothic and Jacobean windows. Outside there is a superb modern topiary garden.

Times: Open Apr-30 Sept, Sun, Tue & Wed 2-5

🅿 ✖ ✿ *Details not confirmed for 2000*

🏛 WILTON (near Salisbury)
WILTON HOUSE
SP2 0BJ (3m W of Salisbury, on the A30)
☎ 01722 746720   746729(24 hr line)
📄 01722 744447

Built on the site of a 9th century nunnery founded by King Alfred, the Tudor origins of the house can still be seen in the tower which survived the 1647 fire and is now incorporated within the splendid 17th-century house, based on designs by Inigo Jones. Wilton House boasts a world famous art collection with over 230 paintings on show. Outside are 21 acres of landscaped parkland, rose and water gardens, woodland and riverside walks. There's a huge children's adventure playground, and a wide variety of events take place. Please telephone for details.

Times: Open 15 Apr-29 Oct daily 10.30-5.30. Last admission 5.30.
Fee: *£6.75 (ch 5-15 £4, under 5 free, students & pen £5.75). Family ticket £17.50.
🅿 ☕ ✗ licensed & toilets for disabled shop garden centre ✗ (ex guide dogs) 🥢

⛪ WOODHENGE
WOODHENGE
(1.5m N of Amesbury, off A345 just S of Durrington)

A Neolithic ceremonial monument dating from about 2300 BC, consisting of six concentric rings of timber posts, now marked by concrete piles. The long axis of the rings, which are oval, points to the rising sun on Midsummer Day.
Times: Open all reasonable times.
🅿 & ♯

Worcestershire

In Worcestershire, the fertile plains of the Vale of Evesham and the Severn Valley climb to the Malvern Hills in the west, and the Cotswolds in the south. To the north of the county lies the industrialised area of the Black Country, in sharp contrast to the south's rural idyll.

Worcester is the county town, and home to the Worcestershire County Cricket Club, which has what some regard as the most attractive grounds in the country, in a delightful setting with views of Worcester Cathedral. Worcester Racecourse is one of the oldest in the country, in Pitchcroft Park, close to the city, beside the River Severn.

Sir Edward Elgar was a Worcester man, and his statue stands in the High Street of the city, facing the cathedral. The cottage where he was born, in Lower Broadheath just west of Worcester, is now open as a museum. He has also recently been commemorated on the new £20 note.

Southeast of Worcester is the Vale of Evesham, the main fruit-growing area of the country, dotted with orchards and market gardens - a picture in the spring with the blossom in the trees. The main town in this area is Evesham, set in a loop of the River Avon.

The Malverns, Great and Little, set on the slopes of the Malvern Hills, are renowned for their refinement. Great Malvern, terraced on its hillside site, came to prominence as a genteel spa for well-to-do Victorians, rivalling the likes of Bath, Buxton and Cheltenham with its glorious surroundings.

EVENTS & FESTIVALS

May
5th-7th Spring Gardening Show, Three Counties Showground, Malvern
27th-28th Oak Apple Celebrations, Worcester

June
16th-18th Three Counties Show, Three Counties Showground, Malvern

July
tbc Worcester Carnival

September
23rd-24th The Malvern Autumn Show, Three Counties Showground, Malvern
tbc St John's Medieval Fayre, Worcester

October
tbc Worcester Male Voice Concert, Worcester Cathedral

December
tbc Victorian Christmas Fayre

Top: Worcester Guildhall

🏛 BEWDLEY
SEVERN VALLEY RAILWAY
Comberton Hill (on A448 (Comberton Hill), it is
clearly signposted from all major roads)
☎ 01299 403816 📄 01299 400839

This standard gauge steam railway has one of
the largest collections of locomotives and rolling
stock in the country. Services operate from
Kidderminster and Bewdley to Bridgnorth
through 16 miles of picturesque scenery along
the River Severn. Special steam galas and
Friends of Thomas Weekends take place along
with Saturday evening `Wine and Dine' and
`Sunday Luncheon' trains. There are footplate
courses for those wishing to experience the thrill
of driving and firing a steam locomotive.

Times: Trains operate wknds throughout year, daily early May
to end Sep, plus school holidays & half terms, Santa Specials,
phone for details.

Fee: *Subject to Review.(Train fares vary according to journey.
Main through ticket £9.20 return, Family ticket £20)

🅿 💺 ♿ (wc Kidderminster/Bridgnorth) toilets for disabled
shop 🍴

See advert under Kidderminster.

WEST MIDLAND SAFARI & LEISURE PARK
Spring Grove DY12 1LF (on A456)
☎ 01299 402114 📄 01299 404519

A drive-around wild animal safari park with over
40 species of exotic animals to see. Pets' corner,
Sealion show, Reptile House, Goat Walk and
Deer Park. Other attractions include a variety of
rides in the leisure area.

Times: Open Apr-Oct, daily from 10am including BH's.
Fee: *£5.25 (ch 4 free). Multi ride wristband £6.50. Junior
restricted £4.50 (restricted rides only). Ride tickets £1 each
from machines (various no of tickets per ride).
🅿 💺 ✕ licensed ♿ (most area accessible with
slopes/tarmac patha) shop 🍴

🏛 BROADWAY
BROADWAY TOWER COUNTRY PARK
WR12 7LB (off A44)
☎ 01386 852390 📄 01386 858829

The 65ft tower was designed by James Wyatt for
the 6th Earl of Coventry, and built in 1799. The
unique building now houses exhibitions on three
floors, depicting its colourful past and various
uses such as holiday retreat to the famous artist
and designer William Morris. The viewing
platform is equipped with a telescope, giving
wonderful views over 13 counties. Around the
Tower is a Country Park with adventure
playground, BBQs, nature walks, giant chess and
draughts, and animal enclosures. The park also
specialises in breeding Red Deer, which can be
seen in an environment very close to their
natural habitat. Ring for details of special events.

Times: Open Apr-Oct, daily 10.30-5. Nov-Mar (tower only)
weekends weather permitting 11-4 or by prior booking.
Fee: *£3.20 (ch £2.20, pen £2.50). Family ticket £9. Party.
🅿 💺 ✕ licensed ♿ toilets for disabled shop 🍴

🏛 BROMSGROVE
AVONCROFT MUSEUM OF HISTORIC BUILDINGS
Stoke Heath B60 4JR (2m S, off A38)
☎ 01527 831886 & 831363
📄 01527 876934

A visit to Avoncroft takes you through nearly 700
years of history. Here you can see 25 buildings
rescued from destruction and authentically
restored on a 15 acre rural site. The magnificent
timbered roof of Worcester Cathedral's original
Guest Hall dates from 1330. There are 15th and
16th century timber framed buildings, 18th
century agricultural buildings and a cockpit.
There are industrial buildings and a working
windmill from the 19th century, and from the
20th a fully furnished pre-fab. The National
Telephone Kiosk Collection is also housed here,
with 13 working kiosks dating from 1922. Most
buildings are accessible to the disabled and there
is a wheelchair available.

Times: Open Jul-Aug daily 10.30-5; Apr-Jun & Sep-Oct 10.30-
4.30 (wknds 5.30). Closed Mon. Mar & Nov 10.30-4. Closed
Mon & Fri. Open BHs.
Fee: *£4.50 (ch £2.25, pen £3.60). Family ticket £12.50.
🅿 💺 ♿ (ramps, wheelchair available) toilets for disabled
shop 🍴

🏛 EVESHAM
THE ALMONRY HERITAGE CENTRE
Abbey Gate WR11 4BG (on A4184, opposite
Merstow Green, main North/South route
through Evesham)
☎ 01386 446944 📄 01386 442348

The 14th-century stone and timber building was
the home of the Almoner of the Benedictine
Abbey in Evesham. It now houses exhibitions
relating to the history of Evesham Abbey, the
Battle of Evesham, and the culture and trade of
Evesham. Evesham Tourist Information Centre is
also located here.

Times: Open all year, Mon-Sat & BHs (ex Xmas) 10-5,
Sun 2-5.
Fee: *£2 (ch 16 free, pen & students £1)
🅿 (110yds) shop 🦅

⛪ HANBURY
HANBURY HALL
WR9 7EA (4.5m E of Droitwich, 1m N of B4090 and 1.5m W of B4091)
☎ 01527 821214 ▤ 01527 821251

This William and Mary style red-brick house, completed in 1701, was built by a prosperous local family. The house contains outstanding painted ceilings and a staircase by Thornhill, and the Watney collection of porcelain, while outside there are both a contemporary orangery and an ice house. The 18th century garden has also been reopened. Please telephone for details of various events.

Times: Open 14 Mar-17-Oct, Sun-Wed 2-6. Last admission 5.30 (dusk if earlier).
Fee: *House & Garden £4.40 (ch £2.50). Family ticket £11. Garden only £2.50 (ch £1)
🅿 ♨ ♿ (Braille guide) toilets for disabled shop ✖ (ex in park) 🐾 ◥

⛪ KIDDERMINSTER
WORCESTERSHIRE COUNTY MUSEUM
Hartlebury Castle, Hartlebury DY11 7XZ (4m S of Kidderminster clearly signed from A449)
☎ 01299 250416 ▤ 01299 251890

Housed in the north wing of Hartlebury Castle, the County Museum contains a delightful display of crafts and industries. There are unique collections of toys, costume, domestic life, room settings and horse-drawn vehicles as well as a reconstructed forge, schoolroom, wheelwright's and tailor's shop. Throughout the museum's season there is access to three splendid State Rooms - the Great Hall, Saloon and Hurd Library, please ring for details of this and other special events..

Times: Open Feb-Nov, Mon-Thu 10-5, BH's 11-5, Fri & Sun 2-5. (Closed Sat & Good Fri).
Fee: *£2.20 (ch & pen £1.10). Family ticket £6.
🅿 ♨ ♿ (car parking close to main building) toilets for disabled shop ✖ (ex guide dogs & in grounds) ◥

⛪ REDDITCH
FORGE MILL NEEDLE MUSEUM & BORDESLEY ABBEY VISITOR CENTRE
Forge Mill, Needle Mill Ln, Riverside B98 8HY (N side of Redditch, off A441)
☎ 01527 62509 ▤ 01527 584619

The museum is housed in the only remaining water-driven, needle-scouring mill, with machinery from the 18th century which is demonstrated regularly. Displays of finds from the nearby 12th-century Cistercian Abbey are shown in the Visitor Centre. Temporary exhibitions on local history and textile themes. Textile workshop programme, and events, including craft demonstrations (1st Sunday of the month Apr-Sep), and weekly concerts in June. Please telephone for details.

Times: Open Etr-Sep, Mon-Fri 11-4.30, Sat-Sun 2-5; Feb-Etr & Oct-Nov, Mon-Thu 11-4 & Sun 2-5. Parties by arrangement.
Fee: *£2.25 (ch 90p, pen £1.80). Family ticket £5. Reduced admission charge for holders of a Reddicard.
🅿 ♿ (wheelchairs with advance notice) toilets for disabled shop ✖ (ex guide dogs) ◥

⛪ SPETCHLEY
SPETCHLEY PARK GARDENS
Spetchley Park WR5 1RS (3m E of Worcester, off A422)
☎ 01905 345213 or 345224

The 110-acre deer park and the 30-acre gardens surround an early 19th-century mansion (not open), with sweeping lawns and herbaceous borders, a rose lawn and enclosed gardens with low box and yew hedges. There is a large collection of trees (including 17th-century Cedars of Lebanon), shrubs and plants, many of which are rare or unusual. A new garden within the old Kitchen Garden is now open. Specialist Plant Fair (26 Apr).

Times: Open Apr-Sep, Tue-Fri 11-5, Sun 2-5; BH Mons 11-5. Other days by appointment.
Fee: *£3 (ch £1.50). Party 25+.
🅿 ♨ ♿ ✖

WORCESTER

The ancient city of Worcester, with its beautiful cathedral, is built either side of the River Severn, mostly on the steeper eastern bank because of a problem with flooding. In the Civil War it was the first city to declare for the King and the last to surrender, and suffered considerable damage as a result. Charles II had his headquarters in the city during the Battle of Worcester in 1651, which led to his defeat.

The city is probably best known for its two famous products, Royal Worcester Porcelain and Worcester Sauce. The latter made from a recipe written by an early Governor of Bengal, himself a Worcester man.

STONE

STONE HOUSE COTTAGE GARDENS

DY10 4BG (2m SE of Kidderminster, on A448)

☎ 01562 69902   ▤ 01562 69960

A beautiful walled garden with towers provides a sheltered area of about one acre for rare shrubs, climbers and interesting herbaceous plants. Adjacent to the garden is a nursery with a large selection of unusual plants. Send an SAE for details of special events.

Times: Open Gardens & nursery Mar-18 Oct, Wed-Sat 10-5.30.
Fee: £2 (ch free).
P ♿ garden centre ✶

WICHENFORD

DOVECOTE

(5.5m NW of Worcester, off B4204)

☎ 01684 850051

This large 17th-century dovecote has nearly 600 nesting boxes and is unusual in its timber-framed, wattle and daub construction, which was rarely used for dovecotes. The gabled roof appears to have a chimney, but it is actually an entrance for the birds.

Times: Open Apr-1 Nov, daily 9-6 or sunset. (Closed Good Fri). Other times by prior appointment.
P (on street parking) ✶ ♆ *Details not confirmed for 2000*

WORCESTER

CITY MUSEUM & ART GALLERY

Foregate St WR1 1DT

☎ 01905 25371   ▤ 01905 616979

The gallery has temporary art exhibitions from both local and national sources. Museum exhibits cover geology, local and natural history, including River Severn displays and activities. Of particular interest is a complete 19th-century chemists shop. There are collections relating to the Worcestershire Regiment and the Worcestershire Yeomanry Cavalry.

Times: Open all year, Mon, Tue Wed & Fri 9.30-6, Sat 9.30-5.(Closed 25-26 Dec & 1 Jan also Good Fri)
P 🖢 ♿ (lift (Taylors Lane ent) induction loop Art Gallery) toilets for disabled shop ✶ *Details not confirmed for 2000*

THE COMMANDERY

Sidbury WR1 2HU (M5 junc 7, A44, signposted)

☎ 01905 361821   ▤ 01905 361822

This fine 15th-century, timber-framed building was the headquarters of Charles II's army during the Battle of Worcester in 1651. It has an impressive Great Hall with some good 15th-century stained glass, and the building is now England's only Civil War centre. Special events throughout the year, many based on the Civil War and Tudor periods. Living history a speciality. Please ring for details.

Times: Open all year, Mon-Sat 10-5, Sun 1.30-5. (Closed 25-26 Dec & 1 Jan)
Fee: *£3.50 (concessions £2.35). Family ticket £9.30.
P (100yds) 🖢 shop ✶ (ex guide dogs) 🍴

ELGAR'S BIRTHPLACE MUSEUM

Crown East Ln, Lower Broadheath WR2 6RH (3m W, off A44 to Leominster).
☎ 01905 333224 🗎 01905 333224

The cottage where Sir Edward Elgar, the composer, was born in 1857 is now a museum. Housed here is a unique collection of photographs, manuscripts and personal memorabilia recording his life and achievements.
Times: Open daily ex Wed, May-Sep 10.30-6. Oct-15 Jan & 16 Feb-Apr 1.30-4.30.
Fee: *£3 (ch 50p, students £1 & pen £2). Party.
🅿 🕭 shop 🐾 (ex guide dogs & in gardens) 🍴

HAWFORD DOVECOTE

(3m N on A449)
☎ 01684 850051

An unusual square, half-timbered 16th-century dovecote. Access on foot only via the entrance drive to the adjoining house.
Times: Open Apr-1 Nov, daily 9-6 or sunset. (Closed Good Fri). Other times by prior appointment only.
🅿 (on street parking) 🐾 🌿 *Details not confirmed for 2000*

MUSEUM OF LOCAL LIFE

Friar St WR1 2NA
☎ 01905 722349

This interesting 500-year-old timber-framed house has a squint and an ornate plaster ceiling. It is now a museum of local life and displays show life here over the last 200 years. A variety of exhibitions and events are held throughout the year. Ring for details.
Times: Open all year, Mon-Wed & Fri-Sat 10.30-5. Also BH's. (Closed 25-26 Dec & 1 Jan).
Fee: Free.
🅿 (200yds) 🕭 toilets for disabled shop 🐾

MUSEUM OF WORCESTER PORCELAIN

Severn St WR1 2NE (M5, J7, next to Worcester Cathedral)
☎ 01905 23221 🗎 01905 617807

Royal Worcester is Britain's oldest continuous producer of porcelain. The extended and refurbished museum takes you on a design journey through time, with room settings, dining scenes and shop fronts in the Georgian, Victorian and twentieth century galleries showing how fine porcelain was used and displayed.

Times: Open Mon-Sat 9-5. Sun 11-5. Closed Etr Sun.
🅿 (charged) 🍴 🕭 (ex factory) toilets for disabled shop 🐾 *Details not confirmed for 2000* 🍴

WORCESTER CATHEDRAL

WR1 2LH
☎ 01905 28854 & 21004
🗎 01905 611139

Worcester Cathedral with its 200 foot tower stands majestically beside the River Severn. The Crypt, built by St Wulstan in 1084, is a classic example of Norman architecture. The 12th century Chapter House and Cloisters are a reminder of the cathedral's monastic past. King John (who signed the Magna Carta) and Prince Arthur (elder brother of Henry VIII) are buried near the High Altar. There are exhibitions and guided tours. The cathedral choir sings during the school term at 5.30 evensong (not Thurs) and 11.00am and 4.00pm Sundays.
Times: Open all year, daily 7.30-6.
🅿 (500yds) 🍴 🕭 (limited access due to nature of building) toilets for disabled shop 🐾 (ex guide dogs) *Details not confirmed for 2000*

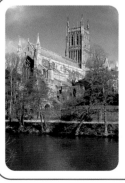

East Riding of Yorkshire

From the imposing chalk cliffs at Flamborough, to the rolling green pastures of the Yorkshire Wolds, and the flourishing port of Hull, the East Riding of Yorkshire boasts some of the finest unspoilt countryside in England, and some wonderful places to visit.

Beverley Minster is big enough to be a cathedral. Among its treasures are a 1000-year old sanctuary chair and some wonderfully intricate wooden carvings. The magnificent Percy Tomb is a fine example of 14th-century stonemasonry. Beverley is also home to the Museum of Army Transport.

Driffield is known as the 'Capital of the Wolds', and is home to a livestock auction that attracts farmers from all around. Close by is Sledmere House, an impressive manor house set among parkland designed by Capability Brown.

Coastal areas of the East Riding can be a little daunting. Flamborough Head is a plateau of rolling turf 150ft high and surrounded on three sides by the sea. The Heritage Coast Project puts on a wide range of events which includes lectures, guided walks and nature expeditions. The lighthouse has defied the elements since 1806.

Further down the coast, Spurn Head is an unusual sand and shingle peninsula curving across the mouth of the Humber, formed of deposits washed from the crumbling cliffs of Holderness a few miles to the north. The earliest record of Spurn is from 670 AD, when a monastery was established there. Since then the spit has been broken down and rebuilt by the sea three times.

EVENTS & FESTIVALS

January
1st Millennium Humber Bridge 10K Fun Run, Hessle

April
24th (provisional) Medieval Jousting, Seweby Hall, Bridlington
30th RSPCA Dog Show, Driffield Showground
30th-1st May East Riding Garden & Kite Festival, Beverley

May
1st-6th May Bridlington Open Golf Festival
20th-21st East Riding of Yorkshire Classic Cycle Race, Beverley
tbc Beverley & East Riding Early Music Festival

June
16th-18th Beverley & East Riding Folk Festival
26th-1st July Bridlington Choral Festival

July
6th-8th Hornsea Music Festival
19th Driffield Agricultural Show

August
2nd-6th (provisional) Hull Jazz Festival
12th-13th Driffield Steam & Vintage Rally
13th Bridlington Harbour Gala 2000

Top: Groynes at Spurn Head

BRIDLINGTON

One of Yorkshire's most popular family seaside resorts, Bridlington has been boosted by a recent £20 million investment. As well as award-winning promenades and gardens, the town now boasts a superb shopping centre and an 18-hole golf course. All the traditional attractions, including fun fairs and amusement arcades, can now be visited using a new seafront road train.

A mile inland, set among the suburbs of the town, stands the priory church of St Mary, the focus of the old town centre. The church dates from the 13th century and contains some charming carvings of mice running up the woodwork.

‌ BEMPTON
RSPB NATURE RESERVE

YO15 1JF (take cliff road from B1229, Bempton Village)
☎ 01262 851179

Part of the spectacular chalk cliffs that stretch from Flamborough Head to Speeton, the reserve is approached up the cliff road from Bempton village. This is one of the sites in England to see thousands of nesting seabirds including gannets and puffins at close quarters. Viewpoints overlook the cliffs which are best visited from April to July. Over two miles of chalk cliffs rising to 400ft with numerus cracks and ledges provide nesting sites for enormous numbers of seabirds including guillemots, razorbills, kittiwakes, fulmars, herring gulls and several pairs of shag. This is the only gannetry on the mainland of England and is growing annually. Many migrants pass off-shore including terns, skuas and shearwaters. Wheatears, ring ouzels, merlins and bluethroats frequent the clifftop on migration. Grey seal and porpoise are sometimes seen offshore. Please phone for details of events.

Times: Open for visitor centre daily, Apr-Sep 10-5.
P (charged) ⬛ & toilets for disabled shop ✖ *Details not confirmed for 2000* ⬛

‌ BRIDLINGTON
SEWERBY HALL & GARDENS

YO15 1EA
☎ 01262 673769 (Park) & 677874 (Hall)
🖹 01262 400189

Sewerby Hall and Gardens, set in 50 acres of parkland overlooking Bridlington Bay, dates back to 1715. The Georgian House, with its 19th century Orangery, contains art galleries, archaeological displays and an Amy Johnson Room with a collection of her trophies and mementoes. The grounds include magnificent walled Old English and Rose gardens and host many events throughout the year including medieval jousting, horse pageant, classic cars etc. Activities for all the family include a Children's Zoo and play areas, golf, putting, bowls, plus woodland and clifftop walks. Please ring for further details of special events.

Times: Gardens & zoo open daily all year. Hall open Mar-Apr & Oct-Dec, Sat-Tue 11-4; May-Sep, daily 10-6.
P ⬛ ✖ & toilets for disabled shop *Details not confirmed for 2000*

‌ BURTON AGNES
BURTON AGNES HALL

Estate Office YO25 0ND (on A166)
☎ 01262 490324 🖹 01262 490513

Built in 1598, this is a magnificent Elizabethan house, with furniture, pictures and china amassed by the family owners over four centuries. There is a walled garden with maze, potager, herbaceous borders, clematis, campanula and geranium collections, and jungle garden, as well as woodland walks.

Times: Open Apr-Oct, daily 11-5.
Fee: *Hall & grounds £4.50 (ch £2.25, pen £4). Grounds only £2.25 (ch £1, pen £2). Party 30+.
P ☕ ♿ (scented garden for the blind) toilets for disabled shop garden centre

NORMAN MANOR HOUSE

This rare survivor from Norman times was replaced by Burton Agnes Hall. Some interesting Norman architectural features can still be seen, but the building was encased in brick at a later period.
Times: Open all year.
⌗

HULL
MAISTER HOUSE
160 High St HU1 1NQ
☎ 01482 324114

The house is a mid-18th-century rebuilding, notable for its splendid stone and wrought-iron staircase, ornate stucco work and finely carved doors. Only the staircase and entrance hall are open.
Times: Open all year, Mon-Fri 10-4 (Closed BH).
P ✈ ♿ ♨ *Details not confirmed for 2000*

'STREETLIFE' - HULL MUSEUM OF TRANSPORT
High St (A63 from M62, follow signs for Old Town)
☎ 01482 613902   ▤ 01482 613710

This purpose built museum uses a 'hands-on' approach to trace 200 years of transport history. With a vehicle collection of national importance, state of the art animatronic displays and stunningly authentic scenarios, you are swept back in time to see Hull's Old Town brought vividly to life. The unique mail coach ride uses the very latest in computer technology to recreate a Victorian journey by four in hand, and

other displays recreate the golden age of steam, public transport and the bicycle.
Times: Open all year, Mon-Sat 10-5, Sun 1.30-4.30. (Closed 24-25 Dec & Good Fri).
Fee: Free.
P (500m) ☕ ♿ toilets for disabled shop ✈ (ex guide dogs)

WILBERFORCE HOUSE
23-25 High St HU1 1NE (A63 from M62, follow signs for Old Town)
☎ 01482 613902   ▤ 01482 613710

The early 17th-century Merchants house was the birthplace of William Wilberforce, who went on to become a leading campaigner against slavery. There are Jacobean and Georgian rooms and displays on Wilberforce, the anti-slavery campaign, silver, costume, historic rooms settings, decorative art and dolls. The house also has secluded gardens. There is a special exhibition The A-Z of Costume, with displays of Hull Museum's extensive costume collection. Christmas event - Victorian Christmas. Telephone for details.
Times: Open all year, Mon-Sat 10-5 & Sun 1.30-4.30. (Closed 25-26 Dec, 1 Jan & Good Fri).
Fee: Free.
P (500m) ♿ (large print) shop ✈ (ex guide dogs)

POCKLINGTON
BURNBY HALL GARDEN & STEWART COLLECTION
The Balk YO42 2QF (off A1079 at turning for Pocklington off B1247)
☎ 01759 302068

The two lakes in this garden have an outstanding collection of 80 varieties of hardy water lilies, designated a National Collection. The lakes stand within seven acres of beautiful gardens including a lovely walled garden, heather beds, a rock garden and a spring and summer bedding area. The museum contains sporting trophies and ethnic material gathered on world-wide travels.
Times: Open 2 Apr-3 Oct, daily 10am-6pm. (last admission 5pm)
Fee: *£2.40 (ch 5-15 £1, pen £1.90). Party 20+.
P ☕ ♿ (free wheelchair hire) toilets for disabled shop ✈ (ex guide dogs)

SPROATLEY
BURTON CONSTABLE HALL
HU11 4LN (1.5m N of Sproatley)
☎ 01964 562400   ▤ 01964 563229

This superb Elizabethan house was built in 1570, but much of the interior was remodelled in the 18th century. There are magnificent reception rooms and a Tudor long gallery with a pendant roof: the contents range from pictures and furniture (much of it by Thomas Chippendale) to a unique collection of 18th-century scientific instruments. Outside are 200 acres of parkland landscaped by 'Capability' Brown, with oaks and chestnuts, and a lake with an island. Camping

contd.

and caravanning sites are available in the park and there is also seasonal fishing.

Times: Open, Hall & grounds Etr Sun-31 Oct, Sat-Thu. Grounds noon-5, Hall 1-5. Last admission 4.15pm.

Fee: *House £4 (ch £1.50, pen £3.70). Family £9.

🅿 💺 ♿ toilets for disabled shop ✈

⛪ THORNTON
THORNTON ABBEY
☎ 01469 40357

A magnificent 14th-century gatehouse and the ruins of the church and other buildings survive from the 12th-century Augustinian abbey. The approach is across a long bridge, spanning a dry moat.

Times: Open all year, Apr-Sep, daily 10-6; Oct-Mar 10-4 or dusk if earlier.

🅿 ♿ ✈ (in certain areas) ⌗

North Yorkshire

England's largest county, North Yorkshire has a stunning natural landscape, encompassing part of the Pennines, the rolling farmlands of the Vale of York, the Cleveland Hills and the North York Moors, plus the Yorkshire Dales National Park, which includes Swaledale and Wensleydale.

The coastline offers its own treasures, from the fishing villages of Staithes and Robin Hood's Bay to Scarborough, one time Regency spa and Victorian bathing resort.

York, traditionally the capital of the North of England, was second only to London prior to the Industrial Revolution. It is a city of immense historical significance: capital of the British province under the Romans in AD 71 and a Viking settlement in the 10th century. In the Middle Ages its prosperity depended on the wool trade. The city's earliest surviving building is the Roman Multangular Tower, and the city walls, dating from the 14th century, are among the finest in Europe, including four gates or 'bars'. However, the gothic Minster is York's crowning glory, built between 1220 and 1470.

Northallerton, rather than York, is the administrative centre of the county. Harrogate, another celebrated North Yorkshire town, is a traditional spa resort renowned for its gentility and excellent tea rooms. Its handsome stone buildings and lovely gardens have earned it the title of Floral Resort of England. To the south of the town, an area of some 200 acres of common land known as The Stray is popular for walking and picnicking.

The Georgian Theatre
BUILT BY
ACTOR-MANAGER
Samuel Butler
1788

EVENTS & FESTIVALS

February
19th-21st Jorvik Viking Festival, York

March
March-December Science City York Festival, York

April
27th-30th Harrogate Spring Flower Show

June
tbc Waterfront Festival, York
17th-25th Millennium Cycling Festival, York
22nd-22nd July Mystery Plays, York Minster

July
7th-16th York Early Music Festival
11th-13th Great Yorkshire Show, Harrogate
15th-21st The Christian Millennia in Northern Europe, York

August
York City Symphony

September
tbc, Lord Mayor's Procession
23rd-1st October York Festival of Food & Drink

November
30th-3rd December St Nicholas Christmas Festival, York

Top: Askrigg

ALDBOROUGH
ROMAN TOWN
(0.75m SE of Boroughbridge, on minor road off
B6265 within 1m of junction of A1 & A6055)
☎ 01423 322768

The pretty present-day village occupies the site of
the northernmost civilian Roman town in Britain.
Remains include two mosaic pavements and
excavated objects in the small museum.
Times: Open Apr-Oct, daily 10-6 (closed 1-2pm).
Fee: £1.70 (ch 90p).
✱ ♯

AYSGARTH
NATIONAL PARK CENTRE
DL8 3TH
☎ 01969 663424

A visitor centre for the Yorkshire Dales National
Park, with maps, guides, walks and local
information. Displays explain the history and
natural history of the area.
Times: Open Apr-Oct, daily 10-5. Nov-Mar limited wknd
opening.
P (charged) ▣ & shop ✱ *Details not confirmed for 2000*
♥

YORKSHIRE CARRIAGE MUSEUM
Yore Mill DL8 3SR (1.75m E on unclass rd N of
A684.Turn rt at Palmer Flatt Hotel, museum
300yds)
☎ 01969 663399

A Grade II listed building at Aysgarth Falls which
houses a varied collection of Victorian horse
drawn vehicles including the 'Woman of
Substance' carriage, a mail coach, a marston
hearse, a 'haunted' carriage, and a fire engine,
among others.
Times: Open Apr-Oct, daily 9.30-7.30, other times 9.30-dusk.
Closed 24 Dec-12 Jan.
Fee: *£2 (ch 75p). Family ticket £5.
P (150 yds) ▣ shop

BEDALE
BEDALE HALL
DL8 1AA (On A684, 1.5m W of A1 at Leeming
Bar)
☎ 01677 424604   ▤ 01677 427146

Housed in a building of 17th-century origin, with
Palladian and Georgian extensions, the centre of
this fascinating museum is the Bedale fire engine
dated 1742. Old documents, photographs,
clothing, toys, craft tools and household utensils
give an absorbing picture of the life of ordinary
people.
Times: Open Etr-Sep, Mon, Tue & Wed-Fri 2-4, Sat 10-2.
Other times by prior arrangement.
Fee: *Donation box available.
P & toilets for disabled shop ✱

BENINGBROUGH
BENINGBROUGH HALL
YO6 1DD (off A19, 8m NW of York. Entrance at
Newton Lodge)
☎ 01904 470666   ▤ 01904 470002

Beningbrough was built around 1716. It houses
100 pictures from the National Portrait Gallery in
London. Ornately carved wood panelling is a
feature of several of the rooms. The other side of
country house life can be seen in the restored
Victorian laundry. The gardens include formal
areas, a conservatory and a wilderness play area.
Times: Open 4 Apr-1 Nov, Sat-Wed & Good Fri. Also Fris
during Jul & Aug. House 11am-5pm. Last admission 4.30pm.
Grounds 11am-5.30pm. Last admission 5pm.
P ✕ licensed & (access to Victorian laundry, shop &
restaurant) toilets for disabled shop ✱ ♥ *Details not
confirmed for 2000*

BRIMHAM
BRIMHAM ROCKS
Brimham House, Summerbridge HG3 4DW (off
B6265)
☎ 01423 780688   ▤ 01423 781020

A Victorian guidebook describes the rocks as `a
place wrecked with grim and hideous forms
defying all description and definition'. The rocks
have remained a great attraction, and stand on
National Trust open moorland at a height of
950ft. An old shooting lodge in the area is now
an information point and shop.
Times: Info centre 28 Mar-1 Nov. June-Sept 11am-5pm daily,
Bank Hols and local school hols. Mar-May & Oct-Dec:
weekends, BHs and local school hols 11am-5pm-weather
permitting.
P & (specially adapted path) toilets for disabled shop ♥
Details not confirmed for 2000

CLAPHAM
YORKSHIRE DALES NATIONAL PARK CENTRE
LA2 8ED
☎ 015242 51419

A comprehensive information centre with
displays on the local countryside and limestone
scenery. A wide range of maps, guides,
information leaflets, gifts and souvenirs are
stocked and knowledgeable staff are on duty to
answer questions.
Times: Open Apr-Oct, daily 10-5.Limited opening Nov-Mar.
P (charged) (Radar key scheme) shop *Details not confirmed
for 2000* ♥

COXWOLD
BYLAND ABBEY
YO6 4BD (2m S of A170 between Thirsk &
Helmsley, near Coxwold village)
☎ 01347 868614

The abbey was built for the Cistercians in the
12th and 13th centuries and enough remains of
the buildings to show how beautiful it must have

been. There are well preserved floor tiles, carved stones and other finds.

Times: Open Apr-Oct, daily 10-6 (or dusk if earlier), closed 1-2pm.

Fee: £1.60 (ch 80p).

P & toilets for disabled ‡ *Details not confirmed for 2000*

DANBY
MOORS CENTRE
Lodge Ln YO21 2NB
☎ 01287 660654 ▤ 01287 660308

The former shooting lodge provides information on the North York Moors National Park, with an exhibition, video, bookshop and information desk. There are riverside and woodland grounds, with terraced gardens, a children's play area and a brass-rubbing centre. Special events are held in summer - telephone 01287 660654 to request information.

Times: Open all year, Apr-Oct, daily 10-5. Nov, Dec & Mar daily 11-4. Jan & Feb wknds only 11-4.

Fee: Free.

P ▆ & (woodland & garden trails, motorised & manual wheelchairs) toilets for disabled shop ✖ (ex in grounds) ▄

EASBY
EASBY ABBEY
(1m SE of Richmond off B6271)

Set beside the River Swale, the Premonstratensian Abbey was founded in 1155 and dedicated to St Agatha. Extensive remains of the monks' domestic buildings can be seen.

Times: Open Apr-Oct 10-6 (or dusk if earlier).

P ‡

FAIRBURN
RSPB NATURE RESERVE
2 Springholme, Caudie Hill WF11 9JQ (W of A1, N of Ferrybridge)
☎ 01767 680551

One-third of the 618-acre RSPB reserve is open water, and over 260 species of birds have been recorded. A visitor centre provides information, and there is an elevated boardwalk, suitable for disabled visitors.

Times: Access to the reserve from the village at all times. Visitor Centre only open Sat, Sun & BHs 10-5. (Closed 25 & 26 Dec). Car park & walkway at centre open daily 9-6 or dusk.

P & (raised boardwalk for wheelchair) toilets for disabled shop *Details not confirmed for 2000*

GRASSINGTON
NATIONAL PARK CENTRE
Colvend, Hebden Rd BD23 5LB
☎ 01756 752774 ▤ 01756 752745

The centre is a useful introduction to the Yorkshire Dales National Park. It has a video and a display on 'Wharfedale - Gateway to the Park', and maps, guides and local information are available. There is also a 24-hr public access information service through computer screens and a full tourist information service.

Times: Open Apr-Oct daily, 10-5. Also limited wknds Nov-Mar.

P (charged) & (Radar key scheme) toilets for disabled shop ✖ *Details not confirmed for 2000* ▄

GUISBOROUGH
GISBOROUGH PRIORY
(next to parish church)
☎ 01287 633801

The remains of the east end of the 14th-century church make a dramatic sight here. The priory was founded in the 12th century for Augustinian canons.

Times: Open all year Apr-Oct, daily 9-5; Oct-Mar 9-5. Closed 24 Dec-1 Jan.

& ✖ ‡

HARROGATE
HARLOW CARR BOTANICAL GARDENS
Crag Ln, Otley Rd HG3 1QB (off B6162, 1.5 miles from Harrogate centre)
☎ 01423 565418 ▤ 01423 530663

The gardens were begun in 1950 on a rough site of pasture and woodland. Today there are 68 impressive acres of ornamental and woodland gardens, including the northern trial grounds. Courses, demonstrations and practical workshops are held in the Study Centre. Prospectus and full programme of events available on application.

Times: Open all year, Mar-Oct, daily 9.30-6. Nov-Feb, daily 9.30-5 or dusk if earlier.

Fee: *£3.60 (ch 16 free, pen £2.70). Party 20+.

P ▆ ✖ licensed & (electric wheelchairs available) toilets for disabled shop garden centre ✖ (ex guide dogs) ▄

THE ROYAL PUMP ROOM MUSEUM
Royal Pde HG1 2RY
☎ 01423 503340 ▤ 01423 840026

The octagonal Pump Room building houses changing exhibitions from the museum's own collections. This part of the building still houses the original sulphur wells, now below modern street level. The wells are enclosed by glass to contain their pungent smell, but the water can be tasted, by those brave enough, at the original spa counter.

Times: Open all year, Apr-Oct, Mon-Sat 10-5, Sun 2-5, (Nov-Mar close at 4pm). (Closed 25-26 Dec & 1 Jan).

P (restricted to 3hrs) & toilets for disabled shop ✖ *Details not confirmed for 2000*

HELMSLEY
DUNCOMBE PARK
YO62 5EB (1m from town centre, off A170)
☎ 01439 770213 & 771115
▤ 01439 771114

Duncombe Park stands at the heart of a spectacular 30-acre early 18th-century landscape garden which is set in 300 acres of dramatic parkland around the River Rye. The house, originally built in 1713, was gutted by fire in 1879 and rebuilt in 1895. Its principal rooms are a fine example of the type of grand interior popular at the turn of the century. Home of the Duncombes for 300 years, for much of this century the house was a girls' school. In 1985 the present Lord and Lady Feversham decided to make it a family

contd.

home again and after major restoration, opened the house to the public in 1990. Part of the garden and parkland were designated a 250-acre National Nature Reserve in 1994. Special events include a Country Fair (May), an Antiques Fair (June), Steam Fair (July), Antiques Fair (November). Please telephone for details.

Times: Open: Apr & Oct Sun-Thu; May-Sep Sun-Fri 10.30-6 (tours every hour).

Fee: *House & Gardens £5.75 (ch 10-16, £2.75, pen £4.75) Gardens & Parkland £3.75 (ch £1.75, pen £3.75) Parkland only £2 (ch £1, pen £2).

🅿 🖭 ✕ licensed ♿ toilets for disabled shop ✖ (ex park) ➾

HELMSLEY CASTLE
☎ 01439 770442

The ruined castle dates from the 12th century and later, and stands within enormous earthworks. It was besieged in the Civil War, and destroyed in 1644.

Times: Open all year, Apr-Oct, daily 10-6 (or dusk if earlier); Nov-mid Mar, Wed-Sun 10-4 (or dusk if earlier). Closed 1-2pm all year.

Fee: £2.30 (ch £1.20).

🅿 (charged) ✖ (in certain areas) ⌗

KIRBY MISPERTON
FLAMINGO LAND THEME PARK & ZOO
The Rectory YO17 6UX (off the A169 Malton to Pickering rd, off A64)
☎ 01653 668287   🖹 01653 668280

Set in 375 acres of lovely North Yorkshire countryside, there are rides and attractions for everyone.

Times: Open 28 Mar-26 Sep, as well as weekends and full half term week in Oct.

Fee: *£10.50 (ch under 4 free, pens £5.30). Family ticket £36.

🅿 🖭 ✕ ♿ (parking) toilets for disabled shop ➾

KIRKHAM
KIRKHAM PRIORY
(5m SW of Malton on minor road off A64)
☎ 01653 618768

The ruins of this former house of Augustinian canons stand on an entrancing site on the banks of the River Derwent. The remains of the finely sculpted 13th-century gatehouse and lavatorium,

where the monks washed in leaded troughs, are memorable.

Times: Open Apr-Sep, daily noon-5.

🅿 ♿ ✖ ⌗ *Details not confirmed for 2000*

KNARESBOROUGH
KNARESBOROUGH CASTLE
HG5 8AE
☎ 01423 503340   🖹 01423 840026

High above the town of Knaresborough, the ruins of this 14th-century castle look down over the gorge of the River Nidd. This imposing fortress was once the hiding place of Thomas Becket's murderers and it also served as a prison for Richard II. Remains include the keep, the sally-port, parts of the curtain wall and the Old Court of Knaresborough, part of which also dates from the 14th century. It now houses a local history museum, and entrance is part of the combined ticket price. A new gallery is devoted to the Civil War in Knaresborough.

Times: Open Etr, May-Sep, daily 10.30-5. Guided tours regulary available.

🅿 (100 metres) ♿ toilets for disabled shop ✖ (ex grounds) *Details not confirmed for 2000*

MALHAM
YORKSHIRE DALES NATIONAL PARK CENTRE
BD23 4DA
☎ 01729 830363

The National Park centre has maps, guides and local information together with displays on the remarkable natural history of the area, local community and work of conservation bodies. Audio-visuals are provided for groups and a 24-hour teletext information service is available..

Times: Open Apr-Oct, daily 10-5. Limited winter opening.

🅿 (charged) ♿ (Radar key scheme for toilet) toilets for disabled shop ✖ *Details not confirmed for 2000* ➾

MALTON
CASTLE HOWARD
YO60 7DA (15m NE of York, off A64)
☎ 01653 648333   648444
🖹 01653 648462

In its dramatic setting of lakes, fountains and extensive gardens, this 18th-century palace was designed by Sir John Vanbrugh. Castle Howard was begun in 1699 for the 3rd Earl of Carlisle, Charles Howard, whose descendants still call the place 'home'. The interior has a 192ft Long Gallery, as well as a Chapel with magnificent stained glass windows by the 19th-century artist, Edward Burne-Jones. The Castle contains a number of important paintings, including a portrait of Henry VIII by Holbein and works by Rubens, Reynolds and Gainsborough. The grounds include the domed Temple of the Four Winds by Vanbrugh, and the richly designed family Mausoleum by Hawksmoor. The Rose

Garden contains both old-fashioned and modern varieties of roses.

© June Buck, Photographer

Times: Open 1-11 Mar Grounds only. 12 Mar-31 Oct, Grounds & Plant Centre 10, House 11. Last admissions 4.30pm.
Fee: *£7 (ch £4.50, pen £6.50). Party 12+.
P ⏿ ✕ licensed ⅋ (chairlift, free adapted transport to house) toilets for disabled shop garden centre ✖ (ex guide dogs in house) 🔔

EDEN CAMP MODERN HISTORY THEME MUSEUM
Eden Camp YO17 6RT (junc of A64 & A169)
☎ 01653 697777   📄 01653 698243

The story of the peoples' war - the drama, the hardships, the humour - unfolds in this museum devoted to civilian life in World War II. The displays, covering the blackout, rationing, the Blitz, the Homeguard and others, are housed in a former prisoner-of-war camp built in 1942 for German and Italian soldiers. Voted Yorkshire and Humberside's Visitor Attraction of the Year 1998. Hut 29 depicts the military and political events of 1944, with a special section covering D-Day.
Times: Open 2nd Mon in Jan-13 Feb wkdays only; 14 Feb-23 Dec, daily 10-5. Last admission 4pm. Allow at least 3-4hrs for a visit.
Fee: *£3.50 (ch & pen £2.50) Party 10+.
P ⏿ ⅋ (taped tours, Braille guides) toilets for disabled shop

MALTON MUSEUM
Old Town Hall, Market Place YO17 7LP (leave A64, follow signs for Malton town centre)
☎ 01653 695136

The extensive Roman settlements in the area are represented and illustrated in this museum, including collections from the Roman fort of Derventio. There are also displays of local prehistoric and medieval finds plus changing exhibitions of local interest.
Times: Open Etr Sat-Oct, Mon-Sat 10-4.
Fee: *£1.50 (ch, pen & students £1) Family ticket(2+2) £4.
P (adjacent) (pay & display-2hrs) ⅋ shop ✖ (ex guide dogs)

🏛 MIDDLEHAM
MIDDLEHAM CASTLE
(2m S of Leyburn on A6108)
☎ 01969 623899

The historic town of Middleham is dominated by the 12th-century keep which saw its great days during the Wars of the Roses. The seat of the Neville family, Earls of Warwick, it was the home for a time of the young King Richard III, then Duke of Gloucester.
Times: Open all year, Apr-Oct, daily 10-6 (or dusk if earlier); Nov-Mar, Wed-Sun 10-4 (or dusk if earlier). Closed 1-2pm during winter season.
Fee: £2.30 (ch £1.20).
P ⅋ (ex tower) shop ⌗

🏛 MIDDLESBROUGH
CAPTAIN COOK BIRTHPLACE MUSEUM
Stewart Park, Marton TS7 6AS (3m S on A172 at Stewart Park, Marton)
☎ 01642 311211   📄 01642 813781

Opened to mark the 250th anniversary of the birth of the voyager in 1728, this museum illustrates the early life of James Cook and his discoveries with temporary exhibitions. Located in spacious and rolling parkland, the site also offers outside attractions for the visitor. A special resource centre is equipped with computers and educational aids. There are Captain Cook Birthday Celebrations in October. Recently refurbished the museum boasts computer interactives and hand-on displays. Educational facilities and workshops.
Times: Open all year: Tues-Sun, Summer hrs 10am-5.30pm. Winter hrs 9am-4pm. Last entry 45 mins before closure. Closed Mon except BH, 25-26 Dec & 1 Jan.
Fee: *£2.40 (ch & pen £1.20). Family ticket £6.
P ⏿ ⅋ (lift to all floors, car parking) toilets for disabled shop ✖ (ex guide dogs)

🏛 NEWBY HALL & GARDENS
NEWBY HALL & GARDENS
HG4 5AE (4m SE of Ripon & 2m W of A1M, off B6265, between Boroughbridge and Ripon)
☎ 01423 322583   📄 01423 324452

This late 17th-century house had its interior and additions designed by Robert Adam, and contains an important collection of classical sculpture and Gobelin tapestries. Twenty-five acres of award-winning gardens include a miniature railway, an adventure garden for children, and a woodland discovery walk. Special events take place throughout the year, including: Spring Plant Fair (May); Rainbow Craft Fair (June & Sept); Yorkshire Craft Pavilion (July), Historic Vehicle Rally (July), Autumn Plant Fair (Sept).
Times: Open Apr-Sep, Tue-Sun & BH's; Gardens 11-5.30; House 12-5. Last admission 5pm (gardens), 4.30pm (house).
Fee: *House & Garden £6.30, (ch & disabled £3.80, pen £5.20). Gardens only £4.50 (ch & disabled £3, pen £3.90). Party rates and family tickets on application. Under 4's go free.
P ✕ licensed ⅋ (wheelchairs available, maps of wheelchair routes) toilets for disabled shop garden centre ✖ (ex guide dogs & some puppies) 🔔
See advert under Ripon.

🏛 NUNNINGTON
NUNNINGTON HALL
YO6 5UY (4.5m SE of Helmsley)
☎ 01439 748283   🖹 01439 748284

This large 16th-to 17th-century house has panelled rooms and a magnificent staircase. The Carlisle collection of miniature rooms is on display.

Times: Open Apr-1 Nov Wed-Sun except BH Mon in Aug and Tuesdays in Jun, Jul & Aug. 1.30-6pm. (1.30-5.30 Apr & Oct) Also open Good Fri. Last admission 1hr before closing time.

🅿 💷 ﺝ toilets for disabled shop 🎇 💥 *Details not confirmed for 2000*

🏛 ORMESBY
ORMESBY HALL
TS7 9AS (3m SE of Middlesborough)
☎ 01642 324188   🖹 01642 300937

An 18th-century mansion, Ormesby Hall has stables attributed to John Carr of York. Plasterwork, furniture and 18th-century pictures are on view.

Times: Open 1 Apr-1 Nov; Tues (guided tours, lat tour 3.30pm), Wed, Thurs, Sun 2-5.30pm. BH Mons and Good Friday.

🅿 💷 ﺝ toilets for disabled shop 🎇 💥 *Details not confirmed for 2000*

🏛 OSMOTHERLEY
MOUNT GRACE PRIORY
DL6 3JG (1m NW)
☎ 01609 883494

A ruined 14th-century Carthusian priory, next to a 17th-century house. One of the monks cells has been fully restored to show how what monastic life was like here, and there are also interesting remains of the cloister, church and outer court.

Times: Open all year, Apr-Oct, daily 10-6 (or dusk if earlier in Oct). Nov-Mar, Wed-Sun 10-4. Closed 1-2pm during winter season.

Fee: £2.80 (ch £1.40).

🅿 ﺝ shop 🎇 ♯ 💥

🏛 PARCEVALL HALL GARDENS
PARCEVALL HALL GARDENS
BD23 6DE (Off B6265 between Grassington and Pateley Bridge)
☎ 01756 720311

Enjoying a hillside setting east of the main Wharfedale Valley, these beautiful gardens belong to an Elizabethan house which is used as the Bradford Diocesan Retreat House (not open to the public).

Times: Open Good Fri-31 Oct, daily 10-6. Winter visitors by appointment.

Fee: *£2 (ch 5-12 50p).

🅿 💷

🏛 PICKERING
NORTH YORKSHIRE MOORS RAILWAY
Pickering Station YO18 7AJ
☎ 01751 472508   🖹 01751 476970

Operating through the heart of the North York Moors National Park between Pickering and Grosmont, steam trains cover a distance of 18 miles. Beautiful Newtondale Halt gives walkers easy access to forest and moorland. The locomotive sheds at Grosmont are open to the public. Events throughout the year include Friends of Thomas the Tank Engine, Steam Gala, Santa Specials. Please telephone for details of these and more.

Times: Open 20 Mar-Oct, daily; Dec, Santa specials and Christmas to New Year running. Further information available from Pickering Station, North Yorkshire.

Fee: *Return: £9.20 (ch £4.60, pen 7.80). Single: £7.10 (ch £3.50, pen £5.70). Family ticket (2 Adults 3 Children £25.70, others on request). All-line ticket £9.20 (ch £4.60, pen £7.80).

🅿 (charged) 💷 ✕ licensed ﺝ (ramp for trains) toilets for disabled shop 🍴

PICKERING CASTLE
☎ 01751 474989

Standing upon its mound high above the town, the 12th-century keep and baileys are among the interesting remains of what was once a favourite royal hunting lodge. An exhibition tells the castle's history.

Times: Open all year, Apr-Oct, daily 10-6 (or dusk if earlier); Nov-Mar, Wed-Sun 10-4 (or dusk if earlier). Closed 24-26 Dec & 1 Jan.

Fee: £2.30 (ch £1.20).

🅿 ﺝ (ex motte) shop 🎇 ♯

🏛 REDCAR
RNLI ZETLAND MUSEUM
5 King St TS10 3AH (on corner of King St and The Promenade)
☎ 01642 485370 & 471813

The museum portrays the lifeboat, maritime, fishing and local history of the area, including its main exhibit 'The Zetland' - the oldest lifeboat in the world dating from 1802. There is also a replica of a fisherman's cottage c1900 and almost

2000 other exhibits. The museum is housed in an early lifeboat station, now a listed building.
Times: Open May-Sep, daily 11-4. Also Etr. Other times by appointment.
Fee: Free.
P (20m) (50p per hour) & (ground floor accessible only) shop

RICHMOND
GREEN HOWARDS MUSEUM
Trinity Church Square, Market Place DL10 4QN
☎ 01748 822133 🖹 01748 826561

This award-winning museum traces the military history of the Green Howards from the late 17th century onwards. The exhibits include uniforms, weapons, medals and a special Victoria Cross exhibition. Regimental and civic plate is displayed, and there is CD ROM and touch screen video of the First World War Western Front. Audio guide available.
Times: Open Feb, Mon-Fri 10-4.30; Mar, Mon-Fri 10-4.30; mid Apr-Oct, Mon-Sat 9.30-4.30 & Sun 2-4.30; Nov, Mon-Sat 10-4.30.
Fee: *£2 (ch 5-16 £1, pen £1.50). Family ticket £5.
P (in market place) & (stairlift for access to all floors) shop ✗

RICHMOND CASTLE
☎ 01748 822493

Built high upon sheer rocks overlooking the River Swale, the castle dates from 1071. Its splendid keep and curtain walls, with two massive towers, are among the impressive remains. Scollard's Hall, built in 1080, may well be the oldest domestic building surviving in Britain.
Times: Open all year, Apr-Oct, daily 10-6 (dusk if earlier); Nov-Mar, daily 10-4 (or dusk if earlier, closed 1-2pm). Closed 24-26 Dec & 1 Jan.
Fee: £2.30 (ch £1.20).
P (800 yds) & shop ✗ ♯ *Details not confirmed for 2000*

RIEVAULX
RIEVAULX ABBEY
YO6 5LB (2.25m W of Helmsley on minor road off B1257)
☎ 01439 798228

The site for this magnificent abbey was given to a small group of Cistercian monks in 1131; building was completed by the end of the century. In its heyday, this was a prosperous foundation, but its fortunes later declined. Surrounded by wooded hills, the site is beautiful, and the remains impressive. From Rievaulx Terrace, at the top of the hill, there is an excellent bird's eye view of the abbey ruins.
Times: Open all year, Apr-Oct, daily 10-6 (or dusk if earlier); Nov-Mar, daily 10-4 (or dusk if earlier. Closed 1-2pm). Closed 24-26 Dec & 1 Jan.
Fee: £3 (ch £1.50).
P & shop ⛝ ♯

RIEVAULX TERRACE & TEMPLES
YO6 5LJ (2m NW of Helmsley on B1257)
☎ 01439 798340

This curved terrace, half a mile long, overlooks the abbey, with views of Ryedale and the Hambleton Hills. It has two mock-Greek temples, one built for hunting parties, the other for quiet contemplation. There are also remarkable frescoes by Borgnis, and an exhibition on English landscape design.
Times: Open April-1 Nov, Apr & Oct daily 10.30-5pm. May-Sept daily 10.30-6pm. Last admission one hour before closing.
P & (runaround vehicle available) shop ✗ *Details not confirmed for 2000*

RIPLEY
RIPLEY CASTLE
HG3 3AY (off A61,Harrogate to Ripon rd)
☎ 01423 770152 🖹 01423 771745

Ripley Castle has been home to the Ingilby family since 1320, and stands at the heart of a delightful estate with deer park, lake and Victorian walled gardens. Groups and tours are invited to experience centuries of English history through the lives of the Ingilby family. The Castle has a rich history and a fine collection of Royalist armour housed in the 1555 tower. Friendly informative tours bring the passage of time to life. There are also walled gardens, tropical hot houses, woodland walks, pleasure grounds and the National Hyacinth collection in spring.
Times: Open Nov-Mar Tue, Thu, Sat & Sun 10.30-3; Apr-Jun Sep-Oct Thu-Sun 10.30-3; Jul-Aug daily 10.30-3, also BH and school holidays. Groups any day by prior arrangement.
Fee: *Castle & Gardens £5 (ch £2.50, pen £4). Gardens only £2.50 (ch £1, pen £2). Party 25+.
P ⚏ ✗ licensed & toilets for disabled shop garden centre ✗ (ex guide dogs) ⬤

RIPON
FOUNTAINS ABBEY & STUDLEY ROYAL
HG4 3DY (4m W off B6265)
☎ 01765 608888 🖹 01765 608889

Founded by Cistercian monks in 1132, Fountains Abbey is the largest monastic ruin in Britain. It was acquired by William Aislabie in 1768, and became the focal point of his landscaped gardens at Studley. Other interesting features include

contd.

Fountains Hall, built between 1598 and 1611 using the stone from the abbey ruins.
Times: Open all year. Jan-Mar,Oct-Dec 10-5;Apr-Sep 10-7;closed at dusk if earlier. Last admissions 1hr before closing time(ex visitor centre,restaurant & shop in Sep,closes at 5).Closed 24-25Dec,Fri in Nov,Dec,Jan.Estate closes early 10 & 11 July and 8 Aug.
🅿 💷 ✗ licensed ♿ toilets for disabled shop ✖ *Details not confirmed for 2000*

NORTON CONYERS HALL
HG4 5EQ (from A61, Ripon to Thirsk, left at top of hill just outside Ripon onto Wath/Norton Conyers)
☎ 01765 640333 📄 01765 69772

This late medieval house with Stuart and Georgian additions has belonged to the Grahams since 1624. The pictures and furniture reflect over 370 years of occupation by the same family. It was visited by James I, Charles I and James II. Another visitor was Charlotte Brontë: a family legend of a mad woman confined in the attics is said to have given her the idea for the mad Mrs Rochester in *Jane Eyre*, and Norton Conyers was an inspiration for Mr Rochester's Thornfield Hall. Family costumes are on display in one of the bedrooms. Please note that ladies are requested not to wear stiletto-heeled shoes. The 18th century walled garden, with its herbaceous borders, small pond and Orangery, is about 100 metres from the house.
Times: Open - House Etr Sun & Mon; BH Sun & Mon; Sun early Jun-mid Sep; daily, 12-17 Jul 2-5. Garden: Etr Sun & Mon; Sun & BH Mon mid Apr-mid Sep, also daily 12-17 July 11.30-5.
Fee: *£3 (ch 10-16, pen, concessions £2.50). Garden entry is free, with donations welcome, although a charge is made at garden charity openings. Parties by arrangement
🅿 ♿ (ramp at entrance) toilets for disabled shop ✖ (ex guide dogs or lead)

⛪ SCARBOROUGH
SCARBOROUGH CASTLE
YO1 1HY (E of town centre)
☎ 01723 372451

The ruins of Scarborough Castle stand on a narrow headland which was once the site of British and Roman encampments. The curtain wall is thought to have pre-dated the keep, the shell of which, with the later barbican and remains of medieval buildings, are all that remain.
Times: Open all year, Apr-Oct, daily 10-6 (or dusk if earlier); Nov-Mar, Wed-Sun, 10-4 (or dusk if earlier, closed 1-2pm). Closed 24-26 Dec & 1 Jan.
Fee: £2.30 (ch £1.20).
🅿 (100 yds) ♿ (ex in keep) ✿

⛪ SKIPTON
SKIPTON CASTLE
BD23 1AQ (Centre of Skipton at the head of the high street)
☎ 01756 792442 📄 01756 796100

Skipton is one of the most complete and best-preserved medieval castles in England. Some of the castle dates from the 1650s when it was rebuilt after being partially damaged following the Civil War. However, the original castle was erected in Norman times, and the gateway with its Norman Arch still exists. The castle became the home of the Clifford family in 1310 and remained so until 1676.

Entrance to the castle is through a massive round-towered gateway with the family motto 'Desormais' carved above it. Other attractions are the Clifford Tearooms and the delightful picnic area with views over Skipton and the woods, situated on the terrace behind the 13th

YORK

King George VI once said that "the history of York is the history of England", and even a cursory glance at the city's past will tend to bear this out. In 306, Constantine was made Emperor here, and the Saxons made the town capital of Deira in the 5th century. The modern name is derived from the Norse, Jorvik, which is what the Vikings called the town when they took over for about a century in 866. York is a compact walled city, and a good way to get a look at it is by taking a cruise up the River Ouse or the River Foss. Not to be missed is the splendour of York Minster, which is the fourth building on this site and took some 250 years to build. It is the largest medieval structure in the UK.

century Chapel of St John the Evangelist, which is now partly restored.
Times: Open all year, daily from 10am (Sun noon). Last admission 6pm (4pm Oct-Feb). (Closed 25 Dec).
Fee: *£4 (inc illustrated tour sheet) (ch under 18 £2, under 5 free, concessions £3.50). Family ticket £11. Party 20+.
P (200m) shop

SUTTON-ON-THE-FOREST
SUTTON PARK
YO61 1DP (on B1363).
☎ 01347 810249 & 811239
🖥 01347 811251

The early Georgian house contains fine furniture, paintings and porcelain. The grounds have superb, award-winning terraced gardens, a lily pond and a Georgian ice house. There are also delightful woodland walks as well as spaces for caravans.
Times: Open - Gardens Etr-end Sept, daily 11am-5pm. House open Good Fri-Etr Mon and all BHs Sun & Mon, Wed & Sun, 7 Apr-29 Sep, 1.30-5. Private parties any day by appointment.
Fee: *Gardens only £2 (ch 50p, pen £1.50). House & Gardens £4 (ch £2.50, pen £3.50)
P ⬛ & ✈ (ex guide dogs in garden)

WHITBY
WHITBY ABBEY
(on clifftop E of Whitby town centre)
☎ 01947 603568

Dominating the skyline above the fishing port of Whitby the haunting ruins of the 13th-century

Benedictine abbey are an impressive sight. St Hilda built the first abbey on the site in 657.
Times: Open all year, Apr-Sep, daily 10-6; Oct-Mar, daily 10-4 or dusk if earlier. Closed 24-26 Dec & 1 Jan.
Fee: £1.70 (ch 90p).
P (charged) shop 🚻

YORK
THE ARC
St Saviourgate YO1 8NN (City centre, follow pedestrian signposts for Archaeological Resource Centre)
☎ 01904 643211

The ARC is a 'hands-on' experience of archaeology, housed in the beautifully restored medieval church of St Saviour. Be an archaeologist yourself - sift through the remains of centuries - bones, shell, pottery and much more. A range of special events and exhibitions of archaeological interest are held all year.
Times: Open: Mon-Fri 10-3.30 (last admission). Sat 1-3.30 (last admission). Closed Sundays & last 2 weeks in December.
Fee: *£3.60. Group rates available on request.
P (50yds) & (induction loop) toilets for disabled shop ✈ 🍴

BORTHWICK INSTITUTE OF HISTORICAL RESEARCH
St Anthony's Hall, Peasholme Green YO1 2PW
☎ 01904 642315

Originally built in the second half of the 15th century for the Guild of St Anthony, the hall was

contd.

later used as an arsenal, a workhouse, a prison and the Bluecoat School from 1705 to 1946. Now part of York University, it houses ecclesiastical archives and exhibitions of documents.

Times: Open all year, Mon-Fri 9.30-12.50 & 2-4.50. Closed Etr & Xmas.

Fee: Free.

P (max 5mins walk) (public car park) 🐕 🦽

CITY ART GALLERY

Exhibition Square YO1 7EW
☎ 01904 551861 ▤ 01904 551866

Six hundred years of painting, from early Italian gold-ground panels to the art of the 20th century, including works by Parmigianino and Bellotto, Frith, Boudin, Lowry, Nash, and nudes by Etty. Outstanding collection of studio pottery. Varied programme of temporary exhibitions and events, including 'Fairytale & Fantasy' - children's book illustrations, 11 December 1999-23 January 2000 and 'Yorkshire Abbeys' in July.

Times: Open all year, daily 9.30-4.30. Closed 25-26 Dec.

Fee: Free.

P (500mtrs) ♿ (chairlift) toilets for disabled shop 🐕 (ex guide dogs)

CLIFFORD'S TOWER

Tower St YO1 1SA
☎ 01904 646940

Named for the unfortunate Roger de Clifford, who was hung in chains from the castle, the tower was unused for centuries, as the first castle burned down and its replacement cracked from top to bottom as a result of subsidence. The walk around the old city walls offers the best way of seeing the ancient city.

Times: Open all year, Apr-Oct, daily 10-6 (or dusk if earlier); Nov-mid Mar, daily 10-4 (or dusk if earlier). Closed 24-26 Dec & 1 Jan.

Fee: £1.80 (ch 90p).

P 🐕 🦽 ♯

FAIRFAX HOUSE

Castlegate YO1 1RN (city centre, close to Jorvik Centre and Cliffords Tower)
☎ 01904 655543 ▤ 01904 652262

An outstanding mid-18th-century house with a richly decorated interior, Fairfax House was acquired by the York Civic Trust in 1983 and restored. Prior to this it had been used as a cinema and a dance hall. The house contains fine examples of Georgian furniture, porcelain, paintings and clocks which form the Terry Collection. This collection was donated by Mr Noel Terry who was the great grandson of Joseph Terry the founder of the York-based confectionery business. There is a special display of a recreated meal dating from 1763 in the dining room and kitchen. The special annual Christmas exhibition, *The Keeping of Christmas*, will be held from 3 December to 6 January. Ring for details of other exhibitions.

Times: Open 20 Feb-5 Jan, Mon-Sat 11-5, (Closed Fri). Sun 1.30-5. Last admission 4.30pm.

P (50yds) (3hr short stay) ♿ (with assistance, phone before visit) shop 🐕 *Details not confirmed for 2000*

JORVIK VIKING CENTRE

Coppergate YO1 9WT (Situated in the Coppergate shopping area follow the signs to Jorvik Viking centre)
☎ 01904 643211 ▤ 01904 627097

Jorvik was the Viking name for York. Between 1976 and 1981 archaeologists made some remarkable discoveries about Jorvik, during a dig in an area known as Coppergate. In 1984 the Jorvik Viking Centre was opened over the site of the original excavations. The dig shed a totally new light on the Viking way of life and has revealed many details of tools, clothing, crafts and trade. The Centre displays the archaeological remains - leather, textiles, metal objects and even timber buildings - in a detailed and vivid reconstruction. `Time-cars' carry visitors through a `time tunnel' from World War II back to Norman times and then to a full-scale reconstruction of 10th-century Coppergate. The busy street scene includes a crowded market, a river wharf with a fully-rigged sailing ship and a family at home. This is all made more authentic by voices speaking in Old Norse and even smells such as cooking, fish, pigsties and rubbish. Finally the tour passes through a reconstruction of Coppergate during the dig of the 1970s. The visit ends in the Skipper Gallery which has a display of some of the 15,000 small objects found during the dig.

Times: Open all year, Apr-Oct daily 9-5.30; Nov-Mar daily 10-4.30 (Closed 25 Dec). Opening times subject to chage, please telephone for up to date details.

Fee: *£5.35 (ch 5-15 £3.99, under 5 free, student/pen £4.60. Family £17.

P (400 yds) (limited to 3 hours) 🍴 ♿ (lift & time car designed to take a wheelchair) toilets for disabled shop 🐕 🦽

MERCHANT ADVENTURERS' HALL

Fossgate YO1 9XD
☎ 01904 654818 ▤ 01904 654818

The medieval guild hall of the powerful Merchant Adventurers' Company was built 1357–61 and is one of the finest in Europe. The Great Hall contains early furniture, one piece dating from the 13th century, paintings, silver, and weights and measures.

Times: Open all year, end Mar-early Nov, daily 8.30-5; early Nov-late Mar, Mon-Sat 8.30-3.30. (Closed 10 days Xmas).
Fee: *£1.90 (ch 7-17 60p, over 62 & students £1.60)
P (500yds) & toilets for disabled ✖

NATIONAL RAILWAY MUSEUM
Leeman Rd YO26 4XJ (Signposted from City Centre)
☎ 01904 621261 ▤ 01904 611112

Among the impressive exhibits are a reconstruction of Stephenson's Rocket; the record-breaking Mallard; a life-size section of the Channel Tunnel; and Royal Palaces on Wheels. The new wing features the Workshop, the Warehouse, and the Working Railway Gallery.
Times: Open all year, Mon-Sun 10-6,(Closed 24-26 Dec).
Fee: *£5.90 (ch under 17 free, pen £4.90, concessions £3.90).
P (charged) 🍽 ✖ licensed & ("Please Touch" evenings) toilets for disabled shop ✖ (ex guide dogs & hearing dogs)

TREASURER'S HOUSE
Chapter House St YO1 2JD
☎ 01904 624247 ▤ 01904 647372

There has been a house on this site since Roman times and in the basement of this elegant 17th-century building is an exhibition of its history. The house was improved during the 18th century with the addition of a fine staircase. Restored between 1897 and 1930, it was left, with its fine furniture, to the National Trust.
Times: Open 28 Mar-1 Nov, daily except Friday. 10.30-5pm. Last admission 4.30pm.
P (400 yds) ✖ licensed ✖ 🐾 *Details not confirmed for 2000*

YORK CASTLE MUSEUM
The Eye of York YO1 IRY (city centre,next to Clifford's Tower)
☎ 01904 653611 ▤ 01904 671078

Fascinating exhibits that bring memories to life, imaginatively displayed through reconstructions of period rooms and two indoor streets, complete with cobbles, a Hansom cab and a park. The museum is housed in the city's former prison and is based on an extensive collection of 'bygones' acquired at the beginning of the century. It was one of the first folk museums to display a huge

range of everyday objects in an authentic scene. The Victorian street includes a pawnbroker, a tallow candle factory and a haberdasher's. There is even a reconstruction of the original sweet shop of the York chocolate manufacturer, Joseph Terry. An extensive collection of many other items ranging from musical instruments to costumes and a gallery of domestic gadgets from Victorian times to the 1960s are further attractions to this remarkable museum. The museum also has one of Britain's finest collections of Militaria; this includes a superb example of an Anglo-Saxon helmet - one of only three known. A special exhibition called 'Seeing it Through' explores the life of York citizens during the Second World War. The museum includes the cell where highwayman Dick Turpin was held. Please contact the museum for details of exhibition and events.
Times: Open all year, Apr-Oct Mon-Sat 9.30-5.30, Sun 10-5.30; Nov-Mar, Mon-Sat 9.30-4, Sun 10-4. (Closed 25-26 Dec & 1 Jan).
🍽 & toilets for disabled shop ✖ *Details not confirmed for 2000* 🐾

YORK MINSTER
Deangate YO1 7HH
☎ 01904 639347 ▤ 01904 613049

It is believed that Edwin King of Northumbria built the first church on this site in 627. Since then both Saxons and Normans built cathedrals here, and parts of the latter survive in many places in the present structure. From 1220 to 1472 the present church was built to replace the romanesque one. It is notable for its size - the largest medieval church north of the Alps - and for its wealth of stained glass, most of which is original to the building. Daily worship has been conducted on this site for 13 centuries. Events include York Mystery Plays (22 Jun-22 Jul).
Times: Open daily, Mon-Sat 7-6 (later in summer), Sun after 1pm.
Fee: *Free admission (donation requested) but following parts charged; Foundations & Treasury £2 (ch £1, pen & students £1.50); Chapter House 70p (ch 30p); Central Tower £2.50 (ch £1); Crypt 70p (ch 30p).
P (440yds) & (loop system, tactile model, braille guide) toilets for disabled shop ✖

YORKSHIRE MUSEUM & GARDENS
Museum Gardens YO1 2DR (Park & Ride services operate from 3 sites near A64 and A19)
☎ 01904 629745 ▤ 01904 651221

The winner of a European award, Yorkshire Museum - set in 10 acres of botanical gardens in the heart of the historic city of York - displays some of the finest Roman, Anglo-Saxon, Viking and Medieval treasures ever discovered in Britain. The Middleham jewel, a fine example of English Gothic jewellery, is on display in the Medieval Gallery and, in the Roman Gallery, visitors can see a fine marble head of Constantine the Great, household utensils

contd.

exhibited in a recreated kitchen and many other artefacts. The Anglo-Saxon Gallery houses the magnificent, delicate silver-gilt Ormside bowl and the skilfully wrought Gilling sword. The Museum also has a fine collection of Rockingham porcelain. Part of York's Roman city walls runs through the Museum Gardens where, amongst a variety of flora and fauna, you can visit a working observatory and the ruins of the medieval St Mary's Abbey with its 14th-century guesthouse - the oldest timber-framed structure in Yorkshire.

Times: Open all year, Apr-Oct, daily 10-5; Nov-Mar, Mon-Sat 10-5, Sun 1-5. Last admission 4.30.

P (5 mins walk) & (ramps & lift) toilets for disabled shop ✖ *Details not confirmed for 2000* ➥

THE YORK STORY

St Mary's, Castlegate YO1 1RN (city centre, near Jorvik Centre)

☎ **01904 628632**

The Heritage Centre is in the predominately 15th-century church of St Mary which has the tallest spire in York, at 152ft. The venue is due to be refurbished as a temporary exhibition centre for major travelling exhibitions. It will reopen to the public in early 1998. Please telephone for details.

Times: Open all year, Mon-Sat 10-5 (Wed 10.30-5), Sun 1-5. (Closed 25-26 Dec & 1 Jan). Subject to closure due to refurbishment.

P (1 min walk) & shop ✖ *Details not confirmed for 2000*

South Yorkshire

South Yorkshire is an industrial area and all the main towns are traditionally steel and coal producing centres. Both of these industries have declined in recent years and have been replaced to some extent by other forms of manufacturing.

Barnsley is the county's administrative centre, located on one Britain's richest coalfields. The town has an entry in the Domesday Book, and was built on land belonging to the priories of Pontefract and Monk Bretton.

Doncaster, originally a Roman station, is set on the River Don. It is known particularly for its racecourse. The best known race on its calender is the celebrated St Leger, which is held in September. In 1875, Charles Dickens watched it from the 18th-century Italianate grandstand at the Town Moor racecourse. The Lincolnshire Handicap is held in March. The town also possesses some fine Georgian architecture, particularly James Paine's house which was built in 1748.

Rotheram, on the outskirts of Sheffield, has a fine 15th-century church, and a bridge with an old chapel over the Don river.

South Yorkshire claims part of the Peak District National park, whose hills and dales provide relief to the millions of city dwellers within its vicinity.

EVENTS & FESTIVALS

December 99
31st Sheffield 2000 Events

January
6th The Ancient Haxey Hood Game, Doncaster

March
tbc Sheffield Irish Festival

April
30th-1st May Open Up, Sheffield studio open days
Embassy World Snooker Championships, Crucible Theatre

May
tbc The Mayfest 2000, Sheffield

June
3rd & 17th Art Hits the Streets, outdoor arts markets, Sheffield
24th Lord Mayor's Parade, Sheffield

July
1st & 15th Art Hits the Streets, outdoor arts markets, Sheffield
tbc South Yorkshire Festival, Wortley Hall

September
tbc Sheffield Show, Graves Park

October
bc Off the Shelf Festival, Sheffield, a celebration of reading and writing

Top: Sheffield

⅏ BARNSLEY
MONK BRETTON PRIORY
(1m E of Barnsley town centre, off A633)
☎ 01226 204089

The priory was an important Cluniac house, founded in 1135. The considerable remains of the gatehouse, church and other buildings can be seen.
Times: Open all year, Apr-Sep, daily 10-6; Oct, 10-4; Nov-Mar, Wed-Sun 10-4 or dusk if earlier. (Closed 24-26 Dec & 1 Jan).
🅿 ❤ ♯

⅏ CONISBROUGH
CONISBROUGH CASTLE
DN12 3HH (NE of town centre off A630)
☎ 01709 863329

The 12th-century keep is one of the country's oldest and best preserved buildings of the period. Surrounded by a curtain wall with round towers, its circular design, with six buttresses, is unique. It features in Sir Walter Scott's *Ivanhoe*.
Times: Open all year, Apr-Sep, Mon-Fri 10-5, Sat & Sun 10-6; Oct-Mar, daily 10-4. Closed 25 Dec & 1 Jan.
🅿 ❤ ✖ ♯

⅏ CUSWORTH
THE MUSEUM OF SOUTH YORKSHIRE LIFE CUSWORTH H HALL
DN5 7TU
☎ 01302 782342   🖹 01302 782342

The Museum of South Yorkshire is located in Cusworth Hall, an 18th-century country house set in a landscaped park. It has displays which illustrate the way local people here lived, worked and entertained themselves over the last 200 years.
Times: Open all year, Mon-Fri 10-5, Sat 11-5 & Sun 1-5. (4pm Dec & Jan) (Closed Good Fri, Xmas & 1 Jan).
🅿 ❤ ❤ (wheelchair available) toilets for disabled shop ✖
Details not confirmed for 2000

⅏ DONCASTER
BRODSWORTH HALL
Brodsworth DN5 7XJ (between A635 & A638)
☎ 01302 722598   🖹 01302 337165

Brodsworth Hall is a Victorian country house which has survived largely intact. The faded grandeur of the family rooms contrasts with the functional austerity of the servant's wing. There are fine gardens.
Times: Open Apr-Oct, Tue-Sun & BH's; gardens and tea rooms noon-6, house 1-6 (last admission 5pm); Group visits mornings by appointment.
Fee: £4.70 (ch £2.40).
🅿 ❤ ❤ toilets for disabled shop ✖ ♯ 🍽

EARTH CENTRE
Denaby Main DN12 4EA
☎ 01709 513933   🖹 01709 512010

Earth Centre is a unique theme park exploring sustainable development. You are encouraged to consider what actions you can take now to shape a sustainable future. The Centre itself has been

SHEFFIELD

Iron smelting has been the main industry in Sheffield since the 12th century, and by the 14th century the city was renowned for its cutlery. Using modern alloys, these skills have been developed to produce precision tools. Sheffield is located on the fast flowing River Don, which powered the industry before the days of the steam engine, and the original weirs can still be seen today. Despite its size, as England's fourth largest city, and its industrial image, Sheffield is the country's greenest city, and a third of it actually lies within the Peak District National Park, with beautiful countryside easily accessible, and excellent walks around and within the city.

built using environmentally sound materials and methods on the regenerated site of two former coalmines.

Times: Open early Apr-early Nov 10-6 (last entry 4pm). During summer holidays 10-8 (last entry 6pm).
Fee: *Adult: by car £8.95 (subsequent adult £4.95), by public transport/on foot £4.95 (ch 5 & concessions £4.95). Ch under 5yrs and essential carers free.
🅿 🍽 ✕ licensed ♿ toilets for disabled shop ✈ (ex guide dogs) ⬤

⛫ MALTBY
ROCHE ABBEY
S66 8NW (1.5m S off A634)
☎ 01709 812739

The walls of the south and north transepts of this 12th-century Cistercian abbey still stand to their full height, providing a dramatic sight for the visitor. There is also a fine gatehouse.
Times: Open Apr-Oct, daily 10-6 (dusk if earlier).
Fee: £1.60 (ch 80p).
🅿 ♿ ⚏

⛫ ROTHERHAM
CLIFTON PARK MUSEUM
Clifton Park, Clifton Ln S65 2AA (Follow directions from inner ring road)
☎ 01709 382121 ext 3635
📠 01709 823631

Housed in a mansion designed by John Carr, the museum is noted for its collection of Rockingham china. Other attractions include the 18th-century rooms, family portraits, the period kitchen, and Victoriana. Regular programme of temporary exhibitions, including `Rotherham Greats' (4 Dec-2 Apr 2000). Please telephone for details.
Times: Open all year, Mon-Thu & Sat 10-5, Sun 1.30-5 (4.30 Oct-Mar). (Closed Xmas & New Year).
Fee: Free.
🅿 ♿ toilets for disabled shop ✈ (ex guide dogs)

⛫ SHEFFIELD
KELHAM ISLAND MUSEUM
Alma St S3 8RY (0.5m NW of city centre, take A61 N to West Bar, follow signposts)
☎ 0114 272 2106 📠 0114 275 7847

The story of Sheffield, its industry and life, with the most powerful working steam engine in Europe, reconstructed workshops, working cutler and craftspeople demonstrating traditional 'made in Sheffield' skills - this is a 'living' museum. During the year Kelham Island stages events, displays and temporary exhibitions culminating in the annual Christmas Victorian Market.
Times: Open Mon-Thu 10-4, Sun 11-4.45.Closed Fri and Sat. Check opening days/times at Christmas & New Year before travelling.
Fee: *£3 (ch £1.50, pen £2). Family ticket £6. Party 12+.
🅿 🍽 ♿ (wheelchair on request) toilets for disabled shop ✈

West Yorkshire

The West Riding has long been industrialised, and not only produced coal but was also home to the traditional wool industry. The tall mill chimneys are characteristic of its industrial heritage, set against the Pennine Hills.

The county includes the towns of Wakefield, Halifax, Huddersfield and Bradford, centres of the wool industry from the 13th century. Huddersfield is known particularly for its fine wool worsted.

Leeds sprawls over its hilly site and includes a great variety of manufacturing and other industries, notably ready-to-wear clothes. It is also home to the celebrated Yorkshire County Cricket Club at Headingley.

Many visitors to the region come in the wake of the extraordinary Brontë family. A motherless family with the curate of Haworth, Patrick Brontë, at its head. The children, Charlotte, Branwell (Patrick), Emily and Anne created a rich fantasy world, feeding their literary imaginations. Their poems and novels evoked the nature of their moorland home, particularly Emily's *Wuthering Heights*, published in December 1847, a year before her death from consumption at the age of 30. The Brontë Society was founded in 1893. In 1926 the American publisher Henry Houston Bonnell bequeathed his collection to the society, who bought the parsonage, the Brontë's former home to accommodate it.

Natural features of the county encompass the wild beauty of Ilkley Moor, Haworth Moor, and parts of the Peak District National Park.

EVENTS & FESTIVALS

March
tbc Bradford Film Festival

April
1st-2nd Complementary Medicine Festival, Ilkley
29th Leeds Dollshouse & Miniatures Fair

May
13th-20th Wharfedale Music Festival, Ilkley

June
tbc Bradford Festival & Mela

July
tbc Bradford Festival & Mela

October
28th-29th Complementary Medicine Festival, Ilkley

November
tbc Scroggling the Holly, Haworth (1st in a series of annual events leading up to Christmas)

Top: The Corn Exchange, Leeds

⛏ BRADFORD
BOLLING HALL
Bowling Hall Rd BD4 7LP (1m from city centre off A650)
☎ 01274 723057 🖹 01274 726220

A classic West Yorkshire manor house, complete with galleried 'housebody' (hall), Bolling Hall dates mainly from the 17th century but has medieval and 18th-century sections. It has panelled rooms, plasterwork in original colours, heraldic glass and a rare Chippendale bed.
Times: Open all year, Wed-Fri 11-4, Sat 10-5, Sun 12-5. (Closed Mon ex BH, Good Fri, 25 & 26 Dec).
Fee: Free.
🅿 ♿ shop ✖

BRADFORD INDUSTRIAL MUSEUM AND HORSES AT WORK
Moorside Rd, Eccleshill BD2 3HP (off A658)
☎ 01274 631756 🖹 01274 636362

Moorside Mills is an original spinning mill, now part of a museum that brings vividly to life the story of the woollen industry in Bradford. The magnificent machinery that once converted raw wool into cloth is on display and the mill yard rings with the sound of iron on stone as shire horses pull trams, haul buses, or give rides. There are changing exhibitions and daily demonstrations.
Times: Open all year, Tue-Sat 10-5, Sun 12-5. (Closed Mon ex BH)
Fee: *Free. Charges made for rides.
🅿 💷 ♿ (induction loop in lecture theatre) toilets for disabled shop ✖

CARTWRIGHT HALL ART GALLERY
Lister Park BD9 4NS (1m from city centre on A650)
☎ 01274 493313 🖹 01274 481045

Built in dramatic Baroque style in 1904, the gallery has permanent collections of 19th-and 20th-century British art, contemporary prints, and older works by British and European masters.
Times: Open all year Apr-Sep, Tue-Sat 10-5, Sun 1-5. (Closed Mon ex BH, Good Fri, 25 & 26 Dec).
Fee: Free.
💷 ♿ (wheelchair available) toilets for disabled shop ✖

COLOUR MUSEUM
1 Providence St BD1 2PW (from city centre follow signs B6144(Haworth)then follow brown tourist information signs)
☎ 01274 390955 🖹 01274 392888

Britain's only Museum of Colour comprises two galleries packed with visitor-operated exhibits demonstrating the effects of light and colour, including optical illusions, and the story of dyeing and textile printing. There is a programme of special exhibitions and events. Please telephone for details.
Times: Open all year, Tue-Fri 2-5, Sat 10-4. Booked parties Tue-Fri mornings. (Closed Sun, Mon & BH's). Hours may be extended during School Hols, phone for details.
Fee: *£1.50 (concessions £1). Family ticket £3.75.
🅿 (300 yds) ♿ (lift from street level) toilets for disabled shop ✖ (ex registered assistant dogs) 🍴

NATIONAL MUSEUM OF PHOTOGRAPHY,FILM & TELEVISION
BD1 1NQ (2 miles from M62, clear signs direct visitors to the location)
☎ 01274 202030 🖹 01274 394540

The past, present and future of the media explored with interactive displays and dramatic reconstructions - ride on a magic carpet, become a newsreader for the day or try your hand at vision mixing. At the heart of the Museum is IMAX, a cinema screen more than five storeys high.
Times: Open all year, Tue-Sun & BH's 10-6. (Closed Mon).
Fee: *Museum free, 2D & 3D IMAX Cinema £5.80 (concessions £4). Groups 20% discount.
🅿 (charged) 💷 ✖ licensed ♿ (tailored tours, cinema seating & hearing services) toilets for disabled shop ✖ (ex guide dogs) 🍴

⛏ BRAMHAM
BRAMHAM PARK
LS23 6ND (on A1 4m S of Wetherby)
☎ 01937 844265 🖹 01937 845923

This fine Queen Anne house was built by Robert Benson and is the home of his descendants. The
contd.

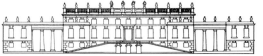

garden has ornamental ponds, cascades, temples and avenues.

Times: Gardens open Etr, May Day & Spring BH wknds 1.15-5.30: House & gardens 21 Jun-6 Sep, Sun, Tue, Wed & Thu also Aug BH Mon, 1.15-5.30. (Last admission 5pm).

🅿 ♿ toilets for disabled ✖ (ex on lead) *Details not confirmed for 2000*

⛫ BRIGHOUSE
SMITH ART GALLERY
Halifax Rd HD6 2EP
☎ 01484 719222   🖹 01484 719222

Established in 1907 with a fine collection of Victorian art, including works by Atkinson Grimshaw and Marcus Stone, the gallery displays works from its founding collection and exhibitions of contemporary art. Lively programme of exhibitions and shows featuring local artists and societies. Please telephone for details.

Times: Open all year, Mon, Tue, Thur & Fri 10-12.30 & 1-6, Sat 10-12.30 & 1-4. (Closed Wed, Sun & BH's).

🅿 (on road) ♿ shop ✖ (ex guide dogs) *Details not confirmed for 2000* 🍽

⛫ HALIFAX
PIECE HALL
HX1 1RE (Well signposted with brown signs from major routes, close to Halifax rail & bus stations)
☎ 01422 358087   🖹 01422 349310

The merchants of Halifax built the elegant and unique hall in 1779, and it has over 300 merchant's rooms around a courtyard, now housing an industrial museum, art galleries and shops selling antiques, books etc. There is an open market on Friday and Saturday, and a flea market on Thursday. There is a lively programe of exhibitions, workshops, activities and events throughout the year, and a festival in the summer, please ring for details.

Times: Open all year daily 8-6 (Closed 25-26 Dec). Industrial Museum Tue-Sat 10-5, Sun 2-5. Art Gallery Tue-Sun 10-5.

Fee: *Free (ex small admission charge for the Industrial Museum & when special events are held).

🅿 (50 yds) 💷 ✖ licensed ♿ (lifts, shopmobility on site & audio guide available) toilets for disabled shop 🍽

SHIBDEN HALL
Lister's Rd HX3 6XG (2km E of Halifax on A58)
☎ 01422 352246 & 321455
🖹 01422 348440

The house dates back to the early 15th century, and its rooms have been laid out to illustrate life in different periods of its history. Craft weekends, featuring over 30 craftworkers demonstrating historic skills, are held, and there's a lively programme of craft events, workshops and family activities. Please apply for details.

Times: Open Mar-Nov, Mon-Sat 10-5, Sun 12-5. Contact for details of winter opening hours.

Fee: *£1.90 (ch & concessions £1) Family £5. Party

🅿 💷 ♿ shop ✖

⛫ HAREWOOD
HAREWOOD HOUSE & BIRD GARDEN
LS17 9LQ (junc A61/A659 Leeds/Harrogate Rd)
☎ 0113 288 6331   🖹 0113 288 6467

The Yorkshire home of the Earl and Countess of Harewood, containing fine furniture, porcelain and paintings, and the landscaped grounds offer lakeside and woodland walks. The Bird Garden has aviaries for over 150 species. Numerous special events take place throughout the year including; regular changing programme of exhibitions; Last Night of the Proms (early Sep); Classic Car Rally (mid Jun) and Jaguar Rally (mid Jul). Telephone for details of these and other events.

Times: Open 9 Mar-Oct, daily Bird Garden from 10am, House from 11am. Grounds & Bird Garden open wknds Nov-Dec.

Fee: *'Freedom ticket'(house, grounds, bird garden, terrace gallery) £6.95 (ch/student £4.75, pen £6.25) Family £22.50. Bird garden, grounds, terrace gallery £5.75 (ch/student £3.25 pen £4.75) Family £17.50. Group rate 15+

🅿 💷 ✖ licensed ♿ (electric ramp to front door of house) toilets for disabled shop garden centre ✖ (in gardens on lead) 🍽

⛫ HAWORTH
BRONTE PARSONAGE MUSEUM
BD22 8DR (leave A629&A6033 follow signs for Haworth, take Rawdon Rd, pass 2 car parks next left, then right)
☎ 01535 642323   🖹 01535 647131

The Brontës were an extraordinary literary family and Haworth Parsonage was their lifelong home. An intensely close-knit family, the Brontës saw the parsonage as the heart of their world from early childhood to the ends of their brief lives, and the moorland setting provided them with inspiration for their writing. The house contains much personal memorabilia, including the furniture Charlotte bought with the proceeds of her literary success, Branwell's portraits of local worthies, Emily's writing desk and Anne's books and drawings.

Times: Open Apr-Sep, daily 10-5.30; Oct-Mar daily 11-5 (final admission 30 min before closing). Closed 11 Jan-5 Feb & 24-27 Dec.

Fee: *£3.80 (ch 5-16 £1.20, concessions £2.80). Family ticket £8.80.

🅿 (charged) ♿ (Information in large type & braille) shop ✖ (ex guide dogs)

KEIGHLEY & WORTH VALLEY RAILWAY & MUSEUM
Keighley, Haworth, Oxenhope & Ingrow West BD22 8NJ
☎ 01535 645214 & 677777
🖹 01535 647317

The line was built mainly to serve the valley's mills, and goes through the heart of Brontë country. It begins at Keighley (also a BR station), and then climbs up to Haworth, and the terminus

is at Oxenhope, which has a museum and restoration building.
Times: All year weekend service, but daily all BH wks & Jul-1st wk Sep.
Fee: *Full line ticket £6 reduced fares for ch & pen. Family ticket £16. Day rover(unlimited travel) £8,Family day rover £20. Party rates.
🅿 (charged) 🚐 ♿ (wheelchairs can be accommodated in brake car). toilets for disabled shop ⬩

⛭ HUDDERSFIELD
HUDDERSFIELD ART GALLERY
Princess Alexandra Walk HD1 2SU
☎ 01484 221964 ext 1962
🖨 01484 221952

The changing displays from the permanent collection include British oil paintings, watercolours, drawings and sculpture from the mid-19th century onwards. Temporary loan art, craft and photography exhibitions are also held throughout the year. Phone for details of current shows and events.
Times: Open all year, Mon-Fri 10-5, Sat 10-4. (Closed Sun & BH's).
Fee: Free.
🅿 ♿ toilets for disabled shop ✘ (ex guide dogs)

TOLSON MEMORIAL MUSEUM
Ravensknowle Park HD5 8DJ (on A629)
☎ 01484 223830 🖨 01484 223843

Displays on the development of the cloth industry and a collection of horse-drawn vehicles, together with natural history, archaeology, toys and folk exhibits. There is a full programme of events and temporary exhibitions.
Times: Open all year. Mon-Fri 11-5, Sat & Sun noon-5. (Closed Xmas).
Fee: Free.
🅿 ♿ toilets for disabled shop ✘

⛭ KEIGHLEY
CLIFFE CASTLE MUSEUM & GALLERY
Spring Gardens Ln BD20 6LH (NW of town off A629)
☎ 01535 618230 🖨 01535 610536

French furniture from the Victoria and Albert Museum is displayed, together with collections of local and natural history, ceramics, dolls, geological items and minerals. The grounds of this 19th-century mansion contain a play area and an aviary.
Times: Open all year, Tue-Sat 10-5, Sun 12-5. Also open BH Mon. (Closed Good Fri & 25-28 Dec).
Fee: Free.
🅿 🚐 ♿ toilets for disabled shop ✘

EAST RIDDLESDEN HALL
Bradford Rd BD20 4EA (1m NE of Keighley on south side of Bradford Rd)
☎ 01535 607075 🖨 01535 691462

This charming 17th-century Yorkshire manor house is typical of its kind, although the plasterwork and oak panelling are contemporary.

contd.

LEEDS

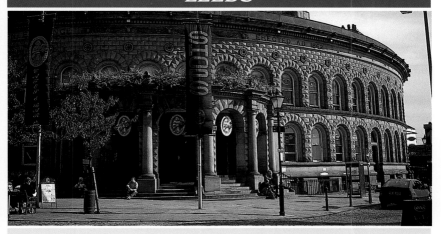

Leeds is fast becoming the 'happening capital' of West Yorkshire. Its fashionable Exchange Quarter is buzzing with clubs, bars, and chic eateries, yet for much of its history, Leeds has been far from fashionable, even though it has been the centre of many things. Medieval Leeds was a market centre, and from the 17th century the wool trade dominated the city, which was a major cloth producer during the Industrial Revolution. Leeds is quick to exploit its productive past, and has converted the Leeds Waterfront into a fine collection of busy tourist attractions. Among these are the Royal Collection of Arms and Armour, and the shopping and craft stalls on Granary Wharf.

A small secluded garden is found in the grounds, which also feature one of the largest medieval tithe barns in the north of England.
Times: Open Apr-1 Nov, Sat-Wed & Good Friday, and Thurs in July & Aug. Sat 1-5pm, Sun and weekdays inc BH 12-5pm.last admission 4.30pm. Shop & tearoom open at 12pm.
🅿 💷 ♿ shop ✖ ✿ *Details not confirmed for 2000*

⛪ LEEDS

CITY ART GALLERY
The Headrow LS1 3AA (city centre, next to town hall and library)
☎ 0113 247 8248   🖳 0113 244 9689

Home to one of the best collections of 20th century British art outside London, as well as Victorian and late 19th century pictures, an outstanding collection of English watercolours, an exceptional display of modern sculpture and temporary exhibitions focusing on the modern and contemporary. Please telephone for details of forthcoming exhibitions.
Times: Open all year, Mon-Sat 10-5, Wed until 8, Sun 1-5.Closed BHs.
🅿 💷 ✖ licensed ♿ (restricted access to upper floor) toilets for disabled shop ✖ (ex guide dogs) *Details not confirmed for 2000* 💷

KIRKSTALL ABBEY & ABBEY HOUSE MUSEUM
Abbey Rd, Kirkstall LS5 3EH (off A65, W of city centre).
☎ 0113 275 5821

The most complete 12th-century Cistercian Abbey in the country stands on the banks of the River Aire. The museum presents a colourful record of Victorian social life.
Times: Open all year, Tue-Sat 10-5, Sun 1-5. Open Bank Hol's. Abbey site open dawn-dusk.
🅿 ♿ toilets for disabled shop ✖ *Details not confirmed for 2000* 💷

MIDDLETON RAILWAY
Moor Rd, Hunslet LS10 2JQ (M621 junc5 or follow signs from A61)
☎ 0113 271 0320 (ansaphone) 🖳 01977 620585

This was the first railway authorised by an Act of Parliament (in 1758) and the first to succeed with steam locomotives (in 1812). Steam trains run each weekend in season from Tunstall Road roundabout to Middleton Park. There is a programme of special events - please telephone for details.
Times: Moor Road Station open for viewing every wknd. Trains run Sat, Sun & BH, Etr-Dec.
Fee: *Entry to station free. £2 (ch £1) Return train fare. Family ticket £5.
🅿 💷 ♿ (ramped access to all areas) toilets for disabled shop 💷

ROYAL ARMOURIES MUSEUM
Armouries Dr LS10 1LT (off A61 close to Leeds centre, follow brown tourist signs)
☎ 0113 220 1999 & 0990 106 666
🖳 0113 220 1997

Situated on the canal waterfront in the heart of Leeds, the museum is designed to bring to life the history and development of arms and armour. Outside on the waterfront there is a 3,000 capacity tilt yard for jousting tournaments and the Beating of the Retreat. A craft court will have demonstrations by skilled armourers and the training of hunting dogs and horses.
Times: Open daily, Mon-Fri 10.30-4.30, Sat-Sun & School hols 11-5.30. Closed 24-25 Dec & 1 Jan.
Fee: *£7.95 (ch 4-15 £4.95, pen & students £6.95). Family ticket £24.95.
🅿 (charged) 💷 ✖ licensed ♿ toilets for disabled shop ✖ 💷

TEMPLE NEWSAM HOUSE & PARK
LS15 0AE (off A63)
☎ 0113 264 7321 (House) & 264 5535 (Park) 🖳 0113 2602285

This Tudor and Jacobean mansion boasts extensive collections of decorative arts in their original room settings, including the incomparable Chippendale collection. Set in 1,200 acres of parkland (landscaped by `Capability' Brown), there's a Rare Breeds Centre, and the gardens have a magnificent display of rhododendrons.
Times: Open all year. House: Tue-Sat 10am-5pm, Sun 1-5pm. 1 Nov-28 Dec & Mar Tues-Sat 10am-4pm Sun 12-5pm. Open Bank Hols. Home Farm 10am-4pm(3pm in winter); Gardens 10-dusk; Estate: daily: dawn-dusk. Closed Jan-Feb re-opens 28 Feb.
Fee: *£2 (concessions £1). Accompanied children 50p. Season ticket £10 (concessions £5, ch £2.50)
🅿 (charged) 💷 ♿ (ramps giving full accesss to parkland) toilets for disabled shop ✖ 💷

TETLEY'S BREWERY WHARF
The Waterfront LS1 1QG
☎ 0113 242 0666 🖳 0113 243 2732

An exploration of the fascinating history of the English pub. With the aid of actors, you will see life in a 14th-century ale-house, through to Elizabethan, Jacobean, Georgian and Victorian hostelries, a 1940s blitzed pub and a futuristic pub.
Times: Open everyday 10.30-5 (except 25-26 Dec & 1 Jan).
Fee: *£3.95 (concesssions £3.25).
🅿 💷 ✖ licensed ♿ (lift & ramps) toilets for disabled shop ✖ (ex guide dogs) 💷

THACKRAY MEDICAL MUSEUM
Beckett St LS9 7LN (next to St James Hospital)
☎ 0113 244 4343 🖳 0113 247 0219

Housed in a large Victorian building, next to the famous St James's Hospital, the Thackray Medical Museum offers a unique hands-on experience. A cow from Gloucester, green mould and smelly toilets - all these things have helped transform our lives. Find out how by walking back in time and exploring the sights, sounds and smells of Victorian slum life.

Times: Open all year, Tue-Sun & BH Mons 10-5.30. Closed 25-26 Dec & 1 Jan.
Fee: *£4.40 (ch 4-16 £3.30, pen, students & unemployed £3.60). Family ticket £14.00. Party 12+.
🅿 (charged) 💷 ♿ (wheelchair loan, induction loop) toilets for disabled shop ✖ (ex guide dogs) 🔔

TROPICAL WORLD
Canal Gardens, Roundhay Park LS8 2ER (3m N of city centre off A58 at Oakwood)
☎ 0113 266 1850

The atmosphere of the tropics is re-created here as visitors walk among banana, citrus, pineapple and other exotic trees. A waterfall cascades into a rock-pool and other pools contain terrapins and carp. There are reptiles, insects and more than 30 species of butterfly. There is also a Nocturnal House, a South American Rainforest, and a Desert House.
Times: Open daily, 10-early evening (dusk in winter), special times at Christmas. Closed 25 Dec
Fee: *£1 (ch 8-15 50p, ch under 8 free).
🅿 💷 ♿ toilets for disabled shop ✖ (ex guide dogs) 🔔

🏛 LOTHERTON HALL
LOTHERTON HALL
Aberford LS25 3EB (off the A1, 0.75m E of Jwith B1217)
☎ 0113 281 3259

Built in Edwardian times, the museum contains furniture, pictures, silver and ceramics from the Gascoigne collection, and works of art on loan from Leeds galleries. Outside, the Edwardian garden, bird garden and deer park are delightful places in which to stroll.
Times: Open Tue-Sat 10-5. Sun 1-5. Bank Hols. Nov-Dec & Mar Tue-Sat 10-4, Sun 12-4.
Fee: *Hall, £2 (ch, pen & students £1, unaccompanied ch 50p). Season ticket £10 (ch £2.50, concessions £5). Party 15+. Free admission to Bird Garden, Gardens & Parkland.
🅿 💷 ✖ licensed ♿ shop ✖ (ex in park)

🏛 MIDDLESTOWN
NATIONAL COAL MINING MUSEUM FOR ENGLAND
Caphouse Colliery, New Rd WF4 4RH (on A642 between Wakefield & Huddersfield)
☎ 01924 848806 📄 01924 840694

A unique opportunity to go 450ft underground down one of Britain's oldest working mine shafts, where models and machinery depict methods and conditions of mining from the early 1800s to the present day. You are strongly advised to wear sensible footwear and warm clothing. Please telephone for details of exhibitions and events
Times: Open all year, daily 10-5. (Closed 24-26 Dec & 1 Jan).
Fee: *£5.75 (ch £4.25, concessions £4.85).
🅿 💷 ✖ licensed ♿ (nature trail not accessible) toilets for disabled shop 🔔

🏛 NOSTELL PRIORY
NOSTELL PRIORY
WF4 1QD (6m SE of Wakefield, off A638)
☎ 01924 863892 📄 01924 865282

Built by Paine in the middle of the 18th century, the priory has an additional wing built by Adam in 1766. It contains a notable saloon and tapestry room and displays pictures and Chippendale

contd.

furniture. There is a lake in the grounds. Events are held here. Please telephone for details.
Times: Open 4 Apr-1 Nov. Apr-Jun, Sept & Oct: Sat & Sun 12pm-5pm. 1 July-3 Sept daily except Friday 12-5. Bank Hols 12-5. Not Good Fri. Last admission 4.30pm.
🅿 💺 ♿ (lift) toilets for disabled shop ✈ 🐾 *Details not confirmed for 2000*

⌂ OAKWELL HALL
OAKWELL HALL
Nutter Ln, Birstall WF17 9LG (6m SE of Bradford, off A652 immediately S of M62)
☎ 01924 326240   🖹 01924 326249

A moated Elizabethan manor house, furnished as it might have looked in the 1690s. Extensive Country Park with countryside centre. There are period gardens, an equestrian arena and an adventure playground.
Times: Open all year, daily (ex Good Fri, 25 Dec-1 Jan).
Fee: *£1.20 (ch 50p). Family ticket £2.50.
🅿 💺 ♿ (herb garden for the blind, large print & braille guide) toilets for disabled shop ✈ (park only ex guide dogs)

⌂ WAKEFIELD
WAKEFIELD ART GALLERY
Wentworth Ter WF1 3QW (N of city centre by Wakefield College and Clayton Hospial)
☎ 01924 305796   🖹 01924 305770

Wakefield was home to two of Britain's greatest modern sculptors - Barbara Hepworth and Henry Moore. The art gallery, which has an important collection of 20th-century paintings and sculptures, has a special room devoted to these two local artists. There are frequent temporary exhibitions of both modern and earlier works covering all aspects of art and crafts.
Times: Open all year, Tue-Sat 10.30-4.30, Sun 2-4.30.
Fee: Free.
🅿 (on street) (on street parking restricted to 2hrs) shop ✈ (ex guide dogs)

⌂ WEST BRETTON
YORKSHIRE SCULPTURE PARK
Bretton Hall WF4 4LG (1 mile from J38 on M1)
☎ 01924 830302   🖹 01924 830044

One of Europe's leading sculpture parks, set in over 100 acres of beautiful parkland. There are changing displays from the loan collection by artists including work by Barbara Hepworth, William Tucker, Grenville Davey and Sol Le Witt. In the adjacent 96 acre Bretton Country Park, there is a permanent exhibition of works by Henry Moore. Various special exhibitions. Please telephone for details.
Times: Open all year 10-6 (summer) 10-4 (winter). (Closed 25-26 & 31 Dec)
Fee: *Free. Car parking £1.50.
🅿 (charged) 💺 ♿ (scooters available for disabled) toilets for disabled shop

Guernsey

If it's sunshine, shopping and sea you're interested in, then the island of Guernsey is the ideal location for a break that combines the feeling of being abroad with the familiarity of the English language and British ways of life.

When William conquered England, he didn't need to conquer Guernsey. It was already part of the Duchy of Normandy. The strategic importance of the island has been recognised through the centuries, from the 13th-century Castle Cornet to the fortifications of the German occupying forces during WWII. There are also many ancient structures, some of which are believed to be among the oldest in Europe.

Guernsey enjoys some 2,000 hours of sunshine a year. This makes its 27 beaches great places to spend time. No matter which way the wind is blowing, you'll be sure to find one that's sheltered.

The island is also known for its conservation efforts. Both the National Trust and the home-grown Société Guernesiaise maintain some beautiful areas, including a wooded valley and a number of fields.

Shopping is a major attraction on Guernsey, not necessarily for what's on sale, although the shops cover a wide variety and some local specialities including Guernsey sweaters and flowers. The real attraction is the low local taxation and lack of VAT, which makes the island a bargain hunter's paradise.

Close to Guernsey are three smaller islands well worth visiting. Sark, Alderney and Aurigny. Sark was the setting for Mervyn Peake's novel, *Mr Pye*. It was also the location for the TV version starring Derek Jacobi.

EVENTS & FESTIVALS

April
Food & Wine Festival, restaurants compete to produce special menus
Guernsey Easter Runs, middle to long distance athletics

May
9th Liberation Day, 55th Anniversary, St Peter Port, cavalcade, entertainments

July
tbc International Folk Festival

August
9th-10th The South Show, Saumarez Manor, St Martins, agricultural show
16th-17th The West Show, L'Erçe Aerodrome, agricultural show
23rd-24th The North Show, Saumarez Park, Castel, agricultural show

September
3rd Church to Church Walk, 19 miles
tbc International Air Rally, Guernsey Aero Club

Top: Jerbourg Point, St Martin

ST PETER PORT

Guernsey's capital, St Peter Port, is imbued with charm - its cobbled streets, steep stairways and fine Regency and Victorian houses overlooking the bustling harbour. The town developed rapidly in the late 18th century as a result of privateering, this was a legally endorsed form of piracy, which permitted privately owned vessels under government license to plunder enemy ships. The pickings were very rich, and St Peter Port flourished. With the development of trade and an influx of residents following the Napoleonic Wars, the harbour was expanded to keep pace, with new jetties begun in 1853 increasing the harbour size dramatically.

🏛 FOREST
GERMAN OCCUPATION MUSEUM
GY8 0BG (Behind Forest Church near the airport)
☎ 01481 238205

The museum has the Channel Islands' largest collection of Occupation items, with tableaux of a kitchen, bunker rooms and a street during the Occupation. Telephone for details of special events.
Times: Open Apr-Oct 10-5. Nov-Mar, daily 10-1. Closed Mons.
Fee: *£2.50 (ch £1.25, ch under 5 free).
🅿 💻 ♿ (ramps & handrails)

🏛 ST ANDREW
GERMAN MILITARY UNDERGROUND HOPSITAL & AMMUNITION STORE
La Vassalerie GY6 8XR
☎ 01481 239100

The largest structure created during the German Occupation of the Channel Islands, a concrete maze of about 75,000sq ft, which took slave workers three-and-a-half years to complete, at the cost of many lives. Most of the equipment has been removed, but the central heating plant, hospital beds and cooking facilities can still be seen.
Times: Open Jul-Aug, daily 10-noon & 2-4.30; May-Jun & Sep, daily 10-noon & 2-4; Apr & Oct, daily 10am-12pm; Mar & Nov, Sun & Thu 2-3.
🅿 ♿ shop *Details not confirmed for 2000*

🏛 ST MARTIN
SAUSMAREZ MANOR
Sausmarez Rd GY4 6SG
☎ 01481 235571   🖷 01481 235572

The Manor has been owned by the same family for centuries. Each room is a happy contrast in style to its neighbour, with collections of Oriental, French and English furniture and paintings. Outside the Formal Garden has herbaceous borders, and the Woodland Garden, set around two small lakes and a stream, is planted with colourful shrubs, bulbs and wild flowers from the subtropics to give a jungle atmosphere. A 7.25-gauge ride-on railway runs for over a quarter of a mile over embankments and through cuttings.
Times: House open last BH in May-last Thu in Sep, Mon-Thur, 10.30-11.30 & 2-3. Also Apr-end of May & Oct, Mon-Thu mornings 10.30-11.30.
Fee: *House £4.50 (ch £2, pen £4). Woodland Garden £1.50(accompanied ch 50p, disabled free). Dolls House Collection £1.95 (ch 75p, concessions £1). Family ticket £5. Railway layout £1 (ch & pen 80p). Train rides £1 (ch & pen 80p). Petland £1.50. Family ticket £5.
🅿 💻 ♿ (free partial access to garden, close parking) shop (Specialises in dolls houses etc) 🐕 (ex dogs for blind and deaf)

🏛 ST PETER PORT
CASTLE CORNET
GY1 1UG (Half mile from St.Peter Port town centre at end of harbour breakwater)
☎ 01481 721657 📄 01481 715177

During the Civil War the castle was garrisoned by the Royalist governor of the island, and did not surrender until 1651. In 1940 the castle was taken over by German troops and adapted for modern warfare. Today it houses the new Maritime Museum, the Spencer collection of uniforms and badges, and the Royal Guernsey Militia Museum, Art Gallery. Special events during the season include outdoor theatre and a Tudor re-enactment camp.
Times: Open Apr-Oct, daily 10-5.
Fee: *£4 (students/pen £2). Joint ticket with Fort Grey & Guernsey Museum. Accompanied children under 12 & educational groups free
P (100 yds) (2 hr time zone, 10hr within 200 yards) 💻 shop ✖ (ex guide dogs) 🍴

GUERNSEY MUSEUM & ART GALLERY
Candie Gardens GY1 1UG
☎ 01481 726518 📄 01481 715177

The museum tells the story of Guernsey and its people, there's an audio-visual theatre and an art gallery, and there are special exhibitions throughout the year. It is surrounded by beautiful gardens with superb views over St Peter Port harbour.
Times: Open all year, daily 10-5 (summer), 10-4 (winter)
Fee: *£2.50 (pen £1.25). Joint ticket with Castle Cornet & Fort Grey £6 (pen £3). Students free.
P (outside museum) (2hr & 5hr) 💻 ♿ toilets for disabled shop ✖ 🍴

🏛 VALE
ROUSSE TOWER
Rousse Tower Headland

One of the original fifteen towers built in 1778-9 in prime defensive positions around the coast of Guernsey. They were designed primarily to prevent the landing of troops on nearby beaches. Musket fire could be directed on invading forces through the loopholes.
Times: Open 9-5.
P ✖

Jersey

The Channel Islands are renowned for their hospitality, prosperity and beauty, with their fine cliffs, sandy beaches, splendid harbours and impressive marinas.

EVENTS & FESTIVALS

April
6th-9th Fifteenth Jersey Jazz Festival, various venues

May
1st-14th (provisional) Environmental Festival 2000, Jersey Environmental Week
13th-21st Jersey International Food Festival

July
10th-15th Jersey Garden Festival

August
10th Jersey Battle of Flowers, parade of flower-festooned floats
11th Jersey Battle of Flowers Moonlight Parade

September
14th (provisional) International Air Display over St Aubins Bay

October
5th-8th Jersey Festival of World Music

The mild climate is conducive to enjoyable holidays, and ensures an abundance of flowers, fruit and vegetables. Notably the Channel Island tomato and the deliciously earthy early Jersey Royal potato, a delicacy in its own right with a knob of Jersey butter.

Like Guernsey, Jersey has its own breed of cow, and its own kind of sweater, the jersey, incorporating an anchor into its design under the neckline at the front. Agriculture and fishing are traditional industries. The conger eel is particularly associated with the island, and conger eel soup is a popular local dish.

Jersey is the largest of the Channel Islands, and the most southerly, just 30 miles (48km) from St Malo. The unique combination of the French and British ways of life contributes much to the island's undoubtable charm. The island is infused with Gallic culture, as you can see by the names of the streets and the baguettes in the bakers'. The local language is traditionally a Norman-French Patois, though this is in decline and English is generally spoken. The islands also have their own banknotes, though the currency is sterling.

The financial industry has transformed the lives of islanders, bringing great prosperity to its economy. Banks of all nationalities are in residence on the island, taking advantage of its low-tax base and proximity to the City of London. Checking out the multi-million pound properties of the rich and famous tax exiles is part of the sightseeing itinerary.

Top: Jersey States chamber, St Helier

⛰ GOREY
Mont Orgueil Castle
JE3 6ET (A3 or coast rd to Gorey)
☎ 01534 853292   ▤ 01534 854303

Standing on a rocky headland, on a site which has been fortified since the Iron Age, this is one of the best-preserved examples in Europe of a medieval concentric castle, and dates from the 12th and 13th centuries.
Times: Open daily throughout the year 9.30-6; Last admission 5pm. Times in winter change (Fri-Mon 10-dusk)
Fee: *£3.50 (ch 10-16, pen & students £2.50, ch 10 free). Three sites for two ticket £6.95 (concessions £4.95).
🅿 (200 yds) (discs required at harbour) shop ✖ (ex guide dogs) ◣

⛰ GROUVILLE
La Hougue Bie
JE2 7UA (A6 or A7 to Five Oaks then prines Tower rd)
☎ 01534 853823   ▤ 01534 856472

This Neolithic burial mound stands 40ft high, and covers a stone-built passage grave which is still intact and may be entered. The passage is 50ft long, and built of huge stones, the mound is made from earth, rubble and limpet shells. On top of the mound are two medieval chapels, one of which has a replica of the Holy Sepulchre in Jerusalem below. Also on the site is an underground bunker built by the Germans as a communications centre. It is now an Occupation museum. Contact the Jersey Museum for information on special events.
Times: Open 29 Mar-Oct daily 10-5.
Fee: *£3.50 (ch 10-16 & pen £2.50, ch 10 free). Discount ticket 3 sites for the price of 2 £6.95 (concessions £4.95).
🅿 ♿ shop ✖ (ex guide dogs) ◣

⛰ ST BRELADE
Jersey Lavender Farm
Rue du Pont Marquet JE3 8DS (on the B25 from St.Aubin's Bay to Redhouses)
☎ 01534 42933   ▤ 01534 45613

Here you can see the complete process of production from cultivation through to harvesting and distillation to the bottling, labelling and packaging of the final product. The National Collection of Lavandula is held here, there's a fine herb garden, an extensive collection of dwarf and slow-growing conifers in the Pygmy Pinetum and a collection of 63 varieties of bamboo.
Times: Open 19 May-20 Sep, Mon-Sat 10-5.
🅿 🍽 ♿ (wheelchair loan, wide doors, grab rails etc) toilets for disabled shop garden centre *Details not confirmed for 2000* ◣

⛰ ST CLEMENT
Samarès Manor
JE2 6QW (2m E of St.Helier on St.Clements inner rd)
☎ 01534 870551   ▤ 01534 768949

The manor stands in 14 acres of beautiful gardens. The Japanese Garden occupies an artificial hill, and has a series of waterfalls

cascading over Cumberland limestone. There's a craft centre, farm animals and a children's play area. Falconry displays mornings and afternoons except Sundays.
Times: Open 3 Apr-16 Oct.
Fee: *£3.70 (ch 16 £1.80, pen £2.95).
🅿 🍽 ✖ licensed ♿ toilets for disabled shop garden centre ✖ (ex guide dogs) ◣

⛰ ST HELIER
Elizabeth Castle
JE2 3WU (access by causeway or amphibious vehicle)
☎ 01534 23971   ▤ 01534 610338

The original Elizabethan fortress was extended in the 17th and 18th centuries, and then refortified by the Germans during the Occupation. Please telephone for details of the living history programme.
Times: Open 29 Mar-Oct, daily 9.30-6. Last admission 5.
Fee: *£3.50 (concessions £2.50, ch 10 free). Three sites for Two ticket £6.95 (concessions £4.95). Pre-booked group 15% discount.
🅿 (20 mins on seafront 🍽 ♿ shop ✖ (ex guide dogs) ◣

Jersey Museum
The Weighbridge JE2 3NF (near bus station on weighbridge)
☎ 01534 633300   ▤ 01534 633301

Home to 'The Story of Jersey', Jersey's art gallery, an exhibition gallery which features a changing programme, a lecture theatre, and an audio-visual theatre. Special exhibitions take place throughout the year.
Times: Open all year, daily 10-5. Winter daily 10-4. (Closed 24-27 & 31 Dec & 1-2 Jan).
Fee: *£3.50 (ch 10 free, concessions £2.50). Discount ticket for 3 sites for the price of 2 £6.95 (concessions £4.95).
🅿 (paycard at most public parking) ✖ licensed ♿ (audio loop, audio guide for partially sighted, car park) toilets for disabled shop ✖ (ex guide dogs) ◣

Occupation Tapestry Gallery
New North Quay JE2 3WD (alongside Marina, opposite Liberation Square)
☎ 01534 811043   ▤ 01534 874099

This converted 19th-century warehouse is home to the acclaimed Occupation Tapestry, and Maritime Museum. The tapestry consists of twelve two-metre panels and tells the story of the occupation of Jersey during World War II. Each of the twelve parishes took responsibility for the stitching of a panel, making it the largest community arts project ever undertaken on the island. The Maritime Museum celebrates the relationship of islanders and the sea.
Times: Open all year, daily 10-5 (winter closing at 4pm).
🅿 (paycards in public car parks) ♿ (braille books, audio guide etc) toilets for disabled shop ✖ *Details not confirmed for 2000* ◣

ST HELIER

The capital of Jersey, St Helier has a large harbour rising into an attractive town overlooked by a massive fortress. The town expanded rapidly in the late 18th century, grown rich on the plunder from enemy ships, liberated under the sanctions of privateering.

The French revolution brought an influx of some 4,000 refugees to Jersey, then the British garrison arrived, and an influx of Irish workers to construct the fort swelled the population further. Interestingly there is still a distinction between the French and Irish Catholics in the town today.

⛏ ST LAWRENCE

GERMAN UNDERGROUND HOSPITAL

Les Charrieres Malorey JE3 1FU

☎ 01534 863442   🖬 01534 865970

On 1 July 1940 the Channel Islands were occupied by German forces, and this vast complex dug deep into a hillside is the most evocative reminder of the Occupation. There is a video presentation which, along with a large collection of memorabilia, brings the experience of the Islanders at war to life and a further exhibition records the impressions of the islanders during 1945, the year of liberation.

Times: Open 15 Mar-8 Nov, daily 9.30-5.30 Last admission 4.15

Fee: *£4.80 (ch £2.40).

🅿 🖭 ✕ licensed ⓹ (ramp to restaurant & lift in Visitor Centre to restaurant) toilets for disabled shop ✖ 🝔

HAMPTONNE COUNTRY LIFE MUSEUM

La Rue de la Patente JE3 1HS (5m from St.Helier on A1, left up A10 and follow signs)

☎ 01534 863955   🖬 01534 863935

Here you will find a medieval 17th-century home, furnished in authentic style and surrounded by 19th-century farm buildings. Guided tours every day. Living history interpretation and daily demonstrations. Special events information is available from the Museum.

Times: Open 29 Mar-Oct, daily 10-4.

Fee: *£3.50 (ch 10-16 & concessions £2.50). Discount ticket 3

sites for the price of 2 available.

🅿 🖭 ⓹ toilets for disabled shop ✖ (ex guide dogs)

⛏ ST PETER

JERSEY MOTOR MUSEUM

St Peter's Village JE3 7AG (Jct off A12 & B41 at St Peters village)

☎ 01534 482966

The museum has a fine collection of motor vehicles from the early 1900s. There are also Allied and German military vehicles of World War II, a Jersey Steam Railway section, aero-engines and other items.

Times: Open end Mar-late Oct, daily 10-5. (Last admission 4.40).

Fee: *£2.50 (ch £1.20). Wheelchair users free.

🅿 ⓹ (access doors avoid turnstyles) shop ✖

ST PETER'S BUNKER MUSEUM

St Peters Village JE3 7AF (at junc of A12 & B41)

☎ 01534 23136   🖬 01534 23136

German uniforms, motorcycles, weapons, documents, photographs and other items from the 1940-45 Occupation are displayed in a wartime bunker which accommodated 36 men and could be sealed in case of attack.

Times: Open 29 Mar-Oct, daily 10-5.

Fee: *£2.50 (ch £1).

🅿 shop ✖

Isle of Man

Going to the Isle of Man is, in many ways, like visiting a foreign country. The island is not ruled by the British monarch, and has its own parliament (the Tynwald) which makes laws that apply only to the island.

The Isle of Man is only 33 miles by 13, yet packs in so much. Celtic crosses, ancient Viking burial grounds and medieval castles are all around, and the history of the island is well chronicled by the award-winning Manx Museum. Inside, visitors can explore the National Art Gallery, the Map Gallery with its large-scale relief map of the island, and see a specially-produced film, 'Story of Mann'.

One of the island's main attractions is its railway network, which began in 1873 and still runs a regular service. 19th-century electric and mountain railways are also still in operation. The Snaefell Mountain Railway is the only electric mountain railway in Britain, and starts its journey from Laxey, home of the Laxey Wheel, the world's largest working waterwheel. Douglas also has horse trams, which have been in operation since 1876, except for wartime breaks.

The island is probably best known for its TT (Tourist Trophy) racing, which is staged in May-June each year. The race, originally for cars only, has been run since 1904, and with motorbikes only since 1911. There are other races too. These include the Ramsey Sprint, the Manx Grand Prix, the Manx International Car Rally, and the Kart Racing Grand Prix.

EVENTS & FESTIVALS

January
1st Castletown Ale Drinkers Society New Year's Day Dip, Castletown

April
16th Passion Sunday Concert with Handel's Messiah, St Matthew's Church, Douglas
29th-1st May Visual Arts Festival, St Johns

May
29th-9th June TT Festival Fortnight

June
11th-17th Christian Celebration Week

July
2nd Rotoraid Fun Day, Ramsey
4th World Manx Gathering, Douglas
6th-10th Festival of the Sea, Peel Harbour

August
13th Isle of Man Marathon, Ramsey
19th Viking Longboat Races, Peel Bay
19th-26th International Viola Competition, Port Erin
26th Laxley Village Gathering

November
8th-12th Manan International Festival of Music & Arts, Port Erin

Top: The Laxey Waterwheel

DOUGLAS

Douglas, the island's capital, is a major centre of the off-shore finance industry and its streets bristle with financial consultancies. The town is also a resort in the Victorian mould, claiming most of the island's hotels and restaurants, an impressive promenade and seafront illuminations. Queen Victoria is commemorated by a statue on the seafront. More remnants of Victoria's reign include horse trams, and an electric railway that goes up Snaefell mountain and round the coast. The sandy beach, which often disappears at high tide, has plenty of rockpools for exploration.

⛪ CASTLETOWN
CASTLE RUSHEN
☎ 01624 648000   🖨 01624 648000

On view to the visitor are the state apartments of this 14th-century stronghold. There is also a Norman keep, flanked by towers from its later rebuilding, with a clock given by Elizabeth I in 1597.
Times: Open Etr-Sep, daily 10-5.
P (100 yds) ⅃ shop ✖ *Details not confirmed for 2000* 🖋

⛪ CREGNEISH
CREGNEASH VILLAGE FOLK MUSEUM
(2m from Port Erin/Port St Mary)
☎ 01624 648000   🖨 01624 648001

A group of traditional Manx cottages with their gardens and walled enclosures. Inside the cottages furniture and the everyday equipment used by typical Manx crofting communities are displayed. Spinning demonstrations are given on certain days and sometimes a blacksmith can be seen at work. In the field adjoining the turner's shed, Manx Loghtan sheep can often be seen - the rams have a tendency to produce four, or even six, horns.
Times: Open Etr-Sep, daily 10-5.
P 🅿 ✖ ⅃ shop ✖ (ex in grounds) *Details not confirmed for 2000* 🖋

⛪ DOUGLAS
MANX MUSEUM
☎ 01624 648000   🖨 01624 648000

The 'Story of Man' begins at Manx Museum, where a specially produced film portrayal of Manx history complements the award-winning gallery displays. This showcase of Manx heritage provides the ideal starting point to a journey of rich discovery embracing the length and breadth of the island.
Times: Open all year, Mon-Sat 10-5. (Closed Sun, Xmas, New Year, am of Tynwald Day 5 Jul).
P ✖ licensed ⅃ toilets for disabled shop ✖ *Details not confirmed for 2000* 🖋

⛪ LAXEY
GREAT LAXEY WHEEL & MINES TRAIL
☎ 01624 648000   🖨 01624 648001

Constructed to keep the lead mines free from water, this big wheel, known as the 'Lady Isabella', is an impressive sight at 72.5ft in diameter. It is the largest working wheel in the world.
Times: Open Etr-Sep, daily 10-5.
P ⅃ shop ✖ *Details not confirmed for 2000*

⛪ PEEL

HOUSE OF MANANNAN
(on quayside)
☎ 01624 648000 🖹 01624 648001

This is an unforgettable experience with interactive displays, using 'state of the art' technology. A visit to the House of Manannan leaves the visitor in awe of Manx heritage and eager to learn more.
Times: Open daily 10-5. Closed Xmas/New Year.
🅿 ♿ toilets for disabled shop ✖ *Details not confirmed for 2000* 🦐

PEEL CASTLE
(on Patricks Isle, facing Peel Bay)
☎ 01624 648000 🖹 01624 648000

The castle was built to protect the cathedral of St German's, perhaps founded by St Patrick, and contains ruins from the 11th century. A phantom black dog, the Moddey Dhoo, is said to haunt the castle.
Times: Open Etr-Sep, daily 10-5.
🅿 shop ✖ *Details not confirmed for 2000* 🦐

⛪ RAMSEY

'THE GROVE' RURAL LIFE MUSEUM
(on W side of Andreas Road)
☎ 01624 648000 🖹 01624 648000

An intimate glimpse into the everyday life of a previous era. Inside are many of the original furnishings and personal belongings of the former owners, the Gibb family, displayed among the minutiae of Victorian life, both upstairs and downstairs.
Times: Open Etr-Sep, daily 10-5.
🅿 💷 ✖ licensed ♿ shop ✖ *Details not confirmed for 2000* 🦐

⛪ SNAEFELL MOUNTAIN

MURRAY'S MUSEUM
Bungalow Corner (Junction A14 & A18)
☎ 01624 861719

The TT races are perhaps the best-known feature of the Isle of Man, and this historic collection of 150 motorcycles and cycles, plus memorabilia, is housed at The Bungalow corner on the TT course.
Times: Open 25 May-Sep daily 10-5.
🅿 💷 ♿ shop *Details not confirmed for 2000*

Scottish Highlands & Islands

Top: Eilean Donan Castle

Here is the Scotland portrayed on a million calendars - a landscape of extraordinary wildness and beauty - in parts barely populated, and sometimes more lunar than earthly in appearance.

The west coastline is a series of mountains and lochs, looking out over the Minches to the Hebrides. Great swathes of treeless moor cover the north. East of the Great Glen, the fault line that slashes across Scotland, the austere Grampian and Cairngorm mountains descend into the fertile coastlands of the Moray Firth and Aberdeenshire.

In the north are Orkney, and further north still, Shetland, islands with a Norse past, where settlers struggle to wrest a living from an inhospitable environment.

In the northeast of the mainland Aberdeen looks out over the North Sea, where the oil platforms pump ashore the wealth that transformed the city. Inland the twin rivers Dee and Don flow past countless castles, most notably Queen Victoria's holiday home, Balmoral.

Throughout the region are reminders of early inhabitants - Stone Age and Bronze Age sites, pre- and post-Christian Celtic stones, and the castles that signified clan strengths and prestige. Later history tends to melancholy and romance; the fate of Bonnie Prince Charlie and the Highland Clearances are still topics of debate.

This area has some incomparable scenery, but be warned: The weather can change quickly, and the midges have a fierce bite!

The directory which follows has been divided into three geographical regions. Counties have not been shown against individual locations as recent legislation has created a number of smaller counties which will be unfamiliar to the visitor. The postal authorities have confirmed that it is no longer necessary to include a county name in addresses, provided a post code is shown.

This region includes the counties of Aberdeen City, Aberdeenshire, Highland, Moray, Orkney, Shetland and Western Isles which reflect the recent national changes.

ABERDEEN
ABERDEEN ART GALLERY
Schoolhill AB10 1FQ
☎ 01224 523700 ▯ 01224 632133

The gallery's 16th to 20th-century Scottish art includes an outstanding collection of modern paintings. Also here are watercolours, sculpture and decorative arts, and a print room and art library.
Times: Open all year, Mon-Sat 10-5, Sun 2-5. (Closed 25-26 Dec & 1-2 Jan).
Fee: Free.
P (500yds) ▰ & toilets for disabled shop ✕

ABERDEEN MARITIME MUSEUM
Provost Ross's House, Shiprow AB11 5BY
☎ 01224 585788 ▯ 01224 632133

The museum is in Provost Ross's House, Aberdeen's oldest building (1593). It highlights the city's maritime history, and its oil industry.
Times: Open all year, Mon-Sat 10-5 (Closed 25-26 Dec & 1,2 Jan).
P 250yds ▰ ✕ licensed & toilets for disabled shop ✕
Details not confirmed for 2000 ▱

CRUICKSHANK BOTANIC GARDEN
University of Aberdeen, St Machar Drive, AB24 3UU (enter by gate in Chanonry, in Old Aberdeen)
☎ 01224 272704 ▯ 01224 272703

Developed at the end of the 19th century, the 11 acres include rock and water gardens, a rose garden, a fine herbaceous border, an arboretum and a patio garden. There are collections of spring bulbs, gentians and alpine plants, and a fine array of trees and shrubs.
Times: Open all year, Mon-Fri 9-4.30; also Sat & Sun, May-Sep 2-5.
P (200metres) (residents only in immediate vicinity) & ✕
Details not confirmed for 2000

PROVOST SKENE'S HOUSE
Guestrow, (off Broad St) AB10 1AS
☎ 01224 641086

The handsome 16th-century town mansion has notable decorated ceilings and panelling, and is now a museum of local history and social life, with rooms furnished in period style. The Costume Gallery presents a changing programme of exhibitions based on the museum's extensive costume collection.
Times: Open all year, Mon-Sat 10-5, Sun 1-4. (Closed 25-26 Dec & 1-2 Jan)
Fee: *£2.50 (concessions £1.50). Family ticket £6.
P (200yds) ▰ & ✕

THE TOLBOOTH
Castle St
☎ 01224 621167

Aberdeen's Museum of Civic history is housed in the city's former Wardhouse, which served as a prison for Aberdeenshire. The Tolbooth tells the stories of prisoners incarcerated there and the ingenious ways in which some of them escaped. Also featured is the story of local government from the 14th century.
Times: Open Apr-Sep, Mon-Sat 10-5, Sun 12.30-3.30.
Fee: *£2.50 (concessions £1.50). Family ticket £6.
P (250yds) (NCP car park) & (lift to top floor) shop ✕

ARNOL
BLACK HOUSE MUSEUM
PA86 9DB
☎ 01851 710395

A traditional Hebridean dwelling, built without mortar and roofed with thatch on a timber framework. It has a central peat fire in the kitchen, no chimney and a byre under the same roof.
Times: Open Apr-Sep, Mon-Sat 9.30-6.30; Oct-Mar, Mon-Thu & Sat 9.30-4.30.
P & shop ✕ ▮ *Details not confirmed for 2000*

AVIEMORE
STRATHSPEY STEAM RAILWAY
Aviemore Station, Dalfaber Rd PH22 1PY (off B970)
☎ 01479 810725

This steam railway covers the five miles from Boat of Garten to Aviemore. The journey takes about 20 minutes, but allow around an hour for the round trip. Timetables are available from the station and the tourist information centre. Special events take place, telephone for details.
Times: Open Jun-Sep daily. Diesel service on Sats & selected days 28 Mar-Oct, (including every weekend, Wed & Thu between these dates)
Fee: *£5 Basic return; £12.50 Family return.
P ▰ & toilets for disabled shop ▱

BALLINDALLOCH
THE GLENLIVET DISTILLERY
AB37 9DB (Off B9008 10m N of Tomintoul).
☎ 01542 783220 ▯ 01542 783218

The visitor centre includes a guided tour of the whisky production facilities and a chance to see inside the vast bonded warehouses where the spirit matures. The new multimedia exhibition and interactive presentations communicate the

contd.

unique history, and traditions of Glenlivet Scotch Whisky.

Times: Open: mid Mar-end Oct, Mon-Sat 10-4, Sun 12.30-4. Jul & Aug remains open until 6 daily.

Fee: *£2.50 for over 18's which includes £2 voucher redeemable in distillery shop against the purchase of a 70cl bottle of whisky. This charge covers entry to exhibition, guided tour of Distillery & a free dram of whisky. (ch18 free, under 8's not admitted to production areas)

🅿 ◾ ♿ toilets for disabled shop 🐕 ⬛

🏛 BALMACARA
BALMACARA (LOCHALSH WOODLAND GARDEN)
IV40 8DN (3m E of Kyle of Lochalsh, off A87)
☎ 01599 566325   📠 01599 566359

The Balmacara estate comprises some 5,600 acres and seven crofting villages, including Plockton, a conservation area. There are excellent views of Skye, Kintail and Applecross. The main attraction is the Lochalsh Woodland Garden, but the whole area is excellent for walking.

Times: Open all year daily 9-sunset.
🅿 ♨ *Details not confirmed for 2000*

🏛 BALMORAL
BALMORAL CASTLE GROUNDS & EXHIBITION
AB35 5TB (on A93 between Ballater & Braemar)
☎ 013397 42334 & 42335
📠 013397 42271

Queen Victoria and Prince Albert first rented Balmoral Castle in 1848, and Prince Albert bought the property four years later. He commissioned William Smith to build a new castle, which was completed by 1856 and is still the Royal Family's Highland residence. Country walks and pony trekking can be enjoyed, and an exhibition of paintings and other works of art can be seen in the castle ballroom, together with a Travel and Carriage exhibition and a wildlife exhibition.

Times: Open 7 Apr-Jul Mon-Sat 10-5.
Fee: *£4 (ch under 16 £1, pen £3)
🅿 (150yds) ◾♿ (wheelchairs available & free parking enquire at main gate) toilets for disabled shop 🐕 (ex guide dogs) ⬛

🏛 BANCHORY
BANCHORY MUSEUM
Bridge St AB31 5SX
☎ 01771 622906   📠 01771 622884

The museum has displays of Scott Skinner (The 'Strathspey King'), natural history, royal commemorative china, local silver artefacts among many other exhibits.

Times: Open Etr-May & Oct, wknds & public holidays 11-1 & 2-5; Jun-Sep, Mon-Sat 10-1 & 2-5, Sun 2-6.
Fee: Free.
🅿 (100yds) (limited) ♿ (toilet in staff area, ask attendant) toilets for disabled shop 🐕 (ex guide dogs)

🏛 BANFF
BANFF MUSEUM
High St AB45 1AE
☎ 01771 622906   📠 01771 622884

Displays of geology and natural history, local history, Banff silver, arms and armour, and displays relating to James Ferguson (18th-century astronomer) and Thomas Edward (19th-century Banff naturalist).

Times: Open Jun-Sep, Fri-Wed 2-5.15.
Fee: Free.
🅿 (200yds) ♿ shop 🐕 (ex guide dogs)

DUFF HOUSE
AB45 3SX (0.5m S, access south of town).
☎ 01261 818181   📠 0131 244 3030

The house was designed by William Adam for William Duff, later Earl of Fife. The main block was roofed in 1739, but the planned wings were never built. Although it is incomplete, the house is still considered one of Britain's finest Georgian baroque buildings.

Times: Under repair, interior not accessible, can be viewed from outside.
🅿 🐕 ⬛

🏛 BIRSAY
EARL'S PALACE
KW15 1PD
☎ 0131 668 8800   📠 0131 668 8888

The gaunt remains of the residence of the late 16th-century Earl of Orkney, constructed round a courtyard.

Times: Open all year.
🐕 ⬛ *Details not confirmed for 2000*

🏛 BOAT OF GARTEN
RSPB NATURE RESERVE ABERNETHY FOREST
Forest Lodge PH25 3EF (signposted from B970)
☎ 01479 831694

Home of the Loch Garten Osprey site, this reserve holds one of most important remnants of Scots Pine forest in the Highlands. Within its 30,760 acres are forest bogs, moorland, mountain top, lochs and crofting land. In addition to the regular pair of nesting ospreys, there are breeding colonies of Scottish crossbill, capercaillies, black grouse and many others. The

ospreys can be viewed through telescopes and there is a live TV link to the nest.
Times: Reserve open at all times. Osprey Centre daily, end Apr-Aug 10-6.
P shop *Details not confirmed for 2000*

BRODIE CASTLE
BRODIE CASTLE
IV36 0TE (4.5m W of Forres, off A96)
☎ 01309 641371 01309 641600

The Brodie family lived here for hundreds of years before passing the castle to the NTS in 1980. It contains many treasures, including furniture, porcelain and paintings. The extensive grounds include a woodland walk and an adventure playground. Wheelchairs for disabled visitors are available. Please telephone for details of recitals, concerts, open air theatre etc.
Times: Open Apr-30 Sep, Mon-Sat 11-5.30, Sun 1.30-5.30; wknds in Oct, Sat 11-5.30, Sun 1.30-5.30. (last admission 4.30). Grounds open all year, 9.30-sunset. Other times by appointment.
P ♿ (audio tape & information sheet in Braille) toilets for disabled shop (ex guide dogs) *Details not confirmed for 2000*

BUCKIE
BUCKIE DRIFTER MARITIME HERITAGE CENTRE
Freuchny Rd AB56 1TT (1m off the A98 between Elgin and Fraserburgh)
☎ 01542 834646 01542 835995

An exciting maritime heritage centre, where you can discover what life was like in the fishing communities of Moray District during the herring boom years of the 1890s and 1930s. Sign on as a crew member of a steam drifter and find out how to catch herring. Try your hand at packing fish in a barrel.
Times: Open Apr-Oct, Mon-Sat 10-5, Sun 12-5.
Fee: *£2.75 (concessions £1.75).
P licensed ♿ (car parking, touch display on lower floor) toilets for disabled shop (ex guide dogs)

CALLANISH
CALLANISH STANDING STONES
PA86 9DY (12m W of Stornoway)
☎ 0131 668 8800 0131 668 8888

An avenue of 19 monoliths leads north from a circle of 13 stones with rows of more stones fanning out to south, east and west. Probably constructed between 3000 and 1500BC, this is a unique cruciform of megaliths.
Times: Open & accessible at all times.
P

CARLOWAY
DUN CARLOWAY BROCH
(1.5m S of Carloway)
☎ 0131 668 8800 0131 668 8888

Brochs are late-prehistoric circular stone towers, and their origins are mysterious. One of the best examples can be seen at Dun Carloway, where the tower still stands about 30ft high.
Times: Open at all reasonable times.
P

CAWDOR
CAWDOR CASTLE
IV12 5RD (on B9090 off A96)
☎ 01667 404615 01667 404674

Home of the Thanes of Cawdor since the 14th century, this lovely castle has a drawbridge, an ancient tower built round a tree, and a freshwater well inside the house. Gardens Weekend takes place in June - guided tours of gardens and Bluebell Walk in Cawdor Big Wood.
Times: Open May-8 Oct, daily 10-5.30. (Last admission 5pm).
Fee: *£5.40 (ch 5-15 £2.80, pen £4.40). Family ticket £14.50. Party 20+. Gardens, grounds & nature trails only £2.80.
P ♿ toilets for disabled shop (ex guide dogs)

CLAVA CAIRNS
CLAVA CAIRNS
(6m E of Inverness)
☎ 0131 668 8800 0131 668 8888

On the south bank of the River Nairn, this group of circular burial cairns is surrounded by three concentric rings of great stones. It dates from around 1600BC, and ranks among Scotland's finest prehistoric monuments.
Times: Open all times.
P

CORGARFF
CORGARFF CASTLE
(8m W of Strathdon village)
☎ 01975 651460

The 16th-century tower was beseiged in 1571 and is associated with the Jacobite risings of 1715 and 1745. It later became a military barracks. Its last military use was to control the smuggling of whisky between 1827 and 1831.
Times: Open Apr-Sep, Mon-Sat 9.30-6.30, Sun 2-6.30; Oct-Mar Sat 9.30-4.30, Sun 2-4.30.
P *Details not confirmed for 2000*

CRAIGELLACHIE

SPEYSIDE COOPERAGE VISITOR CENTRE

Dufftown Rd AB38 9RS (1m S of Craigellachie
on A941)

☎ 01340 871108 ▤ 01340 881437

A working cooperage with unique visitor centre,
where skilled coopers and their apprentices
practise this ancient craft. Each year they repair
around 100,000 oak casks which will be used to
mature many different whiskies. The 'Acorn to
Cask' exhibition traces the history and
development of this industry and includes a
Victorian cooperage with life-size models which
speak in the local dialect.

Times: Open all year ex Christmas and New Year, Mon-Fri
9.30-4.30, also Jun-Sep on Sat 9.30-4.

Fee: *£2.95 (ch £1.75 & pen £2.45). Family ticket £6.75.
Party 15+.

🅿 ♿ (Special picnic table) toilets for disabled shop ✖ (ex
guide dogs)

CRATHES

CRATHES CASTLE & GARDENS

AB31 3QJ (On A93, 3m E of Banchory)

☎ 01330 844525 ▤ 01330 844797

This impressive 16th-century castle with
magnificent interiors has royal associations
dating from 1323. There is a large walled garden
and a notable collection of unusual plants,
including yew hedges dating from 1702. The
grounds contain six nature trails, one suitable for
disabled visitors, and an adventure playground.

Times: Open: Castle & Visitor Centre Apr-Oct, daily 11-5.30.
Last admission 4.45). Garden & grounds open all year, daily
9.30-sunset. Admission to castle by timed ticket arrangement.
(entry may be delayed on busy days)

🅿 ✖ licensed ♿ (tape for visually impaired) toilets for
disabled shop ✖ (ex guide dogs) ❦ *Details not confirmed for
2000*

CROMARTY

HUGH MILLER'S COTTAGE

Church St IV11 8XA

☎ 01381 600245

The cottage houses an exhibition on the life and
work of Hugh Miller, a stonemason born here in
1802 who became an eminent geologist and
writer. It was built by his great-grandfather
around 1698, and now has a charming cottage
garden.

Times: Open May-Sep, Mon-Sat 11-1 & 2-5, Sun 2-5.

🅿 (5mins) (disabled is directly outside) ✖ (ex guide dogs) ❦
Details not confirmed for 2000

CULLODEN MOOR

CULLODEN BATTLEFIELD

1V1 2ED (5m E of Inverness)

☎ 01463 790607 ▤ 01463 794294

A cairn recalls this last battle fought on mainland
Britain, on 16 April 1746, when `Bonnie' Prince
Charles Edward Stuart's army was routed by the
Duke of Cumberland's forces. The battlefield has
been restored to its state on the day of the battle,
and in summer there are 'living history'

enactments. This is a most atmospheric
evocation of tragic events. Telephone for details
of guided tours, etc.

Times: Open - site always. Visitor Centre open Feb-Mar &
Nov-30 Dec, daily 10-4. (Closed 25 & 26 Dec, shop closed 1-7
Nov); Apr-Oct, daily 9-6; Audio visual show closed 30 mins
before Visitor Centre.

🅿 ✖ ♿ (wheelchair, induction loop for hard of
hearing,raised map). toilets for disabled shop ✖ (ex guide
dogs) ❦ *Details not confirmed for 2000*

DOUNBY

BROUGH OF BIRSAY

(6m NW)

☎ 0131 668 8800 ▤ 0131 668 8888

This ruined Romanesque church stands next to
the remains of a Norse village. The nave, chancel
and semicircular apse can be seen, along with
claustral buildings. Crossings must be made on
foot at low-water - there is no boat.

Times: Open at all reasonable times.

🚩

CLICK MILL

(NE of village, off B9057)

☎ 0131 668 8800 ▤ 0131 668 8888

This is an example of the rare Orcadian
horizontal watermill, and is in working condition.

Times: Open at all reasonable time.

🚩

SKARA BRAE

(9m W of Kirkwall on A965)

☎ 01856 841815

Engulfed in drift sand, this remarkable group of
well-preserved Stone Age dwellings is the most
outstanding survivor of its kind in Britain. Stone
furniture and a fireplace can be seen.

Times: Open all year, Apr-Sep, Mon-Sat 9.30-6.30, Sun 2-
6.30; Oct-Mar, Mon-Sat 9.30-4.30, Sun 2-4.30. (Closed 25-26
Dec & 1-3 Jan).

🅿 ✖ 🚩 *Details not confirmed for 2000*

DRUMNADROCHIT

OFFICIAL LOCH NESS MONSTER EXHIBITION

Loch Ness Centre IV3 6TU (on A82)

☎ 01456 450573 & 450218
▤ 01456 450770

A fascinating multi-media presentation lasting 40
minutes. Ten themed areas cover the story from
the pre-history of Scotland, through the cultural
roots of the legend in Highland folklore, and into
the fifty-year controversy which surrounds it.

Times: Open all year; Etr-May 9.30-5.30; Jun-Sep 9.30-6 (9-
8.30 Jul & Aug); Winter 10-4. Last admission 1hr before
closing.

🅿 🅿 ✖ licensed ♿ (parking) toilets for disabled shop ✖
(ex in grounds) *Details not confirmed for 2000*

URQUHART CASTLE
(on A82)
☎ 01456 450551

The castle was once Scotland's biggest and overlooks Loch Ness. It dates mainly from the 14th century, when it was built on the site of an earlier fort, and was destroyed before the 1715 Jacobite rebellion.
Times: Open all year, Apr-Sep, daily 9.30-6.30; Oct-Mar, Mon-Sat 9.30-4.30, Sun 9.30-4.30. (Closed 25-26 Dec & 1-2 Jan).
P shop ✖ ⊪ *Details not confirmed for 2000*

⛫ DUFFTOWN
BALVENIE CASTLE
AB55 4DH
☎ 01340 820121

The ruined castle was the ancient stronghold of the Comyns, and became a stylish house in the 16th century.
Times: Open Apr-Sep, Mon-Sat 9.30-6.30, Sun 2-6.30.
P ⅲ shop ⊪ *Details not confirmed for 2000*

GLENFIDDICH DISTILLERY
AB55 4DH (N of town, off A941)
☎ 01340 820373 ▤ 01340 820805

Set close to Balvenie Castle, the distillery was founded in 1887 by William Grant and has stayed in the hands of the family ever since. Visitors can see the whisky-making process in its various stages, including bottling, and then sample the finished product.
Times: Open all year Mon-Fri 9.30-4.30, also Etr-mid Oct Sat 9.30-4.30, Sun 12-4.30. (Closed Xmas & New Year).
Fee: *Free at the moment, issue of charging currently under review as all other distilleries charge admission.
P ⅲ (ramp access to production area & warehouse gallery) toilets for disabled shop ✖ (ex guide dogs)

⛫ DUFFUS
DUFFUS CASTLE
(off B9012)
☎ 0131 668 8800 ▤ 0131 668 8888

The remains of the mighty motte-and-bailey castle are surrounded by a moat. Within the eight-acre bailey is a 15th-century hall, and the motte is crowned by a 14th-century tower.
Times: Open at all reasonable times.
P ✖ ⊪

⛫ ELGIN
ELGIN CATHEDRAL
North College St IV30 1EL
☎ 01343 547171

Founded in 1224, the cathedral was known as the Lantern of the North and the Glory of the Kingdom because of its beauty. In 1390 it was burnt, along with most of the town. Although it was rebuilt, it fell into ruin after the Reformation. The ruins are quite substantial, however, and there is still a good deal to admire, including the fine west towers and the octagonal chapter house.
Times: Open all year, Apr-Sep, Mon-Sat 9.30-6.30, Sun 2-6.30; Oct-Mar, Mon-Sat 9.30-4.30, Sun 2-4.30. (Closed Thu pm & Fri in winter; 25-26 Dec & 1-3 Jan).
P shop ⊪ *Details not confirmed for 2000*

PLUSCARDEN ABBEY
IV30 8UA (6m SW on unclassified road)
☎ 01343 890257 ▤ 01343 890258

The original monastery was founded by Alexander II in 1230 and then burnt, probably by the Wolf of Badenoch who also destroyed Elgin Cathedral. It was restored in the 14th and 19th centuries, and then reoccupied in 1948 by Benedictines from Prinknash. Once more a religious community, retreat facilities are available for men and women. All services (with Gregorian chant) are open to the public. Pluscarden Pentecost Lectures are held annually on Tuesday, Wednesday and Thursday after Pentecost.
Times: Open all year, daily 4.45-8.30.
Fee: Free.
P ⅲ (induction loop, ramps to shop) toilets for disabled shop

⛫ FETTERCAIRN
FASQUE
AB30 1DN (0.5m N on B974)
☎ 01561 340569 & 340202
▤ 01561 340325 & 340569

Fasque has been the home of the Gladstone family since 1829, and W E Gladstone, four times Prime Minister, lived here from 1830 to 1851. There are impressive state rooms and a handsome, sweeping staircase, as well as extensive servants' quarters. The spacious park has red deer and Soay sheep.
Times: Open May-Sep, daily 11-5.30. (Last admission 5pm).
Fee: *£3.50 (ch £1, concessions £2.50). Party by arrangement.
P ⅷ ⅲ (wheelchairs available) shop ✖

⛫ FINSTOWN
MAES HOWE CHAMBERED CAIRN
(9m W of Kirkwall, on A965)
☎ 01856 761606

The masonry of Britain's finest megalithic tomb is in a remarkable state of preservation. Dating from neolithic times, it contains Viking carvings and runes.
Times: Open all year, Apr-Sep, Mon-Sat 9.30-6.30, Sun 2-6.30; Oct-Mar, Mon-Sat 9.30-4.30, (ex closed Wed & Thur am), Sun 2-4.30. (Closed 25-26 Dec & 1-3 Jan).
P ⅲ shop ✖ ⊪ *Details not confirmed for 2000*

STENNESS STANDING STONES
(3m SW off A965)
☎ 0131 668 8800 ▤ 0131 668 8888

Dating back to the second millennium BC, the remains of this stone circle are near the Ring of Brogar - a splendid circle of upright stones surrounded by a ditch.
Times: Open at any reasonable time.
P ⊪

▦ FORRES
DALLAS DHU DISTILLERY
(1m S of Forres of the Grantown road)
☎ 01309 676548

A perfectly preserved time capsule of the distiller's art. It was built in 1898 to supply malt whisky for Wright and Greig's 'Roderick Dhu' blend. Visitors are welcome to wander at will through this fine old Victorian distillery, or to take a guided tour, dram included.
Times: Open all year, Apr-Sep, Mon-Sat 9.30-6.30, Sun 2-6.30. Oct-Mar, Mon-Sat 9.30-4.30, Sun 2-4.30. (Closed Thu pm & Fri in winter, 25 & 26 Dec, 1 & 3 Jan).
P ♿ toilets for disabled shop ✖ ◪ *Details not confirmed for 2000*

FALCONER MUSEUM
Tolbooth St IV36 1PH (on A96)
☎ 01309 673701   ▤ 01309 675863

Founded by bequests made by two brothers, Alexander and Hugh Falconer. Hugh was a distinguished scientist, friend of Darwin, recipient of many honours and Vice-President of the Royal Society. On display are fossil mammals collected by him, and items relating to his involvement in the antiquity of mankind. Other displays are on local wildlife, geology, archaeology and history. Regular temporary exhibitions are held throughout the year.
Times: Open 12 Mar-16 Apr Mon-Sat 10-5, closed 2 Apr; 19 Apr-30 Apr Mon-Fri 10-5; 4 May-23 Oct Mon-Sat 10-5; 25 Oct-29 Oct Mon-Fri 10-5; Nov-Dec Mon-Thu 11-1 & 2-4.
Fee: Free.
P (100yds) ♿ shop ✖ (ex guide dogs)

SUENOS' STONE
☎ 0131 668 8800   ▤ 0131 668 8888

The 20ft-high stone was elaborately carved in the 9th or 10th century, with a sculptured cross on one side and groups of warriors on the other. Why it stands here no one knows, but it may commemorate a victory in battle.
Times: Open & accessible at all times.
P ✖ ◪

▦ FORT GEORGE
FORT GEORGE
IV1 2TD (11m NE of Inverness)
☎ 01667 462777

Built following the Battle of Culloden as a Highland fortress for the army of George II, this is one of the outstanding artillery fortifications in Europe and still an active army barracks.
Times: Open all year, Apr-Sep, Mon-Sat 9.30-6.30, Sun 2-6.30; Oct-Mar, Mon-Sat 9.30-4.30, Sun 2-4.30. (Closed 25-26 Dec & 1-3 Jan).
P ♿ toilets for disabled shop ✖ ◪ *Details not confirmed for 2000*

QUEEN'S OWN HIGHLANDERS REGIMENTAL MUSEUM COLLECTION
IV1 2TD
☎ 01463 224380   ▤ 01463 224380

Fort George has been a military barracks since it was built in 1748-1769, and was the Depot of the Seaforth Highlanders until 1961. The museum of the Queen's Own Highlanders (Seaforth and Camerons) is sited in the former Lieutenant Governor's house, where uniforms, medals and pictures are displayed.
Times: Open Apr-Sep, Mon-Sat 10-6, Sun 2-6; Oct-Mar, Mon-Fri 10-4. (Closed Good Fri-Etr Mon, Xmas, New Year & BH).
P ♿ (stair lift to 1st floor, wheelchair on 1st floor) toilets for disabled shop ✖ (ex guide dogs) *Details not confirmed for 2000*

▦ FORT WILLIAM
INVERLOCHY CASTLE
PH33 6SN (2m NE)
☎ 0131 668 8800   ▤ 0131 668 8888

The castle was begun in the 13th century and added to later. It is noted in Scottish history for the battle fought nearby in 1645, when Montrose defeated the Campbells.
Times: Open Apr-Sep. Key available from keykeeper.
✖ ◪

▦ GLENCOE
GLENCOE VISITOR CENTRE
PA39 4HX (on A82, 17m S of Fort William)
☎ 01855 811307   ▤ 01855 811772

Glencoe has stunning scenery and some of the most challenging climbs and walks in the Highlands. Red deer, wildcats, eagles and ptarmigan are among the wildlife. It is, however, also forever known as a place of treachery and infamy. The Macdonalds of Glencoe were hosts to a party of troops who, under government orders, fell upon them – men, women and children – in a bloody massacre in 1692. The Visitor Centre tells the story.
Times: Open; Site all year. Visitor Centre Apr-18 May & Sep-Oct, daily 10-5; 19 May-Aug, daily 9.30-5.30. (last admission 30 mins before closing).
P ◪ ♿ (induction loop in video programme room) toilets for disabled shop ✖ (ex guide dogs) ♨ *Details not confirmed for 2000*

HIGHLAND MYSTERYWORLD
PA39 4HL (on A82, 10m S of Fort William)
☎ 01855 811660   ▤ 01855 821463

In a spectacular location at the foot of Glencoe, Highland Mysteryworld explores the myths and legends of the past, with actors and animatronic effects. The indoor attractions include the Astromyth Theatre, Clootie Well and Mysterymall.
Times: Open mid Mar-end Oct, daily, peak 10-6, off peak 10-4.
P ◪ ✖ licensed ♿ toilets for disabled shop ◣

INVERNESS

Geography made Inverness the crossroads of the north. Here the Great Glen emerges from the mountains and meets the sea. The Caledonian Canal, the railways and the roads (civil and military) crossed here. After the Battle of Culloden in 1746, Fort George was built to maintain the crown's grip on the north. The town is still a busy interchange, with port, airport and station. It straddles the River Ness, affording fine walks along the banks under the much rebuilt castle. Easy day trips take you to Loch Ness, Cawdor Castle, the Black Isle and Culloden. If you get the chance, look for the dolphins in the Moray Firth.

GLENFINNAN

GLENFINNAN MONUMENT
PH37 4LT (on A830, 18.5m W of Fort William)
☎ 01397 722250

The monument commemorates Highlanders who fought for Bonnie Prince Charlie in 1745. It stands in an awe-inspiring setting at the head of Loch Shiel. There is a visitor centre with information (commentary in four languages) on the Prince's campaign.
Times: Open - Site all year. Visitor Centre, Apr-18 May & 1 Sep-Oct, daily 10-1 & 2-5; 19 May-Aug, daily 10-6.
🅿 ♿ (information centre only) shop ⚘ *Details not confirmed for 2000*

GOLSPIE

DUNROBIN CASTLE
KW10 6SF (1m NE on A9)
☎ 01408 633177 & 633268
🖨 01408 633800

The ancient seat of the Earls and Dukes of Sutherland is a splendid, gleaming, turreted structure, thanks largely to 19th-century rebuilding, and has a beautiful setting overlooking the sea. Paintings, furniture and family heirlooms are on display, and the gardens are on a grand scale to match the house.
Times: Open Etr-15 Oct, Mon-Sat 10.30-5.30, Sun 12-5.30. Closes 1 hr earlier Etr, May & Oct. Last admission half hour before closing.
Fee: *£5.50 (ch & pen £4). Family ticket £16. Party.
🅿 ♿ (access by arrangement only) shop ✖

HELMSDALE

TIMESPAN
Dunrobin St KW8 6JX (off A9 in centre of village, by Telford Bridge)
☎ 01431 821327

The dramatic story of the Highlands, from Picts and Vikings, to the last burning of a witch and the Highland Clearances, through to crofting, fishing and the present day oil fields. Scenes from the past are re-created using life-size sets, sound effects, and an audio-visual programme.
Times: Open Etr-mid Oct, Mon-Sat 9.30-5, Sun 2-5 (6pm Jul-Aug). Last admission one hour before closing.
Fee: *£3.50 (ch £1.75 pen & student £2.80). Family ticket £8.75.
🅿 ♿ (lifts) toilets for disabled shop garden centre ✖ (ex guide dogs) ▰

HUNTLY

HUNTLY CASTLE
AB54 4SH
☎ 01466 793191

The original medieval castle was rebuilt a number of times and destroyed, once by Mary, Queen of Scots. It was rebuilt for the last time in 1602, in palatial style, and is now an impressive ruin, noted for its ornate heraldic decorations. It stands in wooded parkland.
Times: Open all year, Apr-Sep, Mon-Sat 9.30-6.30, Sun 2-6.30; Oct-Mar, Mon-Sat 9.30-4.30, Sun 2-4.30. (Closed Thu pm & Fri in winter; 25-26 Dec & 1-3 Jan).
🅿 ▯ *Details not confirmed for 2000*

INVERNESS
CASTLE STUART
Petty Parish IV1 2JH (5m E of Inverness, off A96)
☎ 01463 790745   ▤ 01463 792604

Ancient home of the Earls of Moray and the Stuart family, built in 1621, and located within the sound of the cannon's roar from High Culloden Moor, where the last attempt to restore the Stuart monarchy ended in defeat. The interior has been restored, with Jacobean furnishings, armour and historic relics.
Times: Open all year, daily 10-5.
🅿 shop ✖ *Details not confirmed for 2000* ▼

INVERURIE
CARNEGIE MUSEUM
Town House, The Square
☎ 01771 622906   ▤ 01771 622884

This fine museum displays canal relics and items on local history and archaeology.
Times: Open all year, Mon-Tue & Thu-Fri 2-5, Sat 10-1 & 2-4. (Closed Wed & Sun)
Fee: Free.
🅿 (50yds) shop ✖ (ex guide dogs)

KEITH
STRATHISLA DISTILLERY
Seafield Av AB55 5BS (0ff A96, in town)
☎ 01542 783044   ▤ 01542 783039

Tour the oldest distillery in the Highlands, founded in 1786. Discover the art of the blender before sipping a dram in luxurious comfort.
Times: Open Feb-mid Mar, Mon-Fri 9.30-4; mid Mar-end Nov, Mon-Sat 9.30-4, Sun 12.30-4.
Fee: *£4 including £2 voucher redeemable in the distillery shop against the purchase of 70cl bottle of whisky. (ch18 free, children under 8 are not admitted to production areas, but are welcome in the centre)
🅿 (access is very limited) shop ✖ (ex guide dogs) ▼

KEMNAY
CASTLE FRASER
AB51 7LD (off A944, 4m N of Dunecht)
☎ 01330 833463

The massive Z-plan castle was built between 1575 and 1636 and is one of the grandest of the Castles of Mar. The interior was remodelled in 1838 and decoration and furnishings of that period survive in some of the rooms. A formal garden inside the old walled garden, estate trails, a children's play area and a programme of concerts and other events are among the attractions.
Times: Open - Castle Good Fri-Etr Mon, May-Jun & Sep, daily 1.30-5.30; Jul-Aug, daily 11-5.30; wknds in Oct 1.30-5.30 (last admission 4.45). Garden all year, daily 9.30-6; Grounds all year daily 9.30-sunset.
🅿 ⬛ ♿ shop garden centre ✖ (ex guide dogs, certain areas) ♨ *Details not confirmed for 2000*

KILDRUMMY
KILDRUMMY CASTLE
AB54 7XT (10m W of Alford)
☎ 01975 571331

An important part of Scottish history, at least until it was dismantled in 1717, this fortress was the seat of the Earls of Mar. Now it is a ruined, but splendid, example of a 13th-century castle, with four round towers, hall and chapel all discernible. Some parts of the building, including the Great Gatehouse, are from the 15th and 16th centuries.
Times: Open summer only, Apr-Sep, Mon-Sat 9.30-6.30, Sun 2-6.30.
🅿 ♿ toilets for disabled shop ▌ *Details not confirmed for 2000*

KILDRUMMY CASTLE GARDENS
AB33 8RA (on A97)
☎ 019755 71277 & 71203
▤ 019755 71277

With the picturesque ruin as a backdrop, these beautiful gardens include an alpine garden in an ancient quarry and a water garden. There's a small museum and a children's play area.
Times: Open Apr-Oct, daily 10-5.
Fee: *£2 (children go free)
🅿 ⬛ ♿ toilets for disabled shop

KINCRAIG
HIGHLAND WILDLIFE PARK
PH21 1NL (on B9152, 7m S of Aviemore)
☎ 01540 651270   ▤ 01540 651236

As you drive through the main reserve, you can see awe-inspiring European bison grazing alongside wild horses, red deer and highland cattle plus a wide variety of other species. Then in the walk-round forest, woodland and moorland habitats prepare for close encounters with animals such as wolves, capercaillie, arctic foxes, wildcats, pine martens, beavers, otters and owls.
Times: Open throughout the year, weather permitting.
Fee: *£6.30 (child £4.20, pen £5.25)
🅿 ⬛ ♿ toilets for disabled shop ✖ ▼

KINGUSSIE
HIGHLAND FOLK MUSEUM
Duke St PH21 1JG (12m SW of Aviemore off the A9 at Kingussie)
☎ 01540 661307   ▤ 01540 661631

The Museum has a comprehensive highland collection of social history material, displayed in realistic settings and reconstructed buildings. Displays include traditional farming, farm machinery, country crafts, domestic life, costume and furniture.
Times: Open Mar-Oct, Mon-Sat 10-6, Sun 2-6.
🅿 ♿ toilets for disabled shop ✖ (ex guide dogs) *Details not confirmed for 2000*

Ruthven Barracks
(0.5m SE of Kingussie)
☎ 0131 668 8800 🖷 0131 668 8888

Despite being blown up by 'Bonnie' Prince Charlie's Highlanders, these infantry barracks are still the best preserved of the four that were built after the Jacobite uprising. The considerable ruins are the remains of a building completed in 1716 on the site of a fortress of the 'Wolf of Badenoch'.
Times: Open at any reasonable time.
P

KIRKHILL
Moniack Castle (Highland Winery)
IV5 7PQ (7m from Inverness on A862)
☎ 01463 831283 🖷 01463 831419

Commercial wine-making is not a typically Scottish industry, but nevertheless a wide range of country-style wines is produced, including elderflower and silver birch; and mead and sloe gin are also made here.
Times: Open all year, Mon-Sat 10-5. (11-4 in winter).
Fee: *£2. Party.
P shop

MARYCULTER
Storybook Glen
AB12 5FT (5m W of Aberdeen on B9077)
☎ 01224 732941

This is a children's fantasy land, where favourite nursery rhyme and fairytale characters are brought to life. Grown-ups can enjoy the nostalgia and also the 20 acres of Deeside country, full of flowers, plants, trees and waterfalls.
Times: Open Mar-Oct, daily 10-6; Nov-Feb, Sat & Sun only 11-4.
Fee: *£3.60 (ch £1.80, pen £2.70).
P licensed toilets for disabled shop

MARYPARK
Glenfarclas Distillery
AB37 9BD (4m W of Aberlour on A95 to Grantown-on-Spey)
☎ 01807 500245 & 500257
🖷 01807 500234

Home of one of the finest Highland malt whiskies, this distillery provides visitors with comprehensive guided tours illustrating the whisky's history and production. There is also a cask-filling store where you can watch new whisky being poured into oak casks when filling is in progress. A Spirit of Speyside Whisky Festival is held every April.
Times: Open all year; Apr-Sep, Mon-Fri 9.30-5, Sat 10-4 &Sun 12.30-4.30; Oct-Mar, Mon-Fri 10-4. Last tour 1hr before closing time. Coaches by arrangement.
Fee: *£3.50 per adult. Free admission to under 18's.Party.
P (only visitor centre is accessible) toilets for disabled shop (ex guide dogs in vis. centre)

METHLICK
Haddo House
AB41 7EN (off B999, 4m N of Pitmedden)
☎ 01651 851440 🖷 01651 851888

Haddo House is renowned for its association with the Haddo Choral Society and is the venue for international concerts. It is a splendid Palladian-style mansion built in the 1730s to designs by William Adam. Home to the Earls of Aberdeen, the house was refurbished in the 1880s in the 'Adam Revival' style. The adjoining country park, offers beautiful woodland walks.
Times: Open - House Good Fri-Etr Mon & May-Sep, daily 1.30-5.30; wknds in Oct 1.30-5.30 (last admission 45 mins before closing). Garden & country park open all year, daily 9.30-sunset.
P (lift to first floor of house & wheelchair) toilets for disabled shop (ex in grounds, guide dogs ok) *Details not confirmed for 2000*

MINTLAW
Aberdeenshire Farming Museum
Aden Country Park AB42 5FQ (1m W of Mintlaw on A950)
☎ 01771 622906 🖷 01771 622884

Housed in 19th-century farm buildings, once part of the estate which now makes up the Aden Country Park (below). Two centuries of farming history and innovation are illustrated in an exhibition, and the story of the estate is also told. The reconstructed farm of Hareshowe shows how a family in the north-east farmed during the 1950s - access by guided tour only.
Times: Open May-Sep, daily 11-4.30; Apr & Oct, wknds only noon-4.30. Last admission 30 mins before closing. Park open all year, Apr-Sept 7-10, winter 7-7.
Fee: Free.
P (garden for partially sighted) toilets for disabled shop (ex guide dogs)

Aden Country Park
AB42 5FQ (1m W Mintlaw off A950)
☎ 01771 622857 🖷 01771 622884

Over 200 acres of beautiful woodland and open farmland to explore. A network of footpaths winds through specially developed nature trails, and the Ranger Service offers a programme of varied events.
Times: Open all year, summer 7-10, winter 7-7.
P (sensory garden, electric chair, parking) toilets for disabled shop (ex on lead) *Details not confirmed for 2000*

▥ MOUSA ISLAND
Mousa Broch
(Accessible by boat from Sandwick)
☎ 0131 668 8800   ▤ 0131 668 8888

This broch is the best-preserved example of an Iron Age drystone tower in Scotland. The tower is nearly complete and rises to a height of 40ft. The outer and inner walls both contain staircases that may be climbed to the parapet.

Times: Open at all reasonable times.
▮

▥ OLD DEER
Deer Abbey
(10m W of Peterhead)
☎ 0131 668 8800   ▤ 0131 668 8888

The remains of the Cistercian Abbey, founded in 1218, include the infirmary, Abbot's House and the southern claustral range. The University Library at Cambridge now houses the famous Book of Deer.

Times: Open at all reasonable times.
🅿 ✈ ▮ *Details not confirmed for 2000*

▥ ORKNEY

▥ HARRAY (ORKNEY)
Orkney Farm & Folk Museum
KW17 2JR
☎ 01856 771411 & 771268
▤ 01856 874615

The museum consists of two Orkney farmhouses with outbuildings. Kirbuster (Birsay) has the last surviving example of a 'Firehoose' with its central hearth; Corrigall (Harray) represents an improved farmhouse and steading of the late 1800s.

Times: Open Mar-Oct, Mon-Sat 10.30-1 & 2-5, Sun 2-7.
🅿 ㋐ shop ✈ (ex guide dogs) *Details not confirmed for 2000*

▥ KIRKWALL (ORKNEY)
Bishop's & Earl's Palaces
☎ 01856 875461

The Bishop's Palace is a hall-house of the 12th century, later much altered, with a round tower built by Bishop Reid in 1541-48. A later addition was made by the notorious Patrick Stewart, Earl of Orkney, who built the adjacent Earl's Palace between 1600 and 1607 in a splendid Renaissance style.

Times: Open Apr-Sep, Mon-Sat 9.30-6.30, Sun 2-6.30.
㋐ ▮ *Details not confirmed for 2000*

▥ STROMNESS (ORKNEY)
Orkney Maritime & Natural History Museum
52 Alfred St KW16 3DF
☎ 01856 850025

The museum focuses on Orkney's broad maritime connections, including fishing, whaling, the Hudson's Bay Company, the German Fleet in Scapa Flow, and the award winning Pilot's House extension. The Natural History Gallery will be closed for restoration. Summer Exhibition (Apr-

Sep) 'Voices from the Great War' - Orkney's involvement in World War One.

Times: Open May-Sep, Mon-Sun 10-5; Oct-Apr, Mon-Sat 10.30-12.30 & 1.30-5. (Closed Xmas, New Year & 3 wks Feb-Mar).
🅿 (50yds) ㋐ shop ✈ (ex guide dogs) *Details not confirmed for 2000*

Pier Arts Centre
KW16 3AA
☎ 01856 850209   ▤ 01856 851462

The collection is housed in a warehouse standing on its own stone pier. A children's workshop operates during the school summer holidays and there is a constantly changing programme of exhibitions.

Times: Open all year, Tue-Sat 10.30-12.30 & 1.30-5.
🅿 (100 yds) ㋐ shop ✈ (ex guide dogs) *Details not confirmed for 2000*

▥ OYNE
Archaeolink
Berryhill AB52 6QP (1m off A96 on B9002)
☎ 01464 851500   ▤ 01464 851544

A stunning audio-visual show together with a Myths and Legends Gallery and a whole range of interpretation techniques to help you explore what it was like to live 6000 years ago. In addition there are landscaped walkways, and outdoor activity areas including an Iron Age farm, Roman marching camp and Stone Age settlement within the 40 acre park.

Times: Open Apr-Oct, daily 10-5.
Fee: *£3.90 (ch 5-16 & concessions £2.35, ch under 5 free). Family ticket £11. Party 10+.
🅿 ▬ ✕ licensed ㋐ toilets for disabled shop ✈ (ex guide dogs) ▰

▥ PETERCULTER
Drum Castle
AB31 5EY (3m W of 10 m from Aberdeen off A93)
☎ 01330 811204

The great 13th-century Square Tower is one of the three oldest tower houses in Scotland and has associations with Robert the Bruce. The handsome mansion, added in 1619, houses a collection of family memorabilia. The grounds contain the 100-acre Old Wood of Drum, a natural oak wood and an old rose garden. For details of events please telephone.

Times: Open Good Fri-Etr Mon & May-Sep, daily 1.30-5.30; wknds in Oct 1.30-5.30. Last admission 4.45. Grounds open all year 9.30-sunset.
🅿 ▬ ㋐ (wheelchair available) shop ✈ (ex guide dogs) ▰ *Details not confirmed for 2000*

▥ PETERHEAD
Arbuthnot Museum & Art Gallery
St Peter St AB42 1QD
☎ 01771 622906   ▤ 01771 622884

Specialising in local exhibits, particularly those relating to the fishing industry, this museum also displays Arctic and whaling specimens and a British coin collection. The regular programme of exhibitions changes approximately every six weeks.

Times: Open all year, Mon, Tue & Thu-Sat 10.30-1.30 & 2.30-5, Wed 10.30-1. (Closed Sun and PH).

Fee: Free.

P (150 yds) shop ✱ (ex guide dogs)

PITMEDDEN

PITMEDDEN GARDEN

AB41 7PA (1m W of Pitmedden on A920)

☎ 01651 842352   ▤ 01651 843188

The fine 17th-century walled garden, with sundials, pavilions and fountains dotted among the parterres, has been authentically restored, and there is a Museum of Farming Life and a woodland walk.

Times: Open - Garden, Museum of Farming Life & Visitor Centre open May-Sep, daily 10-5.30 last admission 5pm.

P ◼ ♿ (2 wheelchairs available) toilets for disabled shop ♥ *Details not confirmed for 2000*

TOLQUHON CASTLE

(2m NE off B999)

☎ 01651 851286

Now roofless, this late 16th-century quadrangular mansion encloses an early 15th-century tower. There is a fine gatehouse and a splendid courtyard.

Times: Open all year, Apr-Sep, Mon-Sat 9.30-6, Sun 2-6; Oct-Mar wknds only Sat 9.30-4.30, Sun 2-4.30. (Closed 25-26 Dec & 1-2 Jan).

P ♿ toilets for disabled ✱ ▮ *Details not confirmed for 2000*

POOLEWE

INVEREWE GARDEN

IV22 2LG (6m NE of Gairloch, on A832)

☎ 01445 781200   ▤ 01445 781497

The influence of the North Atlantic Drift enables this remarkable garden to grow rare and sub-tropical plants. At its best in early June, but full of beauty from March to October, Inverewe has a backdrop of magnificent mountains and stands to the north of Loch Maree.

Times: Open - Garden all year, Apr-Oct, daily 9.30-9. Nov-14 Mar 9.30-5.30. Visitor Centre Apr-Oct, daily 9.30-5.30. Guided walks 15 Mar-Oct Mon-Fri at 1.30.

P ✕ licensed ♿ (some paths difficult) toilets for disabled shop ✱ (ex guide dogs) ♥ *Details not confirmed for 2000*

RHYNIE

LEITH HALL & GARDEN

Kennethmont AB54 4NQ (on B9002, 1m W of Kennethmont)

☎ 01464 831216

Home of the Leith family for over 300 years, the house dates back to 1650, and has a number of Jacobite relics and fine examples of needlework. It is surrounded by charming gardens and

extensive grounds. Telephone for details of special events.

Times: Open - House Good Fri-Etr Mon & May-Sep, daily 1.30-5.30; wknds in Oct 1.30-5.30. (Last admission 45 mins before closing). Gardens and grounds all year 9.30-sunset.

P ◼ ♿ (parking next to hall, scented garden for the blind) toilets for disabled ✱ (ex guide dogs) ♥ *Details not confirmed for 2000*

ROTHES

GLEN GRANT DISTILLERY

AB38 7BS (On A941, in Rothes)

☎ 01542 783318   ▤ 01542 783304

Founded in 1840, in a sheltered glen, by the two Grant brothers. Discover the secrets of the distillery, including the delightful Victorian garden originally created by Major Grant, recently restored to its former glory, where you can enjoy a dram.

Times: Open mid Mar-end Oct, Mon-Sat 10-4, Sun 11.30-4. Jun-end Sept remains open until 5 daily.

Fee: *£2.50 includes £2 voucher redeemable in the distillery shop against 70cl bottle of whisky. Inclusive charge for garden visit & distillery tour. A free dram is offered to over 18s. (ch18 free, children under 8 not admitted to production areas, but are welcome in centre & garden)

P ♿ (reception centre & still house) toilets for disabled shop ✱ ≡

SCALLOWAY

SCALLOWAY CASTLE

☎ 0131 668 8800   ▤ 0131 668 8888

The ruins of a castle designed on the medieval two-step plan. The castle was actually built in 1600 by Patrick Stewart, Earl of Orkney. When the Earl, who was renowned for his cruelty, was executed in 1615, the castle fell into disuse.

Times: Open at all reasonable time.

P ▮

SHETLAND

LERWICK (SHETLAND)

CLICKHIMIN

ZE1 0QX (1m SW)

☎ 0131 668 8800   ▤ 0131 668 8888

The remains of a prehistoric settlement that was fortified at the beginning of the Iron Age with a stone-built fort. The site was occupied for over 1000 years. The remains include a partially demolished broch (round tower) which still stands to a height of 17ft.

Times: Open at all reasonable time.

▮

FORT CHARLOTTE

ZE1 0JN (overlooking harbour)

☎ 0131 668 8800   ▤ 0131 668 8888

An artillery fort, begun in 1665 to protect the Sound of Bressay during the Anglo-Dutch War. The fort was burned by the Dutch in 1673, together with the town of Lerwick. It was repaired in 1781 during the American War of

contd.

Independence. The fort is pentagonal with high walls and seaward-facing gunports.

Times: Open at all reasonable time.

▌ *Details not confirmed for 2000*

SHETLAND MUSEUM
Lower Hillhead ZE1 0EL
☎ 01595 695057   ▤ 01595 696729

The massive brass propeller blade outside the building is from the 17,000-ton liner *Oceanic*, wrecked off Foula in 1914. The archaeology gallery covers Neolithic burials and axe-making; Bronze Age houses, Iron Age farming and domestic life. There are also agricultural and social history displays, including peat-working, corn harvest, local businesses, medals, bootmaking, and Shetland weddings.

Times: Open all year Mon, Wed, Fri 10-7, Tue, Thu, Sat 10-5.

Fee: Free.

🅿 ♿ (lift, wheelchair available) toilets for disabled shop ✖ (ex guide dogs)

⏚ SKYE, ISLE OF

⏚ ARMADALE (SKYE, ISLE OF)
ARMADALE CASTLE GARDENS & MUSEUM OF THE ISLES
IV45 8RS (1.5km from Armadale Pier)
☎ 01471 844305 & 844227
▤ 01471 844275

Armadale Castle and Gardens were built in 1815 as the home of Lord Macdonald. The sculptured ruins of the castle now house the Museum of the Isles, and a library and study centre offer genealogical research and access to historical records. Surrounding the castle are 40 acres of beautiful woodland gardens and nature trails. The Countryside Ranger Service provides a full summer programme of walks, talks and children's afternoons, and special events take place.

Times: Open daily 9.30-5.30. Garden & Museum open 30 Mar-30 Oct.

Fee: *£3.80 (concessions £2.60). Family ticket £10. Party.

🅿 ☕ ✖ licensed ♿ (wheelchairs available, hearing loop in Audiovisual room) toilets for disabled shop garden centre (on leads) 🍽

⏚ DUNVEGAN
DUNVEGAN CASTLE
IV55 8WF
☎ 01470 521206   ▤ 01470 521205

This fortress stronghold, set on the sea loch of Dunvegan, has been the home of the Chief of Macleod for 790 years. On view are books, pictures, arms and treasured relics of the clan. A pedigree Highland Cattle fold is also an attraction, as is the boat trip to the nearby Seal Colony.

Times: Open 20 Mar-Oct, Mon-Sun 10-5.30 (last admission 5pm. Winter opening: Nov-Mar Castle & Gardens Mon-Sun 11-4, last admission 3.30pm.

Fee: *Castle & Gardens: £5.20 (ch £2.60, OAPs/Students £4.60) Parties. Gardens only: £3.70 (ch £2)

🅿 ☕ ✖ licensed (restaurant has ramps for wheelchair access) shop ✖ (ex guide dogs & in grounds)

⏚ SPEY BAY
TUGNET ICE HOUSE
Tugnet IV32 7PJ (8m E of Elgin on A96, then onto B9104 towards Spey Bay, establishment is 1m further along)
☎ 01309 673701   ▤ 01309 675863

The largest ice house in Scotland, built in 1830, containing exhibitions on the history and techniques of commerical salmon fishing on the River Spey. There are sections on the geography, wildlife and industries of the Lower Spey area, such as ship-building at nearby Kingston.

Times: Open 4 May-26 Sep, Mon-Sun 11-4.

Fee: Free.

🅿 ♿ toilets for disabled shop ✖ (ex guide dogs)

⏚ STONEHAVEN
DUNNOTTAR CASTLE
AB39 2TL (2m S of Stonehaven on A92)
☎ 01569 762173

This once-impregnable fortress, now a spectacular ruin, was the site of the successful protection of the Scottish Crown Jewels from the might of Cromwell.

Times: Open all year, summer Mon-Sat 9-6, Sun 2-5; winter Mon-Fri 9-sunset. Last entry 30 minutes before closing. Closed 25-26 Dec/New Year.

Fee: *£3 (ch 5-15 £1)

🅿 ✖ (ex on lead)

TOLBOOTH MUSEUM
Old Pier
☎ 01771 622906   ▤ 01771 622884

Built in the late 16th centrury as a storehouse for the Earls Marischal at Dunnottar Castle, the building was the Kincardineshire County Tolbooth from 1600-1767. Displays feature local history and fishing.

Times: Open Jun-Sep, Mon & Thu-Sat 10-noon & 2-5; Wed & Sun 2-5.

Fee: Free.

🅿 (20yds) ♿ shop ✖ (ex guide dogs)

SUMBURGH

JARLSHOF PREHISTORIC SITE
(At Sumburgh Head, approx 22m S of Lerwick)
☎ 01950 460112

One of the most remarkable archaeological sites in Europe. There are remains of Bronze Age, Iron Age and Viking settlements as well as a medieval farm. There is also a 16th-century Laird's House, once the home of the Earls Robert and Patrick Stewart, and the basis of 'Jarlshof' in Sir Walter Scott's novel *The Pirate*.
Times: Open Apr-Sep, Mon-Sat 9.30-6.30, Sun 2-6.30.
P & **▮** *Details not confirmed for 2000*

TOMINTOUL

TOMINTOUL MUSEUM
The Square AB37 9ET (on A939, 13m E of Grantown)
☎ 01309 673701 ▤ 01309 675863

Situated in one of the highest villages in Britain, the museum features a reconstructed crofter's kitchen and smiddy, with other displays on the local wildlife, the story of Tomintoul, and the local skiing industry.
Times: Open 7 Apr-1 Jun, Mon-Fri 10-4; 2 Jun-Aug, Mon-Sat 10-4.30; 1-28 Sep, Mon-Sat 10-4; 29 Sep-24 Oct Mon-Fri 10-4.
Fee: Free.
P & (handling display for visually impaired) shop ✗ (ex guide dogs)

TORRIDON

TORRIDON COUNTRYSIDE CENTRE
The Mains IV22 2EZ (N of A896).
☎ 01445 791221 ▤ 01445 791261

Set amid some of Scotland's finest mountain scenery, the centre offers audio-visual presentations on the local wildlife. At the Mains nearby there are deer to be seen.
Times: Open - Countryside Centre May-Sep, Mon-Sat 10-5, Sun 2-5. Estate and Deer Museum daily all year.
P & toilets for disabled ✹ *Details not confirmed for 2000*

TURRIFF

FYVIE CASTLE
Fyvie AB53 8JS (8m SE of Turriff on A947)
☎ 01651 891266

This superb castle, founded in the 13th century, has five towers, each built in a different century, and is one of the grandest examples of Scottish Baronial architecture. It contains the finest wheel stair in Scotland, and a 17th-century morning room, lavishly furnished in Edwardian style. The collection of portraits is exceptional, and there are also displays of arms, armour and tapestries. Telephone for details of events.
Times: Open Apr-Jun & Sep daily 1.30-5.30. Jul-Aug daily 11-5.30, wknds Oct 1.30-5.30. (last admission 4.45). Grounds open all year, daily 9.30-sunset.
P ■ & (small lift, braille sheets) toilets for disabled shop ✗ (ex guide dogs) ✹ *Details not confirmed for 2000*

WESTRAY

NOLTLAND CASTLE
☎ 0131 668 8800 ▤ 0131 668 8888

Started in the 16th century, this ruined castle was never completed. It has a fine hall, vaulted kitchen and a notable winding staircase.
Times: Open all reasonable times. Application to key keeper.
✗ ▮

WICK

CAITHNESS GLASS FACTORY & VISITOR CENTRE
Airport Industrial Estate KW1 5BP (on northern side of Wick, beside airport on A99 to John O'Groats)
☎ 01955 602286 ▤ 01955 605200

All aspects of glassmaking are on view, from the initial processing of the raw materials to the finished article. Visitors can see the jewellery and engraving departments at work and learn about the history of Caithness Glass in the exhibition.
Times: Open all year, Factory shop & Restaurant Mon-Sat 9-5 (Sun, Etr-Dec 11-5). Glassmaking Mon-Fri 9-4.30.
Fee: Free.
P ✗ licensed & toilets for disabled shop ✗ ▱

CASTLE OF OLD WICK
(1m S)
☎ 0131 668 8800 ▤ 0131 668 8888

A ruined four-storey square tower that is probably of the 12th century. It is also known as Castle Oliphant.
Times: Open except when adjoining rifle range is in use.
✗ ▮

Central Scotland

EVENTS & FESTIVALS

March
25th Millennium Champions
Challenge, Blair Castle

April
1st Rugby International,
Scotland v England,
Edinburgh
1st-2nd City of Dundee
Flower Show
8th-23rd Edinburgh
International Science Festival
29th Silk Cup Rugby League
Final, Edinburgh
29th-7th May Water of Leith
Festival, Edinburgh

May
1st-5th Celtic Fayre,
Loch Tay
7th Beltane, Stirling

June
2nd-4th Millennium
Regatta, Isle of Bute

July
20th-23rd The Open Golf
Championship,
St Andrews
22nd-29th Cowal Europe,
Dunoon, Argyll - pan-
European festival

August
4th-26th Edinburgh Military
Tattoo
13th-2nd September
Edinburgh International
Festival
13th-27th Edinburgh
International Film Festival

September
9th Battle of Britain
International Air Show, RAF
Leuchars

*Top: Kenmore on the
banks of Loch Tay*

*The area spans two very different landscapes and histories -
the Highlands (originally Gaelic-speaking and clan-based)
run down to the hills and plains of the industrialised and
more populated Lowlands.*

The map is shaped by the great inlets of the Tay, the Forth
and the Clyde on which the raw materials and the output
of Scotland's industrial revolution were carried to and from
the rest of the world. Now that steel, coal, shipbuilding and
engineering are diminished, Scots are more likely to work in
financial services, micro-electronics or oil.

Along the east coast, many of the fishing villages retain
their charm, particularly on the coast of Fife. Dundee
was once a substantial whaling port. Inland much of
the low land is fertile, being farmed for barley, oats,
potatoes, fruit and cattle.

Volcanoes have left their mark, with lava plugs standing
stark above the landscape. In turbulent times these were
perfect spots to build castles; look at Stirling, Edinburgh or
Dumbarton.

The closeness of the hills to centres of population allowed people
to travel cheaply to outstandingly beautiful areas, which have
been celebrated in song, novel and film. Loch Lomond, The
Trossachs and the Clyde estuary will all repay a visit, even if the
weather is less than perfect.

St Andrews, with Scotland's oldest university; Edinburgh, home
of Scotland's new parliament; Oban, port to the Isles; gracious
Perth, and medieval Culross - the region's towns are diverse,
steeped in history and often very handsome.

This region includes the counties of Angus, Argyll & Bute, City of Edinburgh, Clackmannanshire, Dundee City, East Lothian, Falkirk, Fife, Inverclyde, Midlothian, Perth & Kinross, Stirling and West Lothian which reflect the recent national changes.

ABERDOUR
ABERDOUR CASTLE
KY3 0SL
☎ 01383 860519

The earliest surviving part of the castle is the 14th-century keep. There are also later buildings, and the remains of a terraced garden, a bowling green and a fine 16th-century doocot (dovecote).
Times: Open all year, Apr-Sep, Mon-Sat 9.30-6.30, Sun 2-6.30; Oct-Mar, Mon-Sat 9.30-4.30, Sun 2-4.30. (Closed Thu pm, Fri in winter, 25-26 Dec & 1-3 Jan).
🅿 ♿ toilets for disabled shop ▌ *Details not confirmed for 2000*

ABERLADY
MYRETON MOTOR MUSEUM
EH32 0PZ (1.5m from A198, 2m from A1)
☎ 01875 870288

This is a charming and wide-ranging collection, with cars and motorcycles from 1896, cycles from 1863 and commercial vehicles, historic British military vehicles, advertising signs and automobilia.
Times: Open all year, daily 10-6 (summer); 10-5 (winter). (Closed 25 Dec & 1 Jan).
Fee: *£3 (ch 16 £1).
🅿 ♿ shop ✖ (ex guide dogs)

ALLOA
ALLOA TOWER
Alloa Park FK10 1PP (on A907)
☎ 01259 211701   ▤ 01259 211701

Beautifully restored, the tower, completed in 1467, is the only remaining part of the ancestral home of the Earls of Mar. The structure retains rare medieval features, notably the complete timber roof structure and groin vaulting. A superb loan collection of portraits and chattels of the Erskine family includes paintings by Raeburn. Telephone for details of events.
Times: Open Etr, May-Sep & weekends in Oct, daily 1.30-5.30.
Fee: *£2.50 (concessions £1.70). Family ticket £6.70. Party.
🅿 ♿ toilets for disabled ✖ ❦

ANSTRUTHER
SCOTTISH FISHERIES MUSEUM
St Ayles, Harbour Head KY10 3AB
☎ 01333 310628

A cobbled courtyard by the harbour is the setting for displays which include real and model boats, and a fisherman's cottage.
Times: Open all year, Apr-Oct, Mon-Sat 10-5.30, Sun 11-5; Nov-Mar, Mon-Sat 10-4.30, Sun 2-4.30. (Closed 25-26 Dec & 1-2 Jan). Last admission 45 mins before closing.
Fee: *£3.50 (concessions £2.50). Family ticket £10. Party 12+.
🅿 (20 yds) (charge in summer) 🍴 ♿ (ramps) toilets for disabled shop ✖ (ex guide dogs)

ARBROATH
ARBROATH ABBEY
☎ 01241 878756

The `Declaration of Arbroath' - declaring Robert the Bruce as king - was signed at the 12th-century abbey on 6 April 1320. The abbot's house is well preserved, and the church remains are also interesting.
Times: Open all year, Apr-Sep, Mon-Sat 9.30-6.30, Sun 2-6.30; Oct-Mar, Mon-Sat 9.30-4.30, Sun 2-4.30. (Closed 25-26 Dec & 1-3 Jan)
🅿 ♿ ✖ ▌ *Details not confirmed for 2000*

ARBROATH MUSEUM
Signal Tower, Ladyloan DD11 1PU (On A92)
☎ 01241 875598   ▤ 01241 439263

Fish and Arbroath Smokies, textiles and engineering feature at this local history museum housed in the 1813 shore station of Stevenson's Bell Rock lighthouse.
Times: Open all year, Mon-Sat 10-5; Jul-Aug, Sun 2-5. (Closed 25-26 Dec & 1-2 Jan).
Fee: Free.
🅿 ♿ shop ✖ (ex guide dogs)

BALERNO
MALLENY GARDEN
EH14 7AF (off Lanark Rd (A70))
☎ 0131 449 2283

The delightful gardens are set round a 17th-century house (not open). Shrub roses, a woodland garden, and a group of four clipped yews, survivors of a group planted in 1603, are among its notable features. The National Bonsai Collection for Scotland is also at Malleny. House not open.
Times: Open Apr-Oct, daily 9.30-7; Nov-Mar, daily 9.30-4. House not open.
🅿 ♿ ✖ (ex guide dogs) ❦ *Details not confirmed for 2000*

BANNOCKBURN
BANNOCKBURN HERITAGE CENTRE
Glasgow Rd FK7 0LJ (2m S of Stirling off M80/M9 J9)
☎ 01786 812664

The Heritage Centre stands close to what is traditionally believed to have been Robert the Bruce's command post before the 1314 Battle of Bannockburn, a famous victory for the Scots and a turning point in Scottish history.
Times: Open - Rotunda & site always open. Heritage Centre & Shop; Mar & Nov-23 Dec, daily 11-3; Apr-Oct daily 10-5.30. (Last audio-visual showing half hour before closing).
🅿 ♿ (Induction loop for the hard of hearing) toilets for disabled shop (Closed Nov 1-10) ✖ (ex site only) ❦ *Details not confirmed for 2000*

BARRY
BARRY MILL
DD7 7RJ (2m W of Carnoustie)
☎ 01241 856761

This restored 18th-century mill works on a demonstration basis. Records show that the site has been used for milling since the 16th century.

contd.

Displays highlight the important place the mill held in the community. There is a waymarked walk and picnic area.

Times: Open Good Fri-Etr Mon & May-Sep, daily 11-5; wknds in Oct, 11-5.

P & ramp from car park to mill toilets for disabled (grounds only) 曾 *Details not confirmed for 2000*

⛫ BLAIR ATHOLL
BLAIR CASTLE
PH18 5TL (7m NW of Pitlochry, off A9)

☎ 01796 481207   ▤ 01796 481487

Home of the Dukes of Atholl and the Atholl Highlanders, the Duke's unique private army. The castle dates back to the 13th century but was altered in the 18th century and later given a castellated exterior. The oldest part is Cumming's Tower, built in about 1270. There are paintings, Jacobite relics, lace, tapestries, and Masonic regalia to be seen. The extensive grounds include a deer park, and a restored 18th-century walled garden. Numerous events are held throughout the year, including the annual parade of the Duke's Private Army (ring for details).

Times: Open daily 1 Apr-30 Oct. 10am-6pm. Last admission 5pm.

P (charged) ▄ ✕ licensed & (toilets, but not suitable for severely disabled) shop ✖ (ex in grounds) *Details not confirmed for 2000* ◥

See advert under Pitlochry.

⛫ BLAIR DRUMMOND
BLAIR DRUMMOND SAFARI & LEISURE PARK
FK9 4UR (M9 J10, 4m along A84 towards Callander)

☎ 01786 841456 & 841396
▤ 01786 841491

Drive through the wild animal reserves and see at close range the monkeys, zebras, North American bison, antelope, lions, tigers, white rhino and camels. Other attractions include the sea lion show, a ride on the boat safari through the waterfowl sanctuary and around Chimpanzee Island, an adventure playground, giant astraglide,

and pedal boats. There are also Zimbabwean elephants, giraffes and ostriches.

Times: Open Mar 28-Oct 5, daily 10-5.30. Last admission 4.30.

P ▄ ✕ licensed & (special menus & waitress service if booked in advance) toilets for disabled shop ✖ (ex guide dogs) *Details not confirmed for 2000*

⛫ BO'NESS
BO'NESS & KINNEIL RAILWAY
Bo'ness Station, Union St EH51 9AQ (A904 from all directions, signposted)

☎ 01506 822298   ▤ 01506 828233

Historic railway buildings, including the station and train shed, have been relocated from sites all over Scotland. The Scottish Railway Exhibition tells the story of the development of railways and their impact on the people of Scotland. Take a seven mile return trip by steam train to the tranquil country station at Birkhill. Special events take place throughout the year.

Times: Open 14-28 Mar, Sun; Apr, Sat-Sun; Steam trains depart 12.15, 1.45, 3 & diesel at 4.15. Etr; May-Jun & Sep, Sat-Sun; Jul-Aug, Tue-Sun; Steam trains depart 11.00, 12.15, 1.45, 3 & diesel at 4.15.

Fee: *Return fare £4 (ch 5-15 £2, concessions (disabled & pen) £3). Family ticket £10. Ticket for return train fare and tour of Birkhill Fireclay Mine £6.50 (ch £3.50, concessions £4.80), Family ticket £16.50. Scottish Railway Exhibition £1.50 (accompanied ch free, concessions 70p), Family ticket £2.

P ▄ ✕ & (ramps to stn, and adapted carriage) shop ◥

KINNEIL MUSEUM & ROMAN FORTLET
Duchess Anne Cottages, Kinniel Estate EH51 0PR
☎ 01506 778530

The museum is in a converted stable block of Kinneil House. The ground floor has displays on the industrial history of Bo'ness, while the upper floor looks at the history and environment of the Kinneil estate. The remains of the Roman fortlet can be seen nearby. An audio visual presentation shows 2000 years of history.

Times: Open all year, Mon-Sat 12.30-4.

Fee: Free.

P & shop ✖ (ex guide dogs)

🏛 BUTE, ISLE OF

🏛 ROTHESAY (BUTE, ISLE OF)

ARDENCRAIG

PA20 9HA (1m off A844, S of Rothesay)
☎ 01700 504225 📄 01700 504225

Particular attention has been paid to improving the layout of the garden and introducing rare plants. The greenhouse and walled garden produce plants for floral displays throughout the district. A variety of fish is kept in the ornamental ponds and the aviaries have some interesting birds.
Times: May-Sep.
🅿 🔌 ♿ 🐕 (ex guide dogs) *Details not confirmed for 2000*

BUTE MUSEUM

Stuar St PA20 0BR
☎ 01700 502033 (contact) & 505067 (museum)

Local and natural history displays, including birds, mammals and seashore items; varied collections of recent bygones, a collection of early Christian crosses, and flints and pots from two Neolithic burial cairns. A special exhibition of local interest is held during Highland Week.
Times: Open all year, Apr-Sep, Mon-Sat 10.30-4.30, Sun 2.30-4.30; Oct-Mar, Tue-Sat 2.30-4.30 (Closed Sun & Mon).
Fee: *£1.20 (ch 40p, pen 70p)
🅿 ♿ (touch table for blind) shop 🐕 (ex guide dogs)

ROTHESAY CASTLE

☎ 01700 502691

The focal point of Rothesay is this 13th-century castle. It has lofty curtain walls defended by drum towers that enclose a circular courtyard.
Times: Open all year, Apr-Sep, Mon-Sat 9.30-6.30, Sun 2-6.30; Oct-Mar, Mon-Sat 9.30-4.30 Sun 2-4.30. (Closed Thu pm & Fri in winter; also 25-26 Dec & 1-3 Jan).
🅿 ♿ 🚩 *Details not confirmed for 2000*

🏛 CAUSEWAYHEAD

NATIONAL WALLACE MONUMENT

FK8 2AD (the Monument may be reached by heading along A907, Stirling to Alloa Rd)
☎ 01786 472140 📄 01786 461322

The 220ft tower was completed in 1869, and Sir William Wallace's two-handed sword is preserved inside. Seven battlefields and a fine view towards the Highlands can be seen – one of the most awe inspiring views in Scotland.
Times: Open all year daily. Jan-Feb & Nov-Dec, 10.30-4; Mar-May & Oct, 10-5; Jun & Sep 10-6; Jul-Aug 9.30-6.30.
Fee: *£3.25 (ch & pen £2.25, student £3). Family ticket £9.50.
🅿 🔌 (accessible visitors pavillion at foot of hill) shop 🐕 (ex guide dogs) 🍴

🏛 CRICHTON

CRICHTON CASTLE

(2.5m SW Pathhead)
☎ 01875 320017

The castle dates back to the 14th century, but most of what remains today was built over the following 300 years. A notable feature is the 16th-century wing built by the Earl of Bothwell in Italian style, with an arcade below.
Times: Open Apr-Sep, Mon-Sat 9.30-6.30, Sun 2-6.30.
🅿 shop 🚩 *Details not confirmed for 2000*

🏛 CRIEFF

GLENTURRET DISTILLERY

The Hosh PH7 4HA (1.5m NW off A85)
☎ 01764 656565 📄 01764 654366

The distillery dates from 1775 and is the oldest in Scotland.
Times: Open Feb-Dec, Mon-Sat 9.30-6 (last tour 4.30), Sun 12-6 (last tour 4.30); Jan, Mon-Fri 11.30-4 (last tour 2.30). (Closed 25-26 Dec & 1-2 Jan)
Fee: *Guided tours and Audio visual exhibition £3.50 (ch 12-17 £2.30 ch under 12 Free).
🅿 ✕ licensed ♿ toilets for disabled shop 🐕 🍴

🏛 CULROSS
CULROSS PALACE, TOWN HOUSE & THE STUDY
West Green House KY12 8JH (off A985, 3m E of Kincardine Bridge)
☎ 01383 880359

A royal burgh, Culross dates from the 16th and 17th centuries and has remained virtually unchanged since. It prospered from the coal and salt trades, yet when these declined in the 1700s, Culross stayed as it was. It owes its present appearance to the National Trust for Scotland, which has been gradually restoring it. In the Town House is a visitor centre and exhibition; in the building called The Study can be seen a drawing room with a Norwegian painted ceiling, and The Palace has painted rooms and terraced gardens.

Times: Open - Town House & Study; Apr-Sep daily 1.30-5. Oct Sat & Sun only 11-5. (last admission 4). Palace Apr-Sep daily 11-5.

🅿 ⬛ ♿ toilets for disabled shop ✈ (ex guide dogs) ♨ *Details not confirmed for 2000*

🏛 CUPAR
HILL OF TARVIT MANSIONHOUSE & GARDEN
KY15 5PB (2.5m S of Cupar, off A916)
☎ 01334 653127

Built in the first decade of the 20th century, the mansionhouse is home to a notable collection of paintings, tapestries, furniture and Chinese porcelain. The grounds include formal gardens, and there is a regular programme of concerts and art exhibitions.

Times: Open Good Fri-Etr Mon & May-Sep, daily 1.30-5.30; wknds in Oct 1.30-5.30 (last admission 4.45). Garden & grounds Apr-Oct daily 9.30-9.30. Nov-Mar daily 9.30-4.30.

🅿 ⬛ ♿ toilets for disabled shop ✈ (ex guide dogs) ♨ *Details not confirmed for 2000*

RANKEILOUR PARK - THE SCOTTISH DEER CENTRE
Bow-of-Fife KY15 4NQ (3 miles west of Cupar on A91)
☎ 01337 810391 📄 01337 810477

Guided tours take about 30 minutes and allow you to meet and stroke deer. Children can help with bottle-feeding young fawns, (at certain times of year) and there are indoor and outdoor adventure play areas. Other features include regular falconry displays, a viewing platform and a tree top walkway.

Times: Open daily, Etr-Oct 10-6, Nov-Etr 10-5.

Fee: *£3.95 (ch £2.50, concessions £3.40). Family ticket £11.70. Party 10+.

🅿 ✕ ♿ (special parking bay, loan of wheelchairs) toilets for disabled shop ✈ (ex guide dogs) 🍴

🏛 DIRLETON
DIRLETON CASTLE
EH39 5ER (on A198)
☎ 01620 850330

The oldest part of this romantic castle dates from the 13th century. It was besieged by Edward I in 1298, rebuilt and expanded, and then destroyed in 1650. Now the sandstone ruins have a beautiful mellow quality. Within the castle grounds is a garden established in the 16th century, with ancient yews and hedges around a bowling green.

Times: Open all year, Apr-Sep, Mon-Sat 9.30-6.30, Sun 2-6.30; Oct-Mar, Mon-Sat, 9.30-4.30, Sun 2-4.30. (Closed 25-26 Dec & 1-3 Jan).

🅿 ♿ shop ▌ *Details not confirmed for 2000*

🏛 DOLLAR
CASTLE CAMPBELL
FK14 7PP (10m W of Stirling on A91)
☎ 01259 742408

Traditionally known as the 'Castle of Gloom', the 15th to 17th-century tower stands in the picturesque Ochil Hills and gives wonderful views. It can be reached by a walk through the magnificent Dollar Glen. Care must be taken in, or after, rain when the path may be dangerous.

Times: Open Apr-Sep, Mon-Sat 9.30-6.30, Sun 2-6.30; Oct-Mar, Mon-Sat 9.30-4.30, Sun 2-4.30. (Closed Thu pm & Fri in winter, 25-26 Dec & 1-3 Jan).

🅿 shop ▌ ♨ *Details not confirmed for 2000*

🏛 DOUNE
DOUNE CASTLE
FK16 6EA (8m S of Callander on A84)
☎ 01786 841742

The 14th-century stronghold with its two fine towers has been restored. It stands on the banks of the River Teith, and is associated with Bonnie Prince Charlie and Sir Walter Scott.

Times: Open all year, Apr-Sep, Mon-Sat 9.30-6.30, Sun 2-6.30; Oct-Mar 9.30-4.30, Sun 2-4.30. (Closed Thu pm & Fri in winter; 25-26 Dec & 1-3 Jan).

🅿 ♿ shop ▌ *Details not confirmed for 2000*

🏛 DUNDEE
BROUGHTY CASTLE MUSEUM
Broughty Ferry DD5 2BE (4m E, off A930)
☎ 01382 436916

The 15th-century castle was rebuilt to defend the estuary in the 19th century. It now houses displays on Dundee's whaling history, arms and armour, local history and seashore life. There are superb views across the Tay estuary from the observation room.

Times: Open all year, Mon 11-1 & 2-5, Tue-Thu 10-1 & 2-5. (Sun 2-5 Jul-Sep only). (Closed 25-26 Dec & 1-3 Jan).

🅿 shop ✈ (ex guide dogs) *Details not confirmed for 2000*

CAMPERDOWN COUNTRY PARK

DD2 4TF (A90 to Dundee and turn onto A923 Coupar Angus rd, turn left at 1st rdbt to Camperdown Country Park)

☎ 01382 434296   ▤ 01382 433211

The 19th-century mansion of Camperdown House was built for the son of Admiral Lord Duncan, who defeated the Dutch at the Battle of Camperdown in 1797. The house is set in nearly 400 acres of fine parkland which includes a wildlife centre, an adventure play area and an extensive network of footpaths and forest trails to follow.

Times: Open all year - park. Wildlife Centre - daily, Apr-Sep 10-3.45, Oct-Mar 10-2.45.

▣ ዿ (ramps) toilets for disabled shop ✖ (ex guide dogs) *Details not confirmed for 2000*

DISCOVERY POINT

Discovery Quay DD1 4XA (in Dundee follow signs for Historic Ships)

☎ 01382 201245   ▤ 01382 25891

Discovery Point is the home of *RRS Discovery*, Captain Scott's famous Antarctic ship. Spectacular lighting, graphics and special effects re-create key moments in the *Discovery* story. Learn what happened to the ship after the expedition, during the First World War and the Russian Revolution, and also her involvement in the first survey of the migration patterns of whales.

Times: Open all year, Apr-Oct, Mon-Sat 10-5, Sun 11-5; Nov-Mar, last admission 4pm. Closed 25 Dec & 1-2 Jan

Fee: *£5 (ch £3.75, pen & concessions £3.75). Family ticket £13-£21. Party. Joint ticket with Verdant Works £8.75 (ch £6.75, pen & concessions £6.75). Family ticket £22-£36.

▣ (charged) ▣ ዿ (in-house wheelchairs & lifts, parking, ramps onto ship) toilets for disabled shop ✖ (ex guide dogs)

HM FRIGATE UNICORN

Victory Dock DD1 3JA

☎ 01382 200900 & 200893
▤ 01382 200923

The *Unicorn* is the oldest British-built warship afloat, and Scotland's only example of a wooden warship. Today she houses a museum of life in the Royal Navy during the days of sail, with guns, models and displays.

Times: Open all year, 25 Mar-31 Oct, daily 10-5; Nov-mid Mar open five days a week. Closed 25 Dec & 1 Jan.

Fee: *£3 (concessions £2.50). Party 20+.

▣ ▣ ዿ shop ✖ (no exceptions)

McMANUS GALLERIES

Albert Square DD1 1DA (off A85)

☎ 01382 432020   ▤ 01382 432052

Dundee's main museum has collections of silver, ceramics, glass and furniture, and displays on local archaeology, civic and social history, trades and industries. The major art gallery has an important collection of Scottish and Victorian works of art, and touring exhibitions are a regular feature.

Times: Open all year, Mon 11-5, Tue-Sat 10-5. (Closed 25-26 Dec & 1-3 Jan).

▣ (100 yds) ▣ ዿ (wheelchair available & high arm chairs, audio loop) toilets for disabled shop ✖ (ex guide dogs) *Details not confirmed for 2000*

⛪ DUNFERMLINE

ANDREW CARNEGIE BIRTHPLACE MUSEUM

Moodie St KY12 7PL (400yds S from Dunfermline Abbey)

☎ 01383 724302   ▤ 01383 729002

The museum tells the story of the handloom weaver's son, born here in 1835, who created the biggest steel works in the USA and then became a philanthropist on a huge scale. The present-day work of the philanthropic Carnegie Trust is also explained.

Times: Open all year, Apr, May, Sep & Oct, Mon-Sat 11-5, Sun 2-5; Jun-Aug, Mon-Sat 10-5, Sun 2-5; Nov-Mar, daily 2-4.

▣ ዿ toilets for disabled shop ✖ (ex guide dogs) *Details not confirmed for 2000*

DUNFERMLINE ABBEY

Pittencrieff Park

☎ 01383 739026

The monastery was a powerful Benedictine house, founded by Queen Margaret in the 11th century. The grave of King Robert the Bruce is marked by a modern brass in the choir. The monastery guest house became a royal palace, and was the birthplace of Charles I.

Times: Open all year, Apr-Sep, Mon-Sat 9.30-6.30, Sun 2-6.30; Oct-Mar, Mon-Sat 9.30-4.30, Sun 2-4.30. (Closed Thu pm & Fri in winter; 25-26 Dec & 1-3 Jan).

▣ ዿ shop ✖ ▌ *Details not confirmed for 2000*

PITTENCRIEFF HOUSE MUSEUM

Pittencrieff Park KY12 8QH

☎ 01383 722935 & 313838
▤ 01383 313837

A fine 17th-century mansion house, standing in a park with lawns, hothouses and gardens. In the house are galleries with displays on the history of the house, park and costume. Temporary art exhibitions are shown in the top gallery. The house and park were given to the town by Andrew Carnegie.

Times: Open Apr-Sep 11-5, Oct-Mar 11-4.

Fee: Free.

ዿ (ramp) toilets for disabled shop ✖ (ex guide dogs)

⛪ DUNKELD

THE ELL SHOP & LITTLE HOUSES

The Cross PH8 0AN (off A9, 15m N of Perth)

☎ 01350 727460

The National Trust owns two rows of 20 houses in Dunkeld, and has preserved their 17th/18th-century character. They are not open to the

contd.

public, but there is a display and audio-visual show in the Information Centre.

Times: Open Ell Shop Apr-Sep, Mon-Sat 10-5.30, also Sun Jun-Aug 1.30-5.30; Oct-23 Dec, Mon-Sat 10-4.30. (Closed 1-10 Nov). Exterior of Little Houses can be viewed all year.

P (300yds) & toilets for disabled shop ✖ (ok in village) ❧ *Details not confirmed for 2000*

EAST FORTUNE
MUSEUM OF FLIGHT
East Fortune Airfield EH39 5LF (Signposted from A1 near Haddington)
☎ 01620 880308   ▤ 01620 880355

Situated on 63 acres of one of Britain's best preserved wartime airfields, the museum has three hangars, with more than 50 aeroplanes, plus engines, rockets and memorabilia. Items on display include two Spitfires, a Vulcan bomber and Britain's oldest surviving aeroplane, built in 1896. A special Millennium Air Show will be held on 15/16 July.

Times: Open daily. 10.30-5. Closed 25/31 Dec, 1 Jan.
Fee: *£3 (ch free, concessions £1.50). Season ticket available.
P ■ & toilets for disabled shop

EAST LINTON
HAILES CASTLE
(1m SW on unclass rd).
☎ 0131 668 8800   ▤ 0131 668 8888

The castle was a fortified manor house of the Gourlays and Hepburns. Bothwell brought Mary Queen of Scots here when they were fleeing from Borthwick Castle. The substantial ruins include a 16th-century chapel.

Times: Open at all reasonable times.
✖ ▮ *Details not confirmed for 2000*

PRESTON MILL & PHANTASSIE DOOCOT
EH40 3DS (signposted from A1)
☎ 01620 860426

This attractive mill, with conical, pantiled roof, is the oldest working water-driven meal mill to survive in Scotland, and was last used commercially in 1957. Nearby is the charming Phantassie Doocot (dovecote), built for 500 birds.

Times: Open Good Fri-Easter wknd and May-Sep, Mon-Sat 11-1 & 2-5pm, Sun 1.30-5pm; wknds in Oct, 1.30-4. Last entry 20 mins before closing morning and afternoon.
P & toilets for disabled shop ✖ (ex guide dogs) ❧ *Details not confirmed for 2000*

EDINBURGH
BRASS RUBBING CENTRE
Trinity Apse, Chalmers Close, High St EH1 1SS
☎ 0131 556 4364   ▤ 0131 557 3364

Housed in the 15th-century remnant of Trinity Apse, the Centre offers the chance to make your own rubbing from a wide range of replica monumental brasses and Pictish stones. Tuition is available.

Times: Open Mon-Sat 10-5 (during Edinburgh Festival Sun 12-5).
Fee: *Free.
shop ✖ (ex guide dogs)

EDINBURGH

This is a gem of a city. From the castle on its rock, the Old Town clings to the ridge that drops to Holyrood Palace. Here aristocrat and beggar lived cheek by jowl, within a stone's throw (sometimes literally) of parliament, court and cathedral. In the late 18th century Edinburgh flowered into prominence in the arts, science and philosophy, leaving the legacy of the New Town, with its glorious sweeps of magnificent domestic architecture using the natural contours to great effect. Museums, galleries, restaurants, bars, and concert halls vie for the visitor's attention. If you find accommodation, come for the Festival and the Fringe - there's nothing like it anywhere else.

Camera Obscura

Castlehill, Royal Mile EH1 2LZ (next to Edinburgh castle)
☎ 0131 226 3709 🖷 0131 225 4239

A unique view of Edinburgh - as the lights go down a brilliant moving image of the surrounding city appears. The scene changes as a guide operates the camera's system of revolving lenses and mirrors.
Times: Open all year, daily, Apr-Oct 9.30-6; Nov-Mar 10-5. (Closed 25 Dec). Open later Jul-Aug, phone for details.
Fee: *£3.95 (ch £1.95, students £3.15, pen £2.50) Family £11.50.
P (300mtrs) shop (ex guide dogs)

City Art Centre

2 Market St EH1 1DE
☎ 0131 529 3993 🖷 0131 529 3986

The City Art Centre houses the city's permanent fine art collection and stages a constantly changing programme of temporary exhibitions from all parts of the world. It has six floors of display galleries (linked by an escalator).Please ring for details of special events.
Times: Open Mon-Sat 10-5 (Sun 2-5 during Edinburgh Festival).
Fee: *Free. Admission charged for some exhibitions.
P (500yds) ♿ (induction loop, lifts) toilets for disabled shop (ex guide dogs)

Craigmillar Castle

(2.5m SE)
☎ 0131 661 4445

Mary Queen of Scots retreated to this 14th-century stronghold after the murder of Rizzio, and the plot to murder Darnley, her second husband, was also hatched here. There are 16th and 17th-century apartments.
Times: Open all year, Apr-Sep, Mon-Sat 9.30-6.30, Sun 2-6.30. Oct-Mar, Mon-Sat 9.30-4.30. Sun 2-4.30. (Closed Thu pm & Fri in winter, 25-26 Dec & 1-3 Jan).
P ♿ shop *Details not confirmed for 2000*

Dean Gallery

73 Belford Rd EH4 3DS
☎ 0131 624 6200 🖷 0131 343 3250

Opened in March 1999, the Dean Gallery provides a home for the Eduardo Paolozzi gift of sculpture and graphic art, the Gallery of Modern Art's renowned Dada and Surrealist collections, a major library and archive centre, along with temporary exhibition space for modern and contemporary art.
Times: Open all year, Mon-Sat 10-5, Sun 2-5. (extended opening during Edinburgh Festival).
Fee: Admission to permanent collections free, charge may be made for special exhibitions.
P ♿ (lift) toilets for disabled shop (ex guide dogs)

Dynamic Earth

Holyrood Rd EH8 8LH (on the edge of Holyrood Park, opposite the Palace of Holyrood House)
☎ 0131 550 7800 🖷 0131 550 7801

A new attraction that takes you on a fantastic journey of discovery back through time to learn why the Earth has changed. Amazing interactive displays let you see, hear, smell and feel the planet as it was in the past, as it is today and how it will be in the future.
Times: Open Apr-Oct daily 10-6; Nov-Mar, Wed-Sat 10-5. Closed 24-25 Dec.
P (charged) ✕ licensed ♿ (audio guides, large print transcripts) toilets for disabled shop (ex guide dogs)
Details not confirmed for 2000

Edinburgh Castle

☎ 0131 225 9846

This historic stronghold stands on the precipitous crag of Castle Rock. One of the oldest parts is the 11th-century chapel of the saintly Queen Margaret, but most of the present castle evolved later, during its stormy history of seiges and wars, and was altered again in Victorian times. The Scottish crown and other royal regalia are displayed in the Crown Room. Also notable is the Scottish National War Memorial.
Times: Open Apr-Sep, daily 9.30-6. Oct-Mar, daily 9.30-5. Last ticket sold 45 mins earlier than closing time. Times may occasionally be altered during the Tattoo or for State and military events.
P (charged) ✕ licensed ♿ (free transport to top of Castle Hill lift) toilets for disabled shop *Details not confirmed for 2000*

Former Royal Yacht 'Britannia'

Ocean Dr, Leith EH6 6JJ
☎ 0131 555 5566 🖷 0131 555 8835

The 'Britannia' experience begins in the Visitor Centre where you are provided with an insight into the history of this unique Royal residence. Tour the four main decks and see the bridge, royal apartments and engine room.
Times: Open all year 10.30-4.30 with extended hours in summer and some restrictions in winter.
Fee: *£7.50 (ch £3.75, pen £5.75).
P ♿ (lift to ship, all areas ramped) toilets for disabled shop (ex guide dogs)

Georgian House

7 Charlotte Sq EH2 4DR (2mins walk W end of Princes Street)
☎ 0131 225 2160 🖷 0131 226 3318

The house is part of Robert Adam's splendid north side of Charlotte Square, the epitome of Edinburgh New Town architecture. The lower floors of No 7 have been restored in the style of the early 1800s, when the house was new. There are also videos of life in the New Town, and this house in particular.
Times: Open Apr-Oct, Mon-Sat 10-5, Sun 2-5. Last admission 4.30pm.
P (100 yds) (meters. disabled is directly outside) ♿ (induction loop for hard of hearing) shop (ex guide dogs)
Details not confirmed for 2000

GLADSTONE'S LAND
477b Lawnmarket EH1 2NT (5mins walk from Princes Street via Mound)
☎ 0131 226 5856

Built in 1620, this six-storey tenement, once a merchant's house, still has its arcaded front - a rare feature now. Visitors can also see unusual tempera paintings on the walls and ceilings. It is furnished as a typical 17th-century merchant's home, complete with ground-floor shop front and goods of the period.
Times: Open Apr-Oct, Mon-Sat 10-5, Sun 2-5. Last admission 4.30pm.
P (440yds meters) (outside for disabled) & (tours for the blind can be arranged) shop ✖ (ex guide dofs) ☯ *Details not confirmed for 2000*

HUNTLY HOUSE MUSEUM
142 Canongate EH8 8DD
☎ 0131 529 4143 ▤ 0131 557 3346

This is one of the best-preserved 16th-century buildings in the Old Town. It was built in 1570 and later became the headquarters of the Incorporation of Hammermen. Now a museum of local history, it has collections of silver, glassware, pottery, and other items such as street signs.
Times: Open all year, Mon-Sat 10-5. (During Festival period only, Sun 2-5).
Fee: Free.
P (200yds) meters & shop ✖ (ex guide dogs)

JOHN KNOX HOUSE
The Netherbow, 43-45 High St EH1 1SR (between The Castle and Holyrood House)
☎ 0131 556 9579 ▤ 0131 556 7478

John Knox the Reformer is said to have died in the house, which was built by the goldsmith to Mary, Queen of Scots. Renovation work has revealed the original floor in the Oak Room, and a magnificent painted ceiling.
Times: Open all year, Mon-Sat 10-5 & Sun in Aug 12-4. (Closed Xmas).
Fee: *£1.95 (ch 75p under 7's free, concessions £1.50).
🖥 & (House on 3 levels) toilets for disabled shop ✖ (ex guidance dogs) ☜

LAURISTON CASTLE
Cramond Rd South, Davidson's Mains EH4 6AG (NW outskirts of Edinburgh, 1m E of Cramond)
☎ 0131 336 2060 ▤ 0131 557 3346

The castle is a late 16th-century tower house with 19th-century additions but is most notable as a classic example of the Edwardian age. It has a beautifully preserved Edwardian interior and the feel of a country house, and the spacious grounds are very pleasant. Please telephone for details of special events.
Times: Open all year by guided tour only; Apr-Oct, 11-1 & 2-5; Nov-Mar, wknds 2-4. (Closed Fri).
Fee: *£4 (ch £3). Family ticket £8. Grounds only free.
P & shop ✖ (ex guide dogs)

NATIONAL GALLERY OF SCOTLAND
The Mound EH2 2EL (off Princes Street)
☎ 0131 624 6200 ▤ 0131 343 3250

Occupying a handsome neo-classical building designed by William Playfair, the gallery is home to Scotland's greatest collection of European paintings and sculpture from the Renaissance to Post-Impressionism. It contains notable collections of works by Old Masters, Impressionists and Scottish artists.
Times: Open all year, Mon-Sat 10-5, Sun 2-5; (Extended opening hours during the Edinburgh Festival period).
Fee: Free. Admission charged to some major exhibitions.
P (150yds) & (ramps & lift) toilets for disabled shop ✖ (ex guide dogs)

NELSON MONUMENT
Calton Hill
☎ 0131 556 2716 ▤ 0131 557 3346

Designed in 1807 and erected on Calton Hill, the monument dominates the east end of Princes Street. The views from the top are superb, and every day except Sunday the time ball drops at 1pm as the gun at the castle goes off.
Times: Open all year, Apr-Sep Mon 1-6 Tue-Sat 10-6; Oct-Mar Mon-Sat 10-3.
Fee: *£2
P shop ✖

NEWHAVEN HERITAGE MUSEUM
24 Pier Place, Newhaven EH6 4LP
☎ 0131 551 4165 ▤ 0131 557 3346

The museum tells the story of the village and its people. It looks at fishing, other sea trades, customs and superstitions.
Times: Open all year, Mon-Sun 12-5. (Closed 25-26 Dec & 1-2 Jan).
Fee: Free.
P & shop ✖ (ex guide dogs)

PALACE OF HOLYROODHOUSE
EH8 8DX (at east end of Royal Mile)
☎ 0131 556 7371 & 556 1096 (info)
▤ 0131 557 5256

The Palace grew from the guest house of the Abbey of the Holyrood, said to have been founded by David I after a miraculous apparition. Mary, Queen of Scots had her court here from 1561 to 1567, and Bonnie Prince Charlie held levees at the Palace during his occupation of Edinburgh. The Palace is still used by the Royal Family, but can be visited when they are not in residence. There are fine 17th-century state rooms, and the picture gallery is notable for its series of Scottish monarchs, starting in 330BC with Fergus I.
Times: Open daily. Apr-Oct 9.30-5.15, Nov-Mar 9.30-3.45. Closed 25-26 Dec and when Queen in residence.
Fee: *£5.50 (ch 16 £2.70, pen £4). Family ticket £13.50.
P & (first floor by lift, wheelchair available) toilets for disabled shop ✖ ☜

PARLIAMENT HOUSE

Supreme Courts, 2-11 Parliament Square EH1
1RQ (behind St Giles Cathedral)
☎ 0131 225 2595   📠 0131 240 6755

Scotland's independent parliament last sat in
1707, in this 17th-century building hidden behind
an 1829 façade, now the seat of the Supreme
Law Courts of Scotland. The Parliament Hall has
a fine hammerbeam roof. A large stained glass
window depicts the inauguration of the Court of
Session in 1540.
Times: Open all year, Mon-Fri 10-4.
Fee: Free.
🅿 (400 mtrs) ➍ ✕ ♿ toilets for disabled 🐕 (ex guide
dogs)

THE PEOPLE'S STORY

Canongate Tolbooth, 163 Canongate EH8 8BN
☎ 0131 529 4057   📠 0131 557 3346

The museum, housed in the 16th-century
tolbooth, tells the story of the ordinary people of
Edinburgh from the late 18th century to the
present day. Reconstructions include a prison
cell, 1930's pub and 1940's kitchen supported by
photographs, displays, sounds and smells.
Times: Open, Mon-Sat 10-5. Also, open Sun during
Edinburgh Festival 2-5.
Fee: Free.
♿ (first floor accessible by lift) toilets for disabled shop 🐕

ROYAL BOTANIC GARDEN

Inverleith Row EH3 5LR (1m N of city centre)
☎ 0131 552 7171   📠 0131 552 0382

Established in 1670, on an area the size of a
tennis court, the garden now comprises over 70
acres of beautifully landscaped grounds.
Spectacular features include the Rock Garden,
the Pringle Chinese Collection, and a magnificent
arboretum.
Times: Open all year Nov-Jan, 9.30-4; Feb & Dec 9.30-5; Mar
& Sept 9.30-6; Apr-Jun 9.30am-7pm; Jul-Aug 9.30am-8pm.
(closed 25 Dec & 1 Jan)
🅿 ➍ ✕ (wheelchairs available at east/west
gates) toilets for disabled shop garden centre 🐕 (ex guide
dogs) *Details not confirmed for 2000* ➍

ROYAL MUSEUM OF SCOTLAND (CHAMBERS ST)

Chambers St EH1 1JF
☎ 0131 225 7534   📠 0131 220 4819

This magnificent museum houses extensive
international collections covering the Decorative
Arts, Natural History, Science, Technology and
Working Life, and Geology. A lively programme
of events including temporary exhibitions, films,
lectures and concerts takes place throughout the
year.
Times: Open all year, Mon-Sat 10-5, Sun 12-5 (Tue late
opening till 8). Closed 25 Dec. phone for times on 26 Dec/1 Jan.
Fee: Free.
➍ ✕ licensed ♿ toilets for disabled shop 🐕 (ex guide
dogs)

ROYAL OBSERVATORY VISITOR CENTRE

Blackford Hill EH9 3HJ
☎ 0131 668 8405   📠 0131 668 8429

There are excellent views of Edinburgh from the
rooftop here, and through one of Scotland's
largest telescopes. Play with light, lenses, and
prisms, and learn about the history of the
Observatory, and its current work in Hawaii and
Australia. Public observing on Friday evenings
(end Oct to Mar, weather permitting) 7.30pm
sharp.
Times: Open Mon-Sat 10-5, Sun noon-5.
Fee: *£3 (ch £2, disabled £1). Family ticket £7.
🅿 ♿ (most floors accesible by lift) toilets for disabled shop
🐕 (ex guide dogs) ➍

SCOTCH WHISKY HERITAGE CENTRE

354 Castlehill EH1 2NE
☎ 0131 220 0441   📠 0131 220 6288

Situated beside Edinburgh Castle at the top of the
Royal Mile, the Scotch Whisky Heritage Centre
reveals the mystery of whisky making. The tour
includes a 'ghostly' blender show, barrel ride
through whisky history and a complimentary
dram of blended whisky for adults. There are
over 200 different whiskies available in the Bond
Bar.
Times: Open daily, 10-5.30 (extended in summer). (Closed
25 Dec.)
Fee: *£4.95 (ch 5-17 £2.50, concessions £3.50). Family ticket
£12.
🅿 (.25m) ➍ ♿ toilets for disabled shop 🐕 (ex guide dogs)
➍

SCOTTISH NATIONAL GALLERY OF MODERN ART

Belford Rd EH4 3DR (in the West End of
Edinburgh)
☎ 0131 624 6200   📠 0131 343 3250

An outstanding collection of 20th-century
painting, sculpture and graphic art. Includes
major works by Matisse, Picasso, Bacon, Moore
and Lichtenstein and an exceptional group of
Scottish paintings. Set in leafy grounds with a
sculpture garden.
Times: Open all year, Mon-Sat 10-5 & Sun 2-5. (Extended
opening hours during the Edinburgh Festival).
Fee: Free. Admission charged to some major exhibitions.
🅿 ➍ ♿ (ramps & lift) toilets for disabled shop 🐕 (ex guide
dogs) ➍

SCOTTISH NATIONAL PORTRAIT GALLERY

1 Queen St EH2 1JD (parallel to Princes Street,
just behind St Andrew Square)
☎ 0131 624 6200   📠 0131 558 3691

The collection provides a visual history of
Scotland from the 16th century to the present
day, told through the portraits of the people who
shaped it. Among the most famous are Mary,
Queen of Scots, Ramsay's portrait of David Hume

contd.

and Raeburn's Sir Walter Scott. The building also houses the National Collection of Photography.
Times: Open all year, daily, Mon-Sat 10-5, Sun 2-5. (Extended opening hours during the Edinburgh Festival. (Closed 25-26 Dec & 1 Jan).
Fee: *Free. Admission charged to some major exhibitions.
P (200yds) ⏸ & (ramps & lift) toilets for disabled shop ✶ (ex guide dogs) ⬤

SCOTTISH UNITED SERVICES MUSEUM
Edinburgh Castle EH1 2NG (in Edinburgh Castle)
☎ 0131 225 7534   ▤ 0131 225 3848

The museum is in Edinburgh Castle and after refurbishment will feature a complex of exhibitions illustrating Scottish military history.
Times: Open all year, Apr-Oct, Mon-Sat 9.30-6, Sun 11-6; Nov-Mar, Mon-Sat 9.30-5, Sun 12.30-5 (closed for refurnishment until Apr 2000).
Fee: *Free admission after paying entrance fee to the Castle.
P & toilets for disabled shop ✶

THE WRITERS' MUSEUM
Lady Stair's House, Lady Stair's Close, Lawnmarket EH1 2PA
☎ 0131 529 4901   ▤ 0131 557 3346

Situated in the historic Lady Stair's House which dates from 1622, the museum houses various objects associated with Robert Burns, Sir Walter Scott and Robert Louis Stevenson. Temporary exhibitions are planned throughout the year.
Times: Open all year, Mon-Sat 10-5. (During Festival period only, Sun 2-5).
Fee: Free.
shop ✶ (ex guide dogs)

⛰ EDZELL
EDZELL CASTLE
(on B966)
☎ 01356 648631

The 16th-century castle has a remarkable walled garden built in 1604 by Sir David Lindsay. Flower-filled recesses in the walls are alternated with heraldic and symbolic sculptures of a sort not seen elsewhere in Scotland. There are ornamental and border gardens and a garden house.
Times: Open all year, Apr-Sep, Mon-Sat 9.30-6.30, Sun 2-6.30; Oct-Mar, Mon-Sat 9.30-4.30, Sun 2-4.30. (Closed Thu pm & Fri in winter; 25-26 Dec & 1-3 Jan).
P & toilets for disabled shop garden centre ▮ *Details not confirmed for 2000*

⛰ FALKIRK
CALLENDAR HOUSE
Callendar Park FK1 1YR (from W M80 J4; from E M9 J4/5; A803 to Falkirk, follow signs into Callendar Park)
☎ 01324 503770   ▤ 01324 503771

Mary, Queen of Scots, Oliver Cromwell, Bonnie Prince Charlie, noble earls and wealthy merchants all feature in the the history of Callander House. Costumed interpreters describe early 19th-century life in the kitchens and the

900-year history of the house is illustrated in the 'Story of Callendar House' exhibition. The house is set in parkland, offering boating and woodland walks. Christmas at Callander House will include spitroasting goose in the kitchen, traditional tree and carols in the main hall.
Times: Open all year, Mon-Sat 10-5. Apr-Sep Sun 2-5.
P ⏸ ✗ & (ramps & lift) toilets for disabled shop ✶ (ex guide dogs) *Details not confirmed for 2000* ⬤

ROUGH CASTLE
(1m E of Bonnybridge)
☎ 0131 668 8800   ▤ 0131 668 8888

The impressive earthworks of a large Roman fort on the Antonine Wall can be seen here. The buildings have disappeared, but the mounds and terraces are the sites of barracks, and granary and bath buildings. Running between them is the military road which once linked all the forts on the wall and is still well defined.
Times: Open any reasonable time.
P ✶ ▮

⛰ FALKLAND
FALKLAND PALACE & GARDEN
KY15 7BU (off A912, 11m N of Kirkaldy)
☎ 01337 857397   ▤ 01592 261919

The hunting palace of the Stuart monarchs, this fine building, with a French-Renaissance style south wing, stands in the shelter of the Lomond Hills. The beautiful Chapel Royal and King's Bedchamber are its most notable features, and it is also home to the oldest royal tennis court in Britain (1539). The garden has a spectacular delphinium border. Recorded sacred music is played hourly in the Chapel. Please telephone for details of concerts, recitals etc.
Times: Open Apr-Oct, Mon-Sat 11-5.30, Sun 1.30-5.30. (last admission to palace 4.30, to garden 5). Town Hall by appointment.
P & shop ✶ (ex guide dogs) ♻ *Details not confirmed for 2000*

⛰ GLAMIS
ANGUS FOLK MUSEUM
Kirkwynd Cottages DD8 1RT (off A94, in Glamis)
☎ 01307 840288

A row of stone-roofed, late 18th-century cottages now houses the splendid Angus Folk Collection of domestic equipment and cottage furniture. Across the wynd, an Angus stone steading houses The Life on the Land Exhibition.
Times: Open Good Fri-Etr Mon & May-Sep, daily 11-5; wknds in Oct 11-5. (Last admission 4.30pm).
P & toilets for disabled ✶ (ex guide dogs) ♻ *Details not confirmed for 2000*

GLAMIS CASTLE
DD8 1RJ (5m W of Forfar on A94)
☎ 01307 840393   ▤ 01307 840733

This splendid, turreted and battlemented castle is the family home of the Earls of Strathmore, and was the childhood home of HM The Queen

Mother. The present castle dates from the 15th century, and there are fine collections of china, pictures, tapestries and furniture. Various events during the summer, including Strathmore Vehicle Vintage Club Extravaganza (mid Jul), Grand Scottish Promenade Outdoor (second half Jul).
Times: Open 27 Mar-31 Oct 10.30-5.30 (Jul-Aug open from 10am). Last admission 4.45pm. Other times by prior appointment.
Fee: *Castle & grounds £5.40 (ch £2.80, pen & students £4.20). Grounds only £2.50 (ch & pen £1.40).
🅿 ✗ licensed ♿ toilets for disabled shop ✖ (ex in grounds)

⛰ GLENGOULANDIE DEER PARK
GLENGOULANDIE DEER PARK
PH16 5NL (8m NW of Aberfeldy on B846).
☎ 01887 830261 ▤ 01887 830261

Various native birds and animals are kept in surroundings as similar to their natural environment as possible, and there are herds of red deer and Highland cattle. Pets must not be allowed out of cars.
Times: Open May-Oct, 9am-1hr before sunset.
Fee: *£1. Cars £5.
🅿 shop ✖

⛰ INGLISTON
SCOTTISH AGRICULTURAL MUSEUM
EH28 8NB (at East Gate of Royal Highland Showground)
☎ 0131 333 2674 ▤ 0131 333 2674

A fascinating collection illustrating rural Scotland through the ages: the tools and equipment, the workers and their families. Please telephone for details of the Royal Highland Show.
Times: Open Apr-Sep, daily 10-5; Oct-Mar, Mon-Fri. Closed Xmas & New Year.
🅿 ⬛ ♿ toilets for disabled shop *Details not confirmed for 2000*

⛰ INVERESK
INVERESK LODGE GARDEN
EH21 7TE (A6124 S of Musselburgh)
☎ 0131 665 1855

This charming terraced garden, set in the historic village of Inveresk, specialises in plants, shrubs and roses suitable for growing on small plots. The 17th-century house makes an elegant backdrop.
Times: Open all year, Mon-Fri 10-4.30, Sat-Sun 2-5 (Closed Sat Oct-Mar).
🅿 ♿ ✖ (ex guide dogs) ☙ *Details not confirmed for 2000*

⛰ KELLIE CASTLE & GARDENS
KELLIE CASTLE & GARDENS
KY10 2RF (3m NW of Pittenweem on B9171)
☎ 01333 720271 ▤ 01333 720326

The oldest part dates from about 1360, but it is for its 16th and 17th-century domestic architecture that Kellie is renowned. It has

notable plasterwork and painted panelling, and there are also interesting Victorian gardens.
Times: Open - Castle Good Fri-Etr Mon & May-Sep, daily 1.30-5.30; wknds in Oct 1.30-5.30 (last admission 4.45). Gardens & grounds open all year, Apr-Oct, daily 9.30-sunset.
🅿 ⬛ ♿ (Induction loop for the hard of hearing) shop ✖ (ex guide dogs) ☙ *Details not confirmed for 2000*

⛰ KILLIECRANKIE
KILLIECRANKIE VISITOR CENTRE
NTS Visitor Centre PH16 5LG (3m N of Pitlochry on B8079)
☎ 01796 473233 ▤ 01796 473233

The visitor centre features an exhibition on the battle of 1689, when the Jacobite army routed the English, although the Jacobite leader, `Bonnie Dundee', was mortally wounded in the attack. The wooded gorge is a notable beauty spot, admired by Queen Victoria, and there are some splendid walks.
Times: Visitor Centre, Exhibition, shop & snack bar Apr-Oct, daily 10-5.30. Site all year daily.
🅿 ⬛ ♿ (visitor centre only) toilets for disabled shop ☙ *Details not confirmed for 2000*

⛰ KINROSS
LOCH LEVEN CASTLE
Castle Island (on an Island in Loch Leven accessible by boat from Kinross)
☎ 0131 668 8800 ▤ 0131 668 8888

Mary Queen of Scots was imprisoned here, in this five-storey castle in 1567 - she escaped 11 months later and gave the 14th-century castle its special place in history.
Times: Open Apr-Sep, Mon-Sat 9.30-6.30, Sun 2-6.30.
🅿 shop ✖ ▮ *Details not confirmed for 2000*

RSPB NATURE RESERVE VANE FARM
By Loch Leven KY13 7LX (on southern shore of Loch Leven, entered off B9097 to Glenrothes, 2m E M90 J5)
☎ 01577 862355 ▤ 01577 862013

Well placed beside Loch Leven, with a nature trail and hides overlooking the Loch. Noted for its pink-footed geese, the area also attracts whooper swans, greylag geese, long-eared owls and great spotted woodpeckers amongst others. Details of special events are available from the Visitors Centre.
Times: Open daily, Apr-Xmas, 10-5; Jan-Mar 10-4.
🅿 ⬛ ♿ (ramps into visitor centre) toilets for disabled shop ✖ (ex guide dogs) *Details not confirmed for 2000* ⬛

⛰ KIRKCALDY
KIRKCALDY MUSEUM & ART GALLERY
War Memorial Gardens KY1 1YG (next to Kirkaldy train stn)
☎ 01592 412860 ▤ 01592 412870

Set in lovely grounds, the museum has a superb collection of 19th and 20th-century Scottish

contd.

paintings, a local history exhibition and a changing exhibition programme.

Times: Open all year, Mon-Sat 10.30-5, Sun 2-5. (Closed public hols).

P � & toilets for disabled shop ✶ (ex guide dogs) *Details not confirmed for 2000*

⚏ KIRRIEMUIR
BARRIE'S BIRTHPLACE
9 Brechin Rd DD8 4BX (on A90/A926 6m NW of Forfar)
☎ 01575 572646

The creator of Peter Pan, Sir James Barrie, was born in Kirriemuir in 1860. The upper floors of No 9 Brechin Road are furnished as they may have been when Barrie lived there, and the adjacent house, No 11, houses an exhibition about him.The wash-house outside was his first `theatre' and gave him the idea for Wendy's house in `Peter Pan'.

Times: Open Good Fri-Etr Mon & May-Sep, Mon-Sat 11-5.30 & Sun 1.30-5.30; wknds in Oct 11-5.30, Sun 1.30-5.30. Last admission 5pm.

P (100yds) ▆ & (stairlift, audio programmes) shop ✶ (ex guide dogs) ✽ *Details not confirmed for 2000*

⚏ LINLITHGOW
BLACKNESS CASTLE
EH49 7AL (4m N)
☎ 01506 834807

Once, this was one of the most important fortresses in Scotland. Used as a state prison during covenanting time and in the late 19th century as a powder magazine, it was one of four castles left fortified by the Articles of Union. Most impressive are the massive 17th-century artillery emplacements.

Times: Open all year, Apr-Sep, Mon-Sat 9.30-6.30, Sun 2-6.30. Oct-Mar, Mon-Sat 9.30-4.30, Sun 2-4.30. (Closed Thu pm & Fri in winter; 25-26 Dec & 1-3 Jan).

P shop ✽ *Details not confirmed for 2000*

HOUSE OF THE BINNS
EH49 7NA (4m E of Linlithgow off A904)
☎ 01506 834255

An example of changing architectural tastes from 1612 onwards, the House of The Binns reflects the transition from fortified stronghold to spacious mansion. The original three-storey, grey building, with small windows and twin turrets, finally evolved into a fine U-shaped, crenellated house with beautiful moulded plaster ceilings, ancestral home of the Dalyell family, one of whose members raised the regiment of the Royal Scots Greys. There is a magnificent display of snowdrops and daffodils in spring.

Times: Open: House, May-Sep, daily ex Fri, 1.30-5.30 (last admission 5). Parkland, Apr-Oct, daily 9.30-7; Nov-Mar, daily 9.30-4 (last admission 30 mins before closing).

P & (braille sheets) ✶ (ex guide dogs) ✽ *Details not confirmed for 2000*

LINLITHGOW PALACE
☎ 01506 842896

The magnificent ruin of a great Royal Palace, set in its own park or `peel'. All the Stewart kings lived here, and work commissioned by James I, III, IV, and VI can be seen. The great hall and the chapel are particularly fine. James V was born here in 1512 and Mary, Queen of Scots in 1542.

Times: Open all year, Apr-Sep, Mon-Sat 9.30-6.30, Sun 2-6.30; Oct-Mar, Mon-Sat 9.30-4.30, Sun 2-4.30. (Closed 25-26 Dec & 1-3 Jan).

P & shop ✶ ✽ *Details not confirmed for 2000*

⚏ MILNATHORT
BURLEIGH CASTLE
KY13 7XZ
☎ 0131 668 8800   ▤ 0131 668 8888

Dating from 1582, this tower house has an enclosed courtyard and roofed angle tower.

Times: Open all year, daily.
✶ ✽

⚏ MONTROSE
HOUSE OF DUN
DD10 9LQ (on A935, 3m W of Montrose)
☎ 01674 810264   ▤ 01674 810722

This Georgian house, overlooking the Montrose Basin, was built for Lord Dun in 1730 and is noted for the exuberant plasterwork of the interior. Family portraits, fine furniture and porcelain are on display, and royal mementos connected with a daughter of King William IV and the actress Mrs Jordan, who lived here in the 19th century. There is a walled garden and woodland walks. Telephone for details of events.

Times: Open Good Fri-Etr Mon & May-Sep, daily 1.30-5.30; wknds in Oct 1.30-5.30. (last admission to house 5). Garden & Grounds, all year daily 9.30-sunset.

P ✕ & (braille sheets, house wheelchair & stair lift) toilets for disabled shop ✶ (ex guide dogs) ✽ *Details not confirmed for 2000*

MONTROSE MUSEUM & ART GALLERY
Panmure Place DD10 8HE (opposite Montrose Academy)
☎ 01674 673232 & 875598 (pm)

Extensive local collections cover the history of Montrose from prehistoric times, the maritime history of the port, the natural history of Angus, and local art.

Times: Open all year, Mon-Sat 10-5. (Closed 25-26 Dec & 1-2 Jan).

Fee: Free.
P & shop ✶ (ex guide dogs)

🏛 MULL, ISLE OF

🏛 CRAIGNURE (MULL, ISLE OF)
MULL & WEST HIGHLAND NARROW GAUGE RAILWAY
Craignure (old pier) Station PA65 6AY
☎ 01680 812494 (in season) or
01680 300389 📄 01680 300595

The first passenger railway on a Scottish island, opened in 1984. Both steam and diesel trains operate on the ten-and-a-quarter inch gauge line, which runs from Craignure to Torosay Castle. The line is 1.25 miles long, and there are dramatic woodland and mountain views. Please telephone for details of special events.
Times: Open Easter week to mid Oct.
📆 & (provision to carry person seated in wheelchair on trains) shop *Details not confirmed for 2000*

TOROSAY CASTLE & GARDENS
PA65 6AY (1m S of Ferry Terminal at Craignure)
☎ 01680 812421 📄 01680 812470

The Scottish baronial architecture of this Victorian castle is complemented by the magnificent setting, and inside the house there are displays of portraits and wildlife pictures, family scrapbooks and a study of the Antarctic. The gardens include a statue walk and water garden, an avenue of Australian gum trees, a Japanese garden, many rare shrubs, a narrow gauge steam and diesel railway, a weaver's workshop and a silversmith's.
Times: Open Etr-mid Oct, daily 10.30-5.30. Gardens all year.
Fee: *£4.50 (ch £1.50, pen & students £3.50). Gardens only £3.50. Groups.
📆 🖳 & toilets for disabled shop garden centre (on leads in grounds only) 🍴

🏛 MUTHILL
DRUMMOND CASTLE GARDENS
PH7 4HZ (2m S of Crieff on A822)
☎ 01764 681257 & 681433
📄 01764 681550

The gardens of Drummond Castle were originally laid out in 1630 by John Drummond, 2nd Earl of Perth. In 1830, the parterre was changed to an Italian style. The multi-faceted sundial was designed by John Mylne, Master Mason to Charles I.
Times: Open - Gardens May-Oct, daily 2-6 (Last admission 5pm). Also Etr for 4 days.
Fee: *£3 (ch £1.50 & pen £2).
📆 & toilets for disabled shop (on leads in grounds)

🏛 NEWTONGRANGE
SCOTTISH MINING MUSEUM
Lady Victoria Colliery EH22 4QN (on A7)
☎ 0131 663 7519 📄 0131 654 1618

Based at the Lady Victoria colliery, Scotland's National Coal Mining Museum offers entertaining tours led by ex-miners. Visit the pit-head, Scotland's largest steam winding engine, and a full-scale replica of a modern underground coalface.
Times: Open Feb-Nov, daily 10-5.
Fee: *£4 (ch & concessions £2). Family ticket £10. Party 20+.
📆 🖳 & toilets for disabled shop 🐕 (ex guide dogs)

🏛 NORTH BERWICK
TANTALLON CASTLE
EH39 5PN (3m E on A198)
☎ 01620 892727

A famous 14th-century stronghold of the Douglases facing towards the lonely Bass Rock from the rocky Firth of Forth shore. Nearby 16th and 17th-century earthworks.
Times: Open all year, Apr-Sep, Mon-Sat 9.30-6.30, Sun 2-6.30; Oct-Mar, Mon-Sat 9.30-4.30, Sun 2-4.30. (Closed Thu pm & Fri in winter; 25-26 Dec & 1-3 Jan).
📆 & shop 🐕 📄 *Details not confirmed for 2000*

🏛 NORTH QUEENSFERRY
DEEP-SEA WORLD
KY11 1JR (from N, M90 take exit for Inverkeithing. From S follow signs to Forth Road bridge, first exit left)
☎ 01383 411880 📄 01383 410514

The world's longest underwater tunnel gives you a diver's eye view of an underwater world. Come face to face with Europe's largest collection of Sand Tiger sharks, and watch divers hand feed a wide array of sea life. You can touch live exhibits
contd.

Featured in United Artists *Rob Roy*
Tel: 01764 681257/433 Fax: 01764 681550
Email:
thegardens@drummondcastle.sol.co.uk

Drummond Castle Gardens Perthshire

Scotland's most important formal gardens, among the finest in Europe. The terraces overlook a magnificent parterre celebrating the saltire and family heraldry, surrounding the famous multiplex sundial by John Milne, Master Mason to Charles I.

Open at Eastertime, then daily May 1st to October 31st, 2-6pm (last entry 5pm).

in large rockpools, and see piranhas and other dangerous species in the 'Amazonian Experience'.

Times: Open all year, daily, 27 Mar-Jun Mon-Fri 10-6; Jul-Aug, Mon-Fri 10-6.30; Sep-1 Nov, Mon-Fri 10-6; 2 Nov-26 Mar, Mon-Fri 11-5. Weekends, BH & school holidays 10-6.

Fee: *£6.15 (ch 3-15 £3.75, concessions £4.25). Family ticket available.

🅿 💻 ♿ (ramps) toilets for disabled shop ✈ (ex guide dogs) ⏚

🏛 PENICUIK

EDINBURGH CRYSTAL VISITOR CENTRE

Eastfield Industrial Estate EH26 8HB (on A701)
☎ 01968 675128   📠 01968 674847

A tour around the factory allows you see craftsmen at work during the various stages in the art of glassmaking. An exhibition and video entitled `Capturing the Light' explains the process further. There is also a large collection of Edinburgh Crystal and a factory shop.

Times: Open all year. Factory tours Mon-Fri 9-3.30. Also (Closed 25-26 Dec & 1 Jan). Visitor Centre Mon-Sat 9-5, Sun 11-5.

Fee: *Tours £3 (concessions £2). Family ticket £7.50. Party 15+.

🅿 ✗ licensed ♿ (ramp to first floor) toilets for disabled shop ✈ (ex guide dogs) ⏚

🏛 PERTH

BLACK WATCH REGIMENTAL MUSEUM

Balhousie Castle, Hay St PH1 5HR
☎ 01738 621281 ext 8530
📠 01738 643245

The treasures of the 42nd/73rd Highland Regiment from 1739 to the present day are on show in this museum, together with paintings, silver, colours and uniforms.

Times: Open all year. May-Sep, Mon-Sat 10-4.30 (Closed last Sat in Jun); Oct-Apr, Mon-Fri, 10-3.30 (Closed 23 Dec-6 Jan). Other times & Parties 16+ by appointment.

Fee: *Donations.

🅿 shop ✈ (ex guide dogs)

BRANKLYN GARDEN

116 Dundee Rd PH2 7BB (on Dundee Rd, A85)
☎ 01738 625535

The gardens cover two acres and are noted for their collections of rhododendrons, shrubs and alpines. Garden tours and botanical painting courses are held.

Times: Open Mar-Oct, daily 9.30-sunset.

🅿 ✈ (ex guide dogs) 🏆 *Details not confirmed for 2000*

CAITHNESS GLASS FACTORY & VISITOR CENTRE

Inveralmond Industrial Est PH1 3TZ (on the Perth Western Bypass, A9, at the Inveralmond Roundabout)
☎ 01738 637373   📠 01738 622494

All aspects of paperweight-making can be seen from the viewing gallery at the Visitor Centre. There's a paperweight collectors' gallery, factory shop, children's play area and tourist information centre.

Times: Open all year, Factory shop & restaurant Mon-Sat 9-5, Sun 10-5 (Nov-Mar, Sun 11-5). Glassmaking Mon-Fri 9-4.30.

Fee: Free.

🅿 ✗ licensed ♿ (wheelchair available) toilets for disabled shop ✈ (ex guide dogs) ⏚

HUNTINGTOWER CASTLE

PH1 3JL (2m W)
☎ 01738 627231

Formerly known as Ruthven Castle and famous as the scene of the so-called `Raid of Ruthven' in 1582, this structure was built in the 15th and 16th centuries and features a painted ceiling.

Times: Open all year, Apr-Sep, Mon-Sat 9.30-6.30, Sun 2-6.30; Oct-Mar, Mon-Sat 9.30-4.30, Sun 2-4.30. (Closed Thu pm & Fri in winter; 25-26 Dec & 1-3 Jan).

🅿 ✈ ▉ *Details not confirmed for 2000*

PERTH MUSEUM & ART GALLERY

78 George St PH1 5LB
☎ 01738 632488   📠 01738 443505

This purpose-built museum houses collections of fine and applied art, social and local history,

natural history and archaeology. Temporary exhibitions are held throughout the year.
Times: Open all year, Mon-Sat 10-5. (Closed Xmas-New year).
P (adjacent) & shop ✖ (ex guide dogs) *Details not confirmed for 2000*

🏛 PITLOCHRY

EDRADOUR DISTILLERY
PH16 5JP (2.5m E of Pitlochry on the A924)
☎ 01796 472095 🖥 01796 472002

It was in 1825 that a group of local farmers founded Edradour, naming it after the bubbling burn that runs through it. It is Scotland's smallest distillery and is virtually unchanged since Victorian times. Have a dram of whisky while watching an audio-visual in the malt barn and then take a guided tour through the distillery itself.
Times: Open, early Mar-end Oct, Mon-Sat 9.30-5, Sun 12-5. Winter months, Mon-Sat 10-4, shop only. Tours by arrangement in winter months.
Fee: Free.
P & toilets for disabled shop ✖ (ex guide dogs)

HYDRO-ELECTRIC VISITOR CENTRE, DAM & FISH PASS
PH16 5BX
☎ 01796 473152

The visitor centre features an exhibition showing how electricity is brought from the power station to the customer, and there's access to the turbine viewing gallery. The salmon ladder viewing chamber allows you to see the fish as they travel upstream to their spawning ground.
Times: Open Apr-Oct, daily 10-5.30.
P & (monitor viewing of salmon fish pass) toilets for disabled shop ✖ *Details not confirmed for 2000* ◣

🏛 PORT OF MENTEITH

INCHMAHOME PRIORY
(4m E of Aberfoyle, off A81)
☎ 01877 385294

Walter Comyn founded this Augustinian house in 1238, and it became famous as the retreat of the infant Mary Queen of Scots in 1543. The ruins of the church and cloisters are situated on an island in the Lake of Monteith.
Times: Open Apr-Sep, weekdays 9.30-6.30, Sun 2-6.30. Ferry subject to cancellation in adverse weather conditions.
P shop ◪ *Details not confirmed for 2000*

🏛 PRESTONPANS

PRESTONGRANGE INDUSTRIAL HERITAGE MUSEUM
Prestongrange (on B1348)
☎ 0131 653 2904 🖥 01620 828201

The oldest documented coal mining site in Britain, with 800 years of history, this museum shows a Cornish Beam Engine and on-site evidence of associated industries such as brickmaking and pottery, plus a 16th-century

contd.

customs port. Special Events - weekend events for families and children in July/August, please ring for details.

Times: Open Apr-Oct, daily 11-4. Last tour 3pm.

P ▄▆ & toilets for disabled shop ✖ (ex guide dogs) *Details not confirmed for 2000*

⚏ QUEEN'S VIEW
QUEEN'S VIEW VISITOR CENTRE
PH16 5NR (7m W of Pitlochry on B8019)

☎ 01350 727284   ▤ 01350 728635

Queen Victoria admired the view on a visit here in 1866, and there is a splendid viewpoint which also has access for the disabled. The Visitor Centre has an exhibition describing the history of the area.

Times: Open Apr-Oct, daily 10-6.

P (charged) ▄▆ & toilets for disabled shop *Details not confirmed for 2000* ◥

⚏ ST ANDREWS
BRITISH GOLF MUSEUM
Bruce Embankment KY16 9AB (opposite Royal & Ancient Golf Club)

☎ 01334 478880   ▤ 01334 473306

What do ballooning, music and archery have to do with the game of golf? This museum will show you, tracing the history of the game over 500 years.

Times: Open all year, Etr-mid Oct daily 9.30-5.30; mid Oct-Etr Thu-Mon 11-3. (closed Tue & Wed).

P (charged) & toilets for disabled shop ✖ *Details not confirmed for 2000*

CASTLE & VISITOR CENTRE
☎ 01334 477196

This 13th-century stronghold castle was where Cardinal Beaton was murdered in 1546. The new visitor centre incorporates an exciting multi-media exhibition describing the history of the castle and nearby cathedral.

Times: Open all year, Apr-Sep, Mon-Sat 9.30-6.30, Sun 2-6.30; Oct-Mar, Mon-Sat 9.30-4.30, Sun 2-4.30. (Closed 25-26 Dec & 1-3 Jan).

P & toilets for disabled shop ✖ ▮ *Details not confirmed for 2000*

CATHEDRAL (& MUSEUM)
☎ 01334 472563

The cathedral was the largest in Scotland, and is now an extensive ruin. The remains date mainly from the 12th and 13th centuries, and large parts of the precinct walls have survived intact. Close by is St Rule's church, which the cathedral was built to replace. St Rule's probably dates from before the Norman Conquest, and is considered the most interesting Romanesque church in Scotland.

Times: Open all year, Apr-Sep, Mon-Sat 9.30-6.30, Sun 2-6.30; Oct-Mar, Mon-Sat 9.30-4.30, Sun 2-4.30. (Closed 25-26 Dec & 1-3 Jan).

P & shop ✖ ▮ *Details not confirmed for 2000*

⚏ SCONE
SCONE PALACE
Scone Palace PH2 6BD (2m NE of Perth on A93)

☎ 01738 552300   ▤ 01738 552588

Scottish kings were crowned at Scone until 1651; and it was the site of the famous coronation Stone of Destiny from the 9th century until it was seized by the English in 1296. The castellated edifice of the present palace dates from 1803 but incorporates the 16th-century and earlier buildings. The grounds include a pinetum, woodland garden and brilliant displays of rhododendrons and azaleas in spring. The atmosphere is charming, much-loved and `lived-in' it remains a family home.

Times: Open 2 Apr-25 Oct, daily 9.30-5.15 (last admission 4.45). Special parties outside normal opening hours & during winter by arrangement.

Fee: *Palace & Grounds £5.40 (ch £3.20, pen £4.60). Grounds only £2.70 (ch £1.70) Family £16.50.

P ▄▆ ✖ licensed & toilets for disabled shop ◥

⚏ SOUTH QUEENSFERRY
DALMENY HOUSE
EH30 9TQ

☎ 0131 331 1888   ▤ 0131 331 1788

This is the home of the Earl and the Countess of Rosebery, whose family have lived here for over 300 years. The house, however, dates from 1815 when it was built in Tudor Gothic style. There are examples of fine French furniture, tapestries and porcelain from the Rothschild Mentmore collection. Early Scottish furniture is also shown, with 18th-century portraits, Rosebery racing mementoes and a display of pictures and items associated with Napoleon.

Times: Open July-Aug, Sun 1-5.30, Mon-Tue 12-5.30. Last admission 4.45. Open other times by arrangement for groups.

Fee: *£3.80 (ch 10-16 £2, pen £3.30, students £2.80). Party 20+.

P ▄▆ & toilets for disabled ✖ (ex guide dogs or in grounds)

HOPETOUN HOUSE
EH30 9SL (2m W of Forth Road Bridge, off A904)

☎ 0131 331 2451   ▤ 0131 319 1885

Built in 1699 to a design by William Bruce, but William and Robert Adam in the 18th century. The magnificent reception rooms have paintings by Gainsborough and Raeburn, and there are also fine examples of furniture and a collection of china. The grounds are extensive, and include deer parks with red and fallow deer, and a herd of the rare St Kilda sheep. Special events leaflet available on request.

Times: Open 2 Apr-26 Sep, daily, weekends in Oct 10-5.30 (last admission 4.30).

Fee: *£5 (ch £2.70). Grounds £2.80 (ch £1.70).

P ▄▆ ✖ licensed & toilets for disabled shop (on leads) ◥

INCHCOLM ABBEY

Inchcolm Island (1.5m S of Aberdour. Access by ferry Apr-Sep)

☎ 01383 823332

Situated on a green island on the Firth of Forth, the Augustinian abbey was founded in about 1123 by Alexander I. The well-preserved remains include a fine 13th-century octagonal chapter house and a 13th-century wall painting.

Times: Open Apr-Sep, Mon-Sat 9.30-6.30, Sun 2-6.30.
shop ✖ ♫ Details not confirmed for 2000

QUEENSFERRY MUSEUM

53 High St EH30 9HP

☎ 0131 331 5545   ▤ 0131 557 3346

The museum tells the story of South Queensferry and its people. It looks at the development of the Queensferry Passage, the growth of the former Royal Burgh and the building of the rail and road bridges which span the Forth. There are displays on the life, work and pastimes of Queensferry people and a life-size model of the Burry Man, a centuries-old custom. There are changing exhibitions and a new hands-on display on the natural history of the Forth.

Times: Open all year, Mon & Thu-Sat 10-1, 2.15-5 (Sun noon-5)
Fee: Free.
▣ (0.25m) (mini-induction loop) shop ✖ (ex guide dogs)

🏛 STIRLING

MAR'S WARK

Broad St FK8 1EE

☎ 0131 668 8800   ▤ 0131 668 8888

Now partly ruined, this Renaissance-style mansion was built in 1570 by the lst Earl of Mar, Regent of Scotland. With its gatehouse enriched with sculptures, it is one of several fine buildings on the road to Stirling Castle. The Earls of Mar lived there until the 6th Earl fled the country after leading the 1715 Jacobite Rebellion.

Times: Open at all times.
♫

MUSEUM OF ARGYLL & SUTHERLAND HIGHLANDERS

☎ 01786 75165   ▤ 01786 446038

Situated in the King's Old Building in Stirling Castle, the museum tells the history of the Regiment from 1794 to the present day. Displays include uniforms, silver, paintings, colours, pipe banners and commentaries.

Times: Open Etr-Sep, Mon-Sat 10-5.30, Sun 11-5; Oct-Etr, Mon-Sun 10-4.
▣ (castle esplanade) shop ✖ Details not confirmed for 2000

OLD TOWN JAIL

Saint John St FK8 1EA (follow signs for castle up the hill, jail on left at top of St John's St)

☎ 01786 450050   ▤ 01786 471301

Built in 1847 to replace the old Tolbooth jail, this is an outstanding example of Victorian architecture. A living history performance means the visitor can learn about the daily life of the prisoners and the strict regime practised in the prison.

Times: Open daily, Apr-Sep 9.30-5.30; Oct 9.30-4.30; Nov-Mar 9.30-3.30.
Fee: *£3 (concessions £2.25). Family ticket £8.50.
▣ ✿ (lift to viewpoint) toilets for disabled shop ✖ (ex guide dogs) ◣

ROYAL BURGH OF STIRLING VISITOR CENTRE

Castle Esplanade FK8 1EH (next to Stirling Castle)

☎ 01786 479901 & 462517
▤ 01786 451881

A colourful introduction to Royal Stirling. For centuries, Stirling lay at the centre of Scotland's turbulent history, from the Wars of Independence, through the reign of the Stuart monarchs to a Medieval burgh.

Times: Open all year, Jan-Mar & Nov 9.30-5; Apr-Jun 9.30-6.30; Jul-Aug, 9-6.30; Sep-Oct 9.30-6.
Fee: Free.
▣ ✿ (Induction loop for the hard of hearing) toilets for disabled shop ✖ (ex guide dogs) ❦

SMITH ART GALLERY & MUSEUM

Dumbarton Rd FK8 2RQ (M9 J10, follow town centre signs)

☎ 01786 471917   ▤ 01786 449523

This award-winning museum and gallery presents a variety of exhibitions drawing on its own rich collections and works from elsewhere. A range of programmes and events takes place, ring for details.

Times: Open all year, Tue-Sat 10.30-5, Sun 2-5 (Closed Mon, Xmas day, Boxing day, New Years day).
Fee: Free.
▣ ▬ ✿ (wheelchair lift, induction loop in theatre) toilets for disabled shop ✖ (ex guide dogs)

STIRLING CASTLE

Upper Castle Hill FK8 1EJ

☎ 01786 450000

Sitting on top of a 250ft rock, Stirling Castle has a strategic position on the Firth of Forth. As a result it has been the scene of many events in Scotland's history. James II was born at the castle in 1430. Mary, Queen of Scots spent some years there, and it was James IV's childhood home. Among its finest features are the splendid Renaissance palace built by James V, and the Chapel Royal, rebuilt by James VI.

Times: Open all year, Apr-Sep, daily 9.30-6; Oct-Mar, daily 9.30-5. Last ticket sold 45 mins prior to closing time.
▣ (charged) ✖ licensed ✿ toilets for disabled shop ✖ ♫
Details not confirmed for 2000

⛪ WEEM

CASTLE MENZIES

PH15 2JD (1.5m from Aberfeldy on B846)

☎ **01887 820982**

Restored seat of the Chiefs of Clan Menzies, and a fine example of a 16th-century Z-plan fortified tower house. Prince Charles Edward Stuart stayed here briefly on his way to Culloden in 1746. The whole of the 16th-century building can be explored, and there's a small clan museum.

Times: Open Apr-14 Oct, wkdays 10.30-5, Sun 2-5. Last entry 4.30pm.

Fee: *£3 (ch £1.50, pen £2.50).

🅿 🍽 ♿ toilets for disabled shop 🐕 (ex guide dogs)

Southern Lowlands & Borders

Less dramatic than the Highlands, the border hills present a somewhat austere face to the modern visitor, but in the past this was formidable countryside for the invader.

When no foreigners threatened, the border families often feuded among themselves - consequently most of the old houses are heavily fortified.

Sheep on the hills and tumbling rivers provided wool and power for the textile industries of Galashiels, Selkirk, Hawick and other towns. The rivers are also a magnet for anglers.

Towards the west, the Solway coast and the Galloway hills are quiet interludes on the way to the port of Stranraer and the resort of Ayr. Here Robert Burns' reputation survives some tacky merchandising. Elsewhere in the borders the literary fan can follow in the footsteps of Robert Louis Stevenson, James Hogg and Walter Scott.

Lanarkshire cradles the Clyde on its way to Glasgow, powering the mills of the radical 18th-century industrialist, Robert Owen. Further downstream the river was, in its heyday, an artery on which a massive heavy industrial empire grew.

In general, the region is quieter than the more obvious tourist locations - visitors frequently drive through without stopping. Nevertheless, there is a great deal of interest. The Clyde coast is wonderful; walkers may find that they have great landscapes entirely to themselves; golfers can play world-class courses, and Buddhists (and others) can visit a Tibetan Monastery.

EVENTS & FESTIVALS

January
2nd Millennium Ecumenical Service, Abbey Church, Kilwinning, Ayrshire, 3pm
9th Grand Millennium Fireworks Display, Kilwinning Ayrshire
22nd Burns' Birthday Lantern Event, lantern procession & ceildh, Dumfries

February
11th-13th Scottish Short Mat Bowling Championships, Loreburn Hall, Dumfries

April
1st-9th Curling World Championships, Braehead, Glasgow

May
1st-31st Life In Our Community, exhibition and special events, Lockerbie Town Hall & Lockerbie Ice Rink, Lockerbie, Dumfries & Galloway
26th-4th June Dumfries & Galloway Arts Festival, 11 centres from Moffat to Stranraer

October
12-16th Costa Del Clyde, Govan, Glasgow, large beach environment project for 3-11 year olds of all abilities

Top: Threave Castle on the River Dee

This region includes the counties of City of Glasgow, Dumfries & Galloway, East Ayrshire, East Dunbartonshire, East Renfrewshire, North Ayrshire, North Lanarkshire, Renfrewshire, Scottish Borders, South Ayrshire, South Lanarkshire & West Dunbartonshire which reflect the recent national changes.

ALLOWAY

BURN'S COTTAGE

Burns National Heritage Park KA7 4PY (2m S of Ayr, M77/A77 from Glasgow))
☎ 01292 441215 ▤ 01292 441750

This thatched cottage was built in 1757, and Robert Burns was born here in 1759. The adjacent museum contains a large number of the poets' songs, poems, letters and personal relics. On display are the original manuscripts of 'Auld Lang Syne' and 'Tam O'Shanter'. Special events are held during Burns Week (18-25 Jan).
Times: Open all year, Apr-Oct 9-6; Nov-Mar 10-4 (Sun 12-4).
Fee: Prices under review.
🅿 🖭 ⅋ toilets for disabled shop ✖ (ex guide dogs)

BURN'S MONUMENT

KA7 4PQ (2m S of Ayr, follow signs for Burns' National Heritage Park in Alloway)
☎ 01292 441321

The monument was built in 1823 to a fine design by Thomas Hamilton Junior, with sculptures of characters in Burns' poems by a self-taught artist, James Thom.
Times: Open as for Burns' Cottage.
🅿 ⅋

TAM O'SHANTER EXPERIENCE

Burns National Heritage Park, Murdoch's Lone KA7 4PQ (2m S of Ayr)
☎ 01292 443700 ▤ 01292 441750

An introduction to the life of Robert Burns, with two audio-visual presentations – one about the life of Robert Burns, the other being a multi-screen 3D experience of the Tale of Tam O'Shanter. There are also tranquil landscaped gardens. Please telephone for details.
Times: Open all year, Apr-Oct 9-6, Nov-Mar 9-5.
Fee: Prices under review.
🅿 🖭 ✖ licensed ⅋ toilets for disabled shop ✖ (ex guide dogs)

ARDUAINE

ARDUAINE GARDEN

PA34 4XQ (20m S of Oban, on A816)
☎ 01852 200233 ▤ 01852 200233

An outstanding 18-acre garden on a promontory bounded by Loch Melfort and the Sound of Jura, climatically favoured by the North Atlantic Drift. It is famous for its rhododendrons and azalea species and other rare trees and shrubs.
Times: Open all year, daily 9.30-sunset.
🅿 ⅋ toilets for disabled ✖ (ex guide dogs) ♨ *Details not confirmed for 2000*

ARRAN, ISLE OF

BRODICK (ARRAN, ISLE OF)

BRODICK CASTLE, GARDEN & COUNTRY PARK

KA27 8HY (Ferry from Ardrossan-Brodick. From N end of Arran-Kintyre frequent in Summer, limited in winter)
☎ 01770 302202 ▤ 01770 302312

The site has been fortified since Viking times, but the present castle dates from the 13th century, and was a stronghold of the Dukes of Hamilton. Splendid silver, fine porcelain and paintings acquired by generations of owners can be seen, including many sporting pictures and trophies. There is a magnificent woodland garden, started by the Duchess of Montrose in 1923, world famous for its rhododendrons and azaleas. Ring for details of events, concerts, etc.
Times: Open all year, Garden & Country Park, daily 9.30-sunset. Castle open Good Fri-Oct daily 11.30-5. Last admission 4.30pm.
🅿 ✖ ⅋ (Braille sheets, motorised buggy, wheelchairs & stairlift) toilets for disabled shop ✖ (ex guide dogs) ♨ *Details not confirmed for 2000*

ISLE OF ARRAN HERITAGE MUSEUM

Rosaburn KA27 8DP (Right at Brodick Pier, approx 1m)
☎ 01770 302636

The setting is an 18th-century croft farm, including a cottage restored to its pre-1920 state and a `smiddy' where a blacksmith worked until the late 1960s. There are also occasional demonstrations of horseshoeing, sheepshearing, weaving and spinning, a veteran car rally and a golf tournament - please ring for details.
Times: Open Apr-Oct, Mon-Sat 10-5 high season. Apr-Oct, Mon-Sat 11-4 low season and every Sunday.
🅿 🖭 ⅋ shop *Details not confirmed for 2000*

AUCHINDRAIN

AUCHINDRAIN TOWNSHIP-OPEN AIR MUSEUM

PA32 8XN (5.5m SW of Inverarary)
☎ 01499 500235

Auchindrain is an original West Highland township of great antiquity, and the only communal tenancy township to have survived on its centuries-old site. The buildings are furnished and equipped to present you with a fascinating glimpse of Highland life in the last century.
Times: Open Apr-Sep, daily 10-5.
Fee: *£3 (ch £1.50, pen £2.50). Family ticket £8.
🅿 🖭 shop

BALLOCH

BALLOCH CASTLE COUNTRY PARK

G83 8LX (A82 for Dumbartonshire, Balloch from Glasgow. A811 for Balloch from Stirling.)
☎ 01389 758216 ▤ 01389 755721

Set at the southern end of Loch Lomond, the park encompasses varying habitats, a walled garden, and lawns for picnics giving wonderful views. Overlooking the lawns is Balloch Castle, built in 1808. Its visitor centre gives an introduction to local history and wildlife. Contact park for details of special events.

Times: Open Visitor Centre, Apr-Oct daily 10-5.45 Country Park 8-dusk.

Fee: Free.

P 🚌 ♿ toilets for disabled shop 🛍

🏛 BARCALDINE

BARCALDINE CASTLE

Benderloch PA37 1SA (9m N of Oban on A828 Oban/Fort William road. Take left turn to Tralee in Benderloch)

☎ 01631 720598 📠 01631 720598

16th-century home of the Campbells of Barcaldine. The last of the seven castles built by Black Duncan to be held in Campbell hands, and associated with the Appin Murder and Glencoe Massacre.

Times: Open Etr wk & 24 May-Sep, daily 11-5.30. (Closed Sat in Jun & Sep).

Fee: *£3.25 (ch £1.70, concessions £2.85)

P 🚌 shop ✖ 🐎

🏛 BEARSDEN

ROMAN BATH-HOUSE

Roman Rd G61 2SG

☎ 0131 668 8800 📠 0131 668 8888

Considered to be the best surviving visible Roman building in Scotland, the bath-house was discovered in 1973 during excavations for a construction site. It was originally built for use by the Roman garrison at Bearsden Fort, which is part of the Antonine Wall defences.

Times: Open all reasonable times.

♿ ✖ ∥

🏛 BENMORE

YOUNGER BOTANIC GARDEN

PA23 8QU (7m N of Dunoon on A815)

☎ 01369 706261 & 840599 (shop)

📠 01369 706369

From the formal garden, through the hillside woodlands, follow the paths to a stunning viewpoint with a spectacular outlook across the garden and the Holy Loch to the Firth of Clyde and beyond. Amongst many highlights are the stately conifers, the magnificent avenue of Giant Redwoods, and an extensive magnolia collection. Please telephone for details of special events.

Times: Open Mar-Oct, daily, 9.30-6.

P 🚌 ✖ licensed ♿ toilets for disabled shop garden centre *Details not confirmed for 2000* 🛍

🏛 BLANTYRE

DAVID LIVINGSTONE CENTRE

165 Station Rd G72 9BY (M74 J5 onto A725, to A724, take signs for Blantyre, right at lights, Centre is at foot of hill)

☎ 01698 823140 📠 01698 821424

Share the adventurous life of Scotland's greatest explorer, from his childhood in the Blantyre Mills

to his explorations in the heart of Africa, dramatically illustrated in the historic tenement where he was born. Events are planned throughout the season, contact the centre for details.

Times: Open Mon-Sat 10-5, Sun 12.30-5. (Last admission 4.30). Opening hours may be reduced in winter (contact for details).

Fee: *£2.95 (ch £1.60, concessions £1.95). Family ticket £7.50. Party 10+.

P 🚌 ♿ toilets for disabled shop (ex guide dogs/lead grounds) 🛍

🏛 BOTHWELL

BOTHWELL CASTLE

G71 8BL (approach from Uddingston off B7071)

☎ 01698 816894

Besieged, captured and 'knocked about' several times in the Scottish-English wars, the castle is a splendid ruin. Archibald the Grim built the curtain wall; later, in 1786, the Duke of Buccleuch carved graffiti - a coronet and initials - beside a basement well.

Times: Open all year, Apr-Sep, Mon-Sat 9.30-6.30, Sun 2-6.30; Oct-Mar, Mon-Sat 9.30-4.30, Sun 2-4.30. (Closed Thu pm & Fri in winter; also 25-26 Dec & 1-3 Jan).

P ♿ shop ∥ *Details not confirmed for 2000*

🏛 BROUGHTON

BROUGHTON PLACE

ML12 6HJ (N on A701)

☎ 01899 830234

Designed by Sir Basil Spence in 1938, in the style of a 17th-century Scottish tower house. The drawing room and main hall have paintings and crafts by living British artists for sale. The gardens give fine views of the Tweeddale Hills. There are also national collections of Thalictrum and Tropaeolum. A full programme of exhibitions is available on request.

Times: Open - Gallery 28 Mar-19 Oct & 21 Nov-21 Dec, daily (ex Wed) 10.30-6.

Fee: *Gallery free; Garden donations.

P ♿ shop garden centre ✖ (ex guide dogs)

🏛 CAERLAVEROCK

CAERLAVEROCK CASTLE

Glencaple DG1 4RU (8m SE of Dumfries)

☎ 01387 770244

This ancient seat of the Maxwell family is a splendid medieval stronghold dating back to the 13th century. It has high walls and round towers, with machicolations added in the 15th century.

Times: Open all year, Apr-Sep, Mon-Sat 9.30-6.30, Sun 2-6.30; Oct-Mar 9.30-4.30, Sun 2-4.30. (Closed 25-26 Dec & 1-3 Jan).

P ♿ shop ∥ *Details not confirmed for 2000*

🏛 CARDONESS CASTLE
CARDONESS CASTLE
DG7 2EH (1m SW of Gatehouse of Fleet off A75)
☎ 01557 814427

A 15th-century stronghold overlooking the Water of Fleet. It was once the home of the McCullochs of Galloway. The architectural details inside the tower are of very high quality.
Times: Open all year, Apr-Sep, Mon-Sat 9.30-6.30, Sun 2-6.30; Oct-Mar, wknds only. Sat 9.30-4.30, Sun 2-4.30 (Closed 25-26 Dec & 1-3 Jan).
🅿 shop ▮ *Details not confirmed for 2000*

🏛 CARNASSARIE CASTLE
CARNASSARIE CASTLE
PA31 8RQ (2m N of Kilmartin off A816)
☎ 0131 668 8800 📄 0131 668 8888

Built in the 16th-century by John Carswell, first Protestant Bishop of the Isles, the castle was taken and partly destroyed in Argyll's rebellion of 1685. It consists of a tower house with a courtyard built around.
Times: Open at all reasonable times.
🅿 ✈ ▮

🏛 CASTLE DOUGLAS
THREAVE CASTLE
(3m W on A75)
☎ 01831 168512

Archibald the Grim built this lonely castle in the late 14th century. It stands on an islet in the River Dee, and is four storeys high with round towers guarding the outer wall. The island is reached by boat.
Times: Open Apr-Sep, Mon-Sat 9.30-6.30, Sun 2-6.30.
🅿 ✈ ▮ *Details not confirmed for 2000*

THREAVE GARDEN & ESTATE
DG7 1RX (1m W of Castle Douglas off A75)
☎ 01556 502575 📄 01556 502683

The best time to visit is in spring when there is a dazzling display of daffodils. The garden is a delight in all seasons, however, and is home to the National Trust for Scotland's School of Practical Gardening.
Times: Open all year. Garden, daily 9.30-sunset. Walled garden and glasshouses daily 9.30-5. Visitor centre, Shop & Exhibition Apr-Oct daily 9.30-5.30. (Last entry 30 minutes before closing).
🅿 ✕ licensed ♿ (wheelchairs available incl. electric wheelchair) toilets for disabled shop garden centre ✈ (ex guide dogs) ☙ *Details not confirmed for 2000*

🏛 CLARENCEFIELD ˙
COMLONGON CASTLE
DG1 4NA
☎ 01387 870283 📄 01387 870266

An exceptionally well-preserved 15th-century Border castle. It contains many original features including dungeons, kitchen, great hall, heraldic devices, and bedchambers. Set in gardens and woodland with secluded walks, and is said to be haunted by a 16th-century suicide.

Times: Open Mar-Oct, telephone for opening times.
🅿 ♿ ✈ *Details not confirmed for 2000* ☙

🏛 COATBRIDGE
SUMMERLEE HERITAGE TRUST
Heritage Way, West Canal St ML5 1QD (Follow main routes towards town centre, adjacent to Coatbridge central station)
☎ 01236 431261 📄 01236 440429

A 20-acre museum of social and industrial history centring on the remains of the Summerlee Ironworks which were put into blast in the 1830s. The exhibition hall features displays of social and industrial history including working machinery and recreated workshop interiors. Outside, Summerlee operates the only working tram in Scotland, an underground coalmine and reconstructed miners' rows with interiors dating from 1840. The gallery shows regularly changing exhibitions. Special events throughout the year - ring for details.
Times: Open daily 10-5pm. (Closed 25-26 Dec & 1-2 Jan).
Fee: Free.
🅿 🚊 ♿ (wheelchair available & staff assistance) toilets for disabled shop ✈ (ex guide dogs)

🏛 COLDSTREAM
HIRSEL
Douglas & Angus Estates, Estate Office, The Hirsel TD12 4LP (0.5m W on A697)
☎ 01890 882834 & 882965
📄 01890 882834

The seat of the Home family, the grounds of which are open all year. The focal point is the Homestead Museum, craft centre and workshops. From there, nature trails lead around the lake, along the Leet Valley and into woodland noted for its rhododendrons and azaleas.
Times: Garden & Grounds open all year, daylight hours. Museum 10-5. Craft Centre Mon-Fri, 10-5, wknds noon-5.
Fee: *Etr-Sep: £2 per car. Oct-Etr £1 per car.
🅿 (charged) 🚊 ♿ toilets for disabled shop ✈ (ex on lead)

⚏ CREETOWN
CREETOWN GEM ROCK MUSEUM
Chain Rd DG8 7HJ (follow signs from A75)
☎ 01671 820357 & 820554
🗎 01671 820554

A world famous collection of gems, crystals, minerals and fossils. Interactive computer displays provide an opportunity to learn more, and audio visual displays explain how minerals are formed.
Times: Open Mar-Good Fri, daily 10-4; Good Fri-Sep, daily 9.30-6; Oct-Nov, daily 10-4; (Closed 25 Dec-7 Jan); 8 Jan-Feb, Sat & Sun only 10-4 or by appointment during the week.
Fee: *£2.75 (ch 5-15 £1.75, pen £2.25). Family ticket £7.25. Party 20+.
P ▬ & toilets for disabled shop ✷ (ex guide dogs) ⬤

⚏ CULZEAN CASTLE
CULZEAN CASTLE & COUNTRY PARK
KA19 8LE (4m W of Maybole, off A77)
☎ 01655 760274 & 760269
🗎 01655 760615

The castle and its country park make a fascinating day out. The great 18th-century castle stands on a cliff in spacious grounds and was designed by Robert Adam for the Earl of Cassillis. It is noted for its oval staircase, circular drawing room and plasterwork. The Eisenhower Room explores the American general's links with Culzean. The country park covers 563 acres with a wide range of attractions - shoreline, woodland walks, parkland, an adventure playground, and gardens. Telephone for details of events.
Times: Country park open all year, daily 9.30-sunset. Castle & visitor centre open Apr-Oct, 10.30-5.30. Last admission 5pm. Other times by appointment.
P ▬ ✗ licensed & (wheelchairs available, lift in castle) toilets for disabled shop garden centre (ex castle, ex guide dogs) ☙ *Details not confirmed for 2000*

⚏ DRUMCOLTRAN TOWER
DRUMCOLTRAN TOWER
(7m NE of Dalbeattie)
☎ 0131 668 8800   🗎 0131 668 8888

The 16th-century tower house stands three storeys high and has a simple, functional design.
Times: Open at any reasonable time.
✷ ▮

⚏ DRYBURGH
DRYBURGH ABBEY
(5m SE of Melrose on B6404)
☎ 01835 822381

The abbey was one of the Border monasteries founded by David I, and stands in a lovely setting on the River Tweed. The ruins are equally beautiful, and the church has the graves of Sir Walter Scott and Earl Haig.
Times: Open all year, Apr-Sep, weekdays 9.30-6.30, Sun 2-6.30; Oct-Mar weekdays 9.30-4.30, Sun 2-4.30. (Closed 25-26 Dec & 1-3 Jan).
P & shop ✷ ▮ *Details not confirmed for 2000*

⚏ DUMBARTON
DUMBARTON CASTLE
☎ 01389 732167

The castle is set on the 240ft Dumbarton Rock above the River Clyde, and dominates the town (the capital of the Celtic kingdom of Strathclyde). Most of what can be seen today dates from the 18th and 19th centuries, but there are a few earlier remains, and the rock gives spectacular views.
Times: Open all year, Apr-Sep, Mon-Sat 9.30-6.30, Sun 2-6.30; Oct-Mar, Mon-Sat 9.30-4.30, Sun 2-4.30. (Closed Thu & Fri pm in winter also 25-26 Dec & 1-3 Jan).
P shop ✷ ▮ *Details not confirmed for 2000*

⚏ DUMFRIES
BURNS HOUSE
Burns St DG1 2PS
☎ 01387 255297   🗎 01387 265081

It was here that Robert Burns spent the last three years of his short life; he died here in 1796. The house retains much of its 18th-century character and contains many fascinating items connected with the poet. There is the chair in which he wrote his last poems, many original letters and manuscripts, and the famous Kilmarnock and Edinburgh editions of his work.
Times: Open all year, Apr-Sep, Mon-Sat 10-5, Sun 2-5; Oct-Mar Tue-Sat 10-1 & 2-5.
Fee: Free.
P (100yds) shop

BURNS MAUSOLEUM
St Michael's Churchyard
☎ 01387 255297   🗎 01387 265081

The mausoleum is in the form of a Greek temple, and contains the tombs of Robert Burns, his wife Jean Armour, and their five sons. A sculptured group shows the Muse of Poetry flinging her cloak over Burns at the plough.
Times: Unrestricted access.
Fee: Free.
P (100yds) & (visitors with mobility difficulties tel 01387 255297)

DUMFRIES MUSEUM & CAMERA OBSCURA
The Observatory DG2 7SW
☎ 01387 253374   🗎 01387 265081

Situated in and around the 18th-century windmill tower, the museum's collections were started over 150 years ago and exhibitions trace the history of the people and landscape of Dumfries and Galloway. The Camera Obscura is to be found on the top floor of the windmill tower. Please telephone for details of special events and exhibitions.
Times: Open Apr-Sep Mon-Sat 10-5, Sun, 2-5; Oct-Mar, Tue-Sat 10-1 & 2-5.
Fee: *Free except Camera Obscura £1.50 (concessions 75p)
P & (camera obscura not accessible, parking available) toilets for disabled shop

OLD BRIDGE HOUSE MUSEUM
Mill Rd DG2 7BE
☎ 01387 256904 ▤ 01387 265081

The Old Bridge House was built in 1660, and is
the oldest house in Dumfries. A museum of
everyday life in the town, it has an early 20th-
century dentist's surgery, a Victorian nursery and
kitchens of the 1850s and 1900s.
Times: Open Apr-Sep, Mon-Sat 10-5 & Sun 2-5.
Fee: Free.
▣ & shop

ROBERT BURNS CENTRE
Mill Rd DG2 7BE
☎ 01387 264808 ▤ 01387 265081

This award-winning centre explores the
connections between Robert Burns and the town
of Dumfries. Situated in the town's 18th-century
watermill, the centre tells the story of Burns' last
years spent in the busy streets and lively
atmosphere of Dumfries in the 1790s. In the
evening the centre shows feature films in the
Film Theatre.
Times: Open all year, Apr-Sep, daily 10-8 (Sun 2-5); Oct-Mar,
Tue-Sat 10-1 & 2-5.
Fee: *Free ex audio-visual theatre £1.50 (concessions 75p).
▣ ▆ & (Induction loop hearing system in auditorium)
toilets for disabled shop

▥ DUNDRENNAN
DUNDRENNAN ABBEY
(6.5m SE of Kirkcudbright)
☎ 01557 500262

The now ruined abbey was founded for the
Cistercians. The east end of the church and the
chapter house are of exceptional architectural
quality. Mary, Queen of Scots is thought to have
spent her last night in Scotland here on 15 May
1568, before seeking shelter in England, where
she was imprisoned and eventually executed.
Times: Open summer only, Apr-Sep, Mon-Sat 9.30-6.30, Sun
2-6.30. (Closed Thu pm & Fri).
▣ & ✕ ▮ Details not confirmed for 2000

▥ DUNS
MANDERSTON
TD11 3PP (2m E of Duns on the A6105)
☎ 01361 883450 ▤ 01361 882010

This grandest of grand houses gives a fascinating
picture of Edwardian life above and below stairs.
Completely remodelled for the millionaire
racehorse owner Sir James Miller, the architect
was told to spare no expense, and so the house
boasts the world's only silver staircase. The state
rooms are magnificent, and there are fine formal
gardens, with a woodland garden and lakeside
walks.
Times: Open 13 May-26 Sep, Thu & Sun 2-5.30 (also late
Spring & Aug English BH Mons).
Fee: *Telephone for details.
▣ ▆ & shop ✕ (ex in gardens on lead)

▥ GALASHIELS
LOCHCARRON CASHMERE & WOOL CENTRE
Waverley Mill, Huddersfield St TD1 3BA
☎ 01896 752091 & 751100 ▤ 01896
758833

The museum brings the town's past to life and
the focal point is a display on the woollen
industry. Guided tours of the mill take about 40
minutes.
Times: Open all year, Mon-Sat 9-5, Sun (Jun-Sep) 12-5. Mill
tours Mon-Thu at 10.30, 11.30, 1.30 & 2.30, Fri am only.
Fee: *Museum free. Mill tour £2.50 (ch 14 free).
▣ & toilets for disabled shop ◥

▥ GIGHA ISLAND
ACHAMORE GARDENS
PA41 7AD
☎ 01583 505267 or 505254
▤ 01583 505244

Wonderful woodland gardens of rhododendrons
and azaleas, created by Sir James Horlick, who
bought the little island of Gigha in 1944. Many of
the plants were brought in laundry baskets from
his former home in Berkshire. Sub-tropical plants
flourish in the rich soil and virtually frost-free
climate, and there is a walled garden for some of
the finer specimens.
Times: Open all year, daily.
▣ & Details not confirmed for 2000

▥ GLASGOW
BURRELL COLLECTION
Pollok Country Park G43 1AT (2m S of city
centre)
☎ 0141 649 7151 ▤ 0141 636 0086

Amassed over some 80 years by Sir William
Burrell, who presented it to Glasgow in 1944, the
collection is now beautifully housed in a specially
designed gallery. Among the 8000 items in the
collection are Ancient Egyptian alabaster;
bronzes and jade; Japanese prints; Turkish
pottery; and European medieval art, including
metalwork, sculpture, and illuminated
manuscripts. There are also medieval doorways
and windows, now set in the walls of mellow
sandstone, and paintings and sculptures, ranging
from the 15th to the early 20th centuries, with
work by Cranach, Bellini, Rembrandt, Millet,
Degas, Manet, Cezanne and others.
Times: Open all year, Mon, Wed-Sat 10-5, Sun 11-5. (Closed
Tue, 25-26 Dec & 1-2 Jan).
▣ (charged) ✕ licensed & (wheelchairs available, tape
guides for blind) toilets for disabled shop ✕ Details not
confirmed for 2000

CATHEDRAL
Castle St G4 0QZ
☎ 0141 552 6891

The most complete medieval cathedral surviving
on the Scottish mainland, founded in the 6th
century by St Kentigern, better known as Mungo
('dear one'), Glasgow's patron saint, and dates
from the 13th and 14th centuries. The Cathedral

GLASGOW

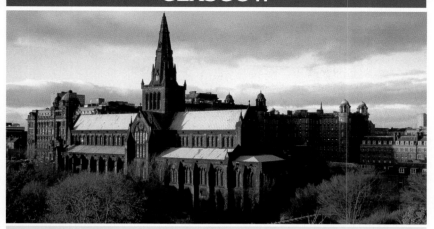

The powerhouse of Queen Victoria's empire, Glasgow was synonymous with heavy engineering, sending its products to virtually every country in the world. Poverty and social problems dogged the city for much of this century, but vigorous efforts have changed the face of Glasgow. There's plenty to enjoy, with abundant parks and museums, particularly Kelvingrove Art Gallery and Museum and the superb Burrell Collection. The School of Art is Charles Rennie Mackintosh's most famous building (guided tours available). The city is close to some of Scotland's loveliest scenery. Loch Lomond, the Clyde Coast, the Trossachs and the Mull of Kintyre are all within reach.

was threatened at the time of the Reformation, but the city's trade guilds formed an armed guard to ensure that no damage was done.
Times: Open all year, Apr-Sep, weekdays 9.30-6.30, Sun 2-6.30; Oct-Mar, weekdays 9.30-4.30, Sun 2-4.30. (Closed 25-26 Dec & 1-3 Jan).
shop ✖ ▮ *Details not confirmed for 2000*

GALLERY OF MODERN ART
Queen St G1 3AZ
☎ 0141 229 1996   📄 0141 204 5316

Set in a magnificent, refurbished neo-classical building in the heart of the city, the gallery houses Glasgow's collection of post-war art and design over four floors of display space, themed to reflect the natural elements of Fire, Earth, Water and Air. The works on display exhibits by Niki De Saint Phalle, Sebastiao Salgado and Eduard Bersudsky. Examples of the work of Scottish artists Peter Howson, John Bellany, Alan Davie, Adrian Wiszniewski and Alison Watt take pride of place. Ring for details of exhibitions.
Times: Open all year, daily 10-5, Sun 11-5.
Fee: Free.
ℙ (200yds) ✖ licensed & toilets for disabled shop ✖ ⬗

GLASGOW ART GALLERY & MUSEUM
Kelvingrove G3 8AG (1m W of city centre)
☎ 0141 287 2699   📄 0141 287 2690

The collection includes works by Giorgione and Rembrandt, and is especially strong on the French Impressionists, Post-Impressionists, and

Scottish artists. Other areas show sculpture, porcelain, silver, and a magnificent display of arms and armour. One section is devoted to the 'Glasgow Style', with furniture by Charles Rennie Mackintosh and others. Ring for details of special events.
Times: Open all year, Mon-Sat 10-5, Sun 11-5. (Closed 25-26 Dec & 1-2 Jan).
ℙ ⬛ ✖ licensed & toilets for disabled shop ✖ *Details not confirmed for 2000*

GLASGOW BOTANIC GARDENS
730 Great Western Rd G12 0UE
☎ 0141 334 2422   📄 0141 339 6964

The gardens were established in 1817 from an older university physic garden, and moved to this site in 1842. There is an outstanding plant collection, but the most remarkable feature is the 23,000 sq ft Kibble Palace, a spectacular glasshouse with soaring tree ferns inside, set off by a number of Victorian sculptures.
Times: Open all year. Gardens open daily 7am-dusk. Kibble Palace & main range of glasshouses Mon-Fri 10-4.45 (4.15 in winter), wknds afternoon only.
& toilets for disabled ✖ (ex in grounds) *Details not confirmed for 2000*

GREENBANK GARDEN
Flenders Rd, Clarkston G76 8RB (off A726 on southern outskirts of the city)
☎ 0141 639 3281

The spacious, walled woodland gardens are attractively laid out in the grounds of an elegant Georgian house (not open), and best seen between April and October. A wide range of flowers and shrubs are grown, with the idea of helping private gardeners to look at possibilities for their own environment. A greenhouse and garden designed for the disabled gardener also displays specialised tools.

Times: Garden open all year, daily 9.30-sunset. (Closed 25-26 Dec & 1-2 Jan). House open Apr-Oct Sun only 2-4. Shop & Tearoom open Apr-Oct, daily 11-5; Nov-Mar, Sat & Sun 2-4.
🅿 💺 ♿ (wheelchairs available) toilets for disabled shop (& plant sales) 🐕 (ex guide dogs) ♨ *Details not confirmed for 2000*

HUNTERIAN ART GALLERY
The University of Glasgow G12 8QQ
☎ 0141 330 5431 📠 0141 330 3618

The core of the collection is a group of paintings bequeathed in the 18th century by Dr William Hunter, but it has grown a good deal since his time. There are important works by James McNeill Whistler, 19th and 20th-century Scottish paintings, contemporary British art and sculpture, and a remarkable re-creation of Charles Rennie Mackintosh's home, including the windows and front door.

Times: Open all year. Main gallery Mon-Sat 9.30-5. Mackintosh House Mon-Sat 9.30-12.30 & 1.30-5. Telephone for PH closures.
🅿 (500 yds) (pay & display) ♿ (lift, wheelchair available) toilets for disabled shop 🐕 (ex guide dogs) *Details not confirmed for 2000* 🔖

HUNTERIAN MUSEUM
The University of Glasgow G12 8QQ (2m W of city centre)
☎ 0141 330 4221 📠 0141 330 3617

Named after the 18th-century physician, Dr William Hunter, who bequeathed his large and important collections of coins, medals, fossils, geological specimens and archaeological and ethnographic items to the university. The exhibits

are shown in the main building of the university, and temporary exhibitions are held.

Times: Open all year, Mon-Sat 9.30-5. (Closed certain PH's phone for details).
🅿 (100yds) ♿ (access by lift, prior arrangement) toilets for disabled shop 🐕 *Details not confirmed for 2000*

HUTCHESONS' HALL
158 Ingram St G1 1EJ
☎ 0141 552 8391 📠 0141 552 7031

This handsome early 19th-century building was designed by David Hamilton and houses a visitor centre and shop. There is a video about Glasgow's merchant city, and the Hall can be booked for functions. Telephone for details, and for concerts, recitals, etc.

Times: Open all year Mon-Sat 10-5. (Closed PH's & 24 Dec-6 Jan). Hall on view subject to functions in progress.)
🅿 (on street) (meters)(outside for disabled) ♿ toilets for disabled shop 🐕 ♨ *Details not confirmed for 2000*

McLELLAN GALLERIES
270 Sauchiehall St G2 3EH
☎ 0141 331 1854 📠 0141 332 9957

With over 1,200 sq metres of top gallery space, the McLellan Galleries provide Glasgow Museums with the opportunity to bring to Glasgow major exhibitions and establish Glasgow as Britain's second art city, with a popular and international exhibition programme.

Times: Open Mon-Sat 10-5, Sun 11-5 during exhibitions.
🅿 (500mtrs) ♿ (assistance available) toilets for disabled shop 🐕 *Details not confirmed for 2000* 🔖

MUSEUM OF TRANSPORT
Kelvin Hall, 1 Bunhouse Rd G3 8DP (1.5m W of city centre)
☎ 0141 287 2628 📠 0141 305 2692

A feast of nostalgia for older Glaswegians and a fascinating look at the past for younger visitors, with Glasgow buses, a reconstruction of a Glasgow side street in the year 1938, and Glasgow trams. There are Scottish-made cars, fire engines, horse-drawn vehicles, cycles, and a walk-in car showroom with vehicles from the 1930s to the present day.

Times: Open all year, Mon, Wed-Sat 10-5, Sun 11-5. (Closed Tue, 25-26 Dec & 1-2 Jan).
🅿 (charged) ✖ licensed ♿ (assistance available) toilets for disabled shop 🐕 *Details not confirmed for 2000*

PEOPLE'S PALACE
Glasgow Green G40 1AT (1m SE of city centre)
☎ 0141 554 0223 📠 0141 550 0892

This museum looks at the work and leisure of the ordinary people of Glasgow, with exhibits ranging from a 2nd-century Roman bowl to mementoes of the Jacobite risings, football games and boxing matches. There are also numerous banners, posters and other material from Glasgow's days of campaigning for wider voting rights, votes for women and recognition of trade unions.

Times: Re-opening after refurbishment April 1998, Mon, Wed-Sat 10-5, Sun 11-5. Closed Tue.

P ▆ & toilets for disabled shop garden centre ✖ *Details not confirmed for 2000*

St Mungo Religious Life & Art Museum

2 Castle St G4 0RH (1m NE of city centre)

☎ 0141 553 2557 ▤ 0141 552 4744

This unique museum, explores the universal themes of life and death and the hereafter through beautiful and evocative art objects associated with different religious faiths. Britain's only authentic Zen garden contributes its own unique sense of peace.

Times: Open all year, Mon, Wed-Sat, Sun 11-5. Closed Tue,25- 26 Dec & 1-2 Jan.

P (charged) ✖ licensed & (taped information & lift) toilets for disabled shop ✖ *Details not confirmed for 2000*

Tenement House

145 Buccleuch St, Garnethill G3 6QN (N of Charing Cross)

☎ 0141 333 0183

This shows an unsung but once-typical side of Glasgow life: it is a first-floor flat, built in 1892, with a parlour, bedroom, kitchen and bathroom, furnished with the original recess beds, kitchen range, sink, and coal bunker, among other articles. The home of Agnes Toward from 1911 to 1965, the flat was bought by an actress who preserved it as a `time capsule'. The contents vividly portray the life of one section of Glasgow society.

Times: Open Mar-Oct, daily 2-5. (Last admission 30 mins before closing); weekday morning visits by educational & other groups (not to exceed 15), by advance booking only.

P (100yds) (v.restricted, recommend parking in town (braille guide) ✖ (ex guide dogs) ❦ *Details not confirmed for 2000*

University of Glasgow Visitor Centre

University Av G12 8QQ

☎ 0141 330 5511 ▤ 0141 330 5225

The Visitor Centre is spacious and pleasant, with leaflets, publications and video displays explaining how the university works, what courses are available and which university events are open to the public. It forms the starting point for guided tours of the university's historic attractions, including the Hunterian Museum, Memorial Chapel, Bute and Randolph Halls, Professors' Square and Lion and Unicorn Staircase.

Times: Open all year, Mon-Sat 9.30-5. Also May-Sep, Sun 2-5.

Fee: *Free. Charge made for tour.

P ▆ & toilets for disabled shop ✖ ➴

⛪ GLENLUCE

Glenluce Abbey

(2m N of village)

☎ 01581 300541

The abbey was founded for the Cistercians in 1192 by Roland, Earl of Galloway. The ruins include a vaulted chapter house, and stand in a beautiful setting.

Times: Open all year, Apr-Sep, Mon-Sat 9.30-6.30, Sun 2-6.30; Oct-Mar, Sat 9.30-4.30, Sun 2-4.30. (Closed 25-26 Dec & 1-3 Jan).

P & shop ✖ ▮ *Details not confirmed for 2000*

⛪ GORDON

Mellerstain House

TD3 6LG (5m E of Earlston, on unclass road)

☎ 01573 410225 ▤ 01573 410636

One of Scotland's finest Georgian houses, begun by William Adam and completed by his son Robert in the 1770s. It has beautiful plasterwork, period furniture and pictures, terraced gardens and a lake.

Times: Open Easter, then May-Sept daily ex Sat. 12.30-5 (Last admission 4.30pm).

Fee: *£4.50 (ch £2, pen £3.50) Party 20+.

P ▆ & shop ✖ (ex guide dogs)

⛪ GREENOCK

McLean Museum & Art Gallery

15 Kelly St PA16 8JX (close to Greenock West Railway Station)

☎ 01475 715624 ▤ 01475 715626

James Watt was born in Greenock, and various exhibits connected with him are shown. The museum also has an art collection, and displays on shipping, natural history, Egyptology and ethnography. Temporary exhibition gallery.

Times: Open all year, Mon-Sat 10-5. Closed local & national PH.

Fee: Free.

P (200mtrs) & toilets for disabled shop ✖ (ex guide dogs)

🏛 HAMILTON
CHATELHERAULT
Ferniegair ML3 7UE (2.5km SE of Hamilton on A72 Hamilton-Larkhall/Lanark Clyde Valley tourist route.)
☎ 01698 426213 🖷 01698 421532

Chatelherault was built by William Adam for the Duke of Hamilton in the 1730s, as a hunting lodge, staff accommodation and kennels. It is set in 500 acres of park, which includes areas of outstanding natural beauty and nature conservation, as well as evidence of land use including mining, quarrying, and Cadzow Castle, a possible hillfort, as well as a herd of white Cadzow cattle.
Times: Open all year, Mon-Sat 10-5, Sun 12-5. House closed all day Friday.
Fee: Free.
P 🖃 ᕔ (architect designed for disabled person) toilets for disabled shop garden centre ✖ (ex grounds, ex guide dogs)

LOW PARKS MUSEUM
129 Muir St ML3 6BJ
☎ 01698 283981 🖷 01698 283479

The museum tells the story of Hamilton and the Clyde Valley, created by linking the former District Museum and The Cameronians (Scottish Rifles) Museum. Housed in the oldest building in the town, dating from 1696, the museum features a restored 18th-century assembly room and exhibitions on Hamilton Palace and The Cameronians.
Times: Open 10-5 Mon-Sat (ex.Fri), 12-5 Sun.
P ᕔ (disabled toilet being built) shop ✖ *Details not confirmed for 2000*

🏛 HERMITAGE
HERMITAGE CASTLE
TD9 0LU (5.5m NE of Newcastleton off A7)
☎ 01387 376222

A vast, eerie ruin of the 14th and 15th centuries, associated with the de Soulis, the Douglases and Mary, Queen of Scots. Much restored in the 19th century.
Times: Apr-Sep, Mon-Sat 9.30-6.30, Sun 2-6.30.
P ᕔ ▌ *Details not confirmed for 2000*

🏛 INNERLEITHEN
ROBERT SMAIL'S PRINTING WORKS
7/9 High St EH44 6HA
☎ 01896 830206

These buildings contain a Victorian office, a paper store with reconstructed waterwheel, a composing room and a press room. The machinery is in full working order and visitors may view the printer at work and experience typesetting in the composing room.
Times: Open May-Sep Mon-Sat 10-1 & 2-5, Sun 2-5; wknds in Oct: Sat 10-1 & 2-5, Sun only 2-5. (Last tour 45mins before closing morning & afternoon).
P (300yds) ᕔ shop ✖ (ex guide dogs) ❦ *Details not confirmed for 2000*

🏛 INVERARAY
INVERARAY CASTLE
PA32 8XE
☎ 01499 302203 🖷 01499 302421

The third Duke of Argyll engaged Roger Morris to build the present castle in 1743; in the process the old Burgh of Inveraray was demolished and a new town built nearby. The beautiful interior decoration was commissioned by the 5th Duke; the great armoury hall and staterooms are of particular note.
Times: Open Apr to mid Oct. Apr-Jun, Oct & Sep, Mon-Thu & Sat 10-1 & 2-5.45. Sun 1-5.45; Jul & Aug, Mon-Sat 10-5.45, Sun 1-5.45. Last admission 12.30 & 5.
P 🖃 ᕔ shop ✖ (ex guide dogs) *Details not confirmed for 2000*

🏛 IRVINE
SCOTTISH MARITIME MUSEUM
Harbourside KA12 8QE (Follow AA signs from Irvine)
☎ 01294 278283 🖷 01294 313211

The museum has displays which reflect all aspects of Scottish maritime history. Vessels can be seen afloat in the harbour and undercover. Experience life in a 1910 shipyard worker's tenement flat. The clipper 'The Carrick' can be boarded to view restoration work underway. There is an annual exhibition and an activity room for children.
Times: Open Apr-Oct, daily 10-5.
P 🖃 ᕔ (audio tapes for blind) toilets for disabled shop ✖ (ex guide dogs)

🏛 JEDBURGH
JEDBURGH ABBEY
4-5 Abbey Bridgend
☎ 01835 863925

Standing as the most complete of the Border monasteries (although it has been sacked and rebuilt many times) Jedburgh Abbey has been described as 'the most perfect and beautiful example of the Saxon and early Gothic in Scotland'. It was founded as a priory in the 12th century by David I and the remains of some of the domestic buildings have been uncovered during excavations.
Times: Open all year, Apr-Sep, Mon-Sat 9.30-6.30, Sun 2-6.30; Oct-Mar, Mon-Sat 9.30-4.30, Sun 2-4.30. (Closed 25-26 Dec & 1-3 Jan).
P ᕔ (limited access) toilets for disabled shop ✖ ▌ *Details not confirmed for 2000*

MARY QUEEN OF SCOTS HOUSE
Queen St TD8 6EW
☎ 01835 863331 🖷 01450 378526

Mary, Queen of Scots visited Jedburgh in 1566, and had to prolong her stay because of ill-health. This splendid house is now a museum devoted to her memory. An unusual feature of this 16th-century fortified dwelling is the left-handed spiral staircase: the Kers, the owners, were left-handed and the special staircase allowed the men to keep their sword hands free.

Times: Open Mar-Nov, daily 10-5 (4.30 Sun).

P (300 yds) & shop ✖ *Details not confirmed for 2000*

⛪ KELSO

FLOORS CASTLE

Roxburghe Estates Office TD5 7SF (from town centre follow Roxburghe Street to main gates)

☎ 01573 223333 ▯ 01573 226056

The home of the 10th Duke of Roxburghe, the Castle's lived-in atmosphere enhances the superb collection of French furniture, tapestries and paintings. The house was designed by William Adam in 1721 and enjoys a magnificent setting overlooking the River Tweed and the Cheviot Hills beyond.

Times: Open 2 Apr-Oct, daily 10-4.30. (last admission 4)

Fee: *£5 (ch 2-15 £3, pen £4.50). Family ticket £14. Grounds only £3. Group rates for 20+.

P ▬ ✖ licensed & (lift) toilets for disabled shop garden centre (must be kept on lead) ➘

KELSO ABBEY

☎ 0131 668 8800 ▯ 0131 668 8888

Founded by David I in 1128 and probably the greatest of the four famous Border abbeys, Kelso became extremely wealthy and acquired extensive lands. In 1545 it served as a fortress when the town was attacked by the Earl of Hertford, but now only fragments of the once-imposing abbey church give any clue to its long history.

Times: Open at any reasonable time.

& ▯

⛪ KILBARCHAN

WEAVER'S COTTAGE

The Cross PA10 2JG (off A737, 12m SW of Glasgow)

☎ 01505 705588

The weaving craft is regularly demonstrated at this delightful 18th-century cottage museum, and there is a collection of weaving equipment and other domestic utensils.

Times: Open Good Fri-Sep, daily, 1.30-5.30; wknds in Oct, 1.30-5.30 (last admission 5).

P ✖ (ex guide dogs) ✹ *Details not confirmed for 2000*

⛪ KILMARNOCK

DEAN CASTLE COUNTRY PARK

Dean Rd KA3 1XB

☎ 01563 522702 ▯ 01563 572552

This fine castle has a 14th-century fortified keep and 15th-century palace. Inside there is an outstanding collection of medieval arms and armour, musical instruments and a display of Burns' manuscripts. The castle is set in a beautiful wooded country park with rivers, gardens, woodlands, adventure playground, children's corner and aviaries. A full programme of events takes place from Apr-Sep.

Times: Open: Country Park all year, dawn to dusk. Dean Castle daily noon-5. Visitor centre & Tearoom 11-5(summer), 11-4(winter). Rare Breeds centre 1-5(summer), 1-4(winter).

Fee: *Country park, visitor centre or rare breeds centre free. Castle £2.50 (ch £1.23, under 5 free, pen £1.25, disabled free)

P ▬ & (disabled garden, car parks, ramps & level paths) toilets for disabled shop ✖ (ex guide dogs inside) ➘

DICK INSTITUTE MUSEUM & ART GALLERY

Elmbank Ave KA1 3BU

☎ 01563 526401 & 555333

▯ 01563 573333

Two museum wings exhibiting geology, natural history, engineering, archaeology and local history, and two art galleries with an important permanent collection of paintings and touring exhibitions of prints, photography and crafts.

Times: Open all year, Gallery & Museum: Mon-Tue, Thu-Fri 10-8, Wed & Sat 10-5. (Closed Sun & PH's).

Fee: *Free except for special exhibitions when a charge may be made.

P & (wheelchair available) toilets for disabled shop ✖ (ex guide dogs) ➘

⛪ KILMARTIN

DUNADD FORT

(1m W of Kilmichael Glassary)

☎ 0131 668 8800 ▯ 0131 668 8888

Dunadd was one of the ancient capitals of Dalriada from which the Celtic kingdom of Scotland was formed. Near to this prehistoric hill fort (now little more than an isolated hillock) are carvings of a boar and a footprint; these probably marked the spot where early kings were invested with their royal power.

Times: Open & accessible at all reasonable times.

✖ ▯

⛪ KILMUN

ARGYLL FOREST PARK

Forest Enterprise PA23 8SE (on A880 1m from junc with A815)

☎ 01369 840666 ▯ 01369 840617

The Argyll Forest Park extends over a large area of hill ground and forest, noted for its rugged beauty. Numerous forest walks and picnic sites allow you to explore, and the Arboretum walks and the route from the Younger Botanic Gardens to Puck's Glen are particularly lovely. A series of guided walks and other ranger-led activites are planned; also deer watches, and 4X4 safaris; please contact for details.

Times: Open all year.

Fee: Free.

P

🏛 KIRKBEAN

ARBIGLAND GARDENS

DG2 8BQ (1m SE, adjacent to Paul Jones cottage).

☎ **01387 880283** 📄 **01387 880 344**

Extensive woodland, formal and water gardens are set around a delightful sandy bay. John Paul Jones, the US Admiral, worked in the gardens as a young boy (his father was the gardener here in the 1740s).

Times: Open Gardens May-Sep, Tue-Sun 2-6. Also open BH Mon. House 22 May-31 May.

🅿 ◖ ⅙ toilets for disabled shop *Details not confirmed for 2000*

🏛 KIRKCUDBRIGHT

BROUGHTON HOUSE & GARDEN

12 High St DG6 4JX (off A711/A755)

☎ **01557 330437**

An 18th-century house where Edward A Hornel, one of the 'Glasgow Boys' group of artists, lived and worked from 1901-1933. It features a collection of his work, an extensive library of local history, including rare editions of Burns' works, and a Japanese-style garden he created.

Times: Open daily, Apr-Oct 1-5.30. (last admission 4.45pm)

🅿 (on street) (limited space) ✈ (ex guide dogs) 🍽 *Details not confirmed for 2000*

MACLELLAN'S CASTLE

☎ **01557 331856**

This handsome structure has been a ruin since the mid-18th century. It was once an imposing castellated mansion, elaborately planned with fine architectural detail. Something of its 16th-century grandeur still remains.

Times: Open summer only, Apr-Sep, Mon-Sat 9.30-6.30, Sun 2-6.30; (Closed 25-26 Dec & 1-3 Jan).

🅿 ⅙ ✈ ▮ *Details not confirmed for 2000*

TOLBOOTH ART CENTRE

High St DG6 4JL

☎ **01557 331556** 📄 **01557 330005**

Dating from 1629, the Tolbooth was converted into an art centre in 1993, and provides an interpretive introduction to the Kirkcudbright artists's colony, which flourished in the town from the 1880s. It also provides studio and exhibition space for contemporary local and visiting artists. There is a programme of exhibitions from March to October and many artists will be working in the studios while exhibiting. Phone for details.

Times: Open Mar & Oct, Mon-Sat 11-4; May-Jun & Sept, Mon-Sat 10-6; Nov-Feb, Mon-Sat 11-4. Open Sun Jun-Sep 2-5.

🅿 (on street parking) ◖ ⅙ (lift) toilets for disabled shop ✈ *Details not confirmed for 2000*

🏛 KIRKOSWALD

SOUTER JOHNNIE'S COTTAGE

Main Rd KA19 8HY (on A77, 4m SW of Maybole)

☎ **01655 760603**

`Souter' means cobbler and the village cobbler who lived in this 18th-century cottage was the inspiration for Burns' character Souter Johnnie, in his ballad *Tam o'Shanter*. The cottage is now a Burns museum and life-size stone figures of the poet's characters can be seen in the restored ale-house in the cottage garden.

Times: Open Good Fri-30 Sept daily 11.30-5; wknds in Oct, 11.30-5. Last admission 4.30

🅿 (75yds) ⅙ (only one small step into cottage) ✈ (ex guide dogs) 🍽 *Details not confirmed for 2000*

🏛 LANGBANK

FINLAYSTONE COUNTRY ESTATE

PA14 6TJ (10m W of Glasgow Airport on A8)

☎ **01475 540285 & 540505**
📄 **01475 540285**

A charming exhibition of Victoriana displayed in a homely family house with historical connections to John Knox and Robert Burns. The house, though, is only a foil to the considerable natural beauty; there are formal gardens, walled gardens, and woodland walks. The 'Dolly Mixture', an international collection of dolls, can be seen in the Visitor Centre.

Times: Open all year. Woodland & Gardens daily, 10-5. House, open Sun: Jul: groups by appointment.

Fee: *Garden & Woods £2.50 (ch & pen £1.50); Guided tour of house (Sun in Jul only), £1.50 (ch, pen: £1).'The Dolly Mixture' Doll Museum 50p.

🅿 ◖ ⅙ (lift to second floor pathways for wheelchairs) toilets for disabled shop (ex on lead)

🏛 LARGS

VIKINGAR!

Greenock Rd KA30 8QL

☎ **01475 689777** 📄 **01475 689444**

A multi-media experience that takes you from the first Viking raids in Scotland to their defeat at the Battle of Largs. Additional facilities include a swimming pool, a 500-seat theatre and cinema, cafe and theatre bar. Phone for information about forthcoming events.

Times: Open all year (closed 25-26 Dec and 1-2 Jan).

🅿 ◖ ✗ licensed ⅙ toilets for disabled shop ✈ (ex guide dogs) *Details not confirmed for 2000* 🍴

🏛 LAUDER

THIRLESTANE CASTLE

TD2 6RU (off A68, follow signs on main road approaches)

☎ **01578 722430** 📄 **01578 722761**

This fairy-tale castle has been the home of the Maitland family, the Earls of Lauderdale, since the 12th century. Some of the most splendid plasterwork ceilings in Britain may be seen in the 17th-century state rooms. The family nurseries house a sizeable collection of antique toys and dolls. The informal grounds, with their riverside setting and views of nearby grouse moors,

include a woodland walk and picnic tables.
Please ring for details of special events.
Times: Open 2-9 Apr, May-Oct daily 11-5 except Sat. Last
admission 4.15
Fee: *£4.50. Family ticket £11. Grounds only £1.50. Party.
🅿 💺 shop 🕱 (ex guide dogs)

⌂ LOCHAWE
CRUACHAN POWER STATION
Dalmally PA33 1AN (A85 18m East of Oban)
☎ 01866 822618   ▤ 01866 822509

A vast cavern hidden 1km inside Ben Cruachan,
which contains a 400,000-kilowatt hydro-electric
power station, driven by water drawn from a
high-level reservoir up the mountain. A guided
tour takes you inside the mountain and reveals
the generators in their underground cavern.
Times: Open Etr-end of Nov, daily 9.30-5 (last tour 4.15). Jul-
Aug 9.30-6 (last tour 5.15)
🅿 💺 � toilets for disabled shop 🕱 (ex guide dogs) *Details
not confirmed for 2000*

⌂ LOCHWINNOCH
RSPB NATURE RESERVE
Largs Rd PA12 4JF (on A760, Largs road,
opposite Lochwinnoch station)
☎ 01505 842663   ▤ 01505 843026

An attractive Norwegian timber building
incorporates an observation tower offering fine
views of the reserve and the surrounding
countryside and an exhibition and lecture room
with a video system and displays. A nature trail
leads through deciduous woodland to two
observation hides. A second trail, featuring a
boardwalk across the marsh, leads to a third
hide; all hides have been designed specifically for
the convenience of disabled visitors. Guided
walks throughout the year. Please telephone for
details.
Times: Open all year, daily 10-5. (Closed Xmas & New Year).
🅿 ⅙ (wheelchairs available,access 3 hides) toilets for
disabled shop 🕱 *Details not confirmed for 2000* 🏴

⌂ MAYBOLE
CROSSRAGUEL ABBEY
(2m S)
☎ 01655 883113

The extensive remains of this 13th-century
Cluniac monastery are impressive and
architecturally important. The monastery was
founded by Duncan, Earl of Carrick and the
church, claustral buildings, abbot's house and an
imposing castellated gatehouse can be seen.
Times: Open Apr-Sep, Mon-Sat 9.30-6.30, Sun 2-6.30. Closed
Thurs pm & Fri.
🅿 ⅙ shop 🕱 ▌ *Details not confirmed for 2000*

⌂ MELROSE
ABBOTSFORD HOUSE
TD6 9BQ (2m W off A6091)
☎ 01896 752043   ▤ 01896 752916

Set on the River Tweed, Sir Walter Scott's
romantic mansion remains much the same as it
was in his day. Inside there are many mementos
and relics of his remarkable life and also his
historical collections, armouries and library, with
some 9000 volumes. The mansion was built by
Scott between 1811 and 1822, and he lived here
until his death ten years after its completion. '
Times: Open daily from 3rd Mon in Mar-Oct, Mon-Sat 10-5.
Sun in Mar-May & Oct 2-5. Sun Jun-Sep 10-5.
Fee: *£3.50 (ch £1.80). Party £2.50 (ch £1.30).
🅿 💺 ⅙ (parking at private entrance) toilets for disabled
shop 🕱 (ex guide dogs & hearing dogs)

HARMONY GARDEN
St Mary's Rd TD6 9LJ
☎ 01721 722502   ▤ 01721 724700

Set around the early 19th-century Harmony Hall
(not open to visitors), this attractive walled
garden has magnificent views of Melrose Abbey
and the Eildon Hills. The garden comprises
lawns, herbaceous and mixed borders, vegetable
and fruit areas, and a rich display of spring bulbs.
Times: Open Apr-Sep, Mon-Sat 10-5.30, Sun 1.30-5.30.
🅿 ⅙ 🕱 ☙ *Details not confirmed for 2000*

MELROSE ABBEY & ABBEY MUSEUM
☎ 01896 822562

The ruin of this Cistercian abbey is probably one
of Scotland's finest, and has been given added
glamour by its connection with Sir Walter Scott.
The abbey was repeatedly wrecked during the
Scottish wars of independence, but parts of the
nave and choir survive from the 14th century.
The heart of Robert the Bruce is buried
somewhere within the church.
Times: Open all year, Apr-Sep Mon-Sat 9.30-6.30, Sun 2-6.30;
Oct-Mar, Mon-Sat 9.30-4.30, Sun 2-4.30.
🅿 ⅙ shop 🕱 ▌ *Details not confirmed for 2000*

PRIORWOOD GARDEN & DRIED FLOWER SHOP
TD6 9PX (off A6091)
☎ 01896 822493

This small garden specialises in flowers suitable
for drying. It is formally designed with
herbaceous and everlasting annual borders, and
the attractive orchard has a display of `apples
through the ages'. Dried flowers are on sale in
the shop.
Times: Open Garden & Shop; Apr-Sep, Mon-Sat 10-5.30, Sun
1.30-5.30; Oct-24 Dec, Mon-Sat 10-4, Sun 1.30-4. Shop in
Abbey St only; 9 Jan-Mar, Mon-Sat 12-4; Apr-24 Dec, Mon-Sat
10-5.30, Sun 1.30-5.30. (Closed 31 Oct-7 Nov).
🅿 ⅙ shop ☙ *Details not confirmed for 2000*

🏛 MILNGAVIE
Mugdock Country Park
Craigallion Rd G62 8EL (N of Glasgow on A81, signed)
☎ 0141 956 6100

This country park incorporates the remains of Mugdock and Craigend castles, set in beautiful landscapes as well as an exhibition centre, craft shops, orienteering course and many walks.
Times: Open all year, daily.
Fee: Free.
🅿 💷 &

🏛 MINARD
Crarae Gardens
PA32 8YA (10m S of Inveraray on A83)
☎ 01546 886614 & 886388
🖥 01546 886388

Set beside Loch Fyne, these gardens are among Scotland's loveliest, noted for their rhododendrons, azaleas, conifers and ornamental shrubs, which include a number of rare species.
Times: Open all year, daily, summer 9-6; winter during daylight hours. Visitor centre, Etr-Oct 10-5.
🅿 💷 & toilets for disabled shop garden centre *Details not confirmed for 2000* 🐕

🏛 MONIAIVE
Maxwelton House Trust
DG3 4DX (A76 from Dumfries to Thornhill, after 2m take B729 to Monavie, 11m along road is Maxwelton House)
☎ 01848 200385

The house dates from the 14th and 15th centuries and was originally the stronghold of the Earls of Glencairn and later, in 1682, the birthplace of Annie Laurie of the famous Scottish ballad.
Times: Open last Sun in May-Sep, Sun-Fri 11-5. Etr-May by booking only.
Fee: *£4 (ch 16 £2 & pen £3)
🅿 shop

🏛 MOTHERWELL
Motherwell Heritage Centre
High Rd ML1 3HU (M74 J6, A723 for town centre. At top of hill, turn left, before railway bridge)
☎ 01698 251000   🖥 01698 268867

This award winning audio-visual experince, 'Technopolis', traces the history of the area from Roman times to the rise of 19th-century industry and the post-industrial era. There is also a fine viewing tower, an exhibition gallery and family history research facilities. A mixed programme of community events and touring exhibitions occur throughout the year.
Times: Open daily 10-5, Sun noon-5pm. Closed Xmas/New Year.
Fee: Free.
🅿 & toilets for disabled shop 🚫 (ex guide dogs)

🏛 NEW ABBEY
New Abbey Corn Mill
(8m S of Dumfries on A710)
☎ 01387 850260

Built in the late 18th century, this water-driven corn mill is still in working order, and regular demonstrations are held.
Times: Open all year, Apr-Sep, Mon-Sat 9.30-6.30, Sun 2-6.30; Oct-Mar, weekdays 9.30-4.30, Sun 2-4.30. (Closed Thu pm & Fri in winter; 25-26 Dec & 1-3 Jan).
🅿 (100yds) 🚫 ⚑ *Details not confirmed for 2000*

Sweetheart Abbey
DG2 8BU
☎ 01387 850397

Lady Devorgilla of Galloway founded Balliol College, Oxford in memory of her husband John Balliol; she also founded this abbey in his memory in 1273. When she died in 1289 she was buried in front of the high altar with the heart of her husband resting on her bosom; hence the name 'Sweetheart Abbey'. The abbey features an unusual precinct wall of enormous boulders.
Times: Open Apr-Sep Mon-Sat 9.30-6.30, Sun 2-6.30.
🅿 & (with assistance) toilets for disabled 🚫 ⚑ *Details not confirmed for 2000*

🏛 OBAN
Caithness Glass Visitor Centre
The Waterfront, Railway Pier PA34 4LW (centre of Oban on the pier beside the train station)
☎ 01631 563386   🖥 01631 563386

Factory shop selling a wide range of perfect and slightly imperfect paperweights and glassware. There is also an audio-visual and interpretive exhibition on glassmaking and the story of Caithness Glass.
Times: Open all year, Factory Shop, Audio visual & interpretative exhibition : Mon-Sat 9-5 (open late Jun-Sep). Etr-Nov Sun 11-5; Nov-Mar 10-5 Mon-Sat.
Fee: Free.
🅿 (100yds) & shop 🚫 (ex guide dogs)

DUNSTAFFNAGE CASTLE
(3m N on peninsula)
☎ 01631 562465

Now ruined, this four-sided stronghold has a gatehouse, two round towers and walls 10ft thick. It was once the prison of Flora MacDonald.
Times: Open Apr-Sep, Mon-Sat 9.30-6.30, Sun 2-6.30.
🅿 shop ▮

🏛 PAISLEY
COATS OBSERVATORY
49 Oakshaw St West PA1 2DE
☎ 0141 889 2013 ▤ 0141 889 9240

Astronomy, meteorology and space flight, along with the history of the building, are the subjects of displays in this observatory built in 1883. More recently, the observatory has resumed an important role in astronomy and meteorology.
Times: Open all year, Tue-Sat 10-5, Sun 2-5. Last entry 15 minutes before closing.
Fee: Free.
shop ✖

🏛 PALNACKIE
ORCHARDTON TOWER
(6m SE of Castle Douglas)
☎ 0131 668 8800 ▤ 0131 668 8888

John Cairns built this rare example of a circular tower in the late 15th century.
Times: Open all reasonable times, on application to key keeper. (Closed 25-26 Dec & 1-2 Jan).
🅿 ✖ ▮

🏛 PEEBLES
KAILZIE
EH45 9HT (2.5m SE on B7062)
☎ 01721 720007 ▤ 01721 720007

These extensive grounds, with their fine old trees, provide a burnside walk flanked by bulbs, rhododendrons and azaleas. A walled garden contains herbaceous, shrub rose borders, greenhouses and a small formal rose garden.
Times: Open 25 Mar-Oct, daily 11-5.30. Grounds close 5.30pm. Garden open all year.
Fee: *Snowdrop day and garden walks £1 during winter months; 31 Oct-31 May £2 (ch 5-12 50p), Jun-Oct £2.50 (ch 5-12 75p). Party 20+.
🅿 ⬤ ✖ licensed ♿ (ramps in garden & gravel paths) toilets for disabled shop

NEIDPATH CASTLE
EH45 8NW (1m W on A72)
☎ 01721 720333 ▤ 01721 720333

Occupying a spectacular position on the Tweed, this 14th-century stronghold has been interestingly adapted to 17th-century living; it contains a rock-hewn well, a pit prison, a small museum, and a tartan display. There are fine walks and a picnic area.
Times: Open Thu before Etr-Sep, Mon-Sat 11-5, Sun 1-5.
🅿 (charged) shop

🏛 PORT GLASGOW
NEWARK CASTLE
☎ 01475 741858

The one-time house of the Maxwells, dating from the 15th and 17th centuries. The courtyard and hall are preserved. Fine turrets and the remains of painted ceilings can be seen, and the hall carries an inscription of 1597.
Times: Open Apr-Sep, Mon-Sat 9.30-6.30, Sun 2-6.30.
🅿 shop ▮ *Details not confirmed for 2000*

🏛 PORT LOGAN
LOGAN BOTANIC GARDEN
DG9 9ND (on B7065)
☎ 01776 860231 ▤ 01776 860333

Logan's exeptionally mild climate allows a colourful array of tender plants to thrive out-of-doors. Amongst the many highlights are tree ferns, cabbage palms, unusual shrubs, climbers and tender perennials found within the setting of the walled, water, terrace and woodland gardens. Please telephone for details of special events.
Times: Open Mar-Oct, 9.30-6, daily.
🅿 ✖ licensed ♿ (wheelchairs available for loan) toilets for disabled shop garden centre ✖ (ex guide dogs) *Details not confirmed for 2000* ◣

🏛 RUTHWELL
RUTHWELL CROSS
(off B724)
☎ 0131 668 8800 ▤ 0131 668 8888

Now in a specially built apse in the parish church, the carved cross dates from the 7th or 8th centuries. Two faces show scenes from the Life of Christ; the others show scroll work, and parts of an ancient poem in Runic characters. It was broken up in the 18th century, but pieced together by a 19th-century minister.
Times: Open all reasonable times. Key from Key Keeper, Kirkyett Cottage, Ruthwell.
🅿 ✖ ▮

SAVINGS BANKS MUSEUM
DG1 4NN (6m W of Annan)
☎ 01387 870640

Housed in the building where Savings Banks first began, the museum traces their growth and development from 1810 up to the present day. The museum also traces the life of Dr Henry Duncan, father of savings banks, and restorer of the Ruthwell Cross. Multi-lingual leaflets available.
Times: Open all year, daily (ex Sun & Mon Oct-Mar), 10-1 & 2-5.
Fee: Free.
🅿 ♿ (touch facilities for blind, guide available) (ex guide dogs)

⌂ SALTCOATS
NORTH AYRSHIRE MUSEUM
Manse St, Kirkgate KA21 5AA
☎ 01294 464174   ▤ 01294 464234

This museum is housed in an 18th-century church, and features a rich variety of artefacts from the North Ayrshire area, including archaeological and social history material. There is a continuing programme of temporary exhibitions.
Times: Open all year, Mon-Sat (ex Wed) 10-1 & 2-5.
P (50 yds) ♿ toilets for disabled ✖ (ex guide dogs) *Details not confirmed for 2000*

⌂ SANQUHAR
SANQUHAR TOLBOOTH MUSEUM
High St DG4 6BN
☎ 01659 250186   ▤ 01387 265081

Housed in the town's fine 18th-century tolbooth, the museum tells the story of the mines and miners of the area, its earliest inhabitants, native and Roman, the history and customs of the Royal Burgh of Sanquhar and local traditions.
Times: Open Apr-Sep, Tue-Sat 10-1 & 2-5, Sun 2-5.
Fee: Free.
P shop

⌂ SELKIRK
BOWHILL HOUSE AND COUNTRY PARK
TD7 5ET (3m W of Selkirk off A708)
☎ 01750 22204   ▤ 01750 22204

An outstanding collection of pictures, including works by Van Dyck, Canaletto, Reynolds, Gainsborough and Claude Lorraine, are displayed here. Memorabilia and relics of people such as Queen Victoria and Sir Walter Scott, and a restored Victorian kitchen add further interest inside the house. Outside, the wooded grounds are perfect for walking.
Times: Open, Park: May-Aug 12-5 (ex Fri). House & park: Jul, daily 1-4.30.
P 💺 ✕ licensed ♿ (guided tours for the blind) toilets for disabled shop (Jul) ✖ (ex in park) *Details not confirmed for 2000* 🍴

⌂ SMAILHOLM
SMAILHOLM TOWER
TD5 7RT (6m W of Kelso on B6937)
☎ 01573 460365

An outstanding example of a classic Border tower-house, probably erected in the 15th century. It is 57ft high and well preserved. The tower has an exhibition of dolls and a display based on Sir Walter Scott's book 'Minstrels of the Border'.
Times: Open Apr-Sep, Mon-Sat 9.30-6.30, Sun 2-6.30. (Closed in winter).
P ✖ ▮ *Details not confirmed for 2000*

⌂ STOBO
DAWYCK BOTANIC GARDEN
EH45 9JU (8m SW of Peebles on B712)
☎ 01721 760254   ▤ 01721 760214

Follow the landscaped walks through this historic arboretum and discover an impressive collection of mature specimen trees - some over 40m tall and including the unique Dawyck beech-stand, majestically towering above a variety of flowering shrubs and herbaceous plants. Notable features include the Swiss Bridge, a fine estate chapel and stonework/terracing produced by Italian craftsmen in the 1820's.
Times: Open Mar-Oct, daily 9.30-6.
P 💺 ♿ toilets for disabled shop garden centre ✖ (ex guide dogs) *Details not confirmed for 2000* 🍴

⌂ STRANRAER
CASTLE KENNEDY GARDENS
Stair Estates DG9 8BX (5m E on A75)
☎ 01776 702024   ▤ 01776 706248

Situated on a peninsula between two lochs, the gardens around the Old Castle were first laid out in the early 18th century. Noted for their rhododendrons and azaleas (at their best May and early Jun) and walled kitchen garden with fine herbaceous borders (best in Aug and Sep). The gardens contain many avenues and walks amid some beautiful scenery.
Times: Open Apr-Sep, daily 10-5.
P 💺 ♿ toilets for disabled shop garden centre *Details not confirmed for 2000*

TARBOLTON
BACHELORS' CLUB
Sandgate St KA5 5RB (on B744, 7.5m NE of Ayr)
☎ 01292 541940

In this 17th-century thatched house, Robert Burns and his friends formed a debating club in 1780. Burns attended dancing lessons and was initiated into freemasonry here in 1781. The house is furnished in the period.

Times: Open Good Friday to 30 Sept, daily 1.30-5.30; wknds in Oct 1.30-5.30.-last admission 5pm.

P (in village) ♿ ✱ (ex guide dogs) ♥ *Details not confirmed for 2000*

TAYNUILT
BONAWE IRON FURNACE
(0.75m NE off B845)
☎ 01866 822432

The furnace is a restored charcoal blast-furnace for iron-smelting and making cast-iron. It was established in 1753 and worked until 1876. The works exploited the Forest of Lorne to provide charcoal for fuel.

Times: Open Apr-Sep, Mon-Sat 9.30-6.30, Sun 2-6.30.

P ♿ toilets for disabled shop ▮ *Details not confirmed for 2000*

THORNHILL
DRUMLANRIG CASTLE
DG3 4AQ (4m N of Thornhill off A76)
☎ 01848 331682 & 330248

This unusual pink sandstone castle was built in the late 17th century in Renaissance style. It contains a collection of paintings by Rembrandt, Da Vinci, Holbein, and many others. There is also French furniture, as well as silver and relics of Bonnie Prince Charlie. The old stable block has a craft centre with resident craft workers, and the grounds offer extensive gardens, a bird of prey centre, and woodland walks. Ring for details of special events.

Times: Open early May-late Aug, Castle open seven days a week. Guided tours and restricted route may operate at various times, please verify before visiting.

P � ♿ (lift for wheelchair users) toilets for disabled shop ✱ (ex in park on lead) *Details not confirmed for 2000* ◀

TONGLAND
GALLOWAY HYDROS VISITOR CENTRE
Tongland Power Station DG6 4LT (on A711 2m N of Kirkcudbright)
☎ 01557 330114

An area of outstanding natural beauty, testimony to the harmonious relationship between hydro power and the environment. This tour of part of the Scottish Power Galloway hydro-electricity scheme includes a video presentation and a visit to the dam and the power station.

Times: Open May-Sep, Mon-Sat, and Sundays during August.

P ♿ (only Fish Pass is not accessible) *Details not confirmed for 2000*

TRAQUAIR
TRAQUAIR HOUSE
EH44 6PW (1m S of Innerleithen on B709).
☎ 01896 830323 & 830785
▤ 01896 830639

This is said to be Scotland's oldest inhabited house. It dates back to the 12th century and 27 Scottish monarchs have stayed here. William the Lion Heart held court at Traquair, and the house has associations with Mary, Queen of Scots and the Jacobite risings. The Bear Gates were closed in 1745, not to be reopened until the Stuarts should once again ascend the throne. Outside there is a maze, croquet, and woodland walks by the River Tweed, as well as craft workshops and an art gallery.

Times: Open Etr-Sep daily, 12.30-5.30 (ex Jun, Jul & Aug 10.30-5.30). Last admission 5pm. Oct, Fri-Sun. Grounds open Apr-Sep, 10.30-5.30.

Fee: *£5 (ch £2.50 pen £4) Family £13. Grounds only £2 (ch £1).

P ▮ ✗ licensed ♿ shop ◀

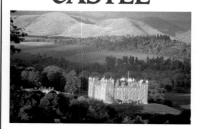

WANLOCKHEAD

Museum of Lead Mining

ML12 6UT (on B797 at N end of Mennock Pass).
☎ 01659 74387 Fax 01659 74481

Wanlockhead is Scotland's highest village, set in the beautiful Lowther Hills. You can visit miners' cottages and the miners' library as well as the 18th-century lead mine, and try your luck at the Gold Panning Centre.

Times: Open Apr-Oct, daily 10-4.30 (last mine tour 4).
Fee: *£3.95 (ch £2, concessions £2.75). Family ticket £9.
P toilets for disabled shop (ex guide dogs)

WHITHORN

Whithorn-Cradle of Christianity

45-47 George St DG8 8NS
☎ 01988 500508

The Whithorn Dig is the site of the first Christian settlement in Scotland - the Candida Casa of St Ninian. Friendly guides explain the excavation, and there's a museum of Early Christian stones.

Times: Open daily, Apr-Oct 10.30-5.
Fee: *£2.70 (ch, pen & UB40's £1.50). Family ticket £7.50. Season ticket. Party.
P (70 yds) (one short staircase with 'stairmatic') toilets for disabled shop

Whithorn Priory

☎ 01988 500508

The first Christian church in Scotland was founded here by St Ninian in 397AD, but the present ruins date from the 12th century. The ruins are sparse but there is a notable Norman door, the Latinus stone of the 5th century and other early Christian monuments.

Times: Open Apr-Sep, Mon-Sat 9.30-6.30, Sun 2-6.30;
P *Details not confirmed for 2000*

North Wales

The evidence of prehistoric movements of liquid rock is obvious when you gaze at the gouged crevasses of tourist attraction Snowdonia, yet the area also owes much of its economic prosperity to mineral deposits formed over millions of years.

Copper, lead and gold in modest quantities. In the south, coal - the best steam coal in the world - and iron; and in the north, slate, which was shipped all over the world.

The region copes with hordes of visitors each year. Approaching from England you pass through the pleasant Marches, and encounter the first of a chain of medieval castles that stretches right across the country. Conwy, Caernarfon, Beaumaris and others, daunting reminders of Edward I's ruthless subjugation of the Welsh.

Along the coast lie a string of brash seaside resorts, and the more genteel Llandudno. A handful of miles inland lie the glories of Snowdon (3650ft/1112mtr) where the vigorous visitor can enjoy strenuous climbs, and the more relaxed can ride the mountain railway.

From Betws-y-Coed explore the falls and gorges of the River Conwy, or travel up to Blaenau Ffestiniog to see a town built of slate, and its remarkable quarries. One of the steam trains of Wales will take you down to the coast by an exceedingly twisty route.

A quieter part is Anglesey, probably the most fervently Welsh part of Wales. The island is reached via the university town of Bangor. Two engineers, Thomas Telford and Robert Stephenson, left their masterpieces here in the form of bridges across the Menai Straits. From Holyhead at the tip, the ferry to Ireland sails.

EVENTS & FESTIVALS

January
23rd-26th Wales Spring Fair, Llandudno

May
28th-29th North Wales Garden Festival, Bodelwyddan Castle, nr St Asaph

June
24th-30th Barmouth to Fort William Three Peaks Yacht Race, Barmouth

July
4th-9th International Musical Eisteddfod, Langollen

August
5th-6th St Asaph Gala Day

October
13th-22nd Llandudno October Festival

Top: Lynnag Mymbyr

BETWS-Y-COED

Even before the train arrived in 1868, Betws-y-Coed drew the tourists. Hemmed in by forested hills and the Rivers Conwy and Llugwy, it is still thronged by visitors in summer. Some are heading for the serious slopes of Snowdonia, while others just want to stroll up the gorges to the Swallow Falls and the Conwy Falls.

There are also easy walks through the forests. The 14th-century Old Church of St Michael and All Angels is of interest, and transport buffs will enjoy the Railway Museum and the Motor Museum. For scenery, the short train trip to Blaenau Ffestiniog is hard to beat.

The directory which follows has been divided into three geographical regions. Counties have not been shown against individual locations as recent legislation has created a number of smaller counties which will be unfamiliar to the visitor. The postal authorities have confirmed that it is no longer necessary to include a county name in addresses, provided a post code is shown.

This region includes the counties of Anglesey, Conwy, Denbighshire, Flintshire, Gwynedd and Wrexham which reflect the recent national changes.

🏛 ANGLESEY, ISLE OF

🏛 BEAUMARIS (ANGLESEY, ISLE OF)

BEAUMARIS CASTLE
LL58 8AP
☎ 01248 810361

Beaumaris was built by Edward I and took from 1295 to 1312 to complete. In later centuries it was plundered for its lead, timber and stone. Despite this it remains one of the most impressive and complete castles built by Edward I. It has a perfectly symmetrical, concentric plan, with a square inner bailey and curtain walls, round corner towers and D-shaped towers in

between. There are also two great gatehouses, but these were never finished.
Times: Open all year, late May-early Oct, daily 9.30-6; late Mar-late May & Oct, daily 9.30-5; Nov-late Mar, Mon-Sat 9.30-4, Sun 11-4. (Closed 24-26 Dec & 1 Jan).
Fee: *£2.20 (ch 5-16, pen & students £1.70, disabled free). Family ticket £6.10.
🅿 ♿ shop ✖ ☺ 🍽

BEAUMARIS GAOL & COURTHOUSE
Steeple Ln LL58 8EW
☎ 01248 810921   🖷 01248 750282

With its treadmill and grim cells, the gaol is a vivid reminder of the tough penalties exacted by 19th-century law. The courthouse, built in 1614 and renovated early in the 19th century, is a unique survival of a Victorian court room.
Times: Open Etr, end Sep, daily 10.30-5. Other times by arrangement only.
Fee: *Gaol £2.75 (ch, pen £1.75). Courthouse £1.50 (ch, pen £1). Combined ticket £3.40 (ch £2.20 & pen £2.20). Family ticket £7.75.
🅿 (500yds) ♿ (narrow gates may restrict some wheelchairs) shop ✖ (ex guide dogs)

MUSEUM OF CHILDHOOD
1 Castle St LL58 8AP (on A545. Opposite Beaumaris Castle)
☎ 01248 712498   🖷 01248 716869

The museum illustrates the life and interests of children and families over 150 years. There are money boxes, dolls, educational toys and games, early clockwork trains, cars and aeroplanes, push toys and cycles.

Times: Open daily 10.30-5.30, Sun 12-5. Last admission 4.30, Sun 4. (Closed Nov-2nd wk Mar).
Fee: *£3 (ch £1.75, pen/students £2.50). Family ticket £8.50. Free entry for wheelchairs.
P (50yds) & shop ✖ (ex guide dogs)

⏚ HOLYHEAD

RSBP NATURE RESERVE SOUTH STACK

South Stack LL65 3HB (A5 to Holyhead then follow brown tourist signs)
☎ 01407 764973

High cliffs with caves and offshore stacks, backed by the maritime heathland of Holyhead Mountain, make this an ideal reserve to watch seabirds. Live video pictures of breeding seabirds are shown in the cliff-top information centre during the summer. Choughs, guillemots, razorbills, fulmars and puffins may be seen.
Times: Open: Visitor Centre daily, Apr-mid Sep, 11-5. Reserve open daily at reasonable times.
P ✖ *Details not confirmed for 2000* 🕭

⏚ BANGOR

PENRHYN CASTLE

LL57 4HN (1m E at Bangor, at Llandegai on A5122, just off A55)
☎ 01248 353084 📠 01248 371281

The splendid castle with its towers and battlements was commissioned in 1827 as a sumptuous family home. Notable rooms include the great hall, the library and the dining room, which is covered with neo-Norman decoration. Among the furniture is a slate bed weighing over a ton, and a decorated brass bed made for Edward VII at the then huge cost of £600. Special events held throughout the year.
Times: Open 24 Mar-Oct, daily (ex Tue) Castle 12-5pm. Grounds and stableblock exhibitions 11-5 (Jul & Aug 10-5.30). Last admission 4.30pm. Last audio tour 4pm.
Fee: *All inclusive ticket: £5 (ch £2.50). Family ticket £12.50. Party 15+. Grounds & stableblock only £4 (ch £1.50).
P ✖ & (wheelchairs & golf buggies pre bookable) toilets for disabled shop ✖ (ex guide dogs) ✤

⏚ BEDDGELERT

SYGUN COPPER MINE

LL55 4NE (1m E of Beddgelert on A498)
☎ 01766 510100 📠 01766 510102

With the help of an expert guide, and an audio-visual underground tour, visitors can explore the workings of this 19th-century copper mine, where magnificent stalactite and stalagmite formations can be seen. The less energetic can enjoy a continuous audio-visual presentation and a display of artefacts found during excavations.

Times: Open most of the year, daily 10-6. (last tour 5pm).
Fee: *£4.75 (ch £3, pen £3.75). Family ticket £14
P & toilets for disabled shop 🕭

⏚ BERRIEW

GLANSEVERN HALL GARDENS

Glansevern SY21 8AH (on A483 between Welshpool and Newtown)
☎ 01686 640200 📠 01686 640829

Built in the Greek Revival style for Arthur Davies Owen, who chose a romantically positioned site on the banks of the River Severn with gentle hills rising in the background. The current owners have developed the gardens, respecting the plantings and features of the past, and added a vast collection of new and interesting species. There are many fine and unusual trees, a lakeside walk, water gardens and a rock garden with lamp-lit grotto.
Times: Open May-Sep, BH Mon, Fri-Sat 2-6. Parties other dates by arrangement
Fee: *£2 (pen £1.50, ch 15 free). Party 20+
P 🍴 & (most areas accessible) shop garden centre

⏚ BODELWYDDAN

BODELWYDDAN CASTLE

LL18 5YA (adjacent to A55, near St Asaph)
☎ 01745 584060 📠 01745 584563

Set in rolling parkland against the impressive background of the Clwydian Hills, this imposing Victorian country house has been magnificently restored. The lavish interiors reflect various periods and design styles from the 19th century and provide a sumptuous setting for a collection of portraits on loan from the National Portrait Gallery in London, complemented by furniture from the Victoria and Albert Museum and sculptures from the Royal Academy of Arts. A programme of events and temporary exhibitions takes place throughout the year. Please telephone for details.
Times: Open Apr-Oct, Sat-Thu 11-5 (last admission 4); Nov-Etr 11-4 (ex Mon or Fri).
Fee: *£4.30 (ch £2.50, pen, UB40, student, disabled £3.80). Family ticket £10.
P & (lift to first floor & Braille Guide) toilets for disabled shop ✖ (ex guide dogs) 🕭

🏛 BRYNCELLI DDU

BRYN CELLI DDU BURIAL CHAMBER
(3m W of Menai Bridge off A4080)
☎ **029 20500200**

Excavated in 1865, and then again in 1925-9, this is a prehistoric circular cairn covering a passage grave with a polygonal chamber.
Times: Open at all times.
Fee: Free.
🅿 ✖ ☺

🏛 CAERNARFON

CAERNARFON CASTLE
LL55 2AY
☎ **01286 677617**

Edward I began building the castle and extensive town walls in 1283 after defeating the last independant ruler of Wales. Completed in 1328, it has unusual polygonal towers, notably the 10-sided Eagle Tower. There is a theory that these features were copied from the walls of Constantinople, to reflect a tradition that Constantine was born nearby. Edward I's son and heir was born and presented to the Welsh people here, setting a precedent that was followed in 1969, when Prince Charles was invested as Prince of Wales.
Times: Open all year, late May-early Oct, daily 9.30-6; late Mar-late May & Oct, daily 9.30-5; Nov-late Mar, Mon-Sat 9.30-4, Sun 11-4. (Closed 24-26 Dec & 1 Jan)
Fee: *£4.20 (ch 5-16, pen & students £3.20, disabled free). Family ticket £11.60.
🅿 shop ✖ ☺ 🔊

🏛 CERRIGYDRUDION

LLYN BRENIG VISITOR CENTRE
LL21 9TT (on B4501)
☎ **01490 420463** 📠 **01490 420694**

The 1800-acre estate has a unique archaeological trail and round-the-lake walk of 10 miles. A hide is available: best viewing is November to March. Disabled anglers are catered for with a specially adapted fishing boat and an annual open day. The centre has an exhibition on geology, archaeology, history and natural history.
Times: Open mid Mar-Nov daily 9am-5pm.
Fee: *Free. (ex water sports & fishing).
🅿 (charged) 🚤 ♿ (boats for disabled & fishing open days) toilets for disabled shop ✖ (ex guide dogs)

🏛 CHIRK

CHIRK CASTLE
LL14 5AF (8m S of Wrexham, signposted off A483)
☎ **01691 777701** 📠 **01691 774706**

Chirk Castle is one of a chain of late 13th-century Marcher castles. Its high walls and drum towers have hardly changed, but the inside shows the varied tastes of 700 years of occupation. One of the least-altered parts is Adam's Tower. Elsewhere, many of the medieval-looking decorations were by Pugin in the 19th century.

Varied furnishings include fine tapestries. Please phone for details of special events.
Times: Open 27 Mar-30 Sep, daily (ex Mon & Tue) (but open BH Mons); 2-31 Oct, Sat & Sun only; Castle 12-5, Grounds 11-6. Last admission 4.30pm.
Fee: *£4.80 (ch £2.40) Family ticket £12. Party. Garden only £2.60 (ch £1.30) National Trust members free.
🅿 ✖ licensed ♿ (Stairclimber) toilets for disabled shop ✖ (ex guide dogs) 🔊

🏛 CONWY

ABERCONWY HOUSE
LL32 8AY (At junction of Castle St & High St)
☎ **01492 592246** 📠 **01492 585153**

This house dates from the 14th century; it is the only medieval merchant's house in Conwy to have survived the centuries of turbulence, fire and pillage in this frontier town. Furnished rooms and an audio-visual presentation show daily life in the house at different periods in its history.
Times: Open Apr-Oct, daily (ex Tues) 10-5, last admission 4.30.
Fee: *£2 (ch £1). Family ticket £5. Prebooked parties £1.80.
🅿 (100yds & 0.5 mile) (public C/P charges) shop ✖ (ex guide dogs) 🔊 🔊

CONWY CASTLE
LL32 8AY (by A55 or B5106)
☎ **01492 592358**

The castle is a magnificent fortress, built from 1283-7 by Edward I. There is an exhibition on castle chapels on the ground floor of the Chapel Tower. The castle forms part of the same defensive system as the extensive town walls, which are among the most complete in Europe. They have 21 towers, and sweep up and down hills as they encircle the town.
Times: Open all year, late May-early Oct, daily 9.30-6; late Mar-late May & Oct, daily 9.30-5; Nov-late Mar, Mon-Sat 9.30-4, Sun 11-4. (Closed 24-26 Dec & 1 Jan)
Fee: *£3.50 (ch 5-16, pen & students £2.50, disabled free). Family ticket £9.50.
🅿 ♿ toilets for disabled shop ✖ ☺ 🔊

CONWY SUSPENSION BRIDGE
LL32 8LO (adjacent to Conwy Castle)
☎ **01492 573282**

Designed by Thomas Telford, one of the greatest engineers of the late 18th and early 19th century, this was the first bridge to span the river at Conwy. The bridge has recently been restored and the toll house furnished as it would have been a century ago.
Times: Open Apr-Oct, daily (ex Tue) 10-5; Jul-Aug daily 10-5. Last admission 30 mins before closing.
Fee: *£1 (ch 50p)
♿ ✖ 🔊

SMALLEST HOUSE
The Quay LL32 8BB (leave A55 at Conwy signpost, through town, at bottom of High St for the quay, turn left)
☎ **01492 593484** 📠 **01492 593484**

The `Guinness Book of Records' lists this as the smallest house in Britain. Just 6ft wide by 10ft high, it is furnished in the style of a mid-Victorian Welsh cottage.

Times: Open Apr-mid Oct daily 10-6 (10-9.30/10pm in Jul & Aug). In winter by arrangement.

Fee: *50p (ch under 16 30p, under 5yrs free admission).

P (100 yds) & shop

CORWEN
RUG CHAPEL
Rug
☎ 01490 412025

Rug Chapel was built in 1637 for Colonel William Salusbury, famous Civil War defender of Denbigh Castle. A rare, little altered example of a 17th-century private chapel, it reflects the Colonel's High Church religious views. Prettily set in a wooded landscape, the chapel's modest exterior gives little hint of the wonders inside - local artists and carvers were given a free reign, with some spectacular results.

Times: Open May-late Sep, Tue-Sat 10-2 & 3-5. (Closed Sun & Mon, ex BH wknds).

Fee: *£2 (ch 5-16, pen & students £1.50, disabled free). Family ticket £5.50.

P & toilets for disabled shop ✂ ☺ ➡

CRICCIETH
CRICCIETH CASTLE
LL52 0DP (off A497)
☎ 01766 522227

The castle dates from the 13th century and was taken and destroyed by Owain Glyndwr in 1404. Evidence of a fierce fire can still be seen. The gatehouse leading to the inner ward remains impressive, and parts of the walls are well preserved.

Times: Open all year, late Mar-late Sep, daily 10-6; site can be viewed at all other times. (Closed 24-26 Dec & 1 Jan).

Fee: *£2.20 (ch 5-16, pen & students £1.70, disabled free). Family ticket £6.10.

P shop ✂ ☺ ➡

CYMER ABBEY
CYMER ABBEY
(2m NW of Dolgellau on A494)
☎ 01341 422854

The abbey was built for the Cistercians in the 13th century. It was never very large, and does not seem to have been finished. The church is the best-preserved building, with ranges of windows and arcades still to be seen. The other buildings have been plundered for stone, but low outlines remain.

Times: Open all year, early Apr-Oct, daily 9.30-6; Nov-early Apr, daily 9.30-4. (Closed 24-26 Dec & 1 Jan)

Fee: *£1.20 (ch 5-16, pen & students 70p, disabled free). Family ticket £3.10.

P & ✂ ☺ ➡

DENBIGH
DENBIGH CASTLE
(via A525, A543 & B5382)
☎ 01745 813385

The castle was begun by Henry de Lacy in 1282 and has an inspiring and impressive gatehouse, with a trio of towers and a superb archway, which is surmounted by a figure believed to be that of Edward I.

Times: Open May-Sep, Mon-Fri 10-5.30, Sat & Sun 9.30-5.30; Site open at all other times. (Closed 24-26 Dec & 1 Jan).

Fee: *£2 (ch 5-16, pen & students £1.50, disabled free). Family ticket £5.50.

P & shop ✂ ☺ ➡

TOWN WALLS & LEICESTER'S CHURCH

Forming an almost complete circuit, the town walls were started in 1282 at the same time as the castle. The remains include one of the gateways and the unfinished Leicester's Church, built by the Earl of Leicester, favourite of Elizabeth I, who wanted it to be the cathedral of the diocese.

Times: Open any reasonable time.

P ✂ ☺ ➡

DOLWYDDELAN
DOLWYDDELAN CASTLE
LL25 0EJ (on A470 Blaenau Ffestiniog to Betws-y-Coed)
☎ 01690 750366

The castle is reputed to be the birthplace of Llywelyn the Great. It was captured in 1283 by Edward I, who immediately began strengthening it for his own purposes. A restored keep of around 1200, and a 13th-century curtain wall can be seen. An exhibition on the castles of the Welsh Princes is located in the keep.

Times: Open all year, early Apr-Oct, daily 9.30-6; Nov-early Apr, daily 9.30-4. (Closed 24-26 Dec & 1 Jan).

Fee: *£2 (ch 5-16, pen & students £1.50, disabled free). Family ticket £5.50

P ✂ ☺ ➡

EWLOE
EWLOE CASTLE
(NW of village on B5125)

Standing in Ewloe Wood are the remains of Ewloe Castle. It was a native Welsh castle, and Henry II was defeated nearby in 1157. Part of the Welsh Tower in the upper ward still stands to its original height, and there is a well in the lower ward. Remnants of walls and another tower can also be seen.

Times: Open at all times.

Fee: Free.

✂ ☺

⛪ FLINT

FLINT CASTLE
CH6 5PH
☎ 01352 733078

The castle was started by Edward I in 1277 and overlooks the River Dee. It is exceptional for its great tower, or Donjon, which is separated by a moat. Other buildings would have stood in the inner bailey, of which parts of the walls and corner towers remain.
Times: Open at all times.
Fee: Free.
🅿 ✈ ☺

⛪ HARLECH

HARLECH CASTLE
LL46 2YH (from A496)
☎ 01766 780552

Harlech Castle was built in 1283-81 by Edward I, with a sheer drop to the sea on one side. Owain Glyndwr starved the castle into submission in 1404 and made it his court and campaigning base. Later, the defence of the castle in the Wars of the Roses inspired the song *Men of Harlech*. Today the sea has slipped away, and the castle's great walls and round towers stand above the dunes.
Times: Open all year, late May-early Oct, daily 9.30-6; late Mar-late May & Oct, daily 9.30-5; Nov-late Mar, Mon-Sat 9.30-4 & Sun 11-4. (Closed 24-26 Dec & 1 Jan).
Fee: *£3 (ch 5-16, pen & students £2, disabled free). Family ticket £8.
🅿 (disabled spaces in car park) shop ✈ ☺ 🍴

⛪ HOLYWELL

BASINGWERK ABBEY
Greenfield Valley Heritage Pk, Greenfield
☎ 01352 714172

The abbey was founded around 1131 by Ranulf de Gernon, Earl of Chester. The first stone church dates from the beginning of the 13th-century. The last abbot surrendered the house to the crown in 1536. The Abbey is close to the Heritage Park Visitor Centre and access to the Museum and Farm Complex at Greenfield Valley.
Times: Open all year, daily 9-6.
Fee: Free.
🅿 ✈ ♿ (disabled facilities in Heritage Park) toilets for disabled shop ✈ ☺

⛪ LLANALLGO

DIN LLUGWY ANCIENT VILLAGE
(1m NW off A5025)

The remains of a 4th-century village can be seen here. There are two circular and seven rectangular buildings, still standing up to head height and encircled by a pentagonal stone wall some 4 to 5ft thick.
Times: Open at all times.
Fee: Free.
✈ ☺

⛪ LLANBERIS

DOLBADARN CASTLE
LL55 4UD (A4086)

Built by Llywelyn the Great in the early 13th century, this Welsh castle overlooks Llyn Padarn in the Llanberis pass.
Times: Open any reasonable time.
🅿 ✈ ☺ 🍴

LLANBERIS LAKE RAILWAY
Padarn Country Park LL55 4TY (off A4086)
☎ 01286 870549

Steam locomotives dating from 1889 to 1948 carry passengers on a four-mile return journey along the shore of Padarn Lake. The terminal station is adjacent to the Welsh Slate Museum, in the Padarn Country Park. The railway was formerly used to carry slate.
Times: Open Easter-late Oct. Trains run frequently every day (ex Sat), 11-4.30 in peak season. Send for free timetable.
🅿 (charged) 🍴 ♿ (Disabled carriage available) toilets for disabled shop ✈ (train & shop)

SNOWDON MOUNTAIN RAILWAY
LL55 4TY (on A4086, Caernarfon to Capel Curig road. 7.5 miles from Caernarfon)
☎ 01286 870223 📠 01286 872518

The journey of just over four-and-a-half miles takes passengers more than 3000ft up to the summit of Snowdon; breathtaking views include, on a clear day, the Isle of Man and the Wicklow Mountains in Ireland. The round trip to the summit and back takes two and a half hours including a half hour at the summit.
Times: Open 15 Mar-1 Nov, daily from 9am (weather permitting).
Fee: *Return £15 (ch £10.80). Single £10.80 (ch £7.70). Family ticket £40. Party 15+.
🅿 (charged) 🍴 ♿ (some carriages suitable for wheelchairs) toilets for disabled shop ✈ (ex off peak) 🍴

WELSH SLATE MUSEUM
Gilfach Ddu, Padarn Country Park LL55 4TY (0.25m off A4086. The Museum is within Padarn Country Park at Llanberis)
☎ 01286 870630 📠 01286 871906

Set among the towering quarries at Llanberis, the Welsh Slate Museum is a living, working site located in the original workshops of Dinorwig Quarry, which once employed 15,000 men and boys. You can see the foundry, smithy, workshops and mess room which make up the old quarry, and view original machinery, much of which is still in working order.
Times: Open Etr-Oct, daily 10-5; Nov-Mar, Sun-Fri 10-4. Last admission 1 hour before closing.
Fee: *£3.50 (ch & concessions £2) Family ticket £7.90.
🅿 (charged) 🍴 ♿ (all parts accessible except patten loft) toilets for disabled shop 🍴

LLANDUDNO JUNCTION
RSPB NATURE RESERVE
LL31 9XZ (off A55)
☎ 01492 584091

The visitor centre has a viewing area which overlooks the estuary and Conwy Castle, and there's a nature trail and three hides for viewing lapwings and shelduck amongst many others. Phone for details of events.
Times: Open daily, 10-5 (or sunset if earlier)
🅿 ♿ toilets for disabled shop ✈ *Details not confirmed for 2000* 🍴

LLANFIHANGEL-Y-PENNANT
CASTELL-Y-BERE
☎ 029 20500200

The castle was begun around 1221 by Prince Llewelyn ap Iorwerth of Gwynedd to guard the southern flank of his principality. It is typically Welsh in design with its D-shaped towers. Although a little off the beaten track, the castle lies in a spectacular setting, overshadowed by the Cader Idris range.
Times: Open all reasonable times.
Fee: Free.
✈ ☺

LLANGOLLEN
HORSE DRAWN BOATS AND CANAL EXHIBITION CENTRE
The Wharf, Wharf Hill LL20 8TA
☎ 01978 860702 & 01691 690322

Take a horsedrawn boat trip along the beautiful Vale of Llangollen, and visit the museum, which illustrates the heyday of canals in Britain. The displays include working and static models, photographs, murals and slides. There is also a narrowboat trip which crosses Pontcysyllte Aqueduct, the largest navigable aqueduct in the world.
Times: Open Etr-Oct, daily (limited opening in Oct).
Fee: *Horse Drawn Boat Trip from £3.50 (ch £2.50). Family ticket £9. Narrowboat Trip £6 (ch £5).
🅿 (400 yrds) 🍴 ✈ licensed ♿ (alighting/pick-up point available) toilets for disabled shop 🍴

LLANGOLLEN STATION
(At the junction of A5 & A539)
☎ 01978 860979 & 860951 timetable
📠 01978 869247

Locomotives and rolling stock are displayed, and passenger trains run on a fourteen-and-a-half-mile round trip between Llangollen and Carrog. A special coach for the disabled is sometimes available. Please ring for details of events.
Times: Open - Station wknds, Steam hauled trains Apr-Oct Sun & daily in Jul & Aug, diesel trains for some off peak services.
Fee: *Station Free, except for special event days when charge of £1 (ch 50p) this is deducted from fare if travelling; 2nd class return fare for full journey £7 (ch £3.50, OAP £5.20) Family ticket £17.50 (2+2). For first class, supplement of £1.50 (ch 75p).
🅿 🍴 ♿ (special coach for disabled parties on some trains) toilets for disabled shop (at Llangollen only) 🍴

PLAS NEWYDD
Hill St
☎ 01978 861314

The 'Ladies of Llangollen', Lady Eleanor Butler and Sarah Ponsonby, lived here from 1780 to 1831. The original stained-glass windows, carved panels, and domestic miscellany of two lives are exhibited along with prints, pictures and letters.
Times: Open Apr-Oct, daily, 10-5.
🅿 ♿ toilets for disabled ✈ (ex guide dogs or in grounds)
Details not confirmed for 2000

VALLE CRUCIS ABBEY
LL29 8DD (on B5103, off A5 W of Llangollen)
☎ 01978 860326

Set in a deep, narrow valley, the abbey was founded for the Cistercians in 1201 by Madog ap Gruffydd. Substantial remains of the church can be seen, and some beautifully carved grave slabs have been found. There is a small exhibition on the Cistercian monks and the abbey.
Times: Open all year, May-late Sep, daily 10-5; Site openrest of year. (Closed 24-26 Dec & 1 Jan)
Fee: *£2 (ch 5-16, pen & students £1.50, disabled free). Family ticket £5.50.
🅿 ♿ shop ✈ ☺ 🍴

LLANGYBI
ST CYBI'S WELL
☎ 01766 810047

Cybi was a 6th-century Cornish saint, known as a healer of the sick, and St Cybi's Well (or Ffynnon Gybi) has been famous for its curative properties through the centuries. The corbelled beehive vaulting inside the roofless stone structure is Irish in style and unique in Wales.
Times: Open at all times.
Fee: Free.
♿ ✈ ☺

LLANRWST
GWYDYR UCHAF CHAPEL
(0.5m SW off B5106)
☎ 01492 640578

Built in the 17th century by Sir John Wynn of Gwydir Castle, the chapel is noted for its painted ceiling and wonderfully varied woodwork.
Times: Open any reasonable time.
Fee: Free.
🅿 ✈ 🚐 ☺

LLANYSTUMDWY
LLOYD GEORGE MEMORIAL MUSEUM & HIGHGATE COTTAGE
LL52 0SH (on A497 between Pwllheli & Criccieth)
☎ 01766 522071

Explore the life and times of David Lloyd George in this museum. His boyhood home is recreated as it would have been when he lived there

contd.

between 1864 and 1880, along with his Uncle Lloyd's shoemaking workshop.

Times: Open Etr, daily 10.30-5; May, Mon-Fri 10.30-5; June, Mon-Sat 10.30-5; Jul-Sep daily 10.30-5; Oct, Mon-Fri, 11-4. Other times by appointment, telephone 01286 679098 or 01766 522071 for details.

Fee: *£3 (ch & pen £2). Family ticket £7.

🅿 ♿ (wheelchair access in garden, with assistance) toilets for disabled shop 🐾 (ex guide dogs) ⬤

⏣ PENARTH FAWR

PENARTH FAWR

(3.5m NE of Pwllheli off A497)

☎ **01766 810880**

The hall, buttery and screen are preserved in this house which was probably built in the 15th century.

Times: Open at all times.

Fee: Free.

♿ 🐾 ⊕

⏣ PENMACHNO

PENMACHNO WOOLLEN MILL

LL24 0PP (2m off A5, between Llangollen/Betws-Y-Coed)

☎ **01690 710545**

The 17th-century quarrymen and farmers wore flannel shirts made from cloth woven by local cottage weavers. The cloth was washed and finished in the Pandy (fulling mill). Power looms introduced in the 19th century now weave lightweight tweed and rug cloth. The Story of Wool exhibition explains the process and its history.

Times: Open daily 10-5.30; Nov-Feb open 10-4.30.

🅿 🍽 shop 🐾 *Details not confirmed for 2000*

TY MAWR

LL25 0HJ (From A5 3m S of Betws-y-Coed take B4406 to Penmachno. House is 2.5m NW of Penmacho by forest road)

☎ **01690 760213**

Situated in the beautiful and secluded Wybrnant Valley, Ty Mawr was the birthplace of Bishop William Morgan (1545-1604), the first translator of the entire Bible into Welsh. The house has been restored to its probable 16th-17th century appearance. The Wybrnant Nature Trail, a short walk, covers approximately one mile.

Times: Open Apr-Sep, Thu-Sun & BH Mons 12-5; Oct, Thu, Fri & Sun 12-4. Last admission 30 mins before closing.

Fee: *£2 (ch £1). Family ticket £5. Party 15+.

🅿 🐾 (ex grounds) 🚐 (minibus access only) ⬤

⏣ PLAS NEWYDD

PLAS NEWYDD

LL61 6DQ (2m S of Llanfairpwll, on A4080)

☎ **01248 714795**   🖷 **01248 713673**

Built by James Wyatt in the 18th century, this house stands on the Menai Strait in unspoilt surroundings. Beautiful lawns and parkland surround the house and there is a fine spring garden, summer garden and later massed hydrangeas and autumn colour. The

Rhododendron Garden is open from April - early June only. An exhibition of Rex Whistler's work is on show including his largest wall painting.

Times: Open 27 Mar-1 Nov, Sat-Wed. House 12-5pm, garden 11am-5.30pm. Last admission 30mins before closing.

Fee: *£4.20 (ch £2.10). Family £10.50. Pre-booked groups (15+). Garden only: £2.20 (ch £1.10).

🅿 ✕ licensed ♿ (Close parking, wheelchairs, stairclimber) toilets for disabled shop 🐾 ⬤

⏣ PORTHMADOG

FFESTINIOG RAILWAY

Harbour Station LL49 9NF (SE end of town, on A487)

☎ **01766 512340**   🖷 **01766 514576**

A narrow gauge steam railway running for 13.5 miles through Snowdonia National Park, with breathtaking views and superb scenery. Buffet service on all trains including licensed bar (in corridor carriages). There's also a museum. Please telephone for details of special events.

Times: Open late Mar-early Nov, daily service and also 26 Dec-1 Jan. Weekend service Nov-Dec (most days). Limited service Feb & Mar. Museum open when trains operating.

🅿 (charged) ✕ licensed ♿ (Wheelchair ramps recently installed) toilets for disabled shop (closed 24/25 Dec) *Details not confirmed for 2000* ⬤

⏣ PORTMEIRION

PORTMEIRION

LL48 6ET (Off A487 at Minffordd)

☎ **01766 770000**   🖷 **01766 771331**

Welsh architect Sir Clough Williams Ellis built his fairy-tale, Italianate village on a rocky, tree-clad peninsula on the shores of Cardigan Bay. A bell-tower, castle and lighthouse mingle with a watch-tower, grottoes and cobbled squares among pastel-shaded picturesque cottages let as holiday accommodation. The 60-acre Gwyllt Gardens include miles of dense woodland paths and are famous for their fine displays of rhododendrons, azaleas, hydrangeas and sub-tropical flora. There is a mile of sandy beach and a playground for children.

Times: Open all year, daily 9.30-5.30.

Fee: *£4 (ch £2, pen £3.30). Party 20+.

🅿 🍽 ✕ licensed ♿ toilets for disabled shop garden centre 🐾 ⬤

⏣ RHUDDLAN

RHUDDLAN CASTLE

LL18 5AD

☎ **01745 590777**

The castle was begun by Edward I in 1277, on a simple `diamond' plan with round towers linked by sections of 9ft thick curtain wall. The moat was linked to a deep-water canal, allowing Edward's ships to sail from the sea right up to the castle.

Times: Open May-late Sep, daily 10-5.

Fee: *£2 (ch 5-16, pen & students £1.50, disabled free). Family ticket £5.50.

🅿 ♿ shop 🐾 ⊕ ⬤

⛫ TAL-Y-CAFN
BODNANT GARDEN
LL28 5RE (8m S of Llandudno & Colwyn Bay on A470. Also signposted from A55)
☎ 01492 650460 ▤ 01492 650448

Set above the River Conwy with beautiful views over Snowdonia, these gardens are a delight. Five terraces in the Italian style were constructed below the house - on the lowest terrace is a canal pool with an open-air stage at one end and a reconstructed Pin Mill at the other. Contact for details of open air theatre.
Times: Open 13 Mar-end Oct, daily 10-5 (last admission half hour before closing)
Fee: *£4.60 (ch £2.30). Party 20+
🅿 ♨ ♿ (steep in places with many steps not easy for wheelchairs) toilets for disabled shop ✈ (ex guide dogs) ♨

⛫ TREFRIW
TREFRIW WOOLLEN MILL
LL27 0NQ (on B5106 in centre of Trefriw)
☎ 01492 640462 ▤ 01492 640462

Established in 1859, the mill is situated beside the fast-flowing Afon Crafnant, which drives two hydro-electric turbines to power the looms. All the machinery of woollen manufacture can be seen here: blending, carding, spinning, dyeing, warping and weaving. In the Weaver's Garden, there are plants traditionally used in the textile industry, mainly for dyeing. Hand-spinning demonstrations.
Times: Mill open Etr-Oct, Mon-Fri 10-5. Weaving demonstrations & turbine house: open all year, Mon-Fri 10-5.
Fee: *Free (ex school parties which must be pre-booked).
🅿 (35 yds) ♨ ♿ shop (Specialises in woven goods) ✈ (in shop & grounds, not mill) ♨

⛫ TYWYN
TALYLLYN RAILWAY
Wharf Station LL36 9EY (A493 Machynlleth to Dolgellau for Tywyn station, B4405 for Abergynolwyn)
☎ 01654 710472 ▤ 01654 711755

The oldest 27in-gauge railway in the world, built in 1865 to run from Tywyn on Cardigan Bay to Abergynolwyn slate mine some seven miles inland. The railway climbs the steep sides of the Fathew Valley and on the way there are stops at Dolgoch Falls and the Nant Gwernol forest. The return trip takes 2.5 hours. All scheduled passenger trains are steam hauled. Please phone for details of special events.
Times: Open 21 Feb-28 Mar, Sun only; 29 Mar-30 Oct, daily. Xmas holiday sevice 18,19,24 & 26 Dec-2 Jan. Timetable available.
Fee: *£8.50 return ticket (ch accompanied £2). Intermediate fares available.
🅿 (charged) ♨ ♿ (prior arrangement useful) toilets for disabled shop ♨

⛫ WREXHAM
ERDDIG
LL13 0YT (off the A525, 2m S of Wrexham and the A483/A5152 Oswestry road)
☎ 01978 355314 ▤ 01978 313333

Built in 1680, the house was enlarged and improved during the next half century by a wealthy London lawyer with a passion for gilt and silver furniture. Original furnishings remain, including a magnificent state bed in Chinese silk. The house is especially notable for the view it gives of both 'upstairs' and 'downstairs' life. The gardens are unusual in that they have been very little changed since the 18th century.
Times: Open 20 Mar-1 Oct, Sat-Wed (open Good Fri), house 12-5, garden 11-6 (Jul-Aug gardens 10-6); 2-31 Oct, Sat-Wed, house 12-4, garden 11-5.
Fee: *All inclusive tickets inc: Family rooms, below stairs, outbuildings & gardens £6 (ch £3). Party 15+. Below stairs, outbuildings & garden £4 (ch £2) Family ticket £10.00. National Trust members free.
🅿 ✗ licensed ♿ toilets for disabled shop ✈ (ex guidance dogs) ♨ ♨

Mid Wales

From the south-west tip of Wales - you can't go farther than St Bride's Bay - right across the country to Offa's Dyke and the English border, there's a bit of everything.

The Pembrokeshire Coast National Park runs 186 miles (299km) from Milford Haven north, embracing some of the finest coastal scenery, which can be tackled in easy or arduous stages, but do take care - the cliffs can be dangerous.

On the south coast are Llanelli and Carmarthen and no literary fan would miss a visit to Laugharne, where Dylan Thomas toiled to produce his most memorable works.

St David's is on most itineraries. For 1500 years pilgrims have trudged to its cathedral, which stands proud in the rather bleak landscape.

Further north, Cardigan Bay sweeps up to Anglesey and Snowdonia, embracing the resorts of Aberporth, New Quay and Aberaeron. The university town of Aberystwyth has plenty to delight visitors, including Devil's Bridge in the Vale of Rheidol. Machynlleth at the mouth of the Dyfi Valley is notable as Owen Glyndwr's parliament, before English supremacy was exerted.

Powys sprawls across the country, taking in the Brecon Beacons and the Black Mountains. The four towns suffixed Wells (Builth, Llangammarch, Llanwrtyd, Llandrindod) are all Victorian spas. The long border with England runs through gentler country.

Top: Brecon Mountain Railway

This region includes the counties of Carmarthenshire, Ceredigion, Pembrokeshire and Powys which reflect recent national changes.

⌂ ABERAERON
LLANERCHAERON
SA48 8DG (2.5m E of Aberaeron off A482)
☎ 01545 570200 ▤ 01545 570200

A rare survivor of the core of a Welsh gentry estate. It was acquired by The National Trust in 1994 having received minimal maintenance in recent decades. Parts of the property are open to visitors.
Times: Open 27 Mar-3 Oct, Thu-Sun & BH Mons 11-5. Last admission 30 mins before closing. Park open all year dawn to dusk.
Fee: *£2 (ch £1). Family ticket £5. Party.
🅿 ⅏ toilets for disabled 🐾 (ex on lead) 🐛

⌂ ABERCRAF
DAN-YR-OGOF SHOWCAVES
SA9 1GJ (M4 J45, midway between Swansea & Brecon on A4067)
☎ 01639 730284 & 730801
▤ 01639 730293

This award winning attraction includes three separate caves, dinosaur park, Iron Age Farm, museum and shire horse centre.
Times: Open Apr-Oct, daily from 10am. Please telephone for Oct.
Fee: *£6.75 (ch £4). Group rates 15+
🅿 ⬛ ⅏ toilets for disabled shop ◥

⌂ ABERGWILI
CARMARTHEN MUSEUM
SA31 2JG (2m E of Carmarthen, on A40)
☎ 01267 231691 ▤ 01267 223830

Housed in the old palace of the Bishop of St David's and set in seven acres of grounds, the museum offers a wide range of local subjects to explore, from geology and prehistory to butter making, Welsh furniture and folk art. Temporary exhibitions are held.
Times: Open all year, Mon-Sat 10-4.30. (Closed Xmas-New Year).
Fee: Free.
🅿 ⬛ ⅏ toilets for disabled shop 🐾 (ex guide dogs)

⌂ ABERYSTWYTH
NATIONAL LIBRARY OF WALES
Penglais Hill SY23 3BU (off Penglais Hill, A487 in the Northern portion of Aberystwyth)
☎ 01970 632800, 623834 & 623837
▤ 01970 615709

This huge library is one of Britain's six copyright libraries, and specialises in Welsh and Celtic literature. It has maps, manuscripts, prints and drawings. A major permanent exhibition 'A Nation's Heritage' is on view and there is a programme of travelling exhibitions. Please telephone for details.
Times: Open all year, exhibitions, library & reading rooms Mon-Fri 9.30-6, Sat until 5. (Closed BH's & first wk Oct).
Fee: Free.
🅿 ⬛ ⅏ toilets for disabled shop 🐾

⌂ AMROTH
COLBY WOODLAND GARDEN
SA67 8PP (1.5 miles inland from Amroth beside Carmarthen Bay, follow brown signs from A477)
☎ 01834 811885

Tranquillity and seclusion abound in this sheltered valley. There are many pleasant meadow and woodland walks. From early spring to the end of June the garden is a blaze of colour, from the masses of daffodils to the rich hues of rhododendrons, azaleas and bluebells.
Times: Open Apr-Oct, daily 10-5. Walled garden Apr-30 Oct 11-5. Last admission 30 mins before closing.
Fee: *£2.80 (ch £1.40). Family ticket £7. Pre-booked parties £2.30 (ch £1.15) NT members free.
🅿 ⬛ ⅏ (Limited due to terrain) toilets for disabled shop garden centre 🐾 (ex on lead) 🐛 ◥

⌂ BRECON
SOUTH WALES BORDERERS (24TH REGIMENT) MUSEUM MUSEUM
The Barracks, The Watton LD3 7EB (close to town centre, well signed)
☎ 01874 613310 ▤ 01874 613275

The museum of the South Wales Borderers and Monmouthshire Regiment, which was raised in 1689 and has been awarded 23 Victoria Crosses. Amongst the collections is the Zulu War Room, devoted to the war and in particular to the events at Rorke's Drift, 1879, when 121 men fought 4500 Zulus.
Times: Open all year, Apr-Sep daily; Oct-Mar, Mon-Fri 9-1 & 2-5. (Closed Xmas & New Year).
Fee: *£2 (ch 16 £1).
🅿 (town centre) ⅏ (Ramp access from main road) shop 🐾 (ex guide dogs) ◥

⌂ CAPEL BANGOR
RHEIDOL HYDRO ELECTRIC POWER STATION & VISITOR CENTRE
Cwm Rheidol SY23 3NF (Off A44 at Capel Bangor)
☎ 01970 880667 ▤ 01970 880670

A guided tour of the power station can be taken. There is a visitor centre.
Times: Open Apr-Oct, daily 10-4 for free tours of the Power Station & visitor centre.
Fee: Free.
🅿 ⬛ ⅏ toilets for disabled

⌂ CAREW
CAREW CASTLE & TIDAL MILL
SA70 8SL (on A4075, 4m E of Pembroke)
☎ 01646 651657 & 651782
▤ 01646 651782

This magnificent Norman castle has royal links with Henry Tudor and was the setting for the Great Tournament of 1508. Nearby is the Carew Cross (Cadw), an impressive 13ft Celtic cross dating from the 11th century. Carew Mill is one of only four restored tidal mills in Britain, with

contd.

records dating back to 1558. Please telephone for details of special events.

Times: Open Etr-Oct, daily 10-5.

🅿 ⚹ (ramps) toilets for disabled shop *Details not confirmed for 2000*

CARREG CENNEN CASTLE

CARREG CENNEN CASTLE

SA19 6UA (unclassified road from A483 to Trapp village)

☎ 01558 822291

A steep path leads up to the castle, which is spectacularly sited on a limestone crag. It was first built as a stronghold of the native Welsh and then rebuilt in the late 13th century. Most remarkable among the impressive remains is a mysterious passage, cut into the side of the cliff and lit by loopholes. The farm at the site has a rare breeds centre.

Times: Open all year, Apr-Sep, daily 9.30-7.30; Oct-Mar, daily, 9.30-4. (Closed 24-26 Dec & 1 Jan).

Fee: *£2.50 (ch 5-16, pen & students £2, disabled free). Family ticket £7.

🅿 ⬛ shop ✖ ☺ 🍴

CILGERRAN

CILGERRAN CASTLE

SA43 2SF (off A484 & A478)

☎ 01239 615007

Set above a gorge of the River Teifi - famed for its coracle fishermen - Cilgerran Castle dates from the 11th to 13th centuries. It decayed gradually after the Civil War, but its great round towers and high walls give a vivid impression of its former strength.

Times: Open all year, early Apr-Oct, daily 9.30-6.30; Nov-early Apr, daily 9.30-4. (Closed 24-26 Dec & 1 Jan).

Fee: *£2 (ch 5-16, pen & students £1.50, disabled free). Family ticket £5.50.

⚹ shop ✖ ☺ 🍴

CRYMYCH

CASTELL HENLLYS FORT

Pant-Glas, Meline SA41 3UT (Off A487 between Eglwyswrw and Newport Pembrokeshire)

☎ 01239 891319   🖷 01239 891319

This Iron Age hill fort is set in the beautiful Pembrokeshire Coast National Park. Excavations began in 1981 and three roundhouses have been reconstructed. A forge, smithy, and looms can be seen, with other attractions such as trails and a herb garden. Please telephone for details of special events.

Times: Open Apr-late Oct, daily 10-5. Last entry 4.30

🅿 ⚹ toilets for disabled shop *Details not confirmed for 2000*
🍴

DRE-FACH FELINDRE

MUSEUM OF THE WELSH WOOLLEN INDUSTRY

SA44 5UP (16m W of Carmarthen off A484, 4m E of Newcastle Emlyn)

☎ 01559 370929   🖷 01559 371592

The museum is housed in the former Cambrian Mills and has a comprehensive display tracing the evolution of the industry from its beginnings to the present day. Demonstrations of the fleece to fabric process are given on 19th-century textile machinery. Special events: please telephone for details.

Times: Open all year, Apr-Sep, Mon-Sat 10-5; Oct-Mar, Mon-Fri 10-5. (Closed 24-26 Dec & 1 Jan).

Fee: *£2.60 (ch/concessions £1.60).

🅿 ⬛ ⚹ (Wheelchair access to ground floor & ample seating) toilets for disabled shop garden centre (ex galleries) 🍴

DRYSLWYN

DRYSLWYN CASTLE

(on B4279)

☎ 029 20500200

The ruined 13th-century castle was a stronghold of the native Welsh. It stands on a lofty mound, and was important in the struggles between English and Welsh. It is gradually being uncovered by excavation.

Times: Open - entrance by arrangement with Dryslwyn Farm.

Fee: Free.

🅿 ✖ ☺

EGLWYSFACH

RSPB NATURE RESERVE

Cae'r Berllan SY20 8TA (6m S of Machynlleth on A487 in Eglwys-Fach. Signposted from main road)

☎ 01654 781265   🖷 01654 781328

Lying at the head of the Dyfi estuary, this grazed saltmarsh is bordered by freshwater marsh and some remnant peat bogs. In the oakwoods are pied flycatchers, redstarts, wood warblers, nut hatches, and both great spotted and lesser spotted woodpeckers. Buzzards, kestrels and sparrowhawks breed in the wood whilst redbreasted mergansers and common sandpipers frequent the river. Peregrines can be seen all year while Merlins and hen harriers hunt over the reserve during the winter. Badgers and polecats live here and there are many species of butterfly. Phone for an events leaflet.

Times: Open daily, 9am-9pm (or sunset if earlier). Visitor Centre & shop: Mar-Oct 9-5; Nov-Feb 10-4 (ex Fri)

🅿 ⚹ shop ✖ *Details not confirmed for 2000* 🍴

FISHGUARD

OCEANLAB

The Parrog, Goodwick SA64 0DE (close to Stena Line ferry terminal at harbour)

☎ 01348 874737   🖷 01348 872528

Overlooking the Pembrokeshire coastline, OceanLab is a multifunctional centre which aims to provide a fun filled experience for the family. A

deep sea time adventure takes the visitor back in time to see marine creatures that lived in the distant past. There is also a hands on science and technology exhibition, a soft play area and a cybercafe where visitors can surf the Internet.
Times: Open Etr-Oct 10-6, winter opening on request.
Fee: *OceanLab/Techniquest £2, Soft Play Area £1, Cyber Cafe £2 per 30 mins.
P 💷 & toilets for disabled shop ✈ (ex guide dogs) 🍽

KIDWELLY
KIDWELLY CASTLE
SA17 5BQ (via A484)
☎ 01554 890104

This is an outstanding example of late 13th-century castle design, with its `walls within walls' defensive system. There were later additions made to the building, the chapel dating from about 1400. Of particular interest are two vast circular ovens.
Times: Open all year, late May-early Oct, daily 9.30-6; late Mar-late May & Oct, daily 9.30-5; Nov-late Mar, Mon-Sat 9.30-4 & Sun 11-4. (Closed 24-26 Dec & 1 Jan).
Fee: *£2.20 (ch 5-16, pen & students £1.70, disabled free). Family ticket £6.10.
P & toilets for disabled shop ✈ ✣ 🍽

LAMPHEY
LAMPHEY PALACE
SA71 5NT (off A4139)
☎ 01646 672224

This ruined 13th-century palace once belonged to the Bishops of St David's.
Times: Open all year, daily 10-5.
Fee: *£2 (ch 5-16, pen & students £1.50, disabled free). Family ticket £5.50.
P & toilets for disabled shop ✈ ✣ 🍽

LAUGHARNE
DYLAN THOMAS' BOAT HOUSE
Dylans Walk SA33 4SD (14m SW of Carmarthen)
☎ 01994 427420   📄 01554 747501

Under Milk Wood was written here by Wales's most prolific 20th-century poet and writer. Set on the `heron priested' shore of the Taf estuary, the house contains original furniture, family photographs, an art gallery and displays on the life and works of Dylan Thomas.
Times: Open all year, May-Oct, daily 10-5; Nov-Apr, daily 10.30-3.
Fee: *£2.75 (ch 7-14 £1, concessions £1.75). Party 5+
P (10mins walk) 💷 shop ✈ (ex guide dogs) 🍽

LAUGHARNE CASTLE
King St SA33 4SA (on A4066)
☎ 01994 427906

Newly opened to the public, picturesque Laugharne Castle stands on a low ridge overlooking the wide Taff Estuary. A medieval fortress converted into an Elizabethan mansion, it suffered a civil war siege and later became the backdrop for elaborate Victorian gardens, now recreated. Laugharne Castle has also inspired

two modern writers - Richard Hughes and Dylan Thomas.
Times: Open May-late Sep, daily 10-5.
Fee: *£2 (ch 5-16, pen & students £1.50, disabled free). Family ticket £5.50.
P (150 mtrs) & toilets for disabled shop ✈ ✣ 🍽

LLANDEILO
DINEFWR PARK
SA19 6RT (off A40 Carmarthenshire, on the western outskirts of Llandeilo)
☎ 01558 823902   📄 01558 822036

At the heart of Welsh history for a thousand years, the Park as we know it today took shape in the years after 1775 when the medieval castle, house, gardens, woods and deer park were integrated into one vast and breathtaking landscape. Access to Church Woods and Dinefwr Castle is through the landscaped park.
Times: Open 27 Mar-Oct, daily (ex Tue & Wed) 11-5. Last admission 30 mins before closing. Park is open during daylight hours in winter.
Fee: Free.
P (charged) 💷 & toilets for disabled shop ✈ (ex outer park on lead) 🐾 🍽

LLANELLI
WWT LLANELLI
Penclacwydd, Llwynhendy SA14 9SH (3m E of Llanelli, off A484)
☎ 01554 741087   📄 01554 741087

A wide variety of wild birds, including oystercatchers, redshanks, curlews, little egrets and occasionally ospreys, can be seen here during the right season. The grounds are beautifully landscaped, and other features include a closed circuit television system transmitting pictures of wild birds on the reserve, a wetland craft area and a flock of colourful Caribbean Flamingos. Facilities for the disabled include easy access on level paths throughout the grounds, special viewing areas, and wheelchair loan. Please ring for details of special events and activities.
Times: Open summer 9.30-5.30, winter 9.30-4.30. Closed 24-25 Dec.
P ✕ & toilets for disabled shop ✈ *Details not confirmed for 2000* 🍽

LLANFAIR CAEREINION
WELSHPOOL & LLANFAIR LIGHT RAILWAY
SY21 0SF (beside A458, Shrewsbury-Dolgellau road)
☎ 01938 810441   📄 01938 810861

The Llanfair Railway is one of the Great Little Trains of Wales. It offers an 8-mile trip through glorious scenery by narrrow-gauge steam train. The line is home to a collection of engines and

contd.

coaches from all round the world. Please ring for details of special events.

Times: Open Etr-26 Sep, wknds; Etr, May Day BH, Spring BH wk; 8 Jun-11 Jul/7-16 Sept, Tue-Thu; 19 Jul-3 Sep, daily. Trains from Llanfair at 10.30, 1.30 & 4.15pm; from Welshpool 11.45, 2.45 & 5.15. Extra trains at BHs.

Fee: *£7.50 return (ch £1, pen £6.50).

P 💺 & (two coaches adapted for wheelchairs) toilets for disabled shop ✈

⬛ LLANRTHNE
NATIONAL BOTANIC GARDEN OF WALES
Middleton Hall SA32 8HG
☎ 01558 668768   📠 01558 668933

This venture will be the first 'national' botanic garden to be created in the United Kingdom this century. The Garden of Wales will be a model to a sustainable way of living in harmony with the natural world. Set in the 18th-century parkland of the former Middleton Hall, the garden is situated within a 568-acre estate on the edge of the beautiful Towy Valley with spectacular views across the surrounding countryside. The garden's centrepiece will be one of the largest single span glasshouses in the world, which, on completion, will house a landscape filled with a living collection of threatened Mediterranean plants and 'Bioverse', a hands-on educational adventure aimed at unlocking the mysteries of plant life.

Times: Opening Spring 2000. Contact for admisssion times.
Fee: Admission charged.

⬛ LLANSTEFFAN
LLANSTEFFAN CASTLE
(off B4312)
☎ 01267 241756

The ruins of this 11th to 13th-century stronghold stand majestically on the west side of the Towy estuary.

Times: Open - access throughout the year.
Fee: Free.
✈ ☺

⬛ LLANYCEFN
PENRHOS COTTAGE
SA66 7XT (Near Maenclochog & Llanycefn, N of Haverfordwest).
☎ 01437 731328   📠 01437 731743

Local tradition has it that cottages built overnight on common land could be claimed by the builders, together with the ground a stone's throw away from the door. This thatched cottage is an example, built with help from friends and family; and it gives an insight into traditional Welsh country life.

Times: Open mid May-Sep Mon-Fri, by appointment only. Tel: 01437-731328.
P (roadside) & shop ✈ (ex in grounds or guide dogs)
Details not confirmed for 2000

⬛ LLAWHADEN
LLAWHADEN CASTLE
☎ 01437 541201

The castle was first built in the 12th century to protect the possessions of the bishops of St David's. The 13th and 14th-century remains of the bishops' hall, kitchen, bakehouse and other buildings can be seen, all surrounded by a deep moat.

Times: Open at all times. Key keeper arrangement.
Fee: Free.
& ✈ ☺

⬛ MACHYNLLETH
CENTRE FOR ALTERNATIVE TECHNOLOGY
SY20 9AZ (2.5m N on A487)
☎ 01654 702400   📠 01654 702782

The Centre for Alternative Technology promotes practical ideas and information on sustainable technologies. The exhibition includes displays of wind, water and solar power, organic gardens, low-energy dwellings, and a unique water-powered railway which ascends a 200ft cliff from the car park. The Wave Tank and the underground 'Mole-Hole' are particularly popular with children. A Festival of the Future is being held as a millennium celebration.

Times: Open Mar-Oct; 10-5.30; Nov-Feb; 11-4. Closed 23-26 Dec & 5-23 Jan.
Fee: *Dec-Mar £4 (ch £2.40, concessions £3.10). Family ticket £11; Apr-Jun, Oct £5.30 (ch £2.90, concessions £4.15). Family ticket £15; Jul-Sep £5.90 (ch 2.90, concessions £4.15). Family ticket £16.25.
P 💺 & (wheelchair available) toilets for disabled shop ✈ (ex guide dogs) ✈

⬛ MONTGOMERY
MONTGOMERY CASTLE
☎ 029 20500200

Initially an earth and timber structure guarding an important ford in the River Severn, Montgomery was considered a 'suitable spot for the erection of an impregnable castle' in the 1220s. Building and modifications continued until 1251-53, but the final conquest of Wales by Edward I meant the castle lost much of its role.

Times: Open all year, any reasonable time.
Fee: Free.
& ✈ ☺

⬛ NEWPORT
PENTRE IFAN BURIAL CHAMBER
(3m SE from B4329 or A487)
☎ 029 20500200

Found to be part of a vanished long barrow when excavated in 1936-37, the remains of this chamber include the capstone, three uprights and a circular forecourt.

Times: Open - access throughout the year.
Fee: Free.
✈ ☺

⌂ PEMBROKE
PEMBROKE CASTLE
SA71 4LA (west end of Main St)
☎ 01646 681510 📋 01646 622260

This 12th to 13th-century fortress has an impressive 80ft-high round keep. There is also an Interpretative Centre with introductory video and Pembroke Yeomanry exhibition. Phone for details of special events which may include archery and falconry displays.

Times: Open all year, daily, Apr-Sep 9.30-6; Mar & Oct 10-5; Nov-Feb, 10.30-4.30; 1 Jan 12.30-4.30 (Closed 24-26 Dec).

Fee: *£3 (ch under16 & pen £2, ch under5 & wheelchairs free). Family ticket £8.

P (200 yds) 📖 ♿ toilets for disabled shop (must be on leads) 🐾

⌂ PONTERWYD
LLYWERNOG SILVER-LEAD MINE
Llywernog Mine SY23 3AB (11m E of Aberystwyth on A44)
☎ 01970 890620 📋 01545 570823

The mine is located high in the beautiful Cambrian Mountains, and you can explore tunnels and chambers dating from the 18th century and see veins of silver-lead ore running through the rocks. At the surface, the old mine buildings contain exhibitions which tell the story of the 'boom days', and there are collections of old tools, working water wheels and quaint machinery. Pan for silver and 'fool's gold' and operate simple pumps and equipment.

Times: Open Etr-Oct, daily 10-6 (Oct 5pm). Nov-Dec by appointment.

Fee: *£4.50 (ch 5-15 £2.95, pen & students £3.95). Family ticket (2 adults, 3 children) £14.

P 📖 ♿ shop 🐾

⌂ PRESTEIGNE
THE JUDGE'S LODGING
Broad St LD8 2AD (on B4362)
☎ 01544 260650/1 📋 01544 260652

A restored Victorian town house with integral courtroom, cells and service areas - step back

contd.

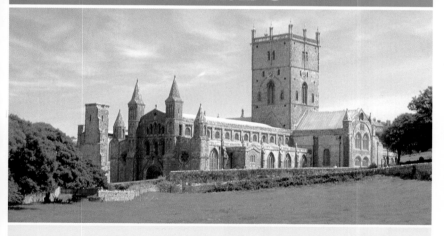

ST DAVID'S

The presence of a cathedral makes a city, so theoretically St David's is a city. In fact it is little more than a village, but the site has been drawing pilgrims for more than 1,500 years, not only to the shrine of one patron saint, but two, for St Patrick was reputedly born near here. The cathedral, like most, is much altered and added to. One medieval gate remains. The tower is 125 ft (38mtr), and curiously has three clocks, not four. Inside look for the carved ceiling, the monarch's stall, and St David's tomb.

Next door are the ruins of Bishop Gower's Palace which was wrecked by a later bishop stealing the lead off the roof!

into the 1870s, accompanied by an 'evesdropping' audiotour of voices from the past.
Times: Open daily, Mar-Apr 10-4; May-Oct 10-6. Closed Nov-Feb.
P & (lift, disabled pack for inaccesible items) shop ✖

⛰ PUMSAINT
DOLAUCOTHI GOLD MINES
SA19 8US (on A482, signposted both directions)
☎ 01558 650359

Here is an opportunity to spend a day exploring the gold mines and to wear a miner's helmet and lamp while touring the underground workings. The information centre and a walk along the Miners' Way disclose the secrets of 2000 years of gold mining. This is the only place in Britain where the Romans mined gold.
Times: Open 20 May-12 Sep, daily 10-5. Guided underground tours daily.
Fee: *£2.60 (ch £1.30) Family ticket £6.50. NT members free. Guided underground tours £3.60 (ch £1.80) Family ticket £9. NT members: £2.60 (ch £1.30). Family ticket £6.50.
P 🅿 & toilets for disabled shop (on leads, but not on tours) 💱 🍴

⛰ ST DAVID'S
ST DAVID'S BISHOP'S PALACE
SA62 6PE (on A487)
☎ 01437 720517

These extensive and impressive ruins are all that remain of the principal residence of the Bishops of St Davids. The palace shares a quiet valley with the cathedral, which was almost certainly built on the site of a monastery founded in the 6th century by St David. The Bishop's Palace houses an exhibition: `Lords of the Palace'.
Times: Open all year, late May-early Oct, daily 9.30-6; late Mar-late May & Oct, daily 9.30-5; Nov-late Mar, Mon-Sat 9.30-4 & Sun 12-4. (Closed 24-26 Dec & 1 Jan).
Fee: *£2 (ch 5-16, pen & students £1.50, disabled free). Family ticket £5.50.
P & toilets for disabled shop ✖ ☺ 🍴

ST DAVID'S CATHEDRAL
The Close SA62 6PE
☎ 01437 720202   🖹 01437 721885

Begun 1181 on the reputed site of St David's 6th century monastic settlement. The present building was altered during the 12th to the 14th

centuries and again in the 16th. The ceilings of oak, painted wood and stone vaulting are of considerable interest.
Times: Open all year 8.30-6.
Fee: *Suggested donation of £2.00.
P (300yds) 🅿 & toilets for disabled shop ✖ (ex guide dogs) 🍴

⛰ STRATA FLORIDA
STRATA FLORIDA ABBEY
SY25 6BT (unclassified road from Pontrhydfendigaid, reached from B4340)
☎ 01974 831261

Little remains of the Cistercian abbey founded in 1164, except the ruined church and cloister. Strata Florida was an important centre of learning in the Middle Ages, and it is believed that the 14th-century poet Dafyd ap Gwilym was buried here.
Times: Open all year, May-late Sep, daily 10-5; Site open rest of year.
Fee: *£2 (ch 5-16, pen & students £1.50, disabled free). Family ticket £5.50.
P & shop ✖ ☺ 🍴

⛰ TALLEY
TALLEY ABBEY
(B4302 from Llandeilo)
☎ 01558 685444

Only beautiful ruins now remain of this once magnificent abbey, including two pointed archways set in the remains of the north and east walls of the central tower. The abbey was founded in 1197 by Rhys ap Gruffudd, and was virtually destroyed in the uprising led by Owain Glyndwr.
Times: Open any reasonable time.
P ✖ ☺ 🍴

⛰ TENBY
TUDOR MERCHANT'S HOUSE
Quay Hill SA70 7BX
☎ 01834 842279

Recalling Tenby's history as a thriving and prosperous port, the Tudor Merchant's house is a fine example of gabled 15th-century architecture. There is a good Flemish chimney and on three walls the remains of frescoes can be seen. A small herb garden has been created.
Times: Open 2 Apr-Sep, Mon-Tue, Thu-Sat 10-5, Sun 1-5. Dec Mon-Tue, Thu-Fri 10-3, Sun 12-3.
Fee: *£1.80 (ch 90p). Groups £1.40 (ch 70p). NT members free.
P (500yds) (no coaches nearby) & (garden could be accessed) ✖ (ex guide or small dogs) 🚗 💱

⛰ TRETOWER
TRETOWER COURT & CASTLE
NP8 2RF (3m NW of Crickhowell, off A479)
☎ 01874 730279

The castle is a substantial ruin of an 11th-century motte and bailey, with a three-storey tower and 9ft-thick walls. Nearby is the Court, a 14th-century fortified manor house which has been altered and extended over the years. The two buildings show the shift from medieval castle to more domestic accommodation over the centuries.

Times: Open late May-early Oct, daily 10-6; late Mar-late May & Oct, daily 10-5; Mar, daily 10-4.

Fee: *£2.20 (ch 5-16, pen & students £1.70, disabled free). Family ticket £6.10.

🅿 ♿ toilets for disabled shop 🐾 ⊕

⛪ WELSHPOOL
POWIS CASTLE
SY21 8RF (1m S of Welshpool, signposted off A483)

☎ 01938 554338 📠 01938 554336

Laid out in the Italian and French styles, the Garden retains its original lead statues, an

Orangery and an aviary on the terraces. The medieval castle contains one of the finest collections of paintings and furniture in Wales and a beautiful collection of treasures from India. Please telephone for details of special events, which include plays, walks, and craft demonstrations.

Times: Castle & museum open: 27 Mar-Jun and Sep-Oct, Wed-Sun 1-5; Jul-Aug Tue-Sun 1-5; Open all Bank Hol's in season. Garden is open same days as castle and museum 11-6. Last admission to all parts is 30 mins before closing.

Fee: *Castle, Museum & Gardens £7.50, (ch under 17 £3.75) Family ticket £18.75. Group member £6.50. Garden only: £5 (ch £2.50) Family £12.50, Group member £4. NT members & ch under 5 free.

🅿 ✗ licensed shop garden centre 🐾 (ex guide dogs) 🐾 ⬛

South Wales

Few places in Britain have been forced to re-invent their identity as abruptly or as completely as South Wales, after the coal and steel and wages ran out. Archetypal images are changing - the pit heads and blast furnaces are gone, and the slag-heaps are being landscaped, but the terraced houses still cling to the sides of the valleys, and you can get a taste of the miner's life in one of the heritage 'experiences'.

The region fought for jobs and investment and now boasts a multitude of high-tech and international companies who have been lured into South Wales, while the creation of the Welsh Assembly has further focused minds on future development.

Many of the coastal towns developed as ports, sending vast tonnages of coal around the world - Swansea, Port Talbot, Barry, Newport, Cardiff. None are exactly tourist territory, but they are interesting and crucial to understanding the history of the area.

The more enticing parts are the Gower Peninsula (west of Swansea, with all the essentials - beaches, cliffs, castles, moors, pretty villages); the Wye Valley meandering up the English border with the massive Chepstow Castle and Tintern Abbey beloved of the English Romantics; and the market town of Abergavenny with its access to the nearby Black Mountains and the Brecon Beacons National Park. Here there is plenty of opportunity for walking, pony trekking and caving.

Top: Blaenavon

This region includes the counties of Blaenau Gwent, Bridgend, Caerphilly, Cardiff, Merthyr Tydfil, Monmouthshire, Neath Port Talbot, Newport, Rhondda Cynon Taff, Swansea, Torfaen and Vale of Glamorgan which reflect the recent national changes.

ABERDULAIS

ABERDULAIS FALLS

SA10 8EU (from M4 J43, take A465, signposted Vale of Neath)
☎ 01639 636674 📄 01639 645069

For over 300 years this famous waterfall has provided energy to drive the wheels of industry. The Turbine House allows visitors access to the top of the falls, with views of the power equipment, fish pass and displays. Please contact for details of special events.

Times: Open: March: Sat & Sun 11am-4pm only. 1 Apr-1Nov Mon-Fri 10am-5pm, Sat, Sun & Bank Hols 11am-6pm (last admission 30 mins before closing).
Fee: *£2.80 (ch £1.40) Family ticket £7. Parties 15+.
📄 💺 ♿ (lifts for disabled to view falls) toilets for disabled shop (on leads) 🐕 🍴

BLAENAVON

BIG PIT MINING MUSEUM

NP4 9XP (M4 J26/25, follow signs along A4042 & A4043 to Pontypool & Blaenavon. Signposted off A465)
☎ 01495 790311 📄 01495 792618

The `Big Pit' closed as a working mine in 1980, but today you can don safety helmets and cap lamps, and descend the 300ft shaft to find out what life was like for generations of miners in South Wales. There is an exhibition in the old pithead baths and a reconstructed miner's cottage can also be seen. Stout shoes and warm clothes are recommended for tours of the mine.
Times: Open Mar-Nov, daily 9.30-5, last tour 3.30. Dec-Feb telephone for opening details.
Fee: *Underground & surface £5.75 (ch £3.95, pen £5.50). Family ticket £17. Surface only £2 (ch £1, OAPs £1.75)
📄 💺 ♿ (underground tours by prior arrangement) toilets for disabled shop (Welsh crafts, books & publications) (not on underground tours) 🍴

BLAENAVON IRONWORKS

North St
☎ 01495 792615

The Blaenavon Ironworks were a milestone in the history of the Industrial Revolution. Constructed in 1788-99, they were the first purpose-built multi-furnace ironworks in Wales. By 1796, Blaenavon was the second largest ironworks in Wales, eventually closing down in 1904.
Times: Open Apr-Sep, Mon-Fri 9.30-4.30, Sat-Sun 10-4. Closed 24-26 Dec & 1 Jan). For details of opening outside this period, telephone 01495 792615.
Fee: *£1.50 (ch 5-16, pen & students £1, disabled free). Family ticket £4.
📄 🐕 ♿ 🍴

BRIDGEND

NEWCASTLE

☎ 01656 659515

The small castle dates back to the 12th century. It is ruined, but a rectangular tower, a richly carved Norman gateway and massive curtain walls, enclosing a polygonal courtyard, can still be seen.
Times: Open - accessible throughout the year. Key keeper arrangement.
Fee: Free.
📄 🐕 ♿

CAERLEON

CAERLEON FORTRESS BATHS, AMPHITHEATRE & BARRACKS

NP6 1AE (on B4236)
☎ 01663 422518

Caerleon was an important Roman military base, with accommodation for thousands of men. The foundations of barrack lines and parts of the ramparts can be seen, with remains of the cookhouse, latrines and baths. The amphitheatre nearby is one of the best examples in Britain.
Times: Open all year, late Mar-Oct daily 9.30-5.15; Nov-late Mar, Mon-Sat 9.30-5, Sun 12-4. (Closed 24-26 Dec & 1Jan).
Fee: *£2 (ch 5-16, pen & students £1.50, disabled free). Family ticket £5.50.
📄 ♿ shop 🐕 ♿ 🍴

ROMAN LEGIONARY MUSEUM

High St NP6 1AE (Situated 10mins from M4/Severn Bridge. Take Junction 25 from M4 onto B4596)
☎ 01633 423134 📄 01633 422869

The museum illustrates the history of Roman Caerleon and the daily life of its garrison. On display are arms, armour and equipment, with a collection of engraved gemstones, a labyrinth mosaic and finds from the legionary base at Usk. Please telephone for details of children's holiday activities.
Times: Open all year, 15 Mar-15 Oct, Mon-Sat 10-6, Sun 2-6; 16 Oct-14 Mar, Mon-Sat 10-4.30, Sun 2-4.30. (Closed 25 & 26 Dec).
Fee: *£2.10 (ch & concessions £1.25). Joint ticket available with Roman Baths & Amphitheatre £3 (ch £1.80)
📄 (100yds) ♿ toilets for disabled shop 🐕 (ex guide dogs) 🍴

CAERPHILLY

CAERPHILLY CASTLE

CF8 1JL (on A469)
☎ 029 20883143

The concentrically planned castle was begun in 1268 by Gilbert de Clare and completed in 1326. It is the largest in Wales, and has extensive land and water defences. A unique feature is the ruined tower - the victim of subsidence - which manages to out-lean even Pisa! The south dam

contd.

platform, once a tournament-field, now displays replica medieval siege-engines.

Times: Open all year, late May-early Oct, daily 9.30-6; late Mar-late May & Oct, daily 9.30-5. Nov-late Mar, Mon-Sat 9.30-4, Sun 11-4. (Closed 24-26 Dec & 1 Jan).

Fee: *£2.50 (ch 5-16, pen & students £2, disabled free). Family ticket £7.

P & shop ✱ ☺ ☟

LLANCAIACH FAWR MANOR

Gelligaer Rd, Nelson CF46 6ER (M4 J32, A470 to Merthyr Tydfil. Then toward Ystrad Mynach A472 follow brown tourist signs)

☎ 01443 412248   ☷ 01443 412688

Step back in time to the Civil War period at this fascinating living history museum. The year is 1645 and you are invited into the Manor to meet the servants of 'Colonel' Edward Prichard - from the puritanical to the gossipy. Please ring for details of special events.

Times: Open all year, Mon-Fri 10-3.30 (last admission), Sat 12-4.30 Sundays 12-4.

P ☟ ✱ licensed & (lift in visitor centre to audio visual show) toilets for disabled shop ✱ (ex in grounds) ☟

⌂ CAERWENT

CAERWENT ROMAN TOWN

(off A48)

☎ 029 20500200

A complete circuit of the town wall of 'Venta Silurum', together with excavated areas of houses, shops and a temple.

Times: Open - access throughout the year.

Fee: Free.

✱ ☺

⌂ CALDICOT

CALDICOT CASTLE, MUSEUM & COUNTRYSIDE PARK

NP6 4HU (from M4 J23 or M48 J2. Signposted from both A48 and B4245)

☎ 01291 420241   ☷ 01291 435094

Caldicot Castle's well-preserved fortifications were founded by the Normans and fully developed by the late 14th century. Restored as a family home by a wealthy Victorian, the castle offers the chance to explore medieval walls and

towers in a setting of tranquil gardens and wooded country park.

Times: Open Mar-Oct, Mon-Fri 10.30-5, Sat & BH 10.30-5, Sun 1.30-5.

P ☟ & toilets for disabled shop *Details not confirmed for 2000* ☟

⌂ CARDIFF

CARDIFF CASTLE

Castle St CF1 2RB (City Centre)

☎ 029 20878100   ☷ 029 20231417

Built on the site of a Roman fort, Roman walls some 10ft thick can still be seen. There is also a Norman keep and a 13th-century tower. The character of the castle comes from its transformation in the 19th century, however, when the immensely rich 3rd Marquess of Bute employed William Burges to restore and rebuild it. Together they created a romantic fantasy of a medieval castle. Also here are the military museums of the Royal Regiment of Wales and Queen's Dragoon Guards.

Times: Open all year, daily (ex 25-26 Dec & 1 Jan) including guided tours, Mar-Oct, 9.30-6 (last tour 5pm); Nov-Feb, 9.30-4.30 (last tour 3.15pm). Royal Regiment of Wales Museum closed Tue. Queen's Dragoon Guards Museum closed Fri.

Fee: *Full conducted tour, military museums, green, Roman Wall & Norman Keep £5 (ch & pen £3). Short tour, military museum, green, Roman Wall & Norman Keep £3 (ch & pen £1.80) Green, Roman Wall, Norman Keep, & military museum £2.50 (ch & pen £1.50).

P (200 yds) ☟ & toilets for disabled shop ✱ (ex in grounds & guide dogs)

DYFFRYN GARDENS

St Nicholas CF5 6SU (6m W of city centre off A48)

☎ 029 20593328   ☷ 029 20591966

One of Wales' finest Edwardian gardens, the beautiful grounds offer an endless variety of colour and form, with many small garden rooms restored with the aid of a Heritage Lottery fund grant. Additional works are still ongoing and some areas may be subject to closure.

Times: Open all year, 10-dusk

Fee: *£3 (ch & pen £2). Family ticket £6.50.

P ☟ & (wheelchairs, parking) toilets for disabled shop garden centre ☟

CARDIFF

The reason for Cardiff's existence is trade. The Bute family saw an opportunity in the early 19th century and built the docks, bringing in builders and craftsmen from far and wide. The mix of peoples was added to by sailors who disembarked and stayed. Tiger Bay (the dock area) was tough, tolerant and colourful. The city is undergoing vigorous changes - the Cardiff Bay Barrage and the Opera House are huge projects and not universally popular. Home of the new Welsh Assembly, Cardiff has many fine municipal buildings and the handsome University College. If you see only one thing here, make for the National Museum of Wales.

LLANDAFF CATHEDRAL
Llandaff CF5 2YF (A48 off M4)
☎ 01222 564554 🖹 01222 564554

A medieval cathedral begun in the 12th century on the site of an early Christian place of worship. The cathedral was severely damaged during the bombing raids on Cardiff during World War II. The interior is dominated by a modernistic post-war 'Christ in Majesty' sculpture by Epstein.
Times: Open all year.
Fee: *£1 per adult (organized tours only). Individuals donations please.
🅿 💺 ✖ ♿ (Wheelchair available) toilets for disabled shop ✖ (ex guide dogs)

NATIONAL MUSEUM & GALLERY
Cathays Park CF1 3NP (Situated in Cathays Park in the heart of Cardiff's Civic Centre)
☎ 029 20397951 🖹 029 20373219

Unique amongst British museums and galleries in its range of art and science displays. 'The Evolution of Wales' exhibition takes you on a spectacular 4,600 million-year journey, tracing the development of Wales and the world from the very beginning of time. There are displays of Bronze Age gold, early Christian monuments,

Celtic treasures, silver, fossils and minerals, as well as temporary exhibitions.
Times: Open all year, Tue-Sun 10-5. (Closed Mon (ex BHs), 24-25 Dec).
Fee: *£4.50 (ch & concessions £2.65). Family ticket £10.25.
🅿 (charged) 💺 ✖ licensed ♿ (wheelchair available) toilets for disabled shop ✖ (ex guide dogs) 🏷

TECHNIQUEST
Stuart St CF1 6BW (J33 from M4, follow A4232 to Cardiff Bay)
☎ 029 20475475

Here in the heart of Cardiff Bay redevelopment area, science and technology are made accessible – and fun – at Britain's leading hands-on discovery science centre. Participate in the

contd.

activities and experiment with the exhibits. See yourself as others see you, instead of the mirror-image you are used to. Understand how aircraft fly . . . Techniquest makes it easy. Please telephone for details of special events.
Times: Open all year (ex Christmas), Mon-Fri 9.30-4.30; Sat, Sun & BH's 10.30-6.
Fee: £5 (ch 5-16 & concessions £3.75). Family ticket £14.50. 🅿 (nearby) 🎧 ♿ toilets for disabled shop ✖ (ex guide dogs) 🌊

⛫ CHEPSTOW
CHEPSTOW CASTLE
NP6 5EZ
☎ 01291 624065

Built by William FitzOsbern, Chepstow is the first recorded Norman stone castle. It stands in a strategic spot above the Wye. The castle was strengthened in the following centuries, but was not besieged (as far as is known) until the Civil War, when it was twice lost to the Parliamentarians. The remains of the domestic rooms and the massive gatehouse with its portcullis grooves and ancient gates are still impressive, as are the walls and towers.
Times: Open all year, late May-early Oct, daily 9.30-6; late Mar-late May & Oct, daily 9.30-5; Nov-late Mar, Mon-Sat 9.30-4, Sun 11-4. (Closed 24-26 Dec & 1 Jan).
Fee: *£3 (ch 5-16, pen & students £2, disabled free). Family ticket £8.
🅿 ♿ shop ✖ ☺ 🌊

⛫ COITY
COITY CASTLE
CF35 6BG
☎ 01656 652021

A 12th to 16th-century stronghold, with a hall, chapel and the remains of a square keep.
Times: Open all year, at all times. Key keeper arrangement.
Fee: Free.
🅿 ✖ ☺

⛫ CWMCARN
CWMCARN FOREST DRIVE
NP6 (8m N of Newport on A467, J28 off M4)
☎ 01633 400205 🖹 01633 400135

A seven-mile scenic drive with spectacular views over the Bristol Channel and surrounding countryside. Facilities include barbecues, picnic

and play areas, and forest and mountain walks. Special events are held throughout the year, please ring for details.
Times: Open Good Friday-Oct, daily 11-7
🅿 ♿ shop *Details not confirmed for 2000*

⛫ GROSMONT
GROSMONT CASTLE
(on B4347)
☎ 01981 240301

Grosmont is one of the 'trilateral' castles of Hubert de Burgh (see also Skenfrith and White Castle). It stands on a mound with a dry moat, and the considerable remains of its 13th-century great hall can be seen. Three towers once guarded the curtain wall, and the western one is well preserved.
Times: Open - access throughout the year.
Fee: Free.
♿ ✖ ☺

⛫ LLANRHIDIAN
WEOBLEY CASTLE
SA3 1HB (from B4271 or B4295)
☎ 01792 390012

A 12th to 14th-century fortified manor house with an exhibition on the history of Weobley and other historic sites on the Gower peninsula.
Times: Open all year, Apr-Oct, daily 9.30-6; Nov-Mar, daily 9.30-5. (Closed 24-26 Dec & 1 Jan).
Fee: *£2 (ch 5-16, pen & students £1.50, disabled free). Family ticket £5.50.
🅿 ♿ shop ✖ ☺ 🌊

⛫ LLANTHONY
LLANTHONY PRIORY
☎ 029 20500200

William de Lacey discovered the remains of a hermitage dedicated to St David. By 1108 a church had been consecrated on the site and just over a decade later the priory was complete. After the priory was brought to a state of seige in an uprising, Hugh de Lacey provided the funds for a new church, and it is this that makes the picturesque ruin seen today. Visitor can still make out the west towers, north nave arcade and south transept.
Times: Open - access throughout the year.
Fee: Free.
🅿 ♿ toilets for disabled ✖ ☺

⛫ LLANTILIO CROSSENNY
HEN GWRT
(off B4233)
☎ 029 20500200

The rectangular enclosure of the former medieval house, still surrounded by a moat.
Times: Open - access throughout the year.
Fee: Free.
✖ 🚆 ☺

⛏ MERTHYR TYDFIL
BRECON MOUNTAIN RAILWAY
Pant Station Dowlais CF48 2UP (2.5m NE. N of
A465)
☎ 01685 722988 🖹 01685 384854

Opened in 1980, this narrow-gauge railway
follows part of an old British Rail route which
closed in 1964 when the iron industry in South
Wales fell into decline. The present route starts at
Pant Station and continues for 3.5 miles through
the beautiful scenery of the Brecon Beacons
National Park, as far as Taf Fechan reservoir. The
train is pulled by a vintage steam locomotive.
Times: Opening times on application to The Brecon
Mountain Railway, Pant Station, Merthyr Tydfil.
Fee: *Fares are under review, please ring for details.
🅿 ➽ ♿ (adapted carriage) toilets for disabled shop

CYFARTHFA CASTLE MUSEUM & ART GALLERY
Cyfarthfa Park CF47 8RE (off A470, N towards
Brecon, follow brown signs)
☎ 01685 723112 🖹 01685 722146

The home of the Crawshay family, this imposing
Gothic mansion was built in 1825 and the
magnificent gardens, designed at around the
same time, still survive. The state rooms are
given over to a museum which covers the social
and industrial life of the area, and also houses
collections of fine and decorative art, natural
history items, archaeology and Egyptology.
Times: Apr-Oct: Mon-Sun 10-6. Oct-Mar: Tue-Fri 10-4.30, Sat-
Sun 12-4.30.
Fee: *£1.60 (concessions 85p).
🅿 ➽ ♿ (stair lift & wheelchair available) toilets for disabled
shop ✖ (ex guide dogs)

⛏ MONMOUTH
NELSON MUSEUM & LOCAL HISTORY CENTRE
New Market Hall, Priory St NP5 3XA (town
centre)
☎ 01600 713519

Commemorative glass, china, silver, medals,
books, models, prints and Admiral Nelson's
fighting sword feature here. The local history
displays deal with Monmouth's past as a fortress

market town, and include a section on the co-
founder of the Rolls Royce company, Charles
Stewart Rolls, who was also a pioneer balloonist,
aviator and, of course, motorist.
Times: Open all year, Mon-Sat 10-1 & 2-5; Sun 2-5. Closed
Xmas & New Year.
🅿 (200 yds) ♿ shop ✖ (ex guide dogs) ➽

⛏ NEATH
NEATH ABBEY
SA10 7DW
☎ 01639 812387

These ruins were originally a Cistercian abbey
founded in 1130 by Richard de Grainville.
Times: Open at all times. Key keeper arrangement.
Fee: Free.
🅿 ♿ ✖ ⌖

⛏ NEWPORT
TREDEGAR HOUSE & PARK
Coedkernew NP1 9YW (2m W, signposted from
A48/M4 J28)
☎ 01633 815880 🖹 01633 815895

Home to one of the greatest of Welsh families,
the Morgans, later Lords Tredegar, for over five
centuries. A tour of the interior gives a
fascinating insight into life above and below
stairs. The house and gardens are set in a 90-
acre landscaped park, where carriage rides,
formal gardens, self-guided trails, craft
workshops, boating, and an adventure
playground provide plenty to do and see.
Times: Open Good Fri-Sep, Wed-Sun & BHs 11-4.(All week in
August. Wknds only in Oct. Special Hallowe'en & Xmas
opening. Also open for group visits at other times.
Fee: *House £3.95 (ch £2 & pen £3). Family ticket £10.50.
🅿 (charged) ➽ ✖ licensed ♿ (wheelchairs for loan) toilets
for disabled shop ✖ (ex grounds & guide dogs all) ➽

⛏ OGMORE
OGMORE CASTLE
☎ 01656 653435

Standing on the River Ogmore, the west wall of
this castle is 40ft high. A hooded fireplace is
preserved in the 12th-century, three-storey keep
and a dry moat surrounds the inner ward.
Times: Open - access throughout the year. Key keeper
arrangement.
Fee: Free.
🅿 ♿ ✖ ⌖

⛏ OXWICH
OXWICH CASTLE
SA3 1NG (A4118 from Swansea)
☎ 01792 390359

Situated on the lovely Gower peninsula, this
Tudor mansion is a striking testament in stone to
the pride and ambitions of the Mansel dynasty of
Welsh gentry. The E-shaped wing houses an
exhibition on historical Gower and 'Chieftains

contd.

and Princes of Wales'. Please telephone for details of special events.

Times: Open May-late Sep, daily 10-5.

Fee: *£2 (ch 5-16, pen & students £1.50, disabled free). Family ticket £5.50.

🅿 ⚬ (Radar key toilet) toilets for disabled ✖ ⚬ 🥤

🏛 PARKMILL

GOWER HERITAGE CENTRE

Y Felin Ddwr SA3 2EM (Follow signs for South Gower on A4118 W from Swansea. W side of Parkmill village)

☎ 01792 371206 📄 01792 371471

Based around a 12th-century water-powered cornmill, the site also contains a number of craft workshops, a museum and a miller's cottage, all set in attractive countryside in an area of outstanding natural beauty. Phone for details of seasonal special events.

Times: Open daily, Mar-Oct 10-7; Nov-Feb 10-5. Closed 25 Dec.

Fee: *£2.60 (ch, students & pen £1.60). Family ticket £6.80. Party.

🅿 💷 ⚬ toilets for disabled shop 🥤

🏛 PENARTH

COSMESTON LAKES COUNTRY PARK & MEDIEVAL VILLA GE

Cosmeston Lakes Country Park, Lavernock Rd CF64 5UY (on B4267 between Barry and Penarth)

☎ 029 20709141 & 20701678
📄 029 20708686

Deserted during the plagues and famines of the 14th century, the original village was rediscovered through archaeological excavations, and the buildings have been faithfully reconstructed on the excavated remains, creating a living museum of medieval village life. Special events throughout the year, including re-enactments and Living History, please ring for details.

Times: Open all year, daily 10.30-5 in Summer, 10.30-4 in Winter. Closed 25 Dec. Country park open at all times.

Fee: *Entry to Village £3, (concessions £2) Family ticket £6.50. Entry to Country Park is free.

🅿 💷 ✖ ⚬ toilets for disabled shop

🏛 PENHOW

PENHOW CASTLE

NP6 3AD (on A48 between Newport & Chepstow. Use M4 J24)

☎ 01633 400800 📄 01633 400990

The oldest inhabited castle in Wales, originally a small border fortress. The building presents a fascinating picture of castle life through nine centuries. Rooms include the Norman bedchamber, the 15th-century Great Hall with its fine screen and minstrels' gallery, the elegant dining room with original panelling and the cosy Victorian housekeeper's room. Please ring for deatails of special events.

Times: Open Good Fri-end Sep, Wed-Sun & BH 10-5.15 last admission; "Candlelit Tours" by arrangement; Aug open daily; Winter Wed 10-4 Sun 1-4. Closed Jan-Feb.

Fee: *£3.60 (ch £2.30). Family ticket £9.50. Party 20+

🅿 (refreshment bar) ⚬ (audio-tours for blind) shop ✖ (ex guide dogs)

🏛 RAGLAN

RAGLAN CASTLE

NP5 2BT (signposted off A40)

☎ 01291 690228

This magnificent 15th-century castle is noted for its `Yellow Tower of Gwent'. It was built by Sir William ap Thomas and destroyed during the Civil War, after a long siege. The ruins are still impressive however, and the castle's history is illustrated in an exhibition situated in the closet tower and two rooms of the gate passage.

Times: Open all year, late May-early Oct, daily 9.30-6; late Mar-late May & Oct, daily 9.30-5; Nov-late Mar, Mon-Sat 9.30-4 & Sun 11-6. (Closed 24-26 Dec & 1 Jan).

Fee: *£2.40 (ch 5-16, pen & students £1.90, disabled free). Family ticket £6.70.

🅿 ⚬ shop ✖ ⚬ 🥤

🏛 ST FAGANS

MUSEUM OF WELSH LIFE

CF5 6XB (4m W of Cardiff, 3m from M4 J33, along A4232)

☎ 029 20573500 📄 029 20573490

A stroll around the indoor galleries and 100 acres of beautiful grounds will give you a fascinating insight into how people in Wales have lived, worked and spent their leisure hours since Celtic times. You can see people practising the traditional means of earning a living, the animals they kept and at certain times of year, the ways in which they celebrated the seasons.

Times: Open all year daily, Jun-Aug 10-6, Sep-May 10-5. Closed 24-26 Dec.

Fee: *Etr-Oct: £5.50 (ch £3.20, OAP/students/UB40 £3.90). Family ticket £14. Nov-Etr: £4.50 (ch £2.65, OAPs/students/UB40 £2.65). Family ticket £10.25.

🅿 💷 ✖ licensed ⚬ (wheelchairs available on a 'first come-first served' basis) toilets for disabled shop ✖ (ex in grounds if on lead) 🥤

ST HILARY
OLD BEAUPRE CASTLE
(1m SW, off A48)
☎ 01446 773034

This ruined manor house was rebuilt during the 16th century. Its most notable features are an Italianate gatehouse and porch. The porch is an unusual three-storeyed structure and displays the Basset arms.
Times: Open - access throughout the year. Key keeper arrangement.
Fee: Free.
P ✕ ♿

SKENFRITH
SKENFRITH CASTLE
☎ 029 20500200

This 13th-century castle has a round keep set inside an imposing towered curtain wall. It was built by Hubert de Burgh as one of three 'trilateral' castles to defend the Welsh Marches.
Times: Open - access throughout the year. Key keeper arrangement.
Fee: Free.
P ✕ ♿ ⚑

SWANSEA
GLYNN VIVAIN ART GALLERY
Alexandra Rd SA1 5DZ
☎ 01792 655006 & 651738
🖷 01792 651713

The gallery has an outstanding collection of Swansea porcelain and pottery, European and Oriental pottery, and glass, including paperweights. There are paintings, drawings and sculptures by British and foreign artists, with the emphasis on Welsh artists. Major exhibition programme all year round (Swansea Festival, Sep-Nov).
Times: Open all year, Tue-Sun & BH Mon 10-5. Closed 25, 26 Dec & 1 Jan.
P (200 yards, NCP) ♿ also sculpture court toilets for disabled shop ✕ (ex guide dogs, hearing dogs) *Details not confirmed for 2000* ⚑

SWANSEA MARITIME & INDUSTRIAL MUSEUM
Museum Square, Maritime Quarter SA1 1SN (M4 J42, on main rd into Swansea city centre)
☎ 01792 650351 & 470371
🖷 01792 654200

This museum complex in the Swansea maritime quarter contains a working woollen mill as well as a selection of floating boats to explore (Apr-Oct). There are displays relating to the Port of Swansea, its industries and environment, transport exhibits, and maritime and agricultural sections. There is a programme of temporary exhibitions.
Times: Open all year, Tue-Sun 10-5.(last admission 4.45pm). Closed Mon except BH Mon, 25, 26 Dec & 1 Jan.
P (50yds) (charged) 🍴 ♿ shop ✕ (ex guide dogs) *Details not confirmed for 2000* ⚑

TINTERN
TINTERN ABBEY
NP6 6SE (via A466)
☎ 01291 689251

The ruins of this Cistercian monastery church are still surprisingly intact. The monastery was established in 1131 and became increasingly wealthy well into the 15th century. During the Dissolution, the monastery was closed and most of the buildings were completely destroyed. During the 18th century many poets and artists came to see the ruins and recorded their impressions.
Times: Open all year, late May-early Oct, daily 9.30-6; late Mar-late May & Oct, daily 9.30-5; Nov-late Mar, Mon-Sat 9.30-4 & Sun 11-6. (Closed 24-26 Dec & 1 Jan).
Fee: *£2.40 (ch 5-16, pen & students £1.90, disabled free). Family ticket £6.70.
P ♿ toilets for disabled shop ✕ ♿ ⚑

TONGWYNLAIS
CASTELL COCH
CF4 7YS (A470 to Tongwynlais junction, then B4262 to castle on top of hill)
☎ 029 20810101

Castell Coch is Welsh for red castle, an appropriate name for this fairy-tale building with its red sandstone walls and conical towers. The castle was originally built in the 13th century but fell into ruins, and the present castle is a late-19th-century creation. Inside, the castle is decorated in fantasy style.
Times: Open all year, late May-early Oct, daily 9.30-6; late Mar-late May & Oct, daily 9.30-5; Nov-late Mar, Mon-Sat 9.30-4, Sun 11-4. (Closed 24-26 Dec & 1 Jan).
Fee: *£2.50 (ch 5-16, pen & students £2, disabled free). Family ticket £7.
P shop ✕ ♿ ⚑

TREHAFOD
RHONDDA HERITAGE PARK
Lewis Merthyr Colliery, Coed Cae Rd CF37 7NP (between Pontypridd & Porth, off A470; follow brown tourist signs from M4 J32)
☎ 01443 682036 🖷 01443 687420

Based at the Lewis Merthyr Colliery, the Heritage Park is a fascinating 'living history' attraction.

contd.

You can take the Cage Ride to 'Pit Bottom' and explore the underground workings of a 1950's pit, guided by men who were miners themselves. There are children's activities, an exhibition gallery and a museum illustrating living conditions in the Rhondda Valley.

Times: Open all year, daily 10-6. Closed Mon from Oct-Etr. Last admission 4.30pm. Closed 25 & 26 Dec.

Fee: *£5.50 (ch & concessions £4.25, pen £4.95). Family ticket £16.25.

🅿 ⬛ ✖ ♿ (Wheelchair available, accessible parking, lifts) toilets for disabled shop ✖ (ex guide dogs) 🍴

🏰 WHITE CASTLE

WHITE CASTLE
NP7 8UD (7m NE of Abergavenny, unclass road N of B4233)
☎ **01600 780380**

The impressive 12th to 13th-century moated stronghold was built by Hubert de Burgh to defend the Welsh Marches. Substantial remains of walls, towers and a gatehouse can be seen. This is the finest of a trio of castles, the others being at Skenfrith and Grosmont.

Times: Open all year, May-late Sep, daily 10-5; site open rest of year.

Fee: *£2 (ch 5-16, pen & students £1.50, disabled free). Family ticket £5.50.

🅿 ♿ ✖ ☺ 🍴

Northern Ireland

The six counties of Ulster are part of the United Kingdom. The greater part of its 1.6 million inhabitants are Protestants, descendants of an influx of settlers from England and Scotland in the 17th century.

Top: Murlough Bay, Co Antrim

Despite recent tensions, the province has consistently drawn tourists, not so much to the cities which are more interesting than attractive, but for the scenery.

The most popular landscapes are linked by the 430 mile (700km) Ulster Way, which takes an intrepid walker though all six counties, taking in the Glens of Antrim with its woods, waterfalls and ruins, and the remarkable Giant's Causeway. Further south near the border with the Republic, the Ulster Way meanders through the Mountains of Mourne, rather gaunt, steep granite hills (highest point Slieve Donard, 2795 ft (852m)). Less strenuous stretches explore the beautiful Lough Erne.

After Belfast, the second city is Londonderry, or Derry, depending on your perspective. The city walls stand virtually complete, a reminder of the siege of 1688 when the Apprentice Boys locked out James II's army. From the walls you can view the sweep of the River Foyle.

Downpatrick, the market town of Down, claims to be the burial place of St Patrick, the patron saint of Ireland. His life is commemorated in the cathedral, and in the converted jail.

For lakes, islands, caves, castles and grand houses, Enniskillen is the place to go. Perched on an island between the Upper and Lower Lough Erne, it offers boat trips, angling, water sports and easy rambling.

BELFAST

Belfast is essentially a Victorian city that prospered on linen, ship-building, rope-making and tobacco, but times change and industries decline. The city centre is on the west bank of the River Lagan, and the most attractive parts lie towards the south around the university and the Botanic Gardens.

Among the sights worth seeing are the opulent interiors of the City Hall on Howard Street, the Grand Opera House in Great Victoria Street, and the Ulster Museum in the Botanic Gardens. At the mouth of the Lagan is the Harland and Wolff shipyard, once the largest shipbuilding operation in the world, where the Titanic was built.

BELFAST

BELFAST CASTLE
Antrim Rd BT15 5GR (2.5m from city centre, take Antrim road towards Glengormley then left into Innisfayle Park, signed)
☎ 028 90776925 ▤ 028 90370228

This Scottish baronial-style castle with its great square six-storey tower and baroque staircase was built in 1870 by the 3rd Marquis of Donegall. There is a Heritage Centre on the second floor. The castle stands on the lower wooded slopes of Cave Hill, an area popular for walks and picnics. Cavehill Carnival family fun day - first Sunday in August.
Times: Open all year, daily. Castle open to public viewing. Food & drink available all day & evening. (closed only 25 Dec)
🅿 💺 ✕ licensed ♿ (lift to all floors, ramps being installed early '98) toilets for disabled shop ✖ (ex guide dogs) *Details not confirmed for 2000* ◥

BOTANIC GARDENS
Stranmillis Rd BT7 1JP
☎ 028 90324902 ▤ 028 90237070

One highlight of the park is the beautiful glass-domed Victorian Palm House, built between 1839-52. This palm house predates the one in Kew Gardens and is one of the earliest curved-glass and iron structures in the world. Another feature is the Tropical Ravine - stand on a balcony to get a wonderful view through a steamy ravine full of exotic plants.
Times: Open all year, Park daily 8-dusk. Tropical ravine and palmhouse Mon-Fri 10-12.30 & 1-5 (summer), closes 4.30 (winter); wknds open 1-5 (summer), 1-4 (winter).
🅿 (street) ♿ *Details not confirmed for 2000*

MALONE HOUSE-BARNETT DEMESNE
Upper Malone Rd BT9 5PB
☎ 028 90681246 ▤ 028 90682197

An early 19th-century Georgian mansion overlooking the River Lagan. Owned by Belfast City Council, the house is now used for trade shows and functions. The Higgin Art Gallery is also open to visitors.
Times: Open all year, Mon-Sat 9.30-5.30. (Closed Xmas Day & Boxing Day)
🅿 ✕ licensed ♿ toilets for disabled ✖ *Details not confirmed for 2000* ◥

ULSTER MUSEUM
Botanic Gardens BT9 5AB (M1/M2 to Balmoral exit)
☎ 028 90383000 ▤ 028 90383003

Both a national museum and an art gallery, the collections are Irish and international in origin and cover antiquities, art, botany and zoology, geology and local history (including industrial

archaeology). A programme of temporary exhibitions and events takes place.
Times: Open all year, Mon-Fri 10-5, Sat 1-5, Sun 2-5. Tel for details of Christmas closures.
Fee: Free.
P (100yds on street) (Clearway 0800-0930 & 1630-1800) 🚌 & (all galleries except one. Loop system, wheelchair lifts) toilets for disabled shop ✖ (ex guide dogs) 🍴

🏛 CO ANTRIM

🏛 BUSHMILLS
OLD BUSHMILLS DISTILLERY
BT57 8XH (on the Castlecatt rd)
☎ 028 20731521 🖪 028 20731339

Old Bushmills was granted its licence in 1608 and is the oldest licenced whiskey distillery in the world. There's a guided tour, and afterwards you can take part in a comparative tasting and become a whiskey expert.
Times: Open Apr-Oct, Mon-Sat 9.30-5.30, Sun noon-5.30; Nov-Mar, Mon-Fri 5 tours daily, hourly from 1030-3.30.
Fee: *£3.50 (pen & student £3, accompanied ch £1.50) Family ticket £9.
P 🚌 & toilets for disabled shop ✖ (ex guide dogs) 🍴

🏛 CARRICK-A-REDE
CARRICK-A-REDE ROPE BRIDGE AND LARRYBANE VISITORS CENTRE
(E of Ballintoy on B15)
☎ 028 20762178 & 20731159

This shaky rope bridge, 80ft above the sea, bridges the 60ft gap between cliffs and a small rocky island. It owes its existence to the salmon who regularly make the dash through the chasm and get netted for their efforts. The bridge has been put across the gap each spring and dismantled every autumn for the last 300 years.
Times: Bridge open Spring-early Sep, daily 10-6; Jul-Aug, daily 10-8. Visitor centre & Tea room open May, wknds & BHs 1-5; Jun-Aug daily 12-6.
Fee: *Parking, cars £2, coaches £6.
P (charged) 🚌 & (information centre) toilets for disabled (NT Ireland)

🏛 GIANT'S CAUSEWAY
GIANT'S CAUSEWAY CENTRE
44 Causeway Rd BT57 8SU (2m N of Bushmills on B146)
☎ 028 20731855 🖪 028 20732537

This dramatic rock formation is undoubtedly one of the wonders of the natural world. The Centre provides an exhibition and audio-visual show, and Ulsterbus provides a minibus service to the

stones and there are guided walks, and special facilities for the disabled.
Times: Open all year, daily 10-4 (6pm Jun & Sep-Oct; 7pm Jul-Aug).
Fee: *Audio-visual show (12 min) £1 (ch 50p). Family ticket £2.50. Causeway coaster fare to Grand causeway currently £1 return, 60p single, (oap & ch 50% reduction). All prices under review.
P (charged) 🚌 ✖ & (mini bus transport with wheelchair hoist, reserved parking) toilets for disabled shop ✖ (ex guide dogs) 🍴

🏛 LISBURN
IRISH LINEN CENTRE & LISBURN MUSEUM
Market Square BT28 1AG (signposted both in and outside the town centre)
☎ 028 92663377 🖪 028 92672624

The centre tells the story of the Irish linen industry past and present. The recreation of individual factory scenes brings the past to life and a series of imaginative hands-on activities describe the linen manufacturing processes. The Museum has regularly changing exhibitions of local interest.
Times: Open all year, Monday-Saturday, 9.30am-5pm.
Fee: Free.
P (200m) (limited for disabled and coaches) 🚌 & (lift, induction loop, staff trained in sign language) toilets for disabled shop ✖ (ex guide dogs)

🏛 TEMPLEPATRICK
PATTERSONS SPADE MILL
751 Antrim Rd BT38 9AP (2m SE of Templepatrick on A6)
☎ 028 94433619 🖪 028 94433619

This is the last surviving water-driven spade mill in Ireland. It has been completely restored by the National Trust and is now back in production. For details of events please telephone (01849) 433619.
Times: Open Etr, Apr-May & Sep, wknds 2-6; Jun-Aug, daily (ex Tue) 2-6, also on BHs.
Fee: *£2.50 (ch £1.25), Family Ticket £6.25. Party £1.75
P & (ramps wheelchair available) toilets for disabled (NT Ireland)

TEMPLETOWN MAUSOLEUM
BT39 (in Castle Upton graveyard on A6, Belfast-Antrim road)

Situated in the graveyard of Castle Upton, this family mausoleum is in the shape of a triumphal arch and was designed by Robert Adam.
Times: Open daily during daylight hours.
Fee: Free.
🚌 (NT Ireland)

⛪ CO ARMAGH

⛪ ARMAGH

ARMAGH COUNTY MUSEUM
The Mall BT61 9BE (on the mall, in the centre of Armagh City)
☎ 028 37523070 ▤ 028 37522631

Housed in a 19th-century schoolhouse, this museum contains an art gallery and library, as well as a collection of local folkcrafts and natural history. Special events are planned thoughout the year, please phone for details.
Times: Open all year, Mon-Fri 10-5, Sat 10-1 & 2-5.
Fee: Free.
🅿 ♿ toilets for disabled shop ✖ (ex guide dogs)

ARMAGH PLANETARIUM & SCIENCE CENTRE
College Hill BT61 9DB (on main Armagh-Belfast rd, close to mall, Armagh City centre)
☎ 028 37523689 & 37524725
▤ 028 37526187

The Planetarium is home to The Star Theatre, a multi-media environment equipped with the latest technology including a virtual reality digital system. Also featured are The Hall of Astronomy, the new Eartharium Building and surrounding the Planetarium is the Astropark, a 25-acre 'hands on' park.
Times: Open all year, Hall of Astronomy Mon-Fri 10-4.45, shows daily at 3. Also open Sat & Sun 1.15-4.45, shows every Sat & Sun 2, 3 & 4. Additional shows during Etr, Xmas & BH's.
Fee: *£3.75 (ch, pens & students £2.75). Family ticket £11. Exhibition area £1.
🅿 ⏺ ♿ (Loop system in theatre) toilets for disabled shop ✖ (ex guide dogs)

NAVAN CENTRE
Killylea Rd BT60 4LD (2m W on A28)
☎ 028 37525550 ▤ 028 37522323

One of Europe's most important Celtic sites - the seat of the ancient Kings of Ulster and setting for the legends of the mythical Cuchulainn. The Centre unveils the history and archaeology of the fort and its landscape in a stunning visual interactive display.
Times: Open all year, Apr-Jun & Sep, Mon-Sat 10-6, Sun 11-6; Jul-Aug, Mon-Sat 10-7, Sun 11-7; Oct-Mar, Mon-Fri 10-5, Sat 11-5, Sun noon-5.
🅿 ⏺ ♿ (loop for hearing aids) toilets for disabled shop ✖ (ex guide dogs) *Details not confirmed for 2000*

PALACE STABLES HERITAGE CENTRE
The Palace Demesne BT60 4EL (located off Friary Road beside council offices)
☎ 028 37529629 ▤ 028 37529630

This picturesque Georgian building, set around a cobbled courtyard, has been lovingly restored and now houses a heritage centre. Living History

- daily Georgian interpretation by authentic costumed characters.
Times: Open all year, May-Aug, Mon-Sat 10-5.30, Sun 1-6; Sep-Apr, Mon-Sat 10-5, Sun 2-5. Last tour 1hr before closing.
Fee: *£3.50 (ch £2, pen £2.70). Family ticket £9.
🅿 ✖ licensed ♿ (Ramps & Lift in stables) toilets for disabled shop (courtyard only)

⛪ MOY

ARGORY
Derrycaw Rd BT71 6NA (4m NE)
☎ 028 8784753 ▤ 028 8789598

Originally the home of the McGeough family, this Regency house is situated on a hillside overlooking the Blackwater River. The house is full of period furniture and bric-a-brac. Of particular interest is the very unusual acetylene lighting, installed by the family in 1906. For details of special events telephone (018687) 84753.
Times: Open Etr, daily; Apr-May & Sep, wknds & BH; Jun-Aug, daily (ex Tue) 2-6. Open from 1pm on BHs. Last tour 5.15.
Fee: *House & grounds £2.60 (ch £1.30). Family ticket £6.50. Car park £1.50. Party £2.
🅿 (charged) ⏺ ♿ (special parking facilities, wheelchair available) toilets for disabled shop ✖ (NT Ireland)

⛪ OXFORD ISLAND

LOUGH NEAGH DISCOVERY CENTRE
Oxford Island National Nature, Reserve BT66 6NJ (signposted from M1 J10)
☎ 028 38322205 ▤ 028 38347438

Learn about the history and wildlife of the Lough through a series of exciting audio-visual shows, interactive games and exhibition. Then experience the Island for yourself: natural history, wildlife, family walks and much more - in a spectacular setting on the water's edge.
Times: Open every day, Apr-Sep 10-7; Oct-Mar 10-5, Wed-Sun.
🅿 ⏺ ♿ (grounds accessible in part, bird watching hides) toilets for disabled shop ✖ (ex guide dogs)

⛪ PORTADOWN

ARDRESS HOUSE
Annaghmore BT62 1SQ (7m W on B28)
☎ 028 38851236 ▤ 028 38851236

A plain 17th-century house, transformed around 1770 by its visionary architect-owner George Ensor, who added elegant wings and superb Adamesque plasterwork. The house has a fine picture gallery on loan from the Earl of Castlestewart. The grounds are beautifully unspoilt and there is a farmyard with livestock and a display of farm implements.
Times: Open Etr, daily; Apr-May & Sep, wknds & BH's; Jun-Aug, daily (ex Tue) 2-6.
Fee: *House, grounds & farm £2.40 (ch £1.20). Family ticket £6.
🅿 ♿ toilets for disabled shop ✖ (ex guide dogs) (NT Ireland)

⚏ CO DOWN

⚏ COMBER
WWT CASTLE ESPIE
Ballydrain Rd BT23 6EA (3m S of Comber, 13m
SE of Belfast. Signed from A22 Comber-
Killyleagh-Downpatrick road)
☎ **028 91874146** 🖹 **028 91873857**

Home to the largest collection of wildfowl in
Ireland. New hides enable you to watch the
splendour of migratory waders and wildfowl.
Beautiful landscaped gardens, a taxidermy
collection and fine paintings by wildlife artists
can also be seen. Thousands of birds migrate to
the reserve in winter and Bird Walks are held on
the last Thursday of every month. The Centre's
effluent is treated in a reed bed filtration system
which can be seen on one walk.
Times: Open all year; summer, Mon-Sat 10.30-5, Sun 11.30-6;
winter Mon-Sat 11.30-4, Sun 11.30-5. (Closed 25 Dec).
Fee: *£3.25 (ch under 4 free, ch £2, pen £2.75); family ticket
£8.50.
P ✕ & (hides have wheelchair platforms) toilets for disabled
shop ✕ 🥤

⚏ DOWNPATRICK
DOWN COUNTY MUSEUM
The Mall BT30 6AH
☎ **028 44615218** 🖹 **028 44615590**

The museum occupies the old county gaol built
between 1789 and 1796. The Saint Patrick
Heritage Centre in the former gatehouse tells the
story of Ireland's patron saint, and the governor's
residence has galleries relating to the human and
natural history of County Down. A Millennium
Exhibition opens December 1999.
Times: Open all year, Jun-Aug, Mon-Fri 10-5, wknds 2-5; rest
of year, Tue-Fri 10-5 & Sat 2-5. Also open all BH's.
Fee: Free.
P (100yds) 🖳 & (wheelchair available, handling boxes on
application) toilets for disabled shop ✕ (ex guide dogs)

⚏ NEWTOWNARDS
MOUNT STEWART HOUSE, GARDEN & TEMPLE OF THE WINDS
Greyabbey BT22 2AD (5m SE off A20)
☎ **028 42788387 & 42788487**
🖹 **028 42788569**

On the east shore of Strangford Lough, this 18th-
century house was the work of three architects.
In the inspired gardens, many rare and
subtropical trees thrive. By the shore of
Strangford Lough is the Temple of the Winds,
built by James Stewart in 1782 for the first
Marquess.
Times: Open House Etr, daily; May-Sep daily (ex Tue); Apr &
Oct wknds, 1-6. Garden: Mar, Sun 2-5; Apr-Sep, daily & Oct,
wknds 11-6. Temple of the Winds Apr-Oct, wknds 2-5.
Fee: *House Garden & Temple: £3.50 (ch £1.75). Family ticket
£8.75. Garden: £3 (ch £1.50) Family ticket £7.50. Party.
P 🖳 & (4 wheelchairs(2 electric) available) toilets for
disabled shop (NT Ireland)

⚏ SAINTFIELD
ROWALLANE GARDEN
BT24 7LH (1m S of Saintfield on A7)
☎ **01238 510131** 🖹 **01238 511242**

Beautiful and exotic 50-acre gardens started by
the Rev John Moore in 1860. The gardens contain
exquisite plants from all over the world. They are
particularly noted for their rhododendrons and
azaleas and for the wonderful floral displays in
spring and summer. There are monthly
demonstrations on The Art of the Gardener.
Events take place throughout the year.
Times: Open Apr-Oct, Mon-Fri 10.30-6, Sat & Sun 2-6; Nov-
Mar, Mon-Fri 10.30-5. (Closed 25-26 Dec & 1 Jan)
Fee: *Apr-Oct £2.50 (ch £1.25); Nov-Mar £1.50 (ch 75p).
P 🖳 & (parking facilities) toilets for disabled (must be on
leads) (NT Ireland)

⚏ STRANGFORD
CASTLE WARD
BT30 7LS (0.5m W of Strangford village on A25)
☎ **028 44881204** 🖹 **028 44881729**

The curious diversity of styles in this house is due
to the fact that its owner and his wife could
never agree; so classical themes and a more
elaborate Gothic look were both incorporated.
The servants' living quarters are separate from
the house and are reached by an underground
passage. The gardens, complete with a small
lake and a classical summerhouse, are richly
planted and especially beautiful in spring.
Times: House open Jun-15 Sep, Fri-Wed 1-6; Apr-May & 18
Sep-Oct, wknds 1-6.
Fee: *House £2.60 (ch £1.30). Estate £3.50 per car (Nov-Mar
£1.75). Family ticket £6.50. Party £2.
P (charged) 🖳 ✕ & (wheelchair available, may be driven
to house) toilets for disabled shop (NT Ireland) 🥤

⚏ CO FERMANAGH

⚏ BELLEEK
BELLEEK POTTERY
3 Main St BT93 3FY
☎ **028 68659300** 🖹 **028 68658625**

Known worldwide for its fine Parian china,
Ireland's oldest pottery was started in 1857 by
the Caldwell family. Meet the craftspeople at
work whilst touring the Pottery and visit the
museum, which has exhibits dating back over
140 years.
Times: Open all year, Apr-Jun, Mon-Fri 9-6, Sat 10-6, Sun 2-6;
Jul-Aug, Mon-Fri 9-8, Sat 10-6, Sun 11-8; Sep, Mon-Fri 9-6, Sat
10-6, Sun 2-6; Oct, Mon-Fri 9-5.30, Sat 10-5.30, Sun 2-6; Nov-
Mar, Mon-Fri 9-5.30.
Fee: *Guided tours £2.00 (ch u12 free, pen £1).
P ✕ & (wheelchairs can be provided) toilets for disabled
shop ✕ (small dogs allowed) 🥤

⛪ ENNISKILLEN
CASTLE COOLE
BT74 (1.5m SE on A4)
☎ 028 66322690 📠 028 66325665

No expense was spared in the building of this mansion. James Wyatt was the architect, the lovely plasterwork ceilings were by Joseph Rose, and the chimneypieces the work of Richard Westmacott. Vast amounts of Portland stone were specially imported, together with an Italian expert in stonework. The house is filled with beautiful Regency furniture.
Times: Open Etr, daily; Apr & Sep, wknds & BH's; May-Aug, daily (ex Thu) 1-6. Last tour 5.15.
Fee: *£2.80 (ch £1.40). Family ticket £7.00. Estate £2.50 per car. Party £2.50.
🅿 (charged) ☕ ♿ (may be driven to house) toilets for disabled shop (NT Ireland)

FLORENCE COURT
BT92 1DB (8m SW via A4 & A32)
☎ 028 66348249 📠 028 66348873

This 18th-century mansion overlooks wild and beautiful scenery towards the Mountains of Cuilcagh. The interior of the house, particularly noted for its flambuoyant rococo plasterwork, was gutted by fire in 1955, but has been miraculously restored. There are pleasure grounds with an Ice House, Summer House and Water Powered Sawmill, also a walled garden and fine views.
Times: Open Etr, daily 1-6; Apr & Sep wknds & BH's 1-6; May-Aug, daily (ex Tue) 1-6.
Fee: *£2.80 (ch £1.40). Family ticket £7. Estate only £2 per car.
🅿 (charged) ☕ ♿ (electric wheelchair available) toilets for disabled shop (NT Ireland)

⛪ NEWTOWNBUTLER
CROM ESTATE
BT92 8AP (3m W)
☎ 028 67738174 & 67738118 📠 028 67738174

Featuring 770 hectares of woodland, parkland and wetland, the Crom Estate is one of Northern Ireland's most important conservation areas. Nature trails are signposted through woodlands to the ruins of the old castle, and past the old boat house and picturesque summer house. Day tickets for pike fishing and boat hire are available from the Visitor Centre. For details of events, telephone (013667) 38118.
Times: Open Apr-Sep, daily 10-6, Sun 12-6.
Fee: *Parking £3
🅿 (charged) ☕ ♿ toilets for disabled shop (NT Ireland)
◣

⛪ CO LONDONDERRY

⛪ COLERAINE
HEZLETT HOUSE
Castlerock BT51 4TN (5m W on Coleraine/Downhill coast road)
☎ 028 70848567

A low, thatched cottage built around 1690 with an interesting cruck truss roof, constructed by using pairs of curved timbers to form arches and infilling around this frame with clay, rubble and other locally available materials.
Times: Open Etr, daily; Apr & Sep wknds & BH's; Jun-Aug, daily (ex Tue) 12-5.
Fee: *£1.80 (ch 90p). Family ticket £4.50.
🅿 ✖ (ex in gardens) (NT Ireland)

⛪ COOKSTOWN
WELLBROOK BEETLING MILL
Corkhill BT80 9RY (4m W in Co Tyrone, 0.5m off A505)
☎ 028 86751735

This 18th-century water-powered linen mill was used for bleaching and, until 1961, for finishing Irish linen. Beetling was the name given to the final process in linen making, when the material was beaten by 30 or so hammers (beetles) to achieve a smooth and slightly shiny finish.
Times: Open Etr, daily; Apr-Jun & Sep, wknds & BH's; Jul-Aug, daily (ex Tue) 2-6.
Fee: *£1.80 (ch 90p). Family ticket £4.50.
🅿 ♿ shop (NT Ireland)

⛪ DOWNHILL
MUSSENDEN TEMPLE BISHOP'S GATE AND BLACK GLEN
Mussenden Rd BT51 4RP (1m W of Castlerock off A2)

Spectacularly placed on a cliff edge overlooking the Atlantic, this perfect 18th-century rotunda was modelled on the Temple of Vesta at Tivoli. Visitors entering by the Bishop's Gate can enjoy a beautiful glen walk up to the headland where the temple stands.
Times: Open Temple: Etr, daily, noon-6; Apr-Jun & Sep, wknds & BH's noon-6; Jul-Aug, daily noon-6.
Fee: Free.
🅿 ♿ (NT Ireland)

⛪ LIMAVADY
ROUGH FORT
(1m W off A2)

Early Christian rath.
Times: Open at all times.
Fee: Free.
🛬 (NT Ireland)

⛏ MONEYMORE

SPRINGHILL

BT45 7NQ (1m from Moneymore on B18)
☎ 028 86748210 🖹 028 86748210

This pleasingly symmetrical manor house dates back to the 17th century. Today much of the family furniture, books and bric-a-brac have been retained. Outside, the laundry, stables, brewhouse, and old dovecote make interesting viewing, as does the excellent costume museum.
Times: Open Etr, Apr-Jun & Sep, wknds & BH's 2-6; Jul-Aug, daily (ex Thu) 2-6.
Fee: *£2.50 (ch £1.25). Family ticket £6.25. Party.£2
🅿 💺 ♿ toilets for disabled shop (must be on leads) (NT Ireland)

⛏ CO TYRONE

⛏ BALLYGAWLEY

U S GRANT ANCESTRAL HOMESTEAD & VISITOR CENTRE

Dergenagh, 190 Ballygawley Rd BT70 1TW (off A4, 3m on Dergenagh road, signposted)
☎ 028 8557133 🖹 028 85767911

Ancestral homestead of Ulysses S Grant, 18th President of the United States of America. The homestead and farmyard have been restored to the style and appearance of a mid 19th-century Irish smallholding.
Times: Open Etr-Sep, Mon-Sat 12-5, Sun 2-6. Other times by arrangement. (Closed 25-26 Dec & 1 Jan).
Fee: *£1 (ch & concessions 50p). Party 10+
🅿 💺 ♿ (wide doorway to audio-visual area/entrances/exits) shop ✈ (ex guide dogs)

⛏ OMAGH

ULSTER AMERICAN FOLK PARK

BT78 5QY (5m NW Omagh)
☎ 028 82243292 🖹 028 82242241

An outdoor museum that traces the history of Ulster's links with America and the emigration of Ulster residents to the US during the 18th and 19th centuries. The 70-acre site is divided into two parts - Old World and New World. There are demonstrations of Old and New World crafts, and a visitor centre, with exhibitions and audio-visual presentations. The Centre for Emigration Studies is based here, with a research library and emigration database - please ring for details.
Times: Open Etr-Sep, daily 11-6.30, Sun & BH 11.30-7; Oct-Etr Mon-Fri 10.30-5. Last admission 1hr 30mins before closing.
Fee: *£4 (ch & pen £2.50). Family ticket £10. Children under 5yrs free.
🅿 ✕ ♿ toilets for disabled shop ✈ (ex guide dogs)

ULSTER HISTORY PARK

Cullion BT79 7SU (7m on B48)
☎ 028 8248188 🖹 028 8248011

The story of settlement in Ireland, told with the aid of full-scale models of the houses and monuments built through the ages. Exhibitions and audio-visual presentations expand the theme.
Times: Open all year, Apr-Sep Mon-Sat 10.30-6.30, Sun 11.30-7, BH's 10.30-7; Oct-Mar Mon-Fri 10.30-5. Last admission 1hr 30mins before closing time.
Fee: *£3.25 (ch, students, pen & registered disabled £1.95). Family ticket (2 adults, 4 children) £10. Group 15+
🅿 💺 ♿ toilets for disabled shop ✈ (ex guide dogs) ⬦

⛏ STRABANE

GRAY'S PRINTING PRESS

49 Main St BT82 8AU
☎ 028 71884094

Strabane was once an important printing and book publishing centre, the only relic of which is a small shop in Main Street. The shop now houses a musem illustrating the history of Strabane, while the Print Museum, housed in a separate building, contains three 19th-century presses, illustrating the development of printing techniques over sixty years.
Times: Open Apr-Sep, Tue-Sat 2-5. Other times by prior arrangement.
Fee: *£1.80 (ch 90p). Family ticket £4.50 Party.
🅿 (100yds) shop ✈ (NT Ireland)

Republic of Ireland

No visitor comes here without preconceptions, and while some of these will be confirmed, there are always plenty of surprises, and more to discover.

To be sure it is green - the Emerald Isle is no misnomer - and you're never far from water, from the craggy Atlantic coast, the countless loughs, rivers and bogs, to the regular falls of rain, or Irish mist. And then there are the people.

Certainly this country with its tiny population has brought us an abundance of world-class literary figures, and you will meet the same love of words and ideas in any street, shop or pub. Music too seems to run in the veins - listening to an Irish band, it soon becomes clear that the musicians are playing as much for their own pleasure as for the tourist's. However, this is no quaint backwater; the Republic has enthusiastically embraced its European identity.

Where to go? It would be hard to miss out on elegant, cosmopolitan Dublin, and in the south there's Cork, vying with the capital for business and cultural supremacy. To explore the west, head for Galway, where Gaelic is still spoken by many inhabitants as a first language, and inland you will not be disappointed by the craft studios and restaurants of Kilkenny.

Further afield there is no end of opportunity for fishing, golfing, walking and relaxing. You can find a quiet charm everwhere you visit, but there are some strikingly unique attractions. The Burren is a naturalist's joy, with exotic flora in every crevice of its strange rockscape, and Newgrange is one of Europe's most important and mysterious prehistoric sites.

EVENTS & FESTIVALS

February
27th-29th Futura Fair, Dublin
International Film Festival, Dublin

March
17th St Patrick's Day
International Music Festival, Dublin
Dublin Maritime Festival

June
16th Bloomsday (James Joyce Festival), Dublin
'The Cat Laughs', International Comedy Festival, Kilkenny
Co Wexford Strawberry Fair
Sligo Arts Festival

July
3rd weekend in July (provisional) Guinness Blues Festival, Dublin
Garden of Ireland Festival, Arklow. Co Wicklow

August
Dublin Regatta
Wicklow Regatta Festival
Kilkenny Arts Festival
Puck Fair, Killorglin
Rose of Tralee Festival

September
All Ireland Hurling Championship Final, Dublin

October
Dublin Theatre Festival
Wexford Festival
Wexford Opera Festival
Cork Jazz Festival

Top: County Kerry

CO CLARE

BUNRATTY

BUNRATTY CASTLE & FOLK PARK
(8 miles from Limerick city on N18 road to Ennis)
☎ 061 361511 & 360788 ▤ 061 361020

Ireland's most complete medieval castle. It houses the Lord Gort collection of furniture, objets d'art, and paintings and tapestries dating from before 1650. One-day tours operate in season from Limerick and include a medieval banquet at the castle. Irish village life at the turn of the century is re-created in the folk park in the grounds.
Times: Open all year, daily 9.30-5.30 (last admission 4.15pm). Folk Park also open Jun-Aug 9-6.30 (last admission 5.30pm).
🅿 🍷 ✕ licensed ♿ toilets for disabled shop *Details not confirmed for 2000* 🐚

LISCANNOR

O'BRIEN'S TOWER & CLIFFS OF MOHER
(6m NW of Lahinch)
☎ 065 81565 & 061 360788
▤ 061 361020

The Cliffs of Moher stand as a giant natural rampart against the aggressive might of the Atlantic Ocean, rising in places to 700ft, and stretch for almost 5 miles. O'Brien's Tower was built in the early 19th century as a viewing point for tourists on the highest point. There is a visitor centre with tourist information.
Times: Open daily Mar-Oct, 10-6 (subject to weather conditions). Visitor centre open all year daily 10am-6pm.
🅿 (charged) 🍷 ♿ toilets for disabled shop *Details not confirmed for 2000* 🐚

QUIN

THE CRAGGAUNOWEN BRONZE AGE PROJECT
(clearly signed from N18, 10km N from village of Sixmilebridge)
☎ 061 367178 & 360788 ▤ 061 361020

Contains a full-scale reconstruction of a crannog, a Bronze Age lake dwelling. The project includes a reconstructed ring fort and replicas of furniture, tools and utensils. Also on display is the *Brendan*, a replica of the leather boat used by St Brendan the Navigator in the 6th century. The boat was sailed across the Atlantic Ocean in 1976 and 1977. Ring for details of special events.
Times: Open Apr-Oct daily 10-6 (last admission 5pm). Mid May-mid Aug 9-6.
🅿 🍷 ♿ toilets for disabled shop *Details not confirmed for 2000* 🐚

CO CORK

BALLINCOLLIG

THE ROYAL GUNPOWDER MILLS
(on Cork/Killarney road)
☎ 021 874430 ▤ 021 874836

An amazing industrial complex on the banks of the River Lee. The mills supplied vast quantities of explosives for the British military forces throughout the world from 1794 to 1903.
Times: Open daily, 18 Apr-30 Sep 10-6. Last tour at 5.15pm.
Fee: *IR£3 (ch IR£1.80, pen & students IR£2.50). Family ticket IR£8.
🅿 🍷 ♿ toilets for disabled shop ✈ (ex guide dogs)

BANTRY

BANTRY HOUSE
(Main gate at harbour wall)
☎ 027 50047 ▤ 027 50795

A Georgian mansion, surrounded by gardens, with a collection of furniture and tapestries. There is an exhibition in the stables.
Times: Open Mar-Oct.
🅿 🍷 ♿ shop ✈ (ex in grounds) *Details not confirmed for 2000* 🐚

BLARNEY

BLARNEY CASTLE & ROCK CLOSE
(5m from Cork on main road towards Limerick)
☎ 021 385252 & 385669 ▤ 021 381518

The site of the famous Blarney Stone, known the world over for the eloquence it is said to impart to those who kiss it. The stone is in the upper tower of the castle, and, held by your feet, you must lean backwards down the inside of the battlements in order to receive the gift of the gab.
Times: Open - Blarney Castle & Rock Close, Jun-Jul Mon-Sat 9-7.30; May Mon-Sat 9-7; Sep Mon-Sat 9-6.30; Apr & Oct Mon-Sat 9-sunset; summer Sun 9.30-5.30; winter Sun 9.30-sunset. Blarney House & Gardens Jun-mid Sep Mon-Sat noon-6.
Fee: *Blarney Castle & Rock Close IR£3.50 (ch IR£1, pen & students IR£2.50).
🅿 ♿ shop ✈ (ex guide dogs)

CARRIGTOHILL

FOTA WILDLIFE PARK
Fota Estate (Turn for Corby from N25, Cork-Waterford road)
☎ 021 812678 ▤ 021 812744

Established with the primary aim of conservation, Fota has more than 70 species of exotic wildlife in open, natural surroundings. Giraffes, zebras, ostrich, antelope and other animals enjoy 40 acres of grassland through which you can walk on an unfenced road in

contd.

complete safety. Monkeys swing through mature trees on lake islands, while kangaroos, macaws and lemurs have complete freedom of the park. Only the cheetahs have a conventional fence.

Times: Open Apr-Oct, Mon-Sat 10-6, Sun 11-6 (last admission 5); Reduced rates and facilities on weekdays in Oct.

P (charged) ᠌╨ 🚸 (Ramps where required) toilets for disabled shop ✈ *Details not confirmed for 2000*

⛪ CLONAKILTY

West Cork Model Village Railway

Inchydoney Rd (signposted at road junction. Village is at Bay side of Clonakilty)

☎ 023 33224   🖷 023 34843

The village depicts the prominent buildings, landmarks and way of life in the six major towns and villages of West Cork. Visitors enter through a lifesize replica of Clonakilty Station as it was in the 1940s. Ring for details of special events.

Times: Open Feb-Oct Mon-Fri   11-5, Sat & Sun 1-5; Jul-Aug, daily, extended hours 10.30-6.

Fee: *IR£3 (concessions IR£2). Family ticket IR£7.50.

P ᠌╨ 🚸 toilets for disabled ✈ (ex guide dogs)

⛪ COBH

The Queentown Story

Cobh Railway Station

☎ 012 813591   🖷 021 813595

A dramatic exhibition of the origins, history and legends of Cobh. Explore conditions on board early emigrant vessels, including life aboard a convict ship leaving Cobh for Australia in 1801. You can also learn about Cobh's special connections with the Titanic.

Times: Open all year 10-6. Last admission 5pm.

Fee: *IR£3.50 (ch12 IR£2, pen & students IR£3). Family ticket IR£10.

P ᠌╨ ✕ 🚸 toilets for disabled shop ✈ (ex guide dogs) ◥

⛪ CORK

Cork Public Museum

Fitzgerald Park, Mardyke (N of University College)

☎ 021 270679   🖷 021 270931

Displays illustrating the history of the city are housed in this museum. The collections cover the economic, social and municipal history from the Mesolithic period. There are fine collections of

Cork Silver and Glass and Youghal Needlepoint Lace.

Times: Open all year, Jun-Aug Mon-Fri 11-1 & 2.15-6, Sun 3-5; Sep-May Mon-Fri 11-1 & 2.15-5, Sun 3-5. (Closed Sat, BH wknds & PH)

P (100 yds) shop ✈ (ex guide dogs)

⛪ MIDLETON

Jameson Heritage Centre

(20m E of Cork towards Waterford)

☎ 021 613594 & 613596   🖷 021 613642

A tour of the Jameson Heritage Centre consists of a 20 minute audio/visual presentation, then a 35 minute guided tour of the Old Distillery and then back to the Jameson Bar for a whiskey tasting - minerals are available for children. The guided tour and audio-visual aids are available in five languages.

Times: Open daily, Mar-Oct 10-6. Last tour 4. Nov-Feb Mon-Fri, two tours 12 & 3. Sat-Sun, two tours 2 & 4. (Closed Xmas).

Fee: *IR£3.95 (ch IR£1.50). Family ticket IR£9.50

P ᠌╨ 🚸 toilets for disabled shop ✈ (ex guide dogs) ◥

⛪ CO DONEGAL

⛪ BALLYSHANNON

The Water Wheels

Abbey Assaroe (cross Abbey River on Rossnowlagh Rd, next turning left & follow signs)

☎ 072 51580

Abbey Assaroe was founded by Cistercian Monks from Boyle Abbey in the late 12th century. The Cistercians excelled in water engineering and canalised the river to turn water wheels for mechanical power.

Times: Open Etr week & May-Aug, 10.30-6.30. Sun 1.30-dusk.

P ᠌╨ ✕ 🚸 toilets for disabled shop garden centre

⛪ BUNCRANA

Guns of Dunree Military Museum

Fort Dunree, Dunree (6m NW, on eastern shore of Lough Swilly)

☎ 077 61817

The first and only permanent and professionally-designed military museum in Ireland. The museum houses a collection of artefacts and an audio-visual display which vividly illustrates the working of a coastal defence battery extending back of 180 years.

Times: Open daily 14 Jun-16 Sep 10.30-6, Sun 1-6.

P ᠌╨ 🚸 shop ✈ *Details not confirmed for 2000*

⛪ LETTERKENNY

Glebe House & Gallery

Church Hill (signposted from Letterkenny)

☎ 074 37071   🖷 074 37072

This Regency house set in beautiful woodland gardens along the shore of Lough Gartan, was given to the nation, along with his art collection, by the artist Derek Hill. The interior of the house

DUBLIN

A million people inhabit the greater Dublin area. Some glorious architecture - in Dublin's case, the inheritance of its Georgian heyday - is interspersed with some pretty uninspired development. The setting is undoubtedly splendid, spanning the River Liffey and spreading round Dublin Bay.

Literature is king in the city which celebrates James Joyce (particularly on June 16th), Becket, Yeats, Shaw, Heaney and many others past and present. The joy of a stay in Dublin is the social life, with the theatres, bars and restaurants buzzing with activity.

is decorated with original wallpapers and textiles by William Morris.

Times: Open Etr & mid May-Sep Sat-Thu 11-6.30. (Last tour of house 5.30).

Fee: *IR£2 (ch & student IR£1, pen IR£1.50). Family ticket IR£5

🅿 💷 ♿ toilets for disabled shop ✖ (ex guide dogs)

🏛 LIFFORD

CAVANACOR HISTORIC HOUSE & CRAFT CENTRE

Ballindrait (1.5m from town off N14 Strabane/Letterkenny road)

☎ (074) 41143   🖹 074 41143

Built in the early 1600s and commanding a view of the Clonleigh Valley and the River Deele, Cavanacor House is the ancestral home of James Knox Polk, 11th President of the USA (1845-1849). King James II dined under the sycamore tree in front of the house in 1689. There is a display of the history of the house and the surrounding area and over 10 acres of landscaped gardens and an old-fashioned walled garden. The Art Gallery will feature exhibitions of new work by national and international artists. Please ring for details.

Times: Open Etr-Aug, Tue-Sat 12-6, Sun 2-6. Closed Mon ex BH's.

Fee: *IR£2.50 (ch & pen IR£1.75). Family ticket IR£7.50.

🅿 💷 ✖ ♿ shop garden centre (on leads)

🏛 CO DUBLIN

🏛 BALBRIGGAN

ARDGILLAN CASTLE

(on R127)

☎ 01 8492212   🖹 01 8492786

A large and elegant country manor house built in 1738, set in 194 acres of parkland overlooking the sea and coast as far as the Mourne Mountains. There is a permanent exhibition of the 17th-century 'Down Survey' maps, various temporary exhibitions. Tours of the Gardens (Jun, Jul and Aug) begin at 3.30pm every Thursday.

Times: Open 20 Dec-Jan, Sun 2-4 (closed 25 Dec); Apr-Sep, Tue-Sun & BH's 11-6; Oct-Mar, Wed-Sun & BH's 11-4.30.

Fee: *IR£3 (pen & students IR£2). Family ticket IR£7. Party.

🅿 💷 ♿ toilets for disabled shop ✖ (ex guide dogs)

🏛 DONABATE

NEWBRIDGE HOUSE AND TRADITIONAL FARM

☎ 01 8436534 & 8462184
🖹 01 8462537

Newbridge House was designed by George Semple and built in 1737 for Charles Cobbe, Archbishop of Dublin. The house contains many splendidly refurbished rooms featuring plasterwork, furniture and paintings. Special events throughout the year include

contd.

demonstrations of sheep shearing, weaving, dying, pottery and harness making.

Times: Open Apr-Sep Tue-Sat 10-5, Sun & PH 2-6; Oct-Mar Sat-Sun & PH 2-5. Parties at other times by arrangement.

P ▣ ⌖ shop ✈ *Details not confirmed for 2000*

▦ DUBLIN

CHRIST CHURCH CATHEDRAL

Christchurch Place (at the top end of Dame St)

☎ 01 6778099   ▤ 01 6798991

Founded in 1038, the cathedral has been largely rebuilt since then, but retains its ancient crypt. There are services daily and choir singing can be heard on Wednesday, Thursday, Saturday and Sunday.

Times: Open 10-5.30.

Fee: *Requested donation IR£2 (children IR£1)

P (100yds) ⌖ shop ✈ (ex guide dogs)

DRIMNAGH CASTLE

Long Mile Rd, Drimnagh

☎ 01 4502530   ▤ 01 4505401

The last surviving medieval castle in Ireland with a flooded moat, Drimnagh dates to the 13th century. The Great Hall and Undercroft have been restored to their medieval grandeur, set off by the 17th-century style formal gardens, all of which are open to the public. Continuously inhabited until 1954, it is now populated by a team of craftsmen, apprentices and young trainees, restoring the later tower, stables and coach-house. Please contact for details of special events, including family fun days etc.

Times: Open Apr-Sep, Wed, wknds & BH's 12-5; Oct-Mar, Sun & BH's 2-5.

P ▣ ⌖ (gravel courtyard and garden. steps) ✈ (ex guide dogs) *Details not confirmed for 2000*

DUBLINIA

St Michael's Hill, Christ Church

☎ 01 6794611   ▤ 01 6797116

The story of medieval Dublin. Housed in the former Synod Hall beside Christ Church Cathedral and developed by the Medieval Trust, DVBLINIA recreates the period from the arrival of Strongbow and the Anglo-Normans in 1170 to the closure of the monasteries by Henry VIII in 1540.

Times: Open Apr-Sep 10-5; Oct-Mar, Mon-Sat 11-4, Sun/BH 10-4.30. Closed 24-26 Dec.

P (100yds) ▣ ⌖ (2 floors accessible, but bridge and tower are not) toilets for disabled shop ✈ (ex guide dogs) ◥

GUINNESS HOP STORE

St.James's Gate

☎ 01 4084800   ▤ 01 4084965

Established in 1876, the Hop Store remained crammed with hopsacks until 1957, when a new hop store came into use. It has now been converted to `The World of Guinness' which shows the history of the famous brewery through museum exhibits and audio-visual presentations.

A gallery dedicated to the world-famous Guinness advertising is a recent addition.

Times: Open all year, daily (Closed 25-26Dec & Good Fri) Jan-Mar & Oct-Dec, Mon-Sat 9.30-4 (Sun & PH 12-4) Apr-Sep Mon-Sat 9.30-5 (Sun & PH 10.30-4.30)

P ▣ ⌖ toilets for disabled shop ✈ *Details not confirmed for 2000* ◥

HOWTH CASTLE RHODODENDRON GARDENS

Howth (9m NE of Dublin city centre, via Fairview Clontarf & Sutton)

☎ 01 8322624 & 8322256

▤ 01 8392405

On the northern boundary of Dublin Bay, the castle is justly famous for its gardens and especially for its rhododendron walk. The walk is open all year, but is at its best in May and June. There are views north to the Mourne Mountains and to the west of Dublin Bay.

Times: Open all year, daily 8am-dusk. (Closed 25 Dec.)

P ▣ ✗ licensed ⌖ (ramped entrance) toilets for disabled ✈ (ex guide dogs) *Details not confirmed for 2000* ◥

HUGH LANE MUNICIPAL GALLERY OF MODERN ART

Charlemont House, Parnell Square

☎ 01 8741903   ▤ 01 8722182

Situated in Charlemont House, one of Dublin's finest Georgian buildings, the gallery's collection comprises an extensive range of Irish and international paintings, sculpture, works on paper and stained glass, and the gallery holds one of the most extensive collections of 20th-century Irish art. There are regular concerts at noon on Sundays throughout the year and public lectures every Sunday. Please contact the Gallery for a Programme of Events.

Times: Open all year, Tue-Thu 9.30-6, Fri-Sat 9.30-5, Sun 11-5. Late night opening Thu until 8, Apr-Aug only. (Closed Mon.) (Closed Good Fri & 24-25 Dec).

P (100 metres) (meter parking) ✗ licensed ⌖ (Ramp & reserved parking) toilets for disabled shop ✈ (ex guide dogs) *Details not confirmed for 2000*

IRISH MUSEUM OF MODERN ART

Royal Hospital Kilmainham, Kilmainham (from City Centre pass Heuston Station, 1st left on St John's Rd)

☎ 01 6718666   ▤ 01 6718695

Housed in the Royal Hospital Kilmainham, an impressive 17th-century building, the museum presents a wide-ranging programme of Irish and International 20th-century art from its own collections and through temporary exhibitions, along with talks, seminars and musical events.

Times: Open all year Tue-Sat 10-5.30, Sun & BH's 12-5.30. (Closed 24-26 Dec & 17 Mar)

P ▣ ⌖ (wheelchair available) toilets for disabled shop ✈ *Details not confirmed for 2000*

JAMES JOYCE CENTRE
35 North Great George's St
☎ 01 8788547   ▤ 01 8788488

Situated in a beautifully restored 18th-century Georgian townhouse, the Centre is dedicated to the promotion of a greater interest in, and understanding, of the life and works of Joyce. There is a well-stocked library open to visitors, exhibition rooms, videos and tapes. Please telephone for details of special events.
Times: Open all year, Mon-Sat 9.30-5, Sun 12.30-5.
P (200 mtrs) ▆ & toilets for disabled shop ✕ *Details not confirmed for 2000* ▚

MARSH'S LIBRARY
St Patrick's Close
☎ 01 4543511   ▤ 01 4543511

The first public library in Ireland, dating from 1701. Designed by William Robinson, the interior has been unchanged for nearly 300 years. The collection is of approximately 25,000 volumes of 16th, 17th and early 18th-century books. Special exhibition until June 2000: 'The Wisdom of the East - Marsh's Oriental Books'.
Times: Open Mon & Wed-Fri, 10-12.45 & 2-5; Sat 10.30-12.45.
P ✕ ⚒

NATIONAL BOTANIC GARDENS
Glasnevin (on Botanic Road, between N1 and N2)
☎ (01) 8374388 & 8377596
▤ 01 8360080

Established in 1795 and covering an area of 48 acres, the gardens contain fine collections of trees and shrubs, as well as renowned herbaceous borders. Separate areas are devoted to annuals and vegetables, and to native Irish plants, arranged according to habitats. The glasshouses contain collections of palms, rare cycads, tropical ferns, cacti and alpines.
Times: Open all year, summer Mon-Sat 9-6, Sun 11-6; winter Mon-Sat 10-4.30, Sun 11-4.30. (Closed 25 Dec).
Fee: *Free entry. Guided tours by arrangement £1.50, telephone for reservations.
P & (Wheelchair available) toilets for disabled ✕ (ex guide dogs)

NATIONAL GALLERY OF IRELAND
Merrion Square (situated 5 mins walk from Pearse Station)
☎ 01 6615133   ▤ 01 6615372

Founded in 1854, the gallery houses the national collection of Irish art, and the national collection of European Old Masters from the 14th to 20th centuries. A Yeats museum has recently opened and a new wing to the existing building will be completed by the end of 2000.
Times: Mon-Sat 10-5.30 (Thu 10-8.30), Sun 2-5. Closed 24-26 Dec & Good Friday.
Fee: Free.
P (5 mins walk) (meter parking, 2hrs max) ▆ ✕ licensed & (braille/audio tours, lifts, ramps, parking bay) toilets for disabled shop ✕

NATURAL HISTORY MUSEUM
Merrion St
☎ 01 6777444   ▤ 01 6766116

Founded by the Royal Dublin Society in 1792, the museum has occupied its present premises since 1857. There are extensive zoological exhibitions and geological specimens, and the Blaschka glass models of marine animals, which are world-famous. The museum is also an important research institute.
Times: Open Tue-Sat 10-5, Sun 2-5.
Fee: Free.
P (parking meters wkdays) & ✕

NEWMAN HOUSE
University College Dublin, 86 St Stephens Green (South side of St Stephen's Green)
☎ 01 7067422 & 4757255
▤ 01 7067211

Newman House consists of two superb Georgian townhouses which contain some of Ireland's finest 18th-century plasterwork and decoration. As the founding home of University College Dublin in 1854, the house has been associated with many famous literary and historical figures.
Times: Open Jun-Aug, Tue-Fri 12-5, Sat 2-5, Sun 11-1. At other times tours by prior arrangement only.
Fee: *IRE2 (concessions IRE1).
P (100yds) ✕ licensed ✕ (ex guide dogs)

NUMBER TWENTY NINE
29 Lower Fitzwilliam St (on the corner of Lower Fitzwilliam St & Upper Mount Sq)
☎ 01 7026165   ▤ 01 6615376

Number Twenty-Nine is an exhibition of the homelife of a middle-class merchant family in late 18th and early 19th-century Dublin.
Times: Open all year, Tue-Sat 10-5, Sun 2-5. (Closed Mon & 2 wks prior to Xmas).
P (charged) ▆ shop ✕ ▚

GEORGE BERNARD SHAW HOUSE
33 Synge St
☎ 01 4750854 & 8722077
▤ 01 8722231

The modest 1840s terrace house where the playwright and Nobel prizewinner George Bernard Shaw was born and spent the first eleven years of his life.
Times: Open May-Oct, Mon-Sat 10-5, Sun & PH's 11-5.
P (charged) shop garden centre ✕ (ex guide dogs) *Details not confirmed for 2000*

▥ MALAHIDE
MALAHIDE CASTLE
☎ 01 8462184 & 8462516
▤ 01 8462537

One of Ireland's oldest castles, this romantic and beautiful structure, set in 250 acres of grounds, has changed very little in 800 years. Tours offer views of Irish period furniture and historical Irish portrait collections. Additional paintings from the
contd.

National Gallery depict Irish life from the last few centuries.

Times: Open all year, Apr-Oct, Mon-Sat 10-5, Sun & PH 11-6; Nov-Mar, Mon-Fri 10-5, Sat-Sun & PH 2-5. Closed for tours 12.45-2pm.

P 🍴 ✕ licensed shop ✖ *Details not confirmed for 2000* 🍺

CO GALWAY

GALWAY

ROYAL TARA CHINA VISITOR CENTRE
Tara Hall, Mervue (off N17 opp Trappers Rest or left off N6 after Ryan's Hotel)
☎ 091 751301   📠 091 757574

Royal Tara China is the country's leading manufacturer of fine bone china, cold cast bronze miniature pubs, castles and cottages, and handpainted pieces. Tours every hour from 9.30 - 3.30.

Times: Open all year, 9-6 (9-8 Jul-Sep, 9-9 Dec). Guided factory tours Mon-Fri 9.30-3.30.

Fee: Free.

P 🍴 ✕ ♿ toilets for disabled shop ✖ (ex guide dogs)

GORT

THOOR BALLYLEE
(1km off N18, 1km off N66)
☎ 091 631436   📠 091 565201

This tower house is the former home of the poet William Butler Yeats and is where he completed most of his literary works. The tower has been restored to appear exactly as it was when he lived there, and houses an Interpretative Centre with audio-visual presentations and displays of his work.

Times: Open Etr-Sep, daily 10-6.

Fee: *IRE3.30 (ch IRE1, pen & students IRE2.80). Family ticket IRE6.60. Party.

P 🍴 ♿ (audio-visual presentation) toilets for disabled shop ✖ 🍺

KINVARRA

DUNGUAIRE CASTLE
☎ 091 37108 & 061 360788
📠 061 361020

The castle has stood for hundreds of years on the site of the 7th-century stronghold of Guaire, the King of Connaught. Today the restored castle gives an insight into the lifestyle of the people who lived there from 1520 to modern times.

Times: Open May-Oct, daily 9.30-5.30 (last admission 5pm).

P shop ✖ (ex guide dogs) *Details not confirmed for 2000* 🍺

ROUNDSTONE

ROUNDSTONE MUSICAL INSTRUMENTS
Craft Centre
☎ 095 35875   📠 095 35980

Situated in an old Franciscan monastry at Roundstone is the craft workshop of Malachy Kearns who makes Ireland's oldest product - the Bodhrán - an 18inch one-side drum made from

goatskin treated by a traditional process. You can see the drums being made and decorated with handpainted designs. A museum dealing with the history of the bodhrán has now opened.

Times: Open all year daily 9-6.

Fee: Free.

P 🍴 ♿ toilets for disabled shop

CO KERRY

CASTLEISLAND

CRAG CAVE
(1m N, signposted off N21)
☎ 066 714244   📠 066 7142352

Crag Cave is one of the longest surveyed cave systems in Ireland, with a total length of 3.81km. It is a spectacular world, where pale forests of stalagmites and stalagtites, thousands of years old, throw eerie shadows around vast echoing caverns complemented by dramatic sound and lighting effects. Tours lasts about 30 minutes.

Times: Open daily, Mar-Nov 10-6 (Jul-Aug until 6.30). Last tour 30 minutes before closing time.

Fee: *IRE4 (ch IRE2, pen & students IRE3). Family ticket IRE12.

P 🍴 ✕ licensed ♿ (ramp to visitor centre) toilets for disabled shop ✖ (ex guide dogs) 🍺

DUNQUIN

THE BLASKET CENTRE
(10m W of Dingle town, on Slea Head Drive)
☎ 066 9156444 & 9156371
📠 066 9156446

In the early part of this century a small group of writers from the remote Blasket Island, just off the coast of County Kerry, achieved world renown. They told their own story in their own language and the centre describes the lives of the Islanders before the sad abandonment of the island in 1953. Research and conference facilities also available.

Times: Open daily, Etr-late Oct 10-6 (7 Jul-Aug). Open on request all year for groups over 30.

Fee: *IRE2.50 (ch & student IRE1, pen IRE1.75). Family ticket IRE6.

P 🍴 ✕ licensed ♿ (reserved parking) toilets for disabled ✖ (ex guide dogs)

⛏ KENMARE
KENMARE HERITAGE CENTRE
The Square
☎ 064 31633   🖹 064 34506

Kenmare has been designated a Bord Failte Heritage Town. The town grew around the mineworks founded in 1670. The Heritage Centre covers the history of Kenmare, including famous visitors, the effects of the Famine, 'historical sites', the Nun of Kenmare and a Kenmare lace exhibition.
Times: Open Apr-Sep, Mon-Sat 9.30-5.30 (also Sun Jul-Aug)
P (400mtrs) ♿ toilets for disabled shop ✖ (ex guide dogs)
Details not confirmed for 2000 ▰

⛏ KILLARNEY
KILLARNEY TRANSPORT MUSEUM
Scotts Hotel Gardens (centre of town, opposite railway station)
☎ 064 34677   🖹 064 32638

A unique collection of Irish veteran, vintage and classic cars, motorcycles, bicycles, carriages and fire engines. Exhibits include the 1907 Silver Stream (reputed to be the rarest car in the world, it was designed and built by an Irishman and he only made one!).For details of special events, please telephone.
Times: Open Apr-Oct, daily 10-6. Open at other times by appointment
Fee: *IR£3 (ch IR£1.50, students & pen IR£2). Family ticket IR£7. Wheelchair visitors free. Party.
P 💺 ✖ licensed ♿ shop

⛏ TRALEE
KERRY THE KINGDOM MUSEUM
Ashe Memorial Hall, Denny St
☎ (066) 27777   🖹 066 27444

The museum tells the story of Kerry (and Ireland) from earliest times. There's an audio-visual presentation on Kerry's spectacular scenery and historic monuments; the priceless treasures of Kerry origin in the Kerry Museum, and Geraldine Tralee - a reconstruction of Tralee during the

Middle Ages when it was the principal seat of the Anglo-Norman FitzGeralds (Geraldines).
Times: Open daily, Mar-Oct 10-6; Aug 10-7; Nov-Dec 12-5. (Closed 24-26 Dec).
P (100mtrs) (disc parking area) 💺 ♿ (enter through tourist office entrance) toilets for disabled shop garden centre ✖
Details not confirmed for 2000

⛏ VALENTIA ISLAND
THE SKELLIG EXPERIENCE
(Ring of Kerry Road, signed after Cahersiveen town then Valentia bridge or ferry from Renard Point)
☎ 064 31633   🖹 064 34506

The Skellig Rocks are renowned for their scenery, sea bird colonies, lighthouses, Early Christian monastic architecture and rich underwater life. The two islands - Skellig Michael and Small Skellig - stand like fairytale castles in the Atlantic Ocean, rising to 218 metres and their steep cliffs plunging 50 metres below the sea. The Heritage Centre, (on Valentia Island, reached from the mainland via a bridge), tells the story of the Skellig Michael monastery.
Times: Open Apr-Jun & Sep 10-7, Jul-Aug 9.30-7.
Fee: *IR£3 (ch IR£1.50, pen & student IR£2.70). Family ticket IR£7.
P 💺 ♿ toilets for disabled shop ✖ (ex guide dogs) ▰

⛏ CO KILDARE

⛏ CELBRIDGE
CASTLETOWN HOUSE
(13m from Dublin, follow signs to Celbridge from N4)
☎ 01 6288252   🖹 01 6271811

Ireland's largest and finest Palladian country house, begun c1722 for William Conolly, speaker of the Irish House of Commons. The state rooms include the 'Pompeian' Long Gallery with its Venetian chandeliers, green silk drawing room and magnificent staircase hall with Lafranchini
contd.

plasterwork. There is a fine collection of 18th-century Irish furniture and paintings.
Times: Opening times expected to be Apr-Sep Mon-Fri 10-6, Sat-Sun & BH 1-6; Oct Mon-Fri 10-5, Sun & BH 1-5; Nov Sun 1-5. Restoration continues, contact before visiting.
Fee: *IRE2.50 (ch & students IRE1, pen IRE1.75). Family ticket IRE6.
P 🍴 ♿ toilets for disabled 🐕 (ex guide dogs)

⚏ KILDARE
JAPANESE GARDENS
Irish National Stud, Tully (Off N7)
☎ 045 521617 & 522963 ▯ 045 522964

Situated in the grounds of the Irish National Stud, the gardens were established by Lord Wavertree between 1906 and 1910, and symbolise `The Life of Man' in a Japanese-style landscape. You can also visit the Horse Museum which includes the skeleton of Arkle. A new attraction is the Commemorative Millennium Garden of St Fiachra, set in a natural setting of woodland, wetland, lakes and islands.
Times: Open 12 Feb-12 Nov, daily 9.30-6, last admission 5.
Fee: *IRE6 (ch 12 IRE3, students & pen IRE4.50). Family ticket IRE14.
P 🐕 licensed ♿ (all parts of stud accessible, only small part of gardens) toilets for disabled shop 🐕 (ex on lead) 🍴

⚏ CO LIMERICK

⚏ FOYNES
FLYING BOAT MUSEUM
(on N69, 23m from Limerick City)
☎ 069 65416 ▯ 069 65416

The museum recalls the era of the flying boats during the 1930s and early 1940s when Foynes was an important airport for air traffic between the United States and Europe. There is a comprehensive range of exhibits, graphic illustrations and a 1940s style cinema featuring a 17 minute film - all original footage from the 30s and 40s.
Times: Open daily, 31 Mar-31 Oct 10-6. Last admissions 5.15pm.
P 🍴 ♿ toilets for disabled shop 🐕 (ex guide dogs) *Details not confirmed for 2000* 🍴

⚏ HOLYCROSS
LOUGH GUR STONE AGE CENTRE
Bruff Rd (17 km S of Limerick City, off R512 rd to Kilmallock)
☎ 061 385186 & 061 360788
▯ 061 361020

Lough Gur introduces visitors to the habitat of Neolithic Man on one of Ireland's most important archaeological sites. Near the lake is an interpretative centre which tells the story of 5000 years of man's presence at Lough Gur.
Times: Open May-Sep, daily 10-6 (last admission 5pm)
P 🍴 ♿ shop 🐕 (ex guide dogs) *Details not confirmed for 2000* 🍴

⚏ KILCORNAN
CELTIC PARK & GARDENS
(N69 Limerick to Tralge rd)
☎ 061 394243 ▯ 353 69 64257

Located on an original Celtic settlement in one of the most important Cromwellian plantations in the south-west of Ireland. As you walk through the park there's plenty to see, including a church built in 1250, a Mass rock, dolmens, a 6/7th century wooden church, a stone circle, lake dwellings, cooking site and a fine example of a ring fort. The gardens contain over 1000 roses, flowering shrubs, a rockery, herbaceous borders, shrubbery and colonnades.
Times: Open daily, Mar-Oct 9-7. Last entry 6pm.
Fee: *IRE3 (pen & students IRE2.50)
P 🍴 shop (on lead)

⚏ LIMERICK
HUNT MUSEUM
The Custom House, Rutland St (a short walk from Arthur's Quay)
☎ 061 312833 ▯ 061 312834

Three floors of galleries exhibit a collection of 2000 pieces of art and antiquity. It includes statues in stone, bronze and wood, crucifixes, panel paintings, metalwork, jewellery, enamels and ceramics. There are drawings by Picasso and da Vinci, and a gold cross worn by Mary, Queen of Scots. Temporary exhibitions are planned throughout the year.
Times: Open daily Mon-Sat 10-5, Sun 2-5.
Fee: *IRE4 (ch IRE2, concwssions IRE3). Family ticket IRE9.50. Party.
P (100mtrs) (parking discs for street parking) 🍴 licensed ♿ toilets for disabled shop 🐕 (ex guide dogs) 🍴

KING JOHN'S CASTLE
Nicholas St
☎ 061 411201 & 360788 ▯ 061 361020

With its imposing twin-towered gatehouse and battle-scarred walls, this 13th-century castle is an impressive Anglo-Norman fortress, where three-dimensional displays demonstrate 800 years of Limerick's and Ireland's history.
Times: Open Apr-Oct daily 9.30-5.30 (last admission 4.30); Nov-Apr, Sun 11-4 (last admission 3pm).
P 🍴 ♿ (lifts and ramps) toilets for disabled shop 🐕 (ex guide dogs) *Details not confirmed for 2000* 🍴

⚏ CO MONAGHAN

⚏ INNISKEEN
PATRICK KAVANAGH RURAL & LITERARY RESOURCE CENTRE
Candlefort (between Carrickmacross N2 & Dundalk N1)
☎ 042 78560 ▯ 042 78560

Birthplace of Patrick Kavanagh, one of Ireland's foremost 20th-century poets. The village grew around the ancient monastery of St Daig MacCairill, founded by 562, and its strong, 10th-century round tower still stands. The centre, housed in the former parish Church, chronicles the ancient history of the region and its role in developing Kavanagh's work. Please telephone for details of special events.

Times: Open all year, Mon Fri 11-5, wknds & BH's 2-6. (Closed 1 Oct-31 May, closed wknds & BH's 1 Dec-16 Mar) P 💺 & toilets for disabled shop *Details not confirmed for 2000* 🗡

🏛 MONAGHAN
MONAGHAN COUNTY MUSEUM
1-2 Hill St (near town centre, opposite Tourist Information office)
☎ (047) 82928 ▤ 047 71189

This is an award-winning museum of local archaeology, history, arts and crafts. Throughout the year various special exhibitions take place.

Times: Open all year, Tue- Sat 11-1 & 2-5.
P (near town centre) (restricted on street parking) & 🐾
Details not confirmed for 2000

🏛 CO OFFALY

🏛 BIRR
BIRR CASTLE DEMESNE
☎ 0509 20336 ▤ 0509 21583

A large, landscaped park with a lake, rivers and waterfalls, with important plant collections including magnolias, maples, limes and oaks. The demesne is particularly colourful in the spring and autumn, and is noted for its formal gardens, containing the tallest box hedges in the world. The Demesne is also home to the Great Birr Telescope, built in 1844.

Times: Open all year. 9am-6pm.
Fee: *IRE4 (ch IRE2.50, pen & students IRE3.20).
P 💺 & toilets for disabled shop garden centre 🗡

🏛 CO ROSCOMMON

🏛 BOYLE
KING HOUSE
(in town centre, turn off N4 (Dublin to Sligo road) at Boyle Abbey, house signposted)
☎ 079 63242 ▤ 079 63243

Built around 1730, King House is of unique architectural and historical importance. Home to the King family until 1788, it then became a military barracks and was home to the famous Connaught Rangers Regiment and latterly the national army. Now magnificently restored, exhibitions tell the stories of the ancient kings of Connaught and explore the Gaelic way of life. Special events include the Boyle Arts Festival and a regular programme of classical music concerts.

Times: Open: wknds Apr & late Oct, daily May-mid Oct, 10-6 (last admission 5pm).
Fee: *IRE3 (ch IRE2, pen/student IRE2.50). Family ticket IRE8. Party.
P 💺 ✗ & (lift to all areas) toilets for disabled shop 🗡 (ex guide dogs)

🏛 STROKESTOWN
STROKESTOWN PARK HOUSE GARDEN & FAMINE MUSEUM
Strokestown Park
☎ 078 33013 ▤ 078 33712

A fine example of an early 18th-century gentleman farmer's country estate. Built in Palladian style the house reflects perfectly the confidence of the newly emergent ruling class. The pleasure garden has also been restored, and the Famine Museum, located in the stable yard, commemorates the Great Irish Famine of the 1840s.

Times: Open daily, Apr-Oct 11-5.30.
P ✗ licensed & (Access for ramps) toilets for disabled shop *Details not confirmed for 2000* 🗡

🏛 CO TIPPERARY

🏛 CASHEL
BR' BOR' HERITAGE CENTRE
☎ 062 61122 ▤ 062 62700

At the foot of the Rock of Cashel, a 4th-century stone fort, this Heritage Centre is dedicated to the study and celebration of native Irish music, song, dance, story telling, theatre and Celtic studies. There's a Folk Theatre where three performances are held daily in the summer, and in the evening, banquets evoke the Court of Brian Bor', 11th-century High King of Ireland with songs, poems and sagas.

Times: Open Jan-May & Oct-Dec, Mon-Fri 9.30-5.30; Jun-Sep Tue-Sat 9.30-11, Sun-Mon 9.30-5.30.
Fee: *Admission to centre free. Night show IRE8.
P (charged) 💺 ✗ licensed & (wheelchair bay in theatre) toilets for disabled shop 🗡 🗡

🏛 CO WATERFORD

🏛 LISMORE
LISMORE CASTLE GARDENS
☎ 058 54424 ▤ 058 54896

Lismore Castle is the Irish home of the Duke of Devonshire. The beautifully situated walled and woodland gardens contain a fine collection of camellias, magnolias and other shrubs and a remarkable Yew Walk. It is said that Spenser wrote part of his *Faerie Queene* in these gardens.

Times: Open 20 Apr-15 Oct, daily 1.45-4.45.
Fee: *IRE3 (ch 16 IRE1.50). Party 20+.
P

🏛 WATERFORD
WATERFORD CRYSTAL VISITOR CENTRE
(on N25, 1m from city centre)
☎ 051 73311 ▤ 051 78539

There are factory tours to see master craftsmen mouth-blow and hand-cut this famous crystal. You can talk to the master engravers and see the

contd.

crystal being sculpted. In the gallery there is the finest display of Waterford crystal in the world.
Times: Tours of factory: Mar-Oct, daily 8.30-4.15; Nov-Feb, Mon-Fri 9-4.
🅿 ⬛ ✕ ♿ (special tours on request) toilets for disabled shop ✖ *Details not confirmed for 2000* 🦢

� CO WEXFORD

� FERRYCARRIG
IRISH NATIONAL HERITAGE PARK
(3m from Wexford, on N11)
☎ 053 20733 🗎 053 20911

Fourteen historical sites set in a magnificent 35-acre mature forest explaining Ireland's history from the Stone and Bronze Ages, through the Celtic period and concluding with the Vikings and Normans. Among the exhibits are a reconstructed Mesolithic camp, a Viking boatyard with 2 full size ships and a Norman motte and bailey. Please ring for details of special events.
Times: Open Apr-Oct daily 9.30-6.30. Last admission 5. Allow 1.5 hour for visit (closing time subject to seasonal change).
Fee: *IR£5 (pen IR£4.50, students IR£4). Family ticket IR£12.50. Group rates available on request.
🅿 ⬛ ✕ licensed ♿ toilets for disabled shop ✖ (ex guide dogs) 🦢

� NEW ROSS
DUNBRODY ABBEY VISITORS CENTRE
Dunbrody Abbey, Campile (10 miles from New Ross at the base of the Hook Peninsular)
☎ 051 88603

The visitor centre is based around the Abbey itself and Dunbrody Castle. There is an intriguing yew hedge maze with 1550 yew trees and a museum. In addition there is a golf pitch and putt course with competitions organised twice a month, and a local craft centre.
Times: Open Apr-Sep 10-6 (7pm Jul-Aug).
Fee: *IR£1.50 (ch IR£1). Family ticket IR£4. Maze/Golf IR£1.50, (ch IR£1). Family IR£4.
🅿 ⬛ ♿ shop garden centre (specialising in conifers & shrubs)

JOHN F KENNEDY ARBORETUM
(12km S of New Ross, off R733)
☎ 051 388171 🗎 051 388172

The Arboretum covers 623 acres across the hill of Slievecoiltia which overlooks the Kennedy ancestral home at Dunganstown. There are 4,500 types of trees and shrubs representing the temperate regions of the world, and laid out in botanical sequence. There's a lake and a visitor centre.
Times: Open daily, May-Aug 10-8; Apr & Sep 10-6.30; Oct-Mar 10-5. Last admission 45 mins before closing. (Closed Good Fri & 25 Dec).
Fee: *IR£2 (ch & student IR£1, pen IR£1.50). Family ticket IR£5. Party 20+. Heritage card (12month) visits all Heritage Service sites. Adult IR£15 (pen IR£10, ch/student IR£6). Family ticket IR£36
🅿 ⬛ ♿ toilets for disabled shop (on lead)

� WEXFORD
THE IRISH AGRICULTURAL MUSEUM
Johnstown Castle Old Farmyard (4m SW, signposted off N25)
☎ 053 42888 🗎 053 42213

This museum has extensive displays on rural transport, farming and the activities of the farmyard and the farmhouse. Large scale replicas of different workshops, including a blacksmith, cooper and basket worker can be seen, and include displays on dairying, cycling, and sugar-beet harvesting and a collection of Irish country furniture.
Times: Open all year, Jun-Aug Mon-Fri 9-5 & Sat-Sun 2-5; Apr-May & Sep-14 Nov Mon-Fri 9-12.30 & 1.30-5, Sat-Sun 2-5; 15 Nov-Mar Mon-Fri 9-12.30 & 1.30-5 (Closed 25 Dec-2 Jan).
Fee: *IR£2.50 (ch & students IR£1.50). Family ticket IR£8. Parking charge May-Sep.
🅿 (charged) ⬛ ♿ toilets for disabled shop ✖ (ex small dogs)

JOHNSTOWN CASTLE GARDENS
Johnstown Castle (4m SW, signposted off N25)
☎ 053 42888 🗎 053 42004

The 19th-century mansion is closed to the public but visitors can explore the 50 acres of grounds containing over 200 different varieties of trees and shrubs, ornamental lakes with wildfowl, and walled gardens and hothouses. The ruins of Rathlannon Castle, a medieval tower house, can also be seen.
Times: Open all year, daily 9-5.30. (Closed 25 Dec).
Fee: *Car (inc passengers) IR£3. Pedestrians IR£1.50 (ch & students IR50p).
🅿 ⬛ ♿ toilets for disabled shop

WEXFORD WILDFOWL RESERVE
North Slob (take coast road over bridge for 3km, signs show turning on right)
☎ 053 23129 🗎 053 24785

The reserve is of international importance for Greenland White-fronted geese (as it has one-third of the world's population), Brent geese, Bewick's swans and widgeon. The reserve is a superb place for birdwatching and there are hides and a tower hide available as well as a visitor centre. Special events take place during the Wexford Festival (last 2 weeks October). Other events also take place - please telephone for details.
Times: Open all year, 15 Apr-Sep 9-6; Oct-14 Apr 10-5.
Fee: Free.
🅿 ♿ ✖ (ex guide dogs)

CO WICKLOW

ENNISKERRY
POWERSCOURT GARDENS EXHIBITION
Powerscourt Estate (just off N11 S of Bray, next to Enniskerry village)
☎ 01 2046000 📠 01 2863561

Begun by Richard Wingfield in the 1740s, the gardens are a blend of formal plantings, sweeping terraces, statuary and ornamental lakes together with secret hollows, rambling walks and walled gardens. The house itself incorporates an exhibition which traces the history of the estate, and tells the story of the disastrous fire of 1974 which gutted the house.
Times: Open - Gardens Mar-Oct daily 9.30-5.30; Nov-Feb daily 9.30-dusk. Waterfall Mar-Oct daily 9.30-7; Nov-Feb daily 10.30-dusk.(Please check winter opening times as they are subject to change)
Fee: *Gardens & House exhibition: IRE5 (ch IRE3, students IRE4.50) House only IRE1.50 (ch IRE1, students IRE1.30) Gardens only IRE3.50 (ch IRE2, students IRE3.20) Waterfall IRE2 (ch IRE1, students IRE1.50) (Winter rates are fairly cheaper)
🅿 💻 ✕ licensed ♿ (Lift to first floor, Wheelchair available) toilets for disabled shop garden centre ✖ (ex guide dogs) 🍽

KILQUADE
NATIONAL GARDENS EXHIBITIONS CENTRE
Calumet Nurseries (7m S of Bray - turn off the N11 at Kilpedder)
☎ 01 2819890 📠 01 2810359

There are 17 different gardens designed by some of Ireland's leading landscapers and designers. There are lectures during the year and guided tours during summer. Ring for details and a calender of events.
Times: Open Feb-22 Dec, Mon-Sat 10-6, Sun 1-6.
Fee: *IRE2.50 (ch under 16 Free, pen IRE2). Party IRE2.
🅿 💻 ♿ garden centre ✖ (ex guide dogs) 🍽

RATHDRUM
AVONDALE HOUSE & FOREST PARK
(1.6km S of town. R752 off N11)
☎ 0404 46111 📠 0404 46111

It was here in 1846 that one of the greatest political leaders of modern Irish history, Charles Stewart Parnell, was born. Parnell spent much of his time at Avondale until his death in October 1891.
Times: House: 17 Mar-Oct, 11-6. Outside of these dates group bookings by appointment. Last admission 1 hour before closure. (Closed Good Fri). Park: Open daily.
Fee: *House IRE3 (pen & students IRE2.50). Family ticket IRE6, extra ch IRE1.50 each. Party. Parking; car IRE3, minibus IRE6, coach IRE12 (if pre booked, no charge).
🅿 (charged) 💻 ♿ (Special carpark & one forest trail accessible) shop ✖ (ex guide dogs & on lead) 🍽

CHRISTIAN BRITAIN

A Guide to Important Christian Locations in the British Isles

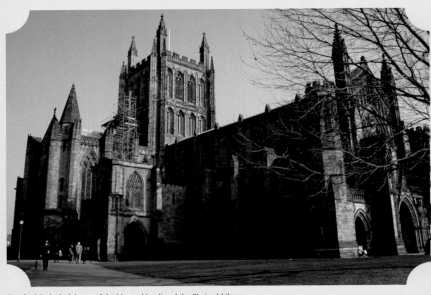

Hereford Cathedral, home of the Mappa Mundi and the Chained Library

Although Christianity began in the 1st century AD, it didn't begin to take hold in Britain until some six centuries later. The history of Christianity as it concerns visitor attractions has three major phases. The early days of missionaries and hermits, the Norman explosion of cathedrals, priories and abbeys, and the collapse of monastic life following the Dissolution of the monasteries by Henry VIII. Due to the third of these events, many of the locations built during the second are little more than a few walls imbued with history. Even so, they are all worth a visit for those interested in the development of one of Britain's most important institutions, the Christian Church.

Details of prices and opening times for all these religious locations may be found in this book.

Centre: A roof boss of Samson and the lion from the Chapter House of Hailes Abbey

Before The Norman Invasion

Probably the most important pre-Norman Christian location in Britain is **Glastonbury Abbey** (p199). Legends claim that Joseph of Arimathea arrived here in 61 AD, planting his staff in the ground, where it flowered at Christmas and Easter. Although it suffered collapse after the Dissolution, during the Middle Ages it was an important pilgrimage centre.

Scotland's first church was **Whithorn Priory** (p348), founded in 397 by St Ninian. The present ruins are 12th century, but the site contains the 5th-century Latinus stone and other early Christian monuments. **Ruthwell parish church** in Dumfries & Galloway (p345) is home to a **carved cross** that dates from the 7th or 8th century. Two sides show scenes from the Life of Christ, while the others contain parts of an ancient Runic poem.

The Benedictine order was founded in the 6th century in Italy, and soon brought to England by St Augustine. **St Augustine's Abbey** (p112) in Canterbury was founded by the Saint himself in 598, and although now ruined, is a fascinating place to visit.

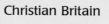

The Ruthwell Cross, Ruthwell, Dumfries & Galloway

One of the few functioning abbeys in this book is also one of the oldest. **Minster Abbey** (p117) was founded in the 7th century, and was one of the first nunneries in England. Although the original buildings are largely ruined, they are open to the public, who can also see a 12th-century carving of Christ.

Much Wenlock Priory in Shropshire (p192) was founded in the 7th century, but destroyed by the Danes. The present ruins date from the rebuilding which took place in the 11th century and after.

Odda's Chapel (p80) in Deerhurst, Gloucestershire, is something of an oddity. Now carefully restored, it is a rare Saxon chapel founded in 1056 by Earl Odda, and spent many years as part of a farmhouse.

Westminster Abbey's history goes back to before the days of St Edward the Confessor, who rebuilt it in the early 11th century (p144). Every Coronation since 1066 has taken place there, and it is the last resting place of many famous historical figures, including Kings and Queens of England, Chaucer and the Unknown Soldier.

David I, King of the Scots, founded a series of Border monasteries in the 12th century. **Dryburgh** (p335), which contains the graves of Sir Walter Scott and Earl Haig; **Jedburgh** (p340), the most complete of the series; and **Kelso** (p341), used as a fortress in the 16th century.

The Norman Explosion

The Cistercian order placed great emphasis on the value of agricultural labour and became very influential in England after the Conquest. Many of the now-ruined abbeys built during the 12th century were under their control.

Furness Abbey in Barrow-in-Furness (p44) is an impressive red sandstone ruin, set in the sinisterly-named but beautiful 'Glen of Deadly Nightshade'. The site museum has some fine stone carving.

During the middle ages, **Hailes Abbey** in Gloucestershire (p82) was a major pilgrimage centre. Its claim to fame was the possession of a phial of blood said to come from Christ Himself.

The largest monastic ruin is that of **Fountains Abbey** in Ripon, North Yorkshire (p273). Founded in 1132, it was aquired by William Aislabie in 1768, and became the focus of his landscaped gardens at Studley. The most complete monastic ruin is **Kirkstall Abbey** in Leeds (p286). It stands on the banks of the River

Gargoyles at Rufford Abbey, Ollerton, Nottinghamshire

Aire and now contains a museum of Victorian life.

The Cistercians' influence continued into the 13th century when they established **Netley Abbey** in Hampshire (p94). The founder was Peter des Roches, who was a tutor to Henry III. Another ruined Cistercian abbey in attractive

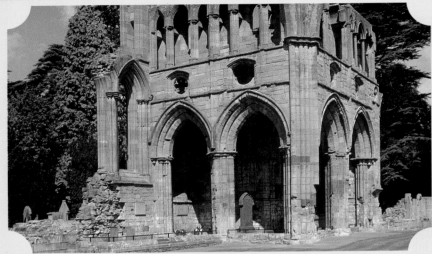

Dryburgh Abbey, founded by David I of Scotland

surroundings is **Rufford Abbey** in Ollerton, Nottinghamshire (p180). **Buildwas Abbey** in Shropshire (p190) was founded in 1135. The church is roofless but has some impressive stout round pillars. **Cleeve Abbey** in Somerset (p201) has a fine timbered roof, traceried windows and wall paintings.

Cistercian influence extended into Scotland and one of the order's abbeys has an important connection outside its monastic history. Mary, Queen of Scots is thought to have spent her last night in Scotland at **Dundrennan Abbey** (p336), before fleeing to England, where she met her grisly end. Mary had a less unpleasant connection with **Inchmahome Priory** in Port of Menteith (p327) which was founded on an island in 1238. She stayed there as a child, before she was sent by her mother to France.

Battle Abbey in East Sussex (p221) also has a gruesome connection. It was founded by William the Conqueror to atone for the slaughter of the Battle of Hastings. The altar stood on the spot where Harold fell, and is still marked with a memorial stone.

The 'Declaration of Arbroath' - which made Robert the Bruce king - was signed in 1320 at **Arbroath Abbey** (p313), which has a well preserved abbot's house and church remains. **Melrose Abbey** (p343), was repeatedly wrecked during the Scottish wars of independence. Legend has it that the heart of Robert the Bruce is buried somewhere in the church. The remaining bits of Robert the Bruce are

buried at **Dunfermline Abbey** (p317), an 11th-century Benedictine abbey, the guest house of which was the birthplace of Charles I.

Inchcolm Abbey is a picturesque Augustinian site, situated on

Much Wenlock Priory, Shropshire

an island on the Firth of Forth (p329), and founded in 1123 by Alexander I of Scotland. Among remains are a 13th-century octagonal chapter house and wall painting. **Whitby Abbey** in Yorkshire (p275) is also worth a look, its haunting ruins sitting above the town. Founded in the 13th century, it was built on the site of a much older abbey.

Mysterious medieval fighting monks, the Knights Templar occupied the site of **Middle Temple Hall** in London (p140), from about 1160. The Hall was completed in 1570 and is a fine example of Tudor architecture. Inside are a 29ft-long table made from a single oak tree from Windsor Forest, and another table made from timbers taken from Francis Drake's ship, the Golden Hind.

In Llangollen, North Wales, **Valle Crucis Abbey** (p355) was founded in 1201 by Madog ap Gruffydd. A relation, Rhy ap Gruffydd, founded **Talley Abbey** (p364) in 1197. It was eventually destroyed in the uprising led by Owain Glyndwr. Another Welsh location is **Strata Florida Abbey** (p364), which was founded in 1164, and was an important centre of learning in the Middle Ages. It is believed that the 14th-century poet, Dafyd ap Gwilym is buried here.

These Welsh ruins are unusual as they were caused by uprisings and rebellion. Most of the religious ruins in Britain were caused in the 15th century when Henry VIII broke from the Catholic Church and had the monasteries dissolved. Some monasteries and abbeys have since been rebuilt but most lie in ruins, as they have for five centuries.

The Norman Cathedrals of Britain

Due to the church-building skills of the Normans, Britain has a fine collection of cathedrals, most of which are still standing and in full working order. **Ely** (p28) was built in the 11th century on the site of a 7th century monastery. It contains a stained glass museum and has a fine Octagon Tower.

Durham (p72) was founded in 1093 as a shrine to St Cuthbert, who had been the prior at Lindisfarne. **St Albans** (p107) was named after, and build on the site of the execution of, the first British martyr, a Roman soldier beheaded for sheltering a Christian priest. **Elgin** (p303) also has a colourful history. Founded in 1224, it was burnt along with the rest of

Elgin in 1390. It was later rebuilt, but then ruined during the Dissolution.

Winchester (p98) is the longest medieval church in Europe, and is founded on a site where Christian worship had been offered for over 400 years. The building contains the famous Illuminated Winchester Bible. More religious treasures can be found at **Hereford** (p101). These include the 13th-Century Mappa Mundi (Map of the World) and the 1400 chained books and 227 manuscripts of the Chained Library.

Chester (p32) was originally a Benedictine monastery, founded in 1092, but didn't become a cathedral until the 16th century. **Salisbury** (p255) was built between 1220 and 1258. It has the highest spire in England, and houses the finest surviving Magna Carta.

Built on the reputed site of St David's 6th century monastic settlement, **St David's** in Pembrokeshire (p364) was begun in 1181. It was altered in the 12th, 13th, 14th and 16th centuries, and is set in a very beautiful location.

After The Dissolution

Founded in 1018, **Buckfast Abbey** (p57) in Buckfastleigh suffered Dissolution and didn't come back to its original use until 1907, when four monks with little building

The remains of the Venerable Bede lie in Durham's Galilee Chapel

experience started making the abbey into a religious community again. The monks make the bracing Buckfast tonic wine.

Aylesford Priory in Kent (p110) was built between the 14th and 15th centuries, and although Dissolved, has since been restored. It is now a house of prayer, guest house and place of pilgrimage, as it would have been centuries ago. Another restored priory is **Brinkburn** at Longframlington (p174). It was founded in 1135 and restored in 1858.

the British church's first real historian and lived in Jarrow, Tyne & Wear, where a museum documents this 8th-century monk's life (p233).

In the 16th century **Bishop William Morgan** followed in the steps of William Tyndale, and set about translating the Bible into his native tongue, in this case Welsh. **Ty Mawr** (p356), near Penmachno in Conwy was Morgan's birthplace.

John Wesley (1703-91) was the

The ruins of Hailes Abbey, Winchcombe, Gloucestershire

Whiteladies Priory (p190) was an Augustinian nunnery founded in 1158. For a change, this suffered destruction during the Civil War when Charles II hid here. **Glasgow Cathedral** (p336) also escaped the wrath of Henry VIII. The city's trade guilds formed an armed guard to defend it from attack.

St George's Chapel in Windsor (p19) was begun in 1475 by Edward IV and completed under Henry VIII. It is a superb building with fan vaulting on the ceiling, large windows, and intricate carving on the choir stalls.

Some of Britain's Christian buildings are much less functional than the abbeys or cathedrals. In the late 16th century, Sir Thomas Tresham built a **triangular lodge** in Rushton, Northants, (p169) which was intended to express his staunch Roman Catholicism. The building is a feast of intriguing religious symbols.

Personalities

As interesting as the architecture of Christianity, are the people who propagated, preached and lived for The Word. **The Venerable Bede** (c673-735) was

founder of Methodism in the 1740s, and the **chapel** he built in 1739 still stands in Bristol (p21). Those interested in Wesley can visit **Wesley's Chapel, House and Museum of Methodism** (p144), which is opposite Bunhill Fields, where Wesley's mother is buried, or the **Old Rectory** in Epworth (p130), where the Wesley brothers were brought up.

Modern Times

Westminster Cathedral (p145) was begun in 1895 but the interior has never been finished. The Christian Byzantine architectural style is stunning, and magnificent views of London can be seen from the 273ft high Campanile Bell Tower.

Coventry Cathedral (p243) suffered German bombing during WWII and is now the most modern ruined cathedral in Britain. The new cathedral was consecrated in 1962, and contains some remarkable modern art. **The Metropolitan Cathedral of Christ the King** (p157), consecrated in 1967, and affectionately known as "Paddy's Wigwam" is one of Liverpool's most memorable landmarks.

AA Hotel Booking Service

The AA Hotel Booking Service - Now you have a free, simple way to reserve a place to stay for a week, weekend, or a one-night stopover.

Do you want to book somewhere in the Lake District that has leisure facilities; a city-centre hotel in Glasgow with parking facilities, or do you need accommodation near Dover which is handy for the Eurotunnel?

The AA Booking Service can take the hassle out of booking the right place for you.

And if you are touring round the UK or Ireland, simply give the AA Hotel Booking Service your list of overnight stops, and from one phone call all your accommodation can be booked for you.

Telephone 0870 5050505

Office hours
Monday-Friday 9am-6pm
Saturday 9am-1pm
Not available Sundays or Bank Holidays

Full listings of AA recognised accommodation available through the Hotel Booking Service can be found and booked at the AA's Internet Site:

http://www.theaa.co.uk/hotels

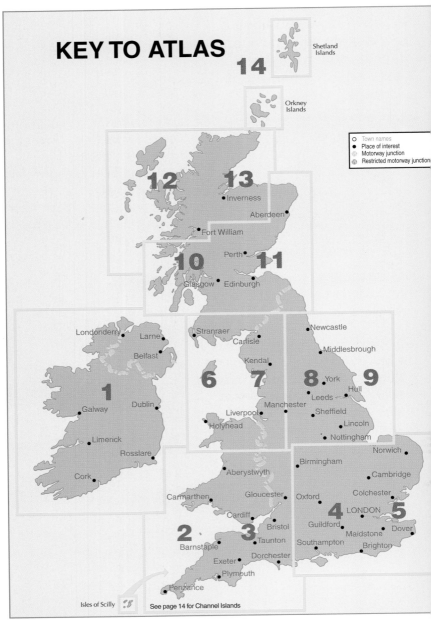

KEY TO ATLAS

14

Shetland Islands

Orkney Islands

○	Town names
●	Place of interest
Ⓙ	Motorway junction
Ⓡ	Restricted motorway junction

12 **13**

Inverness

Aberdeen

Fort William

Perth **11**

10

Glasgow Edinburgh

Londonderry Larne Stranraer Newcastle

Belfast Carlisle Middlesbrough

Kendal

6 **7** **8** York **9**

1 Hull

Galway Dublin Liverpool Manchester Leeds

Holyhead Sheffield

Limerick Lincoln

Rosslare Nottingham

Norwich

Cork Birmingham

Aberystwyth Cambridge

Gloucester Oxford Colchester

Carmarthen **4** LONDON **5**

Cardiff Guildford Dover

2 **3** Bristol Maidstone

Barnstaple Taunton Southampton Brighton

Dorchester

Exeter

Plymouth

Isles of Scilly See page 14 for Channel Islands

Penzance

© The Automobile Association 1999

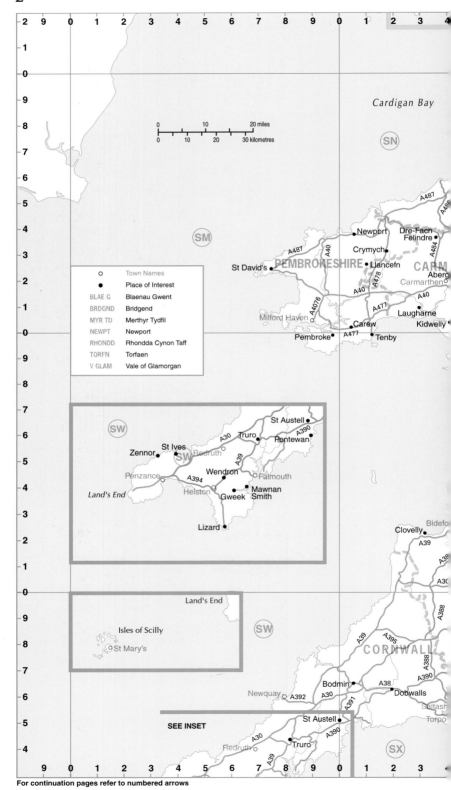

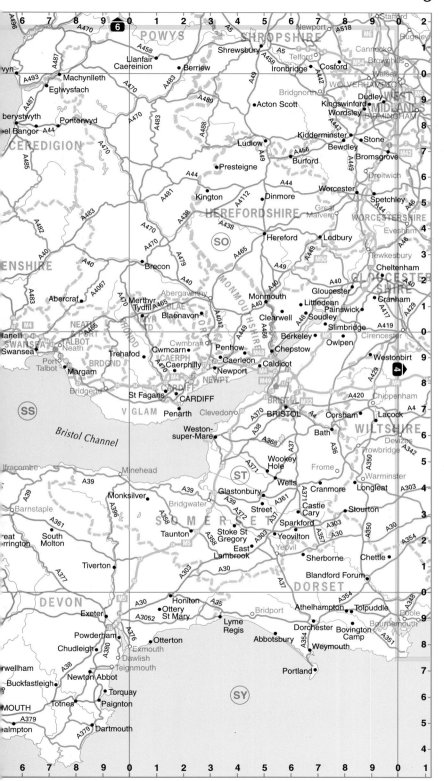

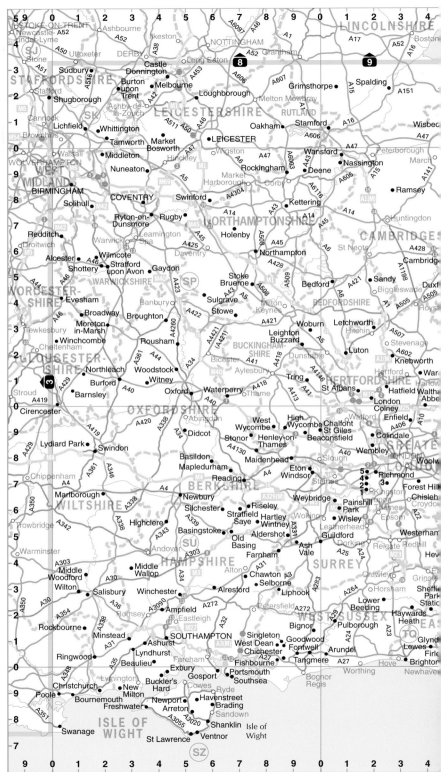

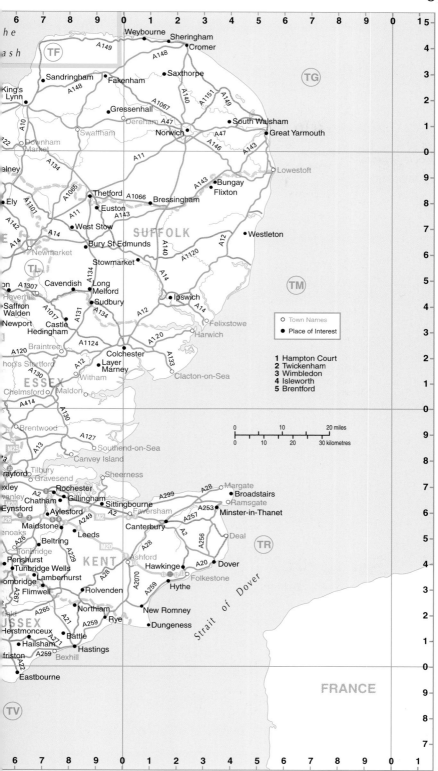

5 6 7 8 9 0 1 2 3 4 5 6 7 8 9 0

0

9

○ Town Names
● Place of Interest

NORTHUMBERLAND

Morpeth

A696
A1

A68

A69

Bardon Mill

A69

doswald

NY

A689

A686

Cowshill

Skelton

Penrith

Dalemain

A689

A68

Gosforth

Whitley Bay
Tynemouth
South Shields

NEWCASTLE UPON TYNE

A695

A692

Gateshead
Jarrow

TYNE & WEAR

SUNDERLAND

Consett

Stanley

A1

Durham

A1(M)

NZ

DURHAM

Bishop Auckland

Spennymoor

Hartlepool

A688

A689

A699

Stockton-on-Tees

Middlesbrough

A66

Darlington

A171

A66

Whitby

UMBRIA

A685

Windermere

dal

Sedbergh

A1

A19

Northallerton

A169

A171

A170

Scarborough

A170

Levens

A684

NORTH YORKSHIRE

A168

SE

A64

A166

Silverdale

Morecambe

Lancaster

sham

A683

A65

Clapham

Ripon

A1(M)

A19

A614

SD

A65

A582

A61

Skipton

Harrogate

York

A64

EAST RIDING OF YORKSHIRE

A59

LANCASHIRE

A56

Ilkley

A65

Otley

A59

A163

Beverley

Clitheroe

M65

Keighley

A660

Bingley

A58

A614

A194

A6

A59

Whalley

Nelson

Shipley

LEEDS

A1(M)

A62

Selby

A63

M62

Salmesbury

Burnley

BRADFORD

Accrington

A646

Halifax

Brighouse

Goole

Scunthorpe

A15

ston

Blackburn

Todmorden

WEST YORKSHIRE

Dewsbury

Pontefract

M18

and

Chorley

Turton Bottoms

Rochdale

Huddersfield

Wakefield

Thorne

rtin

Charnock Richard

Bury

A62

A61

Barnsley

Doncaster

M180

re

Bolton

Middleton

A629

SOUTH

A159

Skelmersdale

Wigan

Oldham

A628

A635

YORKSHIRE

A15

GREATER MANCHESTER

St Helens

A580

Salford

MANCHESTER

A616

Rotherham

Gainsborough

Warrington

M60

Glossop

SHEFFIELD

A1(M)

A631

A57

Altrincham

Stockport

A6

A57

Worksop

Retford

A156

A51

Knutsford

A537

Dronfield

A619

A1

Lincoln

A15

Northwich

A556

Macclesfield

A537

Buxton

A619

Staveley

Chesterfield

A614

A50

CHESHIRE

Jodrell Bank

A60

NOTTINGHAMSHIRE

A51

SJ

Sandbach

A54

A515

Matlock

Mansfield

A617

A534

Kidsgrove

Leek

SK

olmondeley

Crewe

A52

A6097

A46

Nantwich

SJ

A1

STOKE-ON-TRENT

Newcastle-under-Lyme

A52

NOTTINGHAM

A525

A53

Willoughbridge

A50

A38

DERBY

A52

A453

A606

A607

Weston-under-Redcastle

A51

STAFFORDSHIRE

Burton upon Trent

A42

A41

A518

Stafford

A515

LEICESTERSHIRE

RUTLAND

5 6 7 8 9 0 1 2 3 4 5 6 7 8 9 0

Town Names ○
Place of Interest ●

0   10   20 miles
0 10 20 30 kilometres

Whitley Bay
Tynemouth
● South Shields
rrow
○ SUNDERLAND
ashington
(NZ)

A19
● Hartlepool
A689
● Redcar
ockton-
n-Tees ○ ● Middlesbrough
A66
A171
Whitby

● Danby

A19   A169   A171

ORKSHIRE   A170   ○ Scarborough

Helmsley A170
● ● Pickering
● Kirby Misperton
A168 (SE)   A165
ewby   A64 ● Malton
Hall A19   ● Sutton-on-the-Forest   ● Bempton
Burton Agnes ● ● Bridlington
aresborough   A166   A165
A59
York ● ● Pocklington
A64   A165
● Bramham EAST RIDING   A165
● Lotherton Hall OF YORKSHIRE
A58 A1 A163 Beverley ● Sproatley
Selby A614 A1079
● Fairburn A63 A63
M62 A645 A63 ● HULL
○ Pontefract ○ Goole A15
akefield   mmingham ○ ● Grimsby
M18 ○ Thorne ● Scunthorpe ○ Cleethorpes
arnsley ● Cusworth ● Epworth A18
A635 M180
SOUTH ○ Doncaster A46 A16
ORKSHIRE
● Rotherham A159 A15 A1031
A631 ● Gainsborough ○ Louth
SHEFFIELD A1(M) A157 A52
A57 ● Sutton-cum-Lound A16
ronfield Worksop A158
veley A619 ○ Retford A156
○ Chesterfield A1 A57 A158 ● Skegness
A614 ● Ollerton ● Lincoln
A60 Edwinstowe A15
NOTTINGHAMSHIRE A52
Mansfield A617 ○ Coningsby A158
rich ● Farnsfield
● Ripley ● Newstead ● Newark-on-Trent LINCOLNSHIRE (TF)
A6097 A46 The ● Holkham
Denby Eastwood A1 Wash Titchwell ● A149
A38 ● NOTTINGHAM A17 A52 Heacham ●
RBY A52 ● Belvoir A16 ⑤
A15 King's A148
A453 A606 A607 Lynn ○
EICESTERSHIRE A15 A17 NORFOLK
M1 RUTLAND A151

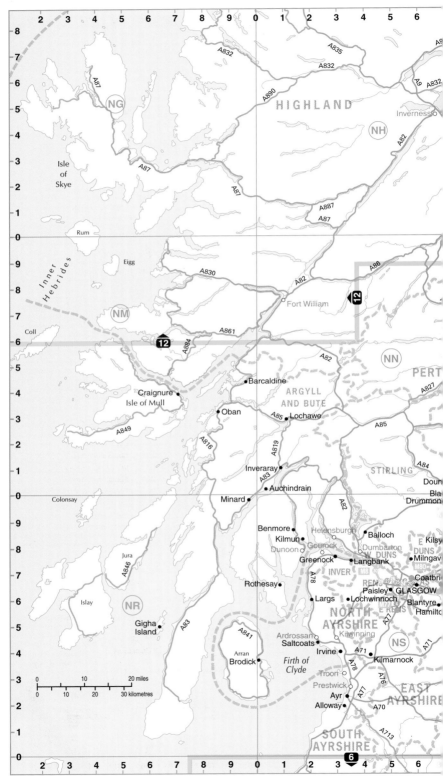

8 9 0 1 2 3 4 5 6 7 8 9 0 1 2 3

Moray Firth

Elgin • Spey Bay • Buckie • Banff ○ Fraserburgh

NK

A96 A940 A941 **12** Keith A95 A98 A90

MORAY

Dufftown A96

A947 Mintlaw A952 A90 • Peterhead

NJ

A95

A938 A939

Aviemore ABEENSHIRE

Oyne • Inverurie A90

• Kildrummy

ABERDEEN CITY
• Aberdeen

13 A93 Maryculter

• Banchory A90

Blair Atholl • Stonehaven

Queen's View • Glengoulandie Deer Park • Weem • Pitlochry

Fettercairn N O R T H

ANGUS S E A

ND KINROSS A826 A93

A90 Montrose

NO SN

Forfar A94 A90 Glamis

A92 • Arbroath

5 Crieff Scone • Muthill Perth Dundee DUNDEE CITY

A92

A90 A91 St Andrews

FIFE Cupar A915

Kinross Glenrothes A917 • Anstruther

CLACKS A977 M90

Causewayhead Alloa A92 ○ Buckhaven

tirling Dunfermline Kirkcaldy
A985

FALKIRK Bo'ness North Queensferry Aberlady
Falkirk South A1
Queensferry Ingliston EDINBURGH East Fortune
imberauld WEST Livingston A71 Musselburgh Prestonpans
Airdrie M8 LOTHIAN Dalkeith EAST
otherwell A702 Newtongrange A68 LOTHIAN

MIDLOTHIAN

A73 Penicuik Duns • Berwick-upon-Tweed

NT A697 NU

A721 A701 A703 Lauder
Peebles Gordon A698 Coldstream
SOUTH Broughton A72 Galashiels A1
ANARKSHIRE Stobo Traquair Melrose Kelso • Ford • Bamburgh

A708 Selkirk
BORDERS (SCOTTISH) • Chillingham
Jedburgh
• Wanlockhead A68 Alnwick
Sanquhar A697 A1 A1068

MRIES AND GALLOWAY NORTHUMBERLAND

8 9 0 1 2 3 4 5 **7** 6 7 8 9 0 1 2 3

○	Town Names
●	Place of Interest
C EDIN	City of Edinburgh
C GLAS	City of Glasgow
CLACKS	Clackmannanshire
W DUNS	West Dunbartonshire
E DUNS	East Dunbartonshire
E RENS	East Renfrewshire
INVER	Inverclyde
N LANS	North Lanarkshire
RENS	Renfrewshire

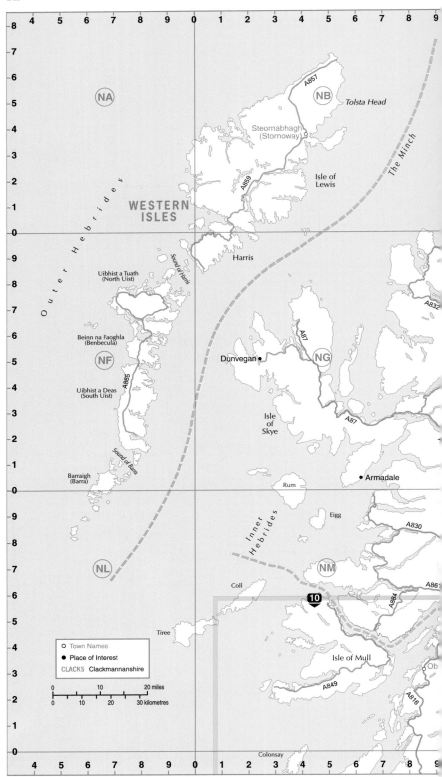

WESTERN
ISLES

Outer Hebrides

NA

NB   Tolsta Head

A857

Steornabhagh
(Stornoway)

A859

Isle of
Lewis

The Minch

Harris

Sound of Harris

Uibhist a Tuath
(North Uist)

A832

Beinn na Faoghla
(Benbecula)

NF

Dunvegan •

NG

A87

A865

Uibhist a Deas
(South Uist)

Isle
of
Skye

A87

Sound of Barra

Barraigh
(Barra)

Rum

• Armadale

Inner Hebrides

Eigg

A830

NL

NM

A861

Coll

10

A884

Tiree

Colonsay

Isle of Mull

Ob

A849

A816

○ Town Names
● Place of Interest
CLACKS Clackmannanshire

0   10   20 miles
0   10   20   30 kilometres

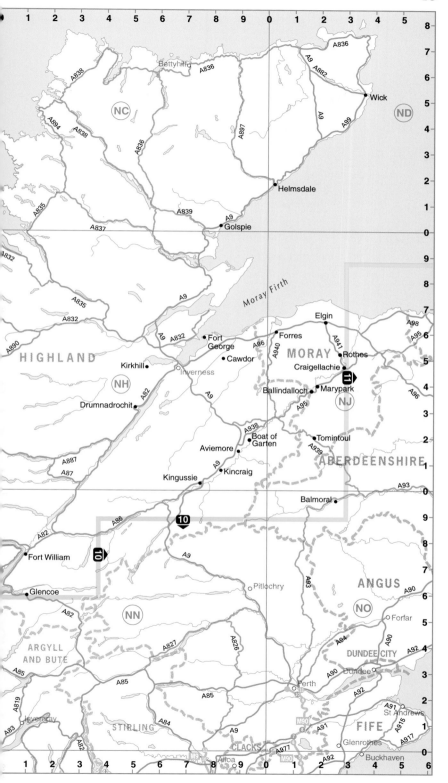

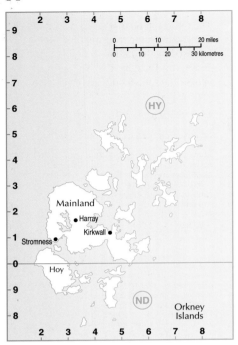

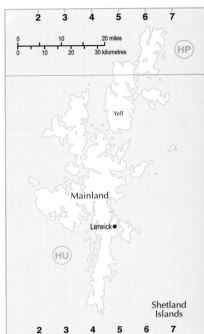

Orkney Islands

HY
HP
HU
ND

9 8 7 6 5 4 3 2 1 0 · 9 · 8

0 10 20 miles
0 10 20 30 kilometres

Mainland
Harray
Kirkwall
Stromness
Hoy

Shetland Islands

Yell
Mainland
Lerwick

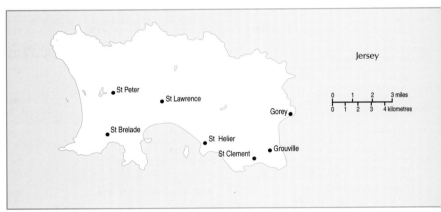

Jersey

St Peter
St Lawrence
Gorey
St Brelade
St Helier
St Clement
Grouville

0 1 2 3 miles
0 1 2 3 4 kilometres

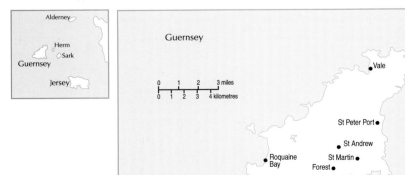

Alderney
Herm
Sark
Guernsey
Jersey

Guernsey

Vale
St Peter Port
St Andrew
Roquaine Bay
St Martin
Forest

0 1 2 3 miles
0 1 2 3 4 kilometres

Index

The figures in bold are map references. These denote the map page number, followed by the National Grid Reference. To find the location, read the first figure across and the second figure vertically within the lettered square.

E

F